AF119785

Special Issue in Honor of the 60th Birthday of Professor Hong-Kun Xu

Special Issue in Honor of the 60th Birthday of Professor Hong-Kun Xu

Editors

Wei-Shih Du
Luigi Muglia
Adrian Petrușel

MDPI

Basel • Beijing • Wuhan • Barcelona • Belgrade • Novi Sad • Cluj • Manchester

Editors

Wei-Shih Du
Department of Mathematics
National Kaohsiung Normal University
Kaohsiung
Taiwan

Luigi Muglia
Department of Mathematics and Computer Science
Universitá della Calabria
Cosenza
Italy

Adrian Petruşel
Faculty of Mathematics and Computer Science
Babeş-Bolyai University
Cluj-Napoca
Cluj-Napoca
Romania

Editorial Office
MDPI
St. Alban-Anlage 66
4052 Basel, Switzerland

This is a reprint of articles from the Special Issue published online in the open access journal *Axioms* (ISSN 2075-1680) (available at: https://www.mdpi.com/journal/axioms/special_issues/hk_xu).

For citation purposes, cite each article independently as indicated on the article page online and as indicated below:

Lastname, A.A.; Lastname, B.B. Article Title. *Journal Name* **Year**, *Volume Number*, Page Range.

ISBN 978-3-7258-1040-6 (Hbk)
ISBN 978-3-7258-1039-0 (PDF)
doi.org/10.3390/books978-3-7258-1039-0

© 2024 by the authors. Articles in this book are Open Access and distributed under the Creative Commons Attribution (CC BY) license. The book as a whole is distributed by MDPI under the terms and conditions of the Creative Commons Attribution-NonCommercial-NoDerivs (CC BY-NC-ND) license.

Contents

Shun-Wei Li, Yu-Lin Chang and Jein-Shan Chen
Plane Section Curves on Surfaces of NCP Functions
Reprinted from: *Axioms* **2022**, *11*, 557, doi:10.3390/axioms11100557 . . . . **159**

Claudia Luminiţa Mihiţ, Ghiocel Moţ and Adrian Petruşel
Fixed Point Theory for Multi-Valued Feng–Liu– Subrahmanyan Contractions
Reprinted from: *Axioms* **2022**, *11*, 563, doi:10.3390/axioms11100563 . . . . **182**

Babar Sultan, Fatima Azmi, Mehvish Sultan, Mazhar Mehmood and Nabil Mlaiki
Boundedness of Riesz Potential Operator on Grand Herz-Morrey Spaces
Reprinted from: *Axioms* **2022**, *11*, 583, doi:10.3390/axioms11110583 . . . . **191**

Yuwen Zhai, Qilin Wang and Tian Tang
Optimality Conditions and Dualities for Robust Efficient Solutions of Uncertain Set-Valued Optimization with Set-Order Relations
Reprinted from: *Axioms* **2022**, *11*, 648, doi:10.3390/axioms11110648 . . . . **205**

Chia-Yu Hsu and Tone-Yau Huang
Second-Ordered Parametric Duality for the Multi-Objective Programming Problem in Complex Space
Reprinted from: *Axioms* **2022**, *11*, 717, doi:10.3390/axioms11120717 . . . . **221**

You Lv and Huaping Huang
The Asymptotic Behavior for Generalized Jiřina Process
Reprinted from: *Axioms* **2023**, *12*, 13, doi:10.3390/axioms12010013 . . . . **231**

About the Editors

Wei-Shih Du

Wei-Shih Du is a Full Professor of Mathematics in the Department of Mathematics, National Kaohsiung Normal University, Kaohsiung 82444, Taiwan. His main research interests include nonlinear analysis and its applications, fixed point theory and its applications, variational principles and inequalities, iterative methods for nonlinear mappings, optimization theory, equilibrium problems, and fractional calculus theory.

Luigi Muglia

Luigi Muglia is an Associate Professor of Mathematics in the Department of Mathematics and Computer Science, Universitá della Calabria, 87036, Arcavacata di Rende, Cosenza, Italy. His main research interests include ordinary differential equations, impulsive equations, and iterative methods for fixed points.

Adrian Petruşel

Adrian Petruşel is a Full Professor of Mathematics in the Faculty of Mathematics and Computer Science, Babeş-Bolyai University Cluj-Napoca and a Full Member of the Academy of Romanian Scientists, Romania. His main research interests include fixed point theory, differential equations and integral equations, and differential and integral inclusions.

Preface

This Special Issue of *Axioms* pays tribute to Professor Hong-Kun Xu's significant contributions and details important recent advances in the theory, methods, and applications of nonlinear analysis, optimization theory, fixed point theory, and algorithms for nonlinear problems. It comprises original, creative, and high-quality research papers that inspire advances in fixed point, coincidence point, and best proximity point theory with applications, set-valued analysis, nonlinear and variational methods for ODEs and PDEs, non-smooth analysis and optimization, inverse and ill-posed problems, convex analysis, matrix theory, and their applications.

The Guest Editors have made every effort to ensure the success of this Special Issue and hope that these efforts will be rewarded. The Guest Editors organized a comprehensive review process for each submission based on the journal's policy, instructions, and guidelines. We received 44 submissions and, after a comprehensive peer-review process, only 16 high-quality articles were accepted for publication (the acceptance rate is around 36%). The accepted papers can be divided according to the following six schemes considering their main purposes:

(1) Fixed point theory and applications;

(2) Algorithms for nonlinear problems;

(3) Nonlinear methods for ODEs and PDEs with applications;

(4) Convex analysis and inequality theory;

(5) Optimization;

(6) Functional analysis.

We hope that interested researchers and practitioners will be inspired by this Special Issue and find it valuable to their own research. This Special Issue highlighted important issues and raised several new problems in these research areas. We would like to heartily thank the Editorial team and the reviewers of *Axioms*, particularly the Editor-in-Chief, Professor Humberto Bustince, and the Assistant Editor, Luna Shen, for their invaluable support and help throughout the editing process.

Wei-Shih Du, Luigi Muglia, and Adrian Petruşel

Editors

axioms MDPI

Editorial

Editorial Conclusion for the Special Issue "Special Issue in Honor of the 60th Birthday of Professor Hong-Kun Xu"

Wei-Shih Du [1,*,†], Luigi Muglia [2] and Adrian Petruşel [3,4]

1 Department of Mathematics, National Kaohsiung Normal University, Kaohsiung 82444, Taiwan
2 Dipartimento di Matematica, Universitá della Calabria, Arcavacata di Rende, 87036 Cosenza, Italy; muglia@mat.unical.it
3 Department of Mathematics, Babeş-Bolyai University Cluj-Napoca, Kogălniceanu Street, No. 1, 400084 Cluj-Napoca, Romania; adrian.petrusel@ubbcluj.ro
4 Academy of Romanian Scientists, Splaiul Independenţei Street No. 54, 050094 Bucharest, Romania
* Correspondence: wsdu@mail.nknu.edu.tw
† Lead Guest editor.

Professor Dr. Hong-Kun Xu

Professor Hong-Kun Xu received his PhD degree from Xi'an Jiaotong University in 1988. He is currently a distinguished professor at Hangzhou Dianzi University, China. In 2004, he received the South African Mathematical Society Research Distinction Award and the Second Prize for Natural Science of the Ministry of Education of China. He is the former Head of the Department of Applied Mathematics and Dean of the College of Science at National Sun Yat-sen University, Taiwan. He was elected as a member of the Academy of Science of South Africa in 2005, and a fellow to the Academy of Sciences for the Developing World (TWAS) in 2012. He was also selected at the "Thousand Talents Program" of Zhejiang Province in 2014 and named as a Thomson Reuters/Clarivate Highly Cited Researcher from 2014 to 2018 and an Elsevier Chinese Highly Cited Researcher from 2019 to 2021. He has published approximately 250 research papers in journals and delivered academic speeches (invited/keynote/plenary) at more than 50 international academic conferences. He is serving on the editorial boards for more than 20 international mathematical journals. His main research interests include nonlinear functional analysis, optimization theory and algorithms, Banach space geometry theory, fixed point theory and applications, nonlinear mapping iteration method, inverse problem and its regularization method, financial mathematics, etc.

Citation: Du, W.-S.; Muglia, L.; Petruşel, A. Editorial Conclusion for the Special Issue "Special Issue in Honor of the 60th Birthday of Professor Hong-Kun Xu". *Axioms* **2023**, *12*, 548. https://doi.org/10.3390/axioms12060548

Received: 26 May 2023
Accepted: 31 May 2023
Published: 1 June 2023

Copyright: © 2023 by the authors. Licensee MDPI, Basel, Switzerland. This article is an open access article distributed under the terms and conditions of the Creative Commons Attribution (CC BY) license (https://creativecommons.org/licenses/by/4.0/).

This Special Issue pays tribute to Professor Hong-Kun Xu's significant contributions to these fields and provides some important recent advances in theory, methods, and applications. It comprises original and high-quality research papers that inspire advances in nonlinear analysis, optimization, and their applications. For more information, please visit the website: https://www.mdpi.com/journal/axioms/special_issues/hk_xu, accessed on 26 February 2021.

The Guest Editors have striven to ensure the success of this Special Issue, and we believe our efforts have been successful. The Guest Editors organized a comprehensive review process for each submission based on the journal's policy and guidelines. We have received 44 submissions and, after a comprehensive review process, 16 high-quality works have been accepted for publication (with an acceptance rate of around 0.36). The accepted papers can be divided according to the following scheme considering their main purposes:

- Fixed point theory and applications (see [1–5]);
- Algorithms for nonlinear problems (see [1,3]);
- Nonlinear methods for ODEs and PDEs with applications (see [6–9]);
- Convex analysis and inequality theory (see [10–13]);
- Optimization (see [1,3,9,12–14]);
- Functional analysis (see [5,6,8,15,16]).

We hope that interested researchers and practitioners will be inspired by this Special Issue and find it valuable to their own research.

This Special Issue has highlighted important issues and raised several new problems in this research area. We would like to express our hearty thanks to the editorial team and the reviewers of *Axioms*, particularly the Editor-in-Chief Prof. Dr. Humberto Bustince and the Assistant Editor Luna Shen, for their invaluable support throughout the editing process.

Author Contributions: Conceptualization, W.-S.D., L.M. and A.P.; methodology, W.-S.D., L.M. and A.P.; software, W.-S.D.; validation, W.-S.D., L.M. and A.P.; formal analysis, W.-S.D., L.M. and A.P.; investigation, W.-S.D., L.M. and A.P.; writing—original draft preparation, W.-S.D.; writing—review and editing, W.-S.D., L.M. and A.P.; visualization, W.-S.D., L.M. and A.P.; supervision, W.-S.D., L.M. and A.P.; project administration, W.-S.D., L.M. and A.P. All authors have read and agreed to the published version of the manuscript.

Funding: The first author is partially supported by Grant No. NSTC 111-2115-M-017-002 of the National Science and Technology Council of the Republic of China.

Institutional Review Board Statement: Not applicable.

Informed Consent Statement: Not applicable.

Data Availability Statement: Not applicable.

Acknowledgments: The authors wish to express their hearty thanks to Hong-Kun Xu for providing his photograph and giving us permission to use it, as shown in the Figure in this manuscript.

Conflicts of Interest: The authors declare no conflict of interest.

References

1. Ceng, L.-C.; Yao, J.-C. Mann-Type Inertial Subgradient Extragradient Rules for Variational Inequalities and Common Fixed Points of Nonexpansive and Quasi-Nonexpansive Mappings. *Axioms* **2021**, *10*, 67. [CrossRef]
2. Huang, H.; Mitrović, Z.D.; Zoto, K.; Radenović, S. On Convex *F*-Contraction in *b*-Metric Spaces. *Axioms* **2021**, *10*, 71. [CrossRef]
3. Li, Y.; Zhang, Y. Bounded Perturbation Resilience of Two Modified Relaxed CQ Algorithms for the Multiple-Sets Split Feasibility Problem. *Axioms* **2021**, *10*, 197. [CrossRef]
4. Mlaiki, N.; Taş, N.; Kaplan, E.; Subhi Aiadi, S.; Karoui Souayah, A. Some Common Fixed-Circle Results on Metric Spaces. *Axioms* **2022**, *11*, 454. [CrossRef]
5. Mihiţ, C.L.; Moţ, G.; Petruşel, A. Fixed Point Theory for Multi-Valued Feng–Liu–Subrahmanyan Contractions. *Axioms* **2022**, *11*, 563. [CrossRef]
6. Tunç, O.; Atan, Ö.; Tunç, C.; Yao, J.-C. Qualitative Analyses of Integro-Fractional Differential Equations with Caputo Derivatives and Retardations via the Lyapunov-Razumikhin Method. *Axioms* **2021**, *10*, 58. [CrossRef]

7. Tunç, O.; Tunç, C.; Wang, Y. Delay-Dependent Stability, Integrability and Boundedeness Criteria for Delay Differential Systems. *Axioms* **2021**, *10*, 138. [CrossRef]
8. Chen, L.; Lin, S.; Zhao, Y. Global Stability of a Lotka-Volterra Competition-Diffusion-Advection System with Different Positive Diffusion Distributions. *Axioms* **2021**, *10*, 166. [CrossRef]
9. Liu, X.-L.; Zhu, C.-C. A Non-Standard Finite Difference Scheme for a Diffusive HIV-1 Infection Model with Immune Response and Intracellular Delay. *Axioms* **2022**, *11*, 129. [CrossRef]
10. Wu, Y.; Yin, H.-P.; Guo, B.-N. Generalizations of Hermite–Hadamard Type Integral Inequalities for Convex Functions. *Axioms* **2021**, *10*, 136. [CrossRef]
11. Huang, H.; Du, W.-S. On a New Integral Inequality: Generalizations and Applications. *Axioms* **2022**, *11*, 458. [CrossRef]
12. Li, S.-W.; Chang, Y.-L.; Chen, J.-S. Plane Section Curves on Surfaces of NCP Functions. *Axioms* **2022**, *11*, 557. [CrossRef]
13. Hsu, C.-Y.; Huang, T.-Y. Second-Ordered Parametric Duality for the Multi-Objective Programming Problem in Complex Space. *Axioms* **2022**, *11*, 717. [CrossRef]
14. Zhai, Y.; Wang, Q.; Tang, T. Optimality Conditions and Dualities for Robust Efficient Solutions of Uncertain Set-Valued Optimization with Set-Order Relations. *Axioms* **2022**, *11*, 648. [CrossRef]
15. Sultan, B.; Azmi, F.; Sultan, M.; Mehmood, M.; Mlaiki, N. Boundedness of Riesz Potential Operator on Grand Herz-Morrey Spaces. *Axioms* **2022**, *11*, 583. [CrossRef]
16. Lv, Y.; Huang, H. The Asymptotic Behavior for Generalized Jiřina Process. *Axioms* **2023**, *12*, 13. [CrossRef]

Disclaimer/Publisher's Note: The statements, opinions and data contained in all publications are solely those of the individual author(s) and contributor(s) and not of MDPI and/or the editor(s). MDPI and/or the editor(s) disclaim responsibility for any injury to people or property resulting from any ideas, methods, instructions or products referred to in the content.

axioms

MDPI

Article

Qualitative Analyses of Integro-Fractional Differential Equations with Caputo Derivatives and Retardations via the Lyapunov–Razumikhin Method

Osman Tunç [1], Özkan Atan [2], Cemil Tunç [3] and Jen-Chih Yao [4,*]

1 Department of Computer Programing, Baskale Vocational School, Van Yuzuncu Yil University, 65080 Van, Turkey; osmantunc89@gmail.com
2 Department of Electric-Electronic Engineering, Faculty of Engineering, Van Yuzuncu Yil University, 65080 Van, Turkey; oatan@yyu.edu.tr
3 Department of Mathematics, Faculty of Sciences, Van Yuzuncu Yil University, 65080 Van, Turkey; cemtunc@yahoo.com
4 Research Center for Interneural Computing, China Medical University Hospital, China Medical University, Taichung 406, Taiwan
* Correspondence: yaojc@mail.cmu.edu.tw

Abstract: The purpose of this paper is to investigate some qualitative properties of solutions of nonlinear fractional retarded Volterra integro-differential equations (FrRIDEs) with Caputo fractional derivatives. These properties include uniform stability, asymptotic stability, Mittag–Leffer stability and boundedness. The presented results are proved by defining an appropriate Lyapunov function and applying the Lyapunov–Razumikhin method (LRM). Hence, some results that are available in the literature are improved for the FrRIDEs and obtained under weaker conditions via the advantage of the LRM. In order to illustrate the results, two examples are provided.

Keywords: nonlinear fractional retarded integro-differential equations; uniform stability; asymptotic stability; Mittag–Leffer stability; boundedness; Lyapunov–Razumikhin method

MSC: 34K20; 34K37; 45J05; 45M10

Citation: Tunç, O.; Atan, Ö.; Tunç, C.; Yao, J.-C. Qualitative Analyses of Integro-Fractional Differential Equations with Caputo Derivatives and Retardations via the Lyapunov–Razumikhin Method. *Axioms* **2021**, *10*, 58. https://doi.org/10.3390/axioms10020058

Academic Editors: Wei-Shih Du, Luigi Muglia and Adrian Petrusel

Received: 19 March 2021
Accepted: 6 April 2021
Published: 9 April 2021

Publisher's Note: MDPI stays neutral with regard to jurisdictional claims in published maps and institutional affiliations.

Copyright: © 2021 by the authors. Licensee MDPI, Basel, Switzerland. This article is an open access article distributed under the terms and conditions of the Creative Commons Attribution (CC BY) license (https://creativecommons.org/licenses/by/4.0/).

1. Introduction

In recent years, a large number of books [1–3] and papers [4–24] have been devoted to the study of various qualitative properties of solutions of scalars and systems of linear and nonlinear Volterra integro-differential equations (IDEs) both without and with delay, and that of some other kinds of differential equations due to their important applications in population growth models, mathematical models of biological species living together, mathematical models in physics, control engineering and signal processing, mathematical models of heat transfer and radiation, standard closed electric RLC circuits, and so on.

In the relevant literature three methods, which are called the second Lyapunov method, Lyapunov–Krasovskiĭ method and Lyapunov–Razumikhin method, come to the forefront to investigate qualitative properties of solutions of linear and nonlinear integro-differential equations both without and with retardation. Among these methods, the second Lyapunov method and Lyapunov–Krasovskiĭ method are extensively used to study various qualitative behaviors of solutions of integro-differential equations of integer order (see, [4–20]). To the best of our knowledge, the Lyapunov–Razumikhin method is less used during that kind of investigation [23,25,26]. However, when it is used for the appropriate problems, it is more effective than the other two methods mentioned, the second Lyapunov method and Lyapunov–Krasovskiĭ method. To the best of our knowledge from the relevant literature, the disadvantages of the Lyapunov second method and Lyapunov–Krasovskiĭ method are that both of these methods require the construction or definition of suitable Lyapunov function(s) and Lyapunov–Krasovskiĭ functional(s), which can include double integrals and additional terms. The construction of suitable Lyapunov function(s) and Lyapunov–Krasovskiĭ functional(s) for nonlinear functional differential equations remains an open problem in the literature at this time. This case is known as a disadvantage. In addition, the time derivatives of double integrals leads to stronger conditions for the negative or negative -semi definite of the time derivative(s) of function(s) or functional(s) used as basic tool(s) in the proof(s).

From this point of view, we would like to present the related work of Du [27]. Indeed, in 1995, the author investigated the uniformly asymptotic stability of trivial solutions of the system of nonlinear RIDEs of the form:

$$\dot{x}(t) = -f(t,x(t)) + g(t,x(t-\tau)) + \int_{t-\tau}^{t} h(t,s,x(s))ds \tag{1}$$

or its equivalent system

$$\dot{x}_i(t) = -f_i(t,x(t)) + g_i(t,x(t-\tau)) + \int_{t-\tau}^{t} h_i(t,s,x(s))ds, (i = 1,2,...,n).$$

In this paper, we consider the following initial value problem (IVP) for the system of nonlinear fractional retarded Volterra integro-differential equations (FrRIDEs) with Caputo derivative:

$$\begin{aligned} {}_{t_0}^{C}D_t^q x(t) = &- f(t,x(t)) + g(t,x(t),x(t-\tau)) + \int_{t-\tau}^{t} h(t,s,x(s))ds \\ &+ \int_{t-\rho}^{t} p(t,s,x(s))ds + q(t,x(t),x(t-\tau),x(t-\rho)), 0 < q < 1, \end{aligned} \tag{2}$$

$$x(t_0+\theta) = \phi(\theta), x(t_0) = \phi(0) = x_0, \theta \in [-\tau,0] \cup [-\rho,0], \tag{3}$$

where $x = (x_1,...,x_n)^T \in \mathbb{R}^n$, $t \in \mathbb{R}$, $s \in [-\tau,\infty) \cup [-\rho,\infty)$, τ and ρ are positive constants, i.e., they are constant retardations, $f = (f_1,...,f_n)^T \in C(\mathbb{R} \times \mathbb{R}^n, \mathbb{R}^n)$, $f_i(t,x(t)) = f_i(t,x_1(t),...,x_n(t))$, $g = (g_1,...,g_n)^T \in C(\mathbb{R} \times \mathbb{R}^n \times C_H, \mathbb{R}^n)$, $C_H = \left\{\phi : \phi \in C \text{ and } \|\phi\|_{t_0} \leq H < \infty\right\}$, $g_i(t,x(t),x(t-\tau)) = g_i(t,x_1(t),...,x_n(t),x_1(t-\tau),...,x_n(t-\tau))$, $h \in C(\mathbb{R} \times [-\tau,\infty) \times C_H, \mathbb{R}^n)$, $p \in C(\mathbb{R} \times [-\rho,\infty) \times C_H, \mathbb{R}^n)$ and $q \in C(\mathbb{R} \times \mathbb{R}^n \times C_H \times C_H, \mathbb{R}^n)$. It is supposed that $f(t,0) = 0$, $g(t,0,0) = 0$, $p(t,s,0) = 0$, and $h(t,s,0) = 0$. Then, the system of Volterra FrRIDEs (2) with a Caputo derivative includes the zero solution, when $q(.) \equiv 0$.

In this article, motivated by the system of nonlinear RIDEs at Equation (1), i.e., the result of Du [27] (Theorem 4), and those in the bibliography of this paper, we consider the system of nonlinear FrRIDEs at Equation (2) with a Caputo derivative. As indicated above, we plan to investigate the uniformly stability, asymptotic stability, and Mittag–Leffler stability of the zero solution of Equation (2) with $q \equiv 0$, and the boundedness of all solutions of Equation (2) with $q \neq 0$, by using the Razumikhin method (see [25,26,28–30]). It should be noted that the Caputo derivative is applicable to continuously differentiable quadratic Lyapunov functions to study qualitative properties of solutions of fractional differential equations and fractional delay differential equations, etc. (see, for example, [25,26,31–37]).

It is known that the presence of the fractional derivatives in the system requires that we use appropriately defined fractional derivatives of Lyapunov functions. In the literature, four types of fractional derivatives are commonly applied to calculate the derivatives of Lyapunov functions; these are the Caputo fractional derivative, the Caputo fractional Dini derivative, the Riemann–Liouville fractional derivative, and the Grünwald–Letnikov fractional derivative [32,36]. Not all of these will be employed here. The results presented below are new contributions to the literature on delay fractional integro-differential equations with Caputo derivatives.

2. Preliminaries

We begin by considering a system of fractional retarded differential equations (FrRDEs) with a Caputo derivative of order $q \in (0,1)$:

$$ {}_{t_0}^{C}D_t^q x(t) = F(t, x_t), t \in J, J = [t_0 - \tau, T), T \leq +\infty, 0 \leq t_0 \leq t, \tag{4} $$

where $x \in \mathbb{R}^n$, $F(t,\phi) \in J \times C([-r,0],\mathbb{R}^n)$, $F(t,0) = 0$, $x(t_0 + s) = \phi(s)$ for $s \in [-r,0]$, $x(t_0^+) = \phi(0)$, $\phi \in C([-r,0],\mathbb{R}^n)$, $r > 0$ is the constant retardation. For $\phi \in C([-r,0],\mathbb{R}^n)$, we use the usual Euclidean norms $\| \,.\, \|$ and $\| \,.\, \|_{t_0}$ defined by

$$ \|x_t\| = \sup_{-r \leq s \leq 0} |x(t+s)| \text{ and } \|\phi\|_{t_0} = \sup_{t_0 - r \leq s \leq t_0} \|\phi(s)\|, $$

respectively.

Since the function F is continuous, for any initial data $(t_0, \phi) \in \mathbb{R}^+ \times C([-r,0],\mathbb{R}^n)$, the initial value problem for the system of FrRDEs in Equation (4) has at the least one solution $x(t) = x(t, t_0, \phi) \in C^1([t_0,\infty),\mathbb{R}^n)$. If the function F satisfies a Lipschitz condition in x, then the solution is unique.

The following lemmas and other concepts are needed in the remainder of this paper. Firstly, we give Lemma 1, which is a consequence of (Theorem 2) [31].

Lemma 1. *Assume that for any initial data $x(t_0, \phi_0) \in \mathbb{R}^+ \times C([-\tau,0],\mathbb{R}^n)$, the system of FrRIDEs in Equation (2) has a solution. If there exists a Lyapunov function V and strictly increasing $u, v \in C(\mathbb{R}^+,\mathbb{R}^+)$ with $u(0) = v(0) = 0$ and*

$$ u(\|x\|) \leq V(t,x) \leq v(\|x\|) \text{ for all } t \geq t_0 - \tau \text{ and all } x \in \mathbb{R}^n $$

and such that for any initial data $(t_0, \phi_0) \in \mathbb{R}^+ \times C([-\tau,0],\mathbb{R}^n)$ and any point $s > t_0$ with

$$ V(s+\xi, x(s+\xi)) < V(s, x(s)) \text{ for all } \xi \in [-\tau, 0), $$

the inequality

$$ {}_{t_0}^{C}D_t^q V(t, x(t)) \leq 0 \text{ for all } t \in (t_0, s] $$

holds, then the zero function of Equation (2) with a zero initial condition is uniformly stable.

Lemma 2 ([31])**.** *The zero solution of the FrRDEs in Equation (4) is asymptotically stable if there exist a continuous function $V(t,x)$, continuous increasing and positive definite functions u, v, ω and a continuous non-decreasing function $p(s) > s$ for $s > 0$ such that the following conditions hold for all $t \in J$:*

$$ V(t,0) \equiv 0, u(|x|) \leq V(t,x) \leq v(|x|) \text{ for all } t \in J \text{ and all } x \in \mathbb{R}^n; $$
$$ {}_{t_0}^{C}D_t^q V(t, x(t)) \leq -\omega(|x(t)|) \text{ for all } t \in (t_0, s]; $$

and

$$ V(t+s, x(t+s)) < pV(t, x(t)) \text{ for all } s \in [-\tau, 0]. $$

Lemma 3 ([38] Lemma 1)**.** *Let $x(t) \in \mathbb{R}^n$ be a vector of differentiable functions. Then for any $t \geq t_0$,*

$$ \frac{1}{2} {}_{t_0}^{C}D_t^q (x^T x) \leq x^T(t) {}_{t_0}^{C}D_t^q x(t) \text{ for all } q \in (0,1], $$

Lemma 4 ([38] Lemma 4). *Let $x(t) \in \mathbb{R}^n$ be a vector of differentiable functions. Then, for any $t \geq t_0$,*

$$\frac{1}{2}{}_{t_0}^{C}D_t^q(x^T P x) \leq x^T(t) P {}_{t_0}^{C}D_t^q x(t) \text{ for all } q \in (0,1],$$

where $P \in \mathbb{R}^{n\times n}$ is a constant, symmetric and positive definite matrix.

Definition 1 ([35] Definiton 3.1). *The trivial solution of the system of FrRIDEs in Equation (2) is said to be Mittag–Leffler stable provided the solution $x(., \phi)$ of (2) satisfies*

$$\|x(t,\phi)\| \leq [m(\|\phi\|_\infty)E_q(-\lambda(t-t_0)^q)]^b,$$

where $q \in (0,1)$, $\lambda \geq 0$, $b > 0$,

$$\|\phi\|_\infty = \max_{\theta\in[-\tau,0]} \|\phi(\theta)\|,$$

$m(0) = 0$, m is a locally Lipschitz function and is non-negative, and

$$E_q(z) = \sum_{k=0}^{\infty} \frac{z^k}{\Gamma(qk+1)}$$

is the one-parameter Mittag–Leffler function, and Γ denotes the Gamma function.

Lemma 5 ([35] Lemma 2.1). *Let $x \in \mathbb{R}^n$be a vector of differentiable functions. If a continuous function $V : [t_0, \infty) \times \mathbb{R}^n \to \mathbb{R}^+$ satisfies*

$${}_{t_0}^{C}D_t^q V(t, x(t)) \leq -\alpha V(t, x(t)),$$

then

$$V(t, x(t)) \leq V(t_0, x(t_0))E_q(-\alpha(t-t_0)^q),$$

where $\alpha > 0$ and $0 < q < 1$.

Lemma 6 ([33] Property 1).

$${}_{t_0}^{C}D_t^q(ax(t) + by(t)) = a{}_{t_0}^{C}D_t^q x(t) + b{}_{t_0}^{C}D_t^q y(t),$$

where $q \in (0,1]$.

The contents of the next lemma are well known.

Lemma 7. *Let $x \in \mathbb{R}^n$, $n \in N$, $n \geq 1$, and $M \in \mathbb{R}^{n\times n}$ be a positive definite symmetric $n \times n$-matrix such that*

$$\lambda_M \geq \lambda_i(M) \geq \lambda_m, (i = 1, 2, ..., n),$$

where $\lambda_i(M)$ denotes the eigenvalues of M. Then

$$\lambda_M\|x\|^2 \geq \langle Mx, x\rangle \geq \lambda_m\|x\|^2,$$

where λ_M and λ_m are the greatest and least eigenvalues of the matrix M, respectively.

We know that λ_M and λ_m are real and positive since M is a positive definite symmetric matrix.

3. Razumikhin Analyses of Solutions

In the system of Volterra FrRIDEs in Equation (2), let $q \equiv 0$, i.e., we consider the system in Equation (2) with Equation (3) replaced by

$$
\begin{aligned}
{}_{t_0}^{C}D_t^q x(t) = &- f(t,x(t)) + g(t,x(t),x(t-\tau)) + \int_{t-\tau}^{t} h(t,s,x(s))ds \\
&+ \int_{t-\rho}^{t} p(t,s,x(s))ds.
\end{aligned} \tag{5}
$$

We will use the following hypotheses in our main results.

Hypothesis 1.

$$
\begin{aligned}
&f(t,0) = g(s,0,0) = h(t,s,0) \equiv 0, \\
&x_i f_i(t,x) > 0 \text{ as } x_i \neq 0, \text{ for } t \in \mathbb{R}^+, \text{ all } x \in \mathbb{R}^n;
\end{aligned}
$$

Hypothesis 2. *The functions H and P satisfy the local Lipschitz condition in x, with*

$$
H(t,s,x) \equiv \int_{t-\tau}^{t} \|h(t,s,x(s))\|ds, h(t,s,0) = 0, \|h(t,s,x(s))\| \leq h_0\|x\| \text{ for } s \leq t
$$

and

$$
P(t,s,x) \equiv \int_{t-\rho}^{t} \|p(t,s,x(s))\|ds, p(t,s,0) = 0, \|p(t,s,x(s))\| \leq p_0\|x\| \text{ for } s \leq t,
$$

where $h_0 > 0$, $p_0 > 0$, h_0, $p_0 \in \mathbb{R}$;

Hypothesis 3.

$$
\begin{aligned}
&\|f(t,x)\| - \|g(t,x,x(t-\tau))\| - (\tau h_0 + \rho p_0)\|x\| \geq 0 \text{ for } t \in \mathbb{R}^+ \\
&\text{and all } x \in \mathbb{R}^n, x(t-\tau) \in C_H;
\end{aligned}
$$

Hypothesis 4.

$$
\begin{aligned}
&\|f(t,x)\| - \|g(t,x,x(t-\tau))\| - (\tau h_0 + \rho p_0)\|x\| \geq \rho_1\|x\| \text{ for } t \in \mathbb{R}^+ \\
&\text{and all } x \in \mathbb{R}^n, x(t-\tau) \in C_H, \text{ where } \rho_1 > 0, \rho_1 \in \mathbb{R};
\end{aligned}
$$

Hypothesis 5. *There exists $q_0 \in C(\mathbb{R}^+, \mathbb{R})$ such that*

$$
\begin{aligned}
&\|q(t,x,x(t-\tau),x(t-\rho))\| \leq |q_0(t)| \, \|x\| \text{ for all } t \geq t_0, x \in \mathbb{R}^n, x(t-\tau), \\
&x(t-\rho) \in C_H,
\end{aligned}
$$

and

$$
\begin{aligned}
&\|f(t,x)\| - \|g(t,x,x(t-\tau))\| - (q_0(t) + \tau h_0 + \rho p_0)\|x\| \geq 0 \text{ for } t \in \mathbb{R}^+ \\
&\text{and all } x \in \mathbb{R}^n, x(t-\tau) \in C_H.
\end{aligned}
$$

Theorem 1. *The zero solution of the system of FrRIDEs in Equation (5) with Caputo derivative is uniformly stable if the conditions of Hypotheses 1–3 hold.*

Proof. We define a Lyapunov function $W := W(t,x) = W(t,x(t))$ by

$$
W(t,x) := \|x\| = \sum_{i=1}^{n} |x_i| = |x_1| + \ldots + |x_n|. \tag{6}
$$

For arbitrary initial data $(t_0, \phi) \in \mathbb{R}^+ \times C([-\tau, 0] \cup [-\rho, 0], \mathbb{R}^n)$ and a point $t > t_0$, it follows that $W(t, x)$ satisfies the Razumikhin condition (see [28–30])

$$W(t, x(t)) > W(t+s, x(t+s))$$

on the initial set $[-\tau, 0] \cup [-\rho, 0]$, i.e.,

$$\|x(t)\| > \|x(t+s)\| \text{ for all } s \in [-\tau, 0] \cup [-\rho, 0].$$

Let $x(t) = x(t, t_0, \phi)$ denote the solution of the IVP of Equation (5) such that $x(t_0^+ + s) = \phi(s)$ for $s \in [-\tau, 0] \cup [-\rho, 0]$. From this point, it is clear that $W(t, x)$ in Equation (6) satisfies the relations

$$W(t, 0) = 0, \frac{1}{2}|x_1| + ... + \frac{1}{2}|x_n| = \frac{1}{2}\|x\| \leq W(t, x),$$

and

$$W(t, x) \leq \frac{5}{4}|x_1| + ... + \frac{5}{4}|x_n| = \frac{5}{4}\|x\|.$$

Taking the Caputo fractional derivative of the Lyapunov function $W(t, x)$ in Equation (6) along the system of FrRIDEs in Equation (5), making use the conditions of Hypotheses 1 and 2 and some elementary calculations, we obtain

$$\begin{aligned}
{}_{t_0}^{C}D_t^q W(t, x(t)) =& {}_{t_0}^{C}D_t^q(|x_1(t)| + |x_2(t)| + ... + |x_n(t)|) \\
=& {}_{t_0}^{C}D_t^q|x_1(t)| + {}_{t_0}^{C}D_t^q|x_2(t)| + ... + {}_{t_0}^{C}D_t^q|x_n(t)| \\
=& (sign x_1(t)){}_{t_0}^{C}D_t^q x_1(t) + (sign x_2(t)){}_{t_0}^{C}D_t^q x_2(t) + ... + (sign x_n(t)){}_{t_0}^{C}D_t^q x_n(t) \\
=& \sum_{i=1}^{n} x_i(t){}_{t_0}^{C}D_t^q x_i(t) \\
=& \sum_{i=1}^{n} x_i(t)[-f_i(t, x(t)) + g_i(t, x(t), x(t-\tau))] \\
&+ \sum_{i=1}^{n} x_i(t)[\int_{t-\tau}^{t} h_i(t, s, x(s))ds + \int_{t-\rho}^{t} p_i(t, s, x(s))ds] \\
\leq& \sum_{i=1}^{n} [-|f_i(t, x(t))| + |g_i(t, x(t), x(t-\tau))|] \\
&+ \sum_{i=1}^{n} [\int_{t-\tau}^{t} |h_i(t, s, x(s))|ds + \int_{t-\rho}^{t} |p_i(t, s, x(s))|ds] \\
=& -\|f(t, x(t))\| + \|g(t, x(t), x(t-\tau))\| + \int_{t-\tau}^{t} \|h(t, s, x(s))\|ds \\
&+ \int_{t-\rho}^{t} \|p(t, s, x(s))\|ds \\
\leq& -\|f(t, x(t))\| + \|g(t, x(t), x(t-\tau))\| \\
&+ h_0 \int_{t-\tau}^{t} \|x(s)\|ds + p_0 \int_{t-\rho}^{t} \|x(s)\|ds. \qquad (7)
\end{aligned}$$

Consider the integral terms such that

$$h_0 \int_{t-\tau}^{t} \|x(s)\| ds + p_0 \int_{t-\rho}^{t} \|x(s)\| ds,$$

which are included in the inequality of Equation (7).

Letting $s - t = \xi$ gives $ds = d\xi$. Hence, for $s = t - \tau$ and $s = t$, it follows that $\xi = -\tau$ and $\xi = 0$, respectively. Similarly, by the same transformation and way, for $s = t - \rho$ and $s = t$, we have $\xi = -\rho$ and $\xi = 0$, respectively. In view of these estimates, using the Razumikhin condition on the set $s \in [-\tau, 0] \cup [-\rho, 0]$, we get

$$\begin{aligned}
h_0 \int_{t-\tau}^{t} \|x(s)\| ds + p_0 \int_{t-\rho}^{t} \|x(s)\| ds &= h_0 \int_{-\tau}^{0} \|x(t+\xi)\| d\xi + p_0 \int_{-\rho}^{0} \|x(t+\xi)\| d\xi \\
&< h_0 \int_{-\tau}^{0} \|x(t)\| d\xi + p_0 \int_{-\rho}^{0} \|x(t)\| d\xi \\
&= h_0 \|x(t)\| \int_{-\tau}^{0} d\xi + p_0 \|x(t)\| \int_{-\rho}^{0} d\xi \\
&= h_0 \tau \|x(t)\| + p_0 \rho \|x(t)\|. \qquad (8)
\end{aligned}$$

Then, from Equations (7) and (8), it follows that

$${}_{t_0}^{C}D_t^q W(t, x(t)) \leq -[\|f(t, x(t))\| - \|g(t, x(t), x(t-\tau))\| - (\tau h_0 + \rho p_0)\|x(t)\|] \leq 0, \qquad (9)$$

that is, using the condition (H3), we have

$${}_{t_0}^{C}D_t^q W(t, x(t)) \leq 0. \qquad (10)$$

Thus, from Lemma 1, the zero solution of the system of FrRIDEs in Equation (5) is uniformly stable. □

Our next result deals with the asymptotic stability of the system in Equation (5).

Theorem 2. *The zero solution of the system of FrRIDEs in Equation (5) is asymptotically stable if the conditions of Hypotheses 1, 2 and 4 hold.*

Proof. With $W(t, x)$ defined as in Equation (6), from the conditions (H1), (H2), and (H4) we easily conclude that

$$\frac{1}{2}\|x\| \leq W(t, x) \leq \frac{5}{4}\|x\|$$

and

$${}_{t_0}^{C}D_t^q W(t, x(t)) \leq -\rho_1 \|x(t)\|.$$

Hence, the zero solution of the system of FrRIDEs in Equation (5) is asymptotically stable by Lemma 2. □

The following theorem shows the Mittag–Leffler stability of the system FrRIDEs in Equation (5).

Theorem 3. *The zero solution of the system of FrRIDEs in Equation (5) is Mittag–Leffler stable if the conditions of Hypotheses 1, 2 and 4 hold*

Proof. Again with the Lyapunov function $W(t,x)$ defined as in Equation (6), from the conditions of Hypotheses 1, 2 and 4, it is clear that

$$ {}_{t_o}^{C}D_t^q W(t,x(t)) \le -\rho_1\|x(t)\| = -\rho_1 W(t,x(t)) $$

holds.

Using Lemma 5, we obtain

$$ \begin{aligned} \|x(t)\| &= W(t,x(t)) \le W(t_0,x(t_0))E_q(-\rho_1(t-t_0)^q) \\ &= \|x(t_0)\|E_q(-\rho_1(t-t_0)^q) \\ &= \left[m(x(t_0))E_q(-\rho_1(t-t_0)^q)\right] \\ &\le \left[m(\|\phi\|_\infty)E_q(-\rho_1(t-t_0)^q)\right] \end{aligned} $$

with $m(x) = \|x(t)\|$, which is locally Lipschitz. Thus, the proof of Theorem 3 is completed by using Definition 1. □

4. Boundedness of Solutions of System in Equation (2)

We now turn our attention to the perturbed system in Equation (2).

Theorem 4. *The solutions of the system of FrRIDEs in Equation (2) are bounded if the conditions of Hypotheses 1, 2 and 5 hold.*

Proof. We again consider the Lyapunov function defined in Equation (6). Calculating the time derivative of the Lyapunov function $W(t,x)$ along the system of FrRIDEs in Equation (2) and using the conditions in Hypotheses 1, 2 and 5, we obtain

$$ \begin{aligned} {}_{t_o}^{C}D_t^q W(t,x(t)) \le &-[\|f(t,x(t))\| - \|g(t,x(t),x(t-\tau))\| - (\tau h_0 + \rho p_0)]\|x\| \\ &+ \|q(t,x,x(t-\tau),x(t-\rho))\| \\ \le &- \|f(t,x(t))\| + \|g(t,x(t),x(t-\tau))\| + (q(t) + \tau h_0 + \rho p_0)\|x\| \le 0. \end{aligned} $$

Hence, we have

$$ W(t,x(t)) \le W(t_0,\phi(t_0)). $$

As a result of this inequality, it follows that

$$ \begin{aligned} W(t,x(t)) &= \|x(t)\| = |x_1(t)| + ... + |x_n(t)| \\ &\le \|x(t_0)\| = |x_1(t_0)| + ... + |x_n(t_0)| = W(t_0,\phi(t_0)). \end{aligned} $$

Let

$$ K_0 = \|x(t_0)\| = |x_1(t_0)| + ... + |x_n(t_0)|. $$

Hence, we obtain

$$ \|x(t)\| = |x_1(t)| + ... + |x_n(t)| \le K_0 \text{ for } t \in \mathbb{R}^+. $$

Hence, it is clear that if $t \to \infty$, then $\|x(t)\| \le K_0$. This inequality completes the proof of Theorem 4. □

Remark 1. *Here, if $q = 1$, the boundedness of solutions as $t \to \infty$ was proved without using the Gronwall inequality, see Theorem 4. By this fact, we have removed some unnecessary conditions, and we can obtain some boundedness results in the literature under less restrictive conditions (see, for example, [12,13] and the bibliography therein). Here, we will not state the details of the discussions.*

We now give the following example and solve the given system using MATLAB software. In fact, the problem was solved using the 4th order Runge–Kutta method in

MATLAB. Here, the graphs of Figures 1–4 show the behaviors of paths of the solutions of Example 1 for different values of fractional order q.

Example 1. *Consider the system of nonlinear Volterra IFrRDEs with Caputo derivative of order $q \in (0,1)$:*

$$\begin{pmatrix} {}^{C}_{t_0}D^q_t x_1(t) \\ {}^{C}_{t_0}D^q_t x_2(t) \end{pmatrix} = \begin{bmatrix} 12x_1(t) + \frac{x_1(t)}{1+t^2+x_1^2(t)} \\ 12x_2(t) + \frac{x_2(t)}{1+t^2+x_2^2(t)} \end{bmatrix} + \begin{bmatrix} \frac{x_1(t)}{1+t^2+x_1^2(t-\frac{1}{10})} \\ \frac{x_2(t)}{1+t^2+x_2^2(t-\frac{1}{10})} \end{bmatrix}$$
$$+ \int_{t-\frac{1}{10}}^{t} \begin{bmatrix} \frac{\sin x_1(s)}{1+t^2+s^2+x_1^2(s)} \\ \frac{\sin x_2(s)}{1+t^2+s^2+x_2^2(s)} \end{bmatrix} ds + \int_{t-\frac{1}{5}}^{t} \begin{bmatrix} \frac{x_1(s)}{1+t^2+s^2+x_1^2(s)} \\ \frac{x_2(s)}{1+t^2+s^2+x_2^2(s)} \end{bmatrix} ds, \quad (11)$$

where $t \geq \frac{1}{10}$, $\tau = \frac{1}{10}$ and $\rho = \frac{1}{5}$ are the constant retardations and $x(t) = x \in \mathbb{R}^2$.

Comparing the system of IFrRDEs with Caputo derivative in Equation (11) with that given by Equation (5), we have the following formulas:

$$f(t,x) = f(t,x_1,x_2) = \begin{bmatrix} 12x_1 + \frac{x_1}{1+t^2+x_1^2} \\ 12x_2 + \frac{x_2}{1+t^2+x_2^2} \end{bmatrix},$$

$$f(t,0) = f(t,0,0) = 0,$$
$$f_1(t,x_1,x_2) = 12x_1 + \frac{x_1}{1+t^2+x_1^2},$$
$$x_1 f_1(t,x_1,x_2) = 12x_1^2 + \frac{x_1^2}{1+t^2+x_1^2} > 0,$$
$$x_1 \neq 0,$$
$$f_2(t,x_1,x_2) = 12x_2 + \frac{x_2}{1+t^2+x_2^2},$$
$$x_2 f_2(t,x_1,x_2) = 12x_2^2 + \frac{x_2^2}{1+t^2+x_2^2} > 0,$$
$$x_2 \neq 0,$$
$$-x_1(t+0)f_1(t,x_1,x_2) - x_2(t+0)f_2(t,x_1,x_2)$$
$$= -12x_1 sgn x_1(t+0) - \frac{x_1 sgn x_1(t+0)}{1+t^2+x_1^2}$$
$$-12x_2 sgn x_2(t+0) - \frac{x_2 sgn x_2(t+0)}{1+t^2+x_2^2}$$
$$\leq -11|x_1| - 11|x_2| = -11\|x\| \leq -\|f(t,x)\|,$$

$$g(t,x,x(t-\tau)) = g(t,x_1,x_2,x_1(t-\frac{1}{10}),x_2(t-\frac{1}{10})) = \begin{bmatrix} \frac{x_1}{1+t^2+x_1^2(t-\frac{1}{10})} \\ \frac{x_2}{1+t^2+x_2^2(t-\frac{1}{10})} \end{bmatrix},$$

$$\|g(t,x,x(t-\tau))\| = \left\|g(t,x_1,x_2,x_1(t-\frac{1}{10}),x_2(t-\frac{1}{10}))\right\| = \left\| \begin{bmatrix} \frac{x_1}{1+t^2+x_1^2(t-\frac{1}{10})} \\ \frac{x_2}{1+t^2+x_2^2(t-\frac{1}{10})} \end{bmatrix} \right\|$$
$$\leq \frac{|x_1|}{1+t^2+x_1^2(t-\frac{1}{10})} + \frac{|x_2|}{1+t^2+x_2^2(t-\frac{1}{10})}$$

$$\leq |x_1| + |x_2| = \|x\|,$$

$$h(t,s,x) = h(t,s,x_1,x_2) = \begin{bmatrix} \frac{\sin x_1}{1+t^2+s^2+x_1^2} \\ \frac{\sin x_2}{1+t^2+s^2+x_2^2} \end{bmatrix},$$

$$h(t,s,0) = h(t,s,0,0) = 0,$$

$$\|h(t,s,x)\| = \|h(t,s,x_1,x_2)\| = \left\| \begin{bmatrix} \frac{\sin x_1}{1+t^2+s^2+x_1^2} \\ \frac{\sin x_2}{1+t^2+s^2+x_2^2} \end{bmatrix} \right\|$$

$$= \frac{|\sin x_1|}{1+t^2+s^2+x_1^2} + \frac{|\sin x_2|}{1+t^2+s^2+x_2^2}$$

$$\leq |\sin x_1| + |\sin x_2| \leq |x_1| + |x_2| = \|x\|,$$

where $h_0 = 1$,

$$H(t,s,x) \equiv \int_{t-\tau}^{t} \|h(t,s,x(s))\| ds = \int_{t-\frac{1}{10}}^{t} \left\| \begin{bmatrix} \frac{\sin x_1(s)}{1+t^2+s^2+x_1^2(s)} \\ \frac{\sin x_2(s)}{1+t^2+s^2+x_2^2(s)} \end{bmatrix} \right\| ds$$

$$= \int_{t-\frac{1}{10}}^{t} \frac{|\sin x_1(s)|}{1+t^2+s^2+x_1^2(s)} ds$$

$$+ \int_{t-\frac{1}{10}}^{t} \frac{|\sin x_2(s)|}{1+t^2+s^2+x_2^2(s)} ds$$

$$\leq \int_{t-\frac{1}{10}}^{t} |\sin x_1(s)| ds + \int_{t-\frac{1}{10}}^{t} |\sin x_2(s)| ds$$

$$\leq \int_{t-\frac{1}{10}}^{t} |x_1(s)| ds + \int_{t-\frac{1}{10}}^{t} |x_2(s)| ds = \int_{t-\frac{1}{10}}^{t} \|x(s)\| ds.$$

Let $s - t = \xi$, which implies $ds = d\xi$. Then, for $s = t - \frac{1}{10}$, we derive $\xi = -\frac{1}{10}$, and similarly for $s = t$, we have $\xi = 0$.

In view of these findings, using the given Razumikhin condition [28–30] on the initial segment $[-\frac{1}{10}, 0]$, it follows that

$$\int_{t-\frac{1}{10}}^{t} \|x(s)\| ds = \int_{-\frac{1}{10}}^{0} \|x(t+\xi)\| d\xi < \int_{-\frac{1}{10}}^{0} \|x(t)\| d\xi = \frac{1}{10}\|x\|.$$

For this step, we consider the term:

$$P(t,s,x) \equiv \int_{t-\rho}^{t} \|p(t,s,x(s))\| ds$$

with

$$p(t,s,x) = p(t,s,x_1,x_2) = \begin{bmatrix} \frac{x_1}{1+t^2+s^2+x_1^2} \\ \frac{x_2}{1+t^2+s^2+x_2^2} \end{bmatrix}, \rho = \frac{1}{5}.$$

In that case, we derive

$$p(t,s,0,0) = 0$$

and

$$\|p(t,s,x)\| = \|p(t,s,x_1,x_2)\| = \left\| \begin{bmatrix} \frac{x_1}{1+t^2+s^2+x_1^2} \\ \frac{x_2}{1+t^2+s^2+x_2^2} \end{bmatrix} \right\|$$

$$= \frac{|x_1|}{1+t^2+s^2+x_1^2} + \frac{|x_2|}{1+t^2+s^2+x_2^2}$$

$$\leq |x_1| + |x_2| = \|x\|, \text{ where } p_0 = 1.$$

For the next step, it follows that

$$P(t,s,x) \equiv \int_{t-\rho}^{t} \|p(t,s,x(s))\| ds = \int_{t-\frac{1}{5}}^{t} \left\| \begin{bmatrix} \frac{x_1(s)}{1+t^2+s^2+x_1^2(s)} \\ \frac{x_2(s)}{1+t^2+s^2+x_2^2(s)} \end{bmatrix} \right\| ds$$

$$\leq \int_{t-\frac{1}{5}}^{t} |x_1(s)| ds + \int_{t-\frac{1}{5}}^{t} |x_2(s)| ds = \int_{t-\frac{1}{5}}^{t} \|x(s)\| ds.$$

Let $s - t = \xi$, which implies $ds = d\xi$. Then, for $s = t - \frac{1}{5}$, we derive $\xi = -\frac{1}{5}$. Similarly, for $s = t$, we have $\xi = 0$. Then,

$$\int_{t-\frac{1}{5}}^{t} \|x(s)\| ds = \int_{-\frac{1}{5}}^{0} \|x(t+\xi)\| d\xi < \int_{-\frac{1}{5}}^{0} \|x(t)\| d\xi = \frac{1}{5}\|x\|.$$

Hence, bringing together the above results, we derive

$$\begin{aligned} &\|f(t,x)\| - \|g(t,x,x(t-\tau))\| - (\tau h_0 + \rho p_0)\|x\| \\ &\geq \|f(t,x)\| - \left\| g(t,x,x(t-\frac{1}{2})) \right\| - (\frac{1}{10} + \frac{1}{5})\|x\| \\ &\geq 11\|x\| - \|x\| - \frac{3}{10}\|x\| = (9.7)\|x\|, \text{ where } \rho_1 = \frac{97}{10}. \end{aligned} \tag{12}$$

In the light of the above discussion, the conditions of Hypotheses 1–3 of Theorem 1, and the conditions of Hypotheses 1, 2 and 4 of Theorems 2 and 3 hold. For this reason, the zero solution of the system of FrRIDEs in Equation (11) with Caputo derivative is uniformly stable, asymptotically stable and Mittag–Leffler stable.

In Figures 1–4, the system of FrRIDEs (11) was solved and the orbits of the solutions $x_1(t)$, $x_2(t)$ were drawn for $\tau = \frac{1}{10}$, $\rho = \frac{1}{5}$ and different initial values when $t \geq \frac{1}{10}$.

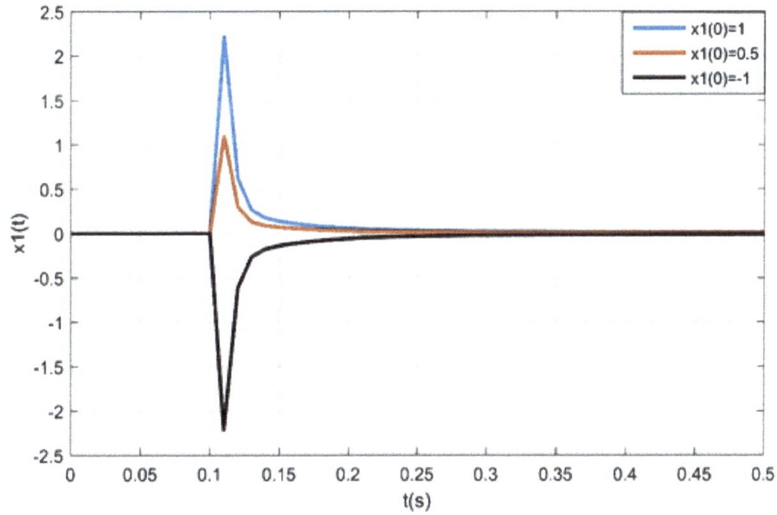

Figure 1. The behaviors of uniformly, asymptotically and Mittag–Leffler stable solution $x_1(t)$ of the system of of fractional retarded Volterra integro-differential equations (FrRIDEs) in Equation (11) for $q = 0.5$, $\tau = \frac{1}{10}$, $\rho = \frac{1}{5}$ and different initial values when $t \geq \frac{1}{10}$.

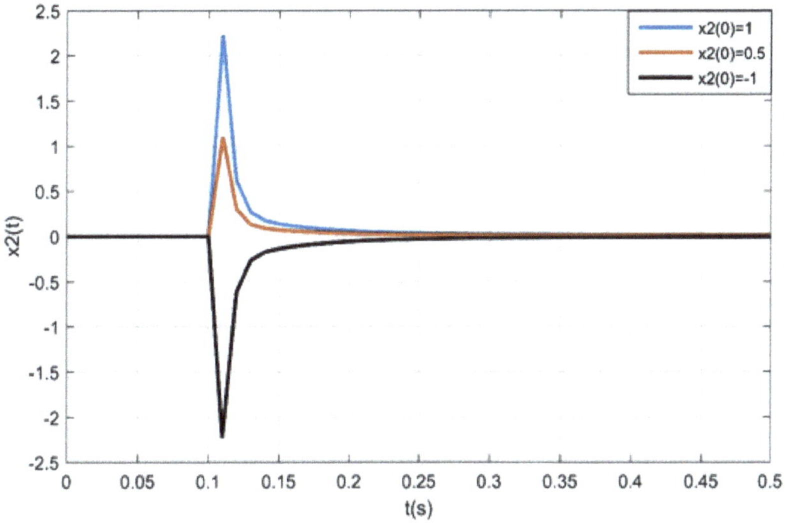

Figure 2. The behaviors of uniformly, asymptotically and Mittag–Leffler stable solution $x_2(t)$ of the system of of FrRIDEs in Equation (11) for $q = 0.5$, $\tau = \frac{1}{10}$, $\rho = \frac{1}{5}$ and different initial values when $t \geq \frac{1}{10}$.

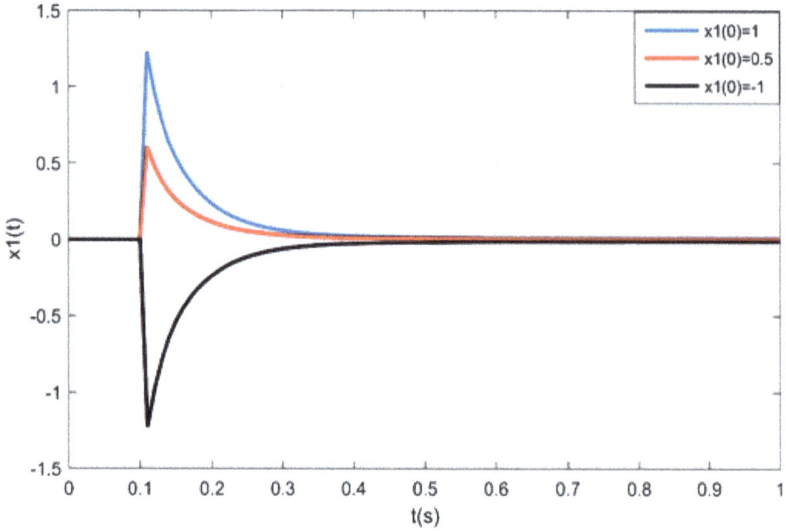

Figure 3. The behaviors of uniformly, asymptotically and Mittag–Leffler stable solution $x_1(t)$ of the system of of FrRIDEs in Equation (11) for $q = 0.9$, $\tau = \frac{1}{10}$, $\rho = \frac{1}{5}$ and different initial values when $t \geq \frac{1}{10}$.

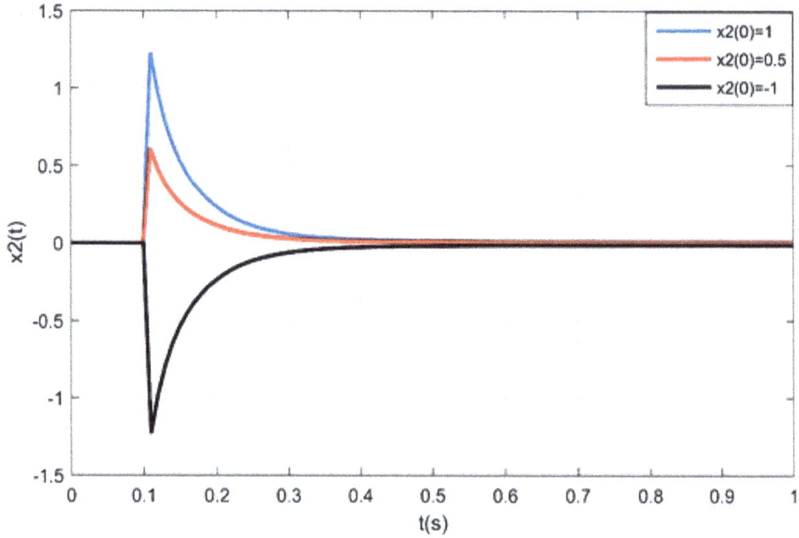

Figure 4. The behaviors of uniformly, asymptotically and Mittag–Leffler stable solution $x_2(t)$ of the system of of FrRIDEs in Equation (11) for $q = 0.9$, $\tau = \frac{1}{10}$, $\rho = \frac{1}{5}$ and different initial values and different initial values when $t \geq \frac{1}{10}$.

For the case $q(.) \neq 0$, we now give the second example and solve it using MATLAB software.

Example 2. *Consider the system of nonlinear Volterra FrRIDEs with Caputo derivative of order $q \in (0,1)$:*

$$\begin{pmatrix} {}^{C}_{t_0}D^q_t x_1(t) \\ {}^{C}_{t_0}D^q_t x_2(t) \end{pmatrix} = \begin{bmatrix} 12x_1(t) + \frac{x_1(t)}{1+t^2+x_1^2(t)} \\ 12x_2(t) + \frac{x_2(t)}{1+t^2+x_2^2(t)} \end{bmatrix} + \begin{bmatrix} \frac{x_1(t)}{1+t^2+x_1^2(t-\frac{1}{10})} \\ \frac{x_2(t)}{1+t^2+x_2^2(t-\frac{1}{10})} \end{bmatrix}$$
$$+ \int_{t-\frac{1}{10}}^{t} \begin{bmatrix} \frac{\sin x_1(s)}{1+t^2+s^2+x_1^2(s)} \\ \frac{\sin x_2(s)}{1+t^2+s^2+x_2^2(s)} \end{bmatrix} ds + \int_{t-\frac{1}{5}}^{t} \begin{bmatrix} \frac{x_1(s)}{1+t^2+s^2+x_1^2(s)} \\ \frac{x_2(s)}{1+t^2+s^2+x_2^2(s)} \end{bmatrix} ds$$
$$+ \begin{pmatrix} \frac{\exp(t)x_1}{1+\exp(2t)+|x_1(t-\frac{1}{10})|+|x_1(t-\frac{1}{5})|} \\ \frac{\exp(t)x_2}{1+\exp(2t)+|x_2(t-\frac{1}{10})|+|x_2(t-\frac{1}{5})|} \end{pmatrix}, \tag{13}$$

where $t \geq \frac{1}{10}$, $\tau = \frac{1}{10}$ and $\rho = \frac{1}{5}$ are the constant delay terms and $x(t) = x \in \mathbb{R}^2$.

Comparing the systems of FrRIDEs in Equation (13) with Caputo derivative and Equation (2), we note that the functions $-f(t,x)$, $g(t,x,x(t-\frac{1}{10}))$, $h(t,s,x)$ and $p(t,s,x)$ are the same as those in Example 1. Then, the satisfaction of the conditions of Hypotheses 1 and 2 have been shown in Example 1. For the verification of the condition of Hypothesis 5, we consider the last term of Equation (13):

$$q(t,x,x(t-\frac{1}{10}),x(t-\frac{1}{5})) = \begin{pmatrix} \frac{\exp(t)x_1}{1+\exp(2t)+|x_1(t-\frac{1}{10})|+|x_1(t-\frac{1}{5})|} \\ \frac{\exp(t)x_2}{1+\exp(2t)+|x_2(t-\frac{1}{10})|+|x_2(t-\frac{1}{5})|} \end{pmatrix}$$

Clearly, it follows that

$$\begin{aligned} \left|q(t,x,x(t-\frac{1}{10}),x(t-\frac{1}{5}))\right| &= \left|\begin{pmatrix} \frac{\exp(t)x_1}{1+\exp(2t)+|x_1(t-\frac{1}{10})|+|x_1(t-\frac{1}{5})|} \\ \frac{\exp(t)x_2}{1+\exp(2t)+|x_2(t-\frac{1}{10})|+|x_2(t-\frac{1}{5})|} \end{pmatrix}\right| \\ &= \frac{\exp(t)|x_1|}{1+\exp(2t)+\left|x_1(t-\frac{1}{10})\right|+\left|x_1(t-\frac{1}{5})\right|} \\ &\quad + \frac{\exp(t)|x_2|}{1+\exp(2t)+\left|x_2(t-\frac{1}{10})\right|+\left|x_2(t-\frac{1}{5})\right|} \\ &\leq \frac{\exp(t)|x_1|}{1+\exp(2t)} + \frac{\exp(t)|x_2|}{1+\exp(2t)} \\ &= \frac{\exp(t)}{1+\exp(2t)}[|x_1|+|x_2|] = |q_0(t)|\|x\|, \end{aligned}$$

where

$$|q_0(t)| = \frac{\exp(t)}{1+\exp(2t)} \leq \frac{1}{2}, |x_1|+|x_2| = \|x\|. \tag{14}$$

In view of Equations (12) and (14), it is clear that

$$\begin{aligned} \|f(t,x)\| - \|g(t,x,x(t-\tau))\| - (q_0(t)+\tau h_0+\rho p_0)\|x\| &\geq (9.7)\|x\| - \frac{\exp(t)}{1+\exp(2t)}\|x\| \\ &\geq (9.7)\|x\| - \frac{1}{2}\|x\| = (9.2)\|x\|. \end{aligned}$$

As a consequence of this inequality, the condition of Hypothesis 5 holds. Thus, the solutions of the system of FrRIDEs in Equation (13) with Caputo derivative are bounded as $t \to \infty$.

The following graphs of Figures 5–8 show the behaviors of paths of the solutions of Example 2 for different values of fractional order q.

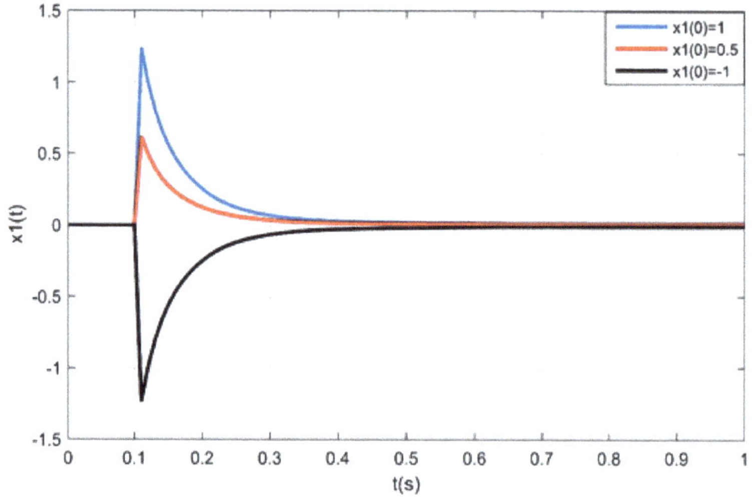

Figure 5. The boundedness of solution $x_1(t)$ of the system of IFrRDEs in Equation (13) for $q = 0.5$, $\tau = \frac{1}{10}$, $\rho = \frac{1}{5}$ and different initial values when $t \geq \frac{1}{10}$.

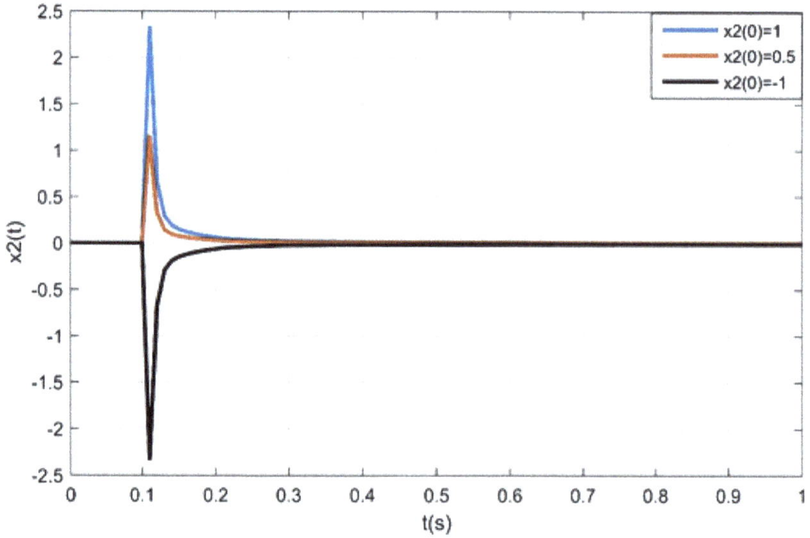

Figure 6. The boundedness of solution $x_2(t)$ of the system of IFrRDEs in Equation (13) for $q = 0.5$, $\tau = \frac{1}{10}$, $\rho = \frac{1}{5}$ and different initial values when $t \geq \frac{1}{10}$.

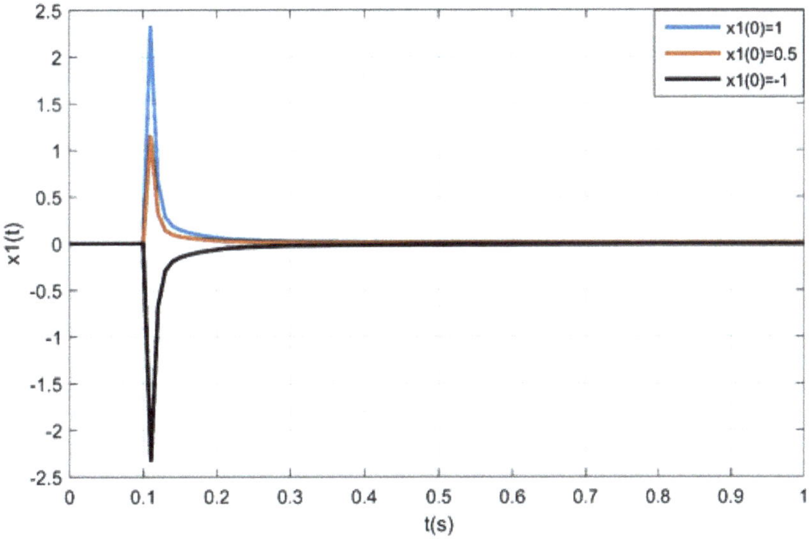

Figure 7. The boundedness of solution $x_1(t)$ of the system of IFrRDEs in Equation (13) for $q = 0.9$, $\tau = \frac{1}{10}$, $\rho = \frac{1}{5}$ and different initial values when $t \geq \frac{1}{10}$.

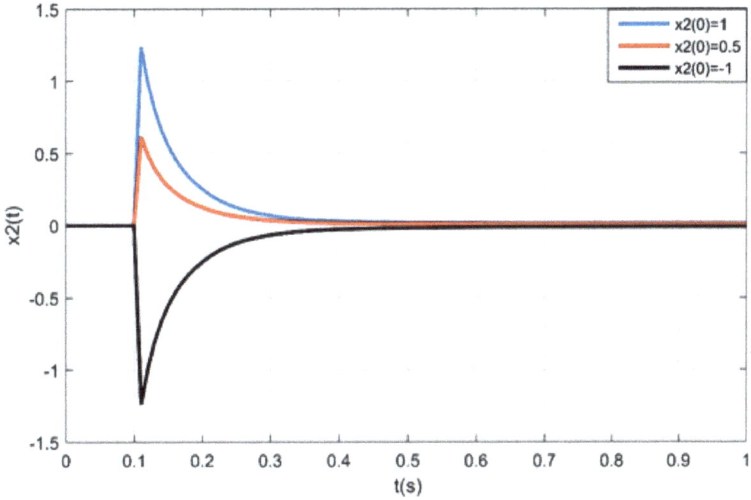

Figure 8. The boundedness of solution $x_2(t)$ of the system of IFrRDEs in Equation (13) for $q = 0.5$, $\tau = \frac{1}{10}$, $\rho = \frac{1}{5}$ and different initial values when $t \geq \frac{1}{10}$.

5. Discussions

We would like to explain the contributions of this paper to the relevant literature as the following.

(1) To the best of our knowledge, in the literature, there are numerous papers on the uniform stability, asymptotic stability, Mittag–Leffer stability and boundedness of fractional differential equations of integer order both with and without delay. However, there are no papers in the literature on the asymptotic stability, Mittag–Leffer stability and boundedness of the FrRIDEs in Equation (2) with Caputo fractional derivative, except the two papers of Hristova and Tunç [25,26], which include some results on

the uniform stability. Next, qualitative behaviors of the FrRIDEs in Equation (2) have not been discussed in the literature yet. Therefore, the results of this paper are new, original and they have scientific novelty.

(2) If $q = 1$ in the FrRIDEs in Equation (2), then we have the system of RIDEs

$$\dot{x}(t) = -f(t, x(t)) + g(t, x(t), x(t-\tau)) + \int_{t-\tau}^{t} h(t, s, x(s))ds$$
$$+ \int_{t-\rho}^{t} p(t, s, x(s))ds + q(t, x(t), x(t-\tau), x(t-\rho)). \tag{15}$$

It is clear that the system of RIDEs in Equation (15) includes, extends and improves the system of RIDEs in Equation (1). This is a contribution to the topic and the relevant literature.

(3) In Du [27] (Theorem 4), the uniform asymptotic stability of the zero solution of the system of RIDEs in Equation (1) was proved using the Lyapunov–Krasovskiĭ functional:

$$V(t, x(.)) := \|x\| + \int_{t-\tau}^{t} \|g(s, x(s))\|ds + \int_{t-\tau}^{t}\int_{t}^{\infty} \|h(u, s, x(s))\|duds.$$

We can prove the same result, [27] (Theorem 4) using the Lyapunov-Razumikhin method and the Lyapunov function

$$W(t, x) := \|x\| = \sum_{i=1}^{n} |x_i| = |x_1| + ... + |x_n|.$$

Clearly, this Lyapunov function does not include the term $\int_{t-\tau}^{t} \|g(s, x(s))\|ds$. The time derivative of this term gives

$$\frac{d}{dt}\int_{t-\tau}^{t} \|g(s, x(s))\|ds = \|g(t, x(t))\| - \|g(t-\tau, x(t-\tau))\|.$$

Based on this approach, we can obtain the result of Du [27] (Theorem 4) under weaker conditions. Namely, we remove the following hypothesis from Du [27] (Theorem 4):

$$\|g(t-\tau, x(t-\tau))\| - \|g(t, x(t-\tau))\| \geq 0, t \in \mathbb{R}^{+}.$$

To the best of our information, this is a stronger condition and the satisfaction of this hypothesis can be difficult. Removing this condition from that of Du [27] (Theorem 4) leads to an important and strong advantage during the applications of that kind of equation.

(4) Du [27] (Theorem 4) proved the related theorem without giving an example in a particular case, which verifies the hypotheses of [27] (Theorem 4). In this paper, we provided two examples and solved them with MATLAB software, which verifies the applicability of the results of this paper.

6. Conclusions

This paper has proposed an effective way to discuss some qualitative properties of solutions of nonlinear Volterra integro-differential equations with Caputo fractional derivatives and multiple constant retardations. Here, a new mathematical model consisting of non-linear fractional Volterra integro-differential equations with Caputo fractional derivatives and two constant retardations was considered. New sufficient conditions for the uniform stability, asymptotic stability and Mittag–Leffer stability of the zero solution, as well as the boundedness of the solutions were obtained. The presented results were proved by defining an appropriate Lyapunov function and applying the Lyapunov–Razumikhin method. An advantage of the new function and method used here is that they eliminate using Gronwall's inequality. Compared to related results in the literature, the conditions here are new, more general, simple and convenient to apply. Examples to show the application of the theorems have been included.

Author Contributions: Investigation, O.T., Ö.A., C.T. and J.-C.Y. Writing—Original Draft: O.T., Ö.A., C.T. and J.-C.Y. All authors have read andagreed to the published version of the manuscript.

Funding: The research of J. C. Yao was partially supported by the Grant MOST 108-2115-M-039-005-MY3.

Institutional Review Board Statement: Not applicable.

Informed Consent Statement: Not applicable.

Data Availability Statement: Not applicable.

Acknowledgments: The authors would like to thank the three anonymous referees and the handling for many useful comments and suggestions, leading to a substantial improvement in the presentation of this article.

Conflicts of Interest: The authors declare no conflict of interest.

References

1. Burton, T.A. Volterra integral and differential equations. In *Mathematics in Science and Engineering*, 2nd ed.; Elsevier: Amsterdam, The Netherlands, 2005; p. 202.
2. Rahman, M. *Integral Equations and Their Applications*; WIT Press: Southampton, UK, 2007.
3. Wazwaz, A.M. Linear and nonlinear integral equations. In *Methods and Applications*; Higher Education Press: Beijing, China; Springer: Heidelberg, Germany, 2011.
4. Alahmadi, F.; Raffoul, Y.; Alharbi, S. Boundedness and stability of solutions of nonlinear Volterra integro-differential equations. *Adv. Dyn. Syst. Appl.* **2018**, *13*, 19–31.
5. Andreev, A.S.; Peregudova, O.A. On the stability and stabilization problems of Volterra integro-differential equations. *Russ. J. Nonlinear Dyn.* **2018**, *14*, 387–407. [CrossRef]
6. Berezansky, L.; Domoshnitsky, A. On stability of a second order integro-differential equation. *Nonlinear Dyn. Syst. Theory* **2019**, *19*, 117–123.
7. Chang, Y.-K.; Ponce, R. Uniform exponential stability and applications to bounded solutions of integro-differential equations in Banach spaces. *J. Integr. Equ. Appl.* **2018**, *30*, 347–369. [CrossRef]
8. Anh, N.P.H.; Tran, A. The New stability criteria for nonlinear Volterra integro-differential equations. *Acta Math. Vietnam.* **2018**, *43*, 485–501.
9. Raffoul, Y.; Rai, H. Uniform stability in nonlinear infinite delay Volterra integro-differential equations using Lyapunov functionals. *Nonauton. Dyn. Syst.* **2016**, *3*, 14–23. [CrossRef]
10. Tunç, C. Properties of solutions to Volterra integro-differential equations with delay. *Appl. Math. Inf. Sci.* **2016**, *10*, 1775–1780. [CrossRef]
11. Tunç, C. Qualitative properties in nonlinear Volterra integro-differential equations with delay. *J. Taibah Univ. Sci.* **2017**, *11*, 309–314. [CrossRef]
12. Tunç, C. Asymptotic stability and boundedness criteria for nonlinear retarded Volterra integro-differential equations. *J. King Saud Univ. Sci.* **2016**, *30*, 3531–3536. [CrossRef]
13. Tunç, C. Stability and boundedness in Volterra-integro differential equations with delays. *Dyn. Syst. Appl.* **2017**, *26*, 121–130.
14. Tunç, O. On the qualitative analyses of integro-differential equations with constant time lag. *Appl. Math. Inf. Sci.* **2020**, *14*, 57–63.
15. Tunç, C.; Tunç, O. New results on the stability, integrability and boundedness in Volterra integro-differential equations. *Bull. Comput. Appl. Math.* **2018**, *6*, 41–58.
16. Tunç, C.; Tunç, O. New qualitative criteria for solutions of Volterra integro-differential equations. *Arab J. Basic Appl. Sci.* **2018**, *25*, 158–165. [CrossRef]
17. Tunç, C.; Tunç, O. A note on the qualitative analysis of Volterra integro-differential equations. *J. Taibah Univ. Sci.* **2019**, *13*, 490–496.
18. Vasundhara, D.J.; Mc Rae, F.A.; Drici, Z. Variational Lyapunov method for fractional differential equations. *Comput. Math. Appl.* **2012**, *64*, 2982–2989.
19. Wang, K. Uniform asymptotic stability in functional-differential equations with infinite delay. *Ann. Differ. Equ.* **1993**, *9*, 325–335.

20. Wang , Q. The stability of a class of functional differential equations with infinite delays. *Ann. Differ. Equ.* **2000**, *16*, 89–97.
21. Wang, Y.; Li, T. Stability analysis of fractional-order nonlinear systems with delay. *Math. Probl. Eng.* **2014**. [CrossRef]
22. Wen, Y.; Zhou, X.F. Zhang, Z.; Liu, S., Lyapunov method for nonlinear fractional differential systems with delay. *Nonlinear Dyn.* **2015**, *82*, 1015–1025. [CrossRef]
23. Zhou, B. Egorov, A.V. Razumikhin and Krasovskii stability theorems for time-varying time-delay systems. *Autom. J. IFAC* **2016**, *71*, 281–291. [CrossRef]
24. Agarwal, R.; Bohner, M.; Domoshnitsky, A.; Goltser, Y. Floquet theory and stability of nonlinear integro-differential equations. *Acta Math. Hung.* **2005**, *109*, 305–330. [CrossRef]
25. Hristova, S.; Tunç, C. Stability of nonlinear Volterra integro-differential equations with Caputo fractional derivative and bounded delays. *Electron. J. Differ. Equ.* **2019**, *30*, 11.
26. Hristova, S.; Tunç, C. On the stability properties of retarded Volterra integro-fractional differential equations with Caputo derivative. *AIP Conf. Proc.* **2021**, *2321*, 030013.
27. Du, X.T. Some kinds of Liapunov functional in stability theory of RFDE. *Acta Math. Appl. Sin.* **1995**, *11*, 214–224. [CrossRef]
28. Hale, J.K.; Verduyn Lunel, S.M. Introduction to functional-differential equations. In *Applied Mathematical Sciences*; Springer: New York, NY, USA, 1993; p. 99.
29. Razumihin, B.S. On stability of systems with retardation. *Russ. Prikl. Mat. Meh.* **1956**, *20*, 500–512.
30. Razumihin, B.S. The application of Lyapunov's method to problems in the stability of systems with delay. *Automat. Remote Control* **1960**, *21*, 515–520.
31. Agarwal, R.; Hristova, S.; O'Regan, D. Lyapunov functions and stability of Caputo fractional differential equations with delays. *Differ. Equ. Dyn. Syst.* **2020**, in press. [CrossRef]
32. Agarwal, R.; O'Regan, D.; Hristova, S. Stability of Caputo fractional differential equations by Lyapunov functions. *Appl. Math.* **2015**, *60*, 653–676. [CrossRef]
33. Hu, J.-B.; Lu, G.-P.; Zhang, S.-B.; Zhao, L.-D. Lyapunov stability theorem about fractional system without and with delay. *Commun. Nonlinear Sci. Numer. Simul.* **2015**, *20*, 905–913. [CrossRef]
34. Li, Y.; Chen, Y.Q.; Podlubny, I. Stability of fractional-order nonlinear dynamic systems: Lyapunov direct method and generalized Mittag-Leffler stability. *Comput. Math. Appl.* **2010**, *59*, 1810–1821. [CrossRef]
35. Liu, S.; Jiang, W.; Li, X.; Zhou, X.-F. Lyapunov stability analysis of fractional nonlinear systems. *Appl. Math. Lett.* **2016**, *51*, 13–19. [CrossRef]
36. Noeiaghdam, S.; Sidorov, D. Caputo-Fabrizio fractional derivative to solve the fractional model of energy supply-demand System. *Math. Model. Eng. Probl.* **2020**, *7*, 359–367. [CrossRef]
37. Podlubny, I. Fractional differential equations. An introduction to fractional derivatives, fractional differential equations, to methods of their solution and some of their applications. In *Mathematics in Science and Engineering;* Academic Press, Inc.: San Diego, CA, USA, 1999; p. 198.
38. Duarte-Mermoud, M.A.; Aguila-Camacho, N.; Gallegos, J.A.; Castro-Linares, R. Using general quadratic Lyapunov functions to prove Lyapunov uniform stability for fractional order systems. *Commun. Nonlinear Sci. Numer. Simul.* **2015**, *22*, 650–659. [CrossRef]

axioms

Article

Mann-Type Inertial Subgradient Extragradient Rules for Variational Inequalities and Common Fixed Points of Nonexpansive and Quasi-Nonexpansive Mappings

Lu-Chuan Ceng [1] and Jen-Chih Yao [2,*]

[1] Department of Mathematics, Shanghai Normal University, Shanghai 200234, China; zenglc@shnu.edu.cn
[2] Research Center for Interneural Computing, China Medical University Hospital, China Medical University, Taichung 40402, Taiwan
* Correspondence: yaojc@mail.cmu.edu.tw

Abstract: Suppose that in a real Hilbert space H, the variational inequality problem with Lipschitzian and pseudomonotone mapping A and the common fixed-point problem of a finite family of nonexpansive mappings and a quasi-nonexpansive mapping with a demiclosedness property are represented by the notations VIP and CFPP, respectively. In this article, we suggest two Mann-type inertial subgradient extragradient iterations for finding a common solution of the VIP and CFPP. Our iterative schemes require only calculating one projection onto the feasible set for every iteration, and the strong convergence theorems are established without the assumption of sequentially weak continuity for A. Finally, in order to support the applicability and implementability of our algorithms, we make use of our main results to solve the VIP and CFPP in two illustrating examples.

Keywords: Mann-type inertial subgradient extragradient rule; variational inequality problem; pseudomonotone mapping; Nonexpansive and quasi-nonexpansive mappings; common fixed point

MSC: 47H09; 47H10; 47J20; 47J25

Citation: Ceng, L.-C.; Yao, J.-C. Mann-Type Inertial Subgradient Extragradient Rules for Variational Inequalities and Common Fixed Points of Nonexpansive and Quasi-Nonexpansive Mappings. *Axioms* **2021**, *10*, 67. https://doi.org/10.3390/axioms10020067

Academic Editor: Alexander Šostak

Received: 16 March 2021
Accepted: 15 April 2021
Published: 19 April 2021

Publisher's Note: MDPI stays neutral with regard to jurisdictional claims in published maps and institutional affiliations.

Copyright: © 2021 by the authors. Licensee MDPI, Basel, Switzerland. This article is an open access article distributed under the terms and conditions of the Creative Commons Attribution (CC BY) license (https://creativecommons.org/licenses/by/4.0/).

1. Introduction

In a real Hilbert space $(H, \|\cdot\|)$, equipped with the inner product $\langle\cdot,\cdot\rangle$, we assume that C is a nonempty closed convex subset and P_C is the metric projection of H onto C. If $S : C \to H$ is a mapping on C, then we denote by $\mathrm{Fix}(S)$ the fixed-point set of S. Moreover, we denote by $\mathbf{R}$ the set of all real numbers. Given a mapping $A : H \to H$. Consider the classical variational inequality problem (VIP) of finding $x^* \in C$ such that $\langle Ax^*, x - x^*\rangle \geq 0$ for all $x \in C$. We denote by VI(C, A) the solution set of the VIP.

To the best of our knowledge, one of the most efficient methods to deal with the VIP is the extragradient method invented by Korpelevich [1] in 1976, that is, for any given $u_0 \in C$, $\{u_m\}$ is the sequence constructed by

$$\begin{cases} v_m = P_C(u_m - \ell A u_m), \\ u_{m+1} = P_C(u_m - \ell A v_m) \quad \forall m \geq 0, \end{cases} \tag{1}$$

with constant $\ell \in (0, \frac{1}{L})$. If VI$(C, A) \neq \emptyset$, one knows that this method has only weak convergence, and only requires that A is monotone and L-Lipschitzian. The literature on the VIP is vast, and Korpelevich's extragradient method has received great attention from many authors, who improved it via various approaches so that some new iterative methods happen to solve the VIP and related optimization problems; see, e.g., [2–12] and the references therein, to name but a few.

It is worth pointing out that the extragradient method needs to calculate two projections onto the feasible set C per iteration. Without question, once one is hard to calculate the projection onto C, the minimum distance problem has to be solved twice per iteration. This perhaps affects the applicability and implementability of the method. To improve Algorithm 1, one has to reduce the number of projections per iteration. In 2011, Censor et al. [13] first suggested the subgradient extragradient method, in which the second projection onto C is replaced by a projection onto a half-space:

$$\begin{cases} v_m = P_C(u_m - \ell A u_m), \\ C_m = \{w \in H : \langle u_m - \ell A u_m - v_m, w - v_m \rangle \le 0\}, \\ u_{m+1} = P_{C_m}(u_m - \ell A v_m) \quad \forall m \ge 0, \end{cases} \tag{2}$$

where A is a L-Lipschitzian monotone mapping and $\ell \in (0, \frac{1}{L})$.

Since then, various modified extragradient-like iterative methods have been investigated by many researchers; see, e.g., [14–19]. In 2014, combining the subgradient extragradient method and Halpern's iteration method, Kraikaew and Saejung [20] proposed the Halpern subgradient extragradient method for solving the VIP, that is, for any given $u_0 \in H$, $\{u_m\}$ is the sequence constructed by

$$\begin{cases} v_m = P_C(u_m - \ell A u_m), \\ C_m = \{v \in H : \langle u_m - \ell A u_m - v_m, v - v_m \rangle \le 0\}, \\ w_m = P_{C_m}(u_m - \ell A v_m), \\ u_{m+1} = \alpha_m u_0 + (1 - \alpha_m) w_m \quad \forall m \ge 0, \end{cases} \tag{3}$$

where $\ell \in (0, \frac{1}{L})$, $\{\alpha_m\} \subset (0,1)$, $\lim_{m\to\infty} \alpha_m = 0$ and $\sum_{m=1}^{\infty} \alpha_m = +\infty$. They proved the strong convergence of $\{u_m\}$ to $P_{\mathrm{VI}(C,A)} u_0$.

In 2018, Thong and Hieu [21] first suggested the inertial subgradient extragradient method, that is, for any given $u_0, u_1 \in H$, the sequence $\{u_m\}$ is generated by

$$\begin{cases} w_m = u_m + \alpha_m(u_m - u_{m-1}), \\ v_m = P_C(w_m - \ell A w_m), \\ C_m = \{v \in H : \langle w_m - \ell A w_m - v_m, v - v_m \rangle \le 0\}, \\ u_{m+1} = P_{C_m}(w_m - \ell A v_m) \quad \forall m \ge 1, \end{cases} \tag{4}$$

with constant $\ell \in (0, \frac{1}{L})$. Under suitable conditions, they proved the weak convergence of $\{u_m\}$ to an element of $\mathrm{VI}(C, A)$. Later, Thong and Hieu [22] designed two inertial subgradient extragradient algorithms with linesearch process for solving a VIP with monotone and Lipschitz continuous mapping A and a FPP of quasi-nonexpansive mapping T with a demiclosedness property in H. Under appropriate conditions, they established the weak convergence results for the suggested algorithms.

Suppose that the notations VIP and CFPP represent a variational inequality problem with Lipschitzian and pseudomonotone mapping $A : H \to H$ and a common fixed-point problem of finitely many nonexpansive mappings $\{T_i\}_{i=1}^N$ and a quasi-nonexpansive mapping T with a demiclosedness property, respectively. Inspired by the research works above, we design two Mann-type inertial subgradient extragradient iterations for finding a common solution of the VIP and CFPP. Our algorithms require only computing one projection onto the feasible set C per iteration, and the strong convergence theorems are established without the assumption of sequentially weak continuity for A on C. Finally, in order to support the applicability and implementability of our algorithms, we make use of our main results to solve the VIP and CFPP in two illustrating examples.

This paper is organized as follows: In Section 2, we recall some definitions and preliminaries for the sequel use. Section 3 deals with the convergence analysis of the proposed algorithms. Finally, in Section 4, in order to support the applicability and implementability of our algorithms, we make use of our main results to find a common solution of the VIP and CFPP in two illustrating examples.

2. Preliminaries

Throughout this paper, we assume that C is a nonempty closed convex subset of a real Hilbert space H. If $\{u_m\}$ is a sequence in H, then we denote by $u_m \to u$ (respectively, $u_m \rightharpoonup u$) the strong (respectively, weak) convergence of $\{u_m\}$ to u. A mapping $F : C \to H$ is said to be nonexpansive if $\|Fu - Fv\| \leq \|u - v\|$ $\forall u, v \in C$. Recall also that $F : C \to H$ is called

(i) L-Lipschitz continuous (or L-Lipschitzian) if $\exists L > 0$ such that $\|Fu - Fv\| \leq L\|u - v\|$ $\forall u, v \in C$;
(ii) monotone if $\langle Fu - Fv, u - v\rangle \geq 0$ $\forall u, v \in C$;
(iii) pseudomonotone if $\langle Fu, v - u\rangle \geq 0 \Rightarrow \langle Fv, v - u\rangle \geq 0$ $\forall u, v \in C$;
(iv) α-strongly monotone if $\exists \alpha > 0$ such that $\langle Fu - Fv, u - v\rangle \geq \alpha\|u - v\|^2$ $\forall u, v \in C$;
(v) quasi-nonexpansive if $\mathrm{Fix}(F) \neq \emptyset$, and $\|Fu - p\| \leq \|u - p\|$ $\forall u \in C$, $p \in \mathrm{Fix}(F)$;
(vi) sequentially weakly continuous on C if for $\{u_m\} \subset C$, the relation holds: $u_m \rightharpoonup u \Rightarrow Fu_m \rightharpoonup Fu$.

It is clear that every monotone operator is pseudomonotone, but the converse is not true. Next, we provide an example of a quasi-nonexpansive mapping which is not nonexpansive.

Example 1. *Let $H = \mathbf{R}$ with the inner product $\langle a, b\rangle = ab$ and induced norm $\|\cdot\| = |\cdot|$. Let $T : H \to H$ be defined as $Tu := \frac{u}{2}\sin u$ $\forall u \in H$. It is clear that $\mathrm{Fix}(T) = \{0\}$ and T is quasi-nonexpansive. However, we claim that T is not nonexpansive. Indeed, putting $u = 2\pi$ and $v = \frac{3\pi}{2}$, we have $\|Tu - Tv\| = \|\frac{2\pi}{2}\sin 2\pi - \frac{3\pi}{4}\sin\frac{3\pi}{2}\| = \frac{3\pi}{4} > \|2\pi - \frac{3\pi}{2}\| = \frac{\pi}{2}$.*

Definition 1 ([23]). *Assume that $T : H \to H$ is a nonlinear operator with $\mathrm{Fix}(T) \neq \emptyset$. Then $I - T$ is said to be demiclosed at zero if for any $\{u_n\}$ in H, the implication holds: $u_n \rightharpoonup u$ and $(I - T)u_n \to 0 \Rightarrow u \in \mathrm{Fix}(T)$.*

Very recently, Thong and Hieu gave an example to illustrate that there exists a quasi-nonexpansive mapping T, but $I - T$ is not demiclosed at zero; see ([22], Example 2). For each $u \in H$, we know that there exists a unique nearest point in C, denoted by $P_C u$, such that $\|u - P_C u\| \leq \|u - v\|$ $\forall v \in C$. P_C is called a metric projection of H onto C.

Lemma 1 ([23]). *The following hold:*

(i) $\langle u - v, P_C u - P_C v\rangle \geq \|P_C u - P_C v\|^2$ $\forall u, v \in H$;
(ii) $\langle u - P_C u, v - P_C u\rangle \leq 0$ $\forall u \in H, v \in C$;
(iii) $\|u - v\|^2 \geq \|u - P_C u\|^2 + \|v - P_C u\|^2$ $\forall u \in H, v \in C$;
(iv) $\|u - v\|^2 = \|u\|^2 - \|v\|^2 - 2\langle u - v, v\rangle$ $\forall u, v \in H$;
(v) $\|\lambda u + (1 - \lambda)v\|^2 = \lambda\|u\|^2 + (1 - \lambda)\|v\|^2 - \lambda(1 - \lambda)\|u - v\|^2$ $\forall u, v \in H$, $\lambda \in [0, 1]$.

Lemma 2 ([24]). *For all $u \in H$ and $\alpha \geq \beta > 0$, the inequalities hold: $\frac{\|u - P_C(u - \alpha Au)\|}{\alpha} \leq \frac{\|u - P_C(u - \beta Au)\|}{\beta}$ and $\|u - P_C(u - \beta Au)\| \leq \|u - P_C(u - \alpha Au)\|$.*

Lemma 3 ([13]). *Suppose that $A : C \to H$ is pseudomonotone and continuous. Then $u^* \in C$ is a solution to the VIP $\langle Au^*, u - u^*\rangle \geq 0$ $\forall u \in C$, if and only if $\langle Au, u - u^*\rangle \geq 0$ $\forall u \in C$.*

Lemma 4 ([25]). *Suppose that $\{a_m\}$ is a sequence of nonnegative numbers satisfying the conditions: $a_{m+1} \leq (1 - \lambda_m)a_m + \lambda_m\gamma_m$ $\forall m \geq 1$, where $\{\lambda_m\}$ and $\{\gamma_m\}$ lie in $\mathbf{R} = (-\infty, \infty)$ such that (i) $\{\lambda_m\} \subset [0, 1]$ and $\sum_{m=1}^{\infty}\lambda_m = \infty$, and (ii) $\limsup_{m\to\infty}\gamma_m \leq 0$ or $\sum_{m=1}^{\infty}|\lambda_m\gamma_m| < \infty$. Then $\lim_{m\to\infty} a_m = 0$.*

Lemma 5 ([23]). *Suppose that $T : C \to C$ is a nonexpansive mapping with $\mathrm{Fix}(T) \neq \emptyset$. Then $I - T$ is demiclosed at zero, that is, if $\{u_m\}$ is a sequence in C such that $u_m \rightharpoonup u \in C$ and $(I - T)u_m \to 0$, then $(I - T)u = 0$, where I is the identity mapping of H.*

Lemma 6 ([25]). *Suppose that $\lambda \in (0, 1]$, $T : C \to H$ is a nonexpansive mapping, and the mapping $T^\lambda : C \to H$ is defined as $T^\lambda u := Tu - \lambda\mu F(Tu)$ $\forall u \in C$, where $F : H \to H$ is κ-Lipschitzian and η-strongly monotone. Then T^λ is a contraction provided $0 < \mu < \frac{2\eta}{\kappa^2}$, that is, $\|T^\lambda u - T^\lambda v\| \leq (1 - \lambda\ell)\|u - v\|$ $\forall u, v \in C$, where $\ell := 1 - \sqrt{1 - \mu(2\eta - \mu\kappa^2)} \in (0, 1]$.*

Lemma 7 ([26]). *Suppose that $\{\Gamma_m\}$ is a sequence of real numbers that does not decrease at infinity in the sense that there exists a subsequence $\{\Gamma_{m_k}\}$ of $\{\Gamma_m\}$ which satisfies $\Gamma_{m_k} < \Gamma_{m_k+1}$ for each integer $k \geq 1$. Define the sequence $\{\tau(m)\}_{m \geq m_0}$ of integers as follows:*

$$\tau(m) = \max\{k \leq m : \Gamma_k < \Gamma_{k+1}\},$$

where integer $m_0 \geq 1$ such that $\{k \leq m_0 : \Gamma_k < \Gamma_{k+1}\} \neq \emptyset$. Then, the following conclusions hold:
(i) $\tau(m_0) \leq \tau(m_0 + 1) \leq \cdots$ *and* $\tau(m) \to \infty$;
(ii) $\Gamma_{\tau(m)} \leq \Gamma_{\tau(m)+1}$ *and* $\Gamma_m \leq \Gamma_{\tau(m)+1}$ $\forall m \geq m_0$.

3. Iterative Algorithms and Convergence Criteria

In this section, let the feasible set C be a nonempty closed convex subset of a real Hilbert space H, and assume always that the following hold:

$T_i : H \to H$ is nonexpansive for $i = 1, ..., N$ and $T : H \to H$ is a quasi-nonexpansive mapping such that $I - T$ is demiclosed at zero;

$A : H \to H$ is L-Lipschitz continuous, pseudomonotone on H, and satisfies the condition that for $\{x_n\} \subset C$, $x_n \rightharpoonup z \Rightarrow \|Az\| \leq \liminf_{n\to\infty} \|Ax_n\|$;

$\Omega = \cap_{i=0}^N \mathrm{Fix}(T_i) \cap \mathrm{VI}(C, A) \neq \emptyset$ with $T_0 := T$;

$f : H \to H$ is a contraction with constant $\delta \in [0, 1)$, and $F : H \to H$ is η-strongly monotone and κ-Lipschitzian such that $\delta < \tau := 1 - \sqrt{1 - \rho(2\eta - \rho\kappa^2)}$ for $\rho \in (0, \frac{2\eta}{\kappa^2})$; $\{\zeta_n\}, \{\beta_n\}, \{\gamma_n\} \subset (0, 1)$, and $\{\tau_n\} \subset (0, \infty)$ are such that

(i) $\beta_n + \gamma_n < 1$ and $\sum_{n=1}^\infty \beta_n = \infty$;
(ii) $\lim_{n\to\infty} \beta_n = 0$ and $\tau_n = o(\beta_n)$, i.e., $\lim_{n\to\infty} \tau_n/\beta_n = 0$;
(iii) $0 < \liminf_{n\to\infty} \gamma_n \leq \limsup_{n\to\infty} \gamma_n < 1$ and $0 < \liminf_{n\to\infty} \zeta_n \leq \limsup_{n\to\infty} \zeta_n < 1$.

In addition, we write $T_n := T_{n \bmod N}$ for integer $n \geq 1$ with the mod function taking values in the set $\{1, 2, ..., N\}$, i.e., if $n = jN + q$ for some integers $j \geq 0$ and $0 \leq q < N$, then $T_n = T_N$ if $q = 0$ and $T_n = T_q$ if $0 < q < N$.

Algorithm 1. Initialization: Let $\lambda_1 > 0$, $\alpha > 0$, $\mu \in (0, 1)$ and $x_0, x_1 \in H$ be arbitrary.
Iterative Steps: Calculate x_{n+1} as follows:
Step 1. Given the iterates x_{n-1} and x_n $(n \geq 1)$, choose α_n such that $0 \leq \alpha_n \leq \bar{\alpha}_n$, where

$$\bar{\alpha}_n = \begin{cases} \min\{\alpha, \frac{\tau_n}{\|x_n - x_{n-1}\|}\} & \text{if } x_n \neq x_{n-1}, \\ \alpha & \text{otherwise.} \end{cases} \tag{5}$$

Step 2. Compute $w_n = x_n + \alpha_n(x_n - x_{n-1})$ and $y_n = P_C(w_n - \lambda_n A w_n)$.
Step 3. Construct the half-space $C_n := \{z \in H : \langle w_n - \lambda_n A w_n - y_n, z - y_n\rangle \leq 0\}$, and compute $z_n = P_{C_n}(w_n - \lambda_n A y_n)$.
Step 4. Calculate $v_n = \zeta_n x_n + (1 - \zeta_n) T_n w_n$ and $x_{n+1} = \beta_n f(x_n) + \gamma_n T z_n + ((1 - \gamma_n)I - \beta_n \rho F) v_n$, and update

$$\lambda_{n+1} = \begin{cases} \min\{\mu \frac{\|w_n - y_n\|^2 + \|z_n - y_n\|^2}{2\langle Aw_n - Ay_n, z_n - y_n\rangle}, \lambda_n\} & \text{if } \langle Aw_n - Ay_n, z_n - y_n\rangle > 0, \\ \lambda_n & \text{otherwise.} \end{cases} \tag{6}$$

Let $n := n + 1$ and return to Step 1.

Remark 1. *It is easy to see that, from (5) we get* $\lim_{n\to\infty} \frac{\alpha_n}{\beta_n}\|x_n - x_{n-1}\| = 0$. *Indeed, we have* $\alpha_n\|x_n - x_{n-1}\| \leq \tau_n\ \forall n \geq 1$, *which together with* $\lim_{n\to\infty} \frac{\tau_n}{\beta_n} = 0$ *implies that* $\frac{\alpha_n}{\beta_n}\|x_n - x_{n-1}\| \leq \frac{\tau_n}{\beta_n} \to 0$ *as* $n \to \infty$.

Lemma 8. *Let* $\{\lambda_n\}$ *be generated by (6). Then* $\{\lambda_n\}$ *is a nonincreasing sequence with* $\lambda_n \geq \lambda := \min\{\lambda_1, \frac{\mu}{L}\}\ \forall n \geq 1$, *and* $\lim_{n\to\infty} \lambda_n \geq \lambda := \min\{\lambda_1, \frac{\mu}{L}\}$.

Proof. First, from (6) it is clear that $\lambda_n \geq \lambda_{n+1}\ \forall n \geq 1$. Furthermore, observe that

$$\left.\begin{array}{r} \frac{1}{2}(\|w_n - y_n\|^2 + \|z_n - y_n\|^2) \geq \|w_n - y_n\|\|z_n - y_n\| \\ \langle Aw_n - Ay_n, z_n - y_n\rangle \leq L\|w_n - y_n\|\|z_n - y_n\| \end{array}\right\} \Rightarrow \lambda_{n+1} \geq \min\{\lambda_n, \frac{\mu}{L}\}.$$

□

Remark 2. *In terms of Lemmas 2 and 8, we claim that if* $w_n = y_n$ *or* $Ay_n = 0$, *then* y_n *is an element of* $\mathrm{VI}(C, A)$. *Indeed, if* $w_n = y_n$ *or* $Ay_n = 0$, *then* $0 = \|y_n - P_C(y_n - \lambda_n Ay_n)\| \geq \|y_n - P_C(y_n - \lambda Ay_n)\|$. *Thus, the assertion is valid.*

The following lemmas are quite helpful for the convergence analysis of our algorithms.

Lemma 9. *Let* $\{w_n\}, \{y_n\}, \{z_n\}$ *be the sequences generated by Algorithm 1. Then*

$$\|z_n - p\|^2 \leq \|w_n - p\|^2 - (1 - \mu\frac{\lambda_n}{\lambda_{n+1}})\|w_n - y_n\|^2 - (1 - \mu\frac{\lambda_n}{\lambda_{n+1}})\|z_n - y_n\|^2\ \forall p \in \Omega. \quad (7)$$

Proof. First, by the definition of $\{\lambda_n\}$ we claim that

$$2\langle Aw_n - Ay_n, z_n - y_n\rangle \leq \frac{\mu}{\lambda_{n+1}}\|w_n - y_n\|^2 + \frac{\mu}{\lambda_{n+1}}\|z_n - y_n\|^2\ \forall n \geq 1. \quad (8)$$

Indeed, if $\langle Aw_n - Ay_n, z_n - y_n\rangle \leq 0$, then inequality (8) holds. Otherwise, from (6) we get (8). Furthermore, observe that for each $p \in \Omega \subset C \subset C_n$,

$$\begin{aligned} \|z_n - p\|^2 &= \|P_{C_n}(w_n - \lambda_n Ay_n) - P_{C_n}p\|^2 \leq \langle z_n - p, w_n - \lambda_n Ay_n - p\rangle \\ &= \tfrac{1}{2}\|z_n - p\|^2 + \tfrac{1}{2}\|w_n - p\|^2 - \tfrac{1}{2}\|z_n - w_n\|^2 - \langle z_n - p, \lambda_n Ay_n\rangle, \end{aligned}$$

which hence yields

$$\|z_n - p\|^2 \leq \|w_n - p\|^2 - \|z_n - w_n\|^2 - 2\langle z_n - p, \lambda_n Ay_n\rangle. \quad (9)$$

From $p \in \mathrm{VI}(C, A)$, we get $\langle Ap, x - p\rangle \geq 0\ \forall x \in C$. By the pseudomonotonicity of A on C we have $\langle Ax, x - p\rangle \geq 0\ \forall x \in C$. Putting $x := y_n \in C$ we get $\langle Ay_n, p - y_n\rangle \leq 0$. Thus,

$$\langle Ay_n, p - z_n\rangle = \langle Ay_n, p - y_n\rangle + \langle Ay_n, y_n - z_n\rangle \leq \langle Ay_n, y_n - z_n\rangle. \quad (10)$$

Substituting (10) for (9), we obtain

$$\|z_n - p\|^2 \leq \|w_n - p\|^2 - \|z_n - y_n\|^2 - \|y_n - w_n\|^2 + 2\langle w_n - \lambda_n Ay_n - y_n, z_n - y_n\rangle. \quad (11)$$

Since $z_n = P_{C_n}(w_n - \lambda_n Ay_n)$, we get $z_n \in C_n := \{z \in H : \langle w_n - \lambda_n Aw_n - y_n, z - y_n\rangle \leq 0\}$, and hence

$$\begin{aligned} 2\langle w_n - \lambda_n A y_n - y_n, z_n - y_n\rangle &= 2\langle w_n - \lambda_n A w_n - y_n, z_n - y_n\rangle + 2\lambda_n\langle A w_n - A y_n, z_n - y_n\rangle \\ &\le 2\lambda_n\langle A w_n - A y_n, z_n - y_n\rangle, \end{aligned}$$

which together with (8), implies that

$$2\langle w_n - \lambda_n A y_n - y_n, z_n - y_n\rangle \le \mu\frac{\lambda_n}{\lambda_{n+1}}\|w_n - y_n\|^2 + \mu\frac{\lambda_n}{\lambda_{n+1}}\|z_n - y_n\|^2.$$

Therefore, substituting the last inequality for (11), we infer that inequality (7) holds. □

Lemma 10. *Suppose that $\{w_n\}, \{x_n\}, \{y_n\}$, and $\{z_n\}$ are bounded sequences generated by Algorithm 1. If $x_n - x_{n+1} \to 0$, $w_n - y_n \to 0$, $w_n - z_n \to 0$, $z_n - T_n z_n \to 0$, and $\exists\{w_{n_k}\} \subset \{w_n\}$ s.t. $w_{n_k} \rightharpoonup z \in H$, then $z \in \Omega$.*

Proof. Utilizing the similar arguments to those in the proof of Lemma 3.3 of [12], we can derive the desired result. □

Lemma 11. *Assume that $\{w_n\}, \{x_n\}, \{y_n\}, \{z_n\}$ are the sequences generated by Algorithm 1. Then they all are bounded.*

Proof. Since $0 < \liminf_{n\to\infty}\gamma_n \le \limsup_{n\to\infty}\gamma_n < 1$ and $0 < \liminf_{n\to\infty}\zeta_n \le \limsup_{n\to\infty}\zeta_n < 1$, we may assume, without loss of generality, that

$$\{\gamma_n\} \subset [a,b] \subset (0,1) \quad \text{and} \quad \{\zeta_n\} \subset [c,d] \subset (0,1). \tag{12}$$

Choose a fixed $p \in \Omega$ arbitrarily. Then we obtain $Tp = p$ and $T_n p = p$ for all $n \ge 1$, and (7) holds. Noticing $\lim_{n\to\infty}(1 - \mu\frac{\lambda_n}{\lambda_{n+1}}) = 1 - \mu > 0$, we might assume that $1 - \mu\frac{\lambda_n}{\lambda_{n+1}} > 0$ for all $n \ge 1$. So it follows from (7) that for all $n \ge 1$,

$$\|z_n - p\| \le \|w_n - p\|. \tag{13}$$

Furthermore, note that

$$\|w_n - p\| \le \|x_n - p\| + \alpha_n\|x_n - x_{n-1}\| = \|x_n - p\| + \beta_n \cdot \frac{\alpha_n}{\beta_n}\|x_n - x_{n-1}\|. \tag{14}$$

In terms of Remark 1, one has $\frac{\alpha_n}{\beta_n}\|x_n - x_{n-1}\| \to 0$ as $n \to \infty$. Hence we deduce that $\exists M_1 > 0$ s.t.

$$M_1 \ge \frac{\alpha_n}{\beta_n}\|x_n - x_{n-1}\| \quad \forall n \ge 1. \tag{15}$$

Using (13)–(15), we obtain that for all $n \ge 1$,

$$\|z_n - p\| \le \|w_n - p\| \le \|x_n - p\| + \beta_n M_1. \tag{16}$$

Noticing $\beta_n + \gamma_n < 1\ \forall n \ge 1$, we have $\frac{\beta_n}{1-\gamma_n} < 1$ for all $n \ge 1$. So, using Lemma 6 and (16) we deduce that

$$\begin{aligned} \|v_n - p\| &\le \zeta_n\|x_n - p\| + (1-\zeta_n)\|T_n w_n - p\| \\ &\le \zeta_n\|x_n - p\| + (1-\zeta_n)\|w_n - p\| \\ &\le \zeta_n(\|x_n - p\| + \beta_n M_1) + (1-\zeta_n)(\|x_n - p\| + \beta_n M_1) \\ &= \|x_n - p\| + \beta_n M_1, \end{aligned}$$

and hence

$$
\begin{aligned}
\|x_{n+1}-p\| &= \|\beta_n f(x_n)+\gamma_n Tz_n+((1-\gamma_n)I-\beta_n\rho F)v_n-p\| \\
&\le \beta_n\|f(x_n)-p\|+\gamma_n\|Tz_n-p\| \\
&\quad +(1-\beta_n-\gamma_n)\|(\tfrac{1-\gamma_n}{1-\beta_n-\gamma_n}I-\tfrac{\beta_n}{1-\beta_n-\gamma_n}\rho F)v_n-p\| \\
&\le \beta_n(\|f(x_n)-f(p)\|+\|f(p)-p\|)+\gamma_n\|z_n-p\| \\
&\quad +(1-\beta_n-\gamma_n)\|(\tfrac{1-\gamma_n}{1-\beta_n-\gamma_n}I-\tfrac{\beta_n}{1-\beta_n-\gamma_n}\rho F)v_n-p\| \\
&\le \beta_n(\delta\|x_n-p\|+\|f(p)-p\|)+\gamma_n\|z_n-p\| \\
&\quad +(1-\gamma_n)\|(I-\tfrac{\beta_n}{1-\gamma_n}\rho F)v_n-(1-\tfrac{\beta_n}{1-\gamma_n})p\| \\
&= \beta_n(\delta\|x_n-p\|+\|f(p)-p\|)+\gamma_n\|z_n-p\| \\
&\quad +(1-\gamma_n)\|(I-\tfrac{\beta_n}{1-\gamma_n}\rho F)v_n-(I-\tfrac{\beta_n}{1-\gamma_n}\rho F)p+\tfrac{\beta_n}{1-\gamma_n}(I-\rho F)p\| \\
&\le \beta_n(\delta\|x_n-p\|+\|f(p)-p\|)+\gamma_n\|z_n-p\| \\
&\quad +(1-\gamma_n)[(1-\tfrac{\beta_n}{1-\gamma_n}\tau)\|v_n-p\|+\tfrac{\beta_n}{1-\gamma_n}\|(I-\rho F)p\|] \\
&= \beta_n(\delta\|x_n-p\|+\|f(p)-p\|)+\gamma_n\|z_n-p\| \\
&\quad +(1-\gamma_n-\beta_n\tau)\|v_n-p\|+\beta_n\|(I-\rho F)p\| \\
&\le \beta_n\delta(\|x_n-p\|+\beta_n M_1)+\beta_n\|f(p)-p\|+\gamma_n(\|x_n-p\|+\beta_n M_1) \\
&\quad +(1-\gamma_n-\beta_n\tau)(\|x_n-p\|+\beta_n M_1)+\beta_n\|(I-\rho F)p\| \\
&\le [1-\beta_n(\tau-\delta)]\|x_n-p\|+\beta_n(M_1+\|f(p)-p\|+\|(I-\rho F)p\|) \\
&= [1-\beta_n(\tau-\delta)]\|x_n-p\|+\beta_n(\tau-\delta)\cdot\tfrac{M_1+\|f(p)-p\|+\|(I-\rho F)p\|}{\tau-\delta} \\
&\le \max\{\|x_n-p\|,\tfrac{M_1+\|f(p)-p\|+\|(I-\rho F)p\|}{\tau-\delta}\}.
\end{aligned}
$$

By induction, we obtain $\|x_n-p\|\le\max\{\|x_1-p\|,\frac{M_1+\|f(p)-p\|+\|(I-\rho F)p\|}{\tau-\delta}\}\ \forall n\ge 1$. Thus, $\{x_n\}$ is bounded, and so are the sequences $\{w_n\},\{y_n\},\{z_n\},\{Tz_n\},\{Fv_n\},\{T_n w_n\}$. □

Theorem 1. *Let the sequence $\{x_n\}$ be constructed by Algorithm 1. Then $\{x_n\}$ converges strongly to the unique solution $x^*\in\Omega$ of the following VIP:*

$$\langle(\rho F-f)x^*,p-x^*\rangle\ge 0\quad\forall p\in\Omega.$$

Proof. First, it is not difficult to show that $P_\Omega(f+I-\rho F)$ is a contraction. In fact, by Lemma 6 and the Banach contraction mapping principle, we obtain that $P_\Omega(f+I-\rho F)$ has a unique fixed point. Say $x^*\in H$, i.e., $x^*=P_\Omega(f+I-\rho F)x^*$. Thus, the following VIP has only a solution $x^*\in\Omega$:

$$\langle(\rho F-f)x^*,p-x^*\rangle\ge 0\quad\forall p\in\Omega. \tag{17}$$

□

We now claim that

$$\gamma_n(1-\mu\frac{\lambda_n}{\lambda_{n+1}})[\|w_n-y_n\|^2+\|z_n-y_n\|^2]\le\|x_n-x^*\|^2-\|x_{n+1}-x^*\|^2+\beta_n M_4,$$

for some $M_4>0$. In fact, observe that

$$
\begin{aligned}
x_{n+1}-x^* &= \beta_n(f(x_n)-x^*)+\gamma_n(Tz_n-x^*)+(1-\beta_n-\gamma_n)\{\tfrac{1-\gamma_n}{1-\beta_n-\gamma_n}[(I-\tfrac{\beta_n}{1-\gamma_n}\rho F)v_n \\
&\quad -(I-\tfrac{\beta_n}{1-\gamma_n}\rho F)x^*]+\tfrac{\beta_n}{1-\beta_n-\gamma_n}(I-\rho F)x^*\} \\
&= \beta_n(f(x_n)-f(x^*))+\gamma_n(Tz_n-x^*)+(1-\gamma_n)[(I-\tfrac{\beta_n}{1-\gamma_n}\rho F)v_n-(I-\tfrac{\beta_n}{1-\gamma_n}\rho F)x^*] \\
&\quad +\beta_n(f-\rho F)x^*.
\end{aligned}
$$

Using Lemma 6 and the convexity of the function $h(t)=t^2\ \forall t\in\mathbf{R}$, we have

$$
\begin{aligned}
&\|x_{n+1}-x^*\|^2\\
&\le \|\beta_n(f(x_n)-f(x^*))+\gamma_n(Tz_n-x^*)+(1-\gamma_n)[(I-\tfrac{\beta_n}{1-\gamma_n}\rho F)v_n-(I-\tfrac{\beta_n}{1-\gamma_n}\rho F)x^*]\|^2\\
&\quad+2\beta_n\langle (f-\rho F)x^*, x_{n+1}-x^*\rangle\\
&\le \beta_n\delta\|x_n-x^*\|^2+\gamma_n\|z_n-x^*\|^2+(1-\beta_n\tau-\gamma_n)\|v_n-x^*\|^2+\beta_n M_2
\end{aligned}
\tag{18}
$$

where $M_2 \ge \sup_{n\ge 1} 2\|f-\rho F)x^*\|\|x_n-x^*\|$ for some $M_2>0$. From (7) and (17), we have

$$
\begin{aligned}
\|x_{n+1}-x^*\|^2 \le{}& \beta_n\delta\|x_n-x^*\|^2+\gamma_n[\|w_n-x^*\|^2-(1-\mu\tfrac{\lambda_n}{\lambda_{n+1}})\|w_n-y_n\|^2-(1-\mu\tfrac{\lambda_n}{\lambda_{n+1}})\|z_n-y_n\|^2]\\
&+(1-\beta_n\tau-\gamma_n)[\zeta_n\|x_n-x^*\|^2+(1-\zeta_n)\|w_n-x^*\|^2]+\beta_n M_2.
\end{aligned}
\tag{19}
$$

Again from (16), we obtain

$$
\|w_n-x^*\|^2 \le (\|x_n-x^*\|+\beta_n M_1)^2 \le \|x_n-x^*\|^2+\beta_n M_3, \tag{20}
$$

where $M_3 \ge \sup_{n\ge 1}(2M_1\|x_n-x^*\|+\beta_n M_1^2)$ for some $M_3>0$. Using (19) and (20), we get

$$
\begin{aligned}
&\|x_{n+1}-x^*\|^2\\
&\le [1-\beta_n(\tau-\delta)](\|x_n-x^*\|^2+\beta_n M_3)-\gamma_n(1-\mu\tfrac{\lambda_n}{\lambda_{n+1}})[\|w_n-y_n\|^2+\|z_n-y_n\|^2]+\beta_n M_2\\
&\le \|x_n-x^*\|^2-\gamma_n(1-\mu\tfrac{\lambda_n}{\lambda_{n+1}})[\|w_n-y_n\|^2+\|z_n-y_n\|^2]+\beta_n M_4,
\end{aligned}
$$

where $M_4 := M_2+M_3$. Consequently,

$$
\gamma_n(1-\mu\frac{\lambda_n}{\lambda_{n+1}})[\|w_n-y_n\|^2+\|z_n-y_n\|^2] \le \|x_n-x^*\|^2-\|x_{n+1}-x^*\|^2+\beta_n M_4. \tag{21}
$$

Next we claim that

$$
\begin{aligned}
\|x_{n+1}-x^*\|^2 \le{}& [1-\beta_n(\tau-\delta)]\|x_n-x^*\|^2\\
&+\beta_n(\tau-\delta)[\tfrac{2}{\tau-\delta}\langle (f-\rho F)x^*, x_{n+1}-x^*\rangle+\tfrac{3M}{\tau-\delta}\cdot\tfrac{\alpha_n}{\beta_n}\cdot\|x_n-x_{n-1}\|]
\end{aligned}
$$

for some $M>0$. In fact, it is easy to see that

$$
\|w_n-x^*\|^2 \le \|x_n-x^*\|^2+\alpha_n\|x_n-x_{n-1}\|[2\|x_n-x^*\|+\alpha_n\|x_n-x_{n-1}\|]. \tag{22}
$$

Using (16), (18), and (22), we get

$$
\begin{aligned}
&\|x_{n+1}-x^*\|^2 \le \beta_n\delta\|x_n-x^*\|^2+\gamma_n\|w_n-x^*\|^2+(1-\beta_n\tau-\gamma_n)[\zeta_n\|x_n-x^*\|^2\\
&\quad+(1-\zeta_n)\|w_n-x^*\|^2]+2\beta_n\langle (f-\rho F)x^*, x_{n+1}-x^*\rangle\\
&\le \beta_n\delta\|x_n-x^*\|^2+\gamma_n[\|x_n-x^*\|^2+\alpha_n\|x_n-x_{n-1}\|(2\|x_n-x^*\|+\alpha_n\|x_n-x_{n-1}\|)]\\
&\quad+(1-\beta_n\tau-\gamma_n)\{\zeta_n\|x_n-x^*\|^2+(1-\zeta_n)[\|x_n-x^*\|^2+\alpha_n\|x_n-x_{n-1}\|(2\|x_n-x^*\|\\
&\quad+\alpha_n\|x_n-x_{n-1}\|)]\}+2\beta_n\langle (f-\rho F)x^*, x_{n+1}-x^*\rangle\\
&\le [1-\beta_n(\tau-\delta)]\|x_n-x^*\|^2+\beta_n(\tau-\delta)\cdot[\tfrac{2\langle (f-\rho F)x^*, x_{n+1}-x^*\rangle}{\tau-\delta}+\tfrac{3M}{\tau-\delta}\cdot\tfrac{\alpha_n}{\beta_n}\cdot\|x_n-x_{n-1}\|],
\end{aligned}
\tag{23}
$$

where $M \ge \sup_{n\ge 1}\{\|x_n-x^*\|, \alpha_n\|x_n-x_{n-1}\|\}$ for some $M>0$.
For each $n\ge 0$, we set

$$
\begin{aligned}
\Gamma_n &= \|x_n-x^*\|^2,\\
\varepsilon_n &= \beta_n(\tau-\delta),\\
\vartheta_n &= \alpha_n\|x_n-x_{n-1}\|3M+2\beta_n\langle (f-\rho F)x^*, x_{n+1}-x^*\rangle.
\end{aligned}
$$

Then (23) can be rewritten as the following formula:

$$
\Gamma_{n+1} \le (1-\varepsilon_n)\Gamma_n+\vartheta_n \quad \forall n\ge 0. \tag{24}
$$

We next show the convergence of $\{\Gamma_n\}$ to zero by the following two cases:

Case 1. *Suppose that there exists an integer $n_0 \geq 1$ such that $\{\Gamma_n\}$ is non-increasing.* Then

$$\Gamma_n - \Gamma_{n+1} \to 0.$$

From (21), we get

$$\gamma_n(1 - \mu\frac{\lambda_n}{\lambda_{n+1}})[\|w_n - y_n\|^2 + \|z_n - y_n\|^2] \leq \Gamma_n - \Gamma_{n+1} + \beta_n M_4.$$

Since $\beta_n \to 0$, $\Gamma_n - \Gamma_{n+1} \to 0$, $1 - \mu\frac{\lambda_n}{\lambda_{n+1}} \to 1 - \mu$ and $\{\gamma_n\} \subset [a, b] \subset (0, 1)$, we have

$$\lim_{n\to\infty} \|w_n - y_n\| = \lim_{n\to\infty} \|z_n - y_n\| = 0. \tag{25}$$

Using Lemma 1 (v), we deduce from (16) that

$$\begin{aligned}
&\|x_{n+1} - x^*\|^2 \\
&= \|\beta_n f(x_n) + \gamma_n T z_n + ((1-\gamma_n)I - \beta_n \rho F)v_n - x^*\|^2 \\
&= \|\beta_n(f(x_n) - \rho F v_n) + \gamma_n(Tz_n - x^*) + (1-\gamma_n)(v_n - x^*)\|^2 \\
&\leq \|\gamma_n(Tz_n - x^*) + (1-\gamma_n)(v_n - x^*)\|^2 + 2\beta_n\langle f(x_n) - \rho F v_n, x_{n+1} - x^*\rangle \\
&= \gamma_n\|Tz_n - x^*\|^2 + (1-\gamma_n)\|v_n - x^*\|^2 - \gamma_n(1-\gamma_n)\|Tz_n - v_n\|^2 \\
&\quad + 2\beta_n\langle f(x_n) - \rho F v_n, x_{n+1} - x^*\rangle \\
&= \gamma_n\|Tz_n - x^*\|^2 + (1-\gamma_n)[\zeta_n\|x_n - x^*\|^2 + (1-\zeta_n)\|T_n w_n - x^*\|^2 - \zeta_n(1-\zeta_n)\|x_n - T_n w_n\|^2] \\
&\quad - \gamma_n(1-\gamma_n)\|Tz_n - v_n\|^2 + 2\beta_n\langle f(x_n) - \rho F v_n, x_{n+1} - x^*\rangle \\
&\leq \gamma_n\|z_n - x^*\|^2 + (1-\gamma_n)[\zeta_n\|x_n - x^*\|^2 + (1-\zeta_n)\|w_n - x^*\|^2 - \zeta_n(1-\zeta_n)\|x_n - T_n w_n\|^2] \\
&\quad - \gamma_n(1-\gamma_n)\|Tz_n - v_n\|^2 + 2\beta_n\langle f(x_n) - \rho F v_n, x_{n+1} - x^*\rangle \\
&\leq \gamma_n(\|x_n - x^*\| + \beta_n M_1)^2 + (1-\gamma_n)(\|x_n - x^*\| + \beta_n M_1)^2 - (1-\gamma_n)\zeta_n(1-\zeta_n)\|x_n - T_n w_n\|^2 \\
&\quad - \gamma_n(1-\gamma_n)\|Tz_n - v_n\|^2 + 2\beta_n\|f(x_n) - \rho F v_n\|\|x_{n+1} - x^*\| \\
&= (\|x_n - x^*\| + \beta_n M_1)^2 - (1-\gamma_n)\zeta_n(1-\zeta_n)\|x_n - T_n w_n\|^2 \\
&\quad - \gamma_n(1-\gamma_n)\|Tz_n - v_n\|^2 + 2\beta_n\|f(x_n) - \rho F v_n\|\|x_{n+1} - x^*\|,
\end{aligned}$$

which immediately yields

$$\begin{aligned}
&(1-\gamma_n)\zeta_n(1-\zeta_n)\|x_n - T_n w_n\|^2 + \gamma_n(1-\gamma_n)\|Tz_n - v_n\|^2 \\
&\leq (\|x_n - x^*\| + \beta_n M_1)^2 - \|x_{n+1} - x^*\|^2 + 2\beta_n\|f(x_n) - \rho F v_n\|\|x_{n+1} - x^*\| \\
&= \Gamma_n - \Gamma_{n+1} + \beta_n M_1(2\|x_n - x^*\| + \beta_n M_1) + 2\beta_n\|f(x_n) - \rho F v_n\|\|x_{n+1} - x^*\|.
\end{aligned}$$

Since $\beta_n \to 0$, $\Gamma_n - \Gamma_{n+1} \to 0$, $\{\gamma_n\} \subset [a, b] \subset (0, 1)$ and $\{\zeta_n\} \subset [c, d] \subset (0, 1)$, we have

$$\lim_{n\to\infty} \|x_n - T_n w_n\| = \lim_{n\to\infty} \|Tz_n - v_n\| = 0. \tag{26}$$

Using Lemma 1 (v) again, we have

$$\begin{aligned}
\|Tz_n - v_n\|^2 &= \|\zeta_n(Tz_n - x_n) + (1-\zeta_n)(Tz_n - T_n w_n)\|^2 \\
&= \zeta_n\|Tz_n - x_n\|^2 + (1-\zeta_n)\|Tz_n - T_n w_n\|^2 - \zeta_n(1-\zeta_n)\|T_n w_n - x_n\|^2.
\end{aligned}$$

So it follows from (26) and $\{\zeta_n\} \subset [c, d] \subset (0, 1)$ that

$$\lim_{n\to\infty} \|Tz_n - x_n\| = \lim_{n\to\infty} \|Tz_n - T_n w_n\| = 0. \tag{27}$$

Therefore, from (25)–(27), we conclude that

$$\|w_n - z_n\| \leq \|w_n - y_n\| + \|y_n - z_n\| \to 0 \quad (n \to \infty), \tag{28}$$

$$\begin{aligned}
\|z_n - T_n z_n\| &\leq \|z_n - w_n\| + \|w_n - x_n\| + \|x_n - T_n w_n\| + \|T_n w_n - T_n z_n\| \\
&\leq 2\|z_n - w_n\| + \|w_n - x_n\| + \|x_n - T_n w_n\| \to 0 \quad (n \to \infty),
\end{aligned} \tag{29}$$

and

$$\begin{array}{l} \|x_{n+1} - x_n\| = \|\beta_n f(x_n) + \gamma_n T z_n + ((1-\gamma_n)I - \beta_n \rho F) v_n - x_n\| \\ = \|\beta_n (f(x_n) - \rho F v_n) + \gamma_n (T z_n - x_n) + (1-\gamma_n)(v_n - x_n)\| \\ \le \beta_n \|f(x_n) - \rho F v_n\| + \gamma_n \|T z_n - x_n\| + (1-\gamma_n)\|v_n - x_n\| \\ \le \beta_n (\|f(x_n)\| + \|\rho F v_n\|) + \gamma_n \|T z_n - x_n\| + (1-\gamma_n)(\|v_n - T z_n\| + \|T z_n - x_n\|) \\ \le \beta_n (\|f(x_n)\| + \|\rho F v_n\|) + \|T z_n - x_n\| + \|v_n - T z_n\| \to 0 \quad (n \to \infty). \end{array} \tag{30}$$

Next, by the boundedness of $\{x_n\}$, we know that $\exists \{x_{n_k}\} \subset \{x_n\}$ s.t.

$$\limsup_{n\to\infty} \langle (f - \rho F)x^*, x_n - x^* \rangle = \lim_{k\to\infty} \langle (f - \rho F)x^*, x_{n_k} - x^* \rangle. \tag{31}$$

Further we might assume that $x_{n_k} \rightharpoonup \hat{x}$. So, from (31) we have

$$\limsup_{n\to\infty} \langle (f - \rho F)x^*, x_n - x^* \rangle = \langle (f - \rho F)x^*, \hat{x} - x^* \rangle. \tag{32}$$

Noticing $w_n - x_n \to 0$ and $x_{n_k} \rightharpoonup \hat{x}$, we obtain $w_{n_k} \rightharpoonup \hat{x}$. Since $x_n - x_{n+1} \to 0$, $w_n - y_n \to 0$, $w_n - z_n \to 0$, $z_n - T_n z_n \to 0$ (due to (25) and (28)–(30)) and $w_{n_k} \rightharpoonup \hat{x}$, by Lemma 10 we get $\hat{x} \in \Omega$. So it follows from (17) and (32) that

$$\limsup_{n\to\infty} \langle (f - \rho F)x^*, x_n - x^* \rangle = \langle (f - \rho F)x^*, \hat{x} - x^* \rangle \le 0, \tag{33}$$

which hence yields

$$\begin{array}{l} \limsup_{n\to\infty} \langle (f - \rho F)x^*, x_{n+1} - x^* \rangle \\ \le \limsup_{n\to\infty} [\|(f - \rho F)x^*\| \|x_{n+1} - x_n\| + \langle (f - \rho F)x^*, x_n - x^* \rangle] \le 0. \end{array} \tag{34}$$

Since $\{\beta_n(\tau - \delta)\} \subset [0,1]$, $\sum_{n=1}^{\infty} \beta_n(\tau - \delta) = \infty$, and

$$\limsup_{n\to\infty} [\frac{2\langle (f - \rho F)x^*, x_{n+1} - x^* \rangle}{\tau - \delta} + \frac{3M}{\tau - \delta} \cdot \frac{\alpha_n}{\beta_n} \cdot \|x_n - x_{n-1}\|] \le 0,$$

by Lemma 4 we conclude from (23) that $\lim_{n\to 0} \|x_n - x^*\| = 0$.

Case 2. *Suppose that* $\exists \{\Gamma_{n_k}\} \subset \{\Gamma_n\}$ *s.t.* $\Gamma_{n_k} < \Gamma_{n_k+1}$ $\forall k \in \mathbf{N}$, *where* $\mathbf{N}$ *is the set of all positive integers.* Define the mapping $\tau : \mathbf{N} \to \mathbf{N}$ by

$$\tau(n) := \max\{k \le n : \Gamma_k < \Gamma_{k+1}\}.$$

Using Lemma 7, we have

$$\Gamma_{\tau(n)} \le \Gamma_{\tau(n)+1} \quad \text{and} \quad \Gamma_n \le \Gamma_{\tau(n)+1}.$$

Putting $\Gamma_n = \|x_n - x^*\|^2$ $\forall n \in \mathbf{N}$ and using the same inference as in Case 1, we can obtain

$$\lim_{n\to\infty} \|x_{\tau(n)+1} - x_{\tau(n)}\| = 0 \tag{35}$$

and

$$\limsup_{n\to\infty} \langle (f - \rho F)x^*, x_{\tau(n)+1} - x^* \rangle \le 0. \tag{36}$$

Because of $\Gamma_{\tau(n)} \le \Gamma_{\tau(n)+1}$ and $\beta_{\tau(n)} > 0$, we conclude from (23) that

$$\|x_{\tau(n)} - x^*\|^2 \le \frac{2}{\tau-\delta} \langle (f - \rho F)x^*, x_{\tau(n)+1} - x^* \rangle + \frac{3M}{\tau-\delta} \cdot \frac{\alpha_{\tau(n)}}{\beta_{\tau(n)}} \cdot \|x_{\tau(n)} - x_{\tau(n)-1}\|,$$

and hence

$$\limsup_{n\to\infty} \|x_{\tau(n)} - x^*\|^2 \le 0.$$

Thus, we have
$$\lim_{n\to\infty} \|x_{\tau(n)} - x^*\|^2 = 0.$$
Using (35), we obtain
$$\begin{aligned}&\|x_{\tau(n)+1} - x^*\|^2 - \|x_{\tau(n)} - x^*\|^2\\ &= 2\langle x_{\tau(n)+1} - x_{\tau(n)}, x_{\tau(n)} - x^*\rangle + \|x_{\tau(n)+1} - x_{\tau(n)}\|^2\\ &\leq 2\|x_{\tau(n)+1} - x_{\tau(n)}\|\|x_{\tau(n)} - x^*\| + \|x_{\tau(n)+1} - x_{\tau(n)}\|^2 \to 0 \quad (n\to\infty).\end{aligned}$$
Taking into account $\Gamma_n \leq \Gamma_{\tau(n)+1}$, we have
$$\begin{aligned}&\|x_n - x^*\|^2 \leq \|x_{\tau(n)+1} - x^*\|^2\\ &\leq \|x_{\tau(n)} - x^*\|^2 + 2\|x_{\tau(n)+1} - x_{\tau(n)}\|\|x_{\tau(n)} - x^*\| + \|x_{\tau(n)+1} - x_{\tau(n)}\|^2.\end{aligned}$$
It is easy to see from (35) that $x_n \to x^*$ as $n \to \infty$. This completes the proof.

Next, we introduce another Mann-type inertial subgradient extragradient algorithm.
Algorithm 2. Initialization: Let $\lambda_1 > 0$, $\alpha > 0$, $\mu \in (0,1)$ and $x_0, x_1 \in H$ be arbitrary.
Iterative Steps: Calculate x_{n+1} as follows:
Step 1. Given the iterates x_{n-1} and x_n $(n \geq 1)$, choose α_n such that $0 \leq \alpha_n \leq \bar{\alpha}_n$, where
$$\bar{\alpha}_n = \begin{cases} \min\{\alpha, \frac{\tau_n}{\|x_n - x_{n-1}\|}\} & \text{if } x_n \neq x_{n-1},\\ \alpha & \text{otherwise.}\end{cases} \tag{37}$$
Step 2. Compute $w_n = x_n + \alpha_n(x_n - x_{n-1})$ and $y_n = P_C(w_n - \lambda_n A w_n)$.
Step 3. Construct the half-space $C_n := \{z \in H : \langle w_n - \lambda_n A w_n - y_n, z - y_n\rangle \leq 0\}$, and compute $z_n = P_{C_n}(w_n - \lambda_n A y_n)$.
Step 4. Calculate $v_n = \zeta_n x_n + (1-\zeta_n)Tz_n$ and $x_{n+1} = \beta_n f(x_n) + \gamma_n T_n w_n + ((1-\gamma_n)I - \beta_n \rho F)v_n$, and update
$$\lambda_{n+1} = \begin{cases} \min\{\mu\frac{\|w_n - y_n\|^2 + \|z_n - y_n\|^2}{2\langle Aw_n - Ay_n, z_n - y_n\rangle}, \lambda_n\} & \text{if } \langle Aw_n - Ay_n, z_n - y_n\rangle > 0,\\ \lambda_n & \text{otherwise.}\end{cases} \tag{38}$$
Let $n := n+1$ and return to Step 1.
It is worth pointing out that Lemmas 8–11 are still valid for Algorithm 2.

Theorem 2. *Let the sequence $\{x_n\}$ be constructed by Algorithm 2. Then $\{x_n\}$ converges strongly to the unique solution $x^* \in \Omega$ of the following VIP:*
$$\langle(\rho F - f)x^*, p - x^*\rangle \geq 0 \quad \forall p \in \Omega.$$

Proof. Utilizing the same arguments as in the proof of Theorem 1, we deduce that there exists a unique solution $x^* \in \Omega = \cap_{i=0}^N \mathrm{Fix}(T_i) \cap \mathrm{VI}(C, A)$ to the VIP (17). □

We now claim that
$$(1-\beta_n\tau - \gamma_n)(1-\zeta_n)(1-\mu\frac{\lambda_n}{\lambda_{n+1}})[\|w_n - y_n\|^2 + \|z_n - y_n\|^2] \leq \|x_n - x^*\|^2 - \|x_{n+1} - x^*\|^2 + \beta_n M_4, \tag{39}$$
for some $M_4 > 0$. In fact, observe that
$$\begin{aligned} x_{n+1} - x^* &= \beta_n(f(x_n) - f(x^*)) + \gamma_n(T_n w_n - x^*)\\ &\quad + (1-\gamma_n)[(I - \tfrac{\beta_n}{1-\gamma_n}\rho F)v_n - (I - \tfrac{\beta_n}{1-\gamma_n}\rho F)x^*] + \beta_n(f - \rho F)x^*,\end{aligned}$$

where $v_n := \zeta_n x_n + (1-\zeta_n)Tz_n$. Using the similar arguments to those of (19) and (20), we have

$$\begin{aligned}\|x_{n+1}-x^*\|^2 \le \beta_n\delta\|x_n-x^*\|^2 + \gamma_n\|w_n-x^*\|^2 + (1-\beta_n\tau-\gamma_n)\{\zeta_n\|x_n-x^*\|^2 \\ + (1-\zeta_n)[\|w_n-x^*\|^2 - (1-\mu\tfrac{\lambda_n}{\lambda_{n+1}})\|w_n-y_n\|^2 - (1-\mu\tfrac{\lambda_n}{\lambda_{n+1}})\|z_n-y_n\|^2]\} + \beta_n M_2.\end{aligned}$$

and

$$\|w_n-x^*\|^2 \le (\|x_n-x^*\| + \beta_n M_1)^2 \le \|x_n-x^*\|^2 + \beta_n M_3,$$

where $M_2 \ge \sup_{n\ge1} 2\|(f-\rho F)x^*\|\|x_n-x^*\|$ for some $M_2 > 0$ and $M_3 \ge \sup_{n\ge1}(2M_1\|x_n - x^*\| + \beta_n M_1^2)$ for some $M_3 > 0$. Combining the last inequalities, we obtain

$$\begin{aligned}&\|x_{n+1}-x^*\|^2 \\ &\le \beta_n\delta\|x_n-x^*\|^2 + \gamma_n(\|x_n-x^*\|^2 + \beta_n M_3) + (1-\beta_n\tau-\gamma_n)(\|x_n-x^*\|^2 + \beta_n M_3) \\ &\quad - (1-\beta_n\tau-\gamma_n)(1-\zeta_n)[(1-\mu\tfrac{\lambda_n}{\lambda_{n+1}})\|w_n-y_n\|^2 + (1-\mu\tfrac{\lambda_n}{\lambda_{n+1}})\|z_n-y_n\|^2] + \beta_n M_2 \\ &\le \|x_n-x^*\|^2 - (1-\beta_n\tau-\gamma_n)(1-\zeta_n)(1-\mu\tfrac{\lambda_n}{\lambda_{n+1}})[\|w_n-y_n\|^2 + \|z_n-y_n\|^2] + \beta_n M_4,\end{aligned}$$

where $M_4 := M_2 + M_3$. This ensures that (39) holds.

Next we claim that

$$\begin{aligned}\|x_{n+1}-x^*\|^2 \ &\le [1-\beta_n(\tau-\delta)]\|x_n-x^*\|^2 \\ &\quad + \beta_n(\tau-\delta)[\tfrac{2}{\tau-\delta}\langle(f-\rho F)x^*, x_{n+1}-x^*\rangle + \tfrac{3M}{\tau-\delta}\cdot\tfrac{\alpha_n}{\beta_n}\cdot\|x_n-x_{n-1}\|]\end{aligned} \tag{40}$$

for some $M > 0$. In fact, using the similar arguments to those of (22) and (23), we have

$$\|w_n-x^*\|^2 \le \|x_n-x^*\|^2 + \alpha_n\|x_n-x_{n-1}\|[2\|x_n-x^*\| + \alpha_n\|x_n-x_{n-1}\|],$$

and

$$\begin{aligned}&\|x_{n+1}-x^*\|^2 \\ &\le \beta_n\delta\|x_n-x^*\|^2 + \gamma_n\|w_n-x^*\|^2 + (1-\beta_n\tau-\gamma_n)[\zeta_n\|x_n-x^*\|^2 + (1-\zeta_n)\|z_n-x^*\|^2] \\ &\quad + 2\beta_n\langle(f-\rho F)x^*, x_{n+1}-x^*\rangle \\ &\le \beta_n\delta\|x_n-x^*\|^2 + (1-\beta_n\tau)[\|x_n-x^*\|^2 + \alpha_n\|x_n-x_{n-1}\|(2\|x_n-x^*\| \\ &\quad + \alpha_n\|x_n-x_{n-1}\|)] + 2\beta_n\langle(f-\rho F)x^*, x_{n+1}-x^*\rangle \\ &\le [1-\beta_n(\tau-\delta)]\|x_n-x^*\|^2 + \alpha_n\|x_n-x_{n-1}\|(2\|x_n-x^*\| + \alpha_n\|x_n-x_{n-1}\|) \\ &\quad + 2\beta_n\langle(f-\rho F)x^*, x_{n+1}-x^*\rangle \\ &\le [1-\beta_n(\tau-\delta)]\|x_n-x^*\|^2 + \beta_n(\tau-\delta)\cdot[\tfrac{2\langle(f-\rho F)x^*, x_{n+1}-x^*\rangle}{\tau-\delta} + \tfrac{3M}{\tau-\delta}\cdot\tfrac{\alpha_n}{\beta_n}\cdot\|x_n-x_{n-1}\|],\end{aligned} \tag{41}$$

where $M \ge \sup_{n\ge1}\{\|x_n-x^*\|, \alpha_n\|x_n-x_{n-1}\|\}$ for some $M > 0$.

For each $n \ge 0$, we set

$$\begin{aligned}\Gamma_n &= \|x_n-x^*\|^2, \\ \varepsilon_n &= \beta_n(\tau-\delta), \\ \vartheta_n &= \alpha_n\|x_n-x_{n-1}\|3M + 2\beta_n\langle(f-\rho F)x^*, x_{n+1}-x^*\rangle.\end{aligned}$$

Then (41) can be rewritten as the following formula:

$$\Gamma_{n+1} \le (1-\varepsilon_n)\Gamma_n + \vartheta_n \quad \forall n \ge 0. \tag{42}$$

We next show the convergence of $\{\Gamma_n\}$ to zero by the following two cases:

Case 3. *Suppose that there exists an integer $n_0 \ge 1$ such that $\{\Gamma_n\}$ is non-increasing.* Then

$$\Gamma_n - \Gamma_{n+1} \to 0.$$

Using the similar arguments to those of (25), we have

$$\lim_{n\to\infty}\|w_n-y_n\| = \lim_{n\to\infty}\|z_n-y_n\| = 0. \tag{43}$$

Using Lemma 1 (v), we get

$$
\begin{aligned}
&\|x_{n+1}-x^*\|^2\\
&=\|\beta_n(f(x_n)-\rho Fv_n)+\gamma_n(T_nw_n-x^*)+(1-\gamma_n)(v_n-x^*)\|^2\\
&\le\|\gamma_n(T_nw_n-x^*)+(1-\gamma_n)(v_n-x^*)\|^2+2\beta_n\langle f(x_n)-\rho Fv_n,x_{n+1}-x^*\rangle\\
&=\gamma_n\|T_nw_n-x^*\|^2+(1-\gamma_n)\|v_n-x^*\|^2-\gamma_n(1-\gamma_n)\|T_nw_n-v_n\|^2\\
&\quad+2\beta_n\langle f(x_n)-\rho Fv_n,x_{n+1}-x^*\rangle\\
&=\gamma_n\|T_nw_n-x^*\|^2+(1-\gamma_n)[\zeta_n\|x_n-x^*\|^2+(1-\zeta_n)\|Tz_n-x^*\|^2-\zeta_n(1-\zeta_n)\|x_n-Tz_n\|^2]\\
&\quad-\gamma_n(1-\gamma_n)\|T_nw_n-v_n\|^2+2\beta_n\langle f(x_n)-\rho Fv_n,x_{n+1}-x^*\rangle\\
&\le\gamma_n\|w_n-x^*\|^2+(1-\gamma_n)[\zeta_n\|x_n-x^*\|^2+(1-\zeta_n)\|z_n-x^*\|^2-\zeta_n(1-\zeta_n)\|x_n-Tz_n\|^2]\\
&\quad-\gamma_n(1-\gamma_n)\|T_nw_n-v_n\|^2+2\beta_n\langle f(x_n)-\rho Fv_n,x_{n+1}-x^*\rangle\\
&\le\gamma_n(\|x_n-x^*\|+\beta_nM_1)^2+(1-\gamma_n)(\|x_n-x^*\|+\beta_nM_1)^2-(1-\gamma_n)\zeta_n(1-\zeta_n)\|x_n-Tz_n\|^2\\
&\quad-\gamma_n(1-\gamma_n)\|T_nw_n-v_n\|^2+2\beta_n\|f(x_n)-\rho Fv_n\|\|x_{n+1}-x^*\|\\
&=(\|x_n-x^*\|+\beta_nM_1)^2-(1-\gamma_n)\zeta_n(1-\zeta_n)\|x_n-Tz_n\|^2\\
&\quad-\gamma_n(1-\gamma_n)\|T_nw_n-v_n\|^2+2\beta_n\|f(x_n)-\rho Fv_n\|\|x_{n+1}-x^*\|,
\end{aligned}
$$

which immediately yields

$$
\begin{aligned}
&(1-\gamma_n)\zeta_n(1-\zeta_n)\|x_n-Tz_n\|^2+\gamma_n(1-\gamma_n)\|T_nw_n-v_n\|^2\\
&\le(\|x_n-x^*\|+\beta_nM_1)^2-\|x_{n+1}-x^*\|^2+2\beta_n\|f(x_n)-\rho Fv_n\|\|x_{n+1}-x^*\|\\
&=\Gamma_n-\Gamma_{n+1}+\beta_nM_1(2\|x_n-x^*\|+\beta_nM_1)+2\beta_n\|f(x_n)-\rho Fv_n\|\|x_{n+1}-x^*\|.
\end{aligned}
$$

Since $\beta_n\to 0$, $\Gamma_n-\Gamma_{n+1}\to 0$, $\{\gamma_n\}\subset[a,b]\subset(0,1)$ and $\{\zeta_n\}\subset[c,d]\subset(0,1)$, we have

$$\lim_{n\to\infty}\|x_n-Tz_n\|=\lim_{n\to\infty}\|T_nw_n-v_n\|=0. \tag{44}$$

Note that

$$
\begin{aligned}
\|T_nw_n-v_n\|^2&=\|\zeta_n(T_nw_n-x_n)+(1-\zeta_n)(T_nw_n-Tz_n)\|^2\\
&=\zeta_n\|T_nw_n-x_n\|^2+(1-\zeta_n)\|T_nw_n-Tz_n\|^2-\zeta_n(1-\zeta_n)\|Tz_n-x_n\|^2.
\end{aligned}
$$

Hence, from (44) we have

$$\lim_{n\to\infty}\|T_nw_n-x_n\|=\lim_{n\to\infty}\|T_nw_n-Tz_n\|=0. \tag{45}$$

So, from (43)–(45) we infer that

$$\|w_n-z_n\|\le\|w_n-y_n\|+\|y_n-z_n\|\to 0\quad(n\to\infty), \tag{46}$$

$$
\begin{aligned}
\|z_n-T_nz_n\|&\le\|z_n-w_n\|+\|w_n-x_n\|+\|x_n-T_nw_n\|+\|T_nw_n-T_nz_n\|\\
&\le 2\|z_n-w_n\|+\|w_n-x_n\|+\|x_n-T_nw_n\|\to 0\quad(n\to\infty),
\end{aligned} \tag{47}
$$

and

$$
\begin{aligned}
&\|x_{n+1}-x_n\|=\|\beta_nf(x_n)+\gamma_nT_nw_n+((1-\gamma_n)I-\beta_n\rho F)v_n-x_n\|\\
&=\|\beta_n(f(x_n)-\rho Fv_n)+\gamma_n(T_nw_n-x_n)+(1-\gamma_n)(v_n-x_n)\|\\
&\le\beta_n\|f(x_n)-\rho Fv_n\|+\gamma_n\|T_nw_n-x_n\|+(1-\gamma_n)\|v_n-x_n\|\\
&\le\beta_n(\|f(x_n)\|+\|\rho Fv_n\|)+\gamma_n\|T_nw_n-x_n\|+(1-\gamma_n)(\|v_n-T_nw_n\|+\|T_nw_n-x_n\|)\\
&\le\beta_n(\|f(x_n)\|+\|\rho Fv_n\|)+\|T_nw_n-x_n\|+\|v_n-T_nw_n\|\to 0\quad(n\to\infty).
\end{aligned} \tag{48}
$$

In addition, using the similar arguments to those of (33) and (34), we have

$$\limsup_{n\to\infty}\langle(f-\rho F)x^*,x_n-x^*\rangle\le 0,$$

and hence

$$\limsup_{n\to\infty}\langle(f-\rho F)x^*,x_{n+1}-x^*\rangle\le 0.$$

Consequently, applying Lemma 4 to (41), we have $\lim_{n\to 0}\|x_n-x^*\|=0$.

Case 4. *Suppose that* $\exists\{\Gamma_{n_k}\} \subset \{\Gamma_n\}$ *s.t.* $\Gamma_{n_k} < \Gamma_{n_k+1}$ $\forall k \in \mathbf{N}$, *where* $\mathbf{N}$ *is the set of all positive integers.* Define the mapping $\tau : \mathbf{N} \to \mathbf{N}$ by $\tau(n) := \max\{k \leq n : \Gamma_k < \Gamma_{k+1}\}$. In the remainder of the proof, using the same arguments as in Case 2 of the proof of Theorem 1, we obtain the desired assertion. This completes the proof.

It is markable that our results improve and extend the corresponding results of Kraikaew and Saejung [20] and Ceng et al. [11], in the following aspects.

(i) Our problem of finding an element of $\cap_{i=0}^N \mathrm{Fix}(T_i) \cap \mathrm{VI}(C, A)$ includes as a special case the problem of finding an element of $\mathrm{VI}(C, A)$ in [20], where $T_1, ..., T_N$ are nonexpansive and $T_0 = T$ is quasi-nonexpansive. It is worth mentioning that Halpern's subgradient extragradient method for solving the VIP in [20] is extended to develop our Mann-type inertial subgradient extragradient rule for solving the VIP and CFPP, in which A is L-Lipschitz continuous, pseudomonotone on H, but it is not required to be sequentially weakly continuous on C.

(ii) Our problem of finding an element of $\cap_{i=0}^N \mathrm{Fix}(T_i) \cap \mathrm{VI}(C, A)$ includes as a special case the problem of finding an element of $\cap_{i=1}^N \mathrm{Fix}(T_i) \cap \mathrm{VI}(C, A)$ in [11], where in [11], A is required to be L-Lipschitz continuous, pseudomonotone on H, and sequentially weakly continuous on C. The modified inertial subgradient extragradient method for solving the VIP and CFPP in [11] is extended to develop our Mann-type inertial subgradient extragradient rule for solving the VIP and CFPP, where T_i is nonexpansive for $i = 1, ..., N$ and $T_0 = T$ is quasi-nonexpansive.

4. Applicability and Implementability of Algorithms

In this section, in order to support the applicability and implementability of our Algorithms 1 and 2, we make use of our main results to find a common solution of the VIP and CFPP in two illustrating examples.

Example 2. *Let* $C = [-1, 1]$ *and* $H = \mathbf{R}$ *with the inner product* $\langle a, b\rangle = ab$ *and induced norm* $\|\cdot\| = |\cdot|$. *Let* $x_0, x_1 \in H$ *be arbitrary. Put* $f(x) = F(x) = \frac{1}{2}x$, $\beta_n = \frac{1}{n+1}$, $\tau_n = \beta_n^2$, $\mu = 0.2$, $\alpha = \lambda_1 = 0.1$, $\gamma_n = \zeta_n = \frac{1}{3}$, $\rho = 2$, *and*

$$\alpha_n = \begin{cases} \min\{\frac{\beta_n^2}{\|x_n - x_{n-1}\|}, \alpha\} & \text{if } x_n \neq x_{n-1}, \\ \alpha & \text{otherwise.} \end{cases}$$

Then we know that $\kappa = \eta = \frac{1}{2}$ *and* $\tau = 1 - \sqrt{1 - \rho(2\eta - \rho\kappa^2)} = 1 \in (0, 1]$. *For* $N = 1$, *we now present Lipschitz continuous and pseudomonotone mapping* A, *quasi-nonexpansive mapping* T *and nonexpansive mapping* T_1 *such that* $\Omega = \mathrm{Fix}(T_1) \cap \mathrm{Fix}(T) \cap \mathrm{VI}(C, A) \neq \emptyset$. *Indeed, let* $A, T, T_1 : H \to H$ *be defined as* $Ax := \frac{1}{1+|\sin x|} - \frac{1}{1+|x|}$, $T_1 x := \sin x$ *and* $Tx := \frac{x}{2} \sin x$ *for all* $x \in H$. *We first show that* A *is pseudomonotone and* L*-Lipschitz continuous with* $L = 2$. *Indeed, it is easy to see that for all* $x, y \in H$,

$$\begin{aligned} \|Ax - Ay\| &= |\tfrac{1}{1+\|\sin x\|} - \tfrac{1}{1+\|x\|} - \tfrac{1}{1+\|\sin y\|} + \tfrac{1}{1+\|y\|}| \\ &\leq |\tfrac{\|y\| - \|x\|}{(1+\|x\|)(1+\|y\|)}| + |\tfrac{\|\sin y\| - \|\sin x\|}{(1+\|\sin x\|)(1+\|\sin y\|)}| \\ &\leq \tfrac{\|x-y\|}{(1+\|x\|)(1+\|y\|)} + \tfrac{\|\sin x - \sin y\|}{(1+\|\sin x\|)(1+\|\sin y\|)} \\ &\leq 2\|x - y\|, \end{aligned}$$

and

$$\langle Ax, y - x\rangle = (\frac{1}{1 + |\sin x|} - \frac{1}{1 + |x|})(y - x) \geq 0 \Rightarrow \langle Ay, y - x\rangle = (\frac{1}{1 + |\sin y|} - \frac{1}{1 + |y|})(y - x) \geq 0.$$

Furthermore, it is clear that $\mathrm{Fix}(T) = \{0\}$, T *is quasi-nonexpansive but not nonexpansive. Meantime,* $I - T$ *is demiclosed at* 0 *due to the continuity of* T. *In addition, it is clear that* T_1 *is nonexpansive and* $\mathrm{Fix}(T_1) = \{0\}$. *Therefore,* $\Omega = \mathrm{Fix}(T_1) \cap \mathrm{Fix}(T) \cap \mathrm{VI}(C, A) = \{0\} \neq \emptyset$. *In this case, Algorithm 1 can be rewritten as follows:*

$$\begin{cases} w_n = x_n + \alpha_n(x_n - x_{n-1}), \\ y_n = P_C(w_n - \lambda_n A w_n), \\ z_n = P_{C_n}(w_n - \lambda_n A y_n), \\ v_n = \frac{1}{3}x_n + \frac{2}{3}T_1 w_n, \\ x_{n+1} = \frac{1}{n+1} \cdot \frac{1}{2}x_n + \frac{1}{3}Tz_n + (\frac{n}{n+1} - \frac{1}{3})v_n \quad \forall n \geq 1, \end{cases} \tag{49}$$

where for each $n \geq 1$, C_n *and* λ_n *are chosen as in Algorithm 1. So, using Theorem 1, we know that* $\{x_n\}$ *converges to* $0 \in \Omega = \mathrm{Fix}(T_1) \cap \mathrm{Fix}(T) \cap \mathrm{VI}(C, A)$. *Meanwhile, Algorithm 2 can be rewritten as follows:*

$$\begin{cases} w_n = x_n + \alpha_n(x_n - x_{n-1}), \\ y_n = P_C(w_n - \lambda_n A w_n), \\ z_n = P_{C_n}(w_n - \lambda_n A y_n), \\ v_n = \frac{1}{3}x_n + \frac{2}{3}Tz_n, \\ x_{n+1} = \frac{1}{n+1} \cdot \frac{1}{2}x_n + \frac{1}{3}T_1 w_n + (\frac{n}{n+1} - \frac{1}{3})v_n \quad \forall n \geq 1, \end{cases} \tag{50}$$

where, for each $n \geq 1$, C_n *and* λ_n *are chosen as in Algorithm 2. So, using Theorem 2, we know that* $\{x_n\}$ *converges to* $0 \in \Omega = \mathrm{Fix}(T_1) \cap \mathrm{Fix}(T) \cap \mathrm{VI}(C, A)$.

Example 3. *Let* $H = L^2([0, 1])$ *with the inner product and induced norm defined by*

$$\langle x, y \rangle = \int_0^1 x(t)y(t)dt \quad \text{and} \quad \|x\| = (\int_0^1 |x(t)|^2 dt)^{1/2} \quad \forall x, y \in H,$$

respectively. Then $(H, \langle \cdot, \cdot \rangle)$ *is a Hilbert space. Let* $C := \{x \in H : \|x\| \leq 1\}$ *be the unit closed ball of H. It is known that*

$$P_C(x) = \begin{cases} \frac{x}{\|x\|} & \text{if } \|x\| > 1, \\ x & \text{if } \|x\| \leq 1. \end{cases}$$

Let $x_0, x_1 \in H$ *be arbitrary. Put* $f(x) = F(x) = \frac{1}{2}x$, $\beta_n = \frac{1}{n+1}$, $\tau_n = \beta_n^2$, $\mu = 0.2$, $\alpha = \lambda_1 = 0.1$, $\gamma_n = \zeta_n = \frac{1}{3}$, $\rho = 2$, *and*

$$\alpha_n = \begin{cases} \min\{\frac{\beta_n^2}{\|x_n - x_{n-1}\|}, \alpha\} & \text{if } x_n \neq x_{n-1}, \\ \alpha & \text{otherwise.} \end{cases}$$

Then we know that $\kappa = \eta = \frac{1}{2}$ *and* $\tau = 1 - \sqrt{1 - \rho(2\eta - \rho\kappa^2)} = 1 \in (0, 1]$. *For* $N = 1$, *we now present Lipschitz continuous and pseudomonotone mapping A, quasi-nonexpansive mapping T and nonexpansive mapping* T_1 *such that* $\Omega = \mathrm{Fix}(T_1) \cap \mathrm{Fix}(T) \cap \mathrm{VI}(C, A) \neq \emptyset$. *Indeed, let* $A, T, T_1 : H \to H$ *be defined as* $(Ax)(t) := \max\{0, x(t)\}$, $(T_1 x)(t) := \frac{1}{2}x(t) - \frac{1}{2}\sin x(t)$ *and* $(Tx)(t) := \frac{1}{2}x(t) + \frac{1}{2}\sin x(t)$ *for all* $x \in H$. *It can be easily verified (see, e.g., [8,9]) that A is monotone and L-Lipschitz continuous with* $L = 1$, *and the solution set of the VIP for A is given by*

$$\mathrm{VI}(C, A) = \{0\} \neq \emptyset.$$

We next show that T and T_1 *are nonexpansive and* $\mathrm{Fix}(T) = \mathrm{Fix}(T_1) = \{0\}$. *Indeed, it is easy to see that for all* $x, y \in H$,

$$\begin{aligned} \|Tx - Ty\| &= (\int_0^1 |\tfrac{1}{2}(x(t) - y(t)) + \tfrac{1}{2}(\sin x(t) - \sin y(t))|^2 dt)^{1/2} \\ &\leq (\int_0^1 (\tfrac{1}{2}|x(t) - y(t)| + \tfrac{1}{2}|x(t) - y(t)|)^2 dt)^{1/2} \\ &= (\int_0^1 |x(t) - y(t)|^2 dt)^{1/2} \\ &= \|x - y\|. \end{aligned}$$

Similarly, we get $\|T_1x - T_1y\| \le \|x - y\|\ \forall x, y \in H$. *Moreover, it is clear that* $\mathrm{Fix}(T) = \mathrm{Fix}(T_1) = \{0\}$. *Therefore,* $\Omega = \mathrm{Fix}(T_1) \cap \mathrm{Fix}(T) \cap \mathrm{VI}(C, A) = \{0\} \neq \emptyset$. *In this case, Algorithm 1 can be rewritten as follows:*

$$\begin{cases} w_n = x_n + \alpha_n(x_n - x_{n-1}), \\ y_n = P_C(w_n - \lambda_n A w_n), \\ z_n = P_{C_n}(w_n - \lambda_n A y_n), \\ v_n = \frac{1}{3}x_n + \frac{2}{3}T_1 w_n, \\ x_{n+1} = \frac{1}{n+1} \cdot \frac{1}{2}x_n + \frac{1}{3}Tz_n + (\frac{n}{n+1} - \frac{1}{3})v_n \quad \forall n \ge 1, \end{cases} \tag{51}$$

where for each $n \ge 1$, C_n *and* λ_n *are chosen as in Algorithm 1. So, using Theorem 1, we know that* $\{x_n\}$ *converges strongly to* $0 \in \Omega = \mathrm{Fix}(T_1) \cap \mathrm{Fix}(T) \cap \mathrm{VI}(C, A)$. *Meantime, Algorithm 2 can be rewritten as follows:*

$$\begin{cases} w_n = x_n + \alpha_n(x_n - x_{n-1}), \\ y_n = P_C(w_n - \lambda_n A w_n), \\ z_n = P_{C_n}(w_n - \lambda_n A y_n), \\ v_n = \frac{1}{3}x_n + \frac{2}{3}Tz_n, \\ x_{n+1} = \frac{1}{n+1} \cdot \frac{1}{2}x_n + \frac{1}{3}T_1 w_n + (\frac{n}{n+1} - \frac{1}{3})v_n \quad \forall n \ge 1, \end{cases} \tag{52}$$

where for each $n \ge 1$, C_n *and* λ_n *are chosen as in Algorithm 2. So, using Theorem 2, we know that* $\{x_n\}$ *converges strongly to* $0 \in \Omega = \mathrm{Fix}(T_1) \cap \mathrm{Fix}(T) \cap \mathrm{VI}(C, A)$.

Author Contributions: All the authors contributed equally to this work. All authors have read and agreed to the published version of the manuscript.

Funding: This research received no external funding.

Institutional Review Board Statement: Not applicable.

Informed Consent Statement: Not applicable.

Data Availability Statement: Not applicable.

Acknowledgments: The research of J. C. Yao was partially supported by the Grant MOST 108-2115-M-039-005-MY3.

Conflicts of Interest: The authors declare no conflict of interest.

References

1. Korpelevich, G.M. The extragradient method for finding saddle points and other problems. *Ekon. Mat. Metod.* **1976**, *12*, 747–756.
2. Cho, S.Y. A monotone Bregan projection algorithm for fixed point and equilibrium problems in a reflexive Banach space. *Filomat* **2020**, *34*, 1487–1497. [CrossRef]
3. Nguyen, L.V.; Ansari, Q.H.; Qin, X. Weak sharpness and finite convergence for solutions of nonsmooth variational inequalities in Hilbert spaces. *Appl. Math. Optim.* **2020**. [CrossRef]
4. Liu, L. A hybrid steepest descent method for solving split feasibility problems involving nonexpansive mappings. *J. Nonlinear Convex Anal.* **2019**, *20*, 471–488.
5. Cho, S.Y. A convergence theorem for generalized mixed equilibrium problems and multivalued asymptotically nonexpansive mappings. *J. Nonlinear Convex Anal.* **2000**, *21*, 1017–1026.
6. Ceng, L.C.; Shang, M. Generalized Mann viscosity implicit rules for solving systems of variational inequalities with constraints of variational inclusions and fixed point problems. *Mathematics* **2019**, *7*, 933. [CrossRef]
7. Cho, S.Y.; Bin Dehaish, B.A. Weak convergence of a splitting algorithm in Hilbert spaces. *J. Appl. Anal. Comput.* **2017**, *7*, 427–438.
8. Alakoya, T.O.; Jolaoso, L.O.; Mewomo, O.T. Two modifications of the inertial Tseng extragradient method with self-adaptive step size for solving monotone variational inequality problems. *Demonstr. Math.* **2020**, *53*, 208–224. [CrossRef]
9. Gebrie, A.G.; Wangkeeree, R. Strong convergence of an inertial extrapolation method for a split system of minimization problems. *Demonstr. Math.* **2020**, *53*, 332–351. [CrossRef]
10. Shehu, Y.; Dong, Q.; Jiang, D. Single projection method for pseudo-monotone variational inequality in Hilbert spaces. *Optimization* **2019**, *68*, 385–409. [CrossRef]
11. Ceng, L.C.; Petrusel, A.; Qin, X.; Yao, J.C. A modified inertial subgradient extragradient method for solving pseudomonotone variational inequalities and common fixed point problems. *Fixed Point Theory* **2020**, *21*, 93–108. [CrossRef]

12. Ceng, L.C.; Shang M.J. Hybrid inertial subgradient extragradient methods for variational inequalities and fixed point problems involving asymptotically nonexpansive mappings. *Optimization* **2021**, *70*, 715–740. [CrossRef]
13. Censor, Y.; Gibali, A.; Reich, S. The subgradient extragradient method for solving variational inequalities in Hilbert space. *J. Optim. Theory Appl.* **2011**, *148*, 318–335. [CrossRef]
14. Tan, B.; Xu, S.; Li, S. Inertial shrinking proection algorithms for solving hierarchical variational inequality problems. *J. Nonlinear Convex Anal.* **2020**, *21*, 871–884.
15. Fan, J. A subgradient extragradient algorithm with inertial effects for solving strongly pseudomonotone variational inequalities. *Optimization* **2020**, *69*, 2199–2215. [CrossRef]
16. Qin, X.; Cho, S.Y.; Wang, L. Strong convergence of an iterative algorithm involving nonlinear mappings of nonexpansive and accretive type. *Optimization* **2018**, *67*, 1377–1388. [CrossRef]
17. Ceng, L.C.; Yuan, Q. Composite inertial subgradient extragradient methods for variational inequalities and fixed point problems. *J. Inequal. Appl.* **2019**, *2019*, 374. [CrossRef]
18. Nguyen, L.V.; Qin, X. Some results on strongly pseudomonotone quasi-variational inequalities. *Set-Valued Var. Anal.* **2020**, *28*, 239–257. [CrossRef]
19. Ceng, L.C.; Postolache, M.; Yao, Y. Iterative algorithms for a system of variational inclusions in Banach spaces. *Symmetry* **2019**, *11*, 811. [CrossRef]
20. Kraikaew, R.; Saejung, S. Strong convergence of the Halpern subgradient extragradient method for solving variational inequalities in Hilbert spaces. *J. Optim. Theory Appl.* **2014**, *163*, 399–412. [CrossRef]
21. Thong, D.V.; Hieu, D.V. Modified subgradient extragradient method for variational inequality problems. *Numer. Alg.* **2018**, *79*, 597–610. [CrossRef]
22. Thong, D.V.; Hieu, D.V. Inertial subgradient extragradient algorithms with line-search process for solving variational inequality problems and fixed point problems. *Numer. Alg.* **2019**, *80*, 1283–1307. [CrossRef]
23. Zhou, H.; Qin, X. *Fixed Points of Nonlinear Operators*; Iterative Methods; De Gruyter: Berlin, Germany, 2020.
24. Denisov, S.V.; Semenov, V.V.; Chabak, L.M. Convergence of the modified extragradient method for variational inequalities with non-Lipschitz operators. *Cybern. Syst. Anal.* **2015**, *51*, 757–765. [CrossRef]
25. Xu, H.K.; Kim, T.H. Convergence of hybrid steepest-descent methods for variational inequalities. *J. Optim. Theory Appl.* **2003**, *119*, 185–201. [CrossRef]
26. Maingé, P.E. Strong convergence of projected subgradient methods for nonsmooth and nonstrictly convex minimization. *Set-Valued Anal.* **2008**, *16*, 899–912. [CrossRef]

axioms

MDPI

Article

On Convex F-Contraction in b-Metric Spaces

Huaping Huang [1,*], Zoran D. Mitrović [2], Kastriot Zoto [3] and Stojan Radenović [4]

1 School of Mathematics and Statistics, Chongqing Three Gorges University, Wanzhou 404020, China
2 Faculty of Electrical Engineering, University of Banja Luka, Patre 5, 78000 Banja Luka, Bosnia and Herzegovina; zoran.mitrovic@etf.unibl.org
3 Department of Mathematics and Computer Sciences, Faculty of Natural Sciences, University of Gjirokastra, 6001 Gjirokastra, Albania; zotokastriot@yahoo.com
4 Faculty of Mechanical Engineering, University of Belgrade, Kraljice Marije 16, 11120 Beograd, Serbia; radens@beotel.net
* Correspondence: huaping@sanxiau.edu.cn

Abstract: In this paper, we introduce a notion of convex F-contraction and establish some fixed point results for such contractions in b-metric spaces. Moreover, we give a supportive example to show that our convex F-contraction is quite different from the F-contraction used in the existing literature since our convex F-contraction does not necessarily contain the continuous mapping but the F-contraction contains such mapping. In addition, via some facts, we claim that our results indeed generalize and improve some previous results in the literature.

Keywords: F-contraction; convex F-contraction; fixed point; b-metric space

MSC: 47H10; 54H25

Citation: Huang, H.; Mitrović, Z.D.; Zoto, K.; Radenović, S. On Convex F-Contraction in b-Metric Spaces. *Axioms* **2021**, *10*, 71. https://doi.org/10.3390/axioms10020071

Academic Editors: Alexander Šostak and Hsien-Chung Wu

Received: 4 March 2021
Accepted: 15 April 2021
Published: 19 April 2021

Publisher's Note: MDPI stays neutral with regard to jurisdictional claims in published maps and institutional affiliations.

Copyright: © 2021 by the authors. Licensee MDPI, Basel, Switzerland. This article is an open access article distributed under the terms and conditions of the Creative Commons Attribution (CC BY) license (https://creativecommons.org/licenses/by/4.0/).

1. Introduction and Preliminaries

In [1], Wardowski introduced the following concept of F-contraction and proved a fixed point theorem that generalizes the classical Banach contraction mapping principle.

Definition 1 ([1]). *Let (X, d) be a metric space and $T : X \to X$ be a mapping. Then T is called an F-contraction if there exists a function $F : (0, +\infty) \to \mathbb{R}$ such that*

(F_1) *F is strictly increasing on $(0, +\infty)$;*

(F_2) *for each sequence $\{\alpha_n\}$ of positive numbers,*

$$\lim_{n\to\infty} \alpha_n = 0 \text{ if and only if } \lim_{n\to\infty} F(\alpha_n) = -\infty;$$

(F_3) *there exists $k \in (0,1)$ such that $\lim_{\alpha\to 0^+} \alpha^k F(\alpha) = 0$;*

(F_4) *there exists $\tau > 0$ such that*

$$\tau + F(d(Tx, Ty)) \le F(d(x, y)) \tag{1}$$

for all $x, y \in X$ with $x \neq y$.

Remark 1. *Definition 1 is the modification of [1] (Definition 2.1). In fact, (2) from [1] says $d(Tx, Ty) > 0$, that is, $Tx \neq Ty$. Note that $Tx \neq Ty$ implies $x \neq y$. Hence, $x \neq y$ in (F_4) is weaker condition than $d(Tx, Ty) > 0$ from (2) of [1]. Moreover, our modification does not disturb the main results of [1]. Clearly, compared with $d(Tx, Ty) > 0$ from [1], our $x \neq y$ is more convenient in applications.*

Otherwise, by (1) *and* (F_1), *we have*

$$d(Tx, Ty) < d(x, y) \tag{2}$$

for all $x, y \in X$ with $x \neq y$. Accordingly, any F-contraction is a contraction.

Remark 2. *It follows immediately from* (2) *that any F-contraction implies that the mapping T is a continuous mapping.*

Wardowski [1] proved that any F-contraction has a unique fixed point.

Theorem 1 ([1])**.** *Let (X, d) be a complete metric space and $T : X \to X$ be an F-contraction. Then, T has a unique fixed point x^* in X. For every $x \in X$, the sequence $\{T^n x\}$ converges to x^*.*

Since then, several authors proved fixed point results for F-contractions (see [2–13]). However, F-contraction has a great limitation since the mapping must be a continuous mapping (see Remark 2). But the continuity is a strong condition. Hence, it restricts the applications greatly.

On the other hand, the concept of b-metric space was introduced by Bakhtin [14] or Czerwik [15] which is a great generalization of usual metric space.

Definition 2. *A b-metric space (X, d, s) $(s \geq 1)$ is a space defined on a nonempty set X with a mapping $d : X \times X \to [0, +\infty)$ satisfying the following conditions:*

(1) $d(x, y) = 0$ if and only if $x = y$;

(2) $d(x, y) = d(y, x)$ for all $x, y \in X$;

(3) $d(x, y) \leq s[d(x, z) + d(z, y)]$ for all $x, y, z \in X$.

In this case, d is called a b-metric on X.

Regarding some other concepts, such as the concepts of b-convergent sequence, b-Cauchy sequence and b-completeness, the reader may refer to [16] and the references therein.

In the sequel, unless there is a special explanation, we always denote by $\mathbb{N}$, the set of positive integers, $\mathbb{R}$, the set of real numbers.

Let (X, d, s) be a b-metric space and T be a self-mapping on X. The Picard sequence of T is given by $\{x_n\}_{n \in \mathbb{N} \cup \{0\}} = \{T^n x\}_{n \in \mathbb{N} \cup \{0\}}$ for any $x \in X$, where $T^0 x = x$. In this case, for the convenience, throughout this paper, we always denote $d(x_{n+1}, x_n)$ by d_n, for all $n \in \mathbb{N} \cup \{0\}$.

In this paper, we introduce the concept of convex F-contraction and give some sufficient conditions when the Picard sequence of convex F-contraction on b-metric space satisfies the Cauchy condition. Our results improve the results of Cosentino and Vetro [17]. Our conclusions are some real generalizations of the results of Popescu and Stan [18]. Moreover, we also expand the main results of Wardowski and Dung [13]. Additionally, we pose two problems at the end of the main text. We aim to continue to work in order to solve the problems in the near future.

2. Main Results

In this section, we first define a notion called convex F-contraction in b-metric spaces. Moreover, we give two examples to illustrate our notion is well-defined. Further, we present a fixed point result for such contraction.

Definition 3. *Let (X, d, s) be a b-metric space and T be a self-mapping on X. We say that T is a convex F-contraction if there exists a function $F : (0, +\infty) \to \mathbb{R}$ such that Condition (F_1) holds and*

(F_2^{α}) for each sequence $\{\alpha_n\}$ of positive numbers, if $\lim_{n\to\infty} F(\alpha_n) = -\infty$, then $\lim_{n\to\infty} \alpha_n = 0$;

(F_3^{s}) there exists $k \in (0, \frac{1}{1+\log_2 s})$ such that $\lim_{\alpha\to 0^+} \alpha^k F(\alpha) = 0$;

(F_4^{λ}) there exist $\tau > 0$ and $\lambda \in [0, 1)$ such that

$$\tau + F(d_n) \leq F(\lambda d_n + (1 - \lambda) d_{n-1}), \tag{3}$$

for all $d_n > 0$, where $n \in \mathbb{N}$.

Remark 3. *Definition 3 improves Definition 1 greatly. Indeed, (F_2^α) is weaker than Condition (F_2). If $s = 1$, then Condition (F_3^s) is Condition (F_3). That is to say, (F_3^s) expands Condition (F_3). Moreover, if $\lambda = 0$, then Condition (F_4^λ) is a consequence of Condition (F_4).*

Example 1. *Let (X, d, s) be a b-metric space and $T : X \to X$ be a mapping. Suppose that T is an F-contraction of Kannan type, i.e., there exists $\tau > 0$ such that*

$$\tau + F(d(Tx, Ty)) \leq F\left(\frac{1}{2}[d(x, Tx) + d(y, Ty)]\right) \tag{4}$$

for all $x, y \in X$ with $x \neq y$.

Choose $F(\alpha) = \ln \alpha$, $\alpha \in (0, +\infty)$, then T is a convex F-contraction. Indeed, it is obvious that F satisfies Conditions (F_1), (F_2^α) and (F_3^s). Moreover, T satisfies Condition (F_4^λ) based on the fact that there exists $\lambda = \frac{1}{2}$ such that

$$\tau + F(d_n) \leq F\left(\frac{d_n}{2} + \frac{d_{n-1}}{2}\right)$$

for all $d_n > 0$, where $n \in \mathbb{N}$. That is, (4) becomes (F_4^λ).

Otherwise, if $F(\alpha) = \ln \alpha$, $\alpha \in (0, +\infty)$, then from (4) we have

$$d(Tx, Ty) \leq K[d(x, Tx) + d(y, Ty)],$$

where $K = \frac{e^{-\tau}}{2} < \frac{1}{2}$, i.e., the contraction of Kannan type (see [19]) holds.

Example 2. *Let T be an F-contraction of Reich type (see [20]), i.e., there exist $\tau > 0$ and $\alpha, \beta, \gamma \in [0, 1], \alpha + \beta + \gamma = 1$ such that*

$$\tau + F(d(Tx, Ty)) \leq F(\alpha d(x, y) + \beta d(x, Tx) + \gamma d(y, Ty)), \tag{5}$$

for all $x, y \in X$ with $x \neq y$.

Choose $F(\alpha) = -\frac{1}{\sqrt{\alpha}}$, $\alpha \in (0, +\infty)$, then T is a convex F-contraction. Indeed, it is clear that F satisfies Conditions (F_1), (F_2^α) and (F_3^s). Moreover, T satisfies Condition (F_4^λ) because there exists $\lambda = \beta$ such that (3) holds. That is, T satisfies Condition (F_4^λ).

Otherwise, if $F(\alpha) = -\frac{1}{\sqrt{\alpha}}$, $\alpha \in (0, +\infty)$, then (5) implies

$$d(Tx, Ty) < \alpha d(x, y) + \beta d(x, Tx) + \gamma d(y, Ty),$$

which is the contraction of Reich type.

Lemma 1. *Let (X, d, s) be a b-metric space and T be a convex F-contraction on X. Then, for every $x \in X$, the sequences $\{T^n x\}_{n \in \mathbb{N} \cup \{0\}}$ is a b-Cauchy sequence.*

Proof. Choose $x \in X$ and construct a sequence $\{x_n\}$ by $x_n = T^n x$ for all $n \in \mathbb{N} \cup \{0\}$. If there exists $n_0 \in \mathbb{N} \cup \{0\}$ such that $x_{n_0+1} = x_{n_0}$, then

$$\{x_n\} = \{x, Tx, T^2x, \ldots, T^{n_0-1}x, x_{n_0}, x_{n_0}, \ldots\}.$$

It is valid that $\{T^n x\}_{n \in \mathbb{N} \cup \{0\}}$ is a b-Cauchy sequence. The proof is completed.

Without loss of generality, assume that $x_{n+1} \neq x_n$ for all $n \in \mathbb{N} \cup \{0\}$. That is to say, assume that $d_n > 0$ for all $n \in \mathbb{N} \cup \{0\}$. From Condition (F_4^λ), we have

$$F(d_n) < \tau + F(d_n) \leq F(\lambda d_n + (1 - \lambda)d_{n-1}).$$

Using Condition (F_1), we obtain

$$d_n < \lambda d_n + (1-\lambda)d_{n-1},$$

then $0 < d_n < d_{n-1}$ for all $n \in \mathbb{N}$. Hence, $\{d_n\}$ is a convergent sequence.

In the following, we show $\lim_{n\to\infty} d_n = 0$. To this end, we show

$$\tau + F(d_n) \le F(d_{n-1}), \tag{6}$$

for all $n \in \mathbb{N}$.

Indeed, if (6) is not true, then

$$\tau + F(d_n) > F(d_{n-1}),$$

for some $n \in \mathbb{N}$. Thus, it establishes that

$$F(d_{n-1}) < \tau + F(d_n) \le F(\lambda d_n + (1-\lambda)d_{n-1}).$$

Using Condition (F_1), we get

$$d_{n-1} < \lambda d_n + (1-\lambda)d_{n-1},$$

which means $d_{n-1} < d_n$. This is a contradiction.

It follows immediately from (6) that

$$F(d_n) \le F(d_0) - n\tau, \tag{7}$$

for all $n \in \mathbb{N}$. (7) implies $\lim_{n\to\infty} F(d_n) = -\infty$. Then by Condition (F_2^{α}), it leads to $\lim_{n\to\infty} d_n = 0$.

In view of $\lim_{n\to\infty} d_n = 0$, then via Condition (F_3^s), there exists $k \in (0, \frac{1}{1+\log_2 s})$ such that

$$\lim_{n\to\infty} d_n^k F(d_n) = 0. \tag{8}$$

From (7) we obtain

$$d_n^k n\tau \le d_n^k F(d_0) - d_n^k F(d_n). \tag{9}$$

Combine (8) and (9), it is easy to see that

$$\lim_{n\to\infty} d_n^k n = 0.$$

Therefore, there exists $n_0 \in \mathbb{N}$ such that

$$d_n \le \frac{1}{n^{\frac{1}{k}}},$$

for all $n \ge n_0$. Finally, using [21] (Lemma 11), we claim that $\{x_n\}$ is a b-Cauchy sequence. □

Theorem 2. *Let (X, d, s) be a b-complete b-metric space and T be a continuous convex F-contraction on X. Then, T has a fixed point in X.*

Proof. For any $x \in X$, by Lemma 1 we deduce that the sequence $\{T^n x\}$ is b-convergent. Write $x^* = \lim_{n\to\infty} T^n x$. Due to the continuity of the mapping T, we conclude that x^* is a fixed point of T. □

Remark 4. *The continuous condition of Theorem 2 is necessary because there exists discontinuous convex F-contraction. See Example 3 in the sequel.*

3. Some Results Related to Convex F-Contractions

In this section, we obtain some results regarding convex F-contractions. We give a supportive example to verify that the mapping T with regard to convex F-contraction is not necessarily continuous. This fact shows that our convex F-contraction is more meaningful than the F-contraction introduced by Wardowski [1] since any F-contraction must contain the continuous mapping T (see Remark 2).

First of all, we present a fixed point theorem for F-contraction of Banach type as follows:

Theorem 3. *Let (X,d,s) be a b-complete b-metric space and T be a self-mapping on X. Suppose that there exists a function $F:(0,+\infty)\to\mathbb{R}$ satisfying Conditions (F_1), (F_2^{α}), (F_3^{s}) and (F_4). Then, T has a unique fixed point x^* in X. Moreover, for any $x\in X$, the sequence $\{T^n x\}$ b-converges to x^*.*

Proof. From Condition (F_4) we obtain Condition (F_4^{λ}) if we choose $\lambda=0$. So, T is a convex F-contraction. Since (F_4) is satisfied, then by Remark 2, T is continuous. Now, from Theorem 2 and Lemma 1, we conclude that for any $x\in X$, there exists $x^*\in X$ such that $Tx^*=x^*$ and $x^*=\lim_{n\to\infty} T^n x$.

In the following, we prove that the fixed point of T is unique. Indeed, assume that T has another fixed point $y^*\in X$, then by (F_4), ones have

$$F(d(x^*,y^*))=F(d(Tx^*,Ty^*))<\tau+F(d(Tx^*,Ty^*))\le F(d(x^*,y^*)),$$

which is a contraction. □

Remark 5. *Note that, from Theorem 3 we get Theorem 1 because in metric spaces $1+\log_2 s=1$ holds, where $s=1$. Therefore, Theorem 3 generalizes Theorem 1.*

Secondly, we give a fixed point theorem for the F-contraction of Kannan type as follows:

Theorem 4. *Let (X,d,s) be a b-complete b-metric space with $s\in[1,2)$. Let T be an F-contraction of Kannan type, i.e., T satisfies (4). Suppose that there exists a function $F:(0,+\infty)\to\mathbb{R}$ satisfying Conditions (F_1), (F_2^{α}) and (F_3^{s}). Then, T has a unique fixed point x^* in X. Moreover, for any $x\in X$, the sequence $\{T^n x\}$ b-converges to x^*.*

Proof. From Example 1 we obtain that T is a convex F-contraction. So, by Lemma 1 we conclude that there exists $x^*\in X$ such that $x^*=\lim_{n\to\infty} x_n$, where $x_n=T^n x$ for any $x\in X$. Next, from Condition (4) and (F_1) we obtain

$$d(Tx,Ty)<\frac{1}{2}[d(x,Tx)+d(y,Ty)] \tag{10}$$

for all $x,y\in X$ with $x\ne y$.

If $x^*\ne Tx^*$, using (10), we have

$$\begin{aligned} d(x^*,Tx^*) &\le s[d(x^*,x_{n+1})+d(x_{n+1},Tx^*)] \\ &\le s\left(d(x^*,x_{n+1})+\frac{1}{2}[d(x_n,x_{n+1})+d(x^*,Tx^*)]\right). \end{aligned}$$

Take the limit as $n\to\infty$ from the above inequality, it follows that

$$d(x^*,Tx^*)\le\frac{s}{2}d(x^*,Tx^*)<d(x^*,Tx^*),$$

which is a contradiction. Hence, $x^*=Tx^*$.

Finally, we prove the fixed point of T is unique. As a matter of fact, if T has two distinct fixed points x^* and y^*, i.e., $x^* \neq y^*$, then by (10), it is easy to see that

$$d(x^*, y^*) = d(Tx^*, Ty^*) < \frac{1}{2}[d(x^*, Tx^*) + d(y^*, Ty^*)] = 0.$$

which is a contradiction. □

Remark 6. *Similar to Theorem 4, the mapping T has a unique fixed point if T from Theorem 4 is replaced by the F-contraction of Chatterjea type (see [22]), i.e., there exists $\tau > 0$ such that*

$$\tau + F(d(Tx, Ty)) \leq F\left(\frac{1}{2s}[d(x, Ty) + d(y, Tx)]\right)$$

for all $x, y \in X$ with $x \neq y$.

Example 3. *Let $X = \mathbb{R}$ and define a mapping $d : X \times X \to [0, +\infty)$ by*

$$d(x, y) = |x - y|^p$$

for all $x, y \in X$, where $p \in [1, 2)$. Then (X, d, s) is a b-metric space with $s = 2^{p-1} \in [1, 2)$. Let $T : X \to X$ be a mapping defined by

$$Tx = \begin{cases} 0, & \text{if } x \in (-\infty, 2], \\ \frac{1}{2}, & \text{if } x \in (2, +\infty). \end{cases}$$

Let $F(\alpha) = \ln \alpha$, $\alpha \in (0, +\infty)$, then F satisfies (F_1), (F_2^α) and (F_3^s). Moreover, there exists $\tau = -\ln(2K) > 0$ such that T is an F-contraction of Kannan type, where $K \in [\frac{1}{3^p}, \frac{1}{2})$ is a constant. Hence, T satisfies (4). Clearly, T is not continuous but by Theorem 4, it has a unique fixed point $x^* = 0$ in X.

Otherwise, it is easy to see that

$$d(Tx, Ty) \leq K[d(x, Tx) + d(y, Ty)]$$

for all $x, y \in X$. Therefore, T is a contraction for Kannan type. However, T is not a contraction for Banach type. Actually, there is not a constant $k \in (0, 1)$ such that

$$d(Tx, Ty) \leq kd(x, y)$$

for all $x, y \in X$.

Remark 7. *By Example 3, we claim that Theorem 4 has a superiority since the mapping T does not necessarily be continuous. Hence, our convex F-contraction can derive more applications than the counterpart of all the results regarding F-contraction. This is because any F-contraction must contain a continuous mapping (see Remark 2).*

Finally, we give a result on F-contraction of Hardy–Rogers type in b-metric spaces. Our result improves the results of [17,18] in b-metric spaces.

Theorem 5. *Let T be a self-mapping on a b-complete b-metric space (X, d, s). Suppose that there exists a function $F : (0, +\infty) \to \mathbb{R}$ satisfying Conditions (F_1), (F_2^α) and (F_3^s). If there exists $\tau > 0$ such that*

$$\begin{aligned} \tau + F(d(Tx, Ty)) \leq F(ad(x, y) &+ b[d(x, Tx) + d(y, Ty)] \\ &+ c[d(x, Ty) + d(y, Tx)]), \end{aligned} \tag{11}$$

for all $x, y \in X$ with $x \neq y$, where $a, b, c \geq 0, a + 2b + 2cs = 1$ and $bs + cs^2 < 1$, then T has a unique fixed point x^* in X. For any $x \in X$, the sequence $\{T^n x\}$ b-converges to x^*.

Proof. Let $x \in X$ and $x_n = T^n x$, for all $n \in \mathbb{N} \cup \{0\}$. If there exists $n_0 \in \mathbb{N} \cup \{0\}$ such that $x_{n_0+1} = x_{n_0}$, that is, $Tx_{n_0} = x_{n_0}$, then x_{n_0} is a fixed point of T.

Without loss of generality, we always assume that $x_{n+1} \neq x_n$ for any $n \in \mathbb{N} \cup \{0\}$. Making full use of (11), we speculate

$$\begin{aligned}\tau + F(d_n) &\leq F(ad_{n-1} + b(d_n + d_{n-1}) + cd(x_{n-1}, x_{n+1})) \\ &\leq F(ad_{n-1} + b(d_n + d_{n-1}) + cs(d_{n-1} + d_n)) \\ &= F((b + cs)d_n + (a + b + cs)d_{n-1}).\end{aligned}$$

That is, (F_4^λ) holds. Consequently, T is a convex F-contraction. Via Lemma 1, there exists $x^* \in X$ such that $x^* = \lim_{n\to\infty} x_n$.

In the following, we prove that x^* is a fixed point of T. To this end, we suppose that $x^* \neq Tx^*$ is absurd. Then

$$d(x^*, Tx^*) \leq s[d(x^*, x_{n+1}) + d(x_{n+1}, Tx^*)]$$

and

$$d(x_{n+1}, Tx^*) \leq s[d(x_{n+1}, x^*) + d(x^*, Tx^*)]$$

imply that

$$\frac{1}{s}d(x^*, Tx^*) \leq \liminf_{n\to\infty} d(x_{n+1}, Tx^*) \leq \limsup_{n\to\infty} d(x_{n+1}, Tx^*) \leq sd(x^*, Tx^*). \tag{12}$$

Put $l = \liminf_{n\to\infty} d(x_{n+1}, Tx^*)$ and $L = \limsup_{n\to\infty} d(x_{n+1}, Tx^*)$. Using Condition (11) and (F_1), we have

$$\begin{aligned}d(Tx_n, Tx^*) &< ad(x_n, x^*) + b[d(x_n, x_{n+1}) + d(x^*, Tx^*)] \\ &\quad + c[d(x_n, Tx^*) + d(x^*, x_{n+1})].\end{aligned} \tag{13}$$

Hence, taking the limit as $n \to \infty$ from both sides of (13) and considering (12), we get

$$l \leq bd(x^*, Tx^*) + cL. \tag{14}$$

Hence, using (12) and (14), we obtain

$$\frac{1}{s}d(x^*, Tx^*) \leq l \leq bd(x^*, Tx^*) + cL \leq bd(x^*, Tx^*) + csd(x^*, Tx^*),$$

which means that $bs + cs^2 \geq 1$. This is a contradiction. Therefore, $x^* = Tx^*$.

Finally, we need to prove the uniqueness of the fixed point. To this end, assume that T has another fixed point y^*. Taking advantage of (11), we arrive at

$$\begin{aligned}F(d(x^*, y^*)) &= F(d(Tx^*, Ty^*)) < \tau + F(d(Tx^*, Ty^*)) \\ &\leq F(ad(x^*, y^*) + b[d(x^*, Tx^*) + d(y^*, Ty^*)] \\ &\quad + c[d(x^*, Ty^*) + d(y^*, Tx^*)]) \\ &= F((a + 2c)d(x^*, y^*)),\end{aligned}$$

which follows immediately from Condition (F_1) that

$$d(x^*, y^*) < (a + 2c)d(x^*, y^*) \leq d(x^*, y^*).$$

This is a contradiction. □

Remark 8. *Theorem 5 generalizes [13] (Corollary 2.5). By virtue of convex F-contractions and Lemma 1, we can get [13] (Theorem 2.4) and [23] (Theorem 3).*

We finally pose the following problems:

Problem 1. Can Condition (F_3^s) be replaced with Condition (F_3) in our all results?

Problem 2. Does Theorem 4 hold if $s \geq 1$ is arbitrary?

Author Contributions: H.H. designed the research and wrote the paper. Z.D.M. and K.Z. wrote the draft preparation and provided the methodology. S.R. co-wrote and made revisions to the paper. H.H. handled funding acquisition. All authors have read and agreed to the published version of the manuscript.

Funding: The first author acknowledges the financial support from the Natural Science Foundation of Chongqing of China (No. cstc2020jcyj-msxmX0762), and the Initial Funding of Scientific Research for High-level Talents of Chongqing Three Gorges University of China (No. 2104/09926601).

Institutional Review Board Statement: Not applicable.

Informed Consent Statement: Not applicable.

Data Availability Statement: Not applicable.

Acknowledgments: The authors thank the editor and the referees for their valuable comments and suggestions which improved greatly the quality of this paper.

Conflicts of Interest: The authors declare no conflict of interest.

References

1. Wardowski, D. Fixed points of a new type of contractive mappings in complete metric spaces. *Fixed Point Theory Appl.* **2012**, *2012*, 94. [CrossRef]
2. Abbas, M.; Nazir, T.; Aleksić, T.L.; Radenović, S. Common fixed points of set-valued F-contraction mappings on domain of sets endowed with directed graph. *Comput. Appl. Math.* **2017**, *36*, 1607–1622. [CrossRef]
3. Altun, I.; Mınak, G.; Dag, H. Multivalued F-contractions on complete metric spaces. *J. Nonlinear Convex Anal.* **2015**, *16*, 659–666. [CrossRef]
4. Altun, I.; Mınak, G.; Olgun, M. Fixed points of multivalued nonlinear F-contractions on complete metric spaces. *Nonlinear Anal. Model. Control.* **2016**, *21*, 201–210. [CrossRef]
5. Chen, L.; Huang, S.; Li, C.; Zhao, Y. Several fixed point theorems for F-Contractions in complete Branciari b-metric spaces and applications. *J. Funct. Spaces* **2020**, *2020*, 7963242.
6. Hussain, A.; Al-Sulami, H.; Hussain, N.; Farooq, H. Newly fixed disc results using advanced contractions on F-metric space. *J. Appl. Anal. Comput.* **2020**, *10*, 2313–2322.
7. Hussain, N.; Latif, A.; Iqbal, I.; Kutbi, M.A. Fixed point results for multivalued F-contractions with application to integral and matrix equations. *J. Nonlinear Convex Anal.* **2019**, *20*, 2297–2311.
8. Kadelburg, Z.; Radenović, S. Notes on some recent papers concerning F-contractions in b-metric spaces. *Constr. Math. Anal.* **2018**, *1*, 108–112. [CrossRef]
9. Mohanta, S.K.; Patra, S. Coincidence points for graph preserving generalized almost F-G-contractions in b-metric spaces. *Nonlinear Stud.* **2020**, *27*, 897–914.
10. Shoaib, M.; Sarwar, M.; Kumam, P. Multi-valued fixed point theorem via F-contraction of Nadler type and application to functional and integral equations. *Bol. Soc. Parana Math.* **2021**, *39*, 83–95. [CrossRef]
11. Taheri, A.; Farajzadeh, A.P. A new generalization of α-type almost-F-contractions and α-type F-Suzuki contractions in metric spaces and their fixed point theorems. *Carpathian Math. Publ.* **2019**, *11*, 475–492. [CrossRef]
12. Tomar, A.; Sharma, R. Almost α-Hardy-Rogers-F-contractions and their applications. *Armen. J. Math.* **2019**, *11*, 1–9.
13. Wardowski, D.; Dung, N.V. Fixed points of F-weak contractions on complete metric spaces. *Demonstr. Math.* **2014**, *47*, 146–155. [CrossRef]
14. Bakhtin, I.A. The contraction principle in quasimetric spaces. *Funct. Anal.* **30**, *1989*, 26–37.
15. Czerwik, S. Contraction mappings in b-metric spaces. *Acta Math. Inform. Univ. Ostrav.* **1993**, *1*, 5–11.
16. Kirk, W.A.; Shahzad, N. *Fixed Point Theory in Distance Spaces*; Springer: Berlin/Heidelberg, Germany, 2014.
17. Cosentino, V.; Vetro, P. Fixed point result for F-contractive mappings of Hardy-Rogers-Type. *Filomat* **2014**, *28*, 715–722. [CrossRef]
18. Popescu, O.; Stan, G. Two fixed point theorems concerning F-contraction in complete metric spaces. *Symmetry* **2020**, *12*, 58. [CrossRef]
19. Kannan, R. Some results on fixed points. *Bull. Calcutta Math. Soc.* **1968**, *60*, 71–76.
20. Reich, S. Some remarks concerning contraction mappings. *Can. Math. Bull.* **1971**, *14*, 121–124. [CrossRef]

21. Tomonari, S. Fixed point theorems for single- and set-valued F-contractions in b-metric spaces. *J. Fixed Point Theory Appl.* **2018**, *20*, 35.
22. Chatterjea, S.K. Fixed-point theorems. *Dokl. Bolg. Akad. Nauk.* **1972**, *25*, 727–730. [CrossRef]
23. Dung, N.V.; Hang, V.T.L. A fixed point theorem for generalized F-contractions on complete metric spaces. *Vietnam. J. Math.* **2015**, *43*, 743–753. [CrossRef]

axioms

Article

Generalizations of Hermite–Hadamard Type Integral Inequalities for Convex Functions

Ying Wu [1], Hong-Ping Yin [1] and Bai-Ni Guo [2,*]

1 College of Mathematics and Physics, Inner Mongolia University for Nationalities, Tongliao 028043, China; nmwuying@163.com (Y.W.); yinhongping008@163.com (H.-P.Y.)
2 School of Mathematics and Informatics, Henan Polytechnic University, Jiaozuo 454010, China
* Correspondence: bai.ni.guo@gmail.com

Abstract: In the paper, with the help of two known integral identities and by virtue of the classical Hölder integral inequality, the authors establish several new integral inequalities of the Hermite–Hadamard type for convex functions. These newly established inequalities generalize some known results.

Keywords: generalization; integral inequality; convex function; Hermite–Hadamard type

MSC: 26A51, 26D15, 26D20, 26E60, 41A55

Citation: Wu, Y.; Yin, H.-P.; Guo, B.-N. Generalizations of Hermite–Hadamard Type Integral Inequalities for Convex Functions. *Axioms* **2021**, *10*, 136. https://doi.org/10.3390/axioms10030136

Academic Editor: Wei-Shih Du

Received: 20 April 2021
Accepted: 25 June 2021
Published: 28 June 2021

Publisher's Note: MDPI stays neutral with regard to jurisdictional claims in published maps and institutional affiliations.

Copyright: © 2021 by the authors. Licensee MDPI, Basel, Switzerland. This article is an open access article distributed under the terms and conditions of the Creative Commons Attribution (CC BY) license (https://creativecommons.org/licenses/by/4.0/).

1. Backgrounds and Motivations

A function $f : I \subseteq \mathbb{R} \to \mathbb{R}$ is said to be convex on an interval I if

$$f(tx + (1-t)y) \le tf(x) + (1-t)f(y)$$

holds for all $x, y \in I$ and $t \in [0,1]$. If $f : I \subseteq \mathbb{R} \to \mathbb{R}$ is a convex function and $a, b \in I$ with $a < b$, then

$$f\left(\frac{a+b}{2}\right) \le \frac{1}{b-a}\int_a^b f(x)\,\mathrm{d}\,x \le \frac{f(a)+f(b)}{2}. \tag{1}$$

The equalities in (1) are valid if and only if $f(x)$ is a linear function on $[a,b]$, as can be seen in [1] (p. 59). In mathematical literature, the double inequality (1) is called the Hermite–Hadamard inequality, named after Charles Hermite (1822–1901) and Jacques Hadamard (1865–1963). The Hermite–Hadamard inequality (1) is a necessary and sufficient condition for a real function to be convex on a closed and bounded real interval. It was extensively studied and generalized over more than one century, since it was first published in [2,3]. Copies of these two papers are available on the Internet since they belong to the fundamental knowledge of the humankind. The monograph [1] is fundamental and can be freely downloaded from the Internet. Other four fundamental monographs are [4–7]. They present the directions of development of the research in this field until now. Since then, the double inequality (1) has attracted many mathematicians' attention. Especially, in the last three decades, numerous generalizations, variants and extensions of this double inequality have been presented. In particular, the Hermite–Hadamard-type inequalities associated with a variety of fractional integral operators have been provided in [8,9] and closely related references therein.

In the paper [10], the Hermite–Hadamard integral inequality (1) was generalized as the following theorems.

Theorem 1 ([10] (Lemma 3)). *Let $f : I \subseteq \mathbb{R} \to \mathbb{R}$ be a differentiable mapping on I°, the interior of an interval I, with $a, b \in I$ and $a < b$. If f is a convex function on I, then*

$$f\left(\frac{a+b}{2}\right) \le \frac{1}{b-a}\int_a^b f(x)\,\mathrm{d}\,x \le \frac{1}{4}\left[f\left(\frac{3b-a}{2}\right) + 2f\left(\frac{a+b}{2}\right) + f\left(\frac{3a-b}{2}\right)\right] \tag{2}$$

and

$$\left|\frac{1}{b-a}\int_a^b f(x)\,\mathrm{d}x-\frac{f\left(\frac{a+b}{2}\right)}{2}\right|\le\left|\frac{f\left(\frac{3b-a}{2}\right)+f\left(\frac{3a-b}{2}\right)}{4}\right|. \tag{3}$$

After carefully verifying the above, we find that the convexity of f should be added to [10] (Theorem 3). The slightly amended version of [10] (Theorem 3) can be stated as follows.

Theorem 2 ([10] (Lemma 3)). *Let $f : I \subseteq \mathbb{R} \to \mathbb{R}$ be a differentiable mapping on I° with $a, b \in I$ and $a < b$, the second derivative $f'' : \left[\frac{3a-b}{2}, \frac{3b-a}{2}\right] \to \mathbb{R}$ be a continuous function on $\left[\frac{3a-b}{2}, \frac{3b-a}{2}\right]$, and $q > 1$. If f and $|f''|^q$ are convex on $\left[\frac{3a-b}{2}, \frac{3b-a}{2}\right]$, then*

$$\begin{aligned}\left|\frac{1}{b-a}\int_a^b f(x)\,\mathrm{d}x-\frac{1}{4}\left[f\left(\frac{3b-a}{2}\right)+2f\left(\frac{a+b}{2}\right)+f\left(\frac{3a-b}{2}\right)\right]\right|&\\ \le\frac{(b-a)^2}{3}\left[\frac{1}{2}\left(\left|f''\left(\frac{3b-a}{2}\right)\right|^q+\left|f''\left(\frac{3a-b}{2}\right)\right|^q\right)\right]^{1/q}&.\end{aligned}$$

In this paper, with the help of two known integral identities (see Lemmas 1 and 2 in the next section) and by virtue of the classical Hölder integral inequality, we aim to generalize those inequalities in Theorems 1 and 2 to several new Hermite–Hadamard-type inequalities for convex functions.

2. Two Lemmas

For establishing new Hermite–Hadamard type inequalities for convex functions and generalizing those inequalities in Theorems 1 and 2, we need the following lemmas.

Lemma 1 ([11] (Lemma 2.1)). *Let $f : I \subset \mathbb{R} \to \mathbb{R}$ be a differentiable mapping on I° and $a, b \in I$ with $a < b$. If $f' \in L_1([a, b])$, then*

$$\frac{f(a)+f(b)}{2}-\frac{1}{b-a}\int_a^b f(x)\,\mathrm{d}x=\frac{b-a}{2}\int_0^1(1-2t)f'(b+t(a-b))\,\mathrm{d}t. \tag{4}$$

Remark 1. *Since*

$$\int_0^{1/2}(1-2t)f'(b+t(a-b))\,\mathrm{d}t=\frac{1}{2}\int_0^1(1-u)f'\left(b+u\frac{a-b}{2}\right)\mathrm{d}u$$

and

$$\int_{1/2}^1(1-2t)f'(b+t(a-b))\,\mathrm{d}t=-\frac{1}{2}\int_0^1 uf'\left(\frac{a+b}{2}+u\frac{a-b}{2}\right)\mathrm{d}u,$$

the identity (4) *is equivalent to*

$$\begin{aligned}\frac{f(a)+f(b)}{2}-\frac{1}{b-a}\int_a^b f(x)\,\mathrm{d}x&\\ =\frac{b-a}{4}\left[\int_0^1(1-t)f'\left(b+t\frac{a-b}{2}\right)\mathrm{d}t-\int_0^1 tf'\left(\frac{a+b}{2}+t\frac{a-b}{2}\right)\mathrm{d}t\right]&.\end{aligned}$$

Lemma 2 ([12] (Lemma 2.1)). *Let $f : I \subseteq \mathbb{R} \to \mathbb{R}$ be a differentiable mapping on I° and $a, b \in I$ with $a < b$. If $f' \in L_1([a, b])$, then*

$$\begin{aligned}\frac{1}{b-a}\int_a^b f(x)\,\mathrm{d}x-f\left(\frac{a+b}{2}\right)&\\ =(b-a)\left[\int_0^{1/2}tf'(b+t(a-b))\,\mathrm{d}t+\int_{1/2}^1(t-1)f'(b+t(a-b))\,\mathrm{d}t\right]&. \end{aligned}\tag{5}$$

Let $u, v \in \mathbb{R}$ with $u < v$ and $\lambda > \mu \geq 0$. For $t \in [0,1]$, it is clear that

$$v + t(u - v) = \left(\frac{\lambda - \mu}{\lambda + \mu}t + \frac{\mu}{\lambda + \mu}\right)\frac{\lambda u - \mu v}{\lambda - \mu} + \left(\frac{\mu - \lambda}{\lambda + \mu}t + \frac{\lambda}{\lambda + \mu}\right)\frac{\lambda v - \mu u}{\lambda - \mu}. \tag{6}$$

3. New Integral Inequalities of Hermite–Hadamard Type

Now, with the help of integral identities (4) and (5), and by virtue of the classical Hölder integral inequality, we begin to establish several new integral inequalities of the Hermite–Hadamard type for convex functions on $\mathbb{R}$ and to generalize integral inequalities in the aforementioned Theorems 1 to 2.

In this section, we use the notations

$$I_{\lambda,\mu}(u,v) = \left[\frac{\lambda u - \mu v}{\lambda - \mu}, \frac{\lambda v - \mu u}{\lambda - \mu}\right] \quad \text{and} \quad I_{\lambda,\mu}^{\circ}(u,v) = \left(\frac{\lambda u - \mu v}{\lambda - \mu}, \frac{\lambda v - \mu u}{\lambda - \mu}\right). \tag{7}$$

Theorem 3. *Suppose that $\lambda > \mu \geq 0$ and $a, b \in \mathbb{R}$ with $a < b$. Let $f : I_{\lambda,\mu}(a,b) \to \mathbb{R}$ be a convex function. Then*

$$\begin{aligned} f\left(\frac{a+b}{2}\right) &\leq \frac{1}{b-a}\int_a^b f(x)\,\mathrm{d}x \\ &\leq \frac{1}{2(\lambda+\mu)}\left[(\lambda-\mu)f\left(\frac{\lambda b - \mu a}{\lambda - \mu}\right) + 4\mu f\left(\frac{a+b}{2}\right) + (\lambda-\mu)f\left(\frac{\lambda a - \mu b}{\lambda - \mu}\right)\right] \end{aligned} \tag{8}$$

and

$$\left|\frac{1}{b-a}\int_a^b f(x)\,\mathrm{d}x - \frac{2\mu}{\lambda+\mu}f\left(\frac{a+b}{2}\right)\right| \leq \frac{\lambda-\mu}{2(\lambda+\mu)}\left|f\left(\frac{\lambda b - \mu a}{\lambda - \mu}\right) + f\left(\frac{\lambda a - \mu b}{\lambda - \mu}\right)\right|, \tag{9}$$

where the equalities in (8) and (9) are valid if $f(x)$ is a linear function on $[a,b]$.

Proof. Using the change of the variable $x = \frac{\lambda}{\lambda+\mu}t + \frac{\mu}{\lambda+\mu}(a+b)$ for $t \in \left[\frac{\lambda a - \mu b}{\lambda}, \frac{\lambda b - \mu a}{\lambda}\right]$ and the convexity of f on $I_{\lambda,\mu}(a,b)$, we have

$$\begin{aligned} \frac{1}{b-a}\int_a^b f(x)\,\mathrm{d}x &= \frac{\lambda}{(\lambda+\mu)(b-a)}\int_{(\lambda a - \mu b)/\lambda}^{(\lambda b - \mu a)/\lambda} f\left(\frac{\lambda}{\lambda+\mu}t + \frac{\mu}{\lambda+\mu}(a+b)\right)\mathrm{d}t \\ &= \frac{\lambda}{(\lambda+\mu)(b-a)}\int_{(\lambda a - \mu b)/\lambda}^{(\lambda b - \mu a)/\lambda} f\left(\frac{\lambda-\mu}{\lambda+\mu}\frac{\lambda}{\lambda-\mu}t + \frac{2\mu}{\lambda+\mu}\left(\frac{a+b}{2}\right)\right)\mathrm{d}t \\ &\leq \frac{\lambda}{(\lambda+\mu)(b-a)}\int_{(\lambda a - \mu b)/\lambda}^{(\lambda b - \mu a)/\lambda}\left[\frac{\lambda-\mu}{\lambda+\mu}f\left(\frac{\lambda}{\lambda-\mu}t\right) + \frac{2\mu}{\lambda+\mu}f\left(\frac{a+b}{2}\right)\right]\mathrm{d}t \\ &= \frac{(\lambda-\mu)^2}{(\lambda+\mu)^2(b-a)}\int_{(\lambda a - \mu b)/(\lambda-\mu)}^{(\lambda b - \mu a)/(\lambda-\mu)} f(t)\,\mathrm{d}t + \frac{2\mu}{\lambda+\mu}f\left(\frac{a+b}{2}\right) \end{aligned} \tag{10}$$

and

$$\frac{(\lambda-\mu)^2}{(\lambda+\mu)^2(b-a)}\int_{(\lambda a - \mu b)/(\lambda-\mu)}^{(\lambda b - \mu a)/(\lambda-\mu)} f(t)\,\mathrm{d}t \leq \frac{\lambda-\mu}{2(\lambda+\mu)}\left[f\left(\frac{\lambda b - \mu a}{\lambda - \mu}\right) + f\left(\frac{\lambda a - \mu b}{\lambda - \mu}\right)\right]. \tag{11}$$

Substituting the inequality (11) into the inequality (10), we have

$$\begin{aligned}0 &\le \frac{1}{b-a}\int_a^b f(x)\,\mathrm{d}\,x - f\left(\frac{a+b}{2}\right)\\ &\le \frac{1}{2(\lambda+\mu)}\left[(\lambda-\mu)f\left(\frac{\lambda b-\mu a}{\lambda-\mu}\right)+4\mu f\left(\frac{a+b}{2}\right)+(\lambda-\mu)f\left(\frac{\lambda a-\mu b}{\lambda-\mu}\right)\right]-f\left(\frac{a+b}{2}\right)\\ &= \frac{1}{2(\lambda+\mu)}\left[(\lambda-\mu)f\left(\frac{\lambda b-\mu a}{\lambda-\mu}\right)-2(\lambda-\mu)f\left(\frac{a+b}{2}\right)+(\lambda-\mu)f\left(\frac{\lambda a-\mu b}{\lambda-\mu}\right)\right].\end{aligned}$$

Therefore, the inequalities (8) and (9) hold.

It is straightforward to verify that, if $f(x) = cx + d$ on $[a, b]$ for c, d being constants, the equalities in (8) and (9) are valid. Theorem 3 is thus proven. □

Remark 2. *If setting $\lambda = 1$ and $\mu = 0$ in Theorem 3, then we recover the double inequality (1).*

If letting $\lambda = 3$ and $\mu = 1$ in Theorem 3, we derive the above inequalities (2) and (3) obtained in [10] (Lemma 3).

Theorem 4. *Suppose that $\lambda > \mu \ge 0$ and $a, b \in \mathbb{R}$ with $a < b$. Let $f : I_{\lambda,\mu}(a,b) \to \mathbb{R}$ be a differentiable mapping on $I^\circ_{\lambda,\mu}(a,b)$. If $|f'|^q$ for $q \ge 1$ is a convex function on $I_{\lambda,\mu}(a,b)$, then*

$$\begin{aligned}&\left|\frac{1}{b-a}\int_a^b f(x)\,\mathrm{d}\,x - f\left(\frac{a+b}{2}\right)\right|\\ &\le \frac{b-a}{8}\left\{\left[\frac{\lambda+2\mu}{3(\lambda+\mu)}\left|f'\left(\frac{\lambda a-\mu b}{\lambda-\mu}\right)\right|^q+\frac{2\lambda+\mu}{3(\lambda+\mu)}\left|f'\left(\frac{\lambda b-\mu a}{\lambda-\mu}\right)\right|^q\right]^{1/q}\right.\\ &\quad\left.+\left[\frac{2\lambda+\mu}{3(\lambda+\mu)}\left|f'\left(\frac{\lambda a-\mu b}{\lambda-\mu}\right)\right|^q+\frac{\lambda+2\mu}{3(\lambda+\mu)}\left|f'\left(\frac{\lambda b-\mu a}{\lambda-\mu}\right)\right|^q\right]^{1/q}\right\}.\end{aligned}\tag{12}$$

Proof. By Lemma 2 and the Hölder integral inequality, we have

$$\begin{aligned}&\left|\frac{1}{b-a}\int_a^b f(x)\,\mathrm{d}\,x - f\left(\frac{a+b}{2}\right)\right|\\ &\le (b-a)\left[\int_0^{1/2} t|f'(b+t(a-b))|\,\mathrm{d}\,t+\int_{1/2}^1(1-t)|f'(b+t(a-b))|\,\mathrm{d}\,t\right]\\ &\le (b-a)\left\{\left(\int_0^{1/2} t\,\mathrm{d}\,t\right)^{1-1/q}\left[\int_0^{1/2} t|f'(b+t(a-b))|^q\,\mathrm{d}\,t\right]^{1/q}\right.\\ &\quad\left.+\left(\int_{1/2}^1(1-t)\,\mathrm{d}\,t\right)^{1-1/q}\left[\int_{1/2}^1(1-t)|f'(b+t(a-b))|^q\,\mathrm{d}\,t\right]^{1/q}\right\}.\end{aligned}\tag{13}$$

Since $(\mu-\lambda)t+\lambda \ge 0$ and

$$\left(\frac{\lambda-\mu}{\lambda+\mu}t+\frac{\mu}{\lambda+\mu}\right)+\left(\frac{\mu-\lambda}{\lambda+\mu}t+\frac{\lambda}{\lambda+\mu}\right)=1$$

for $t \in [0,1]$, letting $u = a$ and $v = b$ in the identity (6) and using the convexity of $|f'|^q$ arrive at

$$|f'(b+t(a-b))|^q \le \frac{(\lambda-\mu)t+\mu}{\lambda+\mu}\left|f'\left(\frac{\lambda a-\mu b}{\lambda-\mu}\right)\right|^q+\frac{(\mu-\lambda)t+\lambda}{\lambda+\mu}\left|f'\left(\frac{\lambda b-\mu a}{\lambda-\mu}\right)\right|^q.\tag{14}$$

Straightforward computation yields

$$\begin{aligned}
&\int_0^{1/2} t|f'(b+t(a-b))|^q \, \mathrm{d}t \\
&\le \int_0^{1/2} t\left[\frac{(\lambda-\mu)t+\mu}{\lambda+\mu}\left|f'\left(\frac{\lambda a-\mu b}{\lambda-\mu}\right)\right|^q + \frac{(\mu-\lambda)t+\lambda}{\lambda+\mu}\left|f'\left(\frac{\lambda b-\mu a}{\lambda-\mu}\right)\right|^q\right]\mathrm{d}t \qquad (15)\\
&= \frac{\lambda+2\mu}{24(\lambda+\mu)}\left|f'\left(\frac{\lambda a-\mu b}{\lambda-\mu}\right)\right|^q + \frac{2\lambda+\mu}{24(\lambda+\mu)}\left|f'\left(\frac{\lambda b-\mu a}{\lambda-\mu}\right)\right|^q
\end{aligned}$$

and

$$\begin{aligned}
&\int_{1/2}^{1} (1-t)|f'(b+t(a-b))|^q \, \mathrm{d}t \\
&\le \int_{1/2}^{1} (1-t)\left[\frac{(\lambda-\mu)t+\mu}{\lambda+\mu}\left|f'\left(\frac{\lambda a-\mu b}{\lambda-\mu}\right)\right|^q + \frac{(\mu-\lambda)t+\lambda}{\lambda+\mu}\left|f'\left(\frac{\lambda b-\mu a}{\lambda-\mu}\right)\right|^q\right]\mathrm{d}t \qquad (16)\\
&= \frac{2\lambda+\mu}{24(\lambda+\mu)}\left|f'\left(\frac{\lambda a-\mu b}{\lambda-\mu}\right)\right|^q + \frac{\lambda+2\mu}{24(\lambda+\mu)}\left|f'\left(\frac{\lambda b-\mu a}{\lambda-\mu}\right)\right|^q.
\end{aligned}$$

It is easy to see that

$$\int_0^{1/2} t \, \mathrm{d}t = \int_{1/2}^{1} (1-t) \, \mathrm{d}t = \frac{1}{8}. \qquad (17)$$

Applying inequalities (15), (16), and (17) into the inequality (13) gives

$$\begin{aligned}
\left|\frac{1}{b-a}\int_a^b f(x)\,\mathrm{d}x - f\left(\frac{a+b}{2}\right)\right| &\le \frac{b-a}{8}\left\{\left[\int_0^{1/2} t|f'(b+t(a-b))|^q \, \mathrm{d}t\right]^{1/q}\right.\\
&\quad \left.+\left[\int_{1/2}^{1}(1-t)|f'(b+t(a-b))|^q \, \mathrm{d}t\right]^{1/q}\right\}\\
&\le \frac{b-a}{8}\left\{\left[\frac{\lambda+2\mu}{3(\lambda+\mu)}\left|f'\left(\frac{\lambda a-\mu b}{\lambda-\mu}\right)\right|^q + \frac{2\lambda+\mu}{3(\lambda+\mu)}\left|f'\left(\frac{\lambda b-\mu a}{\lambda-\mu}\right)\right|^q\right]^{1/q}\right.\\
&\quad \left.+\left[\frac{2\lambda+\mu}{3(\lambda+\mu)}\left|f'\left(\frac{\lambda a-\mu b}{\lambda-\mu}\right)\right|^q + \frac{\lambda+2\mu}{3(\lambda+\mu)}\left|f'\left(\frac{\lambda b-\mu a}{\lambda-\mu}\right)\right|^q\right]^{1/q}\right\}.
\end{aligned}$$

The proof of Theorem 4 is complete. □

Corollary 1. *Under conditions of Theorem 4,*

1. *if* $q = 1$, *then*

$$\left|\frac{1}{b-a}\int_a^b f(x)\,\mathrm{d}x - f\left(\frac{a+b}{2}\right)\right| \le \frac{b-a}{4}\left[\frac{\left|f'\left(\frac{\lambda a-\mu b}{\lambda-\mu}\right)\right| + \left|f'\left(\frac{\lambda b-\mu a}{\lambda-\mu}\right)\right|}{2}\right];$$

2. *if* $\lambda = 1$ *and* $\mu = 0$, *then*

$$\begin{aligned}
&\left|\frac{1}{b-a}\int_a^b f(x)\,\mathrm{d}x - f\left(\frac{a+b}{2}\right)\right|\\
&\qquad \le \frac{b-a}{8}\left\{\left[\frac{|f'(a)|^q + 2|f'(b)|^q}{3}\right]^{1/q} + \left[\frac{2|f'(a)|^q + |f'(b)|^q}{3}\right]^{1/q}\right\}.
\end{aligned}$$

Theorem 5. *Suppose that $\lambda > \mu \geq 0$ and $a, b \in \mathbb{R}$ with $a < b$. Let $f : I_{\lambda,\mu}(a,b) \to \mathbb{R}$ be a differentiable mapping on $I^{\circ}_{\lambda,\mu}(a,b)$, where $I_{\lambda,\mu}(a,b)$ and $I^{\circ}_{\lambda,\mu}(a,b)$ are defined as in (7). If $|f'|^q$ for $q > 1$ is a convex function on $I_{\lambda,\mu}(a,b)$, then*

$$\begin{aligned}\left|\frac{1}{b-a}\int_a^b f(x)\,\mathrm{d}x - f\left(\frac{a+b}{2}\right)\right| &\leq \frac{b-a}{4}\left(\frac{q-1}{2q-1}\right)^{1-1/q}\left\{\left[\frac{\lambda+3\mu}{4(\lambda+\mu)}\left|f'\left(\frac{\lambda a-\mu b}{\lambda-\mu}\right)\right|^q\right.\right.\\ &\quad\left.+\frac{3\lambda+\mu}{4(\lambda+\mu)}\left|f'\left(\frac{\lambda b-\mu a}{\lambda-\mu}\right)\right|^q\right]^{1/q}+\left[\frac{3\lambda+\mu}{4(\lambda+\mu)}\left|f'\left(\frac{\lambda a-\mu b}{\lambda-\mu}\right)\right|^q\right.\\ &\quad\left.\left.+\frac{\lambda+3\mu}{4(\lambda+\mu)}\left|f'\left(\frac{\lambda b-\mu a}{\lambda-\mu}\right)\right|^q\right]^{1/q}\right\}.\end{aligned} \tag{18}$$

Proof. Similar to the proof of the inequality (12) in Theorem 4, making use of Lemma 2 and the Hölder integral inequality reveals

$$\begin{aligned}&\left|\frac{1}{b-a}\int_a^b f(x)\,\mathrm{d}x - f\left(\frac{a+b}{2}\right)\right|\\ &\leq (b-a)\left\{\left[\int_0^{1/2} t^{q/(q-1)}\,\mathrm{d}t\right]^{1-1/q}\left[\int_0^{1/2}|f'(b+t(a-b))|^q\,\mathrm{d}t\right]^{1/q}\right.\\ &\quad\left.+\left[\int_{1/2}^1(1-t)^{q/(q-1)}\,\mathrm{d}t\right]^{1-1/q}\left[\int_{1/2}^1|f'(b+t(a-b))|^q\,\mathrm{d}t\right]^{1/q}\right\},\end{aligned} \tag{19}$$

where

$$\int_0^{1/2} t^{q/(q-1)}\,\mathrm{d}t = \int_{1/2}^1 (1-t)^{q/(q-1)}\,\mathrm{d}t = \frac{q-1}{2q-1}\left(\frac{1}{2}\right)^{(2q-1)/(q-1)}. \tag{20}$$

From the inequality (14) and by the convexity of $|f'|^q$, we obtain

$$\int_0^{1/2}|f'(b+t(a-b))|^q\,\mathrm{d}t \leq \frac{\lambda+3\mu}{8(\lambda+\mu)}\left|f'\left(\frac{\lambda a-\mu b}{\lambda-\mu}\right)\right|^q+\frac{3\lambda+\mu}{8(\lambda+\mu)}\left|f'\left(\frac{\lambda b-\mu a}{\lambda-\mu}\right)\right|^q \tag{21}$$

and

$$\int_{1/2}^1|f'(b+t(a-b))|^q\,\mathrm{d}t \leq \frac{3\lambda+\mu}{8(\lambda+\mu)}\left|f'\left(\frac{\lambda a-\mu b}{\lambda-\mu}\right)\right|^q+\frac{\lambda+3\mu}{8(\lambda+\mu)}\left|f'\left(\frac{\lambda b-\mu a}{\lambda-\mu}\right)\right|^q. \tag{22}$$

Substituting inequalities (20), (21) and (22) into the inequality (19) yields the inequality (18). The proof of Theorem 5 is complete. □

Theorem 6. *Suppose that $\lambda > \mu \geq 0$ and $a, b \in \mathbb{R}$ with $a < b$. Let $f : I_{\lambda,\mu}(a,b) \to \mathbb{R}$ be a differentiable mapping on $I^{\circ}_{\lambda,\mu}(a,b)$, where $I_{\lambda,\mu}(a,b)$ and $I^{\circ}_{\lambda,\mu}(a,b)$ are defined as in (7). If $|f'|^q$ for $q \geq 1$ is a convex function on $I_{\lambda,\mu}(a,b)$, then*

$$\begin{aligned}\left|\frac{f(a)+f(b)}{2}-\frac{1}{b-a}\int_a^b f(x)\,\mathrm{d}x\right| &\leq \frac{b-a}{8}\left\{\left[\frac{\lambda+2\mu}{3(\lambda+\mu)}\left|f'\left(\frac{\lambda a-(2\mu-\lambda)b}{2(\lambda-\mu)}\right)\right|^q\right.\right.\\ &\quad\left.+\frac{2\lambda+\mu}{3(\lambda+\mu)}\left|f'\left(\frac{(2\lambda-\mu)b-\mu a}{2(\lambda-\mu)}\right)\right|^q\right]^{1/q}+\left[\frac{2\lambda+\mu}{3(\lambda+\mu)}\left|f'\left(\frac{(2\lambda-\mu)a-\mu b}{2(\lambda-\mu)}\right)\right|^q\right.\\ &\quad\left.\left.+\frac{\lambda+2\mu}{3(\lambda+\mu)}\left|f'\left(\frac{\lambda b-(2\mu-\lambda)a}{2(\lambda-\mu)}\right)\right|^q\right]^{1/q}\right\}.\end{aligned} \tag{23}$$

Proof. By Lemma 1 and the Hölder integral inequality, we have

$$\begin{aligned}
&\left|\frac{f(a)+f(b)}{2}-\frac{1}{b-a}\int_a^b f(x)\,\mathrm{d}x\right| \\
&\le \frac{b-a}{4}\left[\int_0^1 (1-t)\left|f'\left(b+t\frac{a-b}{2}\right)\right|\mathrm{d}t+\int_0^1 t\left|f'\left(\frac{a+b}{2}+t\frac{a-b}{2}\right)\right|\mathrm{d}t\right] \\
&\le \frac{b-a}{4}\left\{\left(\int_0^1 (1-t)\,\mathrm{d}t\right)^{1-1/q}\left[\int_0^1 (1-t)\left|f'\left(b+t\frac{a-b}{2}\right)\right|^q\mathrm{d}t\right]^{1/q}\right. \\
&\quad \left.+\left(\int_0^1 t\,\mathrm{d}t\right)^{1-1/q}\left[\int_0^1 t\left|f'\left(\frac{a+b}{2}+t\frac{a-b}{2}\right)\right|^q\mathrm{d}t\right]^{1/q}\right\}.
\end{aligned} \tag{24}$$

For $t\in[0,1]$, putting $u=a$ and $v=\frac{a+b}{2}$ in the identity (6) and using the convexity of $|f'|^q$ result in

$$\begin{aligned}
&\left|f'\left(\frac{a+b}{2}+t\frac{a-b}{2}\right)\right|^q \\
&\le \frac{(\lambda-\mu)t+\mu}{\lambda+\mu}\left|f'\left(\frac{(2\lambda-\mu)a-\mu b}{2(\lambda-\mu)}\right)\right|^q+\frac{(\mu-\lambda)t+\lambda}{\lambda+\mu}\left|f'\left(\frac{\lambda b-(2\mu-\lambda)a}{2(\lambda-\mu)}\right)\right|^q.
\end{aligned}$$

Accordingly, we have

$$\begin{aligned}
\int_0^1 t\left|f'\left(\frac{a+b}{2}+t\frac{a-b}{2}\right)\right|^q\mathrm{d}t &\le \int_0^1 t\left[\frac{(\lambda-\mu)t+\mu}{\lambda+\mu}\left|f'\left(\frac{(2\lambda-\mu)a-\mu b}{2(\lambda-\mu)}\right)\right|^q\right. \\
&\quad \left.+\frac{(\mu-\lambda)t+\lambda}{\lambda+\mu}\left|f'\left(\frac{\lambda b-(2\mu-\lambda)a}{2(\lambda-\mu)}\right)\right|^q\right]\mathrm{d}t \\
&=\frac{2\lambda+\mu}{6(\lambda+\mu)}\left|f'\left(\frac{(2\lambda-\mu)a-\mu b}{2(\lambda-\mu)}\right)\right|^q+\frac{\lambda+2\mu}{6(\lambda+\mu)}\left|f'\left(\frac{\lambda b-(2\mu-\lambda)a}{2(\lambda-\mu)}\right)\right|^q.
\end{aligned} \tag{25}$$

Similarly, taking $u=\frac{a+b}{2}$ and $v=b$ in the identity (6) gives

$$\begin{aligned}
&\int_0^1 (1-t)\left|f'\left(b+t\frac{a-b}{2}\right)\right|^q\mathrm{d}t \\
&\le \frac{\lambda+2\mu}{6(\lambda+\mu)}\left|f'\left(\frac{\lambda a-(2\mu-\lambda)b}{2(\lambda-\mu)}\right)\right|^q+\frac{2\lambda+\mu}{6(\lambda+\mu)}\left|f'\left(\frac{(2\lambda-\mu)b-\mu a}{2(\lambda-\mu)}\right)\right|^q.
\end{aligned} \tag{26}$$

Substituting inequalities (25) and (26) into inequality (24) yields (23). The proof of Theorem 6 is complete. □

Corollary 2. *Under conditions of Theorem 6, if* $q=1$, $\lambda=1$, *and* $\mu=0$, *then*

$$\left|\frac{f(a)+f(b)}{2}-\frac{1}{b-a}\int_a^b f(x)\,\mathrm{d}x\right|\le\frac{b-a}{4}\left[\frac{|f'(a)|+|f'(\frac{a+b}{2})|+|f'(b)|}{3}\right].$$

Theorem 7. *Suppose that $\lambda > \mu \ge 0$ and $a, b \in \mathbb{R}$ with $a < b$. Let $f : I_{\lambda,\mu}(a,b) \to \mathbb{R}$ be a differentiable mapping on $I^{\circ}_{\lambda,\mu}(a,b)$, where $I_{\lambda,\mu}(a,b)$ and $I^{\circ}_{\lambda,\mu}(a,b)$ are defined as in (7). If $|f'|^q$ for $q > 1$ is a convex function on $I_{\lambda,\mu}(a,b)$ and $0 \le \ell \le q$, then*

$$\begin{aligned}\left|\frac{f(a)+f(b)}{2} - \frac{1}{b-a}\int_a^b f(x)\,\mathrm{d}x\right| \le{}& \frac{b-a}{4}\left[\frac{q-1}{2q-(\ell+1)}\right]^{1-1/q} \\ &\times\left\{\left[\frac{\lambda+(\ell+1)\mu}{(\ell+1)(\ell+2)(\lambda+\mu)}\left|f'\left(\frac{\lambda a-(2\mu-\lambda)b}{2(\lambda-\mu)}\right)\right|^q\right.\right. \\ &\left.+\frac{(\ell+1)\lambda+\mu}{(\ell+1)(\ell+2)(\lambda+\mu)}\left|f'\left(\frac{(2\lambda-\mu)b-\mu a}{2(\lambda-\mu)}\right)\right|^q\right]^{1/q} \\ &+\left[\frac{(\ell+1)\lambda+\mu}{(\ell+1)(\ell+2)(\lambda+\mu)}\left|f'\left(\frac{(2\lambda-\mu)a-\mu b}{2(\lambda-\mu)}\right)\right|^q\right. \\ &\left.\left.+\frac{\lambda+(\ell+1)\mu}{(\ell+1)(\ell+2)(\lambda+\mu)}\left|f'\left(\frac{\lambda b-(2\mu-\lambda)a}{2(\lambda-\mu)}\right)\right|^q\right]^{1/q}\right\}.\end{aligned} \tag{27}$$

Proof. Similar to the proof of the inequality (23) in Theorem 6 from Lemma 1 and the Hölder integral inequality, we derive

$$\begin{aligned}&\left|\frac{f(a)+f(b)}{2} - \frac{1}{b-a}\int_a^b f(x)\,\mathrm{d}x\right| \\ &\le \frac{b-a}{4}\left[\int_0^1 (1-t)\left|f'\left(b+t\frac{a-b}{2}\right)\right|\mathrm{d}t + \int_0^1 t\left|f'\left(\frac{a+b}{2}+t\frac{a-b}{2}\right)\right|\mathrm{d}t\right] \\ &\le \frac{b-a}{4}\left\{\left[\int_0^1 (1-t)^{(q-\ell)/(q-1)}\,\mathrm{d}t\right]^{1-1/q}\left[\int_0^1 (1-t)^{\ell}\left|f'\left(b+t\frac{a-b}{2}\right)\right|^q\mathrm{d}t\right]^{1/q}\right. \\ &\left.+\left[\int_0^1 t^{(q-\ell)/(q-1)}\,\mathrm{d}t\right]^{1-1/q}\left[\int_0^1 t^{\ell}\left|f'\left(\frac{a+b}{2}+t\frac{a-b}{2}\right)\right|^q\mathrm{d}t\right]^{1/q}\right\}.\end{aligned} \tag{28}$$

It is obvious that

$$\int_0^1 (1-t)^{(q-\ell)/(q-1)}\,\mathrm{d}t = \int_0^1 t^{(q-\ell)/(q-1)}\,\mathrm{d}t = \frac{q-1}{2q-(\ell+1)}. \tag{29}$$

By the identity (6) and the convexity of $|f'|^q$, we obtain

$$\begin{aligned}\int_0^1 (1-t)^{\ell}\left|f'\left(b+t\frac{a-b}{2}\right)\right|^q\mathrm{d}t \le{}& \frac{\lambda+(\ell+1)\mu}{(\ell+1)(\ell+2)(\lambda+\mu)}\left|f'\left(\frac{(\lambda a-(2\mu-\lambda)b}{2(\lambda-\mu)}\right)\right|^q \\ &+\frac{(\ell+1)\lambda+\mu}{(\ell+1)(\ell+2)(\lambda+\mu)}\left|f'\left(\frac{(2\lambda-\mu)b-\mu a}{2(\lambda-\mu)}\right)\right|^q\end{aligned} \tag{30}$$

and

$$\begin{aligned}\int_0^1 t^{\ell}\left|f'\left(\frac{a+b}{2}+t\frac{a-b}{2}\right)\right|^q\mathrm{d}t \le{}& \frac{(\ell+1)\lambda+\mu}{(\ell+1)(\ell+2)(\lambda+\mu)}\left|f'\left(\frac{(2\lambda-\mu)a-\mu b}{2(\lambda-\mu)}\right)\right|^q \\ &+\frac{\lambda+(\ell+1)\mu}{(\ell+1)(\ell+2)(\lambda+\mu)}\left|f'\left(\frac{\lambda b-(2\mu-\lambda)a}{2(\lambda-\mu)}\right)\right|^q.\end{aligned} \tag{31}$$

Substituting inequalities (29), (30) and (31) into the inequality (28) concludes the inequality (27). The proof of Theorem 7 is complete. □

4. Remarks

In this section, we provide several remarks on our main results and related ones

Remark 3. *The facts that inequalities* (8) *and* (9) *in Theorem 3 are sharp were observed and pointed out by an anonymous referee.*

Remark 4. *In fact, the new inequalities in this paper are obtained by using the computation techniques inspired by the papers [11,12] and generalizing ideas from the paper [10]. Similar types of inequalities, or particular cases, are obtained in the literature by other techniques. One may see the Hermite–Hadamard type inequalities from [13]. These texts are excerpted and adapted from valuable comments of an anonymous referee of this paper.*

Remark 5. *The new inequalities for convex and differentiable functions in this paper have particular cases in [10] and some properties make them distinctive from other existing inequalities of the Hermite–Hadamard type under similar hypotheses (for example those from [11]). These texts are excerpted and adapted from valuable comments of an anonymous referee of this paper.*

Remark 6. *The new inequalities* (8) *and* (9) *for convex functions are sharp. But the inequalities involving differentiable functions having derivatives with convexity properties lose the property of sharpness within the class of linear functions. For example, the inequality* (12) *in Theorem 4, the inequality* (18) *in Theorem 5, the inequality* (23) *in Theorem 6, and the inequality* (27) *in Theorem 7 are not sharp for linear functions, as the classical Hermite-Hadamard inequality* (1) *and the inequalities from [11] (for similar types of functions), but they are sharp for constant functions. This solves the problem of sharpness easily. These texts are excerpted and adapted from valuable comments of an anonymous referee of this paper.*

5. Conclusions

In this paper, with the help of two known integral identities and by virtue of the Hölder integral inequality, in Theorems 3–7, and their corollaries, we established several new integral inequalities of the Hermite–Hadamard type for convex functions. These newly established inequalities generalize corresponding ones in the paper [10].

Author Contributions: Writing—original draft, Y.W., H.-P.Y., and B.-N.G. All authors contributed equally to the manuscript and read and approved the final manuscript.

Funding: The first two authors, Y.W. and H.-P.Y., were partially supported by the Natural Science Foundation of Inner Mongolia (Grant No. 2018MS01023) and by the Research Program of Science and Technology at Universities of Inner Mongolia Autonomous Region (Grant No. NJZZ18154 and No. NJZY20119) in China.

Institutional Review Board Statement: Not applicable.

Informed Consent Statement: Not applicable.

Data Availability Statement: Not applicable.

Acknowledgments: The authors appreciate the anonymous referees for their careful corrections to, helpful suggestions to and valuable comments on the original version of this paper.

Conflicts of Interest: The authors declare no conflict of interest.

References

1. Dragomir, Silvestru Sever.; Pearce, C.E.M. Selected Topics on Hermite–Hadamard Type Inequalities and Applications, Amended Version, RGMIA Monographs, Victoria University, 2002. Available online: https://rgmia.org/monographs/hermite_hadamard.html (accessed on 20 June 2021).
2. Hadamard, J. Étude sur les propriétes des fonctions entiéres et en particulier d'une fonction considerée par Riemann. *J. Math. Pures Appl.* **1893**, *58*, 171–215.
3. Hermite, C. Sur deux limites d'une intégrale définie. *Mathesis* **1883**, *3*, 82–82.
4. Mitrinović, D.S.; Pečarić, J.E.; Fink, A.M. *Classical and New Inequalities in Analysis*; Kluwer Academic Publishers: Dordrecht, The Netherlands; Boston, MA, USA; London, UK, 1993. [CrossRef]
5. Niculescu, C.P.; Persson, L.-E. Convex Functions and Their Applications: A Contemporary Approach. In *CMS Books in Mathematics/Ouvrages de Mathématiques de la SMC*, 2nd ed.; Springer: Cham, Switzerland, 2018. [CrossRef]

6. Pachpatte, B.G. Analytic Inequalities: Recent Advances. In *Atlantis Studies in Mathematics, 3*; Atlantis Press: Paris, France, 2012. [CrossRef]
7. Pečarić, J.; Proschan, F.; Tong, Y.L. Convex Functions, Partial Orderings, and Statistical Applications. In *Mathematics in Science and Engineering*; Academic Press, Inc.: Boston, MA, USA, 1992; Volume 187.
8. Cao, J.; Srivastava, H.M.; Liu, Z.-G. Some iterated fractional q-integrals and their applications. *Fract. Calc. Appl. Anal.* **2018**, *21*, 672–695. [CrossRef]
9. Set, E.; Choi, J.; Çelİk, B. Certain Hermite–Hadamard type inequalities involving generalized fractional integral operators. *Rev. R. Acad. Cienc. Exactas Fís. Nat. Ser. A Mat. RACSAM* **2018**, *112*, 1539–1547. [CrossRef]
10. Mehrez, K.; Agarwal, P. New Hermite–Hadamard type integral inequalities for convex functions and their applications. *J. Comput. Appl. Math.* **2019**, *350*, 274–285. [CrossRef]
11. Dragomir, S.S.; Pearce, C.E.M. Two inequalities for differentiable mappings and applications to special means of real numbers and to trapezoidal formula. *Appl. Math. Lett.* **1998**, *11*, 91–95. [CrossRef]
12. Kirmaci, U.S. Inequalities for differentiable mappings and applications to special means of real numbers and to midpoint formula. *Appl. Math. Comput.* **2004**, *147*, 137–146. [CrossRef]
13. Duc, D.T.; Hue, N.N.; Nhan, N.D.V.; Tuan, V.K. Convexity according to a pair of quasi-arithmetic means and inequalities. *J. Math. Anal. Appl.* **2020**, *488*, 124059. [CrossRef]

axioms

MDPI

Article

Delay-Dependent Stability, Integrability and Boundedeness Criteria for Delay Differential Systems

Osman Tunç [1], Cemil Tunç [2] and Yuanheng Wang [3,*]

1 Department of Computer Programing, Baskale Vocational School, Van Yuzuncu Yil University, Van 65080, Turkey; osmantunc89@gmail.com
2 Department of Mathematics, Faculty of Sciences, Van Yuzuncu Yil University, Van 65080, Turkey; cemtunc@yahoo.com
3 Department of Mathematics, Zhejiang Normal University, Jinhua 321004, China
* Correspondence: yaojc@mail.cmu.edu.tw or yhwang@zjnu.cn

Abstract: This paper deals with non-perturbed and perturbed systems of nonlinear differential systems of first order with multiple time-varying delays. Here, for the considered systems, easily verifiable and applicable uniformly asymptotic stability, integrability, and boundedness criteria are obtained via defining an appropriate Lyapunov–Krasovskiĭ functional (LKF) and using the Lyapunov–Krasovskiĭ method (LKM). Comparisons with a former result that can be found in the literature illustrate the novelty of the stability theorem and show new contributions to the qualitative theory of solutions. A discussion of two illustrative examples and the obtained results are presented.

Keywords: system of DDEs; uniformly asymptotically stability; integrability; boundedness at infinity; Lyapunov–Krasovskiĭ functional; multiple time-varying delay

MSC: 34D05; 34K20; 26D15; 45J05

Citation: Tunç, O.; Tunç, C.; Wang, Y. Delay-Dependent Stability, Integrability, and Boundedeness Criteria for Delay Differential Systems. *Axioms* **2021**, *10*, 138. https://doi.org/10.3390/axioms10030138

Academic Editor: Wei-Shih Du

Received: 30 April 2021
Accepted: 23 June 2021
Published: 29 June 2021

Publisher's Note: MDPI stays neutral with regard to jurisdictional claims in published maps and institutional affiliations.

Copyright: © 2021 by the authors. Licensee MDPI, Basel, Switzerland. This article is an open access article distributed under the terms and conditions of the Creative Commons Attribution (CC BY) license (https://creativecommons.org/licenses/by/4.0/).

1. Introduction

The research of systems of delay differential equations (DDEs) with multiple constant and time-varying delays is always a challenging field of study. This is due to the fact that the system of DDEs can be frequently found in many fields such as mechanics, artificial neural networks power systems, medicine, physics, biology, population ecology, engineering, and so forth. For example, the books of Burton [1], Hale and Verduyn Lunel [2], Kiri and Ueda [3], Kolmanovskii and Myshkis [4], Kuang [5], Lakshmikantham et al. [6], and Smith [7] are very important reference books for various fundamental and qualitative results of stability and periodic solutions of functional differential equations of the first and second order. These books also include numerous methods, techniques, their theoretical and real applications in science, engineering, and technology. Indeed, a large number of applications in the theory of artificial neural networks, numerous models for some population dynamics, and ecology problems, etc., can be represented by DDEs with multiple delays, (see, in particular, Berezansky et al. [8], Gil [9], Smith [7], and the bibliography therein). Accordingly, the study of qualitative properties of solutions of scalar DDEs and systems of DDEs with multiple time-varying delays has an important significance in sciences and engineering, and it deserves the attention of researchers.

In recent years, numerous interesting and fruitful results on the qualitative analyses for various differential equations of first and second order both with and without delay have been obtained by applying a linear matrix inequality (LMI) approach, the second Lyapunov method, the LKM, fixed point method, and so on. In particular, some related works on the subject can be summarized briefly as the following.

Berezansky et al. [8] considered a non-autonomous system of first order with time-varying delays. Via the M-matrix method, easily verifiable sufficient stability conditions for the system and its linear version are obtained in [8].

In Berezansky et al. [10], uniform exponential stability of linear systems of first order with time varying coefficients is studied. In [10], a new explicit result is derived with the proof based on the Bohl–Perron theorem. The resulting criterion has advantages over some previous ones.

In Gil [9], the author presents exponential stability results for a nonlinear system of differential equations of first order. Here, the author obtains sharp bounds for the solutions of the system and thus exponential stability can be determined without the use of Lyapunov functions.

Gözen and Tunç [11] investigate an exponential stabilization problem for a class of linear systems of first order with two variable delays. Via a suitable Lyapunov–Krasovskiĭ functional, Leibniz–Newton's formula and linear matrix inequalities, the authors derive some new sufficient conditions for the exponential stability of the zero solution of the system.

Liu [12] studies a class of systems of non-autonomous differential equations of first order with multiple delays. In [12], under proper conditions, several criteria of global stability of a positive equilibrium are obtained.

In Matsunaga [13], for a linear delay differential system of the first order with two coefficients and one delay, some necessary and sufficient conditions on the asymptotic stability of a zero solution, which are composed of delay-dependent and delay-independent stability criteria, are established and the range of the delay is explicitly given.

In Ngoc [14], general nonlinear time-varying differential systems of a first order with two variable delays are considered. Several explicit criteria for exponential stability are given. A discussion of the obtained results and two illustrative examples are presented.

In Petruşel et al. [15], existence, stability, and localization results for a general system of operator equations in complete metric spaces are presented. The approach is based on the application of some fixed point theorems for orbital contractions in a complete metric space.

In Rebenda and Šmarda [16], asymptotic properties of a real two-dimensional differential system with unbounded non-constant delays are investigated. The sufficient conditions for the stability and asymptotic stability of solutions are given. Asymptotic properties of solutions are also studied by means of a Lyapunov–Krasovskiĭ functional.

Shu [17] considers the linear delay system:

$$\dot{x}(t) = Ax(t) + Bx(t-r).$$

The author gives sufficient conditions for the asymptotic stability of the zero solution of this system by deriving a pair of one dimensional delay differential equations from the system and comparing the Lyapunov exponents of the corresponding fundamental solution.

Slyn'ko and Tunç [18] discusses the instability of set differential equations by using some geometric inequalities.

In Tunç [19–21] and Tunç and Tunç [22–25], stability, boundedness, and some other properties of solutions of various non-linear differential systems of second order without or with delay are investigated by the second Lyapunov method and integration techniques.

In Tunç and Golmankhaneh [26], the stability of fractal differentials in the sense of Lyapunov is defined. Sufficient conditions for the stability, uniform boundedness, and convergence of solutions for the suggested fractal differential equations are presented and proven.

Yskak [27] considers a class of linear systems of differential equations of first order with distributed delay and periodic coefficients. The author established sufficient conditions for the asymptotic stability of solutions to this system, obtain estimates of solutions, and study robust stability. On the basis of the obtained results, the author proves an analogue of the Krein's theorem on stability of solutions to the linear system of differential equations with distributed delay.

In Zhang and Jiang [28], by constructing a suitable Lyapunov functional and using some analytical techniques, the authors obtain sufficient conditions for the global exponential stability of zero solution to a class of differential systems of first order with delay.

The results show a relation between the delay time and the coefficients of the equations. In [28], two examples also are given to illustrate the validity of the results.

In Zhang and Wu [29], the authors develop a new technique to study the stability of the delay differential system of first order. In this way, the construction of suitable functionals for a given system with finite delay is easier. The conditions obtained are less restrictive. The main results are three theorems on the stability of the zero solution of the system with finite delay. We also refer readers to the papers of Petruşel and Rus [30], Kien et al. [31], Chadli et al. [32] and the bibliographies of the mentioned sources.

However, to the best of our knowledge, the LKM is the most effective method to investigate various properties of systems of delay DDEs with multiple time-varying delays provided that construct or define a suitable LKF. In fact, from this point of view, constructing, defining, or finding a suitable LKF for a problem under study is a difficult task and an unsolved problem in the literature until this time.

In 2020, Ren and Tian [33] considered the following system of linear DDEs with time-varying delay,

$$\begin{aligned} \dot{x}(t) &= Ax(t) + Bx(t-h(t)), \qquad (1)\\ x(t) &= \phi(t),\ t \in [-h_2, 0], \end{aligned}$$

where $x(t) \in \mathbb{R}^n$ is the system state, $A,\ B \in \mathbb{R}^{n\times n}$, and $h(t) \in C^1(\mathbb{R}^+, (0,\infty))$ is the time-varying delay and satisfies the following conditions:

$$0 \le h_1 \le h(t) \le h_2,\ h_{21} = h_2 - h_1, 0 \le h'(t) \le h_0 < 1.$$

Ren and Tian [33] defined a LKF for the system of DDEs (1). Then, based upon the defined LKF, Ren and Tian [33] proved a theorem, ([33], Theorem 1), on the asymptotically stability of the system of DDEs (1).

The motivation of the results of this paper has been inspired from the paper of Ren and Tian ([33], Theorem 1) and those in the bibliography of this paper. In this paper, we take into consideration a perturbed nonlinear system of DDEs with three multiple time-varying delays as given below:

$$\dot{x}(t) = A(t)x(t) + BF(x(t-h_1(t))) + CG(x(t-h_2(t))) + P(t, x(t), x(t-h_3(t))), \qquad (2)$$

where $x \in \mathbb{R}^n, t \in \mathbb{R}^+ = [0,\infty), h_k(t) \in C^1(\mathbb{R}^+, (0,\infty)),\ k = 1,\ 2,$ and $h_3(t) \in C(\mathbb{R}^+, (0,\infty))$ are the time-varying delays, $A(t) \in C(\mathbb{R}^+, \mathbb{R}^{n\times n}),\ B,\ C \in \mathbb{R}^{n\times n},\ F,\ G \in C(\mathbb{R}^n, \mathbb{R}^n)$, $F(0) = G(0) = 0$ and $P \in C(\mathbb{R}^+ \times \mathbb{R}^n \times \mathbb{R}^n, \mathbb{R}^n)$. We assume that the given time-varying delays $h_1(t)$ and $h_2(t)$ satisfy the following conditions:

$$\begin{aligned} &0 \le h_1 \le h_1(t) \le h_2, 0 \le h_3 \le h_2(t) \le h_4,\\ &0 \le h'_1(t) \le h_5 < 1, 0 \le h'_2(t) \le h_6 < 1,\\ &h = \max\{h_2, h_4\}, h_0 = \max\{h_5, h_6\}. \qquad (3) \end{aligned}$$

We now outline the aim of this paper by the following items, respectively:

(1) We study the uniformly asymptotic stability of zero solution and the integrability of the norm of solutions of the following unperturbed nonlinear system of DDEs via Theorem 3 and Theorem 4, respectively:

$$\dot{x}(t) = A(t)x(t) + BF(x(t-h_1(t))) + CG(x(t-h_2(t))). \qquad (4)$$

To investigate these problems, we define a very different LKF from that in Ren and Tian [16];

(2) We investigate the boundedness of solutions of the perturbed system of nonlinear DDEs (2), see Theorem 5′

(3) In particular cases, two new examples with graphs of their solutions are provided to show applications of Theorems 3–5.

The rest of this paper is organized as follows. Some basic information related to a general functional differential system and a necessary auxiliary theorem, Burton ([1], Theorem 4.2.9), are given in Section 2. A reference theorem of this paper, Ren and Tian ([33], Theorem 1), concerning asymptotic stability of the system of linear DDEs (1) is given in Section 3. Two new results and an example concerning uniformly asymptotic stability and integrability for the unperturbed system (4) are presented in Section 4, while a result and an example for the boundedness of solutions of the perturbed system of DDEs (2) are given in Section 5. Finally, some discussions, contributions, and a conclusion are given in Sections 6 and 7, respectively.

2. Background and Motivation

Consider the system of DDEs:

$$\frac{dx}{dt} = H(t, x_t), \tag{5}$$

where $H \in C(\mathbb{R} \times C_0, \mathbb{R}^n)$, $H(t,0) = 0$ and takes bounded sets into bounded sets. For some $\tau > 0$, $C_0 = C_0([-\tau, 0],\ \mathbb{R}^n)$ denotes the space of continuous functions $\phi : [-\tau, 0] \to \mathbb{R}^n$. For any $a \geq 0$, $\forall t_0 \geq 0$ and $x \in C_0([t_0 - \tau, t_0 + a],\ \mathbb{R}^n)$, we have $x_t = x(t + \theta)$ for $-\tau \leq \theta \leq 0$ and $t \geq t_0$.

Let $x \in \mathbb{R}^n$. The norm $\|.\|$ is defined by $\|x\| = \sum\limits_{i=1}^{n} |x_i|$. Next, let $A \in \mathbb{R}^{n\times n}$. For this case, the matrix norm, $\|A\|$, is defined by $\|A\| = \max\limits_{1\leq j\leq n} \left(\sum\limits_{i=1}^{n} |a_{ij}| \right)$.

In this article, without loss of generality, sometimes instead of $x(t)$, we will simply write x.

For any $\phi \in C_0$, let:

$$\|\phi\|_{C_0} = \sup_{\theta\in[-r,0]} \|\phi(\theta)\| = \|\phi(\theta)\|_{[-r,0]}$$

and

$$C_H = \{\phi : \phi \in C_0 \text{ and } \|\phi\|_{C_0} \leq H < \infty\}.$$

We suppose that the function H satisfies the conditions of the uniqueness of solutions of the system of DDEs (5). We note that the system of DDEs (2) is a particular case of the system of DDEs (5).

Let $x(t) = x(t, t_0, \phi)$ be a solution of the system of DDEs (5) such that $x(t) = \phi(t)$ on $[t_0 - \tau, t_0]$, where $\phi \in C([t_0 - \tau, t_0], \mathbb{R}^n)$ is an initial function.

Let,

$$V_1(t, \phi) : \mathbb{R}^+ \times C_H \to \mathbb{R}^+, \mathbb{R}^+ = [0, \infty),$$

be a continuous functional in t and ϕ with $V_1(t, 0) = 0$. Further, let $\frac{d}{dt}V_1(t, x)$ denote the derivative of $V_1(t, x)$ on the right through any solution $x(t)$ of the system of DDEs (5).

Theorem 1 (Burton ([1], Theorem 4.2.9). *Assume that:*

(A1) *The function $V_1(t, x)$ satisfies the locally Lipschitz in x, i.e., for every compact $S \subset \mathbb{R}^n$ and $\gamma > t_0$, there exists a $K_{\gamma s} \in \mathbb{R}$ with $K_{\gamma s} > 0$ such that:*

$$|V_1(t, x) - V_1(t, y)| \leq K_{\gamma s} \|x - y\|_{[t_0-\tau,t]}$$

for all $t \in [t_0, \gamma]$ and $x, y \in C_0([t_0 - \tau, t_0], S)$;

(A2) *Let $Z(t, \phi)$ be a functional such that it satisfies the one-side locally Lipschitz in t:*

$$Z(t_2, \phi) - Z(t_1, \phi) \leq K(t_2 - t_1), 0 < t_1 < t_2 < \infty, K > 0, K \in \mathbb{R},$$

whenever $\phi \in C_H$, *where* $Z : \mathbb{R}^+ \times C_H \to \mathbb{R}^+$ *is continuous;*

(A3) *There are four strictly increasing functions* $\omega, \omega_1, \omega_2, \omega_3 : \mathbb{R}^+ \to \mathbb{R}^+$ *with value 0 at 0 such that:*

$$\omega(\|\phi(0)\|) + Z(t,\phi) \le V_1(t,\phi) \le \omega_1(\|\phi(0)\|) + Z(t,\phi),$$
$$Z(t,\phi) \le \omega_2(\|\phi\|_C)$$

and

$$\frac{d}{dt}V_1(t, x(.)) \le -\omega_3(\|x(t)\|)$$

whenever $t \in \mathbb{R}^+$ *and* $x \in C_H$. *Then, the solution* $x(t) = 0$ *of the system of DDEs (5) is uniformly asymptotically stable.*

3. Asymptotic Stability

Firstly, we state the main result of Ren and Tian ([33], Theorem 1).

Theorem 2 (Ren and Tian [33], Theorem 1). *For given scalars* h_1 *and* h_2 *, the system (1) with time-varying delays satisfying the condition* $0 \le h_1 \le h_1(t) \le h_2$ *is asymptotically stable if there exist matrices* $P \in S_+^{5n}$, Q_1, Q_2, Q_3,
$Q_4 \in S_+^n$, N_1, $N_2 \in \mathbb{R}^{13n\times 4n}$ *, such that the LMI:*

$$\Psi(\alpha) = \begin{bmatrix} \Phi(\alpha) - \Gamma^T \Re(\alpha)\Gamma - He(\Gamma^T \begin{bmatrix} (1-\alpha)N_1^T \\ \alpha N_2^T \end{bmatrix}) & * \\ \alpha N_1^T + (1-\alpha)N_2^T & -Q \end{bmatrix} < 0$$

holds for $\alpha = \{0, 1\}$, *where:*

$$\begin{aligned}
\Phi(\alpha) =& He(\Sigma_1^T P \Sigma_2) + \varepsilon_1^T Q_1 \varepsilon_1 - \varepsilon_2^T Q_1 \varepsilon_2 + \varepsilon_2^T Q_2 \varepsilon_2 - \varepsilon_4^T Q_2 \varepsilon_4 + h_1^2 \varepsilon_0^T Q_3 \varepsilon_0 \\
&+ h_{12}^2 \varepsilon_0^T Q_4 \varepsilon_0 - \Sigma_3^T Q_3 \Sigma_3 - 3\Sigma_4^T Q_3 \Sigma_4 - 5\Sigma_5^T Q_3 \Sigma_5 - 7\Sigma_6^T Q_3 \Sigma_6, \\
\Sigma_1 =& [\varepsilon_1^T \; h_1\varepsilon_5^T \; \alpha h_{12}\varepsilon_6^T + (1-\alpha)h_{12}\varepsilon_7^T \; h_1^2\varepsilon_8^T \; h_1^3\varepsilon_{11}^T]^T, \\
\Sigma_2 =& \begin{bmatrix} \varepsilon_0^T & \varepsilon_1^T - \varepsilon_2^T & \varepsilon_2^T - \varepsilon_4^T & h_1\varepsilon_1^T - h_1\varepsilon_5^T & \frac{h_1^2}{2}\varepsilon_1^T - h_1^2\varepsilon_8^T \end{bmatrix}^T, \\
\Sigma_3 =& \varepsilon_1 - \varepsilon_2, \\
\Sigma_4 =& \varepsilon_1 + \varepsilon_2 - 2\varepsilon_5, \\
\Sigma_5 =& \varepsilon_1 - \varepsilon_2 + 6\varepsilon_5 - 12\varepsilon_8, \\
\Sigma_6 =& \varepsilon_1 - \varepsilon_2 - 12\varepsilon_5 + 60\varepsilon_8 - 120\varepsilon_{11}, \\
\Sigma_7 =& \varepsilon_2 - \varepsilon_3, \\
\Sigma_8 =& \varepsilon_2 + \varepsilon_3 - 2\varepsilon_6, \\
\Sigma_9 =& \varepsilon_2 - \varepsilon_3 + 6\varepsilon_6 - 12\varepsilon_9, \\
\Sigma_{10} =& \varepsilon_2 + \varepsilon_3 - 12\varepsilon_6 + 60\varepsilon_9 - 120\varepsilon_{12}, \\
\Sigma_{11} =& \varepsilon_3 - \varepsilon_4, \\
\Sigma_{12} =& \varepsilon_3 + \varepsilon_4 - 2\varepsilon_7, \\
\Sigma_{13} =& \varepsilon_3 - \varepsilon_4 + 6\varepsilon_7 - 12\varepsilon_{10}, \\
\Sigma_{14} =& \varepsilon_3 + \varepsilon_4 - 12\varepsilon_7 + 60\varepsilon_{10} - 120\varepsilon_{13},
\end{aligned}$$

$$\begin{aligned}
\varepsilon_0 =& A\varepsilon_1 + B\varepsilon_3, \\
\Gamma =& \begin{bmatrix} \Sigma_7^T & \Sigma_8^T & \Sigma_9^T & \Sigma_{10}^T & \Sigma_{11}^T & \Sigma_{12}^T & \Sigma_{13}^T & \Sigma_{14}^T \end{bmatrix}^T, \\
Q =& diag(Q_4, 3Q_4, 5Q_4, 7Q_4),
\end{aligned}$$

and

$$\varepsilon_i \in \mathbb{R}^{n\times 13n}$$

is defined as:

$$\varepsilon_i = \left[0_{n\times(i-1)n}\; I_n\; 0_{n\times(13-i)n}\right] \text{ for } i = 1, 2, ..., 13.$$

4. Uniformly Asymptotic Stability and Integrability

We now deal with the non-perturbed system of DDEs (4). Here, we first extend and optimize the asymptotic stability result of Ren and Tian ([33], Theorem 1) under very weaker conditions. Next, we give an integrability result for the solutions of the unperturbed non-linear system of DDEs (4). The technique of the proofs is based upon the LKM.

The first main result of this paper is given by Theorem 3.

Theorem 3. *We assume that the following conditions (C1) and (C2) hold:*

(C1) *There exist positive constants a_0, f_0, and g_0 such that:*

$$a_{ii}(t) + \sum_{j=1, j\neq i}^{n} |a_{ji}(t)| \leq -a_0 \text{ for all } t \in \mathbb{R}^+,$$

$$F(0) = 0, \|F(u) - F(v)\| \leq f_0\|u - v\| \text{ for all } u,\ v \in \mathbb{R}^n$$

and

$$G(0) = 0, \|G(v) - G(\omega)\| \leq g_0\|v - \omega\|| \text{ for all } v,\ \omega \in \mathbb{R}^n;$$

(C2) *There exist constants a_0, f_0, g_0 and h_0 from (C1) and (2), respectively, and δ_0 such that:*

$$a_0(1 - h_0) - f_0\|B\| - g_0\|C\| \geq \delta_0.$$

Then zero solution of the unperturbed system of DDEs (4) is uniformly asymptotically stable.

Proof. We define a new LKF $W_1 := W_1(t, x_t)$ by:

$$W_1(t, x_t) := \|x(t)\| + \sum_{i=1}^{2} \lambda_i \int_{t-h_i(t)}^{t} \|x(s)\|ds, \tag{6}$$

where $\lambda_i > 0$, $\lambda_i \in \mathbb{R}$ such that these arbitrary constants will be chosen in the proof later.

The LKF (6) can be expanded as the following:

$$\begin{aligned} W_1(t, x_t) :=& |x_1(t)| + ... + |x_n(t)| + \lambda_1 \int_{t-h_1(t)}^{t} \|x(s)\|ds + \lambda_2 \int_{t-h_2(t)}^{t} \|x(s)\|ds \\ =& |x_1(t)| + ... + |x_n(t)| + \lambda_1 \int_{t-h_1(t)}^{t} |x_1(s)|ds + ... + \lambda_1 \int_{t-h_1(t)}^{t} |x_n(s)|ds \\ &+ \lambda_2 \int_{t-h_2(t)}^{t} |x_1(s)|ds + ... + \lambda_2 \int_{t-h_2(t)}^{t} |x_n(s)|ds. \end{aligned}$$

From (6), it follows that the LKF $W_1(t, x_t)$ satisfies:

$$W_1(t, 0) = 0, \gamma_1\|x\| \leq W_1(t, x_t), \gamma_1 \in (0, 1), \gamma_1 \in \mathbb{R}\,.$$

Let,

$$\gamma_2 \geq 1, \gamma_2 \in \mathbb{R}$$

and

$$Z(t,x) := \sum_{i=1}^{2} \lambda_i \int_{t-h_i(t)}^{t} \|x(s)\| ds.$$

Hence, it is clear that:

$$\gamma_1 \|x\| + Z(t,x) \le W_1(t,x_t) \le \gamma_2 \|x\| + Z(t,x).$$

As for the next step, by some elementary calculations, we derive:

$$\begin{aligned}
|W_1(t,x_t) - W_1(t,y_t)| \le & |\, \|x(t)\| - \|y(t)\|\, | + \sum_{i=1}^{2} \lambda_i \int_{t-h_i(t)}^{t} |\, \|x(s)\| - \|y(s)\|\, | ds \\
\le & \|x(t) - y(t)\| + \sum_{i=1}^{2} \lambda_i \int_{t-h_i(t)}^{t} \|x(s) - y(s)\| ds \\
\le & \|x(t) - y(t)\| + \sum_{i=1}^{2} \lambda_i h_i(t) \sup_{t-h_i(t) \le s \le t} \|x(s) - y(s))\| \\
\le & \|x(t) - y(t)\| + \lambda_1 h_2 \sup_{t-h_1(t) \le s \le t} \|x(s) - y(s))\| \\
& + \lambda_2 h_4 \sup_{t-h_2(t) \le s \le t} \|x(s) - y(s))\|.
\end{aligned}$$

From this point of view, we have:

$$\begin{aligned}
|W_1(t,x_t) - W_1(t,y_t)| \le & (1 + \lambda_1 h_2 + \lambda_2 h_4) \\
& \times \max\left\{ \sup_{t-h_1(t) \le s \le t} \|x(s) - y(s)\|, \sup_{t-h_2(t) \le s \le t} \|x(s) - y(s)\| \right\} \\
= & D_1 \max\left\{ \sup_{t-h_1(t) \le s \le t} \|x(s) - y(s)\|, \sup_{t-h_2(t) \le s \le t} \|x(s) - y(s)\| \right\},
\end{aligned}$$

where:

$$D_1 := 1 + \lambda_1 h_2 + \lambda_2 h_4.$$

Thus, we can conclude that:

$$|W_1(t,x_t) - W_1(t,y_t)| \le D_1 \max\left\{ \|x(s) - y(s)\|_{[t-h_1(t),t]}, \|x(s) - y(s)\|_{[t-h_2(t),t]} \right\}.$$

The last inequality shows that the LKF $W_1(t,x_t)$ satisfies the locally Lipschitz condition. Hence, the satisfaction of the condition (A1) of Burton ([1], Theorem 4. 2.9) was shown.

For the next step, from the definition of $Z(t,x)$, it follows that:

$$\begin{aligned}
Z(t,x) = & \sum_{i=1}^{2} \lambda_i \int_{t-h_i(t)}^{t} \|x(s)\| ds \le \lambda_1 h_1(t) \sup_{t-h_1(t) \le s \le t} \|x(s)\| + \lambda_2 h_2(t) \sup_{t-h_2(t) \le s \le t} \|x(s)\| \\
\le & \lambda_2 h_2 \sup_{t-h_1(t) \le s \le t} \|x(s)\| + \lambda_2 h_4 \sup_{t-h_2(t) \le s \le t} \|x(s)\|.
\end{aligned}$$

Thus, we get:

$$Z(t,x) \le \lambda_1 h_2 \|x(s)\|_{[t-h_1(t),t]} + \lambda_2 h_4 \|x(s)\|_{[t-h_2(t),t]}.$$

As for the next step, using some simple calculations, we find:

$$\begin{aligned}
Z(t_2,x) - Z(t_1,x) =& \sum_{i=1}^{2} \lambda_i \int\limits_{t_2-h_i(t_2)}^{t_2} \|x(s)\|ds - \sum_{i=1}^{2} \lambda_i \int\limits_{t_1-h_i(t_1)}^{t_1} \|x(s)\|ds \\
=& \sum_{i=1}^{2} \lambda_i \int\limits_{t_2-h_i(t_2)}^{t_2} \|x(s)\|ds - \sum_{i=1}^{2} \lambda_i \int\limits_{t_1-h_i(t_1)}^{t_1} \|x(s)\|ds \\
&+ \sum_{i=1}^{2} \lambda_i \int\limits_{t_1-h_i(t_1)}^{t_2-h_i(t_2)} \|x(s)\|ds - \sum_{i=1}^{2} \lambda_i \int\limits_{t_1-h_i(t_1)}^{t_2-h_i(t_2)} \|x(s)\|ds \\
=& \sum_{i=1}^{2} \lambda_i \int\limits_{t_1}^{t_2} \|x(s)\|ds - \sum_{i=1}^{2} \lambda_i \int_{t_1-h_i(t_1)}^{t_2-h_i(t_2)} \|x(s)\|ds \\
\leq& \sum_{i=1}^{2} \lambda_i \int\limits_{t_1}^{t_2} \|x(s)\|ds \\
\leq& (\lambda_1+\lambda_2) \sup_{t_1 \leq s \leq t_2} \|x(s)\|(t_2-t_1) = M(t_2-t_1),
\end{aligned}$$

where:

$$M = (\lambda_1+\lambda_2) \sup_{t_1 \leq s \leq t_2} \|x(s)\|, 0 < t_1 < t_2 < \infty.$$

Thus, the satisfaction of the condition (A2) of Burton ([1], Theorem 4. 2.9) was proven.

As for the next step, we calculate the time derivative of the LKF $W_1(t,x_t)$ in (6) along the system of DDEs (4). Then, we can obtain that:

$$\begin{aligned}
\frac{d}{dt}W_1(t,x_t) =& \sum_{i=1}^{n} x'_i(t)x_i(t+0) + \lambda_1\|x(t)\| - \lambda_1\|x(t-h_1(t))\| \times (1-h'_1(t)) \\
&+ \lambda_2\|x(t)\| - \lambda_2\|x(t-h_2(t))\| \times (1-h'_2(t)).
\end{aligned} \tag{7}$$

We now consider the first term of the equality (7). Via the condition (C1) and some elementary calculations, we have that:

$$\begin{aligned}
\sum_{i=1}^{n} x_i(t+0)x'_i(t) \leq& \sum_{i=1}^{n} a_{ii}|x_i(t)| + \sum_{i=1}^{n} \sum_{j=1,j\neq i}^{n} |a_{ji}|\,|x_i(t)| \\
&+ \sum_{i=1}^{n}\sum_{j=1}^{n} |b_{ij}|\,|F_j(x(t-h_1(t)))| \\
&+ \sum_{i=1}^{n}\sum_{j=1}^{n} |c_{ij}|\,|G_j(x(t-h_2(t)))| \\
=& \sum_{i=1}^{n} \left(a_{ii}(t) + \sum_{j=1,j\neq i}^{n} |a_{ji}(t)| \right) |x_i(t)| \\
&+ \|B\|\,\|F(x(t-h_1(t)))\| + \|C\|\,\|G(x(t-h_2(t)))\| \\
\leq& -a_0\|x(t)\| + \|B\|\,\|F(x(t-h_1(t)))\| + \|C\|\,\|G(x(t-h_2(t)))\|.
\end{aligned} \tag{8}$$

From this point of view, combining (7) and (8) and using the conditions of (3), it follows that:

$$\begin{aligned}\frac{d}{dt}W_1(t,x_t) \le &- a_0\|x(t)\| + \|B\|\,\|F(x(t-h_1(t)))\| + \|C\|\,\|G(x(t-h_2(t)))\| \\ &+ \lambda_1\|x(t)\| - \lambda_1\|x(t-h_1(t))\| \times (1-h'_1(t)) \\ &+ \lambda_2\|x(t)\| - \lambda_2\|x(t-h_2(t))\| \times (1-h'_2(t)) \\ \le &- a_0\|x(t)\| + \|B\|\,\|F(x(t-h_1(t)))\| + \|C\|\,\|G(x(t-h_2(t)))\| \\ &+ \lambda_1\|x(t)\| - \lambda_1\|x(t-h_1(t))\| \times (1-h_5) \\ &+ \lambda_2\|x(t)\| - \lambda_2\|x(t-h_2(t))\| \times (1-h_6) \\ \le &- a_0\|x(t)\| + \|B\|\,\|F(x(t-h_1(t)))\| + \|C\|\,\|G(x(t-h_2(t)))\| \\ &+ \lambda_1\|x(t)\| - \lambda_1(1-h_0)\|x(t-h_1(t))\| \\ &+ \lambda_2\|x(t)\| - \lambda_2(1-h_0)\|x(t-h_2(t))\| \\ \le &- a_0\|x(t)\| + f_0\|B\|\,\|x(t-h_1(t))\| + g_0\|C\|\,\|x(t-h_2(t))\| \\ &+ \lambda_1\|x(t)\| - \lambda_1(1-h_0)\|x(t-h_1(t))\| \\ &+ \lambda_2\|x(t)\| - \lambda_2(1-h_0)\|x(t-h_2(t))\|.\end{aligned}$$

Since λ_1 and λ_2 are arbitrary positive constants, let $\lambda_1 = \frac{f_0\|B\|}{1-h_0}$ and $\lambda_2 = \frac{g_0\|C\|}{1-h_0}$. Then, keeping in the mind the condition (C2), we conclude that:

$$\begin{aligned}\frac{d}{dt}W_1(t,x_t) &\le -\left[a_0 - \frac{f_0\|B\|}{1-h_0} - \frac{g_0\|C\|}{1-h_0}\right]\|x(t)\| \\ &= -\frac{1}{1-h_0}[a_0(1-h_0) - f_0\|B\| - g_0\|C\|]\|x(t)\| \\ &\le -K_0\|x(t)\|, \end{aligned} \tag{9}$$

where:

$$K_0 = \delta_0(1-h_0)^{-1}.$$

Hence, from (9), it is seen that the derivative $\frac{d}{dt}W_1(t,x_t)$ is negative definite. Thus, the condition (A3) of Burton ([1], Theorem 4. 2.9) was satisfied. Hence, all the conditions of (A1)–(A3) of Burton ([1], Theorem 4. 2.9) were satisfied. The whole discussion proves that the zero solution of the nonlinear unperturbed system of DDEs (4) with two multiple time-varying delays is uniformly asymptotically stable. This completes the proof of Theorem 3. □

Theorem 4. *Let the conditions (C1) and (C2) of Theorem 3 hold. Then the norm of solutions of the unperturbed system of DDEs (4) with two multiple time-varying delays are integrable in the sense of Lebesgue on* $\mathbb{R}^+ = [0,\infty)$.

Proof. The proof of this theorem depends upon the LKF $W_1(t,x_t)$. Via the conditions (C1) and (C2), as before we obtain the inequality:

$$\frac{d}{dt}W_1(t,x_t) \le -K_0\|x(t)\|. \tag{10}$$

Since $\frac{d}{dt}W_1(t,x_t)$ is negative definite, the LKF $W_1(t,x_t)$ is decreasing. Keeping in mind this fact and integrating the inequality (10), we obtain:

$$K_0\int_{t_0}^{t}\|x(s)\|ds \le W_1(t_0,\phi(t_0)) - W_1(t,x_t) \le W_1(t_0,\phi(t_0)) \equiv K_1 > 0$$

for all $t \geq t_0$. This inequality clearly implies:

$$\int_{t_0}^{\infty} \|x(s)\|ds \leq K_0^{-1} W_1(t_0, \phi(t_0)) = K_0^{-1} K_1 < \infty.$$

□

Thus, the norm of the solutions of the unperturbed system of DDEs (4) with multiple two time-varying delays is integrable in the sense of Lebesgue on $\mathbb{R}^+ = [0, \infty)$. Hence, the proof of Theorem 4 is completed.

In a particular case of the unperturbed system of DDEs (4) with two multiple time-varying delays, we now give an example, Example 1, to show that the conditions of (C1) and (C2) of Theorem 3 and Theorem 4 can hold.

Example 1. *Consider the following system of non-linear DDEs with two multiple time-varying delays:*

$$\begin{pmatrix} x_1' \\ x_2' \end{pmatrix} = \begin{pmatrix} -25 - \frac{t}{t+1} & \frac{t}{t+1} \\ \frac{t}{t+1} & -25 - \frac{t}{t+1} \end{pmatrix} \begin{pmatrix} x_1 \\ x_2 \end{pmatrix} + \begin{pmatrix} 3 & 2 \\ 2 & 3 \end{pmatrix} \begin{pmatrix} \sin x_1 \left(t - \frac{1}{4}|\sin t|\right) \\ \sin x_2 \left(t - \frac{1}{4}|\sin t|\right) \end{pmatrix} + \begin{pmatrix} 2 & 1 \\ 1 & 2 \end{pmatrix} \begin{pmatrix} \sin x_1 \left(t - \frac{1}{2}|\sin t|\right) \\ \sin x_2 \left(t - \frac{1}{2}|\sin t|\right) \end{pmatrix}, \tag{11}$$

where $h_1(t) = \frac{1}{4}|\sin t|$ and $h_2(t) = \frac{1}{2}|\sin t|$ are two multiple time-varying delays, and $t \geq 1$.

From this point of view, we compare both the system of DDEs (11) and DDEs (4) with two multiple time-varying delays. Hence, we derive that:

$$A(t) = \begin{pmatrix} -25 - \frac{t}{t+1} & \frac{t}{t+1} \\ \frac{t}{t+1} & -25 - \frac{t}{t+1} \end{pmatrix},$$

$$B = \begin{pmatrix} 3 & 2 \\ 2 & 3 \end{pmatrix}, C = \begin{pmatrix} 2 & 1 \\ 1 & 2 \end{pmatrix},$$

$$F(x(t - h_1(t))) = F(x(t - \frac{t}{4}|\sin t|)) = \begin{pmatrix} \sin x_1 \left(t - \frac{1}{4}|\sin t|\right) \\ \sin x_2 \left(t - \frac{1}{4}|\sin t|\right) \end{pmatrix},$$

$$F(0) = 0, x = (x_1, x_2)^T,$$

$$G(x(t - h_2(t))) = G(x(t - \frac{1}{2}|\sin t|)) = \begin{pmatrix} \sin x_1 \left(t - \frac{1}{2}|\sin t|\right) \\ \sin x_2 \left(t - \frac{1}{2}|\sin t|\right) \end{pmatrix},$$

$$G(0) = 0, x = (x_1, x_2)^T.$$

Let,

$$u = x(t - \frac{1}{4}|\sin t|), u_1 = x_1(t - \frac{1}{4}|\sin t|), u_2 = x_2(t - \frac{1}{4}|\sin t|),$$
$$v = y(t - \frac{1}{4}|\sin t|, v_1 = y_1(t - \frac{1}{4}|\sin t|), v_2 = y_2(t - \frac{1}{4}|\sin t|)$$

and

$$v = x(t - \frac{1}{2}|\sin t|), v_1 = x_1(t - \frac{1}{2}|\sin t|), v_2 = x_2(t - \frac{1}{2}|\sin t|),$$
$$\omega = y(t - \frac{1}{2}|\sin t|, \omega_1 = y_1(t - \frac{1}{2}|\sin t|), \omega_2 = y_2(t - \frac{1}{2}|\sin t|).$$

In view of the matrix $A(t)$, it is clear that:

$$a_{11}(t) + |a_{21}(t)| = -25 - \frac{t}{t+1} + \frac{t}{t+1} = -25 < -24 = -a_0$$
$$a_{22}(t) + |a_{12}(t)| = -25 - \frac{t}{t+1} + \frac{t}{t+1} = -25 < -24 = -a_0.$$

Then,

$$a_{ii}(t) + \sum_{j=1, j\neq i}^{2} |a_{ji}(t)| < -24 = -a_0 \text{ for all } t \in \mathbb{R}^+.$$

Next, by some simple calculations, we obtain:

$$\|B\| = 5, \|C\| = 3,$$

and

$$\begin{aligned}
\|F(u) - F(v)\| =& \left\| \begin{pmatrix} \sin u_1 - \sin v_1 \\ \sin u_2 - \sin v_2 \end{pmatrix} \right\| \\
=& |\sin u_1 - \sin v_1| + |\sin u_2 - \sin v_2| \\
=& 2\left|\cos\left(\frac{u_1 + v_1}{2}\right) \sin\left(\frac{u_1 - v_1}{2}\right)\right| \\
\leq& |u_1 - v_1| + |u_2 - v_2| \\
=& \|u - v\|, f_0 = 1. \\
h_1(t) =& \frac{1}{4}|\sin t|, \\
& 0 = h_1 \leq \frac{1}{4}|\sin t| \leq \frac{1}{4} = h_2, \\
& 0 \leq h'_1(t) = \frac{1}{4}\frac{d}{dt}|\sin t| = \frac{1}{4}\frac{\sin t}{|\sin t|} \times \cos t \leq \frac{1}{4} = h_5 < 1.
\end{aligned}$$

$$\begin{aligned}
&\|G(v) - G(\omega)\| = \left\| \begin{pmatrix} \sin v_1 - \sin \omega_1 \\ \sin v_2 - \sin \omega_2 \end{pmatrix} \right\| \leq \|v - \omega\|, \ g_0 = 1, \\
&h_2(t) = \frac{1}{2}|\sin t|, \\
&0 = h_3 \leq \frac{1}{2}|\sin t| \leq \frac{1}{2} = h_4, \\
&0 \leq h'_2(t) = \frac{1}{2}\frac{d}{dt}|\sin t| = \frac{1}{2}\frac{\sin t}{|\sin t|} \times \cos t \leq \frac{1}{2} = h_6 < 1.
\end{aligned}$$

Assume that:

$$h_0 = \max\{h_5, h_6\} = \max\left\{\frac{1}{4}, \frac{1}{2}\right\} = \frac{1}{2}.$$

Considering the statement of condition (C2) and the above calculations, we have:

$$a_0(1 - h_0) - f_0\|B\| - g_0\|C\| = 24\left(1 - \frac{1}{2}\right) - 5 - 3 = 4 \geq 4 = \delta_0.$$

From this point of view, it follows that all the conditions of Theorems 3 and 4, i.e., the conditions (C1) and (C2) hold. For this reason, the zero solution of the system of DDEs (11) with two multiple time-varying delays is uniformly asymptotic stable as well as the norm of solutions of the same system are integrable.

Here, Example 1 was solved using MATLAB software. Indeed, the given example was solved using the 4th order Runge–Kutta method in MATLAB. The graphs of Figures 1 and 2 show the behaviors of paths of the solutions $x_1(t)$, $x_2(t)$ of Example 1, respectively, for $h_1(t) = \frac{1}{4}|\sin t|$, $h_2(t) = \frac{1}{2}|\sin t|$, $t \geq 1$, and different initial values.

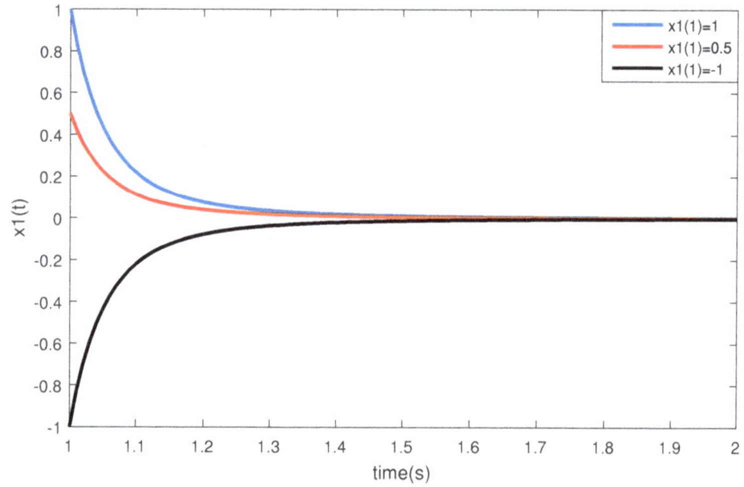

Figure 1. This figure shows that the solution $x_1(t)$ of the system of DDEs (11) with two multiple time-varying delays is uniformly asymptotically stable and the norm of this solution is integrable for $h_1(t) = \frac{1}{4}|\sin t|$, $h_2(t) = \frac{1}{2}|\sin t|$, $t \geq 1$, and different initial values.

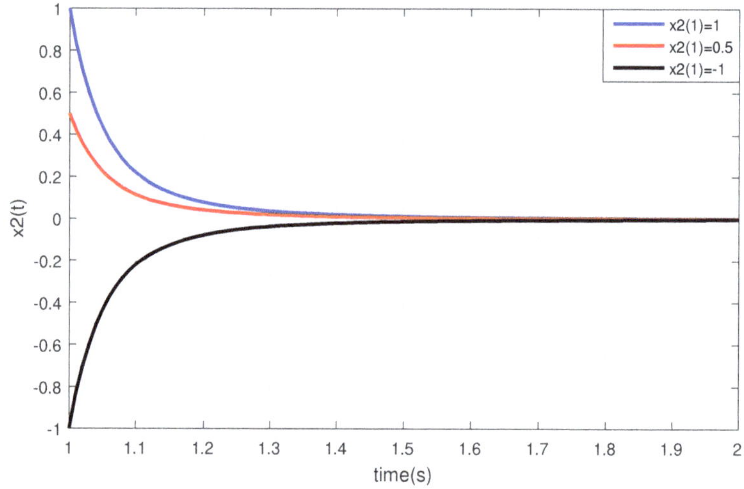

Figure 2. This figure shows that the solution $x_2(t)$ of the system of DDEs (11) with two multiple time-varying delays is uniformly asymptotically stable and the norm of this solution is integrable for $h_1(t) = \frac{1}{4}|\sin t|$, $h_2(t) = \frac{1}{2}|\sin t|$, $t \geq 1$, and different initial values.

We now present our third main result of this paper related to the boundedness of solutions of the perturbed nonlinear system of DDEs (2) with three multiple time-varying delays.

5. Boundedness of Solutions

For the boundedness of solutions of the perturbed system of DDEs (2) with three multiple time-varying delays, in addition to the conditions (C1) and (C2), we need the following condition:

(C3) There exist positive constants $a_0, f_0, g_0, h_0, \delta_0$ from (C1) and (C2), L and a continuous function $p_0 \in C(\mathbb{R}, \mathbb{R})$ such that:

$$\|P(t, x(t), x(t-h_3(t)))\| \le |p_0(t)|\ \|x(t)\| \text{ for all } t \in \mathbb{R}^+, x,\ x(t-h_3(t)) \in \mathbb{R}^n,$$

where:

$$\int_0^\infty |p_0(s)| ds \le L.$$

Theorem 5. *Let conditions (C1)–(C3) hold. Then the solutions of the perturbed system of DDEs (2) with three multiple time-varying delays are bounded as $t \to +\infty$.*

Proof. As in the previous theorems, the proof of this theorem also depends upon the LKF $W_1(t, x_t)$. From the conditions (C1)–(C3), we can derive:

$$\begin{aligned}\frac{d}{dt} W_1(t, x_t) &\le -K_0 \|x(t)\| + \|P(t, x(t), x(t-h_3(t)))\| \\ &\le |p_0(t)|\ \|x(t)\| \\ &\le |p_0(t)| W_1(t, x_t).\end{aligned} \tag{12}$$

□

Integrating the inequality (12) and using the condition (C3), we obtain that:

$$\begin{aligned}W_1(t, x_t) &\le W_1(0, \phi(0)) \exp\Big(\int_0^t |p_0(s)| ds\Big). \\ &\le W_1(0, \phi(0)) \exp\Big(\int_0^\infty |p_0(s)| ds\Big) \\ &\le W_1(0, \phi(0)) \exp(L).\end{aligned}$$

Let,

$$M = W_1(0, \phi(0)) \exp(L) > 0. \tag{13}$$

Using (13) and the definition of the LKF $W_1(t, x_t)$, we have:

$$\|x(t)\| \le \|x(t)\| + \sum_{i=1}^{2} \lambda_i \int_{t-h_i(t)}^{t} \|x(s)\| ds = W_1(t, x_t) \le M,$$

i.e.,

$$\|x(t)\| \le M \text{ for all } t \ge t_0 \ge 0.$$

By calculating the limit of this inequality as $t \to +\infty$, it is derived that:

$$\lim_{t \to +\infty} \||x(t)|\| \le \lim_{t \to +\infty} M = M.$$

Then, we can conclude that the solutions of the perturbed system of nonlinear DDEs (2) with three multiple time-varying delays are bounded as $t \to +\infty$. Thus, Theorem 5 is proven.

In a particular case of the perturbed system of DDEs (2) with three multiple time-varying delays, we now give Example 2, to show that the conditions of (C1)–(C3) of Theorem 5 can be provided.

Here, Example 2 was solved using MATLAB software. Indeed, the given example was solved using the 4th order Runge–Kutta method in MATLAB. The graphs of Figures 3 and 4 show the behaviors of paths of the solutions $x_1(t)$, $x_2(t)$ of Examples 2, respectively, for $h_1(t) = \frac{1}{4}|\sin t|$, $h_2(t) = \frac{1}{2}|\sin t|$, $t \geq 1$, and different initial values.

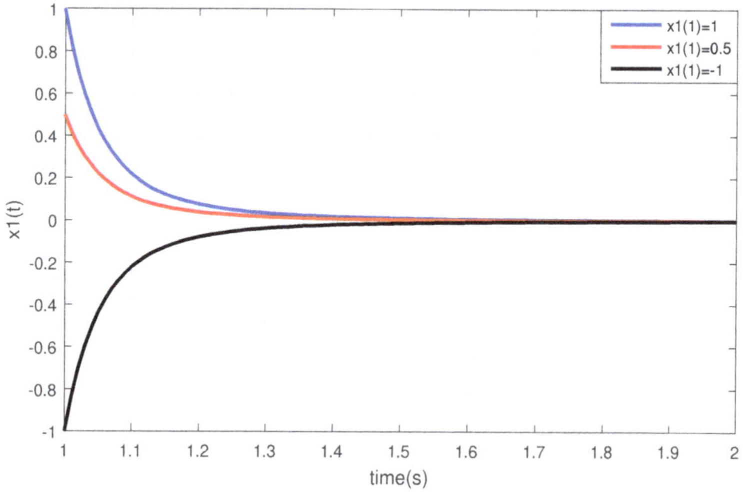

Figure 3. This figure shows that the solution $x_1(t)$ of the perturbed nonlinear system of DDEs (14) with three time-varying delays is bounded for $h_1(t) = \frac{1}{4}|\sin t|$, $h_2(t) = \frac{1}{2}|\sin t|$, $h_3(t) = \frac{1}{6}|\sin t|$, $t \geq 1$, and different initial values.

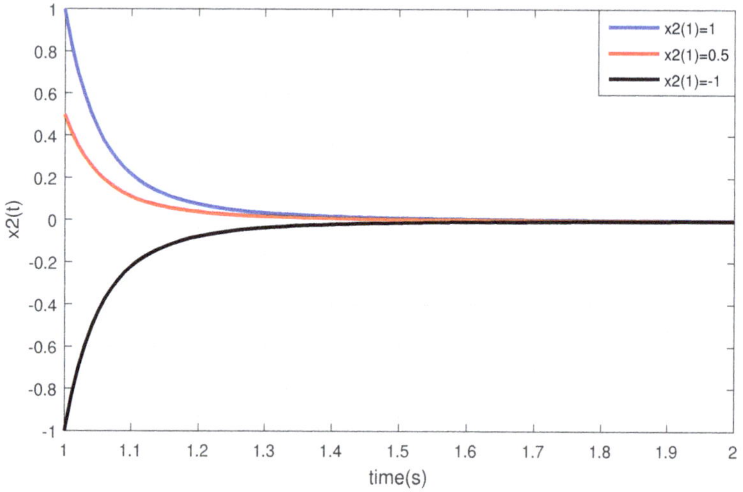

Figure 4. This figure shows that the solution $x_2(t)$ of the perturbed nonlinear system of DDEs (14) with three time-varying delays is bounded for $h_1(t) = \frac{1}{4}|\sin t|$, $h_2(t) = \frac{1}{2}|\sin t|$, $h_3(t) = \frac{1}{6}|\sin t|$, $t \geq 1$, and different initial values.

Example 2. *Consider the following nonlinear system of DDEs with three multiple time-varying delays:*

$$\begin{pmatrix} x_1' \\ x_2' \end{pmatrix} = \begin{pmatrix} -25 - \frac{t}{t+1} & \frac{t}{t+1} \\ \frac{t}{t+1} & -25 - \frac{t}{t+1} \end{pmatrix} \begin{pmatrix} x_1 \\ x_2 \end{pmatrix} + \begin{pmatrix} 3 & 2 \\ 2 & 3 \end{pmatrix} \begin{pmatrix} \sin x_1\left(t - \frac{1}{4}|\sin t|\right) \\ \sin x_2\left(t - \frac{1}{4}|\sin t|\right) \end{pmatrix} + \begin{pmatrix} 2 & 1 \\ 1 & 2 \end{pmatrix} \begin{pmatrix} \sin x_1\left(t - \frac{1}{2}|\sin t|\right) \\ \sin x_2\left(t - \frac{1}{2}|\sin t|\right) \end{pmatrix} + \begin{pmatrix} \frac{x_1 \exp(t)}{1+\exp(2t)+x_1^2(t-\frac{1}{6}|\sin t|)} \\ \frac{x_2 \exp(t)}{1+\exp(2t)+x_2^2(t-\frac{1}{6}|\sin t|)} \end{pmatrix}, \quad (14)$$

where $h_1(t) = \frac{1}{4}|\sin t|$, $h_2(t) = \frac{1}{2}|\sin t|$, and $h_3(t) = \frac{1}{6}|\sin t|$ are three multiple time-varying delays, and $t \geq 1$.

If nonlinear system of DDEs (14) and the perturbed system of DDEs (2) with three multiple time-varying delays are compared, then the condition (C1) and (C2) are satisfied, since they were shown in Example 1. As for the condition (C3), it is clear that:

$$P(t, x(t), x(t - h_3(t))) = P(t, x(t), x(t - \frac{1}{6}|\sin t|)) = \begin{pmatrix} \frac{x_1 \exp(t)}{1+\exp(2t)+x_1^2(t-\frac{1}{6}|\sin t|)} \\ \frac{x_2 \exp(t)}{1+\exp(2t)+x_2^2(t-\frac{1}{6}|\sin t|)} \end{pmatrix}.$$

From this point of view, we derive that:

$$\begin{aligned} \|P(t, x(t), x(t - \frac{1}{6}|\sin t|))\| &= \left\| \begin{pmatrix} \frac{x_1 \exp(t)}{1+\exp(2t)+x_1^2(t-\frac{1}{6}|\sin t|)} \\ \frac{x_2 \exp(t)}{1+\exp(2t)+x_2^2(t-\frac{1}{6}|\sin t|)} \end{pmatrix} \right\| \\ &= \frac{|x_1| \exp(t)}{1 + \exp(2t) + x_1^2(t - \frac{1}{6}|\sin t|)} + \frac{|x_2| \exp(t)}{1 + \exp(2t) + x_2^2(t - \frac{1}{6}|\sin t|)} \\ &\leq \frac{|x_1| \exp(t)}{1 + \exp(2t)} + \frac{|x_2| \exp(t)}{1 + \exp(2t)} \\ &\leq \frac{\exp(t)}{1 + \exp(2t)}[|x_1| + |x_2|] = |p_0(t)|\|x\|, \end{aligned}$$

where:

$$|p_0(t)| = \frac{\exp(t)}{1 + \exp(2t)}, \|x\| = |x_1| + |x_2|.$$

Hence, we obtain:

$$\int_0^\infty |p_0(s)|ds = \int_0^\infty \frac{\exp(s)}{1 + \exp(2s)} ds = \frac{\pi}{4} = L.$$

The obtained results shows that the conditions of (C1)–(C3) of Theorem 5 can hold. Thus, all the solutions of the nonlinear system of DDEs (14) with three multiple time-varying delays are bounded as $t \to \infty$.

In Figures 3 and 4, the system of DDEs (14) was solved by MATLAB software and the trajectories of the solutions were drawn for when $h_1(t) = \frac{1}{4}|\sin t|$, $h_2(t) = \frac{1}{2}|\sin t|$, $h_3(t) = \frac{1}{6}|\sin t|$, $t \geq 1$, and different initial values.

6. Discussion and Contribution

We first compare the conditions Theorems 3 with those of the main result of Ren and Tian ([33], Theorem 1). We also explain the contributions of the next two results, Theorems 4 and 5, of this paper to the relevant literature by the following items, respectively.

(1) The nonlinear perturbed system of DDEs (2) extend and improve the linear system of DDEs (1) (see Tian and Ren [33], Theorem 1) from a linear system of the DDEs with a time-varying delay to the a class of non-linear systems of DDEs with three multiple time-varying delays. Next, in the main result of Tian and Ren ([33], Theorem 1), see the above Theorem 2, the satisfaction of the following LMI is very difficult:

$$\Psi(\alpha) = \begin{bmatrix} \Phi(\alpha) - \Gamma^T\Re(\alpha)\Gamma - He(\Gamma^T\begin{bmatrix}(1-\alpha)N_1^T \\ \alpha N_2^T\end{bmatrix}) & * \\ \alpha N_1^T + (1-\alpha)N_2^T & -Q \end{bmatrix} < 0$$

since the matrix $\Psi(\alpha)$ has numerous terms. This fact can be seen clearly, when we look at ([33], Theorem 1) and the above Theorem 2. Hence, it is clear that this condition can lead conservatism, computational complexity, and difficulty in application fields. However, here, we have very simple conditions, (C1) and (C2) for our stronger result of uniformly asymptotically stability, Theorem 3, instead of asymptotically stability result in ([33], Theorem 1). For sake of brevity, there is no need for more information

(2) To prove Theorem 1, the following LKF $V(x_t)$,

$$\begin{aligned} V(x_t) =& \eta^T(t)P\eta(t) + \int_{t-h_1}^{t} x^T(s)Q_1x(s)ds + \int_{t-h_2}^{t-h_1} x^T(s)Q_2x(s)ds \\ &+ h_1\int_{t-h_1}^{t}\int_{u}^{t} \dot{x}^T(s)Q_3\dot{x}(s)dsdu + h_{12}\int_{t-h_2}^{t-h_1}\int_{u}^{t} \dot{x}^T(s)Q_4\dot{x}(s)dsdu \end{aligned} \tag{15}$$

with

$$\eta(t) = \begin{bmatrix} x^T(t) & \int_{t-h_2}^{t} x^T(s)ds & \int_{t-h_2}^{t-h_1} x^T(s)ds & \int_{t-h_1}^{t}\int_{u}^{t} x^T(s)dsdu & \int_{t-h_1}^{t}\int_{u}^{t}\int_{s}^{t} x^T(r)drdsdu \end{bmatrix}^T$$

is defined by Ren and Tian ([33], Theorem 1). Instead of the LKF (15), we defined the following LKF:

$$W_1(t, x_t) := \|x(t)\| + \sum_{i=1}^{2} \lambda_i \int_{t-h_i(t)}^{t} \|x(s)\|ds. \tag{16}$$

In spite of the non-linear unperturbed system of DDEs (2) having three multiple time-varying delays, the LKF (16) is very simple and more convenient and effective. For the particular case of our theorem, Theorem 3, to get the main result of Ren and Tian ([33], Theorem 1) under very less conservative and optimal conditions, we need the following LKF:

$$W_0(t, x_t) := \|x(t)\| + \lambda \int_{t-h(t)}^{t} \|x(s)\|ds, \tag{17}$$

which is a particular case of the LKF (16).

(3) In Ren and Tian ([33], Theorem 1), differentiating the LKF (15) and using the system of DDEs (1), it was derived that:

$$\begin{aligned}\dot{V}(x_t) =& 2\eta^T(t)P\dot{\eta}(t) + x^T(t)Q_1x(t) - x^T(t-h_1)Q_1x(t-h_1)\\ &+ x^T(t-h_1)Q_2x(t-h_1) - x^T(t-h_2)Q_2x(t-h_2) + h_1^2\dot{x}^T(t)Q_3\dot{x}(t)\\ &+ h_{12}^2\dot{x}^T(t)Q_4\dot{x}(t) - h_1\int_{t-h_1}^{t}\dot{x}^T(s)Q_3\dot{x}(s)ds - h_{12}\int_{t-h_2}^{t-h_1}\dot{x}^T(s)Q_4\dot{x}(s)ds\\ =& \xi^T(t)\{He(\Sigma_1^TP\Sigma_2) + \varepsilon_1^TQ_1\varepsilon_1 - \varepsilon_2^TQ_1\varepsilon_2 + \varepsilon_2^TQ_2\varepsilon_2\\ &- \varepsilon_4^TQ_2\varepsilon_4 + h_1^2\varepsilon_0^TQ_3\varepsilon_0 + h_{12}^2\varepsilon_0^TQ_4\varepsilon_0\}\xi(t)\}\\ &-h_1\int_{t-h_1}^{t}\dot{x}^T(s)Q_3\dot{x}(s)ds - h_{12}\int_{t-h_2}^{t-h_1}\dot{x}^T(s)Q_4\dot{x}(s)ds\end{aligned} \tag{18}$$

with

$$\xi(t) = \left[x^T(t)\; x^T(t-h_1)\; x^T(t-h(t))\; x^T(t-h_2)\;\; \varphi_1^T(t)\;\; \varphi_2^T(t)\;\; \varphi_3^T(t)\right]^T,$$

$$\varphi_1(t) = \left[\frac{1}{h_1}\int_{t-h_1}^{t} x^T(s)ds\; \frac{1}{h(t)-h_1}\int_{t-h(t)}^{t-h_1} x^T(s)ds\; \frac{1}{h_2-h(t)}\int_{t-h_2}^{t-h(t)} x^T(s)ds\right]^T,$$

$$\varphi_2(t) = \left[\frac{1}{h_1^2}\int_{t-h_1}^{t}\int_{u}^{t} x^T(s)dsdu\; \frac{1}{(h(t)-h_1)^2}\int_{t-h(t)}^{t-h_1}\int_{u}^{t-h_1} x^T(s)dsdu\; \frac{1}{(h_2-h(t))^2}\int_{t-h_2}^{t-h(t)}\int_{u}^{t-h(t)} x^T(s)ds\right]^T,$$

$$\begin{aligned}\varphi_3(t) = \Bigg[&\frac{1}{h_1^3}\int_{t-h_1}^{t}\int_{u}^{t}\int_{v}^{t} x^T(s)dsdudv\; \frac{1}{(h(t)-h_1)^3}\int_{t-h(t)}^{t-h_1}\int_{u}^{t-h_1}\int_{v}^{t-h_1} x^T(s)dsdudv\\ &\frac{1}{(h_2-h(t))^3}\int_{t-h_2}^{t-h(t)}\int_{u}^{t-h(t)}\int_{v}^{t-h(t)} x^T(s)dsdvdu\Bigg]^T.\end{aligned} \tag{19}$$

However, let $h_1(t) = h(t)$. It is interesting that calculating the time derivative of the LKF given by (17) and using the system of DDEs (1), we obtain:

$$\frac{d}{dt}W_0(t,x_t) = \sum_{i=1}^{n} x'_i(t)x_i(t+0) + \lambda_1\|x(t)\| - \lambda_1\|x(t-h(t))\| \times (1-h'(t)). \tag{20}$$

The equality (20) has a very simple form than those given by (18) and (19). Indeed, the inequality (20) leads very to less conservative conditions for the negative definiteness of the time derivative $\frac{d}{dt}W_0(t,x_t)$ than those given by Ren and Tian ([33], Theorem 1) for the negative definiteness of $\frac{d}{dt}V(x_t)$. Here, we would not like to give the details of the discussions for the sake of brevity. The less restrictive conditions of Theorem 3 can be followed with a comparison made between the conditions of Ren and Tian ([33], Theorem 1) and our Theorem 3.

(4) To prove Theorem 2, which is given above, firstly, three lemmas, Lemmas 1–3, are given by Ren and Tian [33]. Then, based upon the integral and matrix inequalities therein, a new delay-dependent stability criterion via Theorem 2 is proven in terms of a linear matrix inequality, see Ren and Tian [33], Theorem 1.

In this paper, we define a more suitable LKF (6) and depend upon Burton [1], (Theorem 4. 2.9), to prove Theorems 3–5. From this point of view, Ren and Tian ([33], Theorem 1) investigated the asymptotic stability of the linear system of DDEs (1). Here, we investigate the uniformly asymptotically stability of the zero solution and integrability of the norm of solutions of an unperturbed system of DDEs (4) as well as the boundedness of solutions of the perturbed system of DDEs (2). The result of Theorem

3, the uniformly asymptotically stability includes and implies the asymptotic stability of the linear system of DDEs (1), i.e., but the converse is not true.
As a brief summary, here, we extend and improve the result of Ren and Tian ([33], Theorem 1), and obtain this result under very less conservative conditions and make it more optimal than before. Next, we also obtain two new results on the qualitative properties of the nonlinear unperturbed system of DDEs (4) and as well as the nonlinear perturbed system of DDEs (2), (see Theorems 4 and 5). The applicability of our results can be done easily because of the form of the new less restrictive conditions of Theorems 3–5.

(5) In this particular case, two nonlinear Examples 1 and 2 with two and three time-varying delays, respectively, are given. These examples satisfy the conditions of Theorems 3–5 and they were solved depending upon the 4th order Runge–Kutta method. The trajectories of these examples are plotted by MATLAB software. The stability, integrability, and boundedness of the solutions can be followed clearly.

(6) An advantage of the new and optimal LKF (6) used in the proof of Theorem 5 is to eliminate using Gronwall's inequality for the boundedness of solutions at infinity. A comparison of Theorems 3–5 and those in the literature also shows that the conditions of Theorems 3–5 are more general, simple, and convenient for applications.

7. Conclusions

In this paper, the unperturbed system of DDEs (4) with two multiple time-varying delays and the perturbed system of DDEs (2) with three multiple time-varying delays are taken into consideration. To the best of the authors' knowledge, the qualitative properties of the systems of DDEs (2) and (4) with multiple time-varying delays were not investigated in the relevant literature until this time and the results of this article are new, original, and have scientific novelty.

Indeed, this paper is comprised of three new results, Theorems 3–5, and two new examples, Examples 1 and 2. Theorems 3–5 are related to the uniformly asymptotically stability of zero solution and the integrability of solutions of the non-perturbed system of DDEs (4) as well as the boundedness of solutions of the perturbed system of the DDEs (2), respectively. The technique used to prove Theorems 3–5 depends upon a new LKF and the LKF method. In fact, the real advantage of the new LKF is that it can pioneer to more optimal, general, and less conservative new qualitative results and also eliminate the use of Gronwall's inequality for the boundedness of solutions.

The established sufficient conditions of Theorems 3–5 are more general, simple, less conservative, and more convenient to apply than those available from the literature.

The results of this paper also improve and extend the result of Ren and Tian ([33], Theorem 1) and add two new results on the qualitative properties of solutions and contributes to the topic and relevant literature. The given examples illustrate the particular applications of the new results of this paper.

Author Contributions: Conceptualization, O. T., C.T. and Y.W.; Data curation, O.T.; Formal analysis, O.T., C.T. and Y.W.; Funding acquisition, Y.W.; Methodology, C.T., O.T. and Y.W.; Project administration, C.T.; Supervision, Y.W. and O.T.; Validation, C.T., Y.W.; Visualization, O.T.; Writing—original draft, O.T. All authors have read and agreed to the published version of the manuscript.

Funding: This research was funded by the National Natural Science Foundation of China, grant number 11671365 and the Natural Science Foundation of Zhejiang Province, grant umber LY14A010011.

Institutional Review Board Statement: Not applicable.

Informed Consent Statement: Not applicable.

Data Availability Statement: Not applicable.

Acknowledgments: The authors would like to thank the handling editor and the anonymous referees for their many useful comments and suggestions leading to a substantial improvement of the presentation of this article.

Conflicts of Interest: The authors declare no conflict of interest.

References

1. Burton, T.A. *Stability and Periodic Solutions of Ordinary and Functional Differential Equations*; Corrected Version of the 1985 Original; Dover Publications, Inc.: Mineola, NY, USA, 2005.
2. Hale, J.K.; Lunel, S.M.V. Introduction to functional-differential equations. In *Applied Mathematical Sciences*; Springer: New York, NY, USA, 1993; p. 99.
3. Kiri, Y.; Ueda, Y. Stability criteria for some system of delay differential equations. In *Theory, Numerics and Applications of Hyperbolic Problems II*; Springer Processing In Mathematics amd Statistics, 237; Springer: Cham, Switzerland, 2016; pp. 137–144.
4. Kolmanovskii, V.; Myshkis, A. Applied theory of functional-differential equations. In *Mathematics and Its Applications*; Soviet Series 85; Kluwer Academic Publishers Group: Dordrecht, The Netherlands, 1992.
5. Kuang, Y. Delay differential equations with applications in population dynamics. In *Mathematics in Science and Engineering*; Academic Press, Inc.: Boston, MA, USA, 1993; p. 191.
6. Lakshmikantham, V.; Wen, L.Z.; Zhang, B.G. Theory of differential equations with unbounded delay. In *Mathematics and Its Applications*; Kluwer Academic Publishers Group: Dordrecht, The Netherlands, 1994; p. 298.
7. Smith, H. *An Introduction to Delay Differential Equations with Applications to the Life Sciences*; Texts in Applied Mathematics 57; Springer: New York, NY, USA, 2011.
8. Berezansky, L.; Braverman, E.; Idels, L. New global exponential stability criteria for nonlinear delay differential systems with applications to BAM neural networks. *Appl. Math. Comput.* **2014**, *243*, 899–910. [CrossRef]
9. Gil', M.I. Exponential stability of nonlinear non-autonomous multivariable systems. *Discuss. Math. Differ. Incl. Control Optim.* **2015**, *35*, 89–100. [CrossRef]
10. Berezansky, L.; Diblík, J.; Svoboda, Z.; Šmarda, Z. Simple uniform exponential stability conditions for a system of linear delay differential equations. *Appl. Math. Comput.* **2015**, *250*, 605–614. [CrossRef]
11. Gözen, M.; Tunç, C. A new result on exponential stability of a linear differential system of first order with variable delays. *Nonlinear Stud.* **2020**, *27*, 275–284.
12. Liu, B. Global stability of a class of non-autonomous delay differential systems. *Proc. Am. Math. Soc.* **2010**, *138*, 975–985. [CrossRef]
13. Matsunaga, H. Delay-dependent and delay-independent stability criteria for a delay differential system. *Proc. Am. Math. Soc.* **2008**, *136*, 4305–4312. [CrossRef]
14. Ngoc, P.H.A. Stability of nonlinear differential systems with delay. *Evol. Equ. Control Theory* **2015**, *4*, 493–505. [CrossRef]
15. Petruşel, A.; Petruxsxel, G.; Yao, J. Existence and stability results for a system of operator equations via fixed point theory for non-self orbital contractions. *J. Fixed Point Theory Appl.* **2019**, *21*, 18. [CrossRef]
16. Rebenda, J.; Šmarda, Z. Stability of a functional differential system with a finite number of delays. *Abstr. Appl. Anal.* **2013**, *2013*, 853134. [CrossRef]
17. Shu, F.C. Stability of a 2-dimensional irreducible linear system of delay differential equations. *Appl. Math. E Notes* **2012**, *12*, 36–43.
18. Slyn'ko, V.I.; Tunç, C. Instability of set differential equations. *J. Math. Anal. Appl.* **2018**, *467*, 935–947. [CrossRef]
19. Tunç, C. A note on boundedness of solutions to a class of non-autonomous differential equations of second order. *Appl. Anal. Discrete Math.* **2010**, *4*, 361–372. [CrossRef]
20. Tunç, C. Uniformly stability and boundedness of solutions of second order nonlinear delay differential equations. *Appl. Comput. Math.* **2011**, *10*, 449–462.
21. Tunç, C. Stability to vector Liénard equation with constant deviating argument. *Nonlinear Dynam.* **2013**, *73*, 1245–1251. [CrossRef]
22. Tunç, C.; Tunç, O. A note on certain qualitative properties of a second order linear differential system. *Appl. Math. Inf. Sci.* **2015**, *9*, 953–956.
23. Tunç, C.; Tunç, O. On the boundedness and integration of non-oscillatory solutions of certain linear differential equations of second order. *J. Adv. Res.* **2016**, *7*, 165–168. [CrossRef] [PubMed]
24. Tunç, C.; Tunç, O. A note on the stability and boundedness of solutions to non-linear differential systems of second order. *J. Assoc. Arab Univ. Basic Appl. Sci.* **2017**, *24*, 169–175. [CrossRef]
25. Tunç, C.; Tunç, O. Qualitative analysis for a variable delay system of differential equations of second order. *J. Taibah Univ. Sci.* **2019**, *13*, 468–477. [CrossRef]
26. Tunç, C.; Golmankhaneh, A.K. On stability of a class of second alpha-order fractal differential equations. *AIMS Math.* **2020**, *5*, 2126–2142. [CrossRef]
27. Yskak, T. Stability of solutions to systems of differential equations with distributed delay. *Funct. Differ. Equ.* **2018**, *25*, 97–108.
28. Zhang, H.; Jiang, W. Global exponential stability to a class of differential system with delay. *Ann. Differ. Equ.* **2007**, *23*, 564–569.
29. Zhang, S.; Wu, S. Stability of delay differential systems by several Liapunov functions. *Ann. Differ. Equ.* **2001**, *17*, 86–92.
30. Petruşel, A.; Rus, I.A. The Ulam-Hyers stability of an ordinary differential equation via Gronwall lemmas. *Appl. Set Valued Anal. Optim.* **2020**, *2*, 295–303.
31. Kien, B.T.; Qin, X.; Wen, C.F. L^{∞}-stability for a class of parametric optimal control problems with mixed pointwise constraints. *J. Appl. Numer. Optim.* **2020**, *2*, 297–320.

32. Chadli, O.; Koukkous, A.; Saidi, A. Existence of anti-periodic solutions for nonlinear implicit evolution equations with time dependent pseudomonotone operators. *J. Nonlinear Var. Aanl.* **2017**, *1*, 71–88.
33. Ren, Z.; Tian, J. Stability analysis of systems with interval time-varying delays via a new integral inequality. *Complexity* **2020**, *2020*, 2854293. [CrossRef]

axioms

Article

Global Stability of a Lotka-Volterra Competition-Diffusion-Advection System with Different Positive Diffusion Distributions

Lili Chen, Shilei Lin and Yanfeng Zhao *

College of Mathematics and Systems Science, Shandong University of Science and Technology, Qingdao 266590, China; cll2119@sdust.edu.cm (L.C.); linshilei2021@126.com (S.L.)
* Correspondence: zhaoyf1101@sdust.edu.cm

Abstract: In this paper, the problem of a Lotka–Volterra competition–diffusion–advection system between two competing biological organisms in a spatially heterogeneous environments is investigated. When two biological organisms are competing for different fundamental resources, and their advection and diffusion strategies follow different positive diffusion distributions, the functions of specific competition ability are variable. By virtue of the Lyapunov functional method, we discuss the global stability of a non-homogeneous steady-state. Furthermore, the global stability result is also obtained when one of the two organisms has no diffusion ability and is not affected by advection.

Keywords: competition-diffusion-advection; steady-state solution; spatially heterogeneous; global stability

MSC: 35K51; 35B09; 35B35; 92D25

Citation: Chen, L.; Lin, S.; Zhao, Y. Global Stability of a Lotka-Volterra Competition-Diffusion-Advection System with Different Positive Diffusion Distributions. *Axioms* **2021**, *10*, 166. https://doi.org/10.3390/axioms10030166

Academic Editor: Wei-Shih Du

Received: 22 June 2021
Accepted: 26 July 2021
Published: 28 July 2021

Publisher's Note: MDPI stays neutral with regard to jurisdictional claims in published maps and institutional affiliations.

Copyright: © 2021 by the authors. Licensee MDPI, Basel, Switzerland. This article is an open access article distributed under the terms and conditions of the Creative Commons Attribution (CC BY) license (https://creativecommons.org/licenses/by/4.0/).

1. Introduction

For researchers from the fields of biology and mathematics, advancing the exploration of dynamic systems is a long-term challenge (see [1–3]). The competitive system of two diffusive organisms is often used to simulate population dynamics in biomathematics; for an example, see [1,2,4]. The key to spatial heterogeneity has been discussed in a lot of work, such as [2,5] and its references. In 2020, by proposing a new Lyapunov functional, Ni et al. [6] first studied and proved the global stability of a diffusive, competitive two-organism system, and then extended it to multiple organisms.

Since various methods in the reaction–diffusion–convection system cannot continue to work well, the global dynamics is far from being fully understood. In competitive diffusion advection systems, some progress has been made in [7–11]. Li et al. introduced the weighted Lyapunov functional related to the advection term to study global stability results in 2020 (see [12]), and studied the stability and bifurcation analysis of the model with the time delay term in 2021 (see [11]). Similarly, in 2021, Ma et al. described the overlapping characteristics of bifurcation solutions and studied the influence of advection on the stability of bifurcation solutions. Their results showed that the advection term may change its stability (see [13]). In 2021, Zhou et al. studied the global dynamics of a parabolic system using the competition coefficient (see [14]).

Motivated by the efforts of the aforementioned papers, we will investigate the global stability of a non-homogeneous steady-state solution of a Lotka–Volterra model between two organisms in heterogeneous environments, where two competing organisms have different intrinsic growth rates, advection and diffusion strategies, and follow different positive diffusion distributions.

Hence, we discuss the following advection system:

$$
\begin{cases}
U_t = \nabla\cdot[\mu_1(x)\nabla(\frac{U}{\rho_1(x)}) - R_1(x)\frac{U}{\rho_1(x)}\nabla B_1(x)] + U[\lambda_1(x) - \omega_{11}(x)U - \omega_{12}(x)V], & \\
 & in\ \Omega\times\mathbb{R}^+, \\
V_t = \nabla\cdot[\mu_2(x)\nabla(\frac{V}{\rho_2(x)}) - R_2(x)\frac{V}{\rho_2(x)}\nabla B_2(x)] + V[\lambda_2(x) - \omega_{21}(x)U - \omega_{22}(x)V], & \\
 & in\ \Omega\times\mathbb{R}^+, \\
\mu_1(x)\frac{\partial}{\partial n}(\frac{U}{\rho_1}) - R_1(x)\frac{U}{\rho_1}\frac{\partial B_1(x)}{\partial n} = 0, & on\ \partial\Omega\times\mathbb{R}^+, \\
\mu_2(x)\frac{\partial}{\partial n}(\frac{V}{\rho_2}) - R_2(x)\frac{V}{\rho_2}\frac{\partial B_2(x)}{\partial n} = 0, & on\ \partial\Omega\times\mathbb{R}^+, \\
U(x,0) = U_0(x) \geq, \not\equiv 0, V(x,0) = V_0(x) \geq, \not\equiv 0, & in\ \Omega,
\end{cases} \tag{1}
$$

Here, $U(x,t)$ and $V(x,t)$ are the population densities of biological organisms, location $x \in \Omega$, time $t > 0$, which are supposed to be nonnegative. $\mu_1(x), \mu_2(x) > 0$ correspond to the dispersal rates of two competing biological organisms, respectively. $R_1(x), R_2(x) > 0$ correspond to the advection rates of two competing biological organisms, and $B_1(x), B_2(x) \in C^2(\overline{\Omega})$ are the nonconstant functions and represent the advective directions. Two bounded functions $\lambda_1(x)$ and $\lambda_2(x)$ are the intrinsic growth rates of competing organisms , $\rho_1(x)$, $\rho_2(x) \in C^2(\overline{\Omega})$ are two positive diffusion distributions, respectively. $\omega_{ij}(x) > 0$, $i = 1,2, j = 1,2$ show the strength of competition ability. The spatial habitat $\Omega \subset \mathbb{R}^N$ is a bounded smooth domain, $1 \leq N \in \mathbb{Z}$; n denotes the outward unit normal vector on the boundary $\partial\Omega$. No one can enter or leave the habitat boundary.

The following are our basic assumptions:

Hypothesis 1. $0 < \mu_i(x), R_i(x) \in C^{1+\varrho}(\overline{\Omega}), 0 < \lambda_i(x), \omega_{ij}(x) \in C^{\varrho}(\overline{\Omega}), \varrho \in (0,1)$.

Hypothesis 2. $\frac{\mu_1(x)}{R_1(x)} =: c_1 > 0, \frac{\mu_2(x)}{R_2(x)} =: c_2 > 0,\ x \in \overline{\Omega},$ *where* c_1 *and* c_2 *are constants.*

To simplify the calculation, by letting $u = e^{-c_1B_1(x)}\frac{U}{\rho_1(x)}, v = e^{-c_2B_2(x)}\frac{V}{\rho_2(x)}$, the system (1) converts into the following coupled system

$$
\begin{cases}
u_t = \dfrac{e^{-c_1B_1(x)}}{\rho_1(x)}\nabla[\mu_1(x)e^{c_1B_1(x)}\nabla u] + u[\lambda_1(x) - \omega_{11}(x)ue^{c_1B_1(x)}\rho_1(x) & \\
\quad -\omega_{12}(x)ve^{c_2B_2(x)}\rho_2(x)], & in\ \Omega\times\mathbb{R}^+, \\
v_t = \dfrac{e^{-c_2B_2(x)}}{\rho_2(x)}\nabla[\mu_2(x)e^{c_2B_2(x)}\nabla v] + v[\lambda_2(x) - \omega_{21}(x)ue^{c_1B_1(x)}\rho_1(x) & \\
\quad -\omega_{22}(x)ve^{c_2B_2(x)}\rho_2(x)], & in\ \Omega\times\mathbb{R}^+, \\
\frac{\partial u}{\partial n} = \frac{\partial v}{\partial n} = 0, & on\ \partial\Omega\times\mathbb{R}^+, \\
u(x,0) = e^{-c_1B_1(x)}\frac{U_0(x)}{\rho_1(x)} \geq, \not\equiv 0, v(x,0) = e^{-c_2B_2(x)}\frac{V_0(x)}{\rho_2(x)} \geq, \not\equiv 0, & in\ \Omega,
\end{cases} \tag{2}
$$

when $c_1 = c_2 = 0, \rho_1(x) = \rho_2(x) = 1$, the model (2) has been studied in Ni et al. [6]. $c_1 = c_2, B_1(x) = B_2(x), \rho_1(x) = \rho_2(x) = 1$, the model (2) has been studied in Li et al. [12].

The rest of this article is arranged as follows. In Section 2, we carry out some preparatory work and give four lemmas, where some related properties of the system (1) are deduced from the properties of a single organism model (4). Using the Lyapunov functional method, we will provide and prove our main results in Section 3. In Section 4, one example is given to explain our conclusions.

2. Preliminaries

In order to describe our main results, we present the following uniform estimates for the parabolic equation:

$$\begin{cases} w_t = \varpi_{ij}(x)D_{ij}w + \beta_j(x)D_jw + \lambda(x)w + H(x,t,w), & in\ \Omega \times \mathbb{R}^+, \\ \frac{\partial w}{\partial n} = 0, & on\ \partial\Omega \times \mathbb{R}^+, \\ w(x,0) = w_0(x) \geq, \not\equiv 0, & in\ \Omega, \end{cases} \quad (3)$$

where $\Omega \subset \mathbb{R}^N$ is bounded and $\partial\Omega \in C^{2+\varrho}(\varrho \in (0,1))$ is a smooth boundary. The initial condition $w_0(x) \in W^{2,p}(\Omega), p > 1 + \frac{N}{2}$.

Setting the following assumptions:

(A_1) Let $\varpi_{ij}, \beta_j, \lambda \in C(\overline{\Omega}), \chi_1, \chi_2 > 0$, such that

$$\chi_1|y|^2 \leq \sum_{1\leq i,j\leq N} \varpi_{ij}(x)y_iy_j \leq \chi_2|y|^2, |\beta_j(x)|, |\lambda(x)| \leq \chi_2, for\ all\ x \in \Omega, y \in R^N.$$

(A_2) Let $\Lambda > 0$ be a constant, such that

$$\|\varpi_{ij}\|_{C^\varrho(\overline{\Omega})}, \|\beta_j\|_{C^\varrho(\overline{\Omega})}, \|\lambda\|_{C^\varrho(\overline{\Omega})} \leq \Lambda.$$

(A_3) $H \in L^\infty(\Omega \times [0,\infty) \times [\tau_1, \tau_2])$ for some $\tau_1 < \tau_2$ and there is $\Lambda(\tau_1, \tau_2) > 0$ such that

$$|H(x,t,w_1) - H(x,t,w_2)| \leq \Lambda(\tau_1,\tau_2)|w_1 - w_2|, for\ all\ (x,t) \in \Omega \times [0,\infty), w_1, w_2 \in [\tau_1, \tau_2],$$

and there exists $\Lambda > 0$, satisfying

$$|H(x_1,t_1,w) - H(x_2,t_2,w)| \leq \Lambda(|x_1 - x_2|^\varrho + |t_1 - t_2|^{\frac{\varrho}{2}})\ for\ all (x_1,t_1), (x_2,t_2) \in \overline{\Omega}\times [d, d+3], u \in [\tau_1, \tau_2], d \geq 0.$$

The following lemma (see [15,16]) is the boundedness result of the solution $w(x,t)$ in (3).

Lemma 1. *Let $w(x,t)$ be a solution of (3) with $\tau_1 < w < \tau_2, \tau_1, \tau_2 \in \mathbb{R}$. Suppose that $f, \varpi_{ij}, \beta_j, \lambda$ satisfy the assumptions $(A_1) - (A_3)$, then for any $\kappa \geq 1$, there is a constant $\Lambda(\kappa) > 0$ such that*

$$\max_{x\in\overline{\Omega}} \|w_t(x,\cdot)\|_{C^{\frac{\varrho}{2}}([\kappa,+\infty))} + \max_{t\geq\kappa} \|w_t(\cdot,t)\|_{C(\overline{\Omega})} + \max_{t\geq\kappa} \|w(\cdot,t)\|_{C^{2+\varrho}(\overline{\Omega})} \leq \Lambda(\kappa).$$

In the proof of global stability, the following calculus theory and integral inequality are very important. For details, see [6,17].

Lemma 2 ([17]). *Let $\beta, \lambda > 0$ be constants, $\varphi(t) \geq 0$ in $[\beta,\infty)$. Assume that $\phi \in C^1([\beta,\infty))$ has lower bound, $\phi'(t) \leq -\lambda\varphi(t)$ in $[\beta,\infty)$. If one of the following alternatives holds:*

- *$\varphi \in C^1([\beta,\infty))$ and $\varphi'(t) \leq P$ in $[\beta,\infty)$ for $P > 0$,*
- *$\varphi \in C^\varrho([\beta,\infty))$ and $\|\varphi\|_{C^\varrho([\beta,\infty))} \leq P$ for $0 < m < 1$ and $P > 0$,*

where P and m are constants, then $\lim_{t\to\infty} \varphi(t) = 0$.

Lemma 3 ([6]). *Let $\alpha, \alpha^* \in C^2(\overline{\Omega})$ with $\alpha, \alpha^* > 0$ and $m \in C^1(\overline{\Omega}), b \in C^2(\overline{\Omega})$ with $m, b \geq 0$, α, α^*, m, b are functions. If the following conditions holds:*

- *$q \geq 1$ is a constant, the function $h \in C^{0,1}(\partial\Omega \times [0,\infty))$, $x \in \partial\Omega$, $\frac{h(x,K)}{K}$ is a non-increasing function for $K \in [0,\infty)$,*
- *$\frac{\partial(b(x)\alpha)}{\partial\nu} = h(x,\alpha)$, $\frac{\partial(b(x)\alpha^*)}{\partial\nu} = h(x,\alpha^*)$ on $\partial\Omega$,*

then

$$\int_{\Omega} \frac{b(x)\alpha^*[\alpha^q - \alpha^{*q}]}{\alpha^q} (\nabla\{m(x)\nabla[b(x)\alpha]\} - \frac{\alpha}{\alpha^*}\nabla\{m(x)\nabla[b(x)\alpha^*]\})\,dx \\ \leq - \int_{\Omega} qmb^2\alpha^2 (\frac{\alpha^*}{\alpha})^{q-1} |\nabla \frac{\alpha^*}{\alpha}|^2\,dx \leq 0. \tag{4}$$

Next, we consider the following scalar evolution eqution

$$\begin{cases} u_t = \dfrac{e^{-cB(x)}}{\rho(x)} \nabla[\mu(x)e^{cB(x)}\nabla u] + u[\lambda(x) - \varpi(x)ue^{cB(x)}\rho(x)], & in\ \Omega \times \mathbb{R}^+, \\ \frac{\partial u}{\partial n} = 0, & on\ \partial\Omega \times \mathbb{R}^+, \\ u(x,0) = e^{-cB(x)} \frac{U_0(x)}{\rho(x)} \geq, \not\equiv 0, & in\ \Omega, \end{cases} \tag{5}$$

where $\mu(x), c, \varpi(x), \lambda(x)$ satisty

$$0 < \mu(x), R(x) \in C^{1+\varrho}(\overline{\Omega}), 0 < \lambda(x), \varpi(x) \in C^{\varrho}(\overline{\Omega}), \varrho \in (0,1), \frac{\mu(x)}{R(x)} = c, where\ c\ is\ a\ constant. \tag{6}$$

Now we see the following useful lemma.

Lemma 4 ([1]). *Assume that* $0 < \mu(x), \lambda(x), \rho(x), \varpi(x)$ *on* $\overline{\Omega}$, *then the elliptic problem:*

$$\begin{cases} \dfrac{e^{-cB(x)}}{\rho(x)} \nabla[\mu(x)e^{cB(x)}\nabla u] + u[\lambda(x) - \varpi(x)ue^{cB(x)}\rho(x)] = 0, & in\ \Omega, \\ \frac{\partial u}{\partial n} = 0, & on\ \partial\Omega, \end{cases} \tag{7}$$

has a unique positive solution, denoted by u_θ.

3. Main Results

In this section, firstly, by utilizing the Lyapunov function method, the global stability of the model (5) is obtained, and we can see that the non-constant steady-state for (5) is equivalent to the solution u_θ of (7).

Theorem 1. *Assume that* $u_0(x) \gneqq 0$. *If* $\mu, \rho, c, \lambda, \varpi$ *satisfy* (6), *then Equation (5) has a unique solution* $u(x,t) > 0$ *with* $\lim_{t\to\infty} u(x,t) = u_\theta$ *in* $C^2(\Omega)$.

Proof. According to the upper–lower solutions method [1,18], we obtain (5) with a unique solution $u(x,t) > 0$. Let M be a upper solution of (5), we have $0 < u(x,t) < M$, $(x,t) \in \overline{\Omega} \times (0,\infty)$.

By applying Lemma 1, we can obtain that there exists a constant $\Lambda > 0$ such that

$$\max_{t\geq 1} \|u_t(\cdot,t)\|_{C(\overline{\Omega})} + \max_{t\geq 1} \|u(\cdot,t)\|_{C^{2+\varrho}(\overline{\Omega})} \leq \Lambda. \tag{8}$$

Then, define a function $\Phi : [0,\infty) \to \mathbb{R}$ by

$$\Phi(t) = \int_{\Omega} \rho u_\theta e^{cB}(u - u_\theta - u_\theta \ln \frac{u}{u_\theta})\,dx. \tag{9}$$

Then, $\Phi(t) \geq 0$, $t \geq 0$. By (2) and (4), we have

$$\begin{aligned}
\Phi'(t) &= \int_\Omega \rho u_\theta e^{cB}(1-\frac{u_\theta}{u})u_t \, dx \\
&= \int_\Omega \rho u_\theta e^{cB}(1-\frac{u_\theta}{u})[\frac{e^{-cB}}{\rho}\nabla(\mu e^{cB}\nabla u) + u(\lambda - \varpi u e^{cB}\rho)] \, dx \\
&= \int_\Omega \rho u_\theta e^{cB}(1-\frac{u_\theta}{u})[\frac{e^{-cB}}{\rho}\nabla(\mu e^{cB}\nabla u) - \frac{u e^{-cB}}{u_\theta \rho}\nabla(\mu e^{cB}\nabla u_\theta)] \, dx \\
&+ \int_\Omega \rho u_\theta e^{cB}(1-\frac{u_\theta}{u})[u(\lambda - \varpi u e^{cB}\rho) - \frac{u}{u_\theta}u_\theta(\lambda - \varpi u_\theta e^{cB}\rho)] \, dx \\
&\leq - \int_\Omega \mu e^{cB} u^2 |\nabla \frac{u_\theta}{u}|^2 \, dx - \int_\Omega \rho^2 u_\theta e^{2cB}\varpi(u-u_\theta)^2 \, dx.
\end{aligned} \tag{10}$$

We get

$$\Phi'(t) \leq - \int_\Omega \rho^2 u_\theta e^{2cB}\varpi(u-u_\theta)^2 \, dx =: -\varphi(t) \leq 0. \tag{11}$$

By virtue of (8), we get $|\varphi'(t)| \leq \Lambda$ in $[1,\infty)$ for some $\Lambda > 0$. From Lemma 2, it follows that

$$\lim_{t\to\infty} \varphi(t) = \lim_{t\to\infty} \int_\Omega \rho^2 u_\theta e^{2cB}\varpi(u-u_\theta)^2 \, dx = 0. \tag{12}$$

Applying (8) again, $\{u(\cdot,t) : t \geq 1\}$ is relatively compact in $C^2(\overline{\Omega})$. It can be found that there exists some function $u_\infty(x) \in C^2(\overline{\Omega})$ such that

$$\|u(\cdot,t_s) - u_\infty\|_{C^2(\overline{\Omega})} \to 0 \; as \; t_s \to \infty. \tag{13}$$

Combining with (12), we get $u_\infty(x) = u_\theta(x)$ where $x \in \Omega$. Hence, we deduce

$$\lim_{t\to\infty} u(x,t) = u_\theta(x) \; in \; C^2(\overline{\Omega}).$$

□

In addition, taking advantage of Lyapunov function method, the global stability results of (2) are obtained.

Theorem 2. *Suppose that $u_0(x), v_0(x) \geq, \neq 0$, (H_1) and (H_2) hold, the system (2) admits a non-homogeneous steady-state $(\widetilde{u_\theta}(x), \widetilde{v_\theta}(x)) > 0$ and there exists*

$$\eta_1 > 0, \eta_2 > 0 \; such \; that \; \eta_1 \leq \frac{\widetilde{u_\theta}(x)}{\widetilde{v_\theta}(x)} \leq \eta_2, \; x \in \overline{\Omega}. \tag{14}$$

Suppose that

$$\sqrt{\frac{\eta_2}{\eta_1}} < \min_{\overline{\Omega}} \frac{\varpi_{11}\varpi_{22}}{\varpi_{12}\varpi_{21}}. \tag{15}$$

Then, the system (2) admits a solution $(u(x,t), v(x,t))$ that satisfies

$$\lim_{t\to\infty} u(x,t) = \widetilde{u_\theta}(x), \lim_{t\to\infty} v(x,t) = \widetilde{v_\theta}(x) \; in \; C^2(\overline{\Omega}).$$

Proof. Assume that the inequality (15) holds, let $\Phi : [0,+\infty) \to \mathbb{R}$ defined by

$$\Phi(t) = \int_\Omega \rho_1 \widetilde{u_\theta} e^{c_1 B_1}(u - \widetilde{u_\theta} - \widetilde{u_\theta}\ln\frac{u}{\widetilde{u_\theta}}) \, dx + \int_\Omega \xi \rho_2 \widetilde{v_\theta} e^{c_2 B_2}(v - \widetilde{v_\theta} - \widetilde{v_\theta}\ln\frac{v}{\widetilde{v_\theta}}) \, dx, \tag{16}$$

where $0 < \xi(x) := \dfrac{\varpi_{12}\sqrt{\eta_1\eta_2}}{\varpi_{21}}$. Clearly, $\Phi(t) \geq 0$. By (2) and (4), we have

$$
\begin{aligned}
\Phi'(t) =& \int_\Omega [\rho_1 \widetilde{u}_\theta e^{c_1B_1}(1-\frac{\widetilde{u}_\theta}{u})u_t + \xi\rho_2\widetilde{v}_\theta e^{c_2B_2}(1-\frac{\widetilde{v}_\theta}{v})v_t]\,\mathrm{d}x \\
=& \int_\Omega \rho_1 \widetilde{u}_\theta e^{c_1B_1}(1-\frac{\widetilde{u}_\theta}{u})[\frac{e^{-c_1B_1}}{\rho_1}\nabla(\mu_1 e^{c_1B_1}\nabla u) + u(\lambda_1 - \varpi_{11}ue^{c_1B_1}\rho_1 - \varpi_{12}ve^{c_2B_2}\rho_2)]\,\mathrm{d}x \\
&+\int_\Omega \xi\rho_2\widetilde{v}_\theta e^{c_2B_2}(1-\frac{\widetilde{v}_\theta}{v})[\frac{e^{-c_2B_2}}{\rho_2}\nabla(\mu_2 e^{c_2B_2}\nabla v) + v(\lambda_2 - \varpi_{21}ue^{c_1B_1}\rho_1 - \varpi_{22}ve^{c_2B_2}\rho_2)]\,\mathrm{d}x \\
=& \int_\Omega \rho_1 \widetilde{u}_\theta e^{c_1B_1}(1-\frac{\widetilde{u}_\theta}{u})[\frac{e^{-c_1B_1}}{\rho_1}\nabla(\mu_1 e^{c_1B_1}\nabla u) - \frac{ue^{-c_1B_1}}{\widetilde{u}_\theta\rho_1}\nabla(\mu_1 e^{c_1B_1}\nabla\widetilde{u}_\theta)]\,\mathrm{d}x \\
&+\int_\Omega \xi\rho_2\widetilde{v}_\theta e^{c_2B_2}(1-\frac{\widetilde{v}_\theta}{v})[\frac{e^{-c_2B_2}}{\rho_2}\nabla(\mu_2 e^{c_2B_2}\nabla v) - \frac{ve^{-c_2B_2}}{\widetilde{v}_\theta\rho_2}\nabla(\mu_2 e^{c_2B_2}\nabla\widetilde{v}_\theta)]\,\mathrm{d}x \\
&+\int_\Omega \rho_1 \widetilde{u}_\theta e^{c_1B_1}(1-\frac{\widetilde{u}_\theta}{u})u(\lambda_1 - \varpi_{11}ue^{c_1B_1}\rho_1 - \varpi_{12}ve^{c_2B_2}\rho_2)\,\mathrm{d}x \\
&-\int_\Omega \rho_1 \widetilde{u}_\theta e^{c_1B_1}(1-\frac{\widetilde{u}_\theta}{u})\frac{u}{\widetilde{u}_\theta}\widetilde{u}_\theta(\lambda_1 - \varpi_{11}\widetilde{u}_\theta e^{c_1B_1}\rho_1 - \varpi_{12}\widetilde{v}_\theta e^{c_2B_2}\rho_2)]\,\mathrm{d}x \\
&+\int_\Omega \xi\rho_2\widetilde{v}_\theta e^{c_2B_2}(1-\frac{\widetilde{v}_\theta}{v})v(\lambda_2 - \varpi_{21}ue^{c_1B_1}\rho_1 - \varpi_{22}ve^{c_2B_2}\rho_2)\,\mathrm{d}x \\
&-\int_\Omega \xi\rho_2\widetilde{v}_\theta e^{c_2B_2}(1-\frac{\widetilde{v}_\theta}{v})\frac{v}{\widetilde{v}_\theta}\widetilde{v}_\theta(\lambda_2 - \varpi_{21}\widetilde{u}_\theta e^{c_1B_1}\rho_1 - \varpi_{22}\widetilde{v}_\theta e^{c_2B_2}\rho_2)\,\mathrm{d}x \\
\leq& -\int_\Omega \mu_1 e^{c_1B_1}u^2|\nabla\frac{\widetilde{u}_\theta}{u}|^2\,\mathrm{d}x - \int_\Omega \mu_2 e^{c_2B_2}v^2|\nabla\frac{\widetilde{v}_\theta}{v}|^2\,\mathrm{d}x - \int_\Omega \rho_1^2\widetilde{u}_\theta e^{2c_1B_1}\varpi_{11}(u-\widetilde{u}_\theta)^2\,\mathrm{d}x \\
&-\int_\Omega \rho_1\rho_2 e^{c_1B_1+c_2B_2}(\varpi_{12}\widetilde{u}_\theta + \xi\varpi_{21}\widetilde{v}_\theta)(u-\widetilde{u}_\theta)(v-\widetilde{v}_\theta)\,\mathrm{d}x \\
&-\int_\Omega \xi\rho_2^2\widetilde{v}_\theta e^{2c_2B_2}\varpi_{22}(v-\widetilde{v}_\theta)^2\,\mathrm{d}x.
\end{aligned} \tag{17}
$$

Note that (14) and (15) give rise to

$$
\begin{aligned}
&2\sqrt{\rho_1^2\widetilde{u}_\theta e^{2c_1B_1}\varpi_{11}\xi\rho_2^2\widetilde{v}_\theta e^{2c_2B_2}\varpi_{22}} - \rho_1\rho_2 e^{c_1B_1+c_2B_2}(\varpi_{12}\widetilde{u}_\theta + \xi\varpi_{21}\widetilde{v}_\theta) \\
=&2\rho_1\rho_2 e^{c_1B_1+c_2B_2}\sqrt{\xi\widetilde{u}_\theta\widetilde{v}_\theta\varpi_{11}\varpi_{22}} - \rho_1\rho_2 e^{c_1B_1+c_2B_2}(\varpi_{12}\widetilde{u}_\theta + \xi\varpi_{21}\widetilde{v}_\theta) \\
=&\rho_1\rho_2 e^{c_1B_1+c_2B_2}(2\sqrt{\xi\widetilde{u}_\theta\widetilde{v}_\theta}\sqrt{\varpi_{11}\varpi_{22}} - \sqrt{\xi\widetilde{u}_\theta\widetilde{v}_\theta}(\varpi_{12}\sqrt{\frac{\widetilde{u}_\theta}{\xi\widetilde{v}_\theta}} + \varpi_{21}\sqrt{\frac{\xi\widetilde{v}_\theta}{\widetilde{u}_\theta}})) \\
=&\rho_1\rho_2 e^{c_1B_1+c_2B_2}\sqrt{\xi\widetilde{u}_\theta\widetilde{v}_\theta}(2\sqrt{\varpi_{11}\varpi_{22}} - (\varpi_{12}\sqrt{\frac{\eta_2}{\xi}} + \varpi_{21}\sqrt{\frac{\xi}{\eta_1}})) \\
\geq&\rho_1\rho_2 e^{c_1B_1+c_2B_2}\sqrt{\xi\widetilde{u}_\theta\widetilde{v}_\theta}(2\sqrt{\varpi_{11}\varpi_{22}} - 2\sqrt{\varpi_{12}\varpi_{21}\sqrt{\frac{\eta_2}{\eta_1}}}) \\
>&0.
\end{aligned}
$$

Choosing $0 < \varepsilon \ll 1$, we have

$$
2\sqrt{\rho_1^2\widetilde{u}_\theta e^{2c_1B_1}(\varpi_{11}-\varepsilon)\xi\rho_2^2\widetilde{v}_\theta e^{2c_2B_2}(\varpi_{22}-\varepsilon)} - \rho_1\rho_2 e^{c_1B_1+c_2B_2}(\varpi_{12}\widetilde{u}_\theta + \xi\varpi_{21}\widetilde{v}_\theta) > 0.
$$

Combining with (17), we can deduce

$$
\Phi'(t) \leq -\int_\Omega [\rho_1^2\widetilde{u}_\theta e^{2c_1B_1}\varepsilon(u-\widetilde{u}_\theta)^2 + \xi\rho_2^2\widetilde{v}_\theta e^{2c_2B_2}\varepsilon(v-\widetilde{v}_\theta)^2]\,\mathrm{d}x =: -\varphi(t) \leq 0.
$$

From (13), it follows that

$$
\lim_{t\to\infty} u(x,t) = \widetilde{u}_\theta(x),\ \lim_{t\to\infty} v(x,t) = \widetilde{v}_\theta(x)\ in\ C^2(\overline{\Omega}).
$$

□

Finally, we consider that if one of the two organisms has no diffusion ability and is not affected by advection, the Lyapunov function method can also deduce the following global stability results in (2).

Theorem 3. *If $u_0, v_0 \in C(\overline{\Omega})$ satisfy $u_0(x) \geq, \not\equiv 0$ and $v_0(x) > 0$ on $\overline{\Omega}$. Let $\frac{\mu_1(x)}{R_1(x)} =: c_1, \mu_2(x) = R_2(x) = 0$ for $x \in \overline{\Omega}$, and*

$$\varpi_{12}(x)\varpi_{21}(x) < \varpi_{11}(x)\varpi_{22}(x), x \in \overline{\Omega}. \tag{18}$$

(i) If

$$\varpi_{22}(x)\lambda_1(x) - \varpi_{12}(x)\lambda_2(x) > 0, \forall x \in \overline{\Omega}, \tag{19}$$

and

$$\min_{\overline{\Omega}} \frac{\lambda_2(x)}{\rho_1(x)\varpi_{21}(x)e^{c_1 B_1(x)}} > \max_{\overline{\Omega}} \frac{\varpi_{22}(x)\lambda_1(x) - \varpi_{12}(x)\lambda_2(x)}{\rho_1(x)e^{c_1 B_1(x)}(\varpi_{11}(x)\varpi_{22}(x) - \varpi_{12}(x)\varpi_{21}(x))}, \tag{20}$$

then there is a unique non-homogeneous steady-state $(\widetilde{u_\theta}(x), \widetilde{v_\theta}(x)) > 0$ for the model (2) such that

$$\lim_{t\to\infty}(u(x,t), v(x,t)) = (\widetilde{u_\theta}(x), \widetilde{v_\theta}(x)) \text{ in } C^1(\overline{\Omega}) \times L^2(\Omega).$$

(ii) If

$$\frac{\lambda_2(x)}{\rho_1(x)\varpi_{21}(x)e^{c_1 B_1(x)}} \leq \widetilde{u_\theta}(x), x \in \overline{\Omega}, \tag{21}$$

then there exists a semi-trivial steady-state $(\widetilde{u_\theta}(x), 0)$ for the model (2) such that

$$\lim_{t\to\infty}(u(x,t), v(x,t)) = (\widetilde{u_\theta}(x), 0) \text{ in } C^1(\overline{\Omega}) \times L^2(\overline{\Omega}).$$

(iii) Let

$$\frac{\varpi_{22}(x)}{\varpi_{12}(x)} \leq \frac{\lambda_2(x)}{\lambda_1(x)}, x \in \overline{\Omega}, \tag{22}$$

then the model (2) has a semi-trivial steady-state $(0, \widetilde{v_\theta}(x))$,

$$\lim_{t\to\infty}(u(x,t), v(x,t)) = (0, \widetilde{v_\theta}(x)) \text{ in } C^1(\overline{\Omega}) \times L^2(\overline{\Omega}),$$

where $\widetilde{v_\theta}(x) = \dfrac{\lambda_2(x)}{\rho_2(x)\varpi_{22}(x)e^{c_2 B_2(x)}}$.

Proof. (i) When $\mu_2(x) = R_2(x) = 0$, $x \in \overline{\Omega}$, $(\widetilde{u_\theta}(x), \widetilde{v_\theta}(x))$ of the model (2) satisfies

$$\begin{cases} \frac{e^{-c_1 B_1(x)}}{\rho_1(x)}\nabla[\mu_1(x)e^{c_1 B_1(x)}\nabla u] + u[\lambda_1(x) - \frac{\varpi_{12}(x)}{\varpi_{22}(x)}\lambda_2(x) - \rho_1(x)ue^{c_1 B_1(x)} \\ (\varpi_{11}(x) - \frac{\varpi_{12}(x)\varpi_{21}(x)}{\varpi_{22}(x)})] = 0, & x \in \Omega, \\ \frac{\partial u}{\partial n} = 0, & x \in \partial\Omega, \end{cases} \tag{23}$$

and $\widetilde{v_\theta} = \dfrac{\lambda_2 - \varpi_{21}\rho_1\widetilde{u_\theta}e^{c_1 B_1}}{\varpi_{22}\rho_2 e^{c_2 B_2}}$.

If (18) and (19) hold, we see $\mu_1, \lambda_1 - \frac{\varpi_{12}}{\varpi_{22}}\lambda_2, \rho_1 e^{-c_1 B_1}(\varpi_{11} - \frac{\varpi_{12}\varpi_{21}}{\varpi_{22}}) > 0$, then by Lemma 4, the problem (23) has a unique solution $\widetilde{u_\theta}(x) > 0$. By using the maximum principle in elliptic equation, we infer

$$\widetilde{u_\theta} < \max_{\overline{\Omega}} \frac{\varpi_{22}\lambda_1 - \varpi_{12}\lambda_2}{\rho_1 e^{c_1 B_1}(\varpi_{11}\varpi_{22} - \varpi_{12}\varpi_{21})}.$$

According to (20), we can get $\widetilde{v_\theta} = \dfrac{\lambda_2 - \varpi_{21}\rho_1\widetilde{u_\theta}e^{c_1 B_1}}{\varpi_{22}\rho_2 e^{c_2 B_2}} > 0$, hence there exists a unique steady-state for (2), $(\widetilde{u_\theta}(x), \widetilde{v_\theta}(x)) > 0$.

Let us define a function $\Phi : [0,\infty) \to \mathbb{R}$,

$$\Phi(t) = \int_\Omega \rho_1 \widetilde{u}_\theta e^{c_1 B_1}(u - \widetilde{u}_\theta - \widetilde{u}_\theta \ln \frac{u}{\widetilde{u}_\theta})\,\mathrm{d}x + \int_\Omega \xi \rho_2 e^{c_2 B_2}(v - \widetilde{v}_\theta - \widetilde{v}_\theta \ln \frac{v}{\widetilde{v}_\theta})\,\mathrm{d}x,$$

where $\xi(x) = \frac{\varpi_{12}(x)\widetilde{u}_\theta(x)}{\varpi_{21}(x)} > 0$. Clearly, $\Phi(t) \geqslant 0$. From (2) and (4), we get

$$\begin{aligned}
\Phi'(t) &= \int_\Omega [\rho_1 \widetilde{u}_\theta e^{c_1 B_1}(1 - \frac{\widetilde{u}_\theta}{u})u_t + \xi \rho_2 e^{c_2 B_2}(1 - \frac{\widetilde{v}_\theta}{v})v_t]\,\mathrm{d}x \\
&= \int_\Omega \rho_1 \widetilde{u}_\theta e^{c_1 B_1}(1 - \frac{\widetilde{u}_\theta}{u})[\frac{e^{-c_1 B_1}}{\rho_1}\nabla(\mu_1 e^{c_1 B_1}\nabla u) \\
&\quad + u(\lambda_1 - \varpi_{11} u e^{c_1 B_1}\rho_1 - \varpi_{12} v e^{c_2 B_2}\rho_2)]\,\mathrm{d}x \\
&\quad + \int_\Omega \xi \rho_2 \widetilde{v}_\theta e^{c_2 B_2}(1 - \frac{\widetilde{v}_\theta}{v})[v(\lambda_2 - \varpi_{21} u e^{c_1 B_1}\rho_1 - \varpi_{22} v e^{c_2 B_2}\rho_2)]\,\mathrm{d}x \\
&= \int_\Omega \rho_1 \widetilde{u}_\theta e^{c_1 B_1}(1 - \frac{\widetilde{u}_\theta}{u})[\frac{e^{-c_1 B_1}}{\rho_1}\nabla(\mu_1 e^{c_1 B_1}\nabla u) - \frac{u e^{-c_1 B_1}}{\widetilde{u}_\theta \rho_1}\nabla(\mu_1 e^{c_1 B_1}\nabla \widetilde{u}_\theta)]\,\mathrm{d}x \\
&\quad + \int_\Omega \rho_1 \widetilde{u}_\theta e^{c_1 B_1}(1 - \frac{\widetilde{u}_\theta}{u})u(\lambda_1 - \varpi_{11} u e^{c_1 B_1}\rho_1 - \varpi_{12} v e^{c_2 B_2}\rho_2)\,\mathrm{d}x \\
&\quad - \int_\Omega \rho_1 \widetilde{u}_\theta e^{c_1 B_1}(1 - \frac{\widetilde{u}_\theta}{u})\frac{u}{\widetilde{u}_\theta}\widetilde{u}_\theta(\lambda_1 - \varpi_{11}\widetilde{u}_\theta e^{c_1 B_1}\rho_1 - \varpi_{12}\widetilde{v}_\theta e^{c_2 B_2}\rho_2)]\,\mathrm{d}x \\
&\quad + \int_\Omega \xi \rho_2 e^{c_2 B_2}(1 - \frac{\widetilde{v}_\theta}{v})v(\lambda_2 - \varpi_{21} u e^{c_1 B_1}\rho_1 - \varpi_{22} v e^{c_2 B_2}\rho_2)\,\mathrm{d}x \\
&\quad - \int_\Omega \xi \rho_2 e^{c_2 B_2}(1 - \frac{\widetilde{v}_\theta}{v})\frac{v}{\widetilde{v}_\theta}\widetilde{v}_\theta(\lambda_2 - \varpi_{21}\widetilde{u}_\theta e^{c_1 B_1}\rho_1 - \varpi_{22}\widetilde{v}_\theta e^{c_2 B_2}\rho_2)\,\mathrm{d}x \\
&\leq -\int_\Omega \mu_1 e^{c_1 B_1} u^2 |\nabla \frac{\widetilde{u}_\theta}{u}|^2\,\mathrm{d}x - \int_\Omega \rho_1^2 \widetilde{u}_\theta e^{2c_1 B_1}\varpi_{11}(u - \widetilde{u}_\theta)^2\,\mathrm{d}x \\
&\quad - \int_\Omega \rho_1 \rho_2 e^{c_1 B_1 + c_2 B_2}(\varpi_{12}\widetilde{u}_\theta + \xi \varpi_{21})(u - \widetilde{u}_\theta)(v - \widetilde{v}_\theta)\,\mathrm{d}x \\
&\quad - \int_\Omega \xi \rho_2^2 e^{2c_2 B_2}\varpi_{22}(v - \widetilde{v}_\theta)^2\,\mathrm{d}x.
\end{aligned} \tag{24}$$

We can choose $0 < \varepsilon \ll 1$ and use (18), such that

$$2\sqrt{\rho_1^2 \widetilde{u}_\theta e^{2c_1 B_1}(\varpi_{11} - \varepsilon)\xi \rho_2^2 e^{2c_2 B_2}(\varpi_{22} - \varepsilon)} - \rho_1 \rho_2 e^{c_1 B_1 + c_2 B_2}(\varpi_{12}\widetilde{u}_\theta + \xi \varpi_{21}) > 0.$$

Combining this with (24), we can deduce

$$\Phi'(t) \leq -\int_\Omega [\rho_1^2 \widetilde{u}_\theta e^{2c_1 B_1}\varepsilon(u - \widetilde{u}_\theta)^2 + \xi \rho_2^2 e^{2c_2 B_2}\varepsilon(v - \widetilde{v}_\theta)^2]\,\mathrm{d}x =: -\varphi(t) \leq 0.$$

Applying the Lemma 1 and Sobolev embedding theorem, we deduce that u and v are bounded in $\Omega \times [0,\infty)$ and there is a constant $\Lambda > 0$ such that

$$\max_{t \geq 1} \|u(\cdot,t)\|_{C^{1+\varrho}(\overline{\Omega})} \leq \Lambda \ for\ some\ 0 < \varrho < 1.$$

Combining with (2) and $|\varphi'(t)| < \Lambda_1$ in $[1,\infty)$ for some $\Lambda_1 > 0$, and making use of Lemma 2, we get $\lim_{t\to\infty} \varphi(t) = 0$ and we deduce that

$$\lim_{t\to\infty} u(x,t) = \widetilde{u}_\theta(x), \lim_{t\to\infty} v(x,t) = \widetilde{v}_\theta(x)\ in\ L^2(\Omega).$$

Applying Theorem 2, we get $\lim_{t\to\infty} u(x,t) = \widetilde{u}_\theta(x)$ in $C^1(\overline{\Omega})$.

(ii) Let's define a function $\Phi : [0, \infty) \to \mathbb{R}$,

$$\Phi(t) = \int_\Omega \rho_1 \widetilde{u_\theta} e^{c_1 B_1} (u - \widetilde{u_\theta} - \widetilde{u_\theta} \ln \frac{u}{\widetilde{u_\theta}}) \,dx + \int_\Omega \xi \rho_2 e^{c_2 B_2} v \,dx,$$

where $\xi(x) = \frac{\omega_{12}(x)\widetilde{u_\theta}(x)}{\omega_{21}(x)} > 0$. From (4) and (21), we have

$$\begin{aligned}
\Phi'(t) = & \int_\Omega \rho_1 \widetilde{u_\theta} e^{c_1 B_1} (1 - \frac{\widetilde{u_\theta}}{u})[\frac{e^{-c_1 B_1}}{\rho_1} \nabla (\mu_1 e^{c_1 B_1} \nabla u) - \frac{u e^{-c_1 B_1}}{\widetilde{u_\theta} \rho_1} \nabla (\mu_1 e^{c_1 B_1} \nabla \widetilde{u_\theta})] \,dx \\
& + \int_\Omega \rho_1 \widetilde{u_\theta} e^{c_1 B_1} (1 - \frac{\widetilde{u_\theta}}{u}) u (\lambda_1 - \omega_{11} u e^{c_1 B_1} \rho_1 - \omega_{12} v e^{c_2 B_2} \rho_2) \,dx \\
& - \int_\Omega \rho_1 \widetilde{u_\theta} e^{c_1 B_1} (1 - \frac{\widetilde{u_\theta}}{u}) \frac{u}{\widetilde{u_\theta}} \widetilde{u_\theta} (\lambda_1 - \omega_{11} \widetilde{u_\theta} e^{c_1 B_1} \rho_1)] \,dx \\
& + \int_\Omega \xi \rho_2 e^{c_2 B_2} v (\lambda_2 - \omega_{21} u e^{c_1 B_1} \rho_1 - \omega_{22} v e^{c_2 B_2} \rho_2) \,dx \\
\leq & - \int_\Omega \mu_1 e^{c_1 B_1} u^2 |\nabla \frac{\widetilde{u_\theta}}{u}|^2 \,dx \\
& - \int_\Omega \rho_1 \widetilde{u_\theta} e^{c_1 B_1} (u - \widetilde{u_\theta})(-\omega_{11} e^{c_1 B_1} \rho_1 (u - \widetilde{u_\theta}) - \omega_{12} v e^{c_2 B_2} \rho_2) \,dx \\
& + \int_\Omega \xi \rho_2 e^{c_2 B_2} v [(\lambda_2 - \omega_{21} \widetilde{u_\theta} e^{c_1 B_1} \rho_1) - \omega_{21} e^{c_1 B_1} \rho_1 (u - \widetilde{u_\theta}) - \omega_{22} v e^{c_2 B_2} \rho_2] \,dx \\
\leq & - \int_\Omega \rho_1^2 \widetilde{u_\theta} e^{2c_2 B_2} \omega_{11} (u - \widetilde{u_\theta})^2 \,dx - \int_\Omega \xi \rho_2^2 e^{2c_2 B_2} \omega_{22} v^2 \,dx \\
& - \int_\Omega \rho_1 \rho_2 e^{c_1 B_1 + c_2 B_2} (\omega_{12} \widetilde{u_\theta} + \xi \omega_{21})(u - \widetilde{u_\theta}) v \,dx.
\end{aligned}$$

The following discussion will refer to the part (i), then we will not repeat it.

(iii) Clearly, (2) has a semi-trivial steady-state $(0, \frac{\lambda_2(x)}{\rho_2(x)\omega_{22}(x)e^{c_2 B_2(x)}})$. Let us define a function $\Phi : [0, \infty) \to R$,

$$\Phi(t) = \int_\Omega \rho_1 e^{c_1 B_1} u \,dx + \int_\Omega \xi \rho_2 e^{c_2 B_2} (v - \widetilde{v_\theta} - \widetilde{v_\theta} \ln \frac{v}{\widetilde{v_\theta}}) \,dx,$$

where $\xi(x) = \frac{\omega_{12}(x)}{\omega_{21}(x)} > 0$ and $\widetilde{v_\theta}(x) = \frac{\lambda_2(x)}{\rho_2(x)\omega_{22}(x)e^{c_2 B_2(x)}}$. From (22), we have

$$\begin{aligned}
\Phi'(t) = & \int_\Omega \rho_1 e^{c_1 B_1} u (\lambda_1 - \omega_{11} u e^{c_1 B_1} \rho_1 - \omega_{12} v e^{c_2 B_2} \rho_2) \,dx \\
& + \int_\Omega \xi \rho_2 e^{c_2 B_2} v (\lambda_2 - \omega_{21} u e^{c_1 B_1} \rho_1 - \omega_{22} v e^{c_2 B_2} \rho_2) \,dx \\
& - \int_\Omega \xi \rho_2 e^{c_2 B_2} \frac{v}{\widetilde{v_\theta}} \widetilde{v_\theta} (\lambda_2 - \omega_{22} \widetilde{v_\theta} e^{c_2 B_2} \rho_2)] \,dx \\
= & \int_\Omega \rho_1 e^{c_1 B_1} u [(\lambda_1 - \omega_{12} \widetilde{v_\theta} e^{c_2 B_2} \rho_2) - \omega_{11} u e^{c_1 B_1} \rho_1 - \omega_{12} e^{c_2 B_2} \rho_2 (v - \widetilde{v_\theta})] \,dx \\
& - \int_\Omega \xi \rho_2 e^{2c_2 B_2} (v - \widetilde{v_\theta})[-\omega_{21} u e^{c_1 B_1} \rho_1 - \omega_{22} e^{c_2 B_2} \rho_2 (v - \widetilde{v_\theta})] \,dx \\
\leq & - \int_\Omega \rho_1^2 e^{2c_2 B_2} \omega_{11} u^2 \,dx - \int_\Omega \xi \rho_2^2 e^{2c_2 B_2} \omega_{22} (v - \widetilde{v_\theta})^2 \,dx \\
& - \int_\Omega \rho_1 \rho_2 e^{c_1 B_1 + c_2 B_2} (\omega_{12} + \xi \omega_{21})(v - \widetilde{v_\theta}) u \,dx.
\end{aligned}$$

The following discussion is similar to the part (i), so we omit it. □

4. Example

See the following parabolic problem:

$$\begin{cases} u_t = \dfrac{e^{-cB(x)}}{\rho(x)}\nabla[\mu_1(x)e^{cB(x)}\nabla u] + u[\bar{\lambda}_1\varphi(x)e^{cB(x)}\rho(x) + \varepsilon_1 g_1(x) \\ \quad -\bar{\varpi}_{11}\varphi(x)ue^{cB(x)}\rho(x) - \bar{\varpi}_{12}\varphi(x)ve^{cB(x)}\rho(x)], & in\ \Omega\times\mathbb{R}^+, \\ v_t = \dfrac{e^{-cB(x)}}{\rho(x)}\nabla[\mu_2(x)e^{cB(x)}\nabla v] + v[\bar{\lambda}_2\varphi(x)e^{cB(x)}\rho(x) + \varepsilon_2 g_2(x) \\ \quad -\bar{\varpi}_{21}\varphi(x)ue^{cB(x)}\rho(x) - \bar{\varpi}_{22}\varphi(x)ve^{cB(x)}\rho(x)], & in\ \Omega\times\mathbb{R}^+, \\ \frac{\partial u}{\partial n} = \frac{\partial v}{\partial n} = 0, & on\ \partial\Omega\times\mathbb{R}^+, \\ u(x,0) = e^{-cB(x)}\frac{U_0(x)}{\rho(x)} \geq, \not\equiv 0, v(x,0) = e^{-cB(x)}\frac{V_0(x)}{\rho(x)} \geq, \not\equiv 0, & in\ \Omega, \end{cases} \tag{25}$$

where $\bar{\lambda}_i, \bar{\varpi}_{ij}, \varepsilon_i$ are all positive constants, $B, \rho \in C^2(\overline{\Omega}), \mu_i \in C^{1+\varrho}(\overline{\Omega}), \varphi, g_i \in C^{\varrho}(\overline{\Omega})$ and $\varphi(x), \mu_i(x) > 0$ on $\overline{\Omega}$.

Proposition 1. *If $0 \leq \varepsilon_i \ll 1$ and $\frac{\bar{\varpi}_{21}}{\bar{\varpi}_{11}} < \frac{\bar{\lambda}_2}{\bar{\lambda}_1} < \frac{\bar{\varpi}_{22}}{\bar{\varpi}_{12}}, \dfrac{\bar{\varpi}_{11}\bar{\varpi}_{22}}{\bar{\varpi}_{12}\bar{\varpi}_{21}} > 1$, then there exists $\eta_1 > 0, \eta_2 > 0$ such that*

$$\frac{\bar{\varpi}_{11}\bar{\varpi}_{22}}{\bar{\varpi}_{12}\bar{\varpi}_{21}} > \sqrt{\frac{\eta_2}{\eta_1}} \tag{26}$$

and the system (25) admits a positive non-homogeneous steady-state $(\widetilde{u_\theta}(x), \widetilde{v_\theta}(x))$, which satisfies $\eta_1 \leq \frac{\widetilde{u_\theta}(x)}{\widetilde{v_\theta}(x)} \leq \eta_2$.

Proof. The steady-state of (25) satisfies the following elliptic problem

$$\begin{cases} \dfrac{e^{-cB(x)}}{\rho(x)}\nabla[\mu_1(x)e^{cB(x)}\nabla u] + u[\bar{\lambda}_1\varphi(x)e^{cB(x)}\rho(x) + \varepsilon_1 g_1(x) \\ -\bar{\varpi}_{11}\varphi(x)ue^{cB(x)}\rho(x) - \bar{\varpi}_{12}\varphi(x)ve^{cB(x)}\rho(x)] = 0, & in\ \Omega, \\ \dfrac{e^{-cB(x)}}{\rho(x)}\nabla[\mu_2(x)e^{cB(x)}\nabla v] + v[\bar{\lambda}_2\varphi(x)e^{cB(x)}\rho(x) + \varepsilon_2 g_2(x) \\ -\bar{\varpi}_{21}\varphi(x)ue^{cB(x)}\rho(x) - \bar{\varpi}_{22}\varphi(x)ve^{cB(x)}\rho(x)] = 0, & in\ \Omega, \\ \frac{\partial u}{\partial n} = \frac{\partial v}{\partial n} = 0, & on\ \partial\Omega. \end{cases} \tag{27}$$

Set $\bar{k}_i = \max_{\overline{\Omega}} \dfrac{g_i(x)}{\varphi(x)e^{cB(x)}\rho(x)}, \underline{k_i} = \min_{\overline{\Omega}} \dfrac{g_i(x)}{\varphi(x)e^{cB(x)}\rho(x)}$ for $i = 1, 2$. Applying $0 < \varepsilon_i \ll 1$ and $\frac{\bar{\varpi}_{21}}{\bar{\varpi}_{11}} < \frac{\bar{\lambda}_2}{\bar{\lambda}_1} < \frac{\bar{\varpi}_{22}}{\bar{\varpi}_{12}}$, we have the linear system

$$\begin{cases} \bar{\lambda}_1 + \varepsilon_1\underline{k}_1 - \bar{\varpi}_{11}\underline{u} - \bar{\varpi}_{12}\bar{v} = 0, \\ \bar{\lambda}_2 + \varepsilon_2\bar{k}_2 - \bar{\varpi}_{21}\underline{u} - \bar{\varpi}_{22}\bar{v} = 0, \\ \bar{\lambda}_1 + \varepsilon_1\bar{k}_1 - \bar{\varpi}_{11}\bar{u} - \bar{\varpi}_{12}\underline{v} = 0, \\ \bar{\lambda}_2 + \varepsilon_2\underline{k}_2 - \bar{\varpi}_{21}\bar{u} - \bar{\varpi}_{22}\underline{v} = 0. \end{cases}$$

Then

$$\bar{u} = \frac{\bar{\varpi}_{22}(\bar{\lambda}_1 + \varepsilon_1\bar{k}_1) - \bar{\varpi}_{12}(\bar{\lambda}_2 + \varepsilon_2\underline{k}_2)}{\bar{\varpi}_{11}\bar{\varpi}_{22} - \bar{\varpi}_{12}\bar{\varpi}_{21}}, \underline{u} = \frac{\bar{\varpi}_{22}(\bar{\lambda}_1 + \varepsilon_1\underline{k}_1) - \bar{\varpi}_{12}(\bar{\lambda}_2 + \varepsilon_2\bar{k}_2)}{\bar{\varpi}_{11}\bar{\varpi}_{22} - \bar{\varpi}_{12}\bar{\varpi}_{21}},$$

$$\bar{v} = \frac{\bar{\varpi}_{11}(\bar{\lambda}_2 + \varepsilon_2\bar{k}_2) - \bar{\varpi}_{21}(\bar{\lambda}_1 + \varepsilon_1\underline{k}_1)}{\bar{\varpi}_{11}\bar{\varpi}_{22} - \bar{\varpi}_{12}\bar{\varpi}_{21}}, \underline{v} = \frac{\bar{\varpi}_{11}(\bar{\lambda}_2 + \varepsilon_2\underline{k}_2) - \bar{\varpi}_{21}(\bar{\lambda}_1 + \varepsilon_1\bar{k}_1)}{\bar{\varpi}_{11}\bar{\varpi}_{22} - \bar{\varpi}_{12}\bar{\varpi}_{21}}.$$

Hence, the system (25) has a positive non-homogeneous steady-state $(\widetilde{u_\theta}(x), \widetilde{v_\theta}(x))$ and $0 < \underline{u} < \widetilde{u_\theta}(x) < \bar{u}$ and $0 < \underline{v} < \widetilde{v_\theta}(x) < \bar{v}$. Let

$$\eta_1 = \frac{\underline{u}}{\bar{v}}, \eta_2 = \frac{\bar{u}}{\underline{v}}. \tag{28}$$

we have $\eta_1 \leq \frac{\widetilde{u_\theta}(x)}{\widetilde{v_\theta}(x)} \leq \eta_2$. Applying (28), we get $\lim_{\varepsilon_1,\varepsilon_2\to 0} \frac{\eta_2}{\eta_1} = 1$. Hence, for $0 < \varepsilon_i \ll 1$,

$$\min_{\overline{\Omega}} \frac{\bar{\omega}_{11}\varphi(x)\bar{\omega}_{22}\varphi(x)}{\bar{\omega}_{12}\varphi(x)\bar{\omega}_{21}\varphi(x)} = \frac{\bar{\omega}_{11}\bar{\omega}_{22}}{\bar{\omega}_{12}\bar{\omega}_{21}} > \sqrt{\frac{\eta_2}{\eta_1}}.$$

The proof is completed. □

Example 1. *In the above (25), let $c = 2, B(x) = x, \rho(x) = e^{-x}, \mu_1(x) = \mu_2(x) = e^{-x}, R_1(x) = R_2(x) = \frac{1}{2}e^{-x}, \varphi(x) = e^{-x}, g_1(x) = g_2(x) = 1 + \cos(\frac{\pi}{2}x), \bar{\lambda}_1 = 1, \bar{\lambda}_2 = 2, \bar{\omega}_{11} = \bar{\omega}_{12} = \bar{\omega}_{21} = 1, \bar{\omega}_{22} = 3$, and $\varepsilon_1 = \varepsilon_2 = \frac{1}{3}, x \in \Omega = [0,10]$. Then the problem (25) becomes the following model*

$$\begin{cases} u_t = e^{-x}\nabla[e^x\nabla u] + u[1 + \frac{1}{3}(1+\cos(\frac{\pi}{2}x)) - u - v], & in\ \Omega \times \mathbb{R}^+, \\ v_t = e^{-x}\nabla[e^x\nabla v] + v[2 + \frac{1}{3}(1+\cos(\frac{\pi}{2}x)) - u - 3v], & in\ \Omega \times \mathbb{R}^+, \\ \frac{\partial u}{\partial n} = \frac{\partial v}{\partial n} = 0, & on\ \partial\Omega \times \mathbb{R}^+, \\ u(x,0) = e^{-x}(2+\cos(\pi x)) \geq, \not\equiv 0, v(x,0) = e^{-x}(2+\cos(\pi x)) \geq, \not\equiv 0, & in\ \Omega, \end{cases} \tag{29}$$

where $u_0(x), v_0(x) \geq, \neq 0$. It is not difficult to verify that (H_1) and (H_2) hold. We can find $\eta_1 = 1 > 0, \eta_2 = \frac{7}{3} > 0$, such that $\eta_1 \leq \frac{\widetilde{u_\theta}(x)}{\widetilde{v_\theta}(x)} \leq \eta_2$ and $\sqrt{\frac{\eta_2}{\eta_1}} < \min_{\overline{\Omega}} \frac{\bar{\omega}_{11}\bar{\omega}_{22}}{\bar{\omega}_{12}\bar{\omega}_{21}}$. According to Theorem 2, the model (29) admits a solution $(u(x,t), v(x,t))$ that satisfies

$$\lim_{t\to\infty} u(x,t) = \widetilde{u_\theta}(x), \lim_{t\to\infty} v(x,t) = \widetilde{v_\theta}(x)\ in\ C^2(\overline{\Omega}).$$

Indeed, the steady-state of (29) satisfies the following elliptic problem

$$\begin{cases} e^{-x}\nabla[e^x\nabla u] + u[1 + \frac{1}{3}(1+\cos(\frac{\pi}{2}x)) - u - v] = 0, & in\ \Omega, \\ e^{-x}\nabla[e^x\nabla v] + v[2 + \frac{1}{3}(1+\cos(\frac{\pi}{2}x)) - u - 3v] = 0, & in\ \Omega, \\ \frac{\partial u}{\partial n} = \frac{\partial v}{\partial n} = 0, & on\ \partial\Omega. \end{cases} \tag{30}$$

It is not difficult to see that $\bar{k}_1 = \bar{k}_2 = 2, \underline{k}_1 = \underline{k}_2 = 0$. By calculation, we can obtain

$$\begin{cases} 1 - \underline{u} - \bar{v} = 0, \\ 2 + 2\varepsilon_2 - \underline{u} - 3\bar{v} = 0, \\ 1 + 2\varepsilon_1 - \bar{u} - \underline{v} = 0, \\ 2 - \bar{u} - 3\underline{v} = 0. \end{cases}$$

Then

$$\bar{u} = \frac{1+6\varepsilon_1}{2} = \frac{3}{2} > 0,\ \underline{u} = \frac{1-2\varepsilon_2}{2} = \frac{1}{6} > 0,$$
$$\bar{v} = \frac{1+2\varepsilon_2}{2} = \frac{5}{6} > 0,\ \underline{v} = \frac{1-2\varepsilon_1}{2} = \frac{1}{6} > 0.$$

Hence, $0 < \underline{u} < \widetilde{u_\theta}(x) < \bar{u}$ and $0 < \underline{v} < \widetilde{v_\theta}(x) < \bar{v}$, which yield that there exists a positive non-homogeneous steady-state $(\widetilde{u_\theta}(x), \widetilde{v_\theta}(x))$ of (29).

5. Discussion

In this paper, by using the Lyapunov functional method, we mainly analyzed the global stability of non-homogeneous steady-state for the Lotka–Volterra competition–diffusion–advection system between two competing biological organisms in heterogeneous environments, where two biological organisms are competing for different fundamental resources, their advection and diffusion strategies follow different positive diffusion distributions, and the functions of specific competition ability are variable. Moreover, we also obtained the global stability result when one of the two organisms has no diffusion ability and is not affected by advection.

At the end of this section, we propose an interesting research problem. To the best of our knowledge, for the Lotka–Volterra competition–diffusion–advection system between two competing biological organisms in heterogeneous environments, we did not obtain any results under the condition of cross-diffusion, such as the existence and stability of nontrivial positive steady state. We leave this challenge to future investigations.

Author Contributions: All authors contributed equally and significantly in writing this article. Conceptualization, L.C.; Formal analysis, Y.Z.; Funding acquisition, L.C.; Writing—original draft, S.L. All authors have read and agreed to the published version of the manuscript.

Funding: This research was funded by Shandong Provincial Natural Science Foundation under grant ZR2020MA006 and the Introduction and Cultivation Project of Young and Innovative Talents in Universities of Shandong Province.

Institutional Review Board Statement: Not applicable.

Informed Consent Statement: Not applicable.

Data Availability Statement: Not applicable.

Acknowledgments: We would like to express our thanks to the anonymous referees and the editor for their constructive comments and suggestions, which greatly improved this article.

Conflicts of Interest: The authors declare no conflict of interest.

References

1. Cantrell, R.; Cosner, C. *Spatial Ecology via Reaction-Diffusion Equations*; Wiley: New York, NY, USA, 2003.
2. He, X.; Ni, W. Global dynamics of the Lotka-Volterra competition-diffusion system: Diffusion and spatial heterogeneity I. *Commun. Pure Appl. Math.* **2016**, *69*, 981–1014. [CrossRef]
3. Korobenko, L.; Braverman, E. On evolutionary stability of carrying capacity driven dispersal in competition with regularly diffusing populations. *J. Math. Biol.* **2014**, *69*, 1181–1206. [CrossRef] [PubMed]
4. Hsu, S.; Waltman, P. On a system of reaction-diffusion equations arising from competition in an unstirred chemostat. *SIAM J. Appl. Math.* **1993**, *53*, 1026–1044. [CrossRef]
5. Lam, K.; Ni, W. Uniqueness and complete dynamics in heterogeneous competition–diffusion systems. *SIAM J. Appl. Math.* **2012**, *72*, 1695–1712. [CrossRef]
6. Ni, W.; Shi, J.; Wang, M. Global stability of nonhomogeneous equilibrium solution for the diffusive Lotka-Volterra competition model. *Calc. Var. Partial Differ. Equ.* **2020**, *59*, 267–270. [CrossRef]
7. Cosner, C. Reaction-diffusion-advection models for the effects and evolution of dispersal. *Discret. Contin. Dyn. Syst.* **2014**, *34*, 1701–1745. [CrossRef]
8. Lou, Y.; Zhao, X.; Zhou, P. Global dynamics of a Lotka-Volterra competition-diffusion-advection system in heterogeneous environments. *J. Math. Pures Appl.* **2019**, *121*, 47–82. [CrossRef]
9. Zhou, P.; Xiao, D. Global dynamics of a classical Lotka-Volterra competition-diffusion-advection system. *J. Funct. Anal.* **2018**, *275*, 356–380. [CrossRef]
10. Wang, Q. On a Lotka-Volterra competition-diffusion-advection model in general heterogeneous environments. *J. Math. Anal. Appl.* **2020**, *489*, 124127. [CrossRef]
11. Li, Z.; Dai, B. Stability and Hopf bifurcation analysis in a Lotka–Volterra competition–diffusion–advection model with time delay effect. *Nonlinearity* **2021**, *34*, 3271–3313. [CrossRef]
12. Li, Z.; Dai, B.; Dong, X. Global stability of nonhomogeneous steady-state solution in a Lotka-Volterra competition-diffusion-advection model. *Appl. Math. Lett.* **2020**, *107*, 106480. [CrossRef]
13. Ma, L.; Guo, S. Bifurcation and stability of a two-species reaction-diffusion-advection competition model. *Nonlinear Anal-Real* **2021**, *59*, 103241. [CrossRef]
14. Zhou, P.; Tang, D.; Xiao, D. On Lotka-Volterra competitive parabolic systems: Exclusion, coexistence and bistability. *J. Differ. Equ.* **2021**, *282*, 596–625. [CrossRef]
15. Wang, M. A diffusive logistic equation with a free boundary and sign-changing coefficient in time-periodic environment. *J. Funct. Anal.* **2016**, *270*, 483–508. [CrossRef]
16. Wang, M.; Zhang, Y. Dynamics for a diffusive prey-predator model with different free boundaries. *J. Differ. Equ.* **2018**, *264*, 3527–3558. [CrossRef]
17. Wang, M. Note on the Lyapunov functional method. *Appl. Math. Lett.* **2018**, *75*, 102–107. [CrossRef]
18. Pao, C. *Nonlinear Parabolic and Elliptic Equations*; Plenum Press: New York, NY, USA, 1992.

axioms

Article

Bounded Perturbation Resilience of Two Modified Relaxed CQ Algorithms for the Multiple-Sets Split Feasibility Problem

Yingying Li and Yaxuan Zhang *

College of Science, Civil Aviation University of China, Tianjin 300300, China; yingyl99@163.com
* Correspondence: bunnyxuan@tju.edu.cn

Abstract: In this paper, we present some modified relaxed CQ algorithms with different kinds of step size and perturbation to solve the Multiple-sets Split Feasibility Problem (MSSFP). Under mild assumptions, we establish weak convergence and prove the bounded perturbation resilience of the proposed algorithms in Hilbert spaces. Treating appropriate inertial terms as bounded perturbations, we construct the inertial acceleration versions of the corresponding algorithms. Finally, for the LASSO problem and three experimental examples, numerical computations are given to demonstrate the efficiency of the proposed algorithms and the validity of the inertial perturbation.

Keywords: multiple-sets split feasibility problem; CQ algorithm; bounded perturbation; armijo-line search; self-adaptive step size

MSC: 47J20; 47J25; 49J40

Citation: Li, Y.; Zhang, Y. Bounded Perturbation Resilience of Two Modified Relaxed CQ Algorithms for the Multiple-Sets Split Feasibility Problem. *Axioms* **2021**, *10*, 197. https://doi.org/10.3390/axioms10030197

Academic Editor: Chris Goodrich

Received: 16 July 2021
Accepted: 20 August 2021
Published: 23 August 2021

Publisher's Note: MDPI stays neutral with regard to jurisdictional claims in published maps and institutional affiliations.

Copyright: © 2021 by the authors. Licensee MDPI, Basel, Switzerland. This article is an open access article distributed under the terms and conditions of the Creative Commons Attribution (CC BY) license (https://creativecommons.org/licenses/by/4.0/).

1. Introduction

In this paper, we focus on the Multiple-sets Split Feasibility Problem (MSSFP), which is formulated as follows.

$$\text{Find a point } x^* \in C = \bigcap_{i=1}^{t} C_i \text{ such that } Ax^* \in Q = \bigcap_{j=1}^{r} Q_j, \tag{1}$$

where $A : \mathcal{H}_1 \to \mathcal{H}_2$ is a bounded and linear operator, $C_i \subset \mathcal{H}_1$, $i = 1, \cdots, t$, and $Q_j \subset \mathcal{H}_2$, $j = 1, \cdots, r$ are nonempty closed and convex sets, and $\mathcal{H}_1$ and $\mathcal{H}_2$ are Hilbert spaces. When $t = 1$, $r = 1$, it is the Split Feasibility Problem (SFP). Byrne in [1,2] introduced the following CQ algorithm to solve the SFP,

$$x^{k+1} = P_C(x^k - \alpha_k A^*(I - P_Q)Ax^k), \tag{2}$$

where $\alpha_k \in (0, \frac{2}{\|A\|^2})$. It is proven that the iterates $\{x^k\}$ converge to a solution of the SFP. When P_C and P_Q have explicit expressions, the CQ algorithm is easy to carry out. However, P_C and P_Q have no explicit formulas in general; thus the computation of P_C and P_Q is itself an optimization problem.

To avoid the computation of P_C and P_Q, Yang [3] proposed the relaxed CQ algorithm in finite dimensional spaces. The algorithm is

$$x^{k+1} = P_{C^k}(x^k - \alpha_k A^*(I - P_{Q^k})Ax^k), \tag{3}$$

where $\alpha_k \in (0, \frac{2}{\|A\|^2})$, C^k and Q^k are sequences of closed half spaces containing C and Q, respectively.

As for the MSSFP (1), Censor et al. in [4] proposed the following algorithm,

$$x^{k+1} = P_{\Omega}(x^k - \alpha \nabla p(x^k)), \tag{4}$$

where Ω is an auxiliary closed subset, and $p(x)$ is a function to measure the distance from a point to all the sets C_i and Q_j,

$$p(x) = \frac{1}{2}\sum_{i=1}^{t} \lambda_i \|x - P_{C_i}(x)\|^2 + \frac{1}{2}\sum_{j=1}^{r} \beta_j \|Ax - P_{Q_j}(Ax)\|^2, \tag{5}$$

where $\lambda_i > 0$, $\beta_j > 0$ for every i and j, and $\sum_{i=1}^{t} \lambda_i + \sum_{j=1}^{r} \beta_j = 1$, $0 < \alpha < 2/L$, $L = \sum_{i=1}^{t} \lambda_i + \|A\|^2 \sum_{j=1}^{r} \beta_j$. The convergence of the algorithm (4) is proved in finite dimensional spaces.

Later, He et al. [5] introduced a relaxed self-adaptive CQ algorithm,

$$x^{k+1} = \tau_k \mu + (1 - \tau_k)(x^k - \alpha_k \nabla p_k(x^k)), \tag{6}$$

where the sequence $\{\tau_k\} \subset (0,1)$, $\mu \in \mathcal{H}$, $p_k(x) = \frac{1}{2}\sum_{i=1}^{t} \lambda_i \|x - P_{C_i^k}(x)\|^2 + \frac{1}{2}\sum_{j=1}^{r} \beta_j \|Ax - P_{Q_j^k}(Ax)\|^2$, where the closed convex sets C_i^k and Q_j^k are level sets of some convex functions containing C_i and Q_j, and self-adaptive step size $\alpha_k = \frac{\rho_k p_k(x^k)}{\|\nabla p_k(x^k)\|^2}$, $0 < \rho_k < 4$. They proved that the sequence $\{x^k\}$ generated by algorithm (6) converges in norm to $P_S(\mu)$, where S is the solution set of the MSSFP.

In order to improve the rate of convergence, many scholars have investigated the choice of the step size of the algorithms. Based on the CQ algorithm (2), Yang [6] proposed the step size

$$\alpha_k = \frac{\rho_k}{\|\nabla f(x^k)\|},$$

where $\{\rho_k\}$ is a sequence of positive real numbers satisfying $\sum_{n=0}^{\infty} \rho_k = \infty$ and $\sum_{n=0}^{\infty} \rho_k^2 < +\infty$, and $f(x) = \frac{1}{2}\|(I - P_Q)Ax\|^2$. Assuming that Q is bounded and A is a matrix with full column rank, Yang proved the convergence of the underlying algorithm in finite dimensional spaces. In 2012, López et al. [7] introduced another choice of the step size sequence $\{\alpha_k\}$ in the algorithm (3) as follows

$$\alpha_k = \frac{\rho_k f_k(x^k)}{\|\nabla f_k(x^k)\|^2},$$

where $0 < \rho_k < 4$, $f_k(x) = \frac{1}{2}\|(I - P_{Q^k})Ax\|^2$, and they proved the weak convergence of the iteration sequence in Hilbert spaces. The advantage of this choice of the step size lies in the fact that neither prior information about the matrix norm A nor any other conditions on Q and A are required. Recently, Gibali et al. [8] and Chen et al. [9] used step size determined by Armijo-line search and proved the convergence of the algorithm. For more information on the relaxed CQ algorithm and the selection of step size, please refer to references [10–12].

On the other hand, in order to make the algorithms converge faster, specific perturbations have been introduced into the iterative format, since the perturbations guide the iteration to a lower objective function value without losing the overall convergence. So far, bounded perturbation recovery has been used in many problems.

Consider the usage of the bounded perturbation for the non-smooth optimization problems, $\min_{x \in H} \phi(x) = f(x) + g(x)$, where f and g are proper lower semicontinuous convex functions in real Hilbert spaces, f is differentiable, g is not necessarily differentiable, and ∇f is L-Lipschitz continuous. One of the classic algorithms is the proximal gradient (PG) algorithm, based on which Guo et al. [13] proposed the following PG algorithm with perturbations,

$$x^{k+1} = \mathrm{prox}_{\lambda_k g}(I - \lambda_k D \nabla f + e)(x^k). \tag{7}$$

Assume that (i) D is a bounded linear operator, (ii) $0 < \inf \lambda_k \leq \lambda_k \leq \sup \lambda_k < \frac{2}{L}$, (iii) $e(x^k)$ satisfies $\sum_{k=0}^{\infty} \|e(x^k)\| < +\infty$, and (iv) $\theta_k = \nabla f(x^k) - D(x^k)\nabla f(x^k)$ satisfies $\sum_{k=0}^{\infty} \|\theta_k\| < +\infty$. They asserted that the generated sequence $\{x^k\}$ converges weakly to a solution. Later, Guo and Cui [14] proposed the modified PG algorithm for solving this problem,

$$x^{k+1} = \tau_k h(x^k) + (1-\tau_k)\text{prox}_{\lambda_k g}(I - \lambda_k \nabla f)(x^k) + e(x^k), \tag{8}$$

where $\tau_k \subset [0,1]$, h is a $\rho \in (0,1)$-contractive operator. They proved that the sequence $\{x^k\}$ generated by the algorithm (8) converges strongly to a solution x^*. In 2020, Pakkaranang et al. [15] considered PG algorithm combined with inertial technique

$$\begin{cases} y^k = x^k + \theta_k(x^k - x^{k-1}), \\ x^{k+1} = \tau_k h(y^k) + (1-\tau_k)\text{prox}_{\lambda_k g}(I - \lambda_k \nabla f)(y^k) + e(y^k), \end{cases} \tag{9}$$

and they proved its strong convergence under suitable conditions.

For the convex minimization problem, $\min_{x \in \Omega} f(x)$, where Ω is a nonempty closed convex subset in finite dimensional space and the objective function f is convex, Jin et al. [16] presented the following projected scaled gradient (PSG) algorithm with errors

$$x^{k+1} = P_\Omega(x^k - \lambda_k D(x^k)\nabla f(x^k) + e(x^k)). \tag{10}$$

Assume that (i) $\{D(x^k)\}_{k=0}^{\infty}$ is a sequence of diagonal scaling matrices, and that (ii) (iii) (iv) are the same as the conditions in algorithm (7); then the generated sequence $\{x^k\}$ converges weakly to a solution.

In 2017, Xu [17] applied the superiorization techniques to the relaxed PSG. The iterative form is

$$x^{k+1} = (1-\tau_k)x^k + \tau_k P_\Omega(x^k - \lambda_k D(x^k)\nabla f(x^k) + e(x^k)), \tag{11}$$

where τ_k is a sequence in $[0,1]$, and $D(x^k)$ is a diagonal scaling matrix. He established weak convergence of the above algorithm under appropriate conditions imposed on $\{\tau_k\}$ and $\{\lambda_k\}$.

For the variational inequality problem (VIP for short) $\langle F(x^*), x - x^* \rangle \geq 0$, $\forall x \in C$, where F is a nonlinear operator, Dong et al. [18] considered the external gradient algorithm with perturbations

$$\begin{cases} \bar{x}^k = P_C(x^k - \alpha_k F(x^k) + e_1(x^k)), \\ x^{k+1} = P_C(x^k - \alpha_k F(\bar{x}^k) + e_2(x^k)). \end{cases} \tag{12}$$

where $\alpha_k = \gamma l^{m_k}$ with m_k the smallest non-negative integer such that

$$\alpha_k \|F(x^k) - F(\bar{x}^k)\| \leq \mu \|x^k - \bar{x}^k\|.$$

Assume that F is monotonous and L-Lipschitz is continuous and that the error sequence is summable; the sequence $\{x^k\}$ generated by the algorithm converges weakly to a solution of the VIP.

For the split variational inclusion problem, Duan and Zheng [19] in 2020 proposed the following algorithm

$$x^{k+1} = \tau_k h(x^k) + (1-\tau_k)J_\gamma^{B_1}(I - \lambda_k A^*(I - J_\gamma^{B_2})A)(x^k) + e(x^k), \tag{13}$$

where A is a bounded linear operator, B_1 and B_2 are maximal monotone operators. Assuming that $\lim_{k\to\infty} \tau_k = 0$, $\sum_{k=0}^{\infty} \tau_k = \infty$, $0 < \inf_{k\to\infty} \lambda_k \leq \sup_{k\to\infty} \lambda_k < \frac{2}{L}$, $L = \|A\|^2$ and $\sum_{k=0}^{\infty} \|e(x^k)\| < +\infty$, they proved that the sequence $\{x^k\}$ strongly converges to a solution of the split variational inclusion problem, which is also the unique solution of some variational inequality problem.

For the convex feasibility problem, Censor and Zaslavski [20] considered the perturbation resilience and convergence of dynamic string-averaging projection method.

Adding an inertial term can improve the convergence rate, which is also a perturbation. Recently, for a common solution of the split minimization problem and the fixed point problem, Kaewyong and Sitthithakerngkiet [21] combined the proximal algorithm and a modified Mann's iterative method with the inertial extrapolation and improved related results. Shehu et al. [22] and Li et al. [23] added alternated inertial perturbation to the algorithms for solving the SFP and improved the convergence rate.

At present, the (multiple-sets) split feasibility problem is widely used in application fields, such as CT tomography, image restoration, and image reconstruction, etc. There are many related literatures on the iterative algorithms for solving the (multiple-sets) split feasibility problem. However, there are relatively fewer documents studying the algorithms of the (multiple-sets) split feasibility problem with perturbations, especially with self-adaptive step size. In fact, the latter also has a bounded disturbance recovery property. Motivated by [9,18], we focus on the modified relaxed CQ algorithms to solve the MSSFP (1) in real Hilbert spaces and assert that the proposed algorithms are also bounded-perturbation-resilient.

The rest of the paper is arranged as follows. In Section 2, definitions and notions that will be useful for our analysis are presented. In Section 3, we present our algorithms and prove their weak convergence. In Section 4, we prove that the proposed algorithms have bounded perturbation resilience and construct the inertial modification of the algorithms. Furthermore, finally, in Section 5, we present some numerical simulations to show the validity of the proposed algorithms.

2. Preliminaries

In this section, we first define some symbols and then review some definitions and basic results that will be used in this paper.

Throughout this paper, $\mathcal{H}$ denotes a real Hilbert space endowed with an inner product $\langle \cdot, \cdot \rangle$ and its deduced norm $\| \cdot \|$, and I is the identity operator on $\mathcal{H}$. We denote by S the solution set of the MSSFP (1). Moreover, $x^k \to x$ ($x^k \rightharpoonup x$) represents that the sequence $\{x^k\}$ converges strongly (weakly) to x. Finally, we denote by $\omega_\omega(x^k)$ all the weak cluster points of $\{x^k\}$.

An operator $T : \mathcal{H} \to \mathcal{H}$ is said to be nonexpansive if for all $x, y \in \mathcal{H}$,

$$\|Tx - Ty\| \leq \|x - y\|;$$

$T : \mathcal{H} \to \mathcal{H}$ is said to be firmly nonexpansive if for all $x, y \in \mathcal{H}$,

$$||Tx - Ty||^2 \leq ||x - y||^2 - ||(I - T)x - (I - T)y||^2,$$

or equivalently

$$||Tx - Ty||^2 \leq \langle Tx - Ty, x - y \rangle.$$

It is well known that T is firmly nonexpansive if and only if $I - T$ is firmly nonexpansive.

Let C be a nonempty closed convex subset of $\mathcal{H}$. Then the metric projection P_C from $\mathcal{H}$ onto C is defined as

$$P_C(x) = \underset{y \in C}{\operatorname{argmin}} ||x - y||^2, \quad x \in \mathcal{H}.$$

The metric projection P_C is a firmly nonexpansive operator.

Definition 1 ([24]). *A function $f : \mathcal{H} \to \mathbf{R}$ is said to be weakly lower semicontinuous at $\hat{x}$ if x^k converges weakly to $\hat{x}$ implies*

$$f(\hat{x}) \leq \liminf_{k\to\infty} f(x^k).$$

Definition 2. *If $\varphi : \mathcal{H} \to \mathbf{R}$ is a convex function, the subdifferential of φ at x is defined as*

$$\partial\varphi(x) = \{\xi \in \mathcal{H} \mid \varphi(y) \geq \varphi(x) + \langle \xi, y - x\rangle,\ \forall y \in \mathcal{H}\}.$$

Lemma 1 ([24]). *Let C be a nonempty closed and convex subset of $\mathcal{H}$; then for any $x,\ y \in \mathcal{H},\ z \in C$, the following assertions hold:*
(i) $\langle x - P_C x, z - P_C x\rangle \leq 0$;
(ii) $\|P_C x - z\|^2 \leq \|x - z\|^2 - \|P_C x - x\|^2$;
(iii) $2\langle x, y\rangle \leq \|x\| + \|x\|\|y\|^2$;
(iv) $2\langle x, y\rangle \leq \|x\|^2 + \|y\|^2$.

Lemma 2 ([25]). *Assume that $\{a^k\}_{k=0}^{\infty}$ is a sequence of nonnegative real numbers such that*

$$a^{k+1} \leq (1 + \sigma_k)a^k + \delta_k, \forall k \geq 0,$$

where the nonnegative sequences $\{\sigma_k\}_{k=0}^{\infty}$ and $\{\delta_k\}_{k=0}^{\infty}$ satisfies $\sum_{k=0}^{\infty} \sigma_k < +\infty$ and $\sum_{k=0}^{\infty} \delta_k < +\infty$, respectively. Then $\lim_{k\to\infty} a^k$ exists.

Lemma 3 ([25]). *Let S be a nonempty closed and convex subset of $\mathcal{H}$ and $\{x^k\}$ be a sequence in $\mathcal{H}$ that satisfies the following properties:*
(i) $\lim_{k\to\infty} \|x^k - x\|$ exists for each $x \in S$;
(ii) $\omega_\omega(x^k) \subset S$.
Then $\{x^k\}$ converges weakly to a point in S.

Definition 3. *An algorithmic operator P is said to be bounded perturbations resilient if the iteration $x^{k+1} = P(x^k)$ and $x^{k+1} = P(x^k + \lambda_k v_k)$ all converge, where $\{\lambda_k\}$ is a sequence of nonnegative real numbers, $\{v_k\}$ is a sequence in $\mathcal{H}$, and $M \in \mathbf{R}$ and satisfies*

$$\sum_{k=0}^{\infty} \lambda_k < +\infty, \|v_k\| \leq M.$$

3. Algorithms and Their Convergence

In this section, we introduce two algorithms of the MSSFP (1) and prove their weak convergence. First assume that the following four assumptions hold.

(A1) The solution set S of the MSSFP (1) is nonempty.

(A2) The level sets of convex functions can be expressed by

$$C_i = \{x \in \mathcal{H}_1 \mid c_i(x) \leq 0\} \quad \text{and} \quad Q_j = \{y \in \mathcal{H}_2 \mid q_j(y) \leq 0\},$$

where $c_i : \mathcal{H}_1 \to \mathbf{R}$ $(i = 1, \cdots, t)$ and $q_j : \mathcal{H}_2 \to \mathbf{R}$ $(j = 1, \cdots, r)$ are weakly lower semicontinuous and convex functions.

(A3) For any $x \in \mathcal{H}_1$ and $y \in \mathcal{H}_2$, at least one subgradient $\xi_i \in \partial c_i(x)$ and $\eta_j \in \partial q_j(y)$ can be calculated. The subdifferential ∂c_i and ∂q_j are bounded on the bounded sets.

(A4) The sequences of perturbations $\{e_i(x^k)\}_{k=0}^{\infty}$ $(i = 1, 2, 3)$ is summable, i.e.,

$$\sum_{k=0}^{\infty} \|e_i(x^k)\| < +\infty.$$

Define two sets at point x^k by

$$C_i^k = \{x \in \mathcal{H}_1 \mid c_i(x^k) + \langle \xi_i^k, x - x^k \rangle \leq 0\},$$

and

$$Q_j^k = \{y \in \mathcal{H}_2 \mid q_j(Ax^k) + \langle \eta_j^k, y - Ax^k \rangle \leq 0\},$$

where $\xi_i^k \in \partial c_i(x^k)$ and $\eta_j^k \in \partial q_j(Ax^k)$. Define the function f_k by

$$f_k(x) = \frac{1}{2} \sum_{j=1}^{r} \beta_j \|(I - P_{Q_j^k})Ax\|^2, \tag{14}$$

where $\beta_j > 0$. Then it is easy to verify that the function $f_k(x)$ is convex and differentiable with gradient

$$\nabla f_k(x) = \sum_{j=1}^{r} \beta_j A^*(I - P_{Q_j^k})Ax, \tag{15}$$

and the L-Lipschitz constant of $\nabla f_k(x)$ is $L = \|A\|^2 \sum_{j=1}^{r} \beta_j$.

We see that C_i^k $(i = 1, \cdots, t)$ and Q_j^k $(j = 1, \cdots, r)$ are half spaces such that $C_i \subset C_i^k$, $Q_j \subset Q_j^k$, for all $k \geq 1$. We now present Algorithm 1 with Armijo-line search step size.

Algorithm 1 (The relaxed CQ algorithm with Armijo-line search and perturbation)

Given constant $\gamma > 0$, $l \in (0,1)$, $\mu \in (0,1)$. Let x^0 be arbitrarily chosen, for $k = 0, 1, \cdots$, compute

$$\bar{x}^k = P_{C_{[k]}^k}(x^k - \alpha_k \nabla f_k(x^k) + e_1(x^k)), \tag{16}$$

where $[k] = k \bmod t$ and $\alpha_k = \gamma l^{m_k}$ with m_k the smallest non-negative integer such that

$$\alpha_k \|\nabla f_k(x^k) - \nabla f_k(\bar{x}^k)\| \leq \mu \|x^k - \bar{x}^k\|. \tag{17}$$

Construct the next iterate x^{k+1} by

$$x^{k+1} = P_{C_{[k]}^k}(x^k - \alpha_k \nabla f_k(\bar{x}^k) + e_2(x^k)). \tag{18}$$

Lemma 4 ([6]). *The Armijo-line search terminates after a finite number of steps. In addition,*

$$\frac{\mu l}{L} < \alpha_k \leq \gamma, \ for\ all\ \ k \geq 0. \tag{19}$$

where $L = \|A\|^2 \sum_{j=1}^{r} \beta_j$.

The weak convergence of Algorithm 1 is established below.

Theorem 1. *Let $\{x^k\}$ be the sequence generated by Algorithm 1, and the assumptions (A1)$\sim$(A4) hold. Then $\{x^k\}$ converges weakly to a solution of the MSSFP (1).*

Proof. Let x^* be a solution of the MSSFP. Note that $C \subset C_i \subset C_i^k$, $Q \subset Q_j \subset Q_j^k$, $i = 1, \cdots, t$, $j = 1, \cdots, r$, $k = 0, 1, \cdots$, so $x^* = P_C(x^*) = P_{C_i}(x^*) = P_{C_i^k}(x^*)$ and $Ax^* = P_Q(Ax^*) = P_{Q_j}(Ax^*) = P_{Q_j^k}(Ax^*)$, and thus $f_k(x^*) = 0$ and $\nabla f_k(x^*) = 0$.

First, we prove that $\{x^k\}$ is bounded. Following Lemma 1 (ii), we have

$$\begin{aligned}
& \|x^{k+1} - x^*\|^2 \\
= & \|P_{C^k_{[k]}}(x^k - \alpha_k \nabla f_k(\bar{x}^k) + e_2(x^k)) - x^*\|^2 \\
\leq & \|x^k - \alpha_k \nabla f_k(\bar{x}^k) + e_2(x^k) - x^*\|^2 - \|x^{k+1} - x^k + \alpha_k \nabla f_k(\bar{x}^k) - e_2(x^k)\|^2 \\
= & \|x^k - x^*\|^2 - \|x^{k+1} - x^k\|^2 - 2\langle \alpha_k \nabla f_k(\bar{x}^k) - e_2(x^k), x^k - x^*\rangle \\
& -2\langle \alpha_k \nabla f_k(\bar{x}^k) - e_2(x^k), x^{k+1} - x^k\rangle \\
= & \|x^k - x^*\|^2 - \|x^{k+1} - x^k\|^2 - 2\langle \alpha_k \nabla f_k(\bar{x}^k) - e_2(x^k), x^{k+1} - x^*\rangle \\
= & \|x^k - x^*\|^2 - \|x^{k+1} - x^k\|^2 - 2\langle \alpha_k \nabla f_k(\bar{x}^k), x^{k+1} - x^*\rangle \\
& +2\langle e_2(x^k), x^{k+1} - x^*\rangle \\
= & \|x^k - x^*\|^2 - \|x^{k+1} - \bar{x}^k\|^2 - \|\bar{x}^k - x^k\|^2 - 2\langle x^{k+1} - \bar{x}^k, \bar{x}^k - x^k\rangle \\
& -2\alpha_k\langle \nabla f_k(\bar{x}^k), x^{k+1} - x^*\rangle + 2\langle e_2(x^k), x^{k+1} - x^*\rangle \\
= & \|x^k - x^*\|^2 - \|x^{k+1} - \bar{x}^k\|^2 - \|\bar{x}^k - x^k\|^2 - 2\langle x^{k+1} - \bar{x}^k, \bar{x}^k - x^k\rangle \\
& -2\alpha_k\langle \nabla f_k(\bar{x}^k), x^{k+1} - \bar{x}^k\rangle - 2\alpha_k\langle \nabla f_k(\bar{x}^k), \bar{x}^k - x^*\rangle + 2\langle e_2(x^k), x^{k+1} - x^*\rangle \\
= & \|x^k - x^*\|^2 - \|x^{k+1} - \bar{x}^k\|^2 - \|\bar{x}^k - x^k\|^2 - 2\alpha_k\langle \nabla f_k(\bar{x}^k), \bar{x}^k - x^*\rangle \\
& +2\langle x^k - \bar{x}^k - \alpha_k \nabla f_k(\bar{x}^k), x^{k+1} - \bar{x}^k\rangle + 2\langle e_2(x^k), x^{k+1} - x^*\rangle. \qquad (20)
\end{aligned}$$

From Lemma 1 (iii), we have that

$$2\langle e_2(x^k), x^{k+1} - x^*\rangle \leq \|e_2(x^k)\| + \|e_2(x^k)\|\|x^{k+1} - x^*\|^2. \qquad (21)$$

Since $I - P_C$ is firmly nonexpensive, $\nabla f_k(x^*) = 0$, and Lemma 4, we get that

$$\begin{aligned}
& 2\alpha_k\langle \nabla f_k(\bar{x}^k), \bar{x}^k - x^*\rangle \\
= & 2\alpha_k\langle \sum_{j=1}^{r} \beta_j A^*(I - P_{Q_j^k})A\bar{x}^k - \sum_{j=1}^{r} \beta_j A^*(I - P_{Q_j^k})Ax^*, \bar{x}^k - x^*\rangle \\
= & 2\alpha_k \sum_{j=1}^{r} \beta_j\langle (I - P_{Q_j^k})A\bar{x}^k - (I - P_{Q_j^k})Ax^*, A\bar{x}^k - Ax^*\rangle \\
\geq & 2\frac{\mu l}{L} \sum_{j=1}^{r} \beta_j\|(I - P_{Q_j^k})A\bar{x}^k\|^2. \qquad (22)
\end{aligned}$$

Based on the definition of $\bar{x}^k$ and Lemma 1 (i), we know that

$$\langle \bar{x}^k - x^k + \alpha_k \nabla f_k(x^k) - e_1(x^k), x^{k+1} - \bar{x}^k\rangle \geq 0. \qquad (23)$$

Note that (17), (23), and Lemma 1 (iii) yield that

$$\begin{aligned}
& 2\langle x^k - \bar{x}^k - \alpha_k \nabla f_k(\bar{x}^k), x^{k+1} - \bar{x}^k\rangle \\
\leq & 2\langle -e_1(x^k) + \alpha_k \nabla f_k(x^k) - \alpha_k \nabla f_k(\bar{x}^k), x^{k+1} - \bar{x}^k\rangle \\
= & 2\alpha_k\langle \nabla f_k(x^k) - \nabla f_k(\bar{x}^k), x^{k+1} - \bar{x}^k\rangle - 2\langle e_1(x^k), x^{k+1} - \bar{x}^k\rangle \\
\leq & 2\alpha_k\|\nabla f_k(x^k) - \nabla f_k(\bar{x}^k)\|\|x^{k+1} - \bar{x}^k\| + 2\|e_1(x^k)\|\|x^{k+1} - \bar{x}^k\| \\
\leq & 2\mu\|x^k - \bar{x}^k\|\|x^{k+1} - \bar{x}^k\| + \|e_1(x^k)\| + \|e_1(x^k)\|\|x^{k+1} - \bar{x}^k\|^2 \\
\leq & \mu\|x^k - \bar{x}^k\|^2 + \mu\|x^{k+1} - \bar{x}^k\|^2 + \|e_1(x^k)\| + \|e_1(x^k)\|\|x^{k+1} - \bar{x}^k\|^2 \\
= & \mu\|x^k - \bar{x}^k\|^2 + (\mu + \|e_1(x^k)\|)\|x^{k+1} - \bar{x}^k\|^2 + \|e_1(x^k)\|. \qquad (24)
\end{aligned}$$

From assumption (A4), we know that $\lim_{k\to\infty}\|e_i(x^k)\| = 0$, $i = 1, 2$, and thus $\forall\varepsilon > 0$, $\exists K$, it holds that $\|e_i(x^k)\| < \varepsilon$ for $k > K$. We can therefore assume $\|e_1(x^k)\| \in [0, 1-\mu-\tau)$ and $\|e_2(x^k)\| \in [0, 1/2)$ for $k \geq K$, where $\tau \in (0, 1-\mu)$. Hence, from (24), we get that

$$2\langle x^k - \bar{x}^k - \alpha_k\nabla f_k(\bar{x}^k), x^{k+1} - \bar{x}^k\rangle \leq \mu\|x^k - \bar{x}^k\|^2 + (1-\tau)\|x^{k+1} - \bar{x}^k\|^2 + \|e_1(x^k)\|. \quad (25)$$

Substituting (21), (22), and (25) into (20) yields

$$\begin{aligned}\|x^{k+1} - x^*\|^2 \leq\ & \|x^k - x^*\|^2 - (1-\mu)\|x^k - \bar{x}^k\|^2 - \tau\|x^{k+1} - \bar{x}^k\|^2 \\ & +\|e_1(x^k)\| + \|e_2(x^k)\| + \|e_2(x^k)\|\|x^{k+1} - x^*\|^2 \\ & -2\frac{\mu l}{L}\sum_{j=1}^{r}\beta_j\|(I - P_{Q_j^k})A\bar{x}^k\|^2. \end{aligned} \quad (26)$$

Organizing the above formula we know that

$$\begin{aligned}\|x^{k+1} - x^*\|^2 \leq\ & \frac{1}{1-\|e_2(x^k)\|}\|x^k - x^*\|^2 - \frac{1-\mu}{1-\|e_2(x^k)\|}\|x^k - \bar{x}^k\|^2 \\ & -\frac{\tau}{1-\|e_2(x^k)\|}\|x^{k+1} - \bar{x}^k\|^2 + \frac{\|e_1(x^k)\| + \|e_2(x^k)\|}{1-\|e_2(x^k)\|} \\ & -\frac{2\mu l}{(1-\|e_2(x^k)\|)L}\sum_{j=1}^{r}\beta_j\|(I - P_{Q_j^k})A\bar{x}^k\|^2. \end{aligned} \quad (27)$$

Since $\|e_2(x^k)\| \in [0, 1/2)$ for $k \geq K$, we get

$$1 \leq \frac{1}{1-\|e_2(x^k)\|} \leq 1 + 2\|e_2(x^k)\| < 2. \quad (28)$$

This together with (27) shows that

$$\begin{aligned}\|x^{k+1} - x^*\|^2 \leq\ & (1 + 2\|e_2(x^k)\|)\|x^k - x^*\|^2 - (1-\mu)\|x^k - \bar{x}^k\|^2 + 2\|e_1(x^k)\| \\ & +2\|e_2(x^k)\| - \tau\|x^{k+1} - \bar{x}^k\|^2 - 2\frac{\mu l}{L}\sum_{j=1}^{r}\beta_j\|(I - P_{Q_j^k})A\bar{x}^k\|^2 \\ \leq\ & (1 + 2\|e_2(x^k)\|)\|x^k - x^*\|^2 + 2\|e_1(x^k)\| + 2\|e_2(x^k)\|. \end{aligned} \quad (29)$$

Using Lemma 2 and assumption (A4), we know the existence of $\lim_{k\to\infty}\|x^k - x^*\|^2$ and the boundedness of $\{x^k\}_{k=0}^{\infty}$.

From (29), it follows

$$\begin{aligned} & (1-\mu)\|x^k - \bar{x}^k\|^2 + \tau\|x^{k+1} - \bar{x}^k\|^2 + 2\frac{\mu l}{L}\sum_{j=1}^{r}\beta_j\|(I - P_{Q_j^k})A\bar{x}^k\|^2 \\ \leq\ & (1 + 2\|e_2(x^k)\|)\|x^k - x^*\|^2 - \|x^{k+1} - x^*\|^2 + 2\|e_1(x^k)\| + 2\|e_2(x^k)\|, \end{aligned} \quad (30)$$

which means that

$$\sum_{k=0}^{\infty}\|x^k - \bar{x}^k\| < +\infty, \ \sum_{k=0}^{\infty}\|x^{k+1} - \bar{x}^k\| < +\infty.$$

We therefore have

$$\lim_{k\to\infty}\|x^k - \bar{x}^k\| = 0, \ \lim_{k\to\infty}\|x^{k+1} - \bar{x}^k\| = 0. \quad (31)$$

Thus, by taking $k \to \infty$ in the inequality $\|x^{k+1} - x^k\| \leq \|x^{k+1} - \bar{x}^k\| + \|\bar{x}^k - x^k\|$, we have

$$\lim_{k\to\infty} \|x^{k+1} - x^k\| = 0. \tag{32}$$

From (30), we also know

$$\lim_{k\to\infty} \sum_{j=1}^{r} \beta_j \|(I - P_{Q_j^k})A\bar{x}^k\| = 0. \tag{33}$$

Hence for every $j = 1, 2, \cdots, r$, we have

$$\lim_{k\to\infty} \|(I - P_{Q_j^k})A\bar{x}^k\| = 0. \tag{34}$$

Since $\{x^k\}$ is bounded, the set $\omega_\omega(x^k)$ is nonempty. Let $\widehat{x} \in \omega_\omega(x^k)$; then there exists a subsequence $\{x^{k_n}\}$ of $\{x^k\}$ such that $x^{k_n} \rightharpoonup \widehat{x}$. Next, we show that $\widehat{x}$ is a solution of the MSSFP (1), which will show that $\omega_\omega(x^k) \subset S$. In fact, since $x^{k_n+1} \in C_{[k_n]}^{k_n}$, then by the definition of $C_{[k_n]}^{k_n}$, we have

$$c_{[k_n]}(x^{k_n}) + \langle \xi_{[k_n]}^{k_n}, x^{k_n+1} - x^{k_n} \rangle \leq 0, \tag{35}$$

where $\xi_{[k_n]}^{k_n} \in \partial c_{[k_n]}(x^{k_n})$. For every $i = 1, 2, \cdots, t$, choose a subsequence $\{k_{n_s}\} \subset \{k_n\}$ such that $[k_{n_s}] = i$, then

$$c_i(x^{k_{n_s}}) + \langle \xi_i^{k_{n_s}}, x^{k_{n_s}+1} - x^{k_{n_s}} \rangle \leq 0. \tag{36}$$

Following the assumption (A3) on the boundedness of ∂c_i and (32), there exists M_1 such that

$$\begin{aligned} c_i(x^{k_{n_s}}) &\leq \langle \xi_i^{k_{n_s}}, x^{k_{n_s}} - x^{k_{n_s}+1} \rangle \\ &\leq \|\xi_i^{k_{n_s}}\| \|x^{k_{n_s}} - x^{k_{n_s}+1}\| \\ &\leq M_1 \|x^{k_{n_s}} - x^{k_{n_s}+1}\| \to 0, \; s \to \infty. \end{aligned} \tag{37}$$

From the weak lower semicontinuity of the convex function c_i, we deduce from (37) that $c_i(\widehat{x}) \leq \liminf_{s\to\infty} c_i(x^{k_{n_s}}) \leq 0$, i.e., $\widehat{x} \in C = \bigcap_{i=1}^{t} C_i$.

Noting the fact that $I - P_{Q_j^{k_n}}$ is nonexpansive, together with (31), (34), and A being a bounded and linear operator, we get that

$$\begin{aligned} \|(I - P_{Q_j^{k_n}})Ax^{k_n}\| &\leq \|(I - P_{Q_j^{k_n}})Ax^{k_n} - (I - P_{Q_j^{k_n}})A\bar{x}^{k_n}\| + \|(I - P_{Q_j^{k_n}})A\bar{x}^{k_n}\| \\ &\leq \|Ax^{k_n} - A\bar{x}^{k_n}\| + \|(I - P_{Q_j^{k_n}})A\bar{x}^{k_n}\| \\ &\leq \|A\|\|x^{k_n} - \bar{x}^{k_n}\| + \|(I - P_{Q_j^{k_n}})A\bar{x}^{k_n}\| \to 0, \; n \to \infty. \end{aligned} \tag{38}$$

Since $P_{Q_j^{k_n}}(Ax^{k_n}) \in Q_j^{k_n}$, we have

$$q_j(Ax^{k_n}) + \langle \eta_j^{k_n}, P_{Q_j^{k_n}}(Ax^{k_n}) - Ax^{k_n} \rangle \leq 0, \tag{39}$$

where $\eta_j^{k_n} \in \partial q_j(Ax^{k_n})$. From the boundedness assumption (A3), (38), and (39), there exists M_2 such that

$$
\begin{aligned}
q_j(Ax^{k_n}) &\leq \|\eta_j^{k_n}\|\|Ax^{k_n} - P_{Q_j^{k_n}}(Ax^{k_n})\| \\
&\leq M_2\|(I - P_{Q_j^{k_n}})Ax^{k_n}\| \to 0,\ n \to \infty.
\end{aligned} \tag{40}
$$

Then $q_j(A\widehat{x}) \leq \liminf_{n\to\infty} q_j(Ax^{k_n}) \leq 0$, thus $A\widehat{x} \in Q = \bigcap_{j=1}^{r} Q_j$, and therefore $\widehat{x} \in S$. Using Lemma 3, we conclude that the sequence $\{x^k\}$ converges weakly to a solution of the MSSFP (1). □

Now, we present Algorithm 2 in which the step size is given by the self-adaptive method and prove its weak convergence.

Algorithm 2 (The relaxed CQ algorithm with self-adaptive step size and perturbation)

Take arbitrarily the initial guess x^0, and calculate

$$
x^{k+1} = P_{C_{[k]}^k}(x^k - \alpha_k \nabla f_k(x^k) + e_3(x^k)), \tag{41}
$$

where $\alpha_k = \frac{\rho_k f_k(x^k)}{\|\nabla f_k(x^k)\|^2}$, $0 < \rho_k < 4$, and C_i, Q_j, C_i^k, Q_j^k and $\nabla f_k(x)$ were defined at the beginning of this section.

The convergence result of Algorithm 2 is stated in the next theorem.

Theorem 2. *Let $\{x^k\}$ be the sequence generated by Algorithm 2. Assumptions (A1)∼(A4) hold and ρ_k satisfies $\inf_k \rho_k(4 - \rho_k) > 0$. Then $\{x^k\}$ converges weakly to a solution of the MSSFP (1).*

Proof. First, we prove $\{x^k\}$ is bounded. Let $x^* \in S$. Following Lemma 1 (ii), we have

$$
\begin{aligned}
&\|x^{k+1} - x^*\|^2 \\
= \ &\|P_{C_{[k]}^k}(x^k - \alpha_k \nabla f_k(x^k) + e_3(x^k)) - x^*\|^2 \\
\leq \ &\|x^k - \alpha_k \nabla f_k(x^k) + e_3(x^k) - x^*\|^2 - \|x^{k+1} - x^k + \alpha_k \nabla f_k(x^k) - e_3(x^k)\|^2 \\
= \ &\|x^k - x^*\|^2 - \|x^{k+1} - x^k\|^2 - 2\langle \alpha_k \nabla f_k(x^k) - e_3(x^k), x^k - x^*\rangle \\
&-2\langle \alpha_k \nabla f_k(x^k) - e_3(x^k), x^{k+1} - x^k\rangle \\
= \ &\|x^k - x^*\|^2 - \|x^{k+1} - x^k\|^2 - 2\alpha_k\langle \nabla f_k(x^k), x^k - x^*\rangle \\
&-2\langle \alpha_k \nabla f_k(x^k), x^{k+1} - x^k\rangle + 2\langle e_3(x^k), x^{k+1} - x^*\rangle.
\end{aligned} \tag{42}
$$

From Lemma 1 (iii), it follows

$$
2\langle e_3(x^k), x^{k+1} - x^*\rangle \leq \|e_3(x^k)\| + \|e_3(x^k)\|\|x^{k+1} - x^*\|^2. \tag{43}
$$

Similar with (22), it holds that

$$
2\alpha_k\langle \nabla f_k(x^k), x^k - x^*\rangle \geq 2\alpha_k \sum_{j=1}^{r} \beta_j \|(I - P_{Q_j^k})Ax^k\|^2 = 4\alpha_k f_k(x^k). \tag{44}
$$

From Lemma 1 (iv), one has

$$
-2\langle \alpha_k \nabla f_k(x^k), x^{k+1} - x^k\rangle \leq \alpha_k^2 \|\nabla f_k(x^k)\|^2 + \|x^{k+1} - x^k\|^2. \tag{45}
$$

Substituting (43)–(45) into (42), we get that

$$
\begin{aligned}
\|x^{k+1}-x^*\|^2 \leq\ & \|x^k-x^*\|^2+\alpha_k^2\|\nabla f_k(x^k)\|^2-4\alpha_k f_k(x^k)+\|e_3(x^k)\| \\
& +\|e_3(x^k)\|\|x^{k+1}-x^*\|^2, \\
=\ & \|x^k-x^*\|^2+\frac{\rho_k^2 f_k^2(x^k)}{\|\nabla f_k(x^k)\|^4}\|\nabla f_k(x^k)\|^2-4\frac{\rho_k f_k(x^k)}{\|\nabla f_k(x^k)\|^2}f_k(x^k) \\
& +\|e_3(x^k)\|+\|e_3(x^k)\|\|x^{k+1}-x^*\|^2, \\
=\ & \|x^k-x^*\|^2-\rho_k(4-\rho_k)\frac{f_k^2(x^k)}{\|\nabla f_k(x^k)\|^2}+\|e_3(x^k)\|\|x^{k+1}-x^*\|^2 \\
& +\|e_3(x^k)\|. \qquad (46)
\end{aligned}
$$

Organizing the above formula, we obtain that

$$
\begin{aligned}
& \|x^{k+1}-x^*\|^2 \\
\leq\ & \frac{1}{1-\|e_3(x^k)\|}\|x^k-x^*\|^2-\frac{\rho_k(4-\rho_k)}{1-\|e_3(x^k)\|}\frac{f_k^2(x^k)}{\|\nabla f_k(x^k)\|^2}+\frac{\|e_3(x^k)\|}{1-\|e_3(x^k)\|}. \qquad (47)
\end{aligned}
$$

From assumption (A4), we know that $\lim_{k\to\infty} e_3(x^k)=0$, so we can assume without loss of generality that $\|e_3(x^k)\|\in[0,1/2)$, $k\geq 0$, then

$$
1\leq\frac{1}{1-\|e_3(x^k)\|}\leq 1+2\|e_3(x^k)\|<2. \qquad (48)
$$

So (47) can be reduced as

$$
\|x^{k+1}-x^*\|^2\leq(1+2\|e_3(x^k)\|)\|x^k-x^*\|^2+2\|e_3(x^k)\|. \qquad (49)
$$

Using Lemma 2, we get the existence of $\lim_{k\to\infty}\|x^k-x^*\|^2$ and the boundedness of $\{x^k\}_{k=0}^{\infty}$.

From (47), we know

$$
\begin{aligned}
& \frac{\rho_k(4-\rho_k)}{1-\|e_3(x^k)\|}\frac{f_k^2(x^k)}{\|\nabla f_k(x^k)\|^2} \\
\leq\ & \frac{1}{1-\|e_3(x^k)\|}\|x^k-x^*\|^2-\|x^{k+1}-x^*\|^2+\frac{\|e_3(x^k)\|}{1-\|e_3(x^k)\|}\to 0, \qquad (50)
\end{aligned}
$$

then the fact that $\inf_k \rho_k(4-\rho_k)>0$ asserts that $\frac{f_k^2(x^k)}{\|\nabla f_k(x^k)\|^2}\to 0$. Since ∇f_k is Lipschitz continuity and $\nabla f_k(x^*)=0$, we get that

$$
\|\nabla f_k(x^k)\|^2=\|\nabla f_k(x^k)-\nabla f_k(x^*)\|^2\leq L^2\|x^k-x^*\|^2. \qquad (51)
$$

This implies that $\nabla f_k(x^k)$ is bounded, and thus (50) yields $f_k(x^k)\to 0$. Hence for every $j=1,2,\cdots,r$, we have

$$
\|(I-P_{Q_j^k})Ax^k\|\to 0,\ k\to\infty. \qquad (52)
$$

Let $\{x^{k_n}\}$ be a subsequence of $\{x^k\}$ such that $x^{k_n}\rightharpoonup\widehat{x}\in\omega_\omega(x^k)$, and $\{k_{n_s}\}$ are a subsequence of $\{k_n\}$ such that $[k_{n_s}]=i$. Similar to the proof of Theorem 1, we know that $c_i(\widehat{x})\leq\liminf_{s\to\infty}c_i(x^{k_{n_s}})\leq 0$, i.e., $\widehat{x}\in C=\bigcap_{i=1}^t C_i$. Since (52) indicates that $q_j(A\widehat{x})\leq\liminf_{n\to\infty}q_j(Ax^{k_n})\leq 0$, $A\widehat{x}\in Q=\bigcap_{j=1}^r Q_j$. Therefore $\widehat{x}\in S$. Using Lemma 3, we conclude that the sequence $\{x^k\}$ converges weakly to a solution of the MSSFP (1). □

4. The Bounded Perturbation Resilience

4.1. Bounded Perturbation Resilience of the Algorithms

In this subsection, we consider the bounded perturbation algorithms of Algorithms 1 and 2. Based on Definition 3, in Algorithm 1, let $e_i(x^k) = 0, i = 1, 2$. The original algorithm is

$$\begin{cases} \bar{x}^k = P_{C^k_{[k]}}(x^k - \alpha_k \nabla f_k(x^k)), \\ x^{k+1} = P_{C^k_{[k]}}(x^k - \alpha_k \nabla f_k(\bar{x}^k)), \end{cases} \tag{53}$$

where α_k is obtained by Armijo-line search step size such that $\alpha_k \|\nabla f_k(x^k) - \nabla f_k(\bar{x}^k)\| \leq \mu \|x^k - \bar{x}^k\|$, where $\mu \in (0,1)$. The generated iteration sequence is weakly convergent, which is proved as a special case in Section 3. The algorithm with the bounded perturbation of (53) is that

$$\begin{cases} \bar{x}^k = P_{C^k_{[k]}}(x^k + \lambda_k v_k - \alpha_k \nabla f_k(x^k + \lambda_k v_k)), \\ x^{k+1} = P_{C^k_{[k]}}(x^k + \lambda_k v_k - \alpha_k \nabla f_k(\bar{x}^k)). \end{cases} \tag{54}$$

where $[k] = k \bmod t$ and $\alpha_k = \gamma l^{m_k}$ with m_k the smallest non-negative integer such that

$$\begin{aligned} \alpha_k \|\nabla f_k(x^k + \lambda_k v_k) - \nabla f_k(\bar{x}^k)\| &\leq \mu \|x^k + \lambda_k v_k - \bar{x}^k\| \\ &\leq \mu(\|x^k - \bar{x}^k\| + \lambda_k \|v_k\|). \end{aligned} \tag{55}$$

The following theorem shows that the algorithm (53) is bounded perturbation-resilient.

Theorem 3. *Assume that (A1)∼(A3) are true; the sequence $\{v_k\}_{k=0}^{\infty}$ is bounded and the scalar sequence $\{\lambda_k\}_{k=0}^{\infty}$ satisfies $\lambda_k \geq 0$ and $\Sigma_{k=0}^{\infty} \lambda_k < +\infty$. Then the sequence $\{x^k\}_{k=0}^{\infty}$ generated by iterative scheme (54) converges weakly to a solution of the MSSFP (1). Thus, the algorithm (53) is bounded perturbation-resilient.*

Proof. Let $x^* \in S$. Since $\Sigma_{k=0}^{\infty} \lambda_k < +\infty$ and the sequence $\{v_k\}_{k=0}^{\infty}$ are bounded, we have

$$\sum_{k=0}^{\infty} \lambda_k \|v_k\| < +\infty, \tag{56}$$

thus

$$\lim_{k \to \infty} \lambda_k \|v_k\| = 0. \tag{57}$$

So we can assume that $\lambda_k \|v_k\| \in [0, (1 - \mu - \tau)/2)$, where $\tau \in (0, 1 - \mu)$, without loss of generality. Replacing $e_2(x^k)$ with $\lambda_k v_k$ in (20) and using Lemma 1 (iii) show

$$\begin{aligned} &\|x^{k+1} - x^*\|^2 \\ \leq\ &\|x^k - x^*\|^2 - \|\bar{x}^k - x^k\|^2 - \|x^{k+1} - \bar{x}^k\|^2 - 2\alpha_k \langle \nabla f_k(\bar{x}^k), \bar{x}^k - x^* \rangle \\ &+ 2\langle x^k - \bar{x}^k - \alpha_k \nabla f_k(\bar{x}^k), x^{k+1} - \bar{x}^k \rangle + 2\langle \lambda_k v_k, x^{k+1} - x^* \rangle \\ \leq\ &\|x^k - x^*\|^2 - \|\bar{x}^k - x^k\|^2 - \|x^{k+1} - \bar{x}^k\|^2 - 2\alpha_k \langle \nabla f_k(\bar{x}^k), \bar{x}^k - x^* \rangle \\ &+ 2\langle x^k - \bar{x}^k - \alpha_k \nabla f_k(\bar{x}^k), x^{k+1} - \bar{x}^k \rangle + \lambda_k \|v_k\| + \lambda_k \|v_k\| \|x^{k+1} - x^*\|^2. \end{aligned} \tag{58}$$

Since $I - P_C$ is firmly nonexpensive, $\nabla f_k(x^*) = 0$ and Lemma 4, we get that

$$2\alpha_k \langle \nabla f_k(\bar{x}^k), \bar{x}^k - x^* \rangle \geq 2 \frac{\mu l}{L} \sum_{j=1}^{r} \beta_j \|(I - P_{Q_j^k}) A \bar{x}^k\|^2. \tag{59}$$

Based on the definition of $\bar{x}^k$ and Lemma 1 (i), we know that

$$\langle \bar{x}^k - x^k + \alpha_k \nabla f_k(x^k + \lambda_k \nu_k) - \lambda_k \nu_k, x^{k+1} - \bar{x}^k \rangle \geq 0. \tag{60}$$

Based on (55), the following formulas holds

$$\begin{aligned} & 2\langle \alpha_k \nabla f_k(x^k + \lambda_k \nu_k) - \alpha_k \nabla f_k(\bar{x}^k), x^{k+1} - \bar{x}^k \rangle \\ \leq\ & 2\alpha_k \|\nabla f_k(x^k + \lambda_k \nu_k) - \nabla f_k(\bar{x}^k)\| \|x^{k+1} - \bar{x}^k\| \\ \leq\ & 2\mu \|x^k - \bar{x}^k\| \|x^{k+1} - \bar{x}^k\| + 2\mu\lambda_k \|\nu_k\| \|x^{k+1} - \bar{x}^k\| \\ =\ & \mu \|x^k - \bar{x}^k\|^2 + (\mu + \lambda_k \|\nu_k\|) \|x^{k+1} - \bar{x}^k\|^2 + \mu^2 \lambda_k \|\nu_k\|. \end{aligned} \tag{61}$$

Lemma 1 (iii) reads that

$$-2\lambda_k \langle \nu_k, x^{k+1} - \bar{x}^k \rangle \leq \lambda_k \|\nu_k\| + \lambda_k \|\nu_k\| \|x^{k+1} - \bar{x}^k\|^2. \tag{62}$$

Substituting (60)–(62) into the fifth item of (58), we get

$$\begin{aligned} & 2\langle x^k - \bar{x}^k - \alpha_k \nabla f_k(\bar{x}^k), x^{k+1} - \bar{x}^k \rangle \\ \leq\ & 2\langle x^k - \bar{x}^k - \alpha_k \nabla f_k(\bar{x}^k), x^{k+1} - \bar{x}^k \rangle \\ & + 2\langle \bar{x}^k - x^k + \alpha_k \nabla f_k(x^k + \lambda_k \nu_k) - \lambda_k \nu_k, x^{k+1} - \bar{x}^k \rangle \\ =\ & 2\langle \alpha_k \nabla f_k(x^k + \lambda_k \nu_k) - \alpha_k \nabla f_k(\bar{x}^k), x^{k+1} - \bar{x}^k \rangle - 2\lambda_k \langle \nu_k, x^{k+1} - \bar{x}^k \rangle \\ \leq\ & \mu \|x^k - \bar{x}^k\|^2 + (\mu + 2\lambda_k \|\nu_k\|) \|x^{k+1} - \bar{x}^k\|^2 + (1 + \mu^2) \lambda_k \|\nu_k\| \\ \leq\ & \mu \|x^k - \bar{x}^k\|^2 + (1 - \tau) \|x^{k+1} - \bar{x}^k\|^2 + 2\lambda_k \|\nu_k\|. \end{aligned} \tag{63}$$

Substituting (59) and (63) into (58) we get

$$\begin{aligned} \|x^{k+1} - x^*\|^2 \leq\ & \frac{1}{1 - \lambda_k \|\nu_k\|} \Big[\|x^k - x^*\|^2 + 3\lambda_k \|\nu_k\| - (1 - \mu) \|\bar{x}^k - x^k\|^2 \\ & - \tau \|x^{k+1} - \bar{x}^k\|^2 - 2\frac{\mu l}{L} \sum_{j=1}^{r} \beta_j \|(I - P_{Q_j^k}) A \bar{x}^k\|^2 \Big]. \end{aligned} \tag{64}$$

Since $\lambda_k \|\nu_k\| \in [0,\ (1 - \mu - \tau)/2)$, we get

$$1 \leq \frac{1}{1 - \lambda_k \|\nu_k\|} \leq 1 + 2\lambda_k \|\nu_k\| < 2. \tag{65}$$

This, together with (64), shows that

$$\begin{aligned} \|x^{k+1} - x^*\|^2 \leq\ & (1 + 2\lambda_k \|\nu_k\|) \Big[\|x^k - x^*\|^2 - (1 - \mu) \|x^k - \bar{x}^k\|^2 - \tau \|x^{k+1} - \bar{x}^k\|^2 \\ & - 2\frac{\mu l}{L} \sum_{j=1}^{r} \beta_j \|(I - P_{Q_j^k}) A \bar{x}^k\|^2 \Big] + 6\lambda_k \|\nu_k\| \\ \leq\ & (1 + 2\lambda_k \|\nu_k\|) \|x^k - x^*\|^2 + 6\lambda_k \|\nu_k\|. \end{aligned} \tag{66}$$

Using Lemma 2, we know the existence of $\lim_{k\to\infty} \|x^k - x^*\|^2$ and the boundedness of $\{x^k\}_{k=0}^{\infty}$.

From (64), it follows that

$$\begin{aligned} & (1 - \mu) \|\bar{x}^k - x^k\|^2 + \tau \|x^{k+1} - \bar{x}^k\|^2 + 2\frac{\mu l}{L} \sum_{j=1}^{r} \beta_j \|(I - P_{Q_j^k}) A \bar{x}^k\|^2 \\ \leq\ & \|x^k - x^*\|^2 - (1 - \lambda_k \|\nu_k\|) \|x^{k+1} - x^*\|^2 + 3\lambda_k \|\nu_k\|. \end{aligned} \tag{67}$$

Thus, we have $\lim_{k\to\infty}\|x^k-\bar{x}^k\|=0$, $\lim_{k\to\infty}\|x^{k+1}-\bar{x}^k\|=0$ and $\lim_{k\to\infty}\sum_{j=1}^{r}\beta_j\|(I-P_{Q_j^k})A\bar{x}^k\|^2=0$. Hence,

$$\lim_{k\to\infty}\|x^{k+1}-x^k\|=0, \tag{68}$$

and for every $j=1,2,\cdots,r$,

$$\lim_{k\to\infty}\|(I-P_{Q_j^k})A\bar{x}^k\|=0. \tag{69}$$

Similarly to with Theorem 1, we conclude that the sequence $\{x^k\}$ converges weakly to a solution of the MSSFP (1). □

Remark 1. *When $t=1, r=1$, the MSSFP reduces to the SFP; thus Theorems 1 and 3 guarantee that algorithm (53) is bounded perturbation-resilient with Armijo-line search step size for the SFP.*

Remark 2. *Replace $f_k(x)$ in algorithm (53) by $g_k(x)$, and $\nabla f_k(x)$ by $\nabla g_k(x)$, where $g_k(x)=\frac{1}{2}\|(I-P_{Q_{[k]}^k})Ax\|^2$, and $\nabla g_k(x)=A^*(I-P_{Q_{[k]}^k})Ax$, $[k]=k \bmod r$. The corresponding algorithm is also bounded perturbation-resilient.*

Next, we will prove that Algorithm 2 with self-adaptive step size is bounded perturbation-resilient. Based on Definition 3, let $e_3(x^k)=0$ in Algorithm 2. The original algorithm is

$$x^{k+1}=P_{C_{[k]}^k}(x^k-\alpha_k\nabla f_k(x^k)), \tag{70}$$

where $\alpha_k=\frac{\rho_k f_k(x^k)}{\|\nabla f_k(x^k)\|^2}$, $0<\rho_k<4$. The iterative sequence converges weakly to a solution of the MSSFP (1); see [26]. Consider the algorithm with the bounded perturbation

$$x^{k+1}=P_{C_{[k]}^k}(x^k+\lambda_k v_k-\tilde{\alpha}_k\nabla f_k(x^k+\lambda_k v_k)), \tag{71}$$

where $\tilde{\alpha}_k=\frac{\rho_k f_k(x^k+\lambda_k v_k)}{\|\nabla f_k(x^k+\lambda_k v_k)\|^2}$, $0<\rho_k<4$. The following theorem shows that the algorithm (70) is bounded-perturbation-resilient.

Theorem 4. *Suppose that (A1)∼(A3) are true; the sequence $\{v_k\}_{k=0}^{\infty}$ is bounded and the scalar sequence $\{\lambda_k\}_{k=0}^{\infty}$ satisfies $\lambda_k\geq 0$, $\Sigma_{k=0}^{\infty}\lambda_k<+\infty$, and ρ_k satisfies $\inf_k\rho_k(4-\rho_k)>0$. Then the sequence $\{x^k\}_{k=0}^{\infty}$ generated by iterative scheme (71) converges weakly to a solution of the MSSFP (1). Thus, the algorithm (70) is bounded-perturbation-resilient.*

Proof. Set $e_3(x^k)=\lambda_k v_k+\alpha_k\nabla f_k(x^k)-\tilde{\alpha}_k\nabla f_k(x^k+\lambda_k v_k)$, then (71) can be rewritten as $x^{k+1}=P_{C_{[k]}^k}(x^k-\alpha_k\nabla f_k(x^k)+e_3(x^k))$, which is the form of Algorithm 2. According to Theorem 2, it suffices to prove that $\sum_{k=0}^{\infty}e_3(x^k)<+\infty$. Since $\frac{\rho_k f_k(x^k+\lambda_k v_k)}{\|\nabla f_k(x^k+\lambda_k v_k)\|^2}\nabla f_k(x^k+\lambda_k v_k)$ is continuous, we write

$$\frac{\rho_k f_k(x^k+\lambda_k v_k)}{\|\nabla f_k(x^k+\lambda_k v_k)\|^2}\nabla f_k(x^k+\lambda_k v_k)=\frac{\rho_k f_k(x^k)}{\|\nabla f_k(x^k)\|^2}\nabla f_k(x^k)+O(\lambda_k v_k), \tag{72}$$

where $O(\lambda_k v_k)$ denotes the infinitesimal of the same order of $\lambda_k v_k$. From the expression of $e_3(x^k)$, we obtain

$$\begin{aligned}\|e_3(x^k)\| &\leq \|\lambda_k v_k\| + \left\|\alpha_k \nabla f_k(x^k) - \tilde{\alpha}_k \nabla f_k(x^k + \lambda_k v_k)\right\| \\ &= \|\lambda_k v_k\| + \left\|\frac{\rho_k f_k(x^k)}{\|\nabla f_k(x^k)\|^2}\nabla f_k(x^k) - \frac{\rho_k f_k(x^k + \lambda_k v_k)}{\|\nabla f_k(x^k + \lambda_k v_k)\|^2}\nabla f_k(x^k + \lambda_k v_k)\right\| \\ &= \|\lambda_k v_k\| + \left\|\frac{\rho_k f_k(x^k)}{\|\nabla f_k(x^k)\|^2}\nabla f_k(x^k) - \Big(\frac{\rho_k f_k(x^k)}{\|\nabla f_k(x^k)\|^2}\nabla f_k(x^k) + O(\lambda_k v_k)\Big)\right\| \\ &= \|\lambda_k v_k\| + \|O(\lambda_k v_k)\|. \end{aligned} \tag{73}$$

Since $\{\lambda_k v_k\}$ is summable, we know that $\{e_3(x^k)\}$ is summable, i.e., $\sum_{k=0}^{\infty}\|e_3(x^k)\| \leq +\infty$. Thus, we conclude that the sequence $\{x^k\}$ converges weakly to a solution of the MSSFP (1); i.e., the algorithm (70) is the bounded-perturbation-resilient. □

Remark 3. *When $t = 1$, $r = 1$, the MSSFP reduces to the SFP; thus Theorems 2 and 4 guarantee that algorithm (70) is bounded-perturbation-resilient with the self-adaptive step size for the SFP.*

4.2. Construction of the Inertial Algorithms by Bounded Perturbation Resilience

In this subsection, we consider algorithms with inertial terms as a special case of Algorithms 1 and 2. In Algorithm 1, letting $e_i(x^k) = \theta_k^{(i)}(x^k - x^{k-1})$, $i = 1, 2$, we obtain

$$\begin{cases} \bar{x}^k = P_{C^k_{[k]}}(x^k - \alpha_k \nabla f_k(x^k) + \theta_k^{(1)}(x^k - x^{k-1})), \\ x^{k+1} = P_{C^k_{[k]}}(x^k - \alpha_k \nabla f_k(\bar{x}^k) + \theta_k^{(2)}(x^k - x^{k-1})), \end{cases} \tag{74}$$

where the step size α_k is obtained by Armijo-line search and

$$\theta_k^{(i)} = \begin{cases} \dfrac{\lambda_k^{(i)}}{\|x^k - x^{k-1}\|}, & \|x^k - x^{k-1}\| > 1, \\ \lambda_k^{(i)}, & \|x^k - x^{k-1}\| \leq 1, \end{cases} \quad i = 1, 2. \tag{75}$$

Theorem 5. *Assume that the assumptions (A1)∼(A3) are true, and the sequence $\{\lambda_k\}_{k=0}^{\infty}$ satisfies $\lambda_k \geq 0$, and $\Sigma_{k=0}^{\infty}\lambda_k^{(i)} < +\infty$, $i = 1, 2$. Then, the sequence $\{x^k\}_{k=0}^{\infty}$ generated by iterative scheme (74) converges weakly to a solution of the MSSFP (1).*

Proof. Let $e_i(x^k) = \lambda_k^{(i)} v_k$, $i = 1, 2$, where

$$v_k = \begin{cases} \dfrac{x^k - x^{k-1}}{\|x^k - x^{k-1}\|}, & \|x^k - x^{k-1}\| > 1, \\ x^k - x^{k-1}, & \|x^k - x^{k-1}\| \leq 1. \end{cases} \tag{76}$$

Thus, we know that $\|v_k\| \leq 1$ and $\{e_i(x^k)\}_{k=0}^{\infty}$ satisfies assumption (A4). According to Theorem 1, we conclude that the sequence $\{x^k\}$ converges weakly to a solution of the MSSFP (1). □

Considering the algorithm with inertial bounded perturbation

$$\begin{cases} \bar{x}^k = P_{C^k_{[k]}}(x^k + \theta_k(x^k - x^{k-1}) - \alpha_k \nabla f_k(x^k + \theta_k(x^k - x^{k-1}))), \\ x^{k+1} = P_{C^k_{[k]}}(x^k + \theta_k(x^k - x^{k-1}) - \alpha_k \nabla f_k(\bar{x}^k)). \end{cases} \tag{77}$$

where

$$\theta_k = \begin{cases} \dfrac{\lambda_k}{\|x^k - x^{k-1}\|}, & \|x^k - x^{k-1}\| > 1, \\ \lambda_k, & \|x^k - x^{k-1}\| \leq 1. \end{cases} \tag{78}$$

According to Theorem 3, it is easy to know that the sequence $\{x^k\}$ converges weakly to a solution of the MSSFP (1). More relevant evidence can be found in reference [27].

Similarly, we can get Theorem 6, which asserts that Algorithm 2 with the inertial perturbation is weakly convergent.

Theorem 6. *Assume that (A1)∼(A3) are true; the scalar sequence* $\{\lambda_k\}_{k=0}^{\infty}$ *satisfies* $\lambda_k \geq 0$, *and* $\Sigma_{k=0}^{\infty}\lambda_k < +\infty$, *and* ρ_k *satisfies* $\inf_k \rho_k(4-\rho_k) > 0$. *Then the sequence* $\{x^k\}_{k=0}^{\infty}$ *is generated by each of the following iterative scheme,*

$$x^{k+1} = P_{C^k_{[k]}}(x^k - \alpha_k \nabla f_k(x^k) + \theta_k(x^k - x^{k-1})), \tag{79}$$

$$x^{k+1} = P_{C^k_{[k]}}(x^k - \alpha_k \nabla f_k(x^k + \theta_k(x^k - x^{k-1})) + \theta_k(x^k - x^{k-1})), \tag{80}$$

where θ_k *is the same as (78) and* α_k *is self-adaptive step size which is the same as in Algorithm 2, converges weakly to a solution of the MSSFP (1).*

5. Numerical Experiments

In this section, we compare the asymptotic behavior of algorithms (53) (Chen et al. [9]), (77) (Algorithm 1), (70) (Wen et al. [26]) and (80) (Algorithm 2), denoted by NP1, HP1, NP2, and HP2, respectively. For the sake of convenience, we denote $\mathbf{e}_0 = (0, 0, \cdots, 0)^T$ and $\mathbf{e}_1 = (1, 1, \cdots, 1)^T$, respectively. The codes are written in Matlab 2016a and run on Inter(R) Core(TM) i7-8550U CPU @ 1.80 GHz 2.00 GHz, RAM 8.00 GB. We present two kinds of experiments. One is a real-life problem called LASSO problem, the other kind is some numerical simulation including three examples of the MSSFP.

5.1. LASSO Problem

Let us consider the following LASSO problem [28]

$$\min\{\frac{1}{2}\|Ax-b\|_2^2 \mid x \in \mathbf{R^n}, \|x\|_1 \leq \varepsilon\}$$

where $A \in \mathbf{R^{m\times n}}$, $m < n$, $b \in \mathbf{R^m}$, and $\varepsilon > 0$. The matrix A is generated from a standard normal distribution with mean zero and unit variance. The true sparse signal x^* is generated from uniformly distribution in the interval $[-2, 2]$ with random p position nonzero, while the rest is kept zero. The sample data $b = Ax^*$. For the considered MSSFP, let $r = t = 1$ and $C = \{x \mid \|x\|_1 \leq \varepsilon\}$, $Q = \{b\}$. The objective function is defined as $f(x) = \frac{1}{2}\|Ax-b\|_2^2$.

We report the final error between the reconstructed signal and the true signal. Take $\|x^k - x^*\| < 10^{-4}$ as the stopping criterion, where x^* is the true signal. We compare the algorithms NP1, HP1, NP2 and HP2 with Yang's algorithm [3]. Let $\alpha_k = \gamma l^{m_k}$ for all $k \geq 1$, $\gamma = 1, l = \frac{1}{2}, \mu = \frac{1}{2}, \theta_k = \frac{1}{4}, \rho_k = 0.1$, and $\alpha_k = 0.1 * \dfrac{1}{\|A\|^2}$ of Yang's algorithm [3].

The results are reported in Table 1. Figure 1 shows the objective function value versus iteration numbers when $m = 240, n = 1024, p = 30$.

From Table 1 and Figure 1, we know that the inertial perturbation can improve the convergence of the algorithms and that the algorithms with Armijo-line search or self-adaptive step size perform better than Yang's algorithm [3].

We also measure the restoration accuracy by means of the mean squared error, i.e., MSE= $(1/k)\|x^* - x^k\|$, where x^* is an estimated signal of x. Figure 2 shows a comparison of the accuracy of the recovered signals when $m = 1440, n = 6144, p = 180$. Given the same number of iterations, the recovered signals generated by algorithms in this paper outperform the one generated by Yang's algorithm; NP1 needs more CPU time and presents lower accuracy; algorithms with self-adaptive step size perform better than the algorithms with step size determined by Armijo-line search in CPU time and imposing inertial perturbation accelerates the convergence rate and accuracy of signal recovery.

Table 1. Comparison of algorithms with different step size.

m	n	p		NP1	HP1	NP2	HP2	Yang's alg.
120	512	15	No. of Iter	1588	1119	10,004	7426	10,944
			cpu(time)	0.8560	0.6906	0.6675	0.4991	0.7011
240	1024	30	No. of Iter	1909	1354	10,726	7969	13,443
			cpu(time)	2.1224	1.4836	1.6236	1.2011	1.9789
480	2048	60	No. of Iter	2972	2117	17,338	12,897	22,118
			cpu(time)	22.5140	14.8782	15.4729	11.1033	19.3376
720	3072	90	No. of Iter	3955	2872	21,853	16,244	28,004
			cpu(time)	134.9243	82.6705	79.1640	57.1230	110.0482

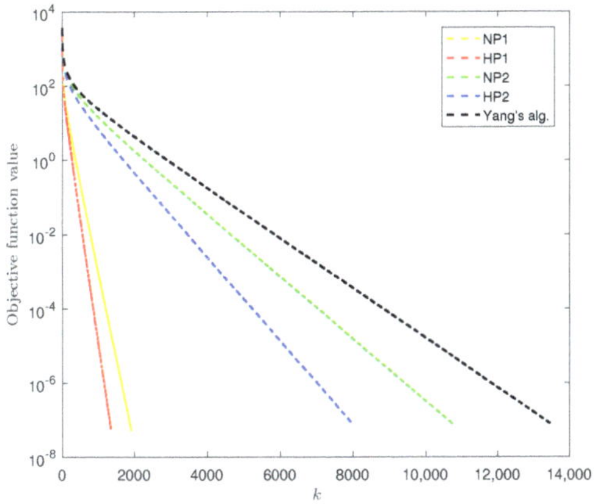

Figure 1. The objective function value versus the iteration number.

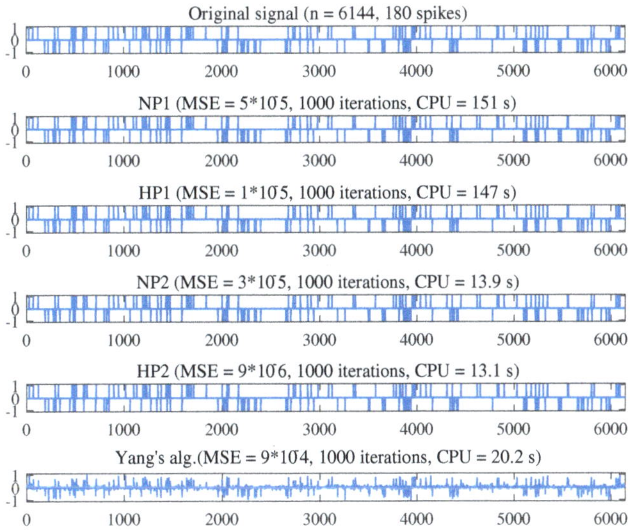

Figure 2. Comparison of signal processing.

5.2. Three MSSFP Problems

Example 1 ([5]). *Take* $\mathcal{H}_1 = \mathcal{H}_2 = \mathbf{R}^3$, $r = t = 2$, $\beta_1 = \beta_2 = \frac{1}{2}$ *and* $\alpha_k = \gamma l^{m_k}$ *for all* $k \geq 1$, $\gamma = 1$, $l = \frac{1}{2}$, $\mu = \frac{1}{2}$, $\theta_k = \frac{1}{4}$, $\rho_k = 0.1$. *Define*

$$\begin{aligned} C_1 &= \left\{x = (x_1, x_2, x_3)^T \in \mathbf{R}^3 \mid x_1 + x_2^2 + 2x_3 \leq 0\right\}, \\ C_2 &= \left\{x = (x_1, x_2, x_3)^T \in \mathbf{R}^3 \mid \frac{x_1^2}{16} + \frac{x_2^2}{9} + \frac{x_3^2}{4} - 1 \leq 0\right\}, \\ Q_1 &= \left\{x = (x_1, x_2, x_3)^T \in \mathbf{R}^3 \mid x_1^2 + x_2 - x_3 \leq 0\right\}, \\ Q_2 &= \left\{x = (x_1, x_2, x_3)^T \in \mathbf{R}^3 \mid \frac{x_1^2}{4} + \frac{x_2^2}{4} + \frac{x_3^2}{9} - 1 \leq 0\right\}, \end{aligned}$$

and

$$A = \begin{pmatrix} 2 & -1 & 3 \\ 4 & 2 & 5 \\ 2 & 0 & 2 \end{pmatrix}.$$

The underlying MSSFP is to find $x^* \in C_1 \bigcap C_2$ *such that* $Ax^* \in Q_1 \bigcap Q_2$.

We use inertial perturbation to accelerate the convergence of the algorithm. For the convenience of comparison, the initial values of the two inertial algorithms are set to be the same. Let $x^0 = x^1$. We use $E_k = \|x^{k+1} - x^k\| / \|x^k\|$ to measure the error of the k-th iterate. If $E_k < 10^{-5}$, then the iteration process stops. We compare our proposed iteration methods HP1 , HP2 with NP1, NP2 and Liu and Tang's Algorithm 2 in [29]. Algorithm 2 is of the form $x^{k+1} = U_{[k]}(x^k - \alpha_k \sum_{j=1}^{r} \beta_j A^*(I - T_j)Ax)$, $\alpha_k \in (0, \frac{2}{\|A\|^2})$. We take $U_{[k]} = P_{C^k_{[k]}}$, $T_j = P_{Q^k_j}$ and $\alpha_k = 0.2 * \frac{1}{\|A\|^2}$, and the algorithm is referred to as LT alg.

The convergence results and the CPU time of the five algorithms are shown in Table 2 and Figure 3. The errors are shown in Figure 4.

The results show that (80) (HP2) outperforms (77) (HP1) for certain initial values. The main reason may be that the self-adaptive step size is more efficient than the one determined by the Armijo-line search. Comparison results of five algorithms and the convergence behavior show that in most cases, the convergence rate of the algorithm can be improved by adding an appropriate perturbation.

Table 2. Numerical results of five algorithms for Example 1.

Choice		NP1	HP1	NP2	HP2	LT alg.
1. $x^0 = (0.1, 0.1, 0.1)^T$	No. of Iter	60	43	219	162	420
	cpu(time)	0.0511	0.0450	0.0362	0.0347	0.0879
2. $x^0 = (-0.4, 0.555, 0.888)^T$	No. of Iter	139	85	195	143	178
	cpu(time)	0.0669	0.0509	0.0342	0.0318	0.0552
3. $x^0 = (1, 2, 3)^T$	No. of Iter	142	89	195	141	178
	cpu(time)	0.0694	0.0490	0.0352	0.0339	0.0551
4. $x^0 = (0.123, 0.745, 0.789)^T$	No. of Iter	149	85	108	77	526
	cpu(time)	0.0590	0.0448	0.0295	0.0268	0.1018

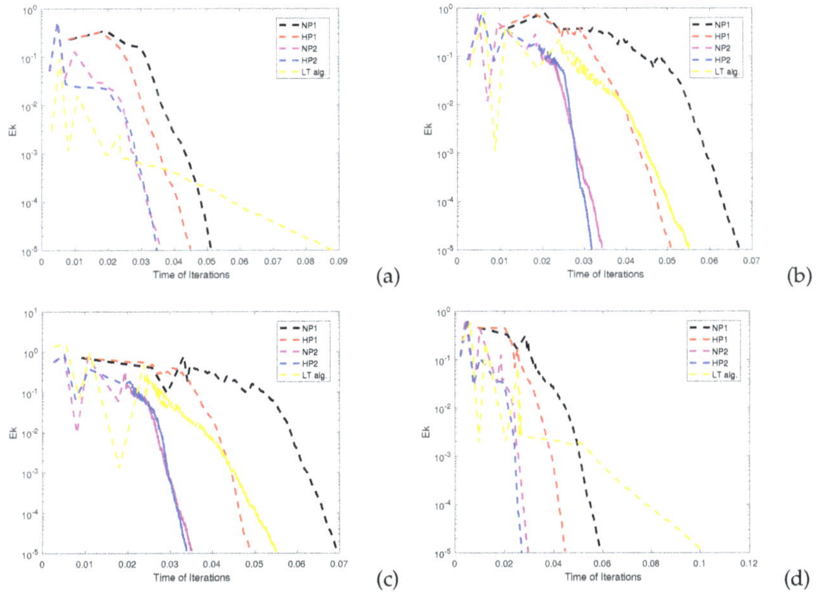

Figure 3. Comparison of CPU times of the algorithms in Example 1: (**a**) Comparison for choice 1. (**b**) Comparison for choice 2. (**c**) Comparison for choice 3. (**d**) Comparison for choice 4.

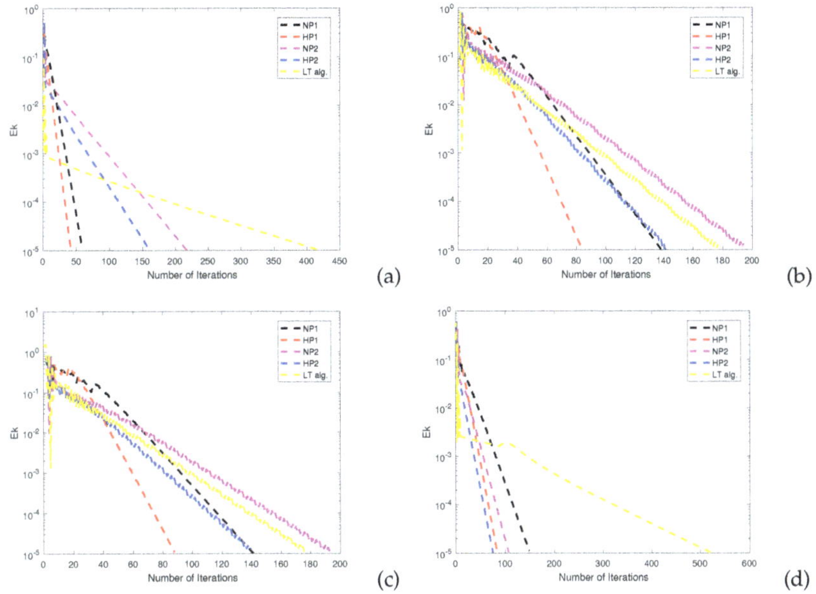

Figure 4. Comparison of iterations of the algorithms in Example 1: (**a**) Comparison for choice 1. (**b**) Comparison for choice 2. (**c**) Comparison for choice 3. (**d**) Comparison for choice 4.

Example 2. *Take* $\mathcal{H}_1 = \mathbf{R}^n$, $\mathcal{H}_2 = \mathbf{R}^m$, $A = (a_{ij})_{m\times n}$ *with* $a_{ij} \in (0,1)$ *generated randomly,* $C_i = \{x \in \mathbf{R}^n \mid \|x - d_i\|_2^2 \le r_i^2\}$, $i = 1, 2, \cdots, t$, $Q_j = \{y \in \mathbf{R}^m \mid \|y - l_j\|_1^2 \le h_j^2\}$, $j = 1, 2, \cdots, r$, *where* $d_i \in [\mathbf{e}_0, 10\mathbf{e}_1]$, $r_i \in [40, 60]$, $l_j \in [\mathbf{e}_0, \mathbf{e}_1]$, $h_j \in [10, 20]$ *are all generated* *randomly. Set* $\beta_1 = \beta_2 = \cdots = \beta_r = \frac{1}{r}$ *and* $\alpha_k = \gamma l^{m_k}$ *for all* $k \geq 1$, $\gamma = 1$, $l = \frac{1}{2}$, $\mu = \frac{1}{2}$, $\theta_k = \frac{1}{4}$, $\rho_k = 0.001$.

We consider using inertial perturbation to accelerate the convergence of the algorithm. If $E_k = \|x^{k+1} - x^k\|/\|x^k\| < 10^{-4}$, then the iteration process stops. Let $x^0 = x^1$. We choose arbitrarily three different initial points and consider iterative steps of the four algorithms with m, n, r, t being different values. See Table 3 for details.

Table 3. Numerical results of the algorithms with and without perturbation for Example 2.

Initial Point		NP1	HP1	NP2	HP2
$r = t = 10$, $m = 15$, $n = 20$					
$x^0 = x^1 = 2 * e_1$	No. of Iter	49	36	1281	999
	cpu(time)	0.1031	0.0669	0.1480	1494
$x^0 = x^1 = 50 * e_1$	No. of Iter	187	121	2297	1669
	cpu(time)	0.2485	0.1536	0.2887	0.1868
$x^0 = x^1 = 100 * rand(n,1)$	No. of Iter	312	225	2357	1811
	cpu(time)	0.4202	0.2908	0.2830	0.2159
$r = t = 10$, $m = n = 40$					
$x^0 = x^1 = 2 * e_1$	No. of Iter	89	66	956	732
	cpu(time)	0.3140	0.1777	0.1534	0.1318
$x^0 = x^1 = 50 * e_1$	No. of Iter	1710	1583	1301	1061
	cpu(time)	4.0390	4.0357	1860	0.1555
$x^0 = x^1 = 100 * rand(n,1)$	No. of Iter	1674	1658	1487	1219
	cpu(time)	4.6581	3.7752	0.2065	0.1762
$r = t = 30$, $m = n = 40$					
$x^0 = x^1 = 2 * e_1$	No. of Iter	136	103	985	753
	cpu(time)	0.6912	0.5174	0.3312	0.2515
$x^0 = x^1 = 50 * e_1$	No. of Iter	1612	1411	1258	968
	cpu(time)	12.3437	11.7164	0.3991	0.3127
$x^0 = x^1 = 100 * rand(n,1)$	No. of Iter	1541	1133	1643	1012
	cpu(time)	11.8273	7.4646	1.0363	0.2965

In this example, we found that the algorithm with Armijo-line search needs fewer iteration steps in relatively low-dimensional spaces. In the case of high-dimensional spaces, the algorithm with self-adaptive step size outperforms in time. Generally, the convergence is improved by inertial perturbations for both algorithms in our paper.

Example 3 ([30]). *Take* $\mathcal{H}_1 = \mathbf{R}^n$, $\mathcal{H}_2 = \mathbf{R}^m$, $A = (a_{ij})_{m\times n}$ *with* $a_{ij} \in (0,1)$ *generated randomly,* $C_i = \{x \in \mathbf{R}^n \mid \|x - d_i\|_2^2 \leq r_i^2\}$, $i = 1,2,\cdots,t$, $Q_j = \{y \in \mathbf{R}^m \mid y^T B_j y + b_j y + c_j \leq 0\}$, $j = 1,2,\cdots,r$, *where* $d_i \in (6\mathbf{e}_0, 16\mathbf{e}_1)$, $r_i \in (100,120)$, $b_j \in (-30\mathbf{e}_1, -20\mathbf{e}_1)$, $c_j \in (-50,-60)$, *and all elements of the matrix* B_j *are all generated randomly in the interval (2,10). Set* $\beta_1 = \beta_2 = \cdots = \beta_r = \frac{1}{r}$ *and* $\alpha_k = \gamma l^{m_k}$ *for all* $k \geq 1$, $\gamma = 1$, $l = \frac{1}{2}$, $\mu = \frac{1}{2}$, $\theta_k = \frac{1}{4}$, $\rho_k = 0.1$.

We consider using inertial perturbation to accelerate the convergence of the algorithm. The stopping criterion is defined by $E_k = \frac{1}{2}\sum_{i=1}^{t} \|x^k - P_{C_i^k} x^k\|^2 + \frac{1}{2}\sum_{j=1}^{r} \|Ax^k - P_{Q_j^k} Ax^k\|^2 < 10^{-4}$. Let $x^0 = x^1$. The details are shown in Table 4.

Table 4. Results of Armijo-line search and self-adaptive algorithms for Example 3.

Initial Point		NP1	HP1	NP2	HP2
$r = t = 10,\ m = n = 20$					
$x^0 = x^1 = e_1$	No. of Iter	477	357	2268	1700
	cpu(time)	1.2453	0.9267	1.0516	0.8038
$x^0 = x^1 = 50 * e_1$	No. of Iter	757	564	3291	2470
	cpu(time)	1.6205	1.2805	1.5623	1.1023
$x^0 = x^1 = 100 * rand(n, 1)$	No. of Iter	996	737	4323	3231
	cpu(time)	1.9087	1.4396	1.9696	1.4493
$r = t = 20,\ m = 40,\ n = 50$					
$x^0 = x^1 = e_1$	No. of Iter	1256	941	5336	4001
	cpu(time)	12.1310	4.0061	5.9165	4.0919
$x^0 = x^1 = 50 * e_1$	No. of Iter	1492	1105	6917	5221
	cpu(time)	12.6430	8.2382	12.9631	9.4880
$x^0 = x^1 = 100 * rand(n, 1)$	No. of Iter	2101	1835	9936	9226
	cpu(time)	16.4070	13.2868	14.9611	12.8079
$r = t = 40,\ m = n = 60$					
$x^0 = x^1 = e_1$	No. of Iter	1758	1317	8328	6245
	cpu(time)	48.2570	38.0668	30.6759	23.4267
$x^0 = x^1 = 50 * e_1$	No. of Iter	2503	1777	12,905	8677
	cpu(time)	59.2127	44.7915	49.5823	32.6868
$x^0 = x^1 = 100 * rand(n, 1)$	No. of Iter	2274	1474	18,781	13,952
	cpu(time)	58.2569	38.1917	72.6622	54.9814

We can see from Table 4 that the convergence rate is improved by inertial perturbations for both algorithms. In most cases, the algorithm with step size determined by Armijo-line search outperforms the one with self-adaptive step size in the number of iterations, whereas the latter outperforms the former in CPU time.

6. Conclusions

In this paper, for the MSSFP, we present two relaxed CQ algorithms with different kinds of self-adaptive step size and discuss their bounded perturbation resilience. Treating appropriate inertial terms as bounded perturbations, we construct the inertial acceleration versions of the corresponding algorithms. For the real-life LASSO problem and three experimental examples, we numerically compare the performance with or without inertial perturbation of the algorithms and also compare the performance of the proposed algorithms with Yang's algorithm [3], and Liu and Tang's algorithm [29]. The results show the efficiency of the proposed algorithms and the validity of the inertial perturbation.

Author Contributions: Both the authors contributed equally to this work. Both authors have read and agreed to the published version of the manuscript.

Funding: The authors was supported by the National Natural Science Foundation under Grant No. 61503385 and No. 11705279, and the Fundamental Research Funds for the Central Universities No. 3122018L004.

Institutional Review Board Statement: Not applicable.

Informed Consent Statement: Not applicable.

Data Availability Statement: Not applicable.

Acknowledgments: The authors would also like to thank the editors and the reviewers for their constructive suggestions and comments, which greatly improved the manuscript.

Conflicts of Interest: The authors declare no conflict of interest.

References

1. Byrne, C. Iterative oblique projection onto convex sets and the split feasibility problem. *Inverse Probl.* **2002**, *18*, 441–453. [CrossRef]
2. Byrne, C. A unified treatment of some iterative algorithms in signal processing and image reconstruction. *Inverse Probl.* **2004**, *20*, 103–120. [CrossRef]
3. Yang, Q.Z. The relaxed CQ algorithm solving the split feasibility problem. *Inverse Probl.* **2004**, *20*, 1261–1266. [CrossRef]
4. Censor, Y.; Elfving, T.; Kopf, N.; Bortfeld, T. The multiple-sets spilt feasibility problem and its applications for inverse problems. *Inverse Probl.* **2005**, *21*, 2071–2084. [CrossRef]
5. He, S.N.; Zhao, Z.Y.; Luo, B. A relaxed self-adaptive CQ algorithm for the multiple-sets split feasibility problem. *Optimization* **2015**, *64*, 1907–1918. [CrossRef]
6. Yang, Q.Z. On variable-step relaxed projection algorithm for variational inequalities. *J. Math. Anal. Appl.* **2005**, *302*, 166–179. [CrossRef]
7. López, G.; Martín-Márquez, V.; Wang, F.H.; Xu, H.K. Solving the split feasibility problem without prior knowledge of matrix norms. *Inverse Probl.* **2012**, *28*, 374–389. [CrossRef]
8. Gibali, A.; Liu, L.W.; Tang, Y.C. Note on the the modified relaxation CQ algorithm for the split feasibility problem. *Optim. Lett.* **2018**, *12*, 817–830. [CrossRef]
9. Chen, Y.; Guo, Y.; Yu, Y.; Chen, R. Self-adaptive and relaxed self-adaptive projection methods for solving the multiple-set split feasibility problem. *Abstr. Appl. Anal.* **2012**, *2012*, 958040. [CrossRef]
10. Xu, H.K. Iterative methods for the split feasibility problem in infinite-dimensional Hilbert spaces. *Inverse Probl.* **2010**, *26*, 105018. [CrossRef]
11. Xu, H.K. A variable Krasnosel'skii-Mann algorithm and the multiple-set split feasibility problem. *Inverse Probl.* **2006**, *22*, 2021–2034. [CrossRef]
12. Yao, Y.H.; Postolache, M.; Liou, Y.C. Strong convergence of a self-adaptive method for the split feasibility problem. *Fixed Point Theory Appl.* **2013**, *2013*, 201. [CrossRef]
13. Guo, Y.N.; Cui, W.; Guo, Y.S. Perturbation resilience of proximal gradient algorithm for composite objectives. *J. Nonlinear Sci. Appl.* **2017**, *10*, 5566–5575. [CrossRef]
14. Guo, Y.N.; Cui, W. Strong convergence and bounded perturbation resilience of a modified proximal gradient algorithm. *J. Inequalities Appl.* **2018**, *2018*, 103. [CrossRef] [PubMed]
15. Pakkaranang, N.; Kumam, P.; Berinde, V.; Suleiman, Y.I. Superiorization methodology and perturbation resilience of inertial proximal gradient algorithm with application to signal recovery. *J. Supercomput.* **2020**, *76*, 9456–9477. [CrossRef]
16. Jin, W.M.; Censor, Y.; Jiang, M. Bounded perturbation resilience of projected scaled gradient methods. *Comput. Optim. Appl.* **2016**, *63*, 365–392. [CrossRef]
17. Xu, H.K. Bound perturbation resilience and superiorization techniques for the projected scaled gradient method. *Inverse Probl.* **2017**, *33*, 044008. [CrossRef]
18. Dong, Q.L.; Gibali, A.; Jiang, D.; Tang, Y. Bounded perturbation resilience of extragradient-type methods and their applications. *J. Inequalities Appl.* **2017**, *2017*, 280. [CrossRef] [PubMed]
19. Duan, P.C.; Zheng, X.B. Bounded perturbation resilience of generalized viscosity iterative algorithm for split variational inclusion problem. *Appl. Set-Valued Anal. Optim.* **2020**, *2*, 49–61.
20. Censor, Y.; Zaslavski, A.J. Convergence and perturbation resilience of dynamic string-averaging projection methods. *Comput. Optim. Appl.* **2013**, *54*, 65–76. [CrossRef]
21. Kaewyong, N.; Sitthithakerngkiet, K. A self-adaptive algorithm for the common solution of the split minimization problem and the fixed point problem. *Axioms* **2021**, *10*, 109. [CrossRef]
22. Shehu, Y.; Dong, Q.L.; Liu, L.L. Global and linear convergence of alternated inertial methods for split feasibility problems. *R. Acad. Sci.* **2021**, *115*, 53.
23. Li, H.Y.; Wu, Y.L.; Wang, F.H. New inertial relaxed CQ algorithms for solving split feasibility problems in Hilbert spaces. *J. Math.* **2021**, *2021*, 6624509. [CrossRef]
24. Bauschke, H.H.; Combettes, P.L. *Convex Analysis and Monotone Operator Theory in Hilbert Space*; Springer: London, UK, 2011.
25. Bauschke, H.H.; Combettes, P.L. A weak-to-strong convergence principle for Fejér-monntone methods in Hilbert spaces. *Math. Oper. Res.* **2001**, *26*, 248–264. [CrossRef]
26. Wen, M.; Peng, J.G.; Tang, Y.C. A cyclic and simultaneous iterative method for solving the multiple-sets split feasibility problem. *J. Optim. Theory Appl.* **2015**, *166*, 844–860. [CrossRef]
27. Sun, J.; Dang, Y.Z.; Xu, H.L. Inertial accelerated algorithms for solving a split feasibility problem. *J. Ind. Manag. Optim.* **2017**, *13*, 1383–1394.
28. Tang, Y.C.; Zhu, C.X.; Yu, H. Iterative methods for solving the multiple-sets split feasibility problem with splitting self-adaptive step size. *Fixed Point Theory Appl.* **2015**, *2015*, 178. [CrossRef]

29. Liu, L.W.; Tang, Y.C. Several iterative algorithms for solving the split common fixed point problem of directed operators with applications. *Optim. A J. Math. Program. Oper. Res.* **2016**, *65*, 53–65.
30. Zhao, J.L.; Yang, Q.Z. Self-adaptive projection methods for the multiple-sets split feasibility problem. *Inverse Probl.* **2011**, *27*, 035009. [CrossRef]

axioms

MDPI

Article

A Non-Standard Finite Difference Scheme for a Diffusive HIV-1 Infection Model with Immune Response and Intracellular Delay

Xiao-Lan Liu [1] and Cheng-Cheng Zhu [2,*]

[1] School of Arts and Science, Suqian University, Suqian 223800, China; xiaolanmathe@126.com
[2] School of Science, Jiangnan University, Wuxi 214122, China
* Correspondence: chengchengzhu@jiangnan.edu.cn

Abstract: In this paper, we propose and study a diffusive HIV infection model with infected cells delay, virus mature delay, abstract function incidence rate and a virus diffusion term. By introducing the reproductive numbers for viral infection R_0 and for CTL immune response number R_1 , we show that R_0 and R_1 act as threshold parameter for the existence and stability of equilibria. If $R_0 \leq 1$, the infection-free equilibrium E_0 is globally asymptotically stable, and the viruses are cleared; if $R_1 \leq 1 < R_0$, the CTL-inactivated equilibrium E_1 is globally asymptotically stable, and the infection becomes chronic but without persistent CTL response; if $R_1 > 1$, the CTL-activated equilibrium E_2 is globally asymptotically stable, and the infection is chronic with persistent CTL response. Next, we study the dynamic of the discreted system of our model by using non-standard finite difference scheme. We find that the global stability of the equilibria of the continuous model and the discrete model is not always consistent. That is, if $R_0 \leq 1$, or $R_1 \leq 1 < R_0$, the global stability of the two kinds model is consistent. However, if $R_1 > 1$, the global stability of the two kinds model is not consistent. Finally, numerical simulations are carried out to illustrate the theoretical results and show the effects of diffusion factors on the time-delay virus model.

Keywords: basic reproduction number; equilibrium; global stability; immune response; nonstandard finite difference scheme; numerical simulation

MSC: 35C07; 35K55; 35K57; 92D25

Citation: Liu, X.-L.; Zhu, C.-C. A Non-Standard Finite Difference Scheme for a Diffusive HIV-1 Infection Model with Immune Response and Intracellular Delay. *Axioms* **2022**, *11*, 129. https://doi.org/10.3390/axioms11030129

Academic Editors: Wei-Shih Du, Luigi Muglia, Adrian Petrusel and Hans J. Haubold

Received: 27 January 2022
Accepted: 10 March 2022
Published: 12 March 2022

Publisher's Note: MDPI stays neutral with regard to jurisdictional claims in published maps and institutional affiliations.

Copyright: © 2022 by the authors. Licensee MDPI, Basel, Switzerland. This article is an open access article distributed under the terms and conditions of the Creative Commons Attribution (CC BY) license (https://creativecommons.org/licenses/by/4.0/).

1. Introduction

In the past few years, host-virus dynamics models have been developed to explain the interactions between virus and target T cells, much attention has been given to the role of the immune response to human immunodeficiency virus (HIV) infection. Many different mechanisms of immune system, defenses against viral infections are of interest because lots of the diseases caused by them, e.g., hepatitis B and AIDS, are chronic and incurable [1,2]. With the new coronavirus epidemic rages around the world [3–5], virus dynamics has become a hot spot again. In the immune response mechanism in vivo for viral infections, the cytotoxic T lymphocyte (CTL) plays a particularly important role, therefore many authors have examined various CTL dynamics.

A virus must take over host cells and use them to replicate because it can not replicate on its own. HIV targets the $CD4^+T$ cells, often referred to as "helper" T cells, when it invades the body. These cells can be considered "messengers" , or the command centres of the immune system. They send signal to other immune cells that an invader is to be fought. Once invaded by the viruses, these infected cells will cause a cytotoxic T-lymphocyte (CTL) response from the immune system. The immune response cells, or cytotoxic lymphocytes, respond to this message and set out to eliminate infection by killing infected cells. Through the lysis of the infected cells, the viruses are prevented from further replication [2]. The

CTL response is also striking in that it sometime does damage to the body when it tries to clear the virus. Over half the tissue damage caused by hepatitis is actually caused by the CTL response [1,6].

If the immune system is functioning normally, these components work together efficiently and an infection is eliminated quickly, causing only temporary discomfort to the host. However, over time HIV is able to deplete the population of $CD4^+T$ cells. What remains unknown is the exact mechanism by which this occurs, but several models have been suggested. For a variety of different hypotheses of how this occurs, we refer the reader to papers [7–9]. The natural killer cells may be fit to eliminate infection, but they are never deployed, which is the the impact of the depletion of $CD4^+T$ cells on the host. This then culminates in a clinical problem wherein the patient becomes vulnerable to infections that a healthy immune system would normally handle.

Quite a lot of mathematical models of HIV have been set up. The classical model is a system with three ordinary differential equations [10,11]. To better understanding the dynamics of these infections, many mathematical models have been proposed by using different kinds of differential equations, see [12–16] and references therein. For example, Yang et al. [15] studied the following model

$$\begin{cases} \frac{\partial T(x,t)}{\partial t} = \lambda - d_1 T(x,t) - \beta_1 T(x,t)V(x,t), \\ \frac{\partial I(x,t)}{\partial t} = \beta_1 T(x,t)V(x,t) - d_2 I(x,t), \\ \frac{\partial V(x,t)}{\partial t} = d\Delta V(x,t) + \gamma I(x,t) - d_3 V(x,t), \end{cases} \tag{1}$$

where $T(x,t), I(x,t)$ and $V(x,t)$ denote the densities of uninfected cells, infected cells and free virus cells at position x at time t, respectively. λ stands for the recruitment rate of the uninfected cells; β_1 is the virus-to-cell infection rate; d_1, d_2 and d_3 represent death rates of uninfected cells, infected cells and free viruses; γ stands for the recruitment rate for free viruses; d stands for the diffusion coefficient and Δ is the Laplacian operator.

To help the body heal, cytotoxic T-lymphocyte effectors ($CTLe$) of the immune system will remove the infected cells to prevent further viral replications. To model these extra dynamics, researchers have studied the model of viral interaction with CTL response [10,17]

$$\begin{cases} \dot{x} = \lambda - dx - \beta xy, \\ \dot{y} = \beta xy - ay - pyz, \\ \dot{z} = cyz - bz, \end{cases} \tag{2}$$

where variables x, y and z denote the density of the healthy cells, the infected cells, and the $CTLs$ populations, respectively. Healthy cells are produced at rate λ and their natural mortality is dx; these cells may come into contact with the virus and become infected cells at rate βxy, infected cells's natural mortality is ay, and they are removed by $CTLs$ at rate pyz; the CTL population increases at the rate cyz and they are removed at the rate bz.

In [18,19], researchers studied a mathematical model for HIV-1 infection with both intracellular delay and cell-mediated immune response:

$$\begin{cases} \frac{dx(t)}{dt} = \lambda - dx(t) - \beta xv, \\ \frac{dy(t)}{dt} = e^{-a\tau}\beta x(t-\tau)v(t-\tau) - ay(t) - py(t)z(t), \\ \frac{dv(t)}{dt} = ky(t) - \mu v(t), \\ \frac{dz(t)}{dt} = cy(t)z(t) - bz(t). \end{cases} \tag{3}$$

Researchers obtain the global stability of the infection-free equilibrium and give many conditions for the local stability of the two infection equilibria: one without $CTLs$ being activated and the other with. There are many references in the dynamics of HIV-1 infection with $CTLs$ response (see, e.g., [17,20–22] and the references therein).

However, there is no diffusion term and only one delay in (3). As we know, the virus is not stationary in space, the movement of the virus in space leads to the spatial spread of the disease, and mostly with general nonlinear incidence rate. Fickian diffusion can reasonably describe the spread of this virus in space and this diffusion process is often represented by the Laplace operator. Inspired by [16,23] , in this paper, we extend the classic model of virus dynamics to a diffusive infection model with intracellular delay and cell-mediated immune response, with two delays and general nonlinear incidence rate, as follows

$$\begin{cases} \frac{\partial T(x,t)}{\partial t} = \lambda - d_1 T(x,t) - \beta_1 T(x,t) f\Big(V(x,t)\Big) - \beta_2 T(x,t) g\Big(I(x,t)\Big), \\ \frac{\partial I(x,t)}{\partial t} = e^{-\mu_1\tau_1}\Big(\beta_1 T(x,t-\tau_1) f\Big(V(x,t-\tau_1)\Big) + \beta_2 T(x,t-\tau_1) g(I(x,t-\tau_1))\Big) \\ \quad -d_2 I(x,t) - p_1 I(x,t) Z(x,t), \\ \frac{\partial V(x,t)}{\partial t} = D\Delta V(x,t) + p_2 e^{-\mu_2\tau_2} I(x,t-\tau_2) - d_3 V(x,t), \\ \frac{\partial Z(x,t)}{\partial t} = q I(x,t) Z(x,t) - d_4 Z(x,t), \end{cases} \tag{4}$$

here $T(x,t), I(x,t), V(x,t)$ and $Z(x,t)$ stand for the densities of uninfected cells, infected cells, virus cells and $CTLs$ at position x at time t, respectively. λ and d_1 denote the natural produce and mortality rate of uninfected cells, and uninfected cells are infected with a rate β_2; and β_1 is the virus-to-cell infection rate; and β_1 is the virus-to-cell infection rate; the natural mortality rate of the infected cells are d_2 and are killed by CTL with a rate p_1 (Note that d_2 reflects the combined effects of natural death rate of uninfected cells, d_1, and any additional cytotoxic effects the virus may have); μ_1 represents the death rate for infected but not yet virus-producing cells, τ_1 represents the latent delay, i.e., the time period from being infected to becoming productive infected cells. Therefore, the probability of surviving from time $t-\tau_1$ to time t is $e^{-\mu_1\tau_1}$; the probability of survival of immature virus is denoted by $e^{-\mu_2\tau_2}$ and the average life time of an immature virus is $\frac{1}{\mu_2}$; where τ_2 represents the time necessary for the newly produced virus to become mature; D is the diffusion coefficient and Δ is the Laplacian operator; p_2 is the recruitment rate for free viruses. Virus particles are removed from the system at rate d_3; q stands for the CTL responsiveness and d_4 denotes decay rate for $CTLs$ in the absence of stimulation.

Here, the incidences are assumed to be the nonlinear responses to the concentrations of virus particles and infected cells, using the forms $\beta_1 Tf(V)$ and $\beta_2 Tg(I)$, where $f(V)$ and $g(I)$ are the force of infection by virus particles and infected cells and satisfy the following properties [24]:

$$f(0) = g(0) = 0, f'(V) > 0, g'(I) > 0, f''(V) \le 0, g''(I) \le 0. \tag{A_1}$$

It follows from (A_1) and the Mean Value Theorem that

$$f'(V)V \le f(V) \le f'(0)V, g'(I)I \le g(I) \le g'(0)I, for I, V \ge 0. \tag{A_2}$$

Epidemiologically, condition (A_1) implies that : (1) the disease cannot spread if there is no infection; (2) the incidences $\beta_1 Tf(V)$ and $\beta_2 Tg(I)$ become faster when the densities of the virus particles and infected cells increase; (3) the per capita infection rates by virus particles and infected cells will slow down as certain inhibiting effect since (A_2) implies that $(\frac{f(V)}{V})' \le 0$ and $(\frac{g(I)}{I})' \le 0$. The incidence rate with condition (A_1) contains the bilinear and the saturation incidences.

In this paper, we will consider the system (4) with initial conditions

$$\begin{aligned} &T(x,s) = \phi_1(x,s) \ge 0, I(x,s) = \phi_2(x,s) \ge 0, \\ &V(x,s) = \phi_3(x,s) \ge 0, Z(x,s) = \phi_4(x,s) \ge 0, (x,s) \in \bar{\Omega} \times [-\tau, 0] \end{aligned} \tag{5}$$

and homogeneous Neumann boundary conditions

$$\frac{\partial V}{\partial n} = 0, t > 0, x \in \partial\Omega. \tag{6}$$

where $\tau = \max\{\tau_1, \tau_2\}$ and Ω is a bounded domain in R^4 with smooth boundary $\partial\Omega$, and $\frac{\partial V}{\partial n}$ stands for the outward normal derivative on $\partial\Omega$.

Usually, the exact solution for a system as (1) is difficult or even impossible to be determined. Hence, researchers seek numerical ones instead. However, how to choose the proper discrete scheme so that the global dynamics of solutions of the corresponding continuous models can be efficiently preserved is still an open problem [25]. Mickens has made an attempt in this connection, by presenting a robust non-standard finite difference (NSFD)scheme [26], which has been widely employed in the study of different epidemic models [23,25–32]. For example, Yang et al. [30] applied the NSFD scheme to discretize system (1) and found that the dynamical behaviors of the discrete model are consistent with the original system. Motivated by the work of [23,25–32], we apply the NSFD scheme to discretize system (4) and obtain:

$$\begin{cases} \frac{T^m_{n+1}-T^m_n}{\Delta t} = \lambda - d_1 T^m_{n+1} - \beta_1 T^m_{n+1} f(V^m_n) - \beta_2 T^m_{n+1} g(I^m_n), \\ \frac{I^m_{n+1}-I^m_n}{\Delta t} = e^{-\mu_1\tau_1}\Big(\beta_1 T^m_{n-m_1+1} f(V^m_{n-m_1}) + \beta_2 T^m_{n-m_1+1} g(I^m_{n-m_1})\Big) \\ \qquad -d_2 I^m_{n+1} - p_1 I^m_{n+1} Z^m_n, \\ \frac{V^m_{n+1}-V^m_n}{\Delta t} = D\frac{V^{m+1}_{n+1} - 2V^m_{n+1} + V^{m-1}_{n+1}}{(\Delta x)^2} + p_2 e^{-\mu_2\tau_2} I^m_{n-m_2+1} - d_3 V^m_{n+1}, \\ \frac{Z^m_{n+1}-Z^m_n}{\Delta t} = q I^m_{n+1} Z^m_n - d_4 Z^m_{n+1}. \end{cases} \tag{7}$$

Here, we assume that $x \in \Omega = [a, b]$, let $\Delta t > 0$ be the time step size and $\Delta x = \frac{b-a}{N}$ be the space step size with N a positive integer. Suppose that there exist two integers $m_1, m_2 \in \aleph$ with $\tau_1 = m_1\Delta t, \tau_2 = m_2\Delta t$. Denote the mesh grid point as $\{(x_m, t_n), m = 0, 1, 2, \cdots, N, n \in N\}$ with $x_m = a + m\Delta x$ and $t_n = n\Delta t$. At each point, we use approximations of $\Big(T(x_m, t_n), I(x_m, t_n), V(x_m, t_n), Z(x_m, t_n)\Big)$ by $(T^m_n, I^m_n, V^m_n, Z^m_n)$. We set all the approximation solutions at the time t_n by the $N + 1$-dimensional vector $U_n = (U^0_n, U^1_n, \cdots, U^N_n)^T$, where $U^{(\cdot)}_n \in \{(T_n, I_n, V_n, Z_n)\}$ and the notation $(\cdot)^T$ is the transposition of a vector. $U_n \geq 0$ means that all components of a vector U_n are nonnegative. The discrete initial conditions of system (7) are given as

$$\begin{array}{l} T^m_s = \phi_1(x_m, t_s) \geq 0, I^m_s = \phi_2(x_m, t_s) \geq 0, \\ V^m_s = \phi_3(x_m, t_s) \geq 0, Z^m_s = \phi_4(x_m, t_s) \geq 0, \end{array} \tag{8}$$

for all $s = -l, -l + 1, \cdots, 0,\ l = \max\{m_1, m_2\}$, and the discrete boundary conditions are

$$V^{-1}_n = V^0_n, V^N_n = V^{N+1}_n, for\ \ n \in \aleph.$$

The main purpose of this paper is to investigate the asymptotic stability of system (4) and (7). Another purpose of this paper is to discuss , whether the discretized system (7) that derived by using NSFD scheme can efficiently preserves the global asymptotic stability of the equilibria to the original system (4) or not.

The paper is organized as follows. In Section 2.1, the model is introduced, and, under some assumptions, positivity and boundedness properties of the solutions are proved by using nonlinear functional analysis methods. In Section 2.2, we consider the existence of infection-free equilibrium, CTL-inactivated equilibrium and infection equilibrium with immunity. In Section 2.3, by introducing the reproductive numbers for viral infection R_0 and for CTL immune response number R_1 , we show that R_0 and R_1 act as threshold parameter for the existence and stability of equilibria. If $R_0 \leq 1$, the infection-free equilibrium E_0 is globally asymptotically stable, and the viruses are cleared; if $R_1 \leq 1 < R_0$, the CTL-inactivated equilibrium E_1 is globally asymptotically stable, and the infection becomes chronic but without persistent CTL response; if $R_1 > 1$, the CTL-activated equilibrium E_2 is globally asymptotically stable, and the infection is chronic with persistent CTL response. In Section 3, we investigate the global dynamics of discrete system (7) correponding to the continuous system (4), by using nonstandard finite difference scheme. We find that the global stability of the equilibria of the continuous model and the discrete model is not always consistent. That is, if $R_0 \leq 1$, or $R_1 \leq 1 < R_0$, the global stability of the two kinds model is consistent. However, if $R_1 > 1$, the global stability of the two kinds model is not consistent. In Section 4, some numerical simulations are given to illustrate the theoretical results and show the effects of diffusion factors on the time-delay virus model. The paper ends with a discussion in Section 5.

2. Dynamical Behaviors of Continuous System

2.1. Positivity and Boundedness of Solutions

In order to study positivity and boundedness of solutions to system (4), we first introduce some notations.

Assume $X = C(\bar{\Omega}, \mathbb{R}^4)$ be the space of continuous functions from the topological space $\bar{\Omega}$ into the space $\mathbb{R}^4$. Let $C = C([-\tau, 0], X)$ be the Banach space of continuous functions from $[-\tau, 0]$ into X with the usual supremum normal. $\phi \in C$ is defined by

$$\phi(x,s) = \phi(s)(x).$$

Define $x_t(s) = x(t+s), s \in [-\tau, 0]$, where $x(\cdot) : [-\tau, \sigma) \to X$ is a continuous function from $[0, \sigma)$ to C.

Theorem 1. *For any $\phi \in C$,*
(a) system (4)–(6) has a unique solution defined on $[0, +\infty)$; and
(b) the solution of (4)–(6) is nonnegative and bounded for all $t \geq 0$.

Proof. For any $\phi = (\phi_1, \phi_2, \phi_3, \phi_4)^T \in C$ and $x \in \bar{\Omega}$, assume

$$F = (F_1, F_2, F_3, F_4) : C \to X$$

by

$$\begin{cases} F_1(\phi)(x) = \lambda - d_1\phi_1(x,0) - \beta_1\phi_1(x,0)f\left(\phi_3(x,0)\right) - \beta_2\phi_1(x,0)g\left(\phi_2(x,0)\right), \\ F_2(\phi)(x) = e^{-\mu_1\tau_1}\left[\beta_1\phi_1(x,-\tau_1)f\left(\phi_3(x,-\tau_1)\right) + \beta_2\phi_1(x,-\tau_1)g\left(\phi_2(x,-\tau_1)\right)\right] \\ \qquad -d_2\phi_2(x,0) - p_1\phi_2(x,0)\phi_4(x,0), \\ F_3(\phi)(x) = p_2e^{-\mu_2\tau_2}k\phi_2(x,-\tau_2) - d_3\phi_3(x,0), \\ F_4(\phi)(x) = q\phi_2(x,0)\phi_4(x,0) - d_4\phi_4(x,0). \end{cases}$$

Then system (4)–(6) can be rewritten as following form

$$\begin{cases} U'(t) = AU + F(U_t), t > 0, \\ U(0) = \phi \in X, \end{cases} \tag{9}$$

where $U = (T, I, V, Z)^T, \phi = (\phi_1, \phi_2, \phi_3, \phi_4)^T$ and $AU = (0, 0, d\Delta v, 0)^T$. It is clear that the operator F is locally Lipschitz in space X. From [27,32–36], we conclude that system (9) has a unique local solution on $t \in [0, T_{max})$, where T_{max} is the maximal existence time for solution of system (4). In addition, it follows from 0 is a sub-solution of each equation of system (4) that $T(x,t) \geq 0, I(x,t) \geq 0, V(x,t) \geq 0, Z(x,t) \geq 0$.

Next, we prove the boundedness of solutions. Let

$$G_1(x,t) = e^{-\mu_1\tau_1}T(x, t-\tau_1) + I(x,t) + \frac{p_1}{q}Z(x,t),$$

then

$$\begin{aligned} \frac{\partial G_1(x,t)}{\partial t} &= \lambda e^{-\mu_1\tau_1} - d_1 e^{-\mu_1\tau_1} T(x,t-\tau_1) - d_2 I(x,t) - \frac{p_1 d_4}{q} Z(x,t) \\ &\le \lambda - \tilde{d} G_1(x,t), \end{aligned}$$

where $\tilde{d} = min\{d_1, d_2, d_4\}$, then

$$G_1(x,t) \le max\left\{\frac{\lambda}{\tilde{d}}, max_{x\in\bar{\Omega}}\left\{e^{-\mu_1\tau_1}\phi_1(x,-\tau_1) + \phi_2(x,0) + \frac{p_1}{q}\phi_3(x,0)\right\}\right\} = \xi_1,$$

so $T(x,t)$,$I(x,t)$ and $Z(x,t)$ are bounded.

From the boundedness of $I(x,t)$ and system (4)–(6), $V(x,t)$ satisfies the following system

$$\begin{cases} \frac{\partial V}{\partial t} - D\Delta V \le p_2 e^{-\mu_2\tau_2}\xi_1 - d_3 V, \\ \frac{\partial V}{\partial n} = 0, \\ V(x,0) = \phi_3(x,0) \ge 0. \end{cases} \tag{2}$$

Assume $V_1(t)$ be a solution to the ordinary differential equation

$$\begin{cases} \frac{dV_1}{dt} = p_2 e^{-\mu_2\tau_2}\xi_1 - d_3 V_1, \\ V_1(0) = max_{x\in\bar{\Omega}}\phi_3(x,0), \end{cases} \tag{3}$$

then

$$V_1(t) \le max\left\{\frac{p_2 e^{-\mu_2\tau_2}\xi_1}{d_3}, max_{x\in\bar{\Omega}}\phi_3(x,0)\right\}, \quad \forall t \in [0, T_{max}).$$

It follows from the comparison principle [37] that $V(x,t) \le V_1(t)$. Therefore

$$V(x,t) \le max\left\{\frac{p_2 e^{-\mu_2\tau_2}\xi_1}{d_3}, max_{x\in\bar{\Omega}}\phi_3(x,0)\right\} = \xi_2, \quad \forall (x,t) \in \bar{\Omega} \times [0, T_{max}).$$

From the above, $T(x,t), I(x,t), V(x,t)$ and $Z(x,t)$ are bounded in $\bar{\Omega} \times [0, T_{max})$. Furthermore, it follows from the standard theory for semilinear parabolic systems [38] that $T_{max} = +\infty$. □

2.2. Existence of Equilibria

It is clear that system (4) always has an infection-free equilibrium

$$E_0 = (T_0, 0, 0, 0),$$

where $T_0 = \frac{\lambda}{d}$, corresponding to the maximal level of healthy CD_4^+T cells. It is the only biologically meaningful equilibrium if

$$R_0 = \frac{\lambda e^{-\mu_1\tau_1}(\beta_1 p_2 f'^{-\mu_2\tau_2} + \beta_2 d_3 g'(0))}{d_1 d_2 d_3} < 1,$$

where R_0 is basic reproduction number.

At an equilibrium of model (4), we have

$$\begin{cases} \lambda = d_1 T + \beta_1 T f(V) + \beta_2 T g(I), \\ e^{-\mu_1\tau_1}\left(\beta_1 T f(V) + \beta_2 T g(I)\right) = d_2 I + p_1 I Z, \\ p_2 e^{-\mu_2\tau_2} I = d_3 V, \\ q I Z = d_4 Z, \end{cases} \tag{4}$$

if $Z = 0$, then a short calculation

$$\lambda - d_1 T = \frac{d_2 d_3 e^{\mu_1\tau_1+\mu_2\tau_2}}{p_2} V, I = \frac{d_3 e^{\mu_2\tau_2}}{p_2} V,$$

which implies that in order to have $T \geq 0$ and $V > 0$ at an equilibrium, then $V \in (0, \frac{\lambda p_2}{d_2 d_3 e^{\mu_1\tau_1+\mu_2\tau_2}}]$. From the second equation of (4), we have

$$T = \frac{d_2 d_3 e^{\mu_1\tau_1+\mu_2\tau_2}}{p_2\Big(\beta_1 f(V) + \beta_2 g(\frac{d_3 e^{\mu_2\tau_2}}{p_2} V)\Big)} V,$$

then substituting T into the first equation of (4)

$$\lambda = \frac{d_1 d_2 d_3 e^{\mu_1\tau_1+\mu_2\tau_2}}{p_2\Big(\beta_1 f(V) + \beta_2 g(\frac{d_3 e^{\mu_2\tau_2}}{p_2} V)\Big)} V + \frac{d_2 d_3 \mu e^{\mu_1\tau_1+\mu_2\tau_2}}{p_2} V = H(V).$$

According to (A_2), for all $V > 0$, we have

$$\begin{aligned} H'(V) &= \frac{d_1 d_2 d_3 e^{\mu_1\tau_1+\mu_2\tau_2}\Big(\beta_1(f(V) - Vf'(V)) + \beta_2\Big(g(\frac{d_3 e^{\mu_2\tau_2}}{p_2}V) - \frac{d_3 e^{\mu_2\tau_2}}{p_2} V g'(\frac{d_3 e^{\mu_2\tau_2}}{p_2}V)\Big)\Big)}{p_2(\beta_1 f(V) + \beta_2 g(\frac{d_3 e^{\mu_2\tau_2}}{p_2}V))^2} \\ &+ \frac{d_2 d_3 e^{\mu_1\tau_1+\mu_2\tau_2}}{p_2} > 0, \end{aligned}$$

further, from (A_1)

$$\lim_{V \to 0^+} H(V) = \frac{d_1 d_2 d_3 e^{\mu_1\tau_1+\mu_2\tau_2}}{p_2\beta_1 f'(0) + d_3\beta_2 e^{\mu_2\tau_2} g'(0)} = \frac{\lambda}{R_0},$$

and

$$H(\frac{\lambda p_2}{d_2 d_3 e^{\mu_1\tau_1+\mu_2\tau_2}}) = \lambda + \frac{\lambda d_1}{\beta_1 f\Big(\frac{\lambda p_2}{d_2 d_3 e^{\mu_1\tau_1+\mu_2\tau_2}}\Big) + \beta_2 g\Big(\frac{\lambda}{d_2 e^{\mu_1\tau_1}}\Big)} > \lambda,$$

this implies that there exists a CTL-inactivated equilibrium $E_1 = (T_1, I_1, V_1, 0)$ when $R_0 > 1$.

Define

$$R_1 = \frac{\lambda q e^{-\mu_1\tau_1}\Big(\beta_1 f(\frac{d_4 p_2 e^{-\mu_2\tau_2}}{d_3 q}) + \beta_2 g(\frac{d_4}{q})\Big)}{d_2 d_4\Big(d_1 + \beta_1 f(\frac{d_4 p_2 e^{-\mu_2\tau_2}}{d_3 q}) + \beta_2 g(\frac{d_4}{q})\Big)},$$

which stands for the immune response activation number and determines whether a persistent immune response can be established or not. If $Z \neq 0$, then from (4), we have

$$T_2 = \frac{\lambda}{d_1 + \beta_1 f(V_2) + \beta_2 g(I_2)}, \quad I_2 = \frac{d_4}{q},$$

$$V_2 = \frac{d_4 p_2 e^{-\mu_2\tau_2}}{d_3 q}, \quad Z_2 = \frac{d_2}{p_1}(R_1 - 1),$$

then, the infection equilibrium with immunity $E_2 = (T_2, I_2, V_2, Z_2)$ exists if $R_1 > 1$. From the above, we have the following result.

Lemma 1. *For system (4),*

(1) *if $R_0 < 1$, then there exists a unique infection-free equilibrium E_0.*
(2) *if $R_1 \leq 1 < R_0$, then there exists a unique infection equilibrium without immunity E_1 besides E_0.*
(3) *if $R_1 > 1$, then there exists a unique infection equilibrium with immunity E_2 besides E_0 and E_1.*

2.3. Global Asymptotic Stability

In this section, we will investigate the global asymptotic stability of the system (4). Assume $\varphi(u) = u - 1 - \ln u$ for $u \in (0, +\infty)$, then $\varphi(x) \geq \varphi(1) = 0$.

Theorem 2. *For system (4), if $R_0 \leq 1$, the infection-free equilibrium E_0 is globally asymptotically stable.*

Proof. Define the Lyapunov function as follows

$$\begin{aligned} L_1 &= \int_\Omega \left\{ T_0\varphi(\frac{T}{T_0}) + e^{\mu_1\tau_1} I + \frac{\beta_1 p_2 T_0 e^{-\mu_2\tau_2} f'(0)}{R_0 d_3} \int_{t-\tau_2}^{t} I(s)ds + \frac{\beta_1 T_0 f'(0)}{R_0 d_3} V \right. \\ &+ \left. \frac{p_1 e^{\mu_1\tau_1}}{q} Z + \int_{t-\tau_1}^{t} \left[\beta_1 T(s) f(V(s)) + \beta_2 T(s) g\Big(I(s)\Big)\right] ds \right\} dx, \end{aligned}$$

then $L_1 \geq 0$, calculating $\frac{dL_1}{dt}$ along the solutions of system (4) and using $\lambda = d_1 T_0$, we have

$$\begin{aligned} \frac{dL_1}{dt} &= \int_\Omega \left\{ \left(1 - \frac{T_0}{T(x,t)}\right)\left(d_1 T_0 - d_1 T(x,t) - \beta_1 T(x,t) f\Big(V(x,t)\Big)\right) \right. \\ &- \beta_2 T(x,t) g\Big(I(x,t)\Big) + \beta_1 T(x,t-\tau_1) f\Big(V(x,t-\tau_1)\Big) \\ &+ \beta_2 T(x,t-\tau_1) g\Big(I(x,t-\tau_1)\Big) - d_2 e^{\mu_1\tau_1} I(x,t) - p_1 e^{\mu_1\tau_1} I(x,t) Z(x,t) \\ &+ \frac{\beta_1 T_0 f'(0)}{R_0 d_3}\Big[D\Delta V(x,t) + p_2 e^{-\mu_2\tau_2} I(x,t-\tau_2) - d_3 V(x,t)\Big] \\ &+ \frac{p_1 e^{\mu_1\tau_1}}{q}\Big[qI(x,t)Z(x,t) - d_4 Z(x,t)\Big] + \beta_1 T(x,t) f\Big(V(x,t)\Big) \\ &+ \beta_2 T(x,t) g\Big(I(x,t)\Big) - \beta_1 T(x,t-\tau_1) f\Big(V(x,t-\tau_1)\Big) \\ &- \left. \beta_2 T(x,t-\tau_1) g\Big(I(x,t-\tau_1)\Big) + \frac{\beta_1 p_2 T_0 e^{-\mu_2\tau_2} f'(0)}{R_0 d_3}\Big[I(x,t) - I(x,t-\tau_2)\Big] \right\} dx, \\ &= \int_\Omega \left\{ d_1 T_0\left(2 - \frac{T_0}{T(x,t)} - \frac{T(x,t)}{T_0}\right) + \left(\frac{T_0}{T(x,t)} - 1\right)\Big[\beta_1 T(x,t) f\Big(V(x,t)\Big) \right. \\ &+ \beta_2 T(x,t) g\Big(I(x,t)\Big)\Big] - d_2 e^{\mu_1\tau_1} I(x,t) + \frac{\beta_1 T_0 f'(0)}{R_0 d_3} D\Delta V(x,t) \\ &+ \frac{\beta_1 T_0 f'(0) p_2 e^{-\mu_2\tau_2}}{R_0 d_3} I(x,t-\tau_2) - \frac{\beta_1 T_0 f'(0)}{R_0} V(x,t) - \frac{p_1 d_4 e^{\mu_1\tau_1}}{q} Z(x,t) \\ &+ \beta_1 T(x,t) f\Big(V(x,t)\Big) + \beta_2 T(x,t) g\Big(I(x,t)\Big) + \frac{\beta_1 T_0 f'(0) p_2 e^{-\mu_2\tau_2}}{R_0 d_3} I(x,t) \\ &- \left. \frac{\beta_1 T_0 f'(0) p_2 e^{-\mu_2\tau_2}}{R_0 d_3} I(x,t-\tau_2) \right\} dx, \end{aligned}$$

from $\int_\Omega \Delta V(x,t)dx = 0$ and condition (A_2), we obtain

$$d_2 e^{\mu_1\tau_1} - \frac{\beta_1 p_2 T_0 f'^{-\mu_2\tau_2}}{R_0 d_3} = \frac{\beta_2 T_0 g'(0)}{R_0},$$

therefore

$$
\begin{aligned}
\frac{dL_1}{dt} &= \int_\Omega \Big\{ d_1 T_0 \Big[2 - \frac{T_0}{T(x,t)} - \frac{T(x,t)}{T_0}\Big] + \beta_1 T_0 f\Big(V(x,t)\Big) + \beta_2 T_0 g\Big(I(x,t)\Big) \\
&- d_2 e^{\mu_1 \tau_1} I(x,t) - \frac{\beta_1 T_0 f'(0)}{R_0} V - \frac{p_1 d_4 e^{\mu_1 \tau_1}}{q} Z(x,t) \\
&+ \frac{\beta_1 T_0 f'(0) p_2 e^{-\mu_2 \tau_2}}{R_0 d_3} I(x,t) \Big\} dx. \\
&\leq \int_\Omega \Big\{ d_1 T_0 \Big[2 - \frac{T_0}{T(x,t)} - \frac{T(x,t)}{T_0}\Big] + \frac{\beta_1 T_0 f'(0)}{R_0} V(x,t)(R_0 - 1) \\
&+ \frac{\beta_2 T_0 g'(0)}{R_0} I(x,t)(R_0 - 1) - \frac{d_4 p_1 e^{\mu_1 \tau_1}}{q} Z(x,t) \Big\} dx.
\end{aligned}
$$

It is follows from $R_0 \leq 1$ that $\frac{dL_1}{dt} \leq 0$. Furthermore, the largest invariant set of $\{\frac{dL_1}{dt} = 0\}$ is the singleton $\{E_0\}$. Then, the classical LaSalle's invariance principle implies that E_0 is globally asymptotically stable. This completes the proof. □

Theorem 3. *For system (4), if $R_1 \leq 1 < R_0$, the CTL-inactivated infection equilibrium E_1 is globally asymptotically stable.*

Proof. Define the Lyapunov function as follows

$$
\begin{aligned}
L_2 &= \int_\Omega \Big\{ T_1 \varphi\Big(\frac{T}{T_1}\Big) + e^{\mu_1 \tau_1} I_1 \varphi\Big(\frac{I}{I_1}\Big) + \frac{\beta_1 T_1 f(V_1)}{p_2 e^{-\mu_2 \tau_2} I_1} V_1 \varphi\Big(\frac{V}{V_1}\Big) + \frac{p_1 e^{\mu_1 \tau_1}}{q} Z \\
&+ \beta_1 T_1 f(V_1) \int_{t-\tau_1}^{t} \varphi\Bigg(\frac{T(\theta) f\Big(V(\theta)\Big)}{T_1 f(V_1)}\Bigg) d\theta + \beta_2 T_1 g(I_1) \int_{t-\tau_1}^{t} \varphi\Bigg(\frac{T(\theta) g\Big(I(\theta)\Big)}{T_1 g(I_1)}\Bigg) d\theta \\
&+ \beta_1 T_1 f(V_1) \int_{t-\tau_2}^{t} \varphi\Big(\frac{I(\theta)}{I_1}\Big) d\theta \Big\} dx.
\end{aligned}
$$

The Lyapunov derivative along system (4) is

$$
\begin{aligned}
\frac{dL_2}{dt} &= \int_\Omega \Big\{ \Big(1 - \frac{T_1}{T(x,t)}\Big) \Big[\lambda - d_1 T(x,t) - \beta_1 T(x,t) f\Big(V(x,t)\Big) - \beta_2 T(x,t) g\Big(I(x,t)\Big) \\
&+ \Big(1 - \frac{I_1}{I(x,t)}\Big) \Big[\beta_1 T(x,t-\tau_1) f\Big(V(x,t-\tau_1)\Big) + \beta_2 T(x,t-\tau_1) g\Big(I(x,t-\tau_1)\Big)\Big] \\
&- d_2 e^{\mu_1 \tau_1} I(x,t) - p_1 e^{\mu_1 \tau_1} I(x,t) Z(x,t)] \\
&+ \frac{\beta_1 T_1 f(V_1)}{p_2 e^{-\mu_2 \tau_2} I_1} \Big(1 - \frac{V_1}{V(x,t)}\Big) \Big[D\Delta V(x,t) + p_2 e^{-\mu_2 \tau_2} I(x,t-\tau_2) - d_3 V(x,t)\Big] \\
&+ \frac{p_1 e^{\mu_1 \tau_1}}{q} \Big[q I(x,t) Z(x,t) - d_4 Z(x,t)\Big] \\
&+ \beta_1 T_1 f(V_1) \Bigg[\frac{T(x,t) f\Big(V(x,t)\Big)}{T_1 f(V_1)} - \frac{T(x,t-\tau_1) f\Big(V(x,t-\tau_1)\Big)}{T_1 f(V_1)} \\
&+ \ln \frac{T(x,t-\tau_1) f\Big(V(x,t-\tau_1)\Big)}{T(x,t) f\Big(V(x,t)\Big)}\Bigg] + \beta_2 T_1 g(I_1) \Bigg[\frac{T(x,t) g\Big(I(x,t)\Big)}{T_1 g(I_1)} \\
&- \frac{T(x,t-\tau_1) g\Big(I(x,t-\tau_1)\Big)}{T_1 g(I_1)} + \ln \frac{T(x,t-\tau_1) g\Big(I(x,t-\tau_1)\Big)}{T(x,t) g\Big(I(x,t)\Big)}\Bigg] \\
&+ \beta_1 T_1 f(V_1) \Big[\frac{I(x,t)}{I_1} - \frac{I(x,t-\tau_2)}{I_1} + \ln \frac{I(x,t-\tau_2)}{I_1}\Big] \Big\} dx.
\end{aligned}
$$

According to the equilibrium conditions of E_1, that

$$\lambda = d_1T_1 + \beta_1T_1f(V_1) + \beta_2T_1g(I_1),$$

$$\beta_1T_1f(V_1) + \beta_2T_1g(I_1) = d_2e^{\mu_1\tau_1}I_1, p_2e^{-\mu_2\tau_2}I_1 = d_3V_1,$$

also recall $\int_\Omega \Delta V(x,t)dx = 0$ and $\int_\Omega \frac{\Delta V(x,t)}{V(x,t)}dx = \int_\Omega \frac{\|\nabla V(x,t)\|^2}{V^2(x,t)}dx$, we have

$$\begin{aligned}
\frac{dL_2}{dt} &= \int_\Omega \Big\{ d_1T_1\Big(1-\frac{T_1}{T(x,t)}\Big)\Big(1-\frac{T(x,t)}{T_1}\Big) + \Big(1-\frac{T_1}{T(x,t)}\Big)\Big[\beta_1T_1f(V_1)+\beta_2T_1g(I_1) \\
&- \beta_1T(x,t)f\Big(V(x,t)\Big) - \beta_2T(x,t)g\Big(I(x,t)\Big)\Big] \\
&+ \Big(1-\frac{I_1}{I(x,t)}\Big)\Big[\beta_1T(x,t-\tau_1)f\Big(V(x,t-\tau_1)\Big) + \beta_2T(x,t-\tau_1)g\Big(I(x,t-\tau_1)\Big)\Big] \\
&- \Big(1-\frac{I_1}{I(x,t)}\Big)\frac{I(x,t)}{I_1}\Big(\beta_1T_1f(V_1)+\beta_2T_1g(I_1)\Big) \\
&- p_1e^{\mu_1\tau_1}I(x,t)Z(x,t) + p_1e^{\mu_1\tau_1}I_1Z(x,t) + \beta_1T_1f(V_1)\Big(1-\frac{V_1}{V(x,t)}\Big)\Big(\frac{I(x,t-\tau_2)}{I_1} \\
&- \frac{V(x,t)}{V_1}\Big) + p_1e^{\mu_1\tau_1}I(x,t)Z(x,t) - \frac{p_1e^{\mu_1\tau_1}d_4}{q}Z(x,t) \\
&+ \beta_1T_1f(V_1)\Big[\frac{T(x,t)f\Big(V(x,t)\Big)}{T_1f(V_1)} - \frac{T(x,t-\tau_1)f\Big(V(x,t-\tau_1)\Big)}{T_1f(V_1)} + \ln\frac{T(x,t-\tau_1)f\Big(V(x,t-\tau_1)\Big)}{T(x,t)f\Big(V(x,t)\Big)}\Big] \\
&+ \beta_2T_1g(I_1)\Big[\frac{T(x,t)g\Big(I(x,t)\Big)}{T_1g(I_1)} - \frac{T(x,t-\tau_1)g\Big(I(x,t-\tau_1)\Big)}{T_1g(I_1)} + \ln\frac{T(x,t-\tau_1)g\Big(I(x,t-\tau_1)\Big)}{T(x,t)g\Big(I(x,t)\Big)}\Big] \\
&+ \beta_1T_1f(V_1)\Big[\frac{I(x,t)}{I_1} - \frac{I(x,t-\tau_1)}{I_1} + \ln\frac{I(x,t-\tau_2)}{I(x,t)}\Big]\Big\}dx \\
&- \frac{\beta_1T_1f(V_1)DV_1}{p_2I_1e^{-\mu_2\tau_2}}\int_\Omega \frac{\|\nabla V(x,t)\|^2}{V^2(x,t)}dx \\
&= \int_\Omega \Big\{ d_1T_1\Big(1-\frac{T_1}{T(x,t)}\Big)\Big(1-\frac{T(x,t)}{T_1}\Big) + \beta_1T_1f(V_1)\Big[3-\frac{T_1}{T(x,t)} - \frac{V_1I(x,t-\tau_2)}{I_1V(x,t)} \\
&- \frac{T(x,t-\tau_1)f\Big(V(x,t-\tau_1)\Big)I_1}{T_1f(V_1)I(x,t)} + \frac{f(V)}{f(V_1)} - \frac{V}{V_1} + \ln\frac{T(x,t-\tau_1)f\Big(V(x,t-\tau_1)I(x,t-\tau_2)\Big)}{T(x,t)f\Big(V(x,t)\Big)I(x,t)}\Big] \\
&+ \beta_2T_1g(I_1)\Big[2-\frac{T_1}{T(x,t)} - \frac{T(x,t-\tau_1)g\Big(I(x,t-\tau_1)\Big)I_1}{T_1g(I_1)I(x,t)} + \ln\frac{T(x,t-\tau_1)g\Big(I(x,t-\tau_1)\Big)}{T(x,t)g\Big(I(x,t)\Big)} \\
&+ \frac{g(I)}{g(I_1)} - \frac{I(x,t)}{I_1}\Big] + p_1I_1e^{\mu_1\tau_1}Z(x,t) - \frac{p_1e^{\mu_1\tau_1}d_4}{q}Z(x,t)\Big\}dx \\
&- \frac{\beta_1T_1f(V_1)DV_1}{p_2I_1e^{-\mu_2\tau_2}}\int_\Omega \frac{\|\nabla V(x,t)\|^2}{V^2(x,t)}dx \\
&= \int_\Omega \Big\{ d_1T_1\Big(1-\frac{T_1}{T(x,t)}\Big)\Big(1-\frac{T(x,t)}{T_1}\Big) + \beta_1T_1f(V_1)\Big[-\varphi\Big(\frac{T_1}{T(x,t)}\Big) \\
&- \varphi\Big(\frac{T(x,t-\tau_1)f\Big(V(x,t-\tau_1)\Big)I_1}{T_1f(V_1)I(x,t)}\Big) - \varphi\Big(\frac{V_1I(x,t-\tau_2)}{I_1V(x,t)}\Big) + \frac{f(V(x,t))}{f(V_1)} - \frac{V(x,t)}{V_1} + \ln\frac{f(V_1)V(x,t)}{f\Big(V(x,t)\Big)V_1}\Big] \\
&+ \beta_2T_1g(I_1)\Big[-\varphi(\frac{T_1}{T(x,t)}) - \varphi\Big(\frac{T(x,t-\tau_1)g(I(x,t-\tau_1))I_1}{T_1g(I_1)I(x,t)}\Big) + \frac{g\Big(I(x,t)\Big)}{g(I_1)} - \frac{I(x,t)}{I_1} \\
&+ \ln\frac{g(I_1)I(x,t)}{g\Big(I(x,t)\Big)I_1}\Big] + p_1e^{\mu_1\tau_1}(I_1-I_2)Z(x,t)\Big\}dx \\
&- \frac{\beta_1T_1f(V_1)DV_1}{p_2I_1e^{-\mu_2\tau_2}}\int_\Omega \frac{\|\nabla V(x,t)\|^2}{V^2(x,t)}dx \\
&= \int_\Omega \{ d_1T_1\Big(1-\frac{T_1}{T(x,t)}\Big)(1-\frac{T(x,t)}{T_1}) + \beta_1T_1f(V_1)\Big[-\varphi(\frac{T_1}{T(x,t)}) - \varphi\Big(\frac{V_1I(x,t-\tau_2)}{I_1V(x,t)}\Big) \\
&- \varphi\Big(\frac{T(x,t-\tau_1)f\Big(V(x,t-\tau_1)\Big)I_1}{T_1f(V_1)I(x,t)}\Big) - \varphi\Big(\frac{f(V_1)V(x,t)}{f\Big(V(x,t)\Big)V_1}\Big) + \Big(\frac{f\Big(V(x,t)\Big)}{f(V_1)} - \frac{V(x,t)}{V_1}\Big)\Big(1-\frac{f(V_1)}{f(V(x,t))}\Big)\Big] \\
&+ \beta_2T_1g(I_1)\Big[-\varphi\Big(\frac{T_1}{T(x,t)}\Big) - \varphi\Big(\frac{T(x,t-\tau_1)g(I(x,t-\tau_1))I_1}{T_1g\Big(I_1I(x,t)\Big)}\Big) - \varphi\Big(\frac{g(I_1)I(x,t)}{g(I(x,t))I_1}\Big) \\
&+ \Big(\frac{g\Big(I(x,t)\Big)}{g(I_1)} - \frac{I(x,t)}{I_1}\Big)\Big(1-\frac{g(I_1)}{g(I(x,t))}\Big)\Big] + p_1e^{\mu_1\tau_1}(I_1-I_2)Z(x,t)\}dx \\
&- \frac{\beta_1T_1f(V_1)DV_1}{p_2I_1e^{-\mu_2\tau_2}}\int_\Omega \frac{\|\nabla V(x,t)\|^2}{V^2(x,t)}dx.
\end{aligned}$$

It follows from (A_1) that

$$\Big(\frac{f\big(V(x,t)\big)}{f(V_1)}-\frac{V(x,t)}{V_1}\Big)\Big(1-\frac{f(V_1)}{f\big(V(x,t)\big)}\Big)\le 0,$$

$$\Big(\frac{g\big(I(x,t)\big)}{g(I_1)}-\frac{I(x,t)}{I_1}\Big)\Big(1-\frac{g(I_1)}{g\big(I(x,t)\big)}\Big)\le 0.$$

As $\varphi(u)\ge 0$ for $u>0$, similar to [23], $sgn(I_1-I_2)=sgn(R_1-1)$, then $\frac{dL_2}{dt}\le 0$, therefore E_1 is stable, and $\frac{dL_2}{dt}=0$ holds if and only if $T(x,t)=T_1, I(x,t)=I_1, V(x,t)=V_1$ and $Z(x,t)=0$ when $R_1<1$, or $T(x,t)=T_1, I(x,t)=I_1, V(x,t)=V_1$ when $R_1=1$. The largest invariance set of $\{\frac{dL_2}{dt}=0\}$ is the singleton $\{E_1\}$. It follows from the classical LaSalle's invariance principle that E_1 is globally asymptotically stable when $R_1\le 1<R_0$. This completes the proof. □

Theorem 4. *For system (4), if $R_1>1$, the interior equilibrium E_2 is globally asymptotically stable.*

Proof. Define the Lyapunov function as follows

$$\begin{aligned}
L_3 &= \int_\Omega\Big\{T_2\varphi(\frac{T}{T_2})+e^{\mu_1\tau_1}I_2\varphi(\frac{I}{I_2})+\frac{\beta_1T_2f(V_2)}{p_2I_2e^{-\mu_2\tau_2}}V_2\varphi(\frac{V}{V_2})\\
&+ \frac{p_1e^{\mu_1\tau_1}}{q}Z_2\varphi(\frac{Z}{Z_2})+\beta_1T_2f(V_2)\int_{t-\tau_1}^{t}\varphi\Big(\frac{T(\theta)f(V(\theta))}{T_2f(V_2)}\Big)d\theta\\
&+ \beta_2T_2g(I_2)\int_{t-\tau_1}^{t}\varphi\Big(\frac{T(\theta)g\big(I(\theta)\big)}{T_2g(I_2)}\Big)d\theta+\beta_1T_2f(V_2)\int_{t-\tau_2}^{t}\varphi\Big(\frac{I(\theta)}{I_2}\Big)d\theta\Big\}dx,
\end{aligned}$$

calculating $\frac{dL_3}{dt}$ along the solutions of system (4) , we have

$$\begin{aligned}
\frac{dL_3}{dt} &= \int_\Omega\Big\{\Big(1-\frac{T_2}{T(x,t)}\Big)\Big(\lambda-d_1T(x,t)-\beta_1T(x,t)f\big(V(x,t)\big)-\beta_2T(x,t)g\big(I(x,t)\big)\Big)\\
&+ \Big(1-\frac{I_2}{I(x,t)}\Big)\Big[\beta_1T(x,t-\tau_1)f\big(V(x,t-\tau_1)\big)+\beta_2T(x,t-\tau_1)g\big(I(x,t-\tau_1)\big)\Big]\\
&- e^{\mu_1\tau_1}\Big(1-\frac{I_2}{I(x,t)}\Big)\Big[d_2I(x,t)-p_1I(x,t)Z(x,t)\Big]\\
&+ \frac{\beta_1T_2f(V_2)}{p_2I_2e^{-\mu_2\tau_2}}\Big(1-\frac{V_2}{V(x,t)}\Big)\Big[\Delta V(x,t)+p_2e^{-\mu_2\tau_2}I(x,t-\tau_2)-d_3V(x,t)\Big]\\
&+ \frac{p_1e^{\mu_1\tau_1}}{q}\Big(1-\frac{Z_2}{Z(x,t)}\Big)\Big[qI(x,t)Z(x,t)-d_4Z(x,t)\Big]\\
&+ \beta_1T_2f(V_2)\Big[\frac{T(x,t)f\big(V(x,t)\big)}{T_2f(V_2)}-\frac{T(x,t-\tau_1)f\big(V(x,t-\tau_1)\big)}{T_2f(V_2)}+\ln\frac{T(x,t-\tau_1)f\big(V(x,t-\tau_1)\big)}{T(x,t)f\big(V(x,t)\big)}\Big]\\
&+ \beta_2T_2g(I_2)\Big[\frac{T(x,t)g\big(I(x,t)\big)}{T_2g(I_2)}-\frac{T(x,t-\tau_1)g\big(I(x,t-\tau_1)\big)}{T_2g(I_2)}+\ln\frac{T(x,t-\tau_1)g\big(I(x,t-\tau_1)\big)}{T(x,t)g\big(I(x,t)\big)}\Big]\\
&+ \beta_1T_2f(V_2)\Big[\frac{I(x,t)}{I_2}-\frac{I(x,t-\tau_2)}{I_2}+\ln\frac{I(x,t-\tau_2)}{I(x,t)}\Big]\Big\}dx,
\end{aligned}$$

using the equilibrium conditions of E_2, then

$$\lambda=d_1T_2+\beta_1T_2f(V_2)+\beta_2T_2g(I_2),\ \ p_2e^{-\mu_2\tau_2}I_2=d_3V_2,$$

$$\beta_1 T_2 f(V_2) + \beta_2 T_2 g(I_2) = e^{\mu_1 \tau_1}(d_2 I_2 + p_1 I_2 Z_2), \;\; I_2 = \frac{d_4}{q},$$

also recall $\int_\Omega \Delta V(x,t)dx = 0$ and $\int_\Omega \frac{\Delta V(x,t)}{V(x,t)}dx = \int_\Omega \frac{\|\nabla V(x,t)\|^2}{V^2(x,t)}dx$, we have

$$\begin{aligned}
\frac{dL_3}{dt} &= \int_\Omega \Bigg\{ d_1 T_2\Big(1 - \frac{T_2}{T(x,t)}\Big)\Big(1 - \frac{T(x,t)}{T_2}\Big) + \beta_1 T_2 f(V_2)\Big[3 - \frac{T_2}{T(x,t)} - \frac{V_2 I(x,t-\tau_2)}{I_2 V(x,t)} \\
&- \frac{T(x,t-\tau_1) f\Big(V(x,t-\tau_1)\Big) I_2}{T_2 f(V_2) I(x,t)} + \frac{f\Big(V(x,t)\Big)}{f(V_2)} - \frac{V(x,t)}{V_2} + \ln \frac{T(x,t-\tau_1) f\Big(V(x,t-\tau_1)\Big) I(t-\tau_2)}{T(x,t) f(V(x,t)) I(x,t)}\Big] \\
&+ \beta_2 T_2 g(I_2)\Big[2 - \frac{T_2}{T(x,t)} - \frac{T(x,t-\tau_1) g\Big(I(x,t-\tau_1)\Big) I_2}{T_2 g(I_2) I(x,t)} + \frac{g\Big(I(x,t)\Big)}{g(I_2)} - \frac{I(x,t)}{I_2} \\
&+ \ln \frac{T(x,t-\tau_1) g\Big(I(x,t-\tau_1)\Big)}{T(x,t) g\Big(I(x,t)\Big)}\Big]\Bigg\} dx - \frac{\beta_1 T_2 f(V_2) D V_2}{p_2 I_2 e^{-\mu_2 \tau_2}} \int_\Omega \frac{\|\nabla V(x,t)\|^2}{V^2(x,t)} dx \\
&= \int_\Omega \{ d_1 T_2\Big(1 - \frac{T_2}{T(x,t)}\Big)(1 - \frac{T(x,t)}{T_2}) + \beta_1 T_2 f(V_2)\Big[-\varphi(\frac{T_2}{T(x,t)}) - \varphi(\frac{V_2 I(x,t-\tau_2)}{I_2 V(x,t)}) \\
&- \varphi\Big(\frac{T(x,t-\tau_1) f\Big(V(x,t-\tau_1)\Big) I_2}{T_2 f(V_2) I(x,t)}\Big) + \frac{f\Big(V(x,t)\Big)}{f(V_2)} - \frac{V(x,t)}{V_2} + \ln \frac{f(V_2) V(x,t)}{V_2 f(V(x,t))}\Big] \\
&+ \beta_2 T_2 g(I_2)\Big[-\varphi(\frac{T_2}{T(x,t)}) - \varphi\Big(\frac{T(x,t-\tau_1) g\Big(I(x,t-\tau_1)\Big) I_2}{T_2 g(I_2) I(x,t)}\Big) \\
&+ \frac{g\Big(I(x,t)\Big)}{g(I_2)} - \frac{I(x,t)}{I_2} + \ln \frac{g(I_2) I(x,t)}{I_2 g\Big(I(x,t)\Big)}\Big]\} dx - \frac{\beta_1 T_2 f(V_2) D V_2}{p_2 I_2 e^{-\mu_2 \tau_2}} \int_\Omega \frac{\|\nabla V(x,t)\|^2}{V^2(x,t)} dx \\
&= \int_\Omega \{ d_1 T_2\Big(1 - \frac{T_2}{T(x,t)}\Big)\Big(1 - \frac{T(x,t)}{T_2}\Big) + \beta_1 T_2 f(V_2)\Big[-\varphi\Big(\frac{T_2}{T(x,t)}\Big) - \varphi\Big(\frac{V_2 I(x,t-\tau_2)}{I_2 V(x,t)}\Big) - \\
\varphi &\Big(\frac{T(x,t-\tau_1) f\Big(V(x,t-\tau_1)\Big) I_2}{T_2 f(V_2) I(x,t)}\Big) - \varphi\Big(\frac{f(V_2) V(x,t)}{V_2 f\Big(V(x,t)\Big)}\Big) + \Big(\frac{f(V(x,t))}{f(V_2)} - \frac{V(x,t)}{V_2}\Big)\Big(1 - \frac{f(V_2)}{f\Big(V(x,t)\Big)}\Big)\Big] \\
&+ \beta_2 T_2 g(I_2)\Big[-\varphi\Big(\frac{T_2}{T(x,t)}\Big) - \varphi\Big(\frac{T(x,t-\tau_1) g\Big(I(x,t-\tau_1)\Big) I_2}{T_2 g(I_2) I(x,t)}\Big) - \varphi\Big(\frac{g(I_2) I(x,t)}{I_2 g\Big(I(x,t)\Big)}\Big) \\
&+ \Big(\frac{g\Big(I(x,t)\Big)}{g(I_2)} - \frac{I(x,t)}{I_2}\Big)\Big(1 - \frac{g(I_2)}{g(I(x,t))}\Big)\Big]\Bigg\} dx - \frac{\beta_1 T_2 f(V_2) D V_2}{k I_2} \int_\Omega \frac{\|\nabla V(x,t)\|^2}{V^2(x,t)} dx,
\end{aligned}$$

from (A_1), it is easy to see that

$$\Big(\frac{f(V(x,t))}{f(V_1)} - \frac{V(x,t)}{V_1}\Big)\Big(1 - \frac{f(V_1)}{f(V(x,t))}\Big) \le 0,$$

$$\Big(\frac{g(I(x,t))}{g(I_1)} - \frac{I(x,t)}{I_1}\Big)\Big(1 - \frac{g(I_1)}{g(I(x,t))}\Big) \le 0.$$

As $\varphi(u) \geq 0$ for $u > 0$, then $\frac{dL_3}{dt} \leq 0$. The largest invariant set of $\{\frac{dL_3}{dt} = 0\}$ is the single point $\{E_2\}$, similar to the proof of Theorem 3, E_2 is globally asymptotically stable. This completes the proof. □

3. Dynamical Behaviors of Discrete System

In preceding section, by introducing Lyapunov functions, we have shown by using continuous Lyapunov functionals that the global asymptotic stability of the equilibria of the continuous system (4) is completely determined by the basic reproduction number. R_0 and R_1 act as threshold parameter for the existence and stability of equilibria. This arises a natural question that whether the global asymptotic stability of the equilibria of the discrete system (7) can be preserved. In this section, we will discuss this problem.

Obviously, the discrete system (7) has the same equilibria as system (4). Similarly, $E_0 = (T_0, 0, 0, 0)$ is the infection-free equilibrium, $E_1 = (T_1, I_1, V_1, 0)$ stands for the CTL-inactivated equilibrium and $E_2 = (T_2, I_2, V_2, Z_2)$ is the CTL-activated equilibrium.

Rewriting the discrete system (7) yields

$$\begin{cases} T_{n+1}^m = \frac{\lambda\Delta t+T_n^m}{1+\Delta t(d_1+\beta_1 f(V_n^m+\beta_2 g(I_n^m))}, \\ I_{n+1}^m = \frac{I_n^m+\Delta t e^{-\mu_1\tau_1}(\beta_1 T_{n-m_1+1}^m f(V_{n-m_1}^m)+\beta_2 T_{n-m_1+1}^m g(I_{n-m_1}^m)}{1+\Delta t(d_2+p_1 Z_n^m)}, \\ AV_{n+1} = V_n + \Delta t p_2 e^{-\mu_2\tau_2} I_{n-m_2+1}, \\ Z_{n+1}^m = \frac{(1+\Delta t q I_{n+1}^m)}{1+\Delta t d_4} Z_n^m, \end{cases}, \tag{5}$$

where the square matrix A of dimension $(N+1)\times(N+1)$ is given by

$$\begin{pmatrix} c_1 & c_2 & 0 & \cdots & 0 & 0 & 0 \\ c_2 & c_3 & c_2 & \cdots & 0 & 0 & 0 \\ 0 & c_2 & c_3 & \cdots & 0 & 0 & 0 \\ \vdots & \vdots & \vdots & \ddots & \vdots & \vdots & \vdots \\ 0 & 0 & 0 & \cdots & c_3 & c_2 & 0 \\ 0 & 0 & 0 & \cdots & c_2 & c_3 & c_2 \\ 0 & 0 & 0 & \cdots & 0 & c_2 & c_1 \end{pmatrix}$$

with $c_1 = 1 + D\Delta t/(\Delta x)^2 + d_3\Delta t, c_2 = -D\Delta t/(\Delta x)^2, c_3 = 1 + 2D\Delta t/(\Delta x)^2 + d_3\Delta t$. It is clear that A is strictly diagonally dominant matrix, therefore A is non-singular. From the third equation of the above system, we have

$$V_{n+1} = A^{-1}(V_n + \Delta t p_2 e^{-\mu_2\tau_2} I_{n-m_2+1}).$$

Theorem 5. *For any $\Delta t > 0, \Delta x > 0$, the solutions of the system (7) remain nonnegative and bounded for all $n \in \mathbb{N}$.*

Proof. Since all parameters in (7) are positive, then using the induction , it is easy to deduce from (5) that all solutions of system (7) remain nonnegative provided that the initial value are nonnegative, for all $n \in \aleph$.

Next, we establish the boundedness of solutions. Define a sequence G_n as follows

$$G_n^m = T_n^m + I_n^m + \frac{p_1}{q} Z_n^m + \Delta t \sum_{j=n-m_1}^{n-1} \Big[\beta_1 f(V_j^m) + \beta_2 g(I_j^m)\Big] T_{j+1}^m e^{-\Delta t\mu_1(n-j)},$$

then

$$\begin{aligned} G_{n+1}^m - G_n^m &= \Delta t\Big(\lambda - d_1 T_{n+1}^m - \beta_1 T_{n+1}^m f(V_n^m) - \beta_2 T_{n+1}^m g(I_n^m)\Big) \\ &+ \Delta t\Big[e^{-\mu_1\tau_1}\Big(\beta_1 T_{n-m_1+1}^m f(V_{n-m_1}^m) + \beta_2 T_{n-m_1+1}^m g(I_{n-m_1}^m)\Big) \\ &- d_2 I_{n+1}^m - p_1 I_{n+1}^m Z_n^m\Big] + \frac{p_1}{q}\Delta t(q I_{n+1}^m Z_n^m - d_4 Z_{n+1}^m) \\ &+ \Delta t \sum_{j=n-m_1+1}^{n} \Big[\beta_1 f(V_j^m) + \beta_2 g(I_j^m)\Big] T_{j+1}^m e^{-\Delta t\mu_1(n-j+1)} \\ &- \Delta t \sum_{j=n-m_1}^{n-1} \Big[\beta_1 f(V_j^m) + \beta_2 g(I_j^m)\Big] T_{j+1}^m e^{-\Delta t\mu_1(n-j)} \\ &= \Delta t\Bigg\{\lambda - d_1 T_{n+1}^m - d_2 I_{n+1}^m - \frac{p_1 d_4}{q} Z_{n+1}^m \\ &+ \Big(1 - e^{\Delta t\mu_1}\Big) \sum_{j=n-m_1+1}^{n} \Big[\beta_1 f(V_j^m) + \beta_2 g(I_j^m)\Big] T_{j+1}^m e^{-\Delta t\mu_1(n-j+1)}\Bigg\} \\ &\leq \Delta t(\lambda - \xi G_{n+1}^m), \end{aligned}$$

where $\xi = \min\{d_1, d_2, d_4, \frac{e^{\Delta t \mu_1}-1}{\Delta t}\}$, then we have

$$G_{n+1}^m \leq \frac{1}{1+\Delta t\xi} G_n^m + \frac{\Delta t\lambda}{1+\Delta t\xi},$$

it follows from the induction that

$$G_n^m \leq (\frac{1}{1+\Delta t\xi})^n G_0^m + \frac{\lambda}{\xi}\Big[1-(\frac{1}{1+\Delta t\xi})^n\Big],$$

therefore

$$\limsup_{n\to\infty} G_n^m \leq \frac{\lambda}{\xi}, \ for \ all \ m \in \{0,1,\cdots,N\},$$

this implies that $\{G_n\}$ is bounded, then $\{T_n\}$,$\{I_n\}$ and $\{Z_n\}$ are bounded.

From the third equation of system (7)

$$\sum_{m=0}^{N} V_{n+1}^m = \frac{1}{1+d_3\Delta t}\Big(\sum_{m=0}^{N} V_n^m + \Delta t p_2 e^{-\mu_2\tau_2}\sum_{m=0}^{N} I_{n-m_2+1}^m\Big),$$

since $\{I_n\}$ is bounded, then there exists $\eta > 0$ such that $I_n^m \leq \eta$ for all $n \in \{-m_2, -m_2 + 1, \cdots, 0, 1, \cdots\}$, $m \in \{0, 1, \cdots, \aleph\}$, then

$$\sum_{m=0}^{N} V_{n+1}^m \leq \frac{1}{1+d_3\Delta t}\Big[\sum_{m=0}^{N} V_n^m + \Delta t p_2 e^{-\mu_2\tau_2}\eta(N+1)\Big],$$

by induction, we have

$$\begin{aligned}
\sum_{m=0}^{N} V_n^m &\leq \frac{1}{(1+d_3\Delta t)^n}\sum_{m=0}^{N} V_0^m + \frac{p_2 e^{-\mu_2\tau_2}\eta(N+1)}{d_3}\Big[1-\frac{1}{(1+d_3\Delta t)^n}\Big] \\
&\leq \sum_{m=0}^{N} V_0^m + \frac{p_2 e^{-\mu_2\tau_2}\eta(N+1)}{d_3},
\end{aligned}$$

therefore $\{V_n\}$ is bounded. This completes the proof. □

Global Stability

In this section, we will study the global stability of the equilibria of system (7) .

Theorem 6. *For system (7), if $R_0 \leq 1$, the infection-free equilibrium E_0 is globally asymptotically stable.*

Proof. Define the discrete Lyapunov function as follows

$$\begin{aligned}
W_n &= \sum_{m=0}^{N}\Bigg\{\frac{1}{\Delta t}\Big[T_0\varphi(\frac{T_n^m}{T_0}) + e^{\mu_1\tau_1}\Big(1+\Delta t\frac{\beta_2 T_0 g'(0)}{R_0 e^{\mu_1\tau_1}}\Big)I_n^m + \frac{\beta_1 T_0 f'(0)}{d_3 R_0}\Big(1+\Delta t d_3\Big)V_n^m \\
&+ \frac{p_1 e^{\mu_1\tau_1}}{q}\Big(1+\Delta t d_4\Big)Z_n^m\Big] + \sum_{j=n-m_1}^{n-1}\Big(\beta_1 f(V_j^m) + \beta_2 g(I_j^m)\Big)T_{j+1}^m \\
&+ \frac{\beta_1 p_2 T_0 f'^{-\mu_2\tau_2}}{R_0 d_3}\sum_{j=n-m_2}^{n-1} I_{j+1}^m\Bigg\}.
\end{aligned}$$

It follows from $u - 1 \geq \ln u$ for all $u > 0$, that $W_n \geq 0$ for all $n \in \aleph$. Then, along the trajectory of (7)

$$
\begin{aligned}
W_{n+1}-W_n &= \sum_{m=0}^{N}\Bigg\{\frac{1}{\Delta t}\Big[T_{n+1}^m - T_n^m + T_0\ln\frac{T_n^m}{T_{n+1}^m} + e^{\mu_1\tau_1}\Big(1+\Delta t\frac{\beta_2 T_0 g'(0)}{R_0 e^{\mu_1\tau_1}}\Big)(I_{n+1}^m - I_n^m)\\
&+ \frac{\beta_1 T_0 f'(0)}{d_3 R_0}\Big(1+\Delta t d_3\Big)\Big(V_{n+1}^m - V_n^m\Big) + \frac{p_1 e^{\mu_1\tau_1}}{q}\Big(1+\Delta t d_4\Big)\Big(Z_{n+1}^m - Z_n^m\Big)\Big]\\
&+ \sum_{j=n-m_1+1}^{n}\Big(\beta_1 f(V_j^m)+\beta_2 g(I_j^m)\Big)T_{j+1}^m\\
&- \sum_{j=n-m_1}^{n-1}\Big(\beta_1 f(V_j^m)+\beta_2 g(I_j^m)\Big)T_{j+1}^m\\
&+ \frac{\beta_1 p_2 T_0 f'^{-\mu_2\tau_2}}{R_0 d_3}\Big[\sum_{j=n-m_2+1}^{n} I_{j+1}^m - \sum_{j=n-m_2}^{n-1} I_{j+1}^m\Big]\Bigg\},
\end{aligned}
$$

using the equilibrium condition of E_0, we have

$$
\begin{aligned}
W_{n+1}-W_n &\le \sum_{m=0}^{N}\Bigg\{\Big(1-\frac{T_0}{T_{n+1}^m}\Big)\Big(d_1T_0 - d_1T_{n+1}^m - \Big(\beta_1 f(V_n^m)+\beta_2 g(I_n^m)\Big)T_{n+1}^m\Big)\\
&+ \Big(1+\Delta t\frac{\beta_2 T_0 g'(0)}{R_0 e^{\mu_1\tau_1}}\Big)\Big(\beta_1 T_{n-m_1+1}^m f(V_{n-m_1}^m) + \beta_2 T_{n-m_1+1}^m g(I_{n-m_1}^m)\Big)\\
&+ e^{\mu_1\tau_1}\Big(1+\Delta t\frac{\beta_2 T_0 g'(0)}{R_0 e^{\mu_1\tau_1}}\Big)\Big(-d_2 I_{n+1}^m - p_1 I_{n+1}^m Z_n^m\Big)\\
&+ \frac{\beta_1 T_0 f'(0)}{d_3 R_0}\Big(1+\Delta t d_3\Big)D\frac{V_{n+1}^{m+1} - 2V_{n+1}^m + V_{n+1}^{m-1}}{(\Delta x)^2}\\
&+ \frac{\beta_1 T_0 f'(0)}{d_3 R_0}\Big(1+\Delta t d_3\Big)\Big(p_2 e^{\mu_2\tau_2} I_{n-m_2+1}^m - d_3 V_{n+1}^m\Big)\\
&+ \frac{p_1 e^{\mu_1\tau_1}}{q}\Big(1+\Delta t d_4\Big)\Big(q I_{n+1}^m Z_n^m - d_4 Z_{n+1}^m\Big) + \Big(\beta_1 f(V_n^m)+\beta_2 g(I_n^m)\Big)T_{n+1}^m\\
&- \Big(\beta_1 f(V_{n-m_1}^m)+\beta_2 g(I_{n-m_1}^m)\Big)T_{n-m_1+1}^m\\
&- \frac{\beta_1 p_2 T_0 f'^{-\mu_2\tau_2}}{R_0 d_3}\Big(I_{n+1}^m - I_{n-m_2+1}^m\Big)\Bigg\}\\
&= \sum_{m=0}^{N}\Bigg\{d_1T_0\Big(2-\frac{T_0}{T_{n+1}^m}-\frac{T_{n+1}^m}{T_0}\Big) + \beta_1 T_0 f(V_n^m) + \beta_2 T_0 g(I_n^m)\\
&- \frac{\beta_2 T_0 g'(0)}{R_0} I_n^m - \frac{\beta_1 T_0 f'(0)}{R_0} V_n^m - \frac{d_4 p_1 e^{\mu_1\tau_1}}{q} Z_n^m\Bigg\}\\
&+ \frac{\beta_1 T_0 f'(0) D}{d_3 R_0 (\Delta x)^2}\Big(V_{n+1}^{N+1} - V_{n+1}^N + V_{n+1}^{-1} - V_{n+1}^0\Big)\\
&\le \sum_{m=0}^{N}\Bigg\{d_1T_0\Big(2-\frac{T_0}{T_{n+1}^m}-\frac{T_{n+1}^m}{T_0}\Big) + \frac{\beta_1 T_0 f'(0)}{R_0} V_n^m\Big(R_0-1\Big)\\
&+ \frac{\beta_2 g'(0) T_0}{R_0} I_n^m\Big(R_0-1\Big) - \frac{d_4 p_1 e^{\mu_1\tau_1}}{q} Z_n^m\Bigg\},
\end{aligned}
$$

the last inequality is deduced from condition (A_2), if $R_0 \le 1$, then $W_{n+1}-W_n \le 0$, for all $n \in \aleph$, therefore, $\{W_n\}$ is monotone decreasing sequence. It follows from $W_n \ge 0$ that $\lim_{n\to\infty} W_n \ge 0$, then

$$\lim_{n\to\infty}(W_{n+1}-W_n) = 0,$$

therefore

(1) If $R_0 < 1$, then $\lim_{n\to\infty}(W_{n+1} - W_n) = 0$ implies that $\lim_{n\to\infty} T_n^m = T_0$, $\lim_{n\to\infty} V_n^m = 0$, $\lim_{n\to\infty} Z_n^m = 0$, $\lim_{n\to\infty} I_n^m = 0$.

(2) If $R_0 = 1$, then $\lim_{n\to\infty}(W_{n+1} - W_n) = 0$ implies that $\lim_{n\to\infty} T_n^m = T_0$, $\lim_{n\to\infty} Z_n^m = 0$, from system (7), we obtain $\lim_{n\to\infty} I_n^m = 0$, $\lim_{n\to\infty} V_n^m = 0$.

Hence, E_0 is globally asymptotically stable when $R_0 \leq 1$. This completes the proof. □

Theorem 7. *For system (7), if $R_1 < 1 < R_0$, the CTL-inactivated infection equilibrium E_1 of is globally asymptotically stable .*

Proof. Define the discrete Lyapunov function as follows

$$\begin{aligned}
\widetilde{W}_n &= \sum_{m=0}^{N}\Bigg\{\frac{1}{\Delta t}\Big[T_1\varphi(\frac{T_n^m}{T_1}) + e^{\mu_1\tau_1}I_1\varphi(\frac{I_n^m}{I_1}) + \frac{\beta_1 T_1 f(V_1)}{p_2 e^{-\mu_2\tau_2}I_1}V_1\varphi(\frac{V_n^m}{V_1}) + \frac{p_1 e^{\mu_1\tau_1}}{q}Z_n^m\Big] \\
&+ \beta_1 T_1 f(V_1)\sum_{j=n-m_1}^{n-1}\varphi\Big(\frac{T_{j+1}^m f(V_j^m)}{T_1 f(V_1)}\Big) + \beta_2 T_1 g(I_1)\sum_{j=n-m_1}^{n-1}\varphi\Big(\frac{T_{j+1}^m g(I_j^m)}{T_1 g(I_1)}\Big) \\
&+ \beta_1 T_1 f(V_1)\sum_{j=n-m_2}^{n-1}\varphi\Big(\frac{I_{j+1}^m}{I_1}\Big) + \beta_1 T_1 f(V_1)\varphi\Big(\frac{f(V_n^m)}{f(V_1)}\Big) + \beta_2 T_1 g(I_1)\varphi\Big(\frac{g(I_n^m)}{g(I_1)}\Big)\Bigg\}.
\end{aligned}$$

Since $u - 1 \geq \ln u$ for all $u > 0$, then $\widetilde{W}_n \geq 0$ for all $n \in \aleph$. The Lyapunov derivative along (7) is

$$\begin{aligned}
\widetilde{W}_{n+1} - \widetilde{W}_n &= \sum_{m=0}^{N}\Bigg\{\frac{1}{\Delta t}\Big[T_{n+1}^m - T_n^m + T_1\ln\frac{T_n^m}{T_{n+1}^m} + e^{\mu_1\tau_1}\Big(I_{n+1}^m - I_n^m + I_1\ln\frac{I_n^m}{I_{n+1}^m}\Big) \\
&+ \frac{\beta_1 T_1 V_1}{p_2 e^{-\mu_2\tau_2}I_1}\Big(V_{n+1}^m - V_n^m + V_1\ln\frac{V_n^m}{V_{n+1}^m}\Big) + \frac{p_1 e^{\mu_1\tau_1}}{q}\Big(Z_{n+1}^m - Z_n^m\Big)\Big] \\
&+ \beta_1 T_1 f(V_1)\Big[\sum_{j=n-m_1+1}^{n}\varphi\Big(\frac{T_{j+1}^m f(V_j^m)}{T_1 f(V_1)}\Big) - \sum_{j=n-m_1}^{n-1}\varphi\Big(\frac{T_{j+1}^m f(V_j^m)}{T_1 f(V_1)}\Big)\Big] \\
&+ \beta_2 T_1 g(I_1)\Big[\sum_{j=n-m_1+1}^{n}\varphi\Big(\frac{T_{j+1}^m g(I_j^m)}{T_1 g(I_1)}\Big) - \sum_{j=n-m_1}^{n-1}\varphi\Big(\frac{T_{j+1}^m g(I_j^m)}{T_1 g(I_1)}\Big)\Big] \\
&+ \beta_1 T_1 f(V_1)\Big[\sum_{j=n-m_2+1}^{n}\varphi\Big(\frac{I_{j+1}^m}{I_1}\Big) - \sum_{j=n-m_2}^{n-1}\varphi(\frac{I_{j+1}^m}{I_1})\Big] \\
&+ \beta_1 T_1 f(V_1)\Big(\frac{f(V_{n+1}^m)}{f(V_1)} - \frac{f(V_n^m)}{f(V_1)} + \ln\frac{f(V_n^m)}{f(V_{n+1}^m)}\Big) \\
&+ \beta_2 T_1 g(I_1)\Big(\frac{g(I_{n+1}^m)}{g(I_1)} - \frac{g(I_n^m)}{g(I_1)} + \ln\frac{g(I_n^m)}{g(I_{n+1}^m)}\Big)\Bigg\} \\
&\leq \sum_{m=0}^{N}\Big\{\frac{1}{\Delta t}\Big[\Big(1 - \frac{T_1}{T_{n+1}^m}\Big)\Big(T_{n+1}^m - T_n^m\Big) + e^{\mu_1\tau_1}\Big(1 - \frac{I_1}{I_{n+1}^m}\Big)\Big(I_{n+1}^m - I_n^m\Big) \\
&+ \frac{\beta_1 T_1 f(V_1)}{p_2 e^{-\mu_2\tau_2}I_1}\Big(1 - \frac{V_1}{V_{n+1}^m}\Big)\Big(V_{n+1}^m - V_n^m\Big) + \frac{p_1 e^{\mu_1\tau_1}}{q}(Z_{n+1}^m - Z_n^m)\Big] \\
&+ \beta_1 T_1 f(V_1)\Big[\varphi\Big(\frac{T_{n+1}^m f(V_n^m)}{T_1 f(V_1)}\Big) - \varphi\Big(\frac{T_{n-m_1+1}^m f(V_{n-m_1}^m)}{T_1 f(V_1)}\Big)\Big] \\
&+ \beta_2 T_1 g(I_1)\Big[\varphi(\frac{T_{n+1}^m g(I_n^m)}{T_1 g(I_1)}) - \varphi(\frac{T_{n-m_1+1}^m g(I_{n-m_1}^m)}{T_1 g(I_1)})\Big] \\
&+ \beta_1 T_1 f(V_1)\Big[\varphi(\frac{I_{n+1}^m}{I_1}) - \varphi(\frac{I_{n-m_2+1}^m}{I_1})\Big] \\
&+ \beta_1 T_1 f(V_1)\Big[\frac{f(V_{n+1}^m)}{f(V_1)} - \frac{f(V_n^m)}{f(V_1)} + \ln\frac{f(V_n^m)}{f(V_{n+1}^m)}\Big] \\
&+ \beta_2 T_1 g(I_1)\Big[\frac{g(I_{n+1}^m)}{g(I_1)} - \frac{g(I_n^m)}{g(I_1)} + \ln\frac{g(I_n^m)}{g(I_{n+1}^m)}\Big]\Big\}.
\end{aligned}$$

As E_1 satisfies

$$\lambda = d_1T_1 + \beta_1T_1f(V_1) + \beta_2T_1g(I_1),$$
$$\beta_1T_1f(V_1) + \beta_2T_1g(I_1) = e^{-\mu_1\tau_1}d_2I_1, p_2e^{-\mu_1\tau_1}I_1 = d_3V_1,$$

then

$$\begin{aligned}
\widetilde{W}_{n+1} - \widetilde{W}_n \quad \leq \quad & \sum_{m=0}^{N} \Big\{ d_1T_1\Big(1-\frac{T_1}{T^m_{n+1}}\Big)\Big(1-\frac{T^m_{n+1}}{T_1}\Big) + \Big(1-\frac{T_1}{T^m_{n+1}}\Big)\Big(\beta_1T_1f(V_1)+\beta_2T_1g(I_1)\Big) \\
- \quad & \Big(1-\frac{T_1}{T^m_{n+1}}\Big)\Big(\beta_1T^m_{n+1}f(V^m_n)+\beta_2T^m_{n+1}g(I^m_n)\Big) \\
+ \quad & \Big(1-\frac{I_1}{I^m_{n+1}}\Big)\Big(\beta_1T^m_{n-m_1+1}f(V^m_{n-m_1})+\beta_2T^m_{n-m_1+1}g(I^m_{n-m_1})\Big) \\
- \quad & \beta_1T_1f(V_1)\frac{I^m_{n+1}}{I_1}\Big(1-\frac{I_1}{I^m_{n+1}}\Big) - \beta_2T_1g(I_1)\frac{I^m_{n+1}}{I_1}\Big(1-\frac{I_1}{I^m_{n+1}}\Big) \\
+ \quad & \beta_1T_1f(V_1)\Big(1-\frac{V_1}{V^m_{n+1}}\Big)\Big(\frac{I^m_{n-m_2+1}}{I_1}-\frac{V^m_{n+1}}{V_1}\Big) - \frac{p_1d_4e^{\mu_1\tau_1}}{q}Z^m_{n+1} \\
+ \quad & \beta_1T_1f(V_1)\Big[\varphi\Big(\frac{T^m_{n+1}f(V^m_n)}{T_1f(V_1)}\Big) - \varphi\Big(\frac{T^m_{n-m_1+1}f(V^m_{n-m_1})}{T_1f(V_1)}\Big)\Big] \\
+ \quad & \beta_2T_1g(I_1)\Big[\varphi\Big(\frac{T^m_{n+1}g(I^m_n)}{T_1g(I_1)}\Big) - \varphi\Big(\frac{T^m_{n-m_1+1}g(I^m_{n-m_1})}{T_1g(I_1)}\Big)\Big] \\
+ \quad & \beta_1T_1f(V_1)\Big[\varphi\Big(\frac{I^m_{n+1}}{I_1}\Big) - \varphi\Big(\frac{I^m_{n-m_2+1}}{I_1}\Big)\Big] \\
+ \quad & \beta_1T_1f(V_1)\Big(\frac{f(V^m_{n+1})}{f(V_1)} - \frac{f(V^m_n)}{f(V_1)} + \ln\frac{f(V^m_n)}{f(V^m_{n+1})}\Big) \\
+ \quad & \beta_2T_1g(I_1)\Big(\frac{g(I^m_{n+1})}{g(I_1)} - \frac{g(I^m_n)}{g(I_1)} + \ln\frac{g(I^m_n)}{g(I^m_{n+1})}\Big)\Big\} \\
- \quad & \sum_{m=0}^{N}\frac{\beta_1T_1f(V_1)D}{p_2I_1e^{-\mu_2\tau_2}(\Delta x)^2}\Big(1-\frac{V_1}{V^m_{n+1}}\Big)\Big(V^{m+1}_{n+1}-2V^m_{n+1}+V^{m-1}_{n+1}\Big) \\
= \quad & \sum_{m=0}^{N}\Big\{d_1T_1\Big(1-\frac{T_1}{T^m_{n+1}}\Big)\Big(1-\frac{T^m_{n+1}}{T_1}\Big) + \beta_1T_1f(V_1)\Big[3-\frac{T_1}{T^m_{n+1}} - \frac{V_1I^m_{n-m_2+1}}{V^m_{n+1}I_1} \\
- \quad & \frac{T^m_{n-m_1+1}f(V^m_{n-m_1})I_1}{T_1f(V_1)I^m_{n+1}} + \frac{f(V^m_{n+1})}{f(V_1)} - \frac{V^m_{n+1}}{V_1} + \ln\frac{T_{n-m_1+1}f(V^m_{n-m_1})I^m_{n-m_2+1}}{T^m_{n+1}f(V^m_{n+1})I^m_{n+1}}\Big] \\
+ \quad & \beta_2T_1g(I_1)\Big[2-\frac{T_1}{T^m_{n+1}} - \frac{T^m_{n-m_1+1}g(I^m_{n-m_1})I_1}{T_1g(I_1)I^m_{n+1}} + \frac{g(I^m_{n+1})}{g(I_1)} \\
- \quad & \frac{I^m_{n+1}}{I_1} + \ln\frac{T^m_{n-m_1+1}g(I^m_{n-m_1})}{T^m_{n+1}g(I^m_{n+1})}\Big] \\
- \quad & \frac{p_1d_4e^{\mu_1\tau_1}}{q}Z^m_{n+1}\Big\} - \frac{\beta_1T_1f(V_1)D}{p_2I_1e^{-\mu_2\tau_2}(\Delta x)^2}V_1\sum_{m=0}^{N-1}\frac{(V^{m+1}_{n+1}-V^m_{n+1})^2}{V^{m+1}_{n+1}V^m_{n+1}} \\
= \quad & \sum_{m=0}^{N}\Big\{d_1T_1\Big(1-\frac{T_1}{T^m_{n+1}}\Big)\Big(1-\frac{T^m_{n+1}}{T_1}\Big) + \beta_1T_1f(V_1)\Big[-\varphi(\frac{T_1}{T^m_{n+1}}) \\
- \quad & \varphi\Big(\frac{T^m_{n-m_1+1}f(V^m_{n-m_1})I_1}{T_1f(V_1)I^m_{n+1}}\Big) - \varphi\Big(\frac{V_1I^m_{n-m_2+1}}{V^m_{n+1}I_1}\Big) + \frac{f(V^m_{n+1})}{f(V_1)} - \frac{V^m_{n+1}}{V_1} \\
+ \quad & \ln\frac{f(V^m_1)V^m_{n+1}}{f(V^m_{n+1})V_1}\Big] + \beta_2T_1g(I_1)\Big[-\varphi\Big(\frac{T_1}{T^m_{n+1}}\Big) - \varphi\Big(\frac{T^m_{n-m_1+1}g(I^m_{n-m_1})I_1}{T_1g(I_1)I^m_{n+1}}\Big) \\
+ \quad & \frac{g(I^m_{n+1})}{g(I_1)} - \frac{I^m_{n_1}}{I_1} + \ln\frac{g(I^m_1)I^m_{n+1}}{g(I^m_{n+1})I_1}\Big] \\
- \quad & \frac{p_1d_4e^{\mu_1\tau_1}}{q}Z^m_{n+1}\Big\} - \frac{\beta_1T_1f(V_1)D}{p_2I_1e^{-\mu_2\tau_2}(\Delta x)^2}V_1\sum_{m=0}^{N-1}\frac{(V^{m+1}_{n+1}-V^m_{n+1})^2}{V^{m+1}_{n+1}V^m_{n+1}} \\
= \quad & \sum_{m=0}^{N}\Big\{d_1T_1\Big(1-\frac{T_1}{T^m_{n+1}}\Big)\Big(1-\frac{T^m_{n+1}}{T_1}\Big) + \beta_1T_1f(V_1)\Big[-\varphi(\frac{T_1}{T^m_{n+1}}) \\
- \quad & \varphi\Big(\frac{T^m_{n-m_1+1}f(V^m_{n-m_1})I_1}{T_1f(V_1)I^m_{n+1}}\Big) - \varphi\Big(\frac{V_1I^m_{n-m_2+1}}{V^m_{n+1}I_1}\Big) \\
- \quad & \varphi\Big(\frac{f(V^m_1)V^m_{n+1}}{f(V^m_{n+1})V_1}\Big) + \Big(\frac{f(V^m_{n+1})}{f(V_1)} - \frac{V^m_{n+1}}{V_1}\Big)\Big(1-\frac{f(V^m_{n+1})V_1}{f(V^m_1)V^m_{n+1}}\Big)\Big] \\
+ \quad & \beta_2T_1g(I_1)\Big[-\varphi\Big(\frac{T_1}{T^m_{n+1}}\Big) - \varphi\Big(\frac{T^m_{n-m_1+1}g(I^m_{n-m_1})I_1}{T_1g(I_1)I^m_{n+1}}\Big) - \varphi\Big(\frac{g(I^m_1)I^m_{n+1}}{g(I^m_{n+1})I_1}\Big) \\
+ \quad & \Big(\frac{g(I^m_{n+1})}{g(I_1)} - \frac{I^m_{n+1}}{I_1}\Big)\Big(1-\frac{g(I_1)}{g(I^m_{n+1})}\Big)\Big] - \frac{p_1d_4e^{\mu_1\tau_1}}{q}Z^m_{n+1}\Big\} \\
- \quad & -\frac{\beta_1T_1f(V_1)D}{p_2I_1e^{-\mu_2\tau_2}(\Delta x)^2}V_1\sum_{m=0}^{N-1}\frac{(V^{m+1}_{n+1}-V^m_{n+1})^2}{V^{m+1}_{n+1}V^m_{n+1}}.
\end{aligned}$$

Similar to the proof of Theorem 3, we have

$$\Big(\frac{f(V(x,t))}{f(V_1)}-\frac{V(x,t)}{V_1}\Big)\Big(1-\frac{f(V_1)}{f(V(x,t))}\Big)\leq 0,$$

$$\Big(\frac{g(I(x,t))}{g(I_1)}-\frac{I(x,t)}{I_1}\Big)\Big(1-\frac{g(I_1)}{g(I(x,t))}\Big)\leq 0.$$

It follows from $\varphi(u)\geq 0$ that $(\widetilde{W}_{n+1}-\widetilde{W}_n)\leq 0$, for all $n\in\aleph$, this implies that $\{\widetilde{W}_n\}$ is monotone decreasing sequence. As $\widetilde{W}_n\geq 0$, then $\lim_{n\to\infty}\widetilde{W}_n\geq 0$, $\lim_{n\to\infty}(\widetilde{W}_{n+1}-\widetilde{W}_n)=0$, so that $\lim_{n\to\infty}T_n^m=T_1$. Combined with system (7), we obtain $\lim_{n\to\infty}I_n^m=I_1$, $\lim_{n\to\infty}V_n^m=V_1$ and $\lim_{n\to\infty}Z_n^m=0$, for all $m\in\{0,1,\cdots,N\}$, then E_1 of system (7) is globally asymptotically stable. This completes the proof. □

Theorem 8. *For system (7), if $R_1>1$, the interior equilibrium E_2 is not globally asymptotically stable .*

Proof. Define the discrete Lyapunov function as follows

$$\begin{aligned}
\overline{W}_n &= \sum_{m=0}^{N}\Big\{\frac{1}{\Delta t}\Big[T_2\varphi\Big(\frac{T_n^m}{T_2}\Big)+e^{\mu_1\tau_1}I_2\varphi\Big(\frac{I_n^m}{I_2}\Big)+\frac{\beta_1T_2f(V_2)}{p_2e^{-\mu_2\tau_2}I_2}V_2\varphi\Big(\frac{V_n^m}{V_2}\Big)\\
&+\frac{p_1e^{\mu_1\tau_1}}{q}Z_2\varphi\Big(\frac{Z_n^m}{Z_2}\Big)+\Delta tp_1e^{\mu_1\tau_1}I_2Z_n^m\Big]+\beta_1T_2f(V_2)\sum_{j=n-m_1}^{n-1}\varphi\Big(\frac{T_{j+1}^mf(V_j^m)}{T_2f(V_2)}\Big)\\
&+\beta_2T_2g(I_2)\sum_{j=n-m_1}^{n-1}\varphi\Big(\frac{T_{j+1}^mg(I_j^m)}{T_2g(I_2)}\Big)+\beta_1T_2f(V_2)\sum_{j=n-m_2}^{n-1}\varphi\Big(\frac{I_{j+1}^m}{I_2}\Big)\\
&+\beta_1T_2f(V_2)\varphi\Big(\frac{f(V_n^m)}{f(V_2)}\Big)+\beta_2T_2g(I_2)\varphi\Big(\frac{g(I_n^m)}{g(I_2)}\Big)\Big\},
\end{aligned}$$

it follows from $u-1\geq\ln u$ that $\overline{W}_n\geq 0$ for all $n\in\aleph$. Then, along the trajectory of (7)

$$\begin{aligned}
\overline{W}_{n+1}-\overline{W}_n &= \sum_{m=0}^{N}\Big\{\frac{1}{\Delta t}\Big[T_{n+1}^m-T_n^m+T_2\ln\frac{T_n^m}{T_{n+1}^m}+e^{\mu_1\tau_1}\Big(I_{n+1}^m-I_n^m+I_2\ln\frac{I_n^m}{I_{n+1}^m}\Big)\\
&+\frac{\beta_1T_2f(V_2)}{p_2e^{-\mu_2\tau_2}I_2}\Big(V_{n+1}^m-V_n^m+V_2\ln\frac{V_n^m}{V_{n+1}^m}\Big)+\frac{p_1e^{\mu_1\tau_1}}{q}(Z_{n+1}^m-Z_n^m\\
&+Z_2\ln\frac{Z_n^m}{Z_{n+1}^m})+\Delta tp_1e^{\mu_1\tau_1}I_2\Big(Z_{n+1}^m-Z_n^m\Big)\Big]\\
&+\beta_1T_2f(V_2)\Big[\sum_{j=n-m_1+1}^{n}\varphi\Big(\frac{T_{j+1}^mf(V_j^m)}{T_2f(V_2)}\Big)-\sum_{j=n-m_1}^{n-1}\varphi\Big(\frac{T_{j+1}^mf(V_j^m)}{T_2f(V_2)}\Big)\Big]\\
&+\beta_2T_2g(I_2)\Big[\sum_{j=n-m_1+1}^{n}\varphi\Big(\frac{T_{j+1}^mg(I_j^m)}{T_2g(I_2)}\Big)-\sum_{j=n-m_1}^{n-1}\varphi\Big(\frac{T_{j+1}^mg(I_j^m)}{T_2g(I_2)}\Big)\Big]\\
&+\beta_1T_2f(V_2)\Big[\sum_{j=n-m_2+1}^{n}\varphi\Big(\frac{I_{j+1}^m}{I_2}\Big)-\sum_{j=n-m_2}^{n-1}\varphi\Big(\frac{I_{j+1}^m}{I_2}\Big)\Big]\\
&+\beta_1T_2f(V_2)\Big(\frac{f(V_{n+1}^m)}{f(V_2)}-\frac{f(V_n^m)}{f(V_2)}+\ln\frac{f(V_n^m)}{f(V_{n+1}^m)}\Big)\\
&+\beta_2T_2g(I_2)\Big(\frac{g(I_{n+1}^m)}{g(I_2)}-\frac{g(I_n^m)}{g(I_2)}+\ln\frac{g(I_n^m)}{g(I_{n+1}^m)}\Big)\Big\}
\end{aligned}$$

$$
\begin{aligned}
\leq\ & \sum_{m=0}^{N}\Bigg\{\frac{1}{\Delta t}\Big[\Big(1-\frac{T_2}{T_{n+1}^m}\Big)\Big(T_{n+1}^m-T_n^m\Big)+e^{\mu_1\tau_1}\Big(1-\frac{I_2}{I_{n+1}^m}\Big)\Big(I_{n+1}^m-I_n^m\Big) \\
+\ & \frac{\beta_1T_2f(V_2)}{p_2e^{-\mu_2\tau_2}I_2}\Big(1-\frac{V_2}{V_{n+1}^m}\Big)\Big(V_{n+1}^m-V_n^m\Big) \\
+\ & \frac{p_1e^{\mu_1\tau_1}}{q}\Big(1-\frac{Z_2}{Z_{n+1}^m}\Big)\Big(Z_{n+1}^m-Z_n^m\Big)+\Delta t p_1e^{\mu_1\tau_1}I_2\Big(Z_{n+1}^m-Z_n^m\Big)\Big] \\
+\ & \beta_1T_2f(V_2)\Big[\varphi\Big(\frac{T_{n+1}^mf(V_n^m)}{T_2f(V_2)}\Big)-\varphi\Big(\frac{T_{n-m_1+1}^mf(V_{n-m_1}^m)}{T_2f(V_2)}\Big)\Big] \\
+\ & \beta_2T_2g(I_2)\Big[\varphi\Big(\frac{T_{n+1}^mg(I_n^m)}{T_2g(I_2)}\Big)-\varphi\Big(\frac{T_{n-m_1+1}^mg(I_{n-m_1}^m)}{T_2g(I_2)}\Big)\Big] \\
+\ & \beta_1T_2f(V_2)\Big[\varphi\Big(\frac{I_{n+1}^m}{I_2}\Big)-\varphi\Big(\frac{I_{n-m_2+1}^m}{I_2}\Big)\Big] \\
+\ & \beta_1T_2f(V_2)\Big(\frac{f(V_{n+1}^m)}{f(V_2)}-\frac{f(V_n^m)}{f(V_2)}+\ln\frac{f(V_n^m)}{f(V_{n+1}^m)}\Big) \\
+\ & \beta_2T_2g(I_2)\Big(\frac{g(I_{n+1}^m)}{g(I_2)}-\frac{g(I_n^m)}{g(I_2)}+\ln\frac{g(I_n^m)}{g(I_{n+1}^m)}\Big)\Bigg\}.
\end{aligned}
$$

From the equilibrium condition of E_2, we have

$$
\lambda=d_1T_2+\beta_1T_2f(V_2)+\beta_2T_2g(I_2),\ \ p_2e^{-\mu_2\tau_2}I_2=d_3V_2,
$$

$$
\beta_1T_2f(V_2)+\beta_2T_2g(I_2)=e^{\mu_1\tau_1}(d_2I_2+p_1I_2Z_2),\ \ I_2=\frac{d_4}{q},
$$

then

$$
\begin{aligned}
\overline{W}_{n+1}-\overline{W}_n\ \leq\ & \sum_{m=0}^{N}\Bigg\{d_2T_2\Big(1-\frac{T_2}{T_{n+1}^m}\Big)\Big(1-\frac{T_{n+1}^m}{T_2}\Big)+\Big(1-\frac{T_2}{T_{n+1}^m}\Big)\Big(\beta_1T_2f(V_2) \\
+\ & \beta_2T_2g(I_2)\Big)-\Big(1-\frac{T_2}{T_{n+1}^m}\Big)\Big(\beta_1T_{n+1}^mf(V_n^m)+\beta_2T_{n+1}^mg(I_n^m)\Big) \\
+\ & \Big(1-\frac{I_2}{I_{n+1}^m}\Big)\Big(\beta_1T_{n-m_1+1}^mf(V_{n-m_1}^m)+\beta_2T_{n-m_1+1}^mg(I_{n-m_1}^m)\Big) \\
-\ & d_2e^{\mu_1\tau_1}I_{n+1}^m-p_1e^{\mu_1\tau_1}I_{n+1}^mZ_n^m+\beta_1T_2f(V_2)+\beta_2T_2g(I_2) \\
-\ & p_1e^{\mu_1\tau_1}I_2Z_2+p_1e^{\mu_1\tau_1}I_2Z_n^m+p_1e^{\mu_1\tau_1}I_2(Z_{n+1}^m-Z_n^m) \\
+\ & \beta_1T_2f(V_2)\Big(1-\frac{V_2}{V_{n+1}^m}\Big)\Big(\frac{I_{n-m_2+1}^m}{I_2}-\frac{V_{n+1}^m}{V_2}\Big) \\
+\ & p_1e^{\mu_1\tau_1}I_{n+1}^mZ_n^m-\frac{p_1d_4e^{\mu_1\tau_1}}{q}Z_{n+1}^m-p_1e^{\mu_1\tau_1}Z_2\frac{I_{n+1}^mZ_n^m}{Z_{n+1}^m} \\
+\ & p_1e^{\mu_1\tau_1}I_2Z_2+\beta_1T_2f(V_2)\Big[\varphi\Big(\frac{T_{n+1}^mf(V_n^m)}{T_2f(V_2)}\Big)-\varphi\Big(\frac{T_{n-m_1+1}^mf(V_{n-m_1}^m)}{T_2f(V_2)}\Big)\Big] \\
+\ & \beta_2T_2g(I_2)\Big[\varphi\Big(\frac{T_{n+1}^mg(I_n^m)}{T_2g(I_2)}\Big)-\varphi\Big(\frac{T_{n-m_1+1}^mg(I_{n-m_1}^m)}{T_2g(I_2)}\Big)\Big] \\
+\ & \beta_1T_2f(V_2)\Big[\varphi\Big(\frac{I_{n+1}^m}{I_2}\Big)-\varphi\Big(\frac{I_{n-m_2+1}^m}{I_2}\Big)\Big] \\
+\ & \beta_1T_2f(V_2)\Big(\frac{f(V_{n+1}^m)}{f(V_2)}-\frac{f(V_n^m)}{f(V_2)}+\ln\frac{f(V_n^m)}{f(V_{n+1}^m)}\Big) \\
+\ & \beta_2T_2g(I_2)\Big(\frac{g(I_{n+1}^m)}{g(I_2)}-\frac{g(I_n^m)}{g(I_2)}+\ln\frac{g(I_n^m)}{g(I_{n+1}^m)}\Big)\Bigg\}
\end{aligned}
$$

$$
\begin{aligned}
&- \frac{DV_2\beta_1T_2f(V_2)}{p_2e^{-\mu_2\tau_2}I_2(\Delta x)^2}\sum_{m=0}^{N-1}\frac{(V_{n+1}^{m+1}-V_{n+1}^{m})^2}{V_{n+1}^{m+1}V_{n+1}^{m}} \\
&= \sum_{m=0}^{N}\Big\{ d_1T_2\Big(1-\frac{T_2}{T^m_{n+1}}\Big)\Big(1-\frac{T^m_{n+1}}{T_2}\Big) + \beta_1T_2f(V_2)\Big[3-\frac{T_2}{T^m_{n+1}} - \frac{V_2I^m_{n-m_2+1}}{V^m_{n+1}I_2} \\
&- \frac{T^m_{n-m_1+1}f(V^m_{n-m_1})I_2}{T_2f(V_2)I^m_{n+1}} + \frac{f(V^m_{n+1})}{f(V_2)} - \frac{V^m_{n+1}}{V_2} + \ln\frac{T^m_{n-m_1+1}f(V^m_{n-m_1})I_{n-m_2+1}}{T^m_{n+1}f(V^m_{n+1})I_{n+1}}\Big] \\
&+ \beta_2T_2g(I_2)\Big[2-\frac{T_2}{T^m_{n+1}} - \frac{T^m_{n-m_1+1}g(I^m_{n-m_1})I_2}{T_2g(I_2)I^m_{n+1}} + \frac{g(I^m_{n+1})}{g(I_2)} \\
&- \frac{I^m_{n+1}}{I_2} + \ln\frac{T^m_{n-m_1+1}g(I^m_{n-m_1})}{T^m_{n+1}g(I^m_{n+1})}\Big] - d_2e^{\mu_1\tau_1}I^m_{n+1} - p_1e^{\mu_1\tau_1}Z_2\frac{I^m_{n+1}Z^m_n}{Z^m_{n+1}}\Big\} \\
&- \frac{DV_2\beta_1T_2f(V_2)}{p_2e^{-\mu_2\tau_2}I_2(\Delta x)^2}\sum_{m=0}^{N-1}\frac{(V_{n+1}^{m+1}-V_{n+1}^{m})^2}{V_{n+1}^{m+1}V_{n+1}^{m}} \\
&= \sum_{m=0}^{N}\Big\{ d_1T_2\Big(1-\frac{T_2}{T^m_{n+1}}\Big)\Big(1-\frac{T^m_{n+1}}{T_2}\Big) + \beta_1T_2f(V_2)\Big[-\varphi\Big(\frac{T_2}{T^m_{n+1}}\Big) \\
&- \varphi\Big(\frac{V_2I^m_{n-m_2+1}}{V^m_{n+1}I_2}\Big) - \varphi\Big(\frac{T^m_{n-m_1+1}f(V^m_{n-m_1})I_2}{T_2f(V_2)I^m_{n+1}}\Big) \\
&+ \Big(\frac{f(V_{n+1})}{f(V_2)} - \frac{V_{n+1}}{V_2}\Big)\Big(1-\frac{f(V_2)}{f(V_{n+1})}\Big)\Big] \\
&+ \beta_2T_2g(I_2)\Big[-\varphi\Big(\frac{T_2}{T^m_{n+1}}\Big) - \varphi\Big(\frac{T^m_{n-m_1+1}g(I^m_{n-m_1})I_2}{T_2g(I_2)I^m_{n+1}}\Big) + \Big(\frac{g(I_{n+1})}{g(I_2)} \\
&- \frac{I^m_{n+1}}{I_2}\Big)\Big(1-\frac{g(I_2)}{g(I_{n+1})}\Big)\Big] - d_2e^{\mu_1\tau_1}I^m_{n+1} - p_1e^{\mu_1\tau_1}Z_2\frac{I^m_{n+1}Z^m_n}{Z^m_{n+1}}\Big\} \\
&- \frac{DV_2\beta_1T_2f(V_2)}{p_2e^{-\mu_2\tau_2}I_2(\Delta x)^2}\sum_{m=0}^{N-1}\frac{(V_{n+1}^{m+1}-V_{n+1}^{m})^2}{V_{n+1}^{m+1}V_{n+1}^{m}}.
\end{aligned}
$$

Similar to the proof of Theorem 3, we have

$$
\Big(\frac{f(V(x,t))}{f(V_1)} - \frac{V}{V_1}\Big)\Big(1-\frac{f(V_1)}{f(V(x,t))}\Big) \leq 0,
$$

$$
\Big(\frac{g(I(x,t))}{g(I_1)} - \frac{I(x,t)}{I_1}\Big)\Big(1-\frac{g(I_1)}{g(I(x,t))}\Big) \leq 0,
$$

this implies that $\{\overline{W}_n\}$ is a monotone decreasing sequence, then $\overline{W}_n \geq 0$, $\lim_{n\to\infty}\overline{W}_n \geq 0$, therefore

$$
\lim_{n\to\infty}(\overline{W}_{n+1} - \overline{W}_n) = 0.
$$

According to the system (7), we claim that the CTL-activated equilibrium E_2 is not globally asymptotically stable. In fact, if the CTL-activated equilibrium E_2 is globally asymptotically stable, from the above inequality, we have

$$
0 \leq -d_2e^{\mu_1\tau_1}I_2 - p_1e^{\mu_1\tau_1}Z_2I_2 < 0,
$$

this is a contradiction. This completes the proof. □

4. Numerical Simulation

In this section, we choose $f(V) = V, g(I) = I$, some numerical results of system (4) are presented for supporting our analytic results. Based on biological meanings of virus dynamics model from papers [39,40], we have estimated the values of our model parameters as follows:

If we choose $D = 3$, then we can give a numerical simulation of the stability of system (4). Using the data in Table 1, we first show in a simulation that the interior equilibrium is stable (see Figure 1).

Table 1. State variables and parameters of HIV-1 infection model.

Parameter	Description	
λ	0.9	References [40]
d_1	0.03	Reference [39]
d_2	0.5	Reference [39]
d_3	0.1	Reference [40]
d_4	0.3	Reference [40]
β_1	0.3	Reference [40]
β_2	0.4	Reference [40]
p_1	$0.08\,\text{day}^{-1}$	Estimate
p_2	$0.5\,\text{day}^{-1}$	Reference [40]
q	0.4	Estimate

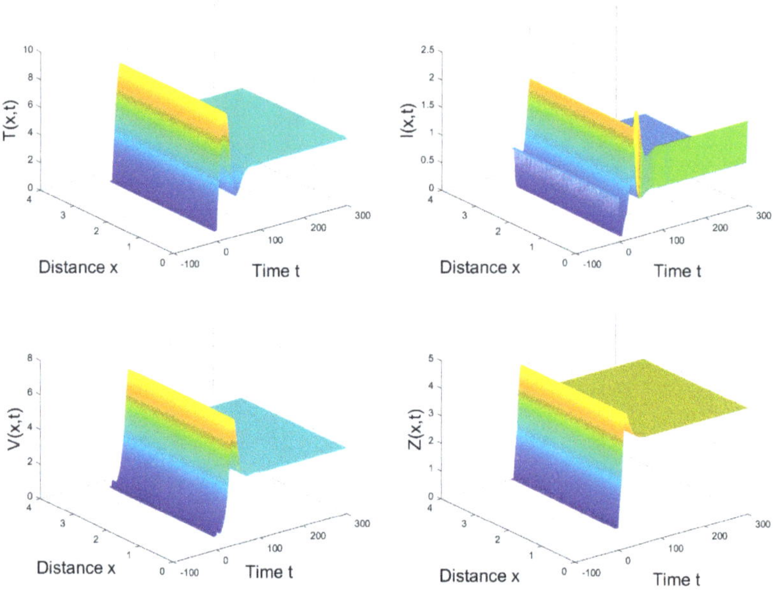

Figure 1. When $D = 3, R_1 > 1$, the interior equilibrium E_2 is globally asymptotically stable.

From Figure 1, we can see that the population has gradually stabilized after a sharp fluctuation.

If we choose $\beta_1 = 0.0003$ and $\beta_2 = 0.004$, then $R_0 < 1$. We can simulate that the infection-free equilibrium is globally asymptotically stable (see Figure 2).

From Figure 2 , we can see that the number of infected cells, virus and CTLs tends to zero, except uninfected cells.

If we choose $q = 0.000004$ and $p_2 = 0.9$, then $R_1 \leq 1 < R_0$. This moment the CTL-inactivated equilibrium is globally asymptotically stable (see Figure 3).

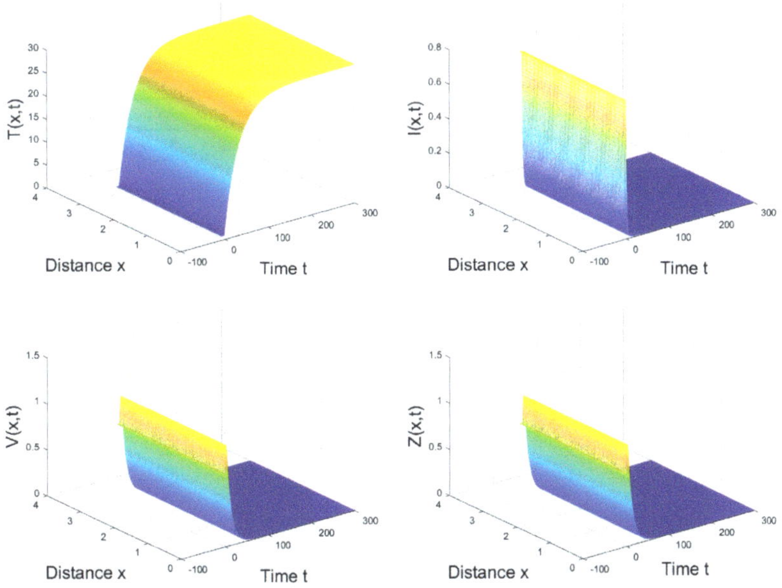

Figure 2. When $D = 3, R_0 < 1$, the infection-free equilibrium E_0 is globally asymptotically stable.

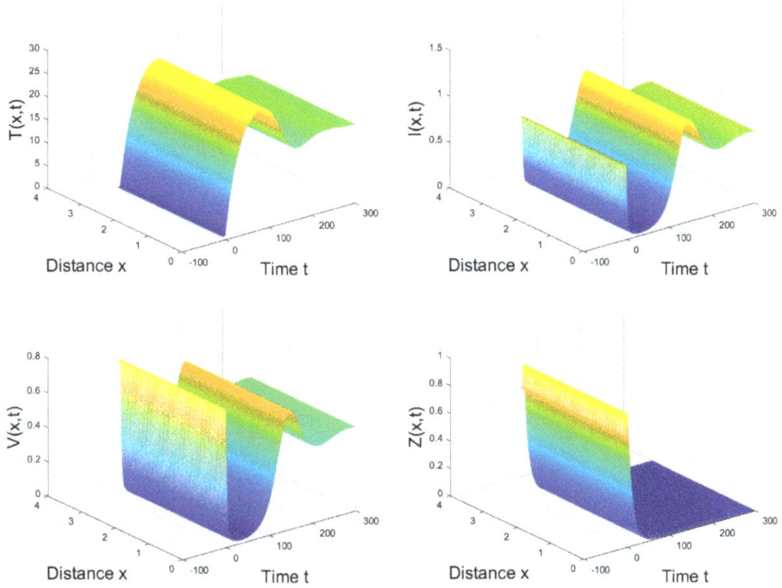

Figure 3. When $D = 3, R_1 \leq 1 < R_0$, the CTL-inactivated equilibrium E_1 is globally asymptotically stable.

From Figure 3, we can see that the population in the compartment $CTLs$ tends to 0. In addition, except for $CTLs$, the number of uninfected cells, infected cells, virus tends to certain constants.

The novelty of this paper is that we consider the effects of diffusion, time delay, and abstract functions on the spread of viruses. In order to see the impact of proliferation on the spread of the virus more intuitively, we first choose $q = 0.04$. Next, we select $D = 0$

and $D = 300$ decibels to simulate the image of I while other parameters keep the values in the Table 1.

The left image in Figure 4 is an image without time delay, and the right image is an image with time delay equal to 300. Since we are simulating long-term dynamic behavior, from the overall image of the two figures, there is no obvious difference in either the stable position or the growth rate. So where is the effect of diffusion reflected? We believe that the effect of diffusion should be reflected in the growth of I. Therefore, we project the two graphs in Figure 4 on the time-quantity axis (Figure 5).

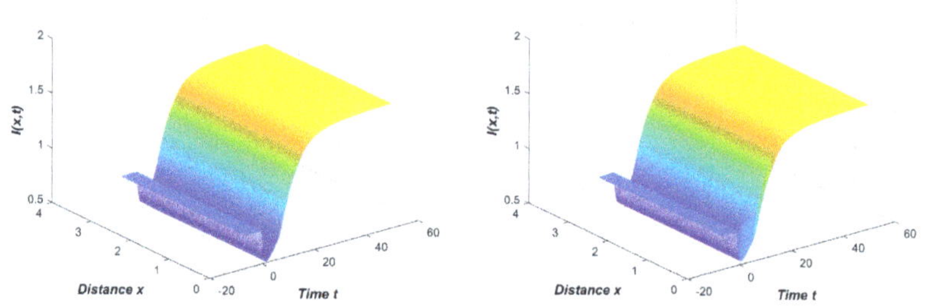

Figure 4. Comparison of compartment I at $D = 0$ and $D = 300$.

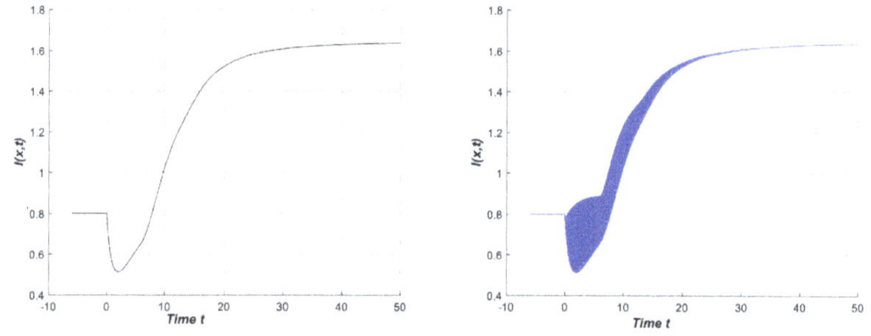

Figure 5. Comparison projection of compartment I when $D = 0$ and $D = 300$.

From the left image of Figure 5, we can clearly see that when there is no time delay, the image rises smoothly and the curve is smooth. When the time lag is equal to 300, the image is not a smooth curve, which shows that the proliferation brings about the proliferation of infected cells and the uneven fluctuation.

5. Conclusions and Discussion

It is necessary to understand the dynamics model for HIV infection since these infected cells usually cause a CTL response from the immune system. In this paper, we first developed a diffusive infection model (4) with general nonlinear incidence rate and two delays on the base of model (3), we show that the global stability of equilibria is completely determined by the reproductive numbers for viral infection R_0 and for CTL immune response R_1. Second, we considered the corresponding discretization of the continuous model by using nonstandard finite difference scheme, and then studied the global stability of the discrete system. Some numerical simulations were also presented to support our analytic results. In general, systems of PDE cannot be solved explicitly, and numerical solutions have to be studied instead. By using the NSFD scheme, we showed that the proposed discrete model partly preserves the global stability of equilibria of the corresponding continuous model. We plan to address how other diffusive terms (for infected and uninfected cells) affect the model in future work.

Author Contributions: X.-L.L.: writing original draft preparation, methodology, formal analysis, editing, validation, funding acquisition; C.-C.Z.: validation, investigation, data curation, visualization. All authors have read and agreed to the published version of the manuscript.

Funding: This project is supported by the Natural Science Foundation of Jiangsu Province, China (Grant No. BK20190578)and the science and technology foundation of Suqian(S201818, Z2021131), China.

Institutional Review Board Statement: Not applicable.

Informed Consent Statement: Not applicable.

Data Availability Statement: Not applicable.

Acknowledgments: The authors are very grateful to the reviewers for their invaluable and expert coments.

Conflicts of Interest: The authors declare no conflict of interest.

References

1. Male, D.; Brostoff, J.; Roth, D.; Roitt, I. *Immunology*, 7th ed.; Elsevier: Amsterdam, The Netherlands, 2006.
2. Nowak, M.; May, R. *Vitus Dynamics*; Oxford University Press: Oxford, UK, 2000.
3. Zhu, C.C.; Zhu, J. Spread trend of COVID-19 epidemic outbreak in China: Using exponential attractor method in a spatial heterogeneous SEIQR model. *Math. Biosci. Eng.* **2020**, *17*, 3062–3087. [CrossRef] [PubMed]
4. Zhu, C.C.; Zhu, J. Dynamic analysis of a delayed COVID-19 epidemic with home quarantine in temporal-spatial heterogeneous via global exponential attractor method. *Chaos Solitons Fractals* **2021**, *143*, 110546. [CrossRef] [PubMed]
5. Zhu, C.C.; Zhu, J. The effect of self-limiting on the prevention and control of the diffuse COVID-19 epidemic with delayed and temporal-spatial heterogeneous. *BMC Infect. Dis.* **2021**, *21*, 1145. [CrossRef] [PubMed]
6. Wodarz, D. *Killer Cell Dynamics: Mathematical and Computational Approaches to Immunology*; Springer: Berlin/Heidelberg, Germany, 2007.
7. Weber, J.N.; Weiss, R.A. HIV infection: The cellular picture. *Sci. Am.* **1988**, *259*, 101–109. [CrossRef] [PubMed]
8. Kirschner, D.E.; Webb, G.; Cloyd, M. Model of HIV-1 disease progression based on virus-induced lymph node homing and homing-induced apotosis of $CD4^+$ lymphocytes. *J. AIDS* **2000**, *24*, 352–362.
9. Anderson, R.; May, R. *Infections Diseases of Humans: Dynamics and Control*; Oxford University Press: Oxford, UK, 1991.
10. Boer, R.D.; Perelson, A. Target cell limited and immune control models of HIV infection: A comparison. *J. Theoret. Biol.* **1998**, *190*, 201–214. [CrossRef] [PubMed]
11. Nowak, M.A.; Bonhoeffer, S.; Hill, A.M.; Boehme, R.; Thomas, H.C.; McDade, H. Viral dynamicss in hepatitis B virus infection. *Proc. Natl. Acad. Sci. USA* **1996**, *93*, 4398–4402. [CrossRef]
12. Lai, X.; Zou, X. Modeling HIV-1 virus dynamics with both virus-to-cell infection and cell-to-cell transimission. *SIAM J. Appl. Math.* **2014**, *74*, 898–917. [CrossRef]
13. Xu, J.; Zhou, Y. Bifurcation analysis of HIV-1 infection model with cell-to-cell transimission and immune response delay. *Math. Biosci. Eng.* **2016**, *13*, 343–367. [CrossRef]
14. Yang, Y.; Zou, L.; Ruan, S. Global dynamics of a delayed within-host viral infection model with both virus-to-cell and cell-to-cell transimissions. *Math. Biosci.* **2015**, *270*, 183–191. [CrossRef] [PubMed]
15. Wang, K.; Wang, W. Propagation of HBV with spatial dependence. *Math. Biosci.* **2007**, *210*, 78–95. [CrossRef]
16. Yang, Y.; Zhou, J.l.; Ma, X.S.; Zhang, T.H. Nonstandard finite difference scheme for a diffusive within-host virus dynamics model with both virus-to-cell and cell-to-cell transmissions. *Comput. Math. Appl.* **2016**, *72*, 1013–1020. [CrossRef]
17. Nowak, M.; Bangham, C. Population dynamics of immune responses to persistent viruses. *Science* **1996**, *272*, 74–79. [CrossRef] [PubMed]
18. Zhu, H.; Zou, X. Dynamics of a HIV-1 infection model with cell-mediated immune response and intracellular delay. *Discrete Contin. Dyn. Syst. Ser. B* **2009**, *12*, 511–524. [CrossRef]
19. Wang, J.L.; Guan, L.J. Global stability for a HIV-1 infection model with cell-mediated immune response and intrecellular delay. *Discret. Contin. Dyn. Syst. Ser. B* **2012**, *17*, 297–302.
20. Arnaout, R.; Nowak, M.; Wodarz, D. HIV-1 dynamics revisited: Biphasic decay by cytotoxic lymphocyte killing. *Proc. R. Soc. Lond. B* **2000**, *265*, 1347–1354. [CrossRef] [PubMed]
21. Culshaw, R.; Ruan, S.; Spiteri, R. Optimal HIV treatment by maxinising immune response. *J. Math. Biol.* **2004**, *48*, 545–562. [CrossRef] [PubMed]
22. Wang, K.; Wang, W.; Liu, X. Global stability in a viral infection model with lytic and nonlytic immune response. *Comput. Math. Appl.* **2006**, *51*, 1593–1610. [CrossRef]
23. Xu, J.H.; Geng, Y. Dynamic consistent NSFD Scheme for a Delayed Viral Infection Model with Immune Response and Nonlinear Incidence. *Discret. Dyn. Nat. Soc.* **2017**, *2017*, 3141736. [CrossRef]
24. Sigdel, R.P.; Mcluskey, C.C. Global stability for an SEI model of infection disease with immigration. *Appl. Math. Comput.* **2014**, *243*, 684–689.

25. Enatsu, Y.; Nakata, Y.; Muroya, Y.; Izzo, G.; Vecchio, A. Global dynamics of difference equations for SIR epidemic models with a class of nonlinear incidence rates. *J. Differ. Equ. Appl.* **2012**, *18*, 1163–1181. [CrossRef]
26. Mickens, R.E. *Nonstandard Finite Difference Models of Differential Equations*; World Scientific: Singapore, 1994.
27. Travis, C.C.; Webb, G.F. Existence and stability for partial functional differential equations. *Trans. Am. Math. Soc.* **1974**, *200*, 395–418. [CrossRef]
28. Shi, P.; Dong, L. Dynamical behaviors of a discrete HIV-1 virus model with bilinear infective rate. *Math. Methods Appl. Sci.* **2014**, *37*, 2271–2280. [CrossRef]
29. Hattaf, K.; Yousfi, N. Global properties of a discrete viral infection model with general incidence rate. *Math. Methods Appl. Sci.* **2016**, *39*, 998–1004. [CrossRef]
30. Yang, Y.; Zhou, J. Global dynamics of a PDE in-host viral model. *Appl. Anal.* **2014**, *93*, 2312–2329.
31. Wang, J.P.; Teng, Z.D.; Miao, H. Global dynamics for discrete-time analog of viral infection model with nonlinear incidence and CTL immune response. *Adv. Differ. Equ.* **2016**, *1*, 143. [CrossRef] [PubMed]
32. Zhu, C.C.; Zhu, J. Stability of a reaction-diffusion alcohol model with the impact of tax policy. *Comput. Math. Appl.* **2017**, *74*, 613–633. [CrossRef]
33. Martin, R.H.; Smith, H.L. Abstract functional differential equations and reaction-diffusion systems. *Trans. Am. Math. Soc.* **1990**, *321*, 1–44.
34. Martin, R.H.; Smith, H.L. Reaction-diffusion systems with time delays: Monotonicity, invariance, comparison and convergence. *J. Reine Angew. Math.* **1991**, *413*, 1–35.
35. Wu, J. *Theory and Applications of Parfunctional Differential Equations*; Springer: New York, NY, USA, 1996.
36. Fitzgibbon, W.E. Semilinear functional differential equations in Banach space. *J. Differ. Equ.* **1978**, *29*, 1–14. [CrossRef]
37. Protter, M.H.; Weinberger, H.F. *Maximum Principles in Differential Equations*; Prentice Hall: Engle-Wood Cliffs, NJ, USA, 1967.
38. Henry, D. *Gerometric Theory of Semilinear Parabolic Equation*; Lecture Notes in Mathematics; Springer: Berlin, Germany, 1993; Volume 840.
39. Nelson, P.; Murray, J.; Perelson, A. A model of HIV-1 pathogenesis that includes an intracellular delay. *Math. Biosci.* **2000**, *163*, 201–215. [CrossRef]
40. Xiang, H.; Tang, Y.L.; Huo, H.F. A viral model with intracellular delay and humoral immunity. *Bull. Malays. Math. Sci. Soc.* **2017**, *40*, 1011–1023. [CrossRef]

axioms

MDPI

Article

Some Common Fixed-Circle Results on Metric Spaces

Nabil Mlaiki [1,*], Nihal Taş [2], Elif Kaplan [3], Suhad Subhi Aiadi [1] and Asma Karoui Souayah [4,5,*]

1 Department of Mathematics and Sciences, Prince Sultan University, Riyadh 11586, Saudi Arabia
2 Department of Mathematics, Balıkesir University, 10145 Balıkesir, Turkey
3 Department of Mathematics, Ondokuz Mayıs University, 55280 Samsun, Turkey
4 Department of Business Administration, College of Science and Humanities, Shaqra University, Dhurma 11961, Saudi Arabia
5 Institut Préparatoire aux Études d'Ingénieurs de Gafsa, Gafsa University, Gafsa 2112, Tunisia
* Correspondence: nmlaiki@psu.edu.sa or nmlaiki2012@gmail.com (N.M.); asma.souayah@yahoo.fr (A.K.S.)

Abstract: Recently, the fixed-circle problems have been studied with different approaches as an interesting and geometric generalization. In this paper, we present some solutions to an open problem CC: what is (are) the condition(s) to make any circle $C_{\varpi_0,\sigma}$ as the common fixed circle for two (or more than two) self-mappings? To do this, we modify some known contractions which are used in fixed-point theorems such as the Hardy–Rogers-type contraction, Kannan-type contraction, etc.

Keywords: metric spaces; fixed circle; common fixed circle

MSC: 54E35; 54E40; 54H25

Citation: Mlaiki, N.; Taş, N.; Kaplan, E.; Subhi Aiadi, S.; Karoui Souayah, A. Some Common Fixed-Circle Results on Metric Spaces. *Axioms* **2022**, *11*, 454. https://doi.org/10.3390/axioms11090454

Academic Editors: Adrian Petrusel, Wei-Shih Du and Luigi Muglia

Received: 6 August 2022
Accepted: 1 September 2022
Published: 4 September 2022

Publisher's Note: MDPI stays neutral with regard to jurisdictional claims in published maps and institutional affiliations.

Copyright: © 2022 by the authors. Licensee MDPI, Basel, Switzerland. This article is an open access article distributed under the terms and conditions of the Creative Commons Attribution (CC BY) license (https://creativecommons.org/licenses/by/4.0/).

1. Introduction

In the recent past, the fixed-circle problem has been introduced as a new geometric generalization of fixed-point theory. After that, some solutions to this problem have been investigated using various techniques (for example, see [1–8], and the references therein). In addition, in [1], the following open problem was given:

Let $(X, \mathfrak{D})$ be a metric space and $C_{\varpi_0,\sigma} = \{\varpi \in X : \mathfrak{D}(\varpi, \varpi_0) = \sigma\}$ be any circle on X.

Open Problem CC: What is (are) the condition(s) to make any circle $C_{\varpi_0,\sigma}$ as the common fixed circle for two (or more than two) self-mappings?

Let ξ and g be two self-mappings on a set X. If $\xi\varpi = g\varpi = \varpi$ for all $\varpi \in C_{\varpi_0,\sigma}$, then $C_{\varpi_0,\sigma}$ is called a common fixed circle of the pair (ξ, g) (see [9] for more details).

Some solutions were given for this open problem (for example, see [8,9]). To obtain new solutions, in this paper, we define new contractions for the pair (ξ, g) and prove new common fixed-circle results on metric spaces. Before moving on to the main results, we recall the following.

Throughout this article, we denote by $\mathbb{R}$ the set of all real numbers and by $\mathbb{R}_+$ the set of all positive real numbers.

Let ξ and g be self-mappings on a set X. If $\xi\varpi = g\varpi = w$ for some ϖ in X, then ϖ is called a coincidence point of ξ and g, w is called a point of coincidence of ξ and g.

Let $C(\xi, g) = \{\varpi \in X : \xi\varpi = g\varpi = \varpi\}$ denote the set of all common fixed-points of self-mappings ξ and g.

In [10], Wardowski introduced the following family of functions to obtain a new type of contraction called $\mathcal{F}$-contraction.

Let $\mathbb{F}$ be the family of all mappings $\mathcal{F} : \mathbb{R}_+ \to \mathbb{R}$ that satisfy the following conditions:

($\mathcal{F}1$) $\mathcal{F}$ is strictly increasing, that is, for all $a, b \in \mathbb{R}_+$ such that $a < b$ implies that $\mathcal{F}(a) < \mathcal{F}(b)$;

($\mathcal{F}2$) For every sequence $\{a_n\}_{n\in N}$ of positive real numbers, $\lim_{n\to\infty} a_n = 0$ and $\lim_{n\to\infty} \mathcal{F}(a_n) = -\infty$ are equivalent;

$(\mathcal{F}3)$There exists $k \in (0,1)$ such that $\lim_{a\to 0^+} a^k\mathcal{F}(a) = 0$.

Some examples of functions that confirm the conditions $(\mathcal{F}1)$, $(\mathcal{F}2)$, and $(\mathcal{F}3)$ are as follows:

- $\mathcal{F}(a) = \ln(a)$;
- $\mathcal{F}(a) = \ln(a) + a$;
- $\mathcal{F}(a) = \ln(a^2 + a)$;
- $\mathcal{F}(a) = -\frac{1}{\sqrt{a}}$ (see [10] for more details).

Definition 1. *[10] Let $(X, \mathfrak{D})$ be a metric space, $\mathcal{F} \in \mathbb{F}$ and $\xi : X \to X$. The mapping ξ is called an $\mathcal{F}$-contraction if there exists $\tau > 0$ such that*

$$\tau + \mathcal{F}(\mathfrak{D}(\xi\varpi, \xi v)) \leq \mathcal{F}(\mathfrak{D}(\varpi, v))$$

for all $\varpi, v \in X$ satisfying $\mathfrak{D}(T\varpi, Tv) > 0$.

2. Main Results

In this section, we prove new common fixed-circle theorems on metric spaces. For this purpose, we modify some well-known contractions such as the Wardowski-type contraction [10], Nemytskii–Edelstein-type contraction [11,12], Banach-type contraction [13], Hardy–Rogers-type contraction [14], Reich-type contraction [15], Chatterjea-type contraction [16], and Kannan-type contraction [17].

At first, we introduce the following new contraction type for two mappings to obtain some common fixed-circle results on metric spaces.

Definition 2. *Let $(X, \mathfrak{D})$ be a metric space and ξ, g be two self-mappings on X. If there exist $\tau > 0, \mathcal{F} \in \mathbb{F}$ and $\varpi_0 \in X$ such that*

$$\tau + \mathcal{F}(\mathfrak{D}(\varpi, \xi\varpi) + \mathfrak{D}(\varpi, g\varpi)) \leq \mathcal{F}(\mathfrak{D}(\varpi_0, \varpi))$$

for all $\varpi \in X$ satisfying $\min\{\mathfrak{D}(\varpi, \xi\varpi), \mathfrak{D}(\varpi, g\varpi)\} > 0$, then the pair (ξ, g) is called a Wardowski-type $\mathcal{F}_{\xi g}$-contraction.

Notice that the point ϖ_0 mentioned in Definition 2 must be a common fixed-point of the mappings ξ and g. In fact, if ϖ_0 is not a common fixed-point of ξ and g, then we have $\mathfrak{D}(\varpi_0, \xi\varpi_0) > 0$ and $\mathfrak{D}(\varpi_0, g\varpi_0) > 0$. Hence, we obtain

$$\min\{\mathfrak{D}(\varpi_0, \xi\varpi_0), \mathfrak{D}(\varpi_0, g\varpi_0)\} > 0 \Longrightarrow \tau + \mathcal{F}(\mathfrak{D}(\varpi_0, \xi\varpi_0) + \mathfrak{D}(\varpi_0, g\varpi_0)) \leq \mathcal{F}(\mathfrak{D}(\varpi_0, \varpi_0)).$$

This gives a contradiction since the domain of $\mathcal{F}$ is $(0, \infty)$. As a result, we receive the following proposition as a consequence of Definition 2.

Proposition 1. *Let $(X, \mathfrak{D})$ be a metric space. If the pair (ξ, g) is a Wardowski-type $\mathcal{F}_{\xi g}$-contraction with $\varpi_0 \in X$, then we have $\xi\varpi_0 = g\varpi_0 = \varpi_0$.*

Using this new type contraction, we give the following fixed-circle theorem.

Theorem 1. *Let $(X, \mathfrak{D})$ be a metric space and the pair (ξ, g) be a Wardowski-type $\mathcal{F}_{\xi g}$-contraction with $\varpi_0 \in X$. Define the number σ by*

$$\sigma = \inf\{\mathfrak{D}(\varpi, \xi\varpi) + \mathfrak{D}(\varpi, g\varpi) : \varpi \neq \xi\varpi, \varpi \neq g\varpi, \varpi \in X\}. \quad (1)$$

Then, $C_{\varpi_0,\sigma}$ is a common fixed circle of the pair (ξ, g). Especially, ξ and g fix every circle $C_{\varpi_0,r}$ where $r < \sigma$.

Proof. We distinguish two cases.

Case 1: Let $\sigma = 0$. Clearly, $C_{\varpi_0,\sigma} = \{\varpi_0\}$ and by Proposition 1, we see that $C_{\varpi_0,\sigma}$ is a common fixed circle of the pair (ξ, g).

Case 2: Let $\sigma > 0$ and $\varpi \in C_{\varpi_0,\sigma}$. If $\xi\varpi \neq \varpi$ and $g\varpi \neq \varpi$, then by (1), we have $\mathfrak{D}(\varpi, \xi\varpi) + \mathfrak{D}(\varpi, g\varpi) \geq \sigma$. Hence, using the Wardowski-type $\mathcal{F}_{\xi g}$-contraction property and the fact that $\mathcal{F}$ is increasing, we obtain

$$\begin{aligned} \mathcal{F}(\sigma) &\leq \mathcal{F}(\mathfrak{D}(\varpi, \xi\varpi) + \mathfrak{D}(\varpi, g\varpi)) \\ &\leq \mathcal{F}(\mathfrak{D}(\varpi_0, \varpi)) - \tau \\ &< \mathcal{F}(\mathfrak{D}(\varpi_0, \varpi)) \\ &= \mathcal{F}(\sigma) \end{aligned}$$

This gives a contradiction. Therefore, we have $\mathfrak{D}(\varpi, \xi\varpi) + \mathfrak{D}(\varpi, g\varpi) = 0$, that is, $\varpi = \xi\varpi$ and $\varpi = g\varpi$. As a consequence, $C_{\varpi_0,\sigma}$ is a common fixed circle of the pair (ξ, g).

Now, we show that ξ and g also fix any circle $C_{\varpi_0,r}$ with $r < \sigma$. Let $\varpi \in C_{\varpi_0,r}$ and suppose that $\mathfrak{D}(\varpi, \xi\varpi) + \mathfrak{D}(\varpi, g\varpi) > 0$. With the Wardowski-type $\mathcal{F}_{\xi g}$-contraction property, we have

$$\begin{aligned} \mathcal{F}(\mathfrak{D}(\varpi, \xi\varpi) + \mathfrak{D}(\varpi, g\varpi)) &\leq \mathcal{F}(\mathfrak{D}(\varpi_0, \varpi)) - \tau \\ &< \mathcal{F}(\mathfrak{D}(\varpi_0, \varpi)) \\ &= \mathcal{F}(r). \end{aligned}$$

Since $\mathcal{F}$ is increasing, then we find

$$\mathfrak{D}(\varpi, \xi\varpi) + \mathfrak{D}(\varpi, g\varpi) < \mathfrak{D}(\varpi_0, \varpi) < r < \sigma.$$

However, $\sigma = \inf\{\mathfrak{D}(\varpi, \xi\varpi) + \mathfrak{D}(\varpi, g\varpi) : \varpi \neq \xi\varpi, \varpi \neq g\varpi, \varpi \in X\}$, so this gives a contradiction. Thus, $\mathfrak{D}(\varpi, \xi\varpi) + \mathfrak{D}(\varpi, g\varpi) = 0$ and $\varpi = \xi\varpi = g\varpi$. Hence, $C_{\varpi_0,r}$ is a common fixed circle of the pair (ξ, g). □

Example 1. *Let* $X = \{0, 1, -e, e, e-1, e+1, -e^2, e^2, e^2-1, e^2+1, e^2-e, e^2+e\}$ *with usual metric. Define* $\xi, g : X \to X$ *by*

$$\xi\varpi = \begin{cases} 1, & \varpi = 0 \\ \varpi, & otherwise \end{cases}$$

and

$$g\varpi = \begin{cases} e-1, & \varpi = 0 \\ \varpi, & otherwise \end{cases}.$$

Take $\mathcal{F}(a) = \ln(a) + a$, $a > 0$, $\tau = e$ *and* $\varpi_0 = e^2$. *Thus, the pair* (ξ, g) *is a Wardowski-type* $\mathcal{F}_{\xi g}$*-contraction. For* $\varpi = 0$, *we have*

$$\begin{aligned} \min\{\mathfrak{D}(\varpi, \xi\varpi), \mathfrak{D}(\varpi, g\varpi)\} &= \min\{\mathfrak{D}(0,1), \mathfrak{D}(0, e-1)\} \\ &= \min\{1, e-1\} \\ &= 1 > 0 \end{aligned}$$

In addition, we can easily see that the following inequality is satisfied:

$$\begin{aligned} \tau + \mathcal{F}(\mathfrak{D}(\varpi, \xi\varpi) + \mathfrak{D}(\varpi, g\varpi)) &\leq \mathcal{F}(\mathfrak{D}(\varpi_0, \varpi)) \\ e + \mathcal{F}(1 + e - 1) &\leq \mathcal{F}\left(e^2\right) \\ e + \ln e + e &\leq \ln e^2 + e^2 \\ 2e + 1 &\leq 2 + e^2 \end{aligned}$$

With Theorem (1), we obtain

$$\sigma = \inf\{\mathfrak{D}(\varpi, \xi\varpi) + \mathfrak{D}(\varpi, g\varpi) : \varpi \neq \xi\varpi, \varpi \neq g\varpi, \varpi \in X\} = \inf\{1 + e - 1\} = e$$

and ξ, g *fix the circle* $C_{e^2,e} = \{e^2 - e, e^2 + e\}$. *Notice that* ξ *and* g *fix also the circle* $C_{e^2,1} = \{e^2 - 1, e^2 + 1\}$.

The converse of Theorem 1 fails. The following example confirms this statement.

Example 2. *Let* $(X, \mathfrak{D})$ *be a metric space with any point* $\varpi_0 \in X$. *Define the self-mappings* ξ *and* g *as follows:*

$$\xi\varpi = \begin{cases} \varpi, & \mathfrak{D}(\varpi, \varpi_0) \leq \mu \\ \varpi_0, & \mathfrak{D}(\varpi, \varpi_0) > \mu \end{cases}$$

and

$$g\varpi = \begin{cases} \varpi, & \mathfrak{D}(\varpi, \varpi_0) \leq \mu \\ \varpi_0, & \mathfrak{D}(\varpi, \varpi_0) > \mu \end{cases},$$

for all $\varpi \in X$ *with any* $\mu > 0$. *Then, it can be easily checked that the pair* (ξ, g) *is not a Wardowski-type* $\mathcal{F}_{\xi g}$*-contraction for the point* ϖ_0 *but* ξ *and* g *fix every circle* $C_{\varpi_0,r}$ *where* $r \leq \mu$.

Example 3. *Let* $\mathbb{C}$ *be the set of complex numbers,* $(\mathbb{C}, \mathfrak{D})$ *be the usual metric space, and define the self-mappings* $\xi, g : \mathbb{C} \to \mathbb{C}$ *as follows:*

$$\xi\varpi = \begin{cases} \varpi, & |\varpi - 2| < e \\ \varpi + \frac{1}{2}, & |\varpi - 2| \geq e \end{cases}$$

and

$$g\varpi = \begin{cases} \varpi, & |\varpi - 2| < e \\ \varpi - \frac{1}{2}, & |\varpi - 2| \geq e \end{cases},$$

for all $\varpi \in C$. *We have* $\sigma = \inf\{\mathfrak{D}(\varpi, \xi\varpi) + \mathfrak{D}(\varpi, g\varpi) : \varpi \neq \xi\varpi, \varpi \neq g\varpi, \varpi \in C\}$. *Thus, the pair* (ξ, g) *is a Wardowski-type* $\mathcal{F}_{\xi g}$*-contraction with* $\mathcal{F} = ln(a), \tau = \ln e$ *and* $\varpi_0 = 2 \in C$. *Obviously, the number of common fixed circles of* ξ *and* g *is infinite.*

Definition 3. *If there exist* $\tau > 0$, $\mathcal{F} \in \mathcal{F}$ *and* $\varpi_0 \in X$ *such that for all* $\varpi \in X$ *the following holds:*

$$\tau + \mathcal{F}(\mathfrak{D}(\xi\varpi, \varpi) + \mathfrak{D}(g\varpi, \varpi)) < \mathcal{F}(\mathfrak{D}(\varpi, \varpi_0))$$

with $\min\{\mathfrak{D}(\xi\varpi, \varpi), \mathfrak{D}(g\varpi, \varpi)\} > 0$, *then the pair* (ξ, g) *is called a Nemytskii–Edelstein-type* $\mathcal{F}_{\xi g}$*-contraction.*

Proposition 2. *Let* $(X, \mathfrak{D})$ *be a metric space. If the pair* (ξ, g) *is a Nemytskii-Edelstein-type* $\mathcal{F}_{\xi g}$*-contraction with* $\varpi_0 \in X$, *then we have* $\xi\varpi_0 = g\varpi_0 = \varpi_0$.

Proof. It can be easily proved from the similar arguments used in Proposition 1. □

Theorem 2. *Let the pair* (ξ, g) *be a Nemytskii–Edelstein-type* $\mathcal{F}_{\xi g}$*-contraction with* $\varpi_0 \in X$ *and* σ *be defined as in* (1). *Then,* $C_{\varpi_0,\sigma}$ *is a common fixed circle of the pair* (ξ, g). *Especially,* ξ *and* g *fix every circle* $C_{\varpi_0,r}$ *where* $r < \sigma$.

Proof. It can be easily seen from the proof of Theorem 1. □

In addition, we inspire the classical Banach contraction principle to give the following definition:

Definition 4. *If there exist $\tau > 0$, $\mathcal{F} \in \mathcal{F}$ and $\varpi_0 \in X$ such that for all $\varpi \in X$, the following holds:*

$$\tau + \mathcal{F}(\mathfrak{D}(\xi\varpi, \varpi) + \mathfrak{D}(g\varpi, \varpi)) \le \mathcal{F}(\eta\mathfrak{D}(\varpi, \varpi_0))$$

with $\min\{\mathfrak{D}(\xi\varpi, \varpi), \mathfrak{D}(g\varpi, \varpi)\} > 0$ *where* $\eta \in [0, 1)$, *then the pair* (ξ, g) *is called a Banach-type* $\mathcal{F}_{\xi g}$*-contraction.*

Proposition 3. *Let $(X, \mathfrak{D})$ be a metric space. If the pair (ξ, g) is a Banach-type $\mathcal{F}_{\xi g}$-contraction with $\varpi_0 \in X$, then we have $\xi\varpi_0 = g\varpi_0 = \varpi_0$.*

Proof. It can be easily proved from the similar arguments used in Proposition 1. □

Theorem 3. *Let the pair (ξ, g) be a Banach-type $\mathcal{F}_{\xi g}$-contraction with $\varpi_0 \in X$ and σ be defined as in (1). Then $C_{\varpi_0,\sigma}$ is a common fixed circle of the pair (ξ, g). Especially, ξ and g fix every circle $C_{\varpi_0,r}$ where $r < \sigma$.*

Proof. It can be easily seen from the proof of Theorem 1. □

If we consider Example 1, then the pair (ξ, g) is both a Nemytskii–Edelstein-type $\mathcal{F}_{\xi g}$-contraction and a Banach-type $\mathcal{F}_{\xi g}$-contraction with $\mathcal{F}(a) = \ln(a) + a$, $a > 0, \tau = e$, $\varpi_0 = e^2$ and so ξ, g have two common fixed circles $C_{e^2,e}$ and $C_{e^2,1}$.

We introduce the notion of Hardy–Rogers-type $\mathcal{F}_{\xi g}$-contraction.

Definition 5. *Let $(X, \mathfrak{D})$ be a metric space and ξ, g be two self-mappings on X. The pair (ξ, g) is called a Hardy–Rogers-type $\mathcal{F}_{\xi g}$-contraction if there exist $\tau > 0$ and $\mathcal{F} \in \mathcal{F}$ such that*

$$\tau + \mathcal{F}(\mathfrak{D}(\varpi, \xi\varpi) + \mathfrak{D}(\varpi, g\varpi)) \le \mathcal{F}\left(\begin{array}{c} \alpha\mathfrak{D}(\varpi, \varpi_0) + \beta\mathfrak{D}(\varpi, \xi\varpi) \\ +\gamma\mathfrak{D}(\varpi, g\varpi) + \delta\mathfrak{D}(\varpi_0, \xi\varpi_0) + \eta\mathfrak{D}(\varpi_0, g\varpi_0) \end{array} \right) \quad (2)$$

holds for any $\varpi, \varpi_0 \in X$ with $min\{\mathfrak{D}(\varpi, \xi\varpi), \mathfrak{D}(\varpi, g\varpi)\} > 0$, where $\alpha, \beta, \gamma, \delta, \eta$ are nonnegative numbers, $\alpha \neq 0$ and $\alpha + \beta + \gamma + \delta + \eta \le 1$.

Proposition 4. *If the pair (ξ, g) is a Hardy–Rogers-type $\mathcal{F}_{\xi g}$-contraction with $\varpi_0 \in X$, then we have $\xi\varpi_0 = g\varpi_0 = \varpi_0$.*

Proof. Suppose that $\xi\varpi_0 \neq \varpi_0$ and $g\varpi_0 \neq \varpi_0$. From the definition of the Hardy–Rogers-type $\mathcal{F}_{\xi g}$-contraction with $\min\{\mathfrak{D}(\varpi_0, \xi\varpi_0), \mathfrak{D}(\varpi_0, g\varpi_0)\} > 0$, we obtain

$$\begin{aligned} \tau + \mathcal{F}(\mathfrak{D}(\varpi_0, \xi\varpi_0) + \mathfrak{D}(\varpi_0, g\varpi_0)) &\le \mathcal{F}\left(\begin{array}{c} \alpha\mathfrak{D}(\varpi_0, \varpi_0) + \beta\mathfrak{D}(\varpi_0, \xi\varpi_0) \\ +\gamma\mathfrak{D}(\varpi_0, g\varpi_0) + \delta\mathfrak{D}(\varpi_0, \xi\varpi_0) + \eta\mathfrak{D}(\varpi_0, g\varpi_0) \end{array} \right) \\ &= \mathcal{F}((\beta + \delta)\mathfrak{D}(\varpi_0, \xi\varpi_0) + (\gamma + \eta)\mathfrak{D}(\varpi_0, g\varpi_0)) \\ &< \mathcal{F}(\mathfrak{D}(\varpi_0, \xi\varpi_0) + \mathfrak{D}(\varpi_0, g\varpi_0)) \end{aligned}$$

a contradiction because of $\tau > 0$. Thus, we have $\xi\varpi_0 = g\varpi_0 = \varpi_0$. □

Using Proposition 4, we rewrite the condition (2) as follows:

$$\tau + \mathcal{F}(\mathfrak{D}(\varpi, \xi\varpi), \mathfrak{D}(\varpi, g\varpi)) \le \mathcal{F}(\alpha\mathfrak{D}(\varpi, \varpi_0) + \beta\mathfrak{D}(\varpi, \xi\varpi) + \gamma\mathfrak{D}(\varpi, g\varpi))$$

with $\min\{\mathfrak{D}(\varpi, \xi\varpi), \mathfrak{D}(\varpi, g\varpi)\} > 0$ where α, β, γ are nonnegative numbers, $\alpha \neq 0$ and $\alpha + \beta + \gamma \le 1$.

Using this inequality, we present the following fixed-circle result.

Theorem 4. *Let the pair (ξ, g) be a Hardy–Rogers-type $\mathcal{F}_{\xi g}$-contraction with $\varpi_0 \in X$ and σ be defined as in (1). If $\beta = \gamma$, then $C_{\varpi_0,\sigma}$ is a common fixed circle of the pair (ξ, g). In addition, ξ and g fix every circle $C_{\varpi_0,r}$ with $r < \sigma$.*

Proof. We distinguish two cases.

Case 1: Let $\sigma = 0$. Clearly, $C_{\varpi_0,\sigma} = \{\varpi_0\}$ and by Proposition 4, we see that $C_{\varpi_0,\sigma}$ is a common fixed circle of the pair (ξ, g).

Case 2: Let $\sigma > 0$ and $\varpi \in C_{\varpi_0,\sigma}$. Using the Hardy–Rogers-type $\mathcal{F}_{\xi g}$-contractive property and the fact that $\mathcal{F}$ is increasing, we have

$$\begin{aligned}\mathcal{F}(\sigma) &\leq \mathcal{F}(\mathfrak{D}(\varpi,\xi\varpi) + \mathfrak{D}(\varpi,g\varpi)) \\ &\leq \mathcal{F}(\alpha\mathfrak{D}(\varpi,\varpi_0) + \beta\mathfrak{D}(\varpi,\xi\varpi) + \gamma\mathfrak{D}(\varpi,g\varpi)) - \tau \\ &< \mathcal{F}(\alpha\sigma + \beta(\mathfrak{D}(\varpi,\xi\varpi) + \mathfrak{D}(\varpi,g\varpi))) \\ &< \mathcal{F}((\alpha+\beta)(\mathfrak{D}(\varpi,\xi\varpi) + \mathfrak{D}(\varpi,g\varpi))) \\ &< \mathcal{F}(\mathfrak{D}(\varpi,\xi\varpi) + \mathfrak{D}(\varpi,g\varpi)).\end{aligned}$$

This gives a contradiction. Therefore, $\mathfrak{D}(\varpi,\xi\varpi) + \mathfrak{D}(\varpi,g\varpi) = 0$ and so $\xi\varpi = \varpi = g\varpi$. As a result, $C_{\varpi_0,\sigma}$ is a common fixed circle of the pair (ξ, g).

Now, we show that ξ and g also fix any circle $C_{\varpi_0,r}$ with $r < \sigma$. Let $\varpi \in C_{\varpi_0,r}$ and suppose that $\mathfrak{D}(\varpi,\xi\varpi) + \mathfrak{D}(\varpi,g\varpi) > 0$. By the Hardy–Rogers-type $\mathcal{F}_{\xi g}$-contraction, we have

$$\begin{aligned}\mathcal{F}(\mathfrak{D}(\varpi,\xi\varpi) + \mathfrak{D}(\varpi,g\varpi)) &\leq \mathcal{F}(\alpha\mathfrak{D}(\varpi,\varpi_0) + \beta\mathfrak{D}(\varpi,\xi\varpi) + \gamma\mathfrak{D}(\varpi,g\varpi)) - \tau \\ &< \mathcal{F}(\alpha\mathfrak{D}(\varpi,\varpi_0) + \beta\mathfrak{D}(\varpi,\xi\varpi) + \gamma\mathfrak{D}(\varpi,g\varpi)) \\ &< \mathcal{F}(\mathfrak{D}(\varpi,\xi\varpi) + \mathfrak{D}(\varpi,g\varpi))\end{aligned}$$

a contradiction. So, we obtain $\mathfrak{D}(\varpi,\xi\varpi) + \mathfrak{D}(\varpi,g\varpi) = 0$ and $\xi\varpi = \varpi = g\varpi$. Thus, $C_{\varpi_0,r}$ is a common fixed circle of the pair (ξ, g). □

Remark 1. *If we take $\alpha = 1$ and $\beta = \gamma = \delta = \eta = 0$ in Definition 5, then we obtain the concept of a Wardowski-type $\mathcal{F}_{\xi g}$-contractive mapping.*

Now, we give the concept of a Reich-type $\mathcal{F}_{\xi g}$-contraction as follows.

Definition 6. *If there exist $\tau > 0$, $\mathcal{F} \in \mathcal{F}$ and $\varpi_0 \in X$ such that for all $\varpi \in X$, the following holds:*

$$\tau + \mathcal{F}(\mathfrak{D}(\xi\varpi,\varpi) + \mathfrak{D}(g\varpi,\varpi)) \leq \mathcal{F}\left(\begin{array}{c}\alpha\mathfrak{D}(\varpi,\varpi_0) + \beta[\mathfrak{D}(\varpi,\xi\varpi) + \mathfrak{D}(\varpi,g\varpi)] \\ +\gamma[\mathfrak{D}(\varpi_0,\xi\varpi_0) + \mathfrak{D}(\varpi_0,g\varpi_0)]\end{array}\right) \quad (3)$$

with $\min\{\mathfrak{D}(\xi\varpi,\varpi), \mathfrak{D}(g\varpi,\varpi)\} > 0$, where $\alpha + \beta + \gamma < 1$, $\alpha \neq 0$ and $\alpha, \beta, \gamma \in [0, \infty)$. Then, the pair (ξ, g) is called a Reich-type $\mathcal{F}_{\xi g}$-contraction on X.

Proposition 5. *If the pair (ξ, g) is a Reich-type $\mathcal{F}_{\xi g}$-contraction with $\varpi_0 \in X$, then we have $\xi\varpi_0 = \varpi_0 = g\varpi_0$.*

Proof. Assume that $\xi\varpi_0 \neq \varpi_0$ and $g\varpi_0 \neq \varpi_0$. From the definition of the Reich-type $\mathcal{F}_{\xi g}$-contraction with $\min\{\mathfrak{D}(\varpi_0,\xi\varpi_0), \mathfrak{D}(\varpi_0,g\varpi_0)\} > 0$, we get

$$\begin{aligned}\tau + \mathcal{F}(\mathfrak{D}(\varpi_0,\xi\varpi_0) + \mathfrak{D}(\varpi_0,g\varpi_0)) &\leq \mathcal{F}\left(\begin{array}{c}\alpha\mathfrak{D}(\varpi_0,\varpi_0) + \beta[\mathfrak{D}(\varpi_0,\xi\varpi_0) + \mathfrak{D}(\varpi_0,g\varpi_0)] \\ +\gamma[\mathfrak{D}(\varpi_0,\xi\varpi_0) + \mathfrak{D}(\varpi_0,g\varpi_0)]\end{array}\right) \\ &= \mathcal{F}((\beta+\gamma)[\mathfrak{D}(\varpi_0,\xi\varpi_0) + \mathfrak{D}(\varpi_0,g\varpi_0)]) \\ &< \mathcal{F}(\mathfrak{D}(\varpi_0,\xi\varpi_0) + \mathfrak{D}(\varpi_0,g\varpi_0))\end{aligned}$$

a contradiction because of $\tau > 0$. Then, we have $\xi\varpi_0 = \varpi_0 = g\varpi_0$. □

Using Proposition 5, we rewrite the condition (3) as follows:

$$\tau + \mathcal{F}(\mathfrak{D}(\xi\varpi,\varpi) + \mathfrak{D}(g\varpi,\varpi)) \leq \mathcal{F}(\alpha\mathfrak{D}(\varpi,\varpi_0) + \beta[\mathfrak{D}(\varpi,\xi\varpi) + \mathfrak{D}(\varpi,g\varpi)])$$

with $\min\{\mathfrak{D}(\xi\varpi,\varpi),\mathfrak{D}(g\varpi,\varpi)\}>0$ where $\alpha+\beta<1$, $\alpha\neq 0$ and $\alpha,\beta\in[0,\infty)$.

Using this inequality, we obtain the following common fixed-circle result.

Theorem 5. *Let the pair (ξ,g) be a Reich-type $\mathcal{F}_{\xi g}$-contraction with $\varpi_0\in X$ and σ be defined as in (1). Then, $C_{\varpi_0,\sigma}$ is a common fixed circle of the pair (ξ,g). Especially, ξ and g fix every circle $C_{\varpi_0,\rho}$ with $\rho<\sigma$.*

Proof. We distinguish two cases.

Case 1: Let $\sigma=0$. Clearly, $C_{\varpi_0,\sigma}=\{\varpi_0\}$ and by Proposition 5, we see that $C_{\varpi_0,\sigma}$ is a common fixed circle of the pair (ξ,g).

Case 2: Let $\sigma>0$ and $\varpi\in C_{\varpi_0,\sigma}$. This case can be easily seen since

$$\begin{aligned}\mathcal{F}(\sigma) &\leq \mathcal{F}(\mathfrak{D}(\xi\varpi,\varpi)+\mathfrak{D}(g\varpi,\varpi))\\ &\leq \mathcal{F}((\alpha+\beta)[\mathfrak{D}(\xi\varpi,\varpi)+\mathfrak{D}(g\varpi,\varpi)])\\ &< \mathcal{F}(\mathfrak{D}(\xi\varpi,\varpi)+\mathfrak{D}(g\varpi,\varpi)).\end{aligned}$$

Consequently, $C_{\varpi_0,\sigma}$ is a common fixed circle of the pair (ξ,g). Especially, ξ and g fix every circle $C_{\varpi_0,\rho}$ with $\rho<\sigma$. □

To obtain, some new common fixed-circle results, we define the following contractions.

Definition 7. *If there exist $\tau>0$, $\mathcal{F}\in\mathcal{F}$ and $\varpi_0\in X$ such that for all $\varpi\in X$, the following holds:*

$$\tau+\mathcal{F}(\mathfrak{D}(\xi\varpi,\varpi)+\mathfrak{D}(g\varpi,\varpi))\leq\mathcal{F}(\eta[\mathfrak{D}(\xi\varpi,\varpi_0)+\mathfrak{D}(g\varpi,\varpi_0)])$$

with $\min\{\mathfrak{D}(\xi\varpi,\varpi),\mathfrak{D}(g\varpi,\varpi)\}>0$ where $\eta\in\left(0,\frac{1}{3}\right)$, then the pair (ξ,g) is called a Chatterjea-type $\mathcal{F}_{\xi g}$-contraction.

Proposition 6. *If the pair (ξ,g) is a Chattereja-type $\mathcal{F}_{\xi g}$-contraction with $\varpi_0\in X$, then we have $\xi\varpi_0=\varpi_0=g\varpi_0$.*

Proof. From the similar arguments used in Proposition 4, it can be easily proved. □

Theorem 6. *Let the pair (ξ,g) be a Chatterjea-type $\mathcal{F}_{\xi g}$-contraction with $\varpi_0\in X$ and σ be defined as in (1). Then, $C_{\varpi_0,\sigma}$ is a common fixed circle of the pair (ξ,g). Especially, ξ and g fix every circle $C_{\varpi_0,\rho}$ with $\rho<\sigma$.*

Proof. We distinguish two cases.

Case 1: Let $\sigma=0$. Clearly, $C_{\varpi_0,\sigma}=\{\varpi_0\}$ and by Proposition 6, we see that $C_{\varpi_0,\sigma}$ is a common fixed circle of the pair (ξ,g).

Case 2: Let $\sigma>0$ and $\varpi\in C_{\varpi_0,\sigma}$. Using the Chatterjea-type $\mathcal{F}_{\xi g}$-contractive property, the fact that $\mathcal{F}$ is increasing, and the triangle inequality property of metric function d, we have

$$\begin{aligned}\mathcal{F}(\sigma) &\leq \mathcal{F}(\mathfrak{D}(\xi\varpi,\varpi)+\mathfrak{D}(g\varpi,\varpi))\\ &\leq \mathcal{F}(\eta[\mathfrak{D}(\xi\varpi,\varpi_0)+\mathfrak{D}(g\varpi,\varpi_0)])-\tau\\ &\leq \mathcal{F}(\eta[\mathfrak{D}(\xi\varpi,\varpi)+\mathfrak{D}(\varpi,\varpi_0)+\mathfrak{D}(g\varpi,\varpi)+\mathfrak{D}(\varpi,\varpi_0)])\\ &= \mathcal{F}(\eta[2\mathfrak{D}(\varpi,\varpi_0)+[\mathfrak{D}(\xi\varpi,\varpi)+\mathfrak{D}(g\varpi,\varpi)]])\\ &= \mathcal{F}(3\eta[\mathfrak{D}(\xi\varpi,\varpi)+\mathfrak{D}(g\varpi,\varpi)])\\ &< \mathcal{F}(\mathfrak{D}(\xi\varpi,\varpi)+\mathfrak{D}(g\varpi,\varpi)).\end{aligned}$$

This gives a contradiction. Thus, $\mathfrak{D}(\xi\varpi,\varpi)+\mathfrak{D}(g\varpi,\varpi)=0$, that is, $\xi\varpi=\varpi=g\varpi$. As a result, $C_{\varpi_0,\sigma}$ is a common fixed circle of the pair (ξ,g). By the similar arguments used in the proof of Theorem 1, ξ and g also fix any circle $C_{\varpi_0,\rho}$ with $\rho<\sigma$. □

Definition 8. *If there exist $\tau>0$, $\mathcal{F}\in\mathcal{F}$ and $\varpi_0\in X$ such that for all $\varpi\in X$ the following holds:*

$$\tau+\mathcal{F}(\mathfrak{D}(\xi\varpi,\varpi)+\mathfrak{D}(g\varpi,\varpi))\leq\mathcal{F}(\eta[\mathfrak{D}(\varpi,\xi\varpi_0)+\mathfrak{D}(\varpi,g\varpi_0)])\tag{4}$$

with $\min\{\mathfrak{D}(\xi\varpi,\varpi),\mathfrak{D}(g\varpi,\varpi)\}>0$ where $\eta\in\left(0,\frac{1}{2}\right)$, then the pair (ξ,g) is called a Kannan-type $\mathcal{F}_{\xi g}$-contraction.

Proposition 7. *If the pair (ξ,g) is a Kannan-type $\mathcal{F}_{\xi g}$-contraction with $\varpi_0\in X$, then we have $\xi\varpi_0=\varpi_0=g\varpi_0$.*

Proof. From the similar arguments used in Proposition 4, it can be easily obtained. □

Theorem 7. *Let the pair (ξ,g) be a Kannan-type $\mathcal{F}_{\xi g}$-contraction with $\varpi_0\in X$ and σ be defined as in (1). Then, $C_{\varpi_0,\sigma}$ is a common fixed circle of the pair (ξ,g). Especially, ξ and g fix every circle $C_{\varpi_0,\rho}$ with $\rho<\sigma$.*

Proof. We distinguish two cases.

Case 1: Let $\sigma=0$. Clearly, $C_{\varpi_0,\sigma}=\{\varpi_0\}$ and by Proposition 7, we see that $C_{\varpi_0,\sigma}$ is a common fixed circle of the pair (ξ,g).

Case 2: Let $\sigma>0$ and $\varpi\in C_{\varpi_0,\sigma}$. Using the Kannan-type $\mathcal{F}_{\xi g}$-contractive property, the fact that $\mathcal{F}$ is increasing, and the triangle inequality property of metric function d, we have

$$\begin{aligned}\mathcal{F}(\sigma)&\leq\mathcal{F}(\mathfrak{D}(\xi\varpi,\varpi)+\mathfrak{D}(g\varpi,\varpi))\\&\leq\mathcal{F}(\eta[\mathfrak{D}(\varpi,\xi\varpi_0)+\mathfrak{D}(\varpi,g\varpi_0)])-\tau\\&\leq\mathcal{F}(\eta[\mathfrak{D}(\varpi,\varpi_0)+\mathfrak{D}(\varpi,\varpi_0)])\\&\leq\mathcal{F}(2\eta\sigma)\\&<\mathcal{F}(\mathfrak{D}(\xi\varpi,\varpi)+\mathfrak{D}(g\varpi,\varpi)).\end{aligned}$$

This gives a contradiction. Thus, $\mathfrak{D}(\xi\varpi,\varpi)+\mathfrak{D}(g\varpi,\varpi)=0$, that is, $\xi\varpi=\varpi=g\varpi$. As a result, $C_{\varpi_0,\sigma}$ is a common fixed circle of the pair (ξ,g). By similar arguments used in the proof of Theorem 1, ξ and g also fix any circle $C_{\varpi_0,\rho}$ with $\rho<\sigma$. □

Now, we present an illustrative example of our obtained results.

Example 4. *Let $X=\{1,2,e^2,e^2-1,e^2+1\}$ be the metric space with the usual metric. Let us define the self-mappings $\xi,g:X\longrightarrow X$ as*

$$\xi\varpi=\begin{cases}2, & \varpi=1\\ \varpi, & otherwise\end{cases}$$

and

$$g\varpi=\begin{cases}2, & \varpi=1\\ \varpi, & otherwise\end{cases},$$

for all $\varpi\in X$.

The pair (ξ,g) is a Hardy–Rogers-type $\mathcal{F}_{\xi g}$-contraction with $\mathcal{F}=lna+a$, $\tau=0.01$, $\alpha=\beta=\gamma=\frac{1}{4}$ and $\varpi_0=e^2$. Indeed, we get

$$\min\{\mathfrak{D}(\varpi,\xi\varpi),\mathfrak{D}(\varpi,g\varpi)\}=\min\{\mathfrak{D}(1,2),\mathfrak{D}(1,2)\}=1>0$$

for $\varpi = 1$ and we get

$$\begin{aligned}\alpha\mathfrak{D}(\varpi,\varpi_0)+\beta\mathfrak{D}(\varpi,\xi\varpi)+\gamma\mathfrak{D}(\varpi,g\varpi) &= \frac{1}{4}\left[\mathfrak{D}\left(1,e^2\right)+\mathfrak{D}(1,2)+\mathfrak{D}(1,2)\right]\\ &= \frac{1}{4}\left[e^2-1+1+1\right]\\ &= \frac{e^2+1}{4}.\end{aligned}$$

Then, we have

$$\begin{aligned}\tau+\mathcal{F}(\mathfrak{D}(\varpi,\xi\varpi)+\mathfrak{D}(\varpi,g\varpi)) &= 0.01+\ln 2+2\\ &\leq \mathcal{F}\left(\frac{e^2+1}{4}\right)\\ &= \ln\left(e^2+1\right)-\ln 4+\frac{e^2+1}{4}.\end{aligned}$$

The pair (ξ, g) is a Reich-type $\mathcal{F}_{\xi g}$-contraction with $\mathcal{F} = \ln a$, $\tau = \ln(e^2+1) - \ln 6$, $\alpha = \beta = \frac{1}{3}$ and $\varpi_0 = e^2$. Indeed, we get

$$\min\{\mathfrak{D}(\varpi,\xi\varpi),\mathfrak{D}(\varpi,g\varpi)\} = \min\{\mathfrak{D}(1,2),\mathfrak{D}(1,2)\} = 1 > 0$$

for $\varpi = 1$ and we have

$$\begin{aligned}\alpha\mathfrak{D}(\varpi,\varpi_0)+\beta[\mathfrak{D}(\varpi,\xi\varpi)+\mathfrak{D}(\varpi,g\varpi)] &= \frac{1}{3}\mathfrak{D}\left(1,e^2\right)+\frac{1}{3}[\mathfrak{D}(1,2)+\mathfrak{D}(1,2)]\\ &= \frac{e^2+1}{3}.\end{aligned}$$

Then, we obtain

$$\begin{aligned}\tau+\mathcal{F}(\mathfrak{D}(\varpi,\xi\varpi)+\mathfrak{D}(\varpi,g\varpi)) &= \ln\left(e^2+1\right)-\ln 6+\ln 2\\ &\leq \mathcal{F}\left(\frac{e^2+1}{3}\right)\\ &= \ln(e^2+1)-\ln 3.\end{aligned}$$

The pair (ξ, g) is both a Chatterjea-type $\mathcal{F}_{\xi g}$-contractions and a Kannan-type $\mathcal{F}_{\xi g}$-contraction with $\mathcal{F} = lna$, $\tau = \ln(e^2-2) - \ln 4$, $\eta = \frac{1}{4}$ and $\varpi_0 = e^2$. Indeed, for Chatterjea-type $\mathcal{F}_{\xi g}$-contractions, we get

$$\min\{\mathfrak{D}(\varpi,\xi\varpi),\mathfrak{D}(\varpi,g\varpi)\} = \min\{\mathfrak{D}(1,2),\mathfrak{D}(1,2)\} = 1 > 0$$

for $\varpi = 1$ and we have

$$\begin{aligned}\eta[\mathfrak{D}(\varpi_0,\xi\varpi)+\mathfrak{D}(\varpi_0,g\varpi)] &= \frac{1}{4}\left[\mathfrak{D}\left(e^2,2\right)+\mathfrak{D}\left(e^2,2\right)\right]\\ &\leq \frac{1}{4}\left[2(e^2-2)\right]\\ &= \frac{e^2-2}{2}.\end{aligned}$$

Then, we obtain

$$\begin{aligned}\tau + \mathcal{F}(\mathfrak{D}(\varpi,\xi\varpi) + \mathfrak{D}(\varpi,g\varpi)) &= \ln\left(e^2 - 2\right) - \ln 4 + \ln 2 \\ &\leq \mathcal{F}\left(\frac{e^2-2}{2}\right) \\ &= \ln\left(e^2 - 2\right) - \ln 2.\end{aligned}$$

For Kannan-type $\mathcal{F}_{\xi g}$-contractions, we have

$$\min\{\mathfrak{D}(\varpi,\xi\varpi),\mathfrak{D}(\varpi,g\varpi)\} = \min\{\mathfrak{D}(1,2),\mathfrak{D}(1,2)\} = 1 > 0$$

for $\varpi = 1$ and we have

$$\begin{aligned}\eta[\mathfrak{D}(\varpi,\xi\varpi_0) + \mathfrak{D}(\varpi,g_0)] &= \frac{1}{4}\left[\mathfrak{D}\left(1,e^2\right) + \mathfrak{D}\left(1,e^2\right)\right] \\ &\leq \frac{1}{4}\left[2(e^2-1)\right] \\ &= \frac{e^2-1}{2}.\end{aligned}$$

Then, we obtain

$$\begin{aligned}\tau + \mathcal{F}(\mathfrak{D}(\varpi,\xi\varpi) + \mathfrak{D}(\varpi,g\varpi)) &= \ln\left(e^2 - 2\right) - \ln 4 + \ln 2 \\ &\leq \mathcal{F}\left(\frac{e^2-1}{2}\right) \\ &= \ln\left(e^2 - 1\right) - \ln 2.\end{aligned}$$

Consequently, ξ and g fix the circle $C_{e^2,1} = \{e^2-1, e^2+1\}$.

If we combine the notions of Banach-type $\mathcal{F}_{\xi g}$-contractions, Chatterjea-type $\mathcal{F}_{\xi g}$-contractions, and Kannan-type $\mathcal{F}_{\xi g}$-contractions, then we get the following corollary. This corollary can be considered as Zamfirescu-type common fixed-circle result [18].

Corollary 1. *Let $(X,\mathfrak{D})$ be a metric space, $\xi, g : X \longrightarrow X$ be two self-mappings and σ be defined as in (1). If there exist $\tau > 0$, $\mathcal{F} \in \mathcal{F}$ and $\varpi_0 \in X$ such that for all $\varpi \in X$, at least one of the followings holds:*

(1) $\tau + \mathcal{F}(\mathfrak{D}(\xi\varpi,\varpi) + \mathfrak{D}(g\varpi,\varpi)) \leq \mathcal{F}(\alpha\mathfrak{D}(\varpi,\varpi_0))$,

(2) $\tau + \mathcal{F}(\mathfrak{D}(\xi\varpi,\varpi) + \mathfrak{D}(g\varpi,\varpi)) \leq \mathcal{F}(\beta[\mathfrak{D}(\xi\varpi,\varpi_0) + \mathfrak{D}(g\varpi,\varpi_0)])$,

(3) $\tau + \mathcal{F}(\mathfrak{D}(\xi\varpi,\varpi) + \mathfrak{D}(g\varpi,\varpi)) \leq \mathcal{F}(\gamma[\mathfrak{D}(\varpi,\xi\varpi_0) + \mathfrak{D}(\varpi,g\varpi_0)])$,

with $\min\{\mathfrak{D}(\xi\varpi,\varpi),\mathfrak{D}(g\varpi,\varpi)\} > 0$ where $0 \leq \alpha < 1$, $0 \leq \beta,\gamma < \frac{1}{2}$, then $C_{\varpi_0,\sigma}$ is a common fixed circle of the pair (ξ, g). Especially, ξ and g fix every circle $C_{\varpi_0,\rho}$ with $\rho < \sigma$.

Proof. It is obvious. □

Author Contributions: N.M.: conceptualization, supervision, writing—original draft; N.T.: writing—original draft, methodology; E.K.: conceptualization, supervision, writing—original draft; S.S.A.: conceptualization, writing—original draft; A.K.S.: methodology, writing—original draft. All authors read and approved the final manuscript.

Funding: This research received no external funding.

Informed Consent Statement: Not applicable.

Data Availability Statement: Not applicable.

Acknowledgments: The authors N. Mlaiki and S. S. Aiadi would like to thank Prince Sultan University for paying the publication fees for this work through TAS LAB.

Conflicts of Interest: The authors declare no conflict of interest.

References

1. Mlaiki, N.; Özgür, N.Y.; Taş, N. New fixed-circle results related to F_c-contractive and F_c-expanding mappings on metric spaces. *arXiv* **2021**, arXiv:2101.10770.
2. Celik, U.; Özgür, N. On the fixed-circle problem. *Facta Univ. Ser. Math. Inform.* **2021**, *35*, 1273–1290. [CrossRef]
3. Bisht, R.K.; Özgür, N. Geometric properties of discontinuous fixed point set of $\epsilon - \delta$ contractions and applications to neural networks. *Aequationes Math.* **2020**, *94*, 847–863. [CrossRef]
4. Joshi, M.; Tomar, A.; Padaliya, S.K. Fixed point to fixed ellipse in metric spaces and discontinuous activation function. *Appl. Math. E-Notes* **2021**, *21*, 225–237.
5. Joshi, M.; Tomar, A. On unique and nonunique fixed points in metric spaces and application to chemical sciences. *J. Funct. Spaces* **2021**, *2021*, 5525472. [CrossRef]
6. Tomar, A.; Joshi, M.; Padaliya, S.K. Fixed point to fixed circle and activation function in partial metric space. *J. Appl. Anal.* **2022**, *28*, 57–66. [CrossRef]
7. Joshi, M.; Tomar, A.; Nabwey, H.A.; George, R. On Unique and Nonunique Fixed Points and Fixed Circles in-Metric Space and Application to Cantilever Beam Problem. *J. Funct. Spaces* **2021**, *2021*, 6681044. [CrossRef]
8. Özgür, N.Y. Fixed-disc results via simulation functions. *Turk. J. Math.* **2019**, *43*, 2794–2805. [CrossRef]
9. Mlaiki, N.; Taş, N.; Özgür, N.Y. On the fixed-circle problem and Khan type contractions. *Axioms* **2018**, *7*, 80. [CrossRef]
10. Wardowski, D. Fixed points of a new type of contractive mappings in complete metric spaces. *Fixed Point Theory Appl.* **2012**, *2012*, 94. [CrossRef]
11. Edelstein, M. On fixed and periodic points under contractive mappings. *J. Lond. Math. Soc.* **1962**, *37*, 74–79. [CrossRef]
12. Nemytskii, V.V. The fixed point method in analysis. *Usp. Mat. Nauk* **1936**, *1*, 141–174. (In Russian)
13. Banach, S. Sur les operations dans les ensembles abstraits et leur application auxequations integrales. *Fund. Math.* **1922**, *3*, 133–181. [CrossRef]
14. Hardy, G.E.; Rogers, T.D. A generalization of a fixed point theorem of Reich. *Canad. Math. Bull.* **1973**, *16*, 201–206. [CrossRef]
15. Reich, S. Some remarks concerning contraction mappings. *Oanad. Math. Bull.* **1971**, *14*, 121–124. [CrossRef]
16. Chatterjea, S.K. Fixed-point theorems. *C. R. Acad. Bulgare Sci.* **1972**, *25*, 727–730. [CrossRef]
17. Kannan, R. Some results on fixed points. *Bull. Calcutta Math. Soc.* **1968**, *60*, 71–76.
18. Zamfirescu, T. A theorem on fixed points. *Atti Acad. Naz. Lincei Rend. Cl. Sei. Fis. Mat. Natur.* **1972**, *52*, 832–834.

axioms

Article

On a New Integral Inequality: Generalizations and Applications

Huaping Huang [1,†] and Wei-Shih Du [2,*,†]

1 School of Mathematics and Statistics, Chongqing Three Gorges University, Wanzhou, Chongqing 404020, China
2 Department of Mathematics, National Kaohsiung Normal University, Kaohsiung 82444, Taiwan
* Correspondence: wsdu@mail.nknu.edu.tw
† These authors contributed equally to this work.

Abstract: In this paper, we present some generalizations and improvements of a new integral inequality from the 29th IMC in 2022. Some applications of our new results are also provided.

Keywords: IMC 2022; quasi-hyperbolic sine function; exponential function; arithmetic mean-geometric mean (AM-GM) inequality; Cauchy-Schwarz inequality; Lagrange mean value theorem

MSC: 26B05; 26B20; 26D10; 26E60; 47G10

Citation: Huang, H.; Du, W.-S. On a New Integral Inequality: Generalizations and Applications. *Axioms* **2022**, *11*, 458. https://doi.org/10.3390/axioms11090458

Academic Editor: Simeon Reich

Received: 23 August 2022
Accepted: 4 September 2022
Published: 6 September 2022

Publisher's Note: MDPI stays neutral with regard to jurisdictional claims in published maps and institutional affiliations.

Copyright: © 2022 by the authors. Licensee MDPI, Basel, Switzerland. This article is an open access article distributed under the terms and conditions of the Creative Commons Attribution (CC BY) license (https://creativecommons.org/licenses/by/4.0/).

1. Introduction and Motivation

As we all know, in the history of the research process of inequality theory, many important generalization studies often come from some simple inequalities that have widespread applications. Over the past more than five decades, rapid developments in inequality theory and its applications have contributed greatly to many branches of mathematics, economics, finance, physics, dynamic systems theory, game theory, and so on; for more details, one can refer to [1–4] and the references therein.

The following new integral inequality (here we regard it as a theorem) arose from the 29th International Mathematics Competition for University Students (for short, IMC 2022), which was held in Blagoevgrad, Bulgaria on 1–7 August 2022. For more information (including proofs), please visit the following official website of IMC 2022: https://www.imc-math.org.uk (accessed on 1 August 2022).

Theorem 1. *Let $f:[0,1]\to(0,+\infty)$ be an integrable function such that $f(x)\cdot f(1-x)=1$ for all $x\in[0,1]$. Then $\int_0^1 f(x)\,\mathrm{d}x \geq 1$.*

Motivated by the above integral inequality, the following questions arise naturally.
Question 1. Can we establish new real generalizations of Theorem 1?
Question 2. Does Theorem 1 still hold if we replace the codomain $(0,+\infty)$ of f with $(-\infty,+\infty)$?

In this work, our questions will be answered affirmatively. In Section 2, we successfully establish a new real generalization (see Theorem 2 below) of Theorem 1, which is a positive answer to Question 1. In Section 3, we first construct a new simple counterexample to show that Question 2 is not always true. Furthermore, we establish an equivalent theorem (see Theorem 3 below) of Theorem 2. Finally, some applications of our new results are given in Section 4. The new results we present in this paper are novel and developmental.

2. New Results for Question 1

The following result is very crucial for answering Question 1.

Lemma 1. *Let $f(x)$ be an integrable function on $[a,b]$. Then*

$$\begin{aligned}\int_a^b f(x)\,\mathrm{d}x &= \int_a^b f(a+b-x)\,\mathrm{d}x \\ &= \frac{1}{2}\int_a^b [f(x)+f(a+b-x)]\,\mathrm{d}x \\ &= \int_a^{\frac{a+b}{2}} [f(x)+f(a+b-x)]\,\mathrm{d}x \\ &= \int_{\frac{a+b}{2}}^b [f(x)+f(a+b-x)]\,\mathrm{d}x.\end{aligned}$$

Proof. By using integration by substitution (see, e.g., [5]), we have

$$\begin{aligned}\int_a^b f(x)\,\mathrm{d}x &\xlongequal{(\text{let } t=a+b-x)} \int_b^a f(a+b-t)\,(-\mathrm{d}t) \\ &= \int_a^b f(a+b-t)\,\mathrm{d}t = \int_a^b f(a+b-x)\,\mathrm{d}x. \end{aligned} \tag{1}$$

Hence, we obtain

$$\begin{aligned}\int_a^b f(x)\,\mathrm{d}x &= \frac{1}{2}\left[\int_a^b f(x)\,\mathrm{d}x + \int_a^b f(a+b-x)\,\mathrm{d}x\right] \\ &= \frac{1}{2}\int_a^b [f(x)+f(a+b-x)]\,\mathrm{d}x. \end{aligned} \tag{2}$$

Note that

$$\begin{aligned}\int_{\frac{a+b}{2}}^b [f(x)+f(a+b-x)]\,\mathrm{d}x &\xlongequal{(\text{let } t=a+b-x)} \int_{\frac{a+b}{2}}^a [f(a+b-t)+f(t)]\,(-\mathrm{d}t) \\ &= \int_a^{\frac{a+b}{2}} [f(a+b-t)+f(t)]\,\mathrm{d}t \\ &= \int_a^{\frac{a+b}{2}} [f(x)+f(a+b-x)]\,\mathrm{d}x, \end{aligned} \tag{3}$$

so it is easy to see that

$$\begin{aligned}&\int_a^b [f(x)+f(a+b-x)]\,\mathrm{d}x \\ &= \int_a^{\frac{a+b}{2}} [f(x)+f(a+b-x)]\,\mathrm{d}x + \int_{\frac{a+b}{2}}^b [f(x)+f(a+b-x)]\,\mathrm{d}x \\ &= 2\int_a^{\frac{a+b}{2}} [f(x)+f(a+b-x)]\,\mathrm{d}x.\end{aligned}$$

Combining (1) and (2) together with (3), we prove the desired conclusion. □

With the help of Lemma 1, we can establish the following generalization of Theorem 1.

Theorem 2. *Let $f:[a,b]\to(0,+\infty)$ be an integrable function such that*

$$f(x)\cdot f(a+b-x) = c \tag{4}$$

for all $x\in[a,b]$, where $c>0$ is a constant. Then

$$\int_a^b f(x)\,\mathrm{d}x \geq (b-a)\sqrt{c}. \tag{5}$$

The case of equality holds in (5) if and only if $f(x) = f(a+b-x) = \sqrt{c}$ for all $x \in [a,b]$.

Proof. We use two methods to show (5).
<u>Method 1</u>. By (4) and using the arithmetic-mean–geometric-mean (AM-GM) inequality, we have

$$f(x) + f(a+b-x) \geq 2\sqrt{f(x)f(a+b-x)} = 2\sqrt{c} \quad \text{for any } x \in [a,b]. \tag{6}$$

By (6) and applying Lemma 1, we arrive at

$$\int_a^b f(x)\,dx = \int_a^{\frac{a+b}{2}} [f(x) + f(a+b-x)]\,dx \geq \int_a^{\frac{a+b}{2}} 2\sqrt{c}\,dx = (b-a)\sqrt{c}.$$

Obviously, the equality holds in (5) if and only if the equality holds in (6) and if and only if $f(x) = f(a+b-x) = \sqrt{c}$ for all $x \in [a,b]$.
<u>Method 2</u>. By applying Lemma 1 and using (4), it follows that

$$\int_a^b f(x)\,dx = \int_a^b f(a+b-x)\,dx = \int_a^b \frac{c}{f(x)}\,dx.$$

Applying Cauchy–Schwarz inequality, we obtain

$$\left(\int_a^b f(x)\,dx\right)^2 = \int_a^b f(x)\,dx \cdot \int_a^b \frac{c}{f(x)}\,dx \geq \left(\int_a^b \sqrt{c}\,dx\right)^2 = (b-a)^2 c.$$

This proves the inequality (5). Clearly, the equality holds in (5) if and only if $f(x) = f(a+b-x) = \sqrt{c}$ for all $x \in [a,b]$. □

Remark 1. *By taking $a = 0$ and $b = c = 1$ in Theorem 2, we can prove Theorem 1.*

Remark 2. *There are many functions satisfying condition (4), as in Theorem 2, such as*

(i) $f(x) = \sqrt{c},\ x \in [a,b]$, *where $c > 0$ is a constant;*
(ii) $f(x) = \alpha^x,\ x \in [a,b]$, *where $\alpha > 0$ with $\alpha \neq 1$;*
(iii) $f(x) = \dfrac{x}{a+b-x},\ x \in [a,b]$;
(iv) $f(x) = \dfrac{a+b-x}{x},\ x \in [a,b]$;
(v) $f(x) = \begin{cases} (a+b-x)^2 + 1, & x \in [a, \frac{a+b}{2}), \\ 1, & x = \frac{a+b}{2}, \\ \frac{1}{x^2+1}, & x \in (\frac{a+b}{2}, b]. \end{cases}$

3. New Results for Question 2

In this section, we first provide a simple counterexample to show that Question 2 is not always true if we replace the codomain $(0,+\infty)$ of f with $(-\infty,+\infty)$.

Example 1. *Let $f : [0,1] \to (-\infty,+\infty)$ be defined by*

$$f(x) = \begin{cases} 1, & x \in [0, \frac{1}{4}) \cup (\frac{3}{4}, 1], \\ -1, & x \in [\frac{1}{4}, \frac{3}{4}]. \end{cases}$$

Then, f is an integrable function on $[0,1]$ but not continuous on $[0,1]$. Clearly, $f(x)$ satisfies $f(x) \cdot f(1-x) = 1$ for all $x \in [0,1]$. However, it is easy to see that

$$\int_0^1 f(x)\,dx = 0 < 1.$$

By applying Theorem 2, we obtain the following result.

Theorem 3. *Let $g : [a,b] \to (-\infty,+\infty)$ be an integrable function such that*

$$g(x) \cdot g(a+b-x) = \lambda \tag{7}$$

for all $x \in [a,b]$, where λ is a nonzero constant. Then

$$\int_a^b |g(x)|\,\mathrm{d}x \geq (b-a)\sqrt{|\lambda|}. \tag{8}$$

The case of equality holds in (8) *if and only if $|g(x)| = |g(a+b-x)| = \sqrt{|\lambda|}$ for all $x \in [a,b]$.*

Proof. Due to (7), we know that $g(x) \neq 0$ for all $x \in [a,b]$. So we can define $f : [a,b] \to (0,+\infty)$ by

$$f(x) = |g(x)| \quad \text{for } x \in [a,b].$$

Since g is integrable, f is integrable. From (7) again, we obtain

$$f(x) \cdot f(a+b-x) = |g(x) \cdot g(a+b-x)| = |\lambda| \quad \text{for all } x \in [a,b].$$

Let $c = |\lambda|$. Then $c > 0$. Hence, all conditions in Theorem 2 are satisfied. By Theorem 2, we obtain

$$\int_a^b |g(x)|\,\mathrm{d}x = \int_a^b f(x)\,\mathrm{d}x \geq (b-a)\sqrt{c} = (b-a)\sqrt{|\lambda|},$$

and the equality holds in (8) if and only if $|g(x)| = |g(a+b-x)| = \sqrt{|\lambda|}$. The proof is completed. □

Remark 3. *We applied Theorem 2 to show Theorem 3. It is obvious that Theorem 2 is a special case of Theorem 3. Therefore, we can conclude that Theorems 2 and 3 are indeed equivalent.*

Taking advantage of Theorem 3, we easily obtain the following results.

Corollary 1. *Let $g : [0,1] \to (-\infty,+\infty)$ be an integrable function such that*

$$g(x) \cdot g(1-x) = \lambda$$

for all $x \in [0,1]$, where λ is a nonzero constant. Then

$$\int_0^1 |g(x)|\mathrm{d}x \geq \sqrt{|\lambda|}. \tag{9}$$

The case of equality holds in (9) *if and only if $|g(x)| = |g(1-x)| = \sqrt{|\lambda|}$ for all $x \in [0,1]$.*

Proof. Taking $a = 0$ and $b = 1$ in Theorem 3, then the desired result is obtained. □

Corollary 2. *Let $m > 0$. Suppose that $g : [-m,m] \to (-\infty,+\infty)$ is an integrable function such that*

$$g(x) \cdot g(-x) = 1$$

for all $x \in [-m,m]$. Then

$$\int_{-m}^m |g(x)|\mathrm{d}x \geq 2m. \tag{10}$$

The case of equality holds in (10) *if and only if $|g(x)| = |g(-x)| = 1$ for all $x \in [-m,m]$.*

Proof. Take $a = -m$, $b = m$, and $\lambda = 1$ in Theorem 3, then the desired conclusion is proved. □

As a consequence of Theorem 3, we obtain the following theorem.

Theorem 4. *Let $h : (-\infty, +\infty) \to (-\infty, +\infty)$ be a function satisfying $\int_{-\infty}^{+\infty} h(x)\,\mathrm{d}x < \infty$. Suppose that there exist $a, b \in (-\infty, +\infty)$ with $a < b$ such that*

$$h(x) \cdot h(a + b - x) = \lambda \tag{11}$$

for all $x \in [a, b]$, where λ is a nonzero constant. Then, for any $u, v \in (-\infty, +\infty)$ with $u \leq a$ and $b \leq v$, we have

$$\int_u^v |h(x)|\,\mathrm{d}x \geq (b-a)\sqrt{|\lambda|},$$

$$\int_u^{+\infty} |h(x)|\,\mathrm{d}x \geq (b-a)\sqrt{|\lambda|},$$

$$\int_{-\infty}^{v} |h(x)|\,\mathrm{d}x \geq (b-a)\sqrt{|\lambda|}$$

and

$$\int_{-\infty}^{+\infty} |h(x)|\,\mathrm{d}x \geq (b-a)\sqrt{|\lambda|}.$$

Proof. Define $g : [a, b] \to (-\infty, +\infty)$ by

$$g(x) = h(x) \quad \text{for } x \in [a, b].$$

Since $\int_{-\infty}^{+\infty} h(x)\,\mathrm{d}x < \infty$, $\int_a^b h(x)\,\mathrm{d}x < \infty$. Hence, h is integrable on $[a, b]$. It follows that g, $|g|$, and $|h|$ are integrable on $[a, b]$ and

$$\int_a^b |g(x)|\,\mathrm{d}x = \int_a^b |h(x)|\,\mathrm{d}x.$$

By (11), we obtain

$$g(x) \cdot g(a+b-x) = h(x) \cdot h(a+b-x) = \lambda \quad \text{for all } x \in [a, b].$$

Hence all conditions in Theorem 3 are satisfied. By utilizing Theorem 3, we obtain

$$\int_u^v |h(x)|\,\mathrm{d}x \geq \int_a^b |h(x)|\,\mathrm{d}x \geq (b-a)\sqrt{|\lambda|},$$

$$\int_u^{+\infty} |h(x)|\,\mathrm{d}x \geq \int_a^b |h(x)|\,\mathrm{d}x \geq (b-a)\sqrt{|\lambda|},$$

$$\int_{-\infty}^{v} |h(x)|\,\mathrm{d}x \geq \int_a^b |h(x)|\,\mathrm{d}x \geq (b-a)\sqrt{|\lambda|}$$

and

$$\int_{-\infty}^{+\infty} |h(x)|\,\mathrm{d}x \geq \int_a^b |h(x)|\,\mathrm{d}x \geq (b-a)\sqrt{|\lambda|}.$$

The proof is completed. □

4. Some Applications

In this section, we first establish the following new useful inequalities, which improve the known inequalities for exponential functions.

Theorem 5. *Let $a > 0$. Then, the following hold.*

(i) *If $0 < a < 1$, then $a^x < 1 + xa^{\frac{x}{2}} \ln a$ for all $x > 0$.*

(ii) *If $a = 1$, then $a^x = 1 + xa^{\frac{x}{2}} \ln a = 1$ for all $x > 0$.*

(iii) *If $a > 1$, then $a^x > 1 + xa^{\frac{x}{2}} \ln a$ for all $x > 0$.*
In particular, we have

$$e^x > xe^{\frac{x}{2}} + 1 > x + 1 \text{ for all } x > 0.$$

Proof. Given $x > 0$. Let $f(y) = a^y$ for $y \in [0, x]$. Then f is integrable on $[0, x]$, and

$$f(y) \cdot f(x - y) = a^x \quad \text{for all } y \in [0, x].$$

Hence, by applying Theorem 2, we have

$$\frac{1}{\ln a}(a^x - 1) = \int_0^x a^y \, dy \geq xa^{\frac{x}{2}}. \tag{12}$$

(i) If $0 < a < 1$, then $\ln a < 0$. Note that $f(y) = f(x - y) = a^{\frac{x}{2}}$ holds for $y = \frac{x}{2}$. So the equality does not hold in (12). From (12), we obtain

$$a^x < 1 + xa^{\frac{x}{2}} \ln a \quad \text{for all } x > 0.$$

(ii) Clearly, if $a = 1$, then $a^x = 1 = 1 + xa^{\frac{x}{2}} \ln a$ for all $x > 0$.
(iii) If $a > 1$, then $\ln a > 0$. Since $f(y) = f(x - y) = a^{\frac{x}{2}}$ holds for $y = \frac{x}{2}$, the equality does not hold in (12). Hence, using (12) again, we obtain

$$a^x > 1 + xa^{\frac{x}{2}} \ln a \quad \text{for all } x > 0.$$

In particular, by taking $a := e$, we have

$$e^x > xe^{\frac{x}{2}} + 1 > x + 1 \quad \text{for all } x > 0.$$

The proof is completed. □

Next, we provide a new simple proof of the following important fundamental inequality for hyperbolic sine functions by applying Theorem 2, Theorem 3, or their corollaries.

Theorem 6. $\sinh x > x$ *for all $x > 0$.*

Proof. Given $x > 0$. Let $f(y) = e^y$ for $y \in [-x, x]$. Then f is integrable on $[-x, x]$ and

$$f(y) \cdot f(-y) = e^0 = 1 \quad \text{for all } y \in [-x, x].$$

By applying Theorem 2 (or Theorem 3 or Corollary 2), we obtain

$$e^x - e^{-x} = \int_{-x}^{x} e^y \, dy \geq 2x.$$

Since $e^x \neq e^{-x}$ for $x \neq 0$, we obtain

$$\sinh x = \frac{e^x - e^{-x}}{2} > x.$$

The proof is completed. □

In this paper, we introduce the concept of quasi-hyperbolic sine function.

Definition 1. *A function q-sinh : $(0, +\infty) \times (-\infty, +\infty) \to (-\infty, +\infty)$ is said to be a quasi-hyperbolic sine function if*

$$q\text{-}\sinh(a, x) = \frac{a^x - a^{-x}}{2} \quad \text{for } a > 0 \text{ and } x \in (-\infty, +\infty).$$

Remark 4. *In [6], Nantomah, Okpoti, and Nasiru defined generalized hyperbolic sine function using*

$$\sinh_a x = \frac{a^x - a^{-x}}{2} \quad \text{for } a > 1 \text{ and } x \in (-\infty, +\infty).$$

It is obvious that a hyperbolic sine function is a generalized hyperbolic sine function, and a generalized hyperbolic sine function is a quasi-hyperbolic sine function, but the converse is not true.

We now give the following new inequalities for quasi-hyperbolic sine functions.

Theorem 7. *Let $a > 0$. Then, the following hold.*

(i) If $0 < a < 1$, then $q\text{-}\sinh(a, x) < x \ln a$ for all $x > 0$.
(ii) If $a = 1$, then $q\text{-}\sinh(a, x) = 0$ for all $x > 0$.
(iii) If $a > 1$, then $q\text{-}\sinh(a, x) = \sinh_a x > x \ln a$ for all $x > 0$.

Proof. Given $x > 0$. Let $f(y) = a^y$ for $y \in [-x, x]$. Thus, f is integrable on $[-x, x]$ and

$$f(y) \cdot f(-y) = a^0 = 1 \quad \text{for all } y \in [-x, x].$$

By applying Theorem 2 (or Theorem 3 or Corollary 2), we obtain

$$\frac{1}{\ln a}(a^x - a^{-x}) = \int_{-x}^{x} a^y \, \mathrm{d}y \geq 2x. \tag{13}$$

(i) If $0 < a < 1$, then $\ln a < 0$. Since $a^x \neq a^{-x}$ for $x \neq 0$, the equality does not hold in (13). Hence (13) yields

$$q\text{-}\sinh(a, x) = \frac{a^x - a^{-x}}{2} < x \ln a.$$

(ii) Clearly, $q\text{-}\sinh(1, x) = \frac{1^x - 1^{-x}}{2} = 0$ for all $x > 0$.
(iii) If $a > 1$, then $\ln a > 0$. Since $a^x \neq a^{-x}$ for $x \neq 0$, the equality does not hold in (13). So, from (13) again, we obtain

$$q\text{-}\sinh(a, x) = \sinh_a x = \frac{a^x - a^{-x}}{2} > x \ln a.$$

The proof is completed. □

Remark 5. *Theorem 6 is a special case of Theorem 7 (iii).*

Theorem 8. *Let $a < b$. Then there exists $\xi \in \left(\frac{a+b}{2}, b\right)$ such that*

$$\mathrm{e}^{\xi} = \frac{\mathrm{e}^b - \mathrm{e}^a}{b - a}.$$

Proof. From the Lagrange mean value theorem or integral mean value theorem, it is easy to see that there exists $\xi \in (a, b)$ such that

$$\mathrm{e}^{\xi} = \frac{\mathrm{e}^b - \mathrm{e}^a}{b - a}. \tag{14}$$

We now claim that $\xi \in \left(\frac{a+b}{2}, b\right)$. Let $f(x) = \mathrm{e}^x$ for $x \in [a, b]$. Then f is integrable on $[a, b]$ and

$$f(x) \cdot f(a + b - x) = \mathrm{e}^{a+b} := c \quad \text{for all } x \in [a, b].$$

Note that $f(x) = f(a+b-x) = \sqrt{c}$ holds for $x = \frac{a+b}{2}$. Accordingly, by applying Theorem 2, we obtain

$$e^b - e^a = \int_a^b e^x \, dx > (b-a)\sqrt{c} = (b-a)e^{\frac{a+b}{2}}, \tag{15}$$

which follows immediately from (14) and (15) that $\xi > \frac{a+b}{2}$. Therefore, $\xi \in \left(\frac{a+b}{2}, b\right)$. $\square$

Theorem 9. *Let $0 < a < b$. Then there exists $\xi \in \left(a, \frac{a+b}{2}\right)$ such that*

$$b - a = \xi(\ln b - \ln a).$$

Proof. Making full use of the Lagrange mean value theorem, we can find $\xi \in (a,b)$, such that

$$\frac{1}{\xi} = \frac{\ln b - \ln a}{b-a}. \tag{16}$$

We now speculate that $\xi \in \left(a, \frac{a+b}{2}\right)$. To this end, put $f(x) = \dfrac{x}{a+b-x}$ for $x \in [a,b]$. Thus f is integrable on $[a,b]$ and

$$f(x) \cdot f(a+b-x) = 1 \quad \text{for all } x \in [a,b].$$

Note that $f(x) = f(a+b-x) = 1$ holds for $x = \frac{a+b}{2}$. So, by utilizing Theorem 2, we obtain

$$(a+b)(\ln b - \ln a) - (b-a) = \int_a^b \frac{x}{a+b-x} \, dx > b - a. \tag{17}$$

Combining (16) and (17), we obtain $\xi < \frac{a+b}{2}$. Therefore, we show $\xi \in \left(a, \frac{a+b}{2}\right)$. $\square$

5. Conclusions

In this paper, we study two questions for Theorem 1 as follows:

Question 1. Can we establish new real generalizations of Theorem 1?

Question 2. Does Theorem 1 still hold if we replace the codomain $(0, +\infty)$ of f with $(-\infty, +\infty)$?

We establish Theorem 2, which is a new real generalization of Theorem 1, and a positive answer to Question 1. A new simple counterexample is given to verify that Question 2 is not always true. Furthermore, we prove Theorem 3, which is equivalent to Theorem 2, and show some applications of our new results. In summary, our new results are original, novel, and developmental in the literature. We hope that our new results can be applied to nonlinear analysis, mathematical physics, and related fields in the future.

Author Contributions: Writing original draft, H.H. and W.-S.D. Both authors contributed equally to the manuscript. All authors have read and agreed to the published version of the manuscript.

Funding: The first author is partially supported by the Natural Science Foundation of Chongqing of China (No. cstc2020jcyj-msxmX0762) and the Initial Funding of Scientific Research for High-level Talents of the Chongqing Three Gorges University of China (No. 2104/09926601). The second author is partially supported by Grant No. MOST 111-2115-M-017-002 of the Ministry of Science and Technology of the Republic of China.

Institutional Review Board Statement: Not applicable.

Informed Consent Statement: Not applicable.

Data Availability Statement: Not applicable.

Acknowledgments: The authors wish to express their hearty thanks to the anonymous referees for their valuable suggestions and comments.

Conflicts of Interest: The authors declare no conflict of interest.

References

1. Kuang, J.-C. *Applied Inequalities (Chang Yong Bu Deng Shi)*, 5th ed.; Shandong Press of Science and Technology: Jinan, China, 2021. (In Chinese)
2. Mitrinović, D.S.; Pečarić, J.E.; Fink, A.M. *Classical and New Inequalities in Analysis*; Kluwer Academic Publishers: Dordrecht, The Netherlands, 1993.
3. Mitrinović, D.S.; Vasić, P.M. *Analytic Inequalities*; Springer: Berlin/Heidelberg, Germany, 1970.
4. Wang,W.L. *Approaches to Prove Inequalities*; Press of Harbin Industrial University: Harbin, China, 2011. (In Chinese)
5. Rudin, W. *Principles of Mathematical Analysis*; McGraw-Hill, Inc.: New York, NY, USA, 1976.
6. Nantomah, K.; Okpoti, C.A.; Nasiru, S.S. On a Generalized Sigmoid Function and its Properties. *Asian J. Math. Appl.* **2020**, *2020*, ama0527.

axioms

Article

Plane Section Curves on Surfaces of NCP Functions

Shun-Wei Li, Yu-Lin Chang * and Jein-Shan Chen

Department of Mathematics, National Taiwan Normal University, Taipei 11677, Taiwan; wonderful9568509@gmail.com (S.-W.L.); jschen@math.ntnu.edu.tw (J.-S.C.)
* Correspondence: ylchang@math.ntnu.edu.tw

Abstract: The goal of this paper is to investigate the curves intersected by a vertical plane with the surfaces based on certain NCP functions. The convexity and differentiability of these curves are studied as well. In most cases, the inflection points of the curves cannot be expressed exactly. Therefore, we instead estimate the interval where the curves are convex under this situation. Then, with the help of differentiability and convexity, we obtain the local minimum or maximum of the curves accordingly. The study of these curves is very useful to binary quadratic programming.

Keywords: NCP functions; section curves; convexity; differentiability; binary quadratic programming

Citation: Li, S.-W.; Chang, Y.-L.; Chen, J.-S. Plane Section Curves on Surfaces of NCP Functions. *Axioms* **2022**, *11*, 557. https://doi.org/10.3390/axioms11100557

Academic Editors: Wei-Shih Du, Luigi Muglia and Adrian Petrusel

Received: 8 September 2022
Accepted: 30 September 2022
Published: 14 October 2022

Publisher's Note: MDPI stays neutral with regard to jurisdictional claims in published maps and institutional affiliations.

Copyright: © 2022 by the authors. Licensee MDPI, Basel, Switzerland. This article is an open access article distributed under the terms and conditions of the Creative Commons Attribution (CC BY) license (https://creativecommons.org/licenses/by/4.0/).

1. Introduction

The nonlinear complementarity problem (NCP) is finding a vector $x \in \mathbb{R}^n$ such that

$$x \geq 0, \quad F(x) \geq 0 \quad \text{and} \quad \langle x, F(x) \rangle = 0,$$

where $\langle \cdot, \cdot \rangle$ is the Euclidean inner product and F is a function from $\mathbb{R}^n$ to $\mathbb{R}^n$. Since a few decades ago, the NCP has attracted significant attention due to its various applications in areas such as economics, engineering, and information engineering [1]. There are many methods proposed for solving the NCP. One popular approach is to reformulate the NCP as a system of nonlinear equations, whereas the other approach is to recast the NCP as an unconstrained minimization problem. Both methods rely on the so-called NCP function. A function $\phi : \mathbb{R}^2 \to \mathbb{R}$ is said to be an NCP function if it satisfies

$$\phi(a,b) = 0 \quad \Longleftrightarrow \quad a \geq 0, \quad b \geq 0 \quad \text{and} \quad ab = 0.$$

In light of the NCP function, one can define the vector-valued function $\Phi_F(x) : \mathbb{R}^n \to \mathbb{R}^n$ by

$$\Phi_F(x) := \begin{pmatrix} \phi(x_1, F_1(x)) \\ \vdots \\ \phi(x_n, F_n(x)) \end{pmatrix},$$

where $F(x) = (F_1(x), \cdots, F_n(x))$ is a mapping from $\mathbb{R}^n$ to $\mathbb{R}^n$. Consequently, solving the NCP is equivalent to solving a system of equation $\Phi_F(x) = 0$. In particular, it also induces a merit function of the NCP which is given by

$$\min_{x \in \mathbb{R}^n} \Psi_F(x) := \frac{1}{2} \|\Phi_F(x)\|^2.$$

It is clear that the global minimizer of $\Psi_F(x)$ is the solution to the NCP. During the past few decades, several NCP functions have been discovered [2–7]. A well-known NCP function is the Fischer–Burmeister function [8,9] $\phi_{\text{FB}} : \mathbb{R}^2 \to \mathbb{R}$, defined as

$$\phi_{\text{FB}}(a,b) = ||(a,b)|| - (a+b),$$

where $||(a,b)|| = \sqrt{a^2+b^2}$. In [10], Tseng did an extension of the Fischer–Burmeister function, in which a 2-norm is relaxed to a general p-norm. In other words, the so-called generalized FB function is defined by

$$\phi^p_{\rm FB}(a,b) = ||(a,b)||_p - (a+b), \tag{1}$$

where $||(a,b)||_p = \sqrt[p]{|a|^p+|b|^p}$ and $p>1$. Similarly, it induces a merit function $\psi^p_{\rm FB} : \mathbb{R}^2 \to \mathbb{R}_+$ given by

$$\psi^p_{\rm FB}(a,b) = \frac{1}{2}|\phi^p_{FB}(a,b)|^2 \tag{2}$$

where $p>1$.

Another popular NCP function is the natural residual function [4], $\phi_{\rm NR} : \mathbb{R} \to \mathbb{R}$ given by

$$\phi_{\rm NR}(a,b) = a - (a-b)_+.$$

Is there a similar extension for the natural residual NCP function? Wu, Ko and Chen answered this question in [4]. The extension is kind of discrete generalization because they defined the function $\phi^p_{\rm NR} : \mathbb{R}^2 \to \mathbb{R}$ by

$$\phi^p_{\rm NR}(a,b) = a^p - (a-b)^p_+, \tag{3}$$

where $p>1$ and p is an odd integer. Recently, the idea of discrete generalization of natural residual function has beei applied to construct discrete Fischer–Burmeister functions. More specifically, $\phi^p_{\rm D-FB} : \mathbb{R}^2 \to \mathbb{R}$ is defined by

$$\phi^p_{\rm D-FB}(a,b) = (\sqrt{a^2+b^2})^p - (a+b)^p, \tag{4}$$

where $p>1$ and p is an odd integer. If $p=1$, then it is exactly the classical Fischer–Burmeister function (see [4,11]). The graph of $\phi^p_{\rm NR}$ is not symmetric. Is it possible to construct a symmetric natural residual NCP function? Chang, Yang, and Chen answered this question in [2]. Note that the function $\phi^p_{\rm NR}$ can also be expressed as a piecewise function:

$$\phi^p_{\rm NR}(a,b) = \begin{cases} a^p - (a-b)^p, & \text{if } a > b, \\ a^p, & \text{if } a \le b, \end{cases}$$

where $p>1$ and p is an odd integer. They use this expression of $\phi^p_{\rm NR}$ to modify the part on $a<b$, and achieve symmetrization of $\phi^p_{\rm S-NR}(a,b)$ as below:

$$\phi^p_{\rm S-NR}(a,b) = \begin{cases} a^p - (a-b)^p, & \text{if } a > b, \\ a^p = b^p, & \text{if } a = b, \\ b^p - (b-a)^p, & \text{if } a < b, \end{cases} \tag{5}$$

where $p>1$ and p is an odd integer. Surprisingly, it is still an NCP function.

How about the merit function induced by $\phi^p_{\rm S-NR}(a,b)$? Observing that the merit function has squared terms, Chang, Yang, and Chen combined a^p and b^p together and constructed $\psi^p_{\rm S-NR}(a,b)$ as

$$\psi^p_{\rm S-NR}(a,b) = \begin{cases} a^pb^p - (a-b)^pb^p, & \text{if } a > b, \\ a^pb^p = a^{2p}, & \text{if } a = b, \\ a^pb^p - (b-a)^pa^p, & \text{if } a < b, \end{cases} \tag{6}$$

where $p>1$ and p is an odd integer.

Recently, more and more NCP functions have been discovered. As mentioned, Wu et al. [4] proposed a discrete type of natural residual function. Regarding this discrete counterpart, Alcantara and Chen [1] consider a continuous type of natural residual function as below:

$$\widetilde{\phi}^p_{\rm NR}(a,b) = {\rm sgn}(a)|a|^p - [(a-b)_+]^p, \tag{7}$$

where $p > 1$ is a real number and

$$\mathrm{sgn}(x) = \begin{cases} 1, & \text{if } x > 0, \\ 0, & \text{if } x = 0, \\ -1, & \text{if } x < 0. \end{cases}$$

The main principle behind their work is described as follows. If $f(\cdot)$ is a bijection mapping and $\phi = \phi_1 - \phi_2$ is a given NCP function, then $f(\phi) = f(\phi_1) - f(\phi_2)$ is also an NCP function. Hence, it can be verified that

$$\widetilde{\phi}^p_{\rm NR}(a,b) = f(a) - f([a-b]_+)$$

is an NCP function by employing the bijective function $f(t) = \mathrm{sgn}(t)|t|^p$, see [12]. Note that when p is an positive odd integer, it reduces to the discrete type of a natural residual function, that is, $\widetilde{\phi}^p_{\rm NR}(a,b) = \phi^p_{\rm NR}(a,b)$.

For further symmetrization, using the above idea in (5) and (6), one can obtain a continuous type of natural residual functions [12]:

$$\widetilde{\phi}^p_{\rm S-NR}(a,b) = \begin{cases} \mathrm{sgn}(a)|a|^p - (a-b)^p, & \text{if } a \geq b, \\ \mathrm{sgn}(b)|b|^p - (b-a)^p, & \text{if } a < b, \end{cases} \tag{8}$$

and its corresponding merit function

$$\widetilde{\psi}^p_{\rm S-NR}(a,b) = \begin{cases} \mathrm{sgn}(a)\mathrm{sgn}(b)|a|^p|b|^p - \mathrm{sgn}(b)(a-b)^p|b|^p, & \text{if } a \geq b, \\ \mathrm{sgn}(a)\mathrm{sgn}(b)|a|^p|b|^p - \mathrm{sgn}(a)(b-a)^p|a|^p, & \text{if } a < b, \end{cases} \tag{9}$$

where $p > 0$. Again, when p is an odd integer, we see the beloe relations,

$$\widetilde{\phi}^p_{\rm S-NR}(a,b) = \phi^p_{\rm S-NR}(a,b), \quad \text{and} \quad \widetilde{\psi}^p_{\rm S-NR}(a,b) = \psi^p_{\rm S-NR}(a,b).$$

The NCP functions can also be constructed by certain invertible functions. What kind of inverse functions can be applied to construct the NCP functions? Lee, Chen, and Hu [6] figured it out in ([6], Proposition 3.8). In particular, let $f : \mathbb{R} \to \mathbb{R}$ be a continuous differentiable function and $g : \mathbb{R} \to \mathbb{R}$ with $g(0) = 1$. They chose functions of $f(t)$ and $g(t)$ satisfying the below conditions to construct new NCP functions:

(i) f is invertible on $[1, \infty)$.
(ii) $(f^{-1})'$ is a strictly monotonically increasing function.
(iii) $g(0) = 1, g(t) \geq 1, \forall t > 0$ and $\frac{-1}{2} < g(t) \leq 1 \; \forall t < 0$.

More specifically, it is shown that the function

$$\phi_{f,g}(a,b) = f(f^{-1}(|a|) + f^{-1}(|b|) - f^{-1}(0)) - (g(b)a + g(a)b)$$

is an NCP function. For example, taking $f(t) = \ln(t)$, we see that $f(t)$ is invertible on $[1, \infty)$ and the inverse function is $f^{-1}(t) = e^t$. It is easy to see that $(f^{-1}(t))' = e^t > 0, \forall t \in \mathbb{R}$. Thus, f^{-1} is strictly monotone increasing on $\mathbb{R}$. For third condition, we take $g(t) = e^t$, which gives $g(t) > 1$ on $(1, \infty)$ and $-\frac{1}{2} < g(t) < 1$ on $(-\infty, 0)$. We list some more examples of f and g as below. Examples of $f(t)$ are

$$f_1(t) = \sqrt{t-1}, \quad f_2(t) = \sqrt[5]{t-1}, \quad f_3(t) = \ln(t),$$

and examples of $g(t)$ are

$$g_1(t) = e^t, \quad g_2(t) = \frac{\sqrt{t^2+4}+t}{2}, \quad g_3(t) = \frac{4-e^{-t}}{1+2e^{-t}}.$$

In summary, nine corresponding NCP functions are generated by using the above $f(t)$ and $g(t)$.

$$\begin{aligned}
\phi_{f_1,g_1}(a,b) &= \sqrt{a^2+b^2} - e^b a - e^a b. \\
\phi_{f_1,g_2}(a,b) &= \sqrt{a^2+b^2} - \left(\frac{\sqrt{b^2+4}+b}{2}\right)a - \left(\frac{\sqrt{a^2+4}+a}{2}\right)b. \\
\phi_{f_1,g_3}(a,b) &= \sqrt{a^2+b^2} - \left(\frac{4-e^{-b}}{1+2e^{-b}}\right)a - \left(\frac{4-e^{-a}}{1+2e^{-a}}\right)b. \\
\phi_{f_2,g_1}(a,b) &= \sqrt[5]{|a|^5+|b|^5} - e^b a - e^a b. \\
\phi_{f_2,g_2}(a,b) &= \sqrt[5]{|a|^5+|b|^5} - \left(\frac{\sqrt{b^2+4}+b}{2}\right)a - \left(\frac{\sqrt{a^2+4}+a}{2}\right)b. \qquad (10) \\
\phi_{f_2,g_3}(a,b) &= \sqrt[5]{|a|^5+|b|^5} - \left(\frac{4-e^{-b}}{1+2e^{-b}}\right)a - \left(\frac{4-e^{-a}}{1+2e^{-a}}\right)b. \\
\phi_{f_3,g_1}(a,b) &= \ln(e^{|a|}+e^{|b|}-1) - e^b a - e^a b. \\
\phi_{f_3,g_2}(a,b) &= \ln(e^{|a|}+e^{|b|}-1) - \left(\frac{\sqrt{b^2+4}+b}{2}\right)a - \left(\frac{\sqrt{a^2+4}+a}{2}\right)b. \\
\phi_{f_3,g_3}(a,b) &= \ln(e^{|a|}+e^{|b|}-1) - \left(\frac{4-e^{-b}}{1+2e^{-b}}\right)a - \left(\frac{4-e^{-a}}{1+2e^{-a}}\right)b.
\end{aligned}$$

In [13], Tsai et al. discussed the geometry of curves on Fischer–Burmeister function surfaces, which are intersected by the plane $a+b=2r$ for $r \in \mathbb{R}$. They parametrized the curves by considering $a = r+t$ and $b = r-t$ and defined the vector valued function $\alpha(t) : \mathbb{R} \to \mathbb{R}^3$ and $\beta(t) : \mathbb{R} \to \mathbb{R}^3$ as $\alpha(t) = (r+t, r-t, \phi(r+t, r-t))$ and $\beta(t) = (r+t, r-t, \psi(r+t, r-t))$, respectively. Tsai et al. also found the local maxima and minima and studied the convexity of curves.

In this paper, we follow a similar idea to the one in [13] to investigate the curves, which are the intersection of a vertical plane $a+b=1$ and surfaces based on NCP functions. We also have to point out that the study on these curves is very useful to binary quadratic programming. See [14] for the details. We parametrize the curves by the vector functions $\tau(x) : \mathbb{R} \to \mathbb{R}^3$ and $\sigma(x) : \mathbb{R} \to \mathbb{R}^3$, where $\tau(x) = (x, 1-x, \phi(x, 1-x))$ and $\sigma(x) = (x, 1-x, \phi(x, 1-x))$. Then, we explore the behavior of the curves when the value p is perturbed. In addition, we discuss the convexity and local minimum and maximum of curves. Although the inflection points cannot be exactly determined, we can still estimate the interval in which the curves are convex such as in ([14], Proposition 2.1(b)). With the convexity or differentiability of a curve, we discuss the local minimum and maximum.

2. Preliminaries

In this section, we review some prerequisite knowledge about the convexity and differentiability of NCP functions which will be applied to investigate the curves. First, it is known that the convexity and differentiability of an NCP function cannot hold simultaneously (see [15]). The convexity of NCP functions has been thoroughly investigated in the literature. We will now quickly recall some results directly.

Lemma 1 ([3], Property 2.1 and Property 2.2, [2], Proposition 2.2). *Let ϕ^p_{FB}, ψ^p_{FB} and $\phi^p_{\text{D-FB}}$ be defined as in (1), (2) and (4) respectively. Then, the following hold.*

(a) *The function $\phi^p_{\text{FB}}(a,b)$ is differentiable everywhere except for the origin, and convex on $\mathbb{R}^2$, provided $p > 1$.*
(b) *The function $\psi^p_{\text{FB}}(a,b)$ is differentiable everywhere, but neither convex nor concave, provided $p > 1$.*
(c) *The function $\phi^p_{\text{D-FB}}(a,b)$ is differentiable everywhere, but neither convex nor concave provided $p > 1$ and is an odd integer.*

Lemma 2 ([4], Proposition 2.4, [2], Proposition 2.2). *Let ϕ^p_{NR}, $\phi^p_{\text{S-NR}}$, and $\psi^p_{\text{S-NR}}$ be defined as in (3), (5) and (6) respectively. Then, when $p > 1$ and is an odd integer, the following hold.*

(a) *The function $\phi^p_{\text{NR}}(a,b)$ is differentiable everywhere, but neither convex nor concave.*
(b) *The function $\phi^p_{\text{S-NR}}(a,b)$ is differentiable everywhere except for $a = b$. but neither convex nor concave.*
(c) *The function $\psi^p_{\text{S-NR}}(a,b)$ is differentiable everywhere, but neither convex nor concave.*

Lemma 3 ([1], Proposition 2). *Let $\widetilde{\phi}^p_{\text{NR}}$, $\widetilde{\phi}^p_{\text{S-NR}}$ and $\widetilde{\psi}^p_{\text{S-NR}}$ be defined as in (7), (8) and (9) respectively. Then, for $p > 1$, the following hold.*

(a) *The function $\widetilde{\phi}^p_{\text{NR}}(a,b)$ is differentiable everywhere, but neither convex nor concave.*
(b) *The function $\widetilde{\phi}^p_{\text{S-NR}}(a,b)$ is differentiable everywhere except for $a = b$, but neither convex nor concave.*
(c) *The function $\widetilde{\psi}^p_{\text{S-NR}}(a,b)$ is differentiable everywhere, but neither convex nor concave.*

Proposition 1 ([12], Proposition 2.3). *Suppose that g is strictly increasing on some interval $I = [0, t_0)$. Then, for $p > 1$, the function $\phi^p_g = \|(a,b)\|_p - (g(b)a + g(a)b)$ is an NCP function, but nonconvex.*

We can apply Proposition 1 to check the convexity of NCP functions as in (10). In particular, based on Proposition 1, the following NCP functions are nonconvex and not differentiable at $(0,0)$.

(a) $\phi_{f_1 g_1}(a,b) = \sqrt{a^2+b^2} - e^b a - e^a b$.
(b) $\phi_{f_1 g_2}(a,b) = \sqrt{a^2+b^2} - \left(\frac{\sqrt{b^2+4}+b}{2}\right)a - \left(\frac{\sqrt{a^2+4}+a}{2}\right)b$.
(c) $\phi_{f_1 g_3}(a,b) = \sqrt{a^2+b^2} - \left(\frac{4-e^{-b}}{1+2e^{-b}}\right)a - \left(\frac{4-e^{-a}}{1+2e^{-a}}\right)b$.
(d) $\phi_{f_2 g_1}(a,b) = \sqrt[5]{|a|^5+|b|^5} - e^b a - e^a b$.
(e) $\phi_{f_2 g_2}(a,b) = \sqrt[5]{|a|^5+|b|^5} - \left(\frac{\sqrt{b^2+4}+b}{2}\right)a - \left(\frac{\sqrt{a^2+4}+a}{2}\right)b$.
(f) $\phi_{f_2 g_3}(a,b) = \sqrt[5]{|a|^5+|b|^5} - \left(\frac{4-e^{-b}}{1+2e^{-b}}\right)a - \left(\frac{4-e^{-a}}{1+2e^{-a}}\right)b$.

Moreover, the below NCP functions are nonconvex as well.

(g) $\phi_{f_3 g_1}(a,b) = \ln(e^{|a|} + e^{|b|} - 1) - e^b a - e^a b$.
(h) $\phi_{f_3 g_2}(a,b) = \ln(e^{|a|} + e^{|b|} - 1) - \left(\frac{\sqrt{b^2+4}+b}{2}\right)a - \left(\frac{\sqrt{a^2+4}+a}{2}\right)b$.
(i) $\phi_{f_3 g_3}(a,b) = \ln(e^{|a|} + e^{|b|} - 1) - \left(\frac{4-e^{-b}}{1+2e^{-b}}\right)a - \left(\frac{4-e^{-a}}{1+2e^{-a}}\right)b$.

3. The Differentiability of the Curves

In this section, we investigate the differentiability of the curves, which are the intersection of surfaces of NCP functions $\phi(a,b)$, (or merit functions $\psi(a,b)$) with the vertical plane $a + b = 1$. To proceed, we set $a = x$ and $b = 1 - x$. Then, the curves are parameterized as

$$\tau(x) = \phi(x, 1-x) \quad \text{and} \quad \sigma(x) = \psi(x, 1-x).$$

From the aforementioned NCP functions in Section 2, the parametrized curves are listed as below:

$$\tau^p_{\rm FB}(x) = \sqrt[p]{|x|^p + |1-x|^p} - 1. \tag{11}$$

$$\sigma^p_{\rm FB}(x) = \frac{1}{2}|\tau^p_{\rm FB}(x)|^2. \tag{12}$$

$$\tau^p_{\rm D-FB}(x) = \left(\sqrt{x^2 + (1-x)^2}\right)^p - 1. \tag{13}$$

$$\tau^p_{\rm NR}(x) = x^p - (2x-1)^p_+. \tag{14}$$

$$\tau^p_{\rm S-NR}(x) = \begin{cases} x^p - (2x-1)^p, & \text{if } x > \frac{1}{2}, \\ (\frac{1}{2})^p, & \text{if } x = \frac{1}{2}, \\ (1-x)^p - (1-2x)^p, & \text{if } x < \frac{1}{2}. \end{cases} \tag{15}$$

$$\sigma^p_{\rm S-NR}(x) = \begin{cases} x^p(1-x)^p - (2x-1)^p(1-x)^p, & \text{if } x > \frac{1}{2}, \\ (\frac{1}{2})^{2p}, & \text{if } x = \frac{1}{2}, \\ x^p(1-x)^p - x^p(1-2x)^p, & \text{if } x < \frac{1}{2}. \end{cases} \tag{16}$$

$$\widetilde{\tau}^p_{\rm NR}(x) = \text{sgn}(x)|x|^p - [(2x-1)_+]^p. \tag{17}$$

$$\widetilde{\tau}^p_{\rm S-NR}(x) = \begin{cases} \text{sgn}(x)|x|^p - (2x-1)^p, & \text{if } x \geq \frac{1}{2}, \\ \text{sgn}(1-x)|1-x|^p - (1-2x)^p, & \text{if } x < \frac{1}{2}. \end{cases} \tag{18}$$

$$\widetilde{\sigma}^p_{\rm S-NR}(x) = \begin{cases} \text{sgn}(x)\text{sgn}(1-x)|x|^p|1-x|^p - \text{sgn}(1-x)(2x-1)^p|1-x|^p, & \text{if } x \geq \frac{1}{2}, \\ \text{sgn}(x)\text{sgn}(1-x)|1-x|^p|x|^p - \text{sgn}(x)(1-2x)^p|x|^p, & \text{if } x < \frac{1}{2}. \end{cases} \tag{19}$$

$$\tau_{f_1,g_1}(x) = \sqrt{x^2 + (1-x)^2} - e^{(1-x)}x - e^x(1-x). \tag{20}$$

$$\tau_{f_1,g_2}(x) = \sqrt{x^2 + (1-x)^2} - \left(\frac{\sqrt{(1-x)^2+4} + (1-x)}{2}\right)x - \left(\frac{\sqrt{x^2+4}+x}{2}\right)(1-x). \tag{21}$$

$$\tau_{f_1,g_3}(x) = \sqrt{x^2 + (1-x)^2} - \left(\frac{4 - e^{-(1-x)}}{1 + 2e^{-(1-x)}}\right)x - \left(\frac{4-e^{-x}}{1+2e^{-x}}\right)(1-x). \tag{22}$$

$$\tau_{f_2,g_1}(x) = \sqrt[5]{|x|^5 + |1-x|^5} - e^{(1-x)}x - e^x(1-x). \tag{23}$$

$$\tau_{f_2,g_2}(x) = \sqrt[5]{|x|^5 + |1-x|^5} - \left(\frac{\sqrt{(1-x)^2+4} + (1-x)}{2}\right)x - \left(\frac{\sqrt{x^2+4}+x}{2}\right)(1-x). \tag{24}$$

$$\tau_{f_2,g_3}(x) = \sqrt[5]{|x|^5 + |1-x|^5} - \left(\frac{4 - e^{-(1-x)}}{1 + 2e^{-(1-x)}}\right)x - \left(\frac{4-e^{-x}}{1+2e^{-x}}\right)(1-x). \tag{25}$$

$$\tau_{f_3,g_1}(x) = \ln\left(e^{|x|} + e^{|1-x|} - 1\right) - e^{(1-x)}x - e^x(1-x). \tag{26}$$

$$\tau_{f_3,g_2}(x) = \ln\left(e^{|x|} + e^{|1-x|} - 1\right) - \left(\frac{\sqrt{(1-x)^2+4} + (1-x)}{2}\right)x - \left(\frac{\sqrt{x^2+4}+x}{2}\right)(1-x). \tag{27}$$

$$\tau_{f_3,g_3}(x) = \ln(e^{|x|} + e^{|1-x|} - 1) - \left(\frac{4 - e^{-(1-x)}}{1 + 2e^{-(1-x)}}\right)x - \left(\frac{4 - e^{-x}}{1 + 2e^{-x}}\right)(1 - x). \tag{28}$$

Proposition 2. *Let τ^p_{FB}, σ^p_{FB} and $\tau^p_{\text{D-FB}}$ be defined as (11), (12) and (13) respectively. Then, the following hold.*

(a) *For $p > 1$, the function $\tau^p_{\text{FB}}(\cdot)$ is differentiable on $\mathbb{R}$.*
(b) *For $p > 1$, the function $\sigma^p_{\text{FB}}(\cdot)$ is differentiable on $\mathbb{R}$.*
(c) *For all odd integers, the function $\tau^p_{\text{D-FB}}(\cdot)$ is differentiable on $\mathbb{R}$.*

Proof. The results follow immediately from Lemma 1. □

Proposition 3. *Let $\tau^p_{\text{NR}}(x)$, $\tau^p_{\text{S-NR}}$ and $\sigma^p_{\text{S-NR}}$ be defined as in (14), (15) and (16), respectively. Then, for $p > 1$ and p is an odd integer, the following hold.*

(a) *The function $\tau^p_{\text{NR}}(\cdot)$ is differentiable on $\mathbb{R}$;*
(b) *The function $\tau^p_{\text{S-NR}}(\cdot)$ is not differentiable at $x = \frac{1}{2}$;*
(c) *The function $\sigma^p_{\text{S-NR}}(\cdot)$ is differentiable on $\mathbb{R}$.*

Proof. The results are immediate consequences of Lemma 2. □

Proposition 4. *Let $\widetilde{\tau}^p_{\text{NR}}$, $\widetilde{\tau}^p_{\text{S-NR}}$, and $\widetilde{\sigma}^p_{\text{S-NR}}$ be defined as in (17), (18) and (19), respectively. Then, for $p > 1$, the following hold.*

(a) *The function $\widetilde{\tau}^p_{\text{NR}}(\cdot)$ is differentiable on $\mathbb{R}$.*
(b) *The function $\widetilde{\tau}^p_{\text{S-NR}}(\cdot)$ is not differentiable at $x = \frac{1}{2}$.*
(c) *The function $\widetilde{\sigma}^p_{\text{S-NR}}(\cdot)$ is differentiable on $\mathbb{R}$.*

Proof. The results follow from Lemma 3 directly. □

Proposition 5. *Let τ_{f_i,g_j} be defined as in (20)–(28) where $i = 1,2,3$ and $j = 1,2,3$. Then, the following hold.*

(a) *For $i = 1,2$ and $j = 1,2,3$, the function $\tau_{f_i,g_j}(\cdot)$ is differentiable on $\mathbb{R}$.*
(b) *For $j = 1,2,3$, The function $\tau_{f_3,g_j}(\cdot)$ is not differentiable at $x = 0$ or $x = 1$.*

Proof. (a) Based on Proposition 2(a), the function $\tau^p_{\text{FB}}(x)$ is differentiable on $\mathbb{R}$. In addition, we know that the exponential function and $\sqrt{(1-x)^2 + 4}$ are differentiable on $\mathbb{R}$. Therefore, $\tau_{f_i,g_j}(x)$ is differentiable on $\mathbb{R}$.

(b) Let $h(x) = \ln(e^{|x|} + e^{|1-x|} - 1)$, which says $h'(x) = \frac{\frac{x}{|x|}e^{|x|} - \frac{(1-x)}{|1-x|}e^{|1-x|}}{e^{|x|} + e^{|1-x|} - 1}$. For $x > 0$, the right derivative at $x = 0$ is $h'(0_+) = \frac{1-e}{e}$. For $x < 0$, the left derivative at $x = 0$ is $h'(0_-) = \frac{-1-e}{e}$. Then, it is clear that $h'(0_+) \neq h'(0_-)$, hence $h(\cdot)$ is not differentiable at $x = 0$. Similarly, it is easy to check the non-differentiability at $x = 1$. To summarize, the function $\tau_{f_3,g_j}(x)$ is not differentiable at $x = 0$ or $x = 1$. □

4. The Convexity of the Curves

In Section 2, we discussed the convexity of NCP functions. It naturally leads to the convexity of the curves. Although we cannot find the inflection points one by one, we focus on estimating the interval where the curves are convex. In addition, with different p, the geometric structure of the curves will be changed. The following lemma will be employed to check the convexity.

Lemma 4. (a) *If $g(x)$ and $h(x)$ are convex on an interval, then $g(x)+h(x)$ is also convex on the interval.*

(b) *Let $g(x): \mathbb{R}^n \to (-\infty, \infty)$ be a convex function and let $h(x): g(\mathbb{R}^n) \to \mathbb{R}$ be a nondecreasing convex function. Then $f(x) = h(g(x))$ is convex on $\mathbb{R}^n$.*

Proof. These are very basic materials which are also well known, see [16]. □

Proposition 6. *Let τ^p_{FB} and $\tau^p_{\text{D-FB}}$ be defined as in (11) and (13), respectively. Then, the following hold. See Figure 1.*

(a) *For $p>1$, the function $\tau^p_{\text{FB}}(\cdot)$ is convex on $\mathbb{R}$.*

(b) *When p is an odd integer, the function $\tau^p_{\text{D-FB}}(\cdot)$ is convex on $\mathbb{R}$.*

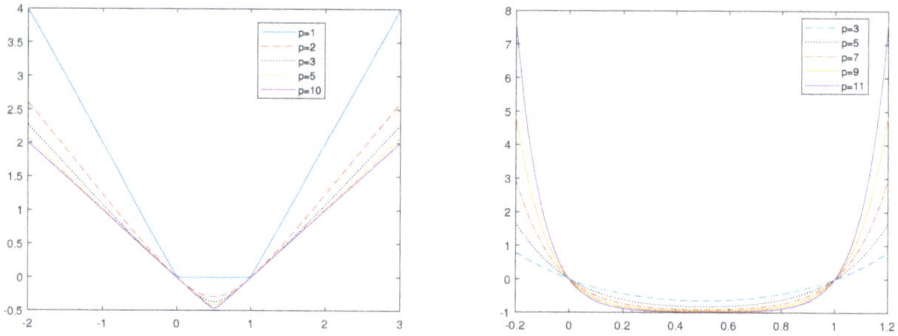

(a) (b)

Figure 1. Graph of $\tau^p_{\text{FB}}(x)$ and $\tau^p_{\text{D-FB}}(x)$ with different p. (**a**) Graph of $\tau^p_{\text{FB}}(x)$ with different values of p; (**b**) Graph of $\tau^p_{\text{D-FB}}(x)$ with different values of p.

Proof. (a) First, as indicated in (11), $\tau^p_{\text{FB}}(x) = \sqrt[p]{|x|^p + |1-x|^p} - 1$. Since the curve $\tau^p_{\text{FB}}(x)$ is the section of a plane with the surface of the function $\phi^p_{\text{FB}}(a,b)$, which is convex on $\mathbb{R}^2$ according to Lemma 1(a). $\tau^p_{\text{FB}}(x)$ is convex on $\mathbb{R}$.

(b) As shown in (13), $\tau^p_{\text{D-FB}}(x) = \left(\sqrt{x^2+(1-x)^2}\right)^p - 1$, where p is an odd integer. Let $g(x) := \sqrt{x^2+(1-x)^2}$ and $h(x) := x^p - 1$. It is clear that $h(x)$ is nondecreasing and convex; moreover, $g(x)$ is positive and convex. Then, according to Lemma 4(b), $\tau^p_{\text{D-FB}}(\cdot)$ is convex on $\mathbb{R}$. □

Proposition 7. *Let σ^p_{FB} be defined as in (12). Then, for any $p>1$, the function $\sigma^p_{\text{FB}}(\cdot)$ is convex on $(-\infty, 0)$ and $(1, \infty)$. See Figure 2.*

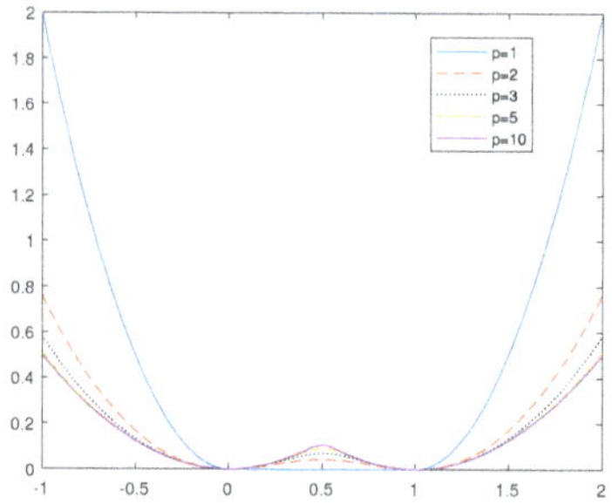

Figure 2. Graphs of σ^p_{FB} with different values of p.

Proof. As given in (12), $\sigma^p_{\mathrm{FB}}(x) = \frac{1}{2}\left(\tau^p_{FB}(x)\right)^2$. Let $g(x) := \tau^p_{\mathrm{FB}}(x)$ and $h(x) := \frac{1}{2}x^2$. It is clear that $h(x)$ is nondecreasing and convex on $(0, \infty)$. Furthermore, $g(x)$ is convex and positive on $(1, \infty)$. Hence, according to Lemma 4(b), $\sigma^p_{\mathrm{FB}}(x)$ is convex on $(1, \infty)$. In addition, due to symmetry, $\sigma^p_{\mathrm{FB}}(x)$ is also convex on $(-\infty, 0)$. □

Remark 1. (i) *Set $p = 2$. The second derivative of $\sigma^2_{\mathrm{FB}}(x) = \frac{1}{2}|\tau^2_{\mathrm{FB}}(x)|^2$ gives*

$$\left(\sigma^2_{\mathrm{FB}}\right)''(x) = 2 - \frac{1}{(2x^2 - 2x + 1)^{\frac{3}{2}}}.$$

From this, we know that $a_{\pm} = \frac{1}{2}\left(1 \pm \sqrt{2^{\left(\frac{1}{3}\right)} - 1}\right)$ are two inflection points of the function $\sigma^p_{\mathrm{FB}}(x)$. Hence, the function $\sigma^p_{\mathrm{FB}}(x)$ is convex on the intervals $(-\infty, a_-)$ and (a_+, ∞). For a general $p > 1$, we have difficulty in determining their infection points. However, let us study their behavior when p goes to ∞ on the interval $(0, 1)$. When $1/2 < x < 1$, we have $|x| > |1 - x|$. Hence, the function $\sigma^p_{\mathrm{FB}}(x)$ approaches $\frac{1}{2}(x - 1)^2$ as p goes to ∞. Similarly, provided $0 < x < 1/2$, the function $\sigma^p_{\mathrm{FB}}(x)$ approaches $\frac{1}{2}x^2$ as p goes to ∞. Note also that $\sigma^p_{\mathrm{FB}}(\frac{1}{2})$ approaches $\frac{1}{8}$ as p goes to ∞.

(ii) *We also examine the behavior of the second derivative of the function $\sigma^p_{\mathrm{FB}}(x)$ at the point 0.55 which is near $\frac{1}{2}$. We present the numerical results in Figure 3. Observe that their inflection points $a^p_{\pm}$ approaches $1/2$, and also that $(\sigma^p_{\mathrm{FB}})''(0.55)$ approaches 1 as p goes to ∞.*

According to Remark 1 and Figure 3, we make a conjecture here.

Conjecture 1. *Let σ^p_{FB} be defined as in (12). Then, for any $p > 1$, the function $\sigma^p_{\mathrm{FB}}(\cdot)$ has two inflection points $0 < a^p_- < \frac{1}{2} < a^p_+ < 1$, and both approach $\frac{1}{2}$ as p goes to ∞.*

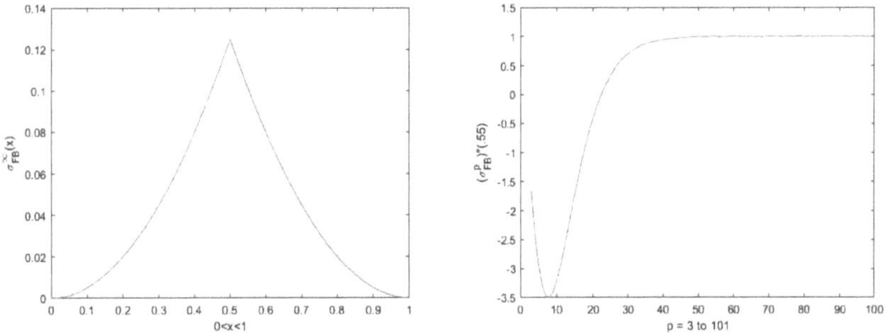

(a) (b)

Figure 3. Graphic evidence regarding Remark 1 and Conjecture 1. (**a**) Graphs of $\sigma^{\infty}_{\mathrm{FB}}(x)$ when $0 < x < 1$; (**b**) Graphs of $(\sigma^p_{\mathrm{FB}})''(0.55)$ for different p.

Proposition 8. *Let τ^p_{NR} and τ^p_{S-NR} be defined as in (14) and (15), respectively. Then, when p is an odd integer, the following hold. See Figure 4.*

(a) *The function $\tau^p_{\mathrm{NR}}(\cdot)$ is convex on $(0, \frac{4}{7})$.*

(b) *The function $\tau^p_{\mathrm{S-NR}}(\cdot)$ is convex on $(\frac{3}{7}, \frac{4}{7})$.*

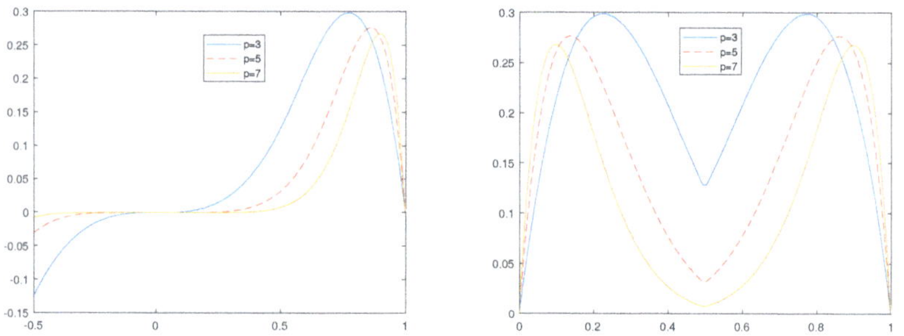

(**a**) (**b**)

Figure 4. Graphs of τ^p_{NR} and $\tau^p_{\mathrm{S-NR}}$ with different values of p. (**a**) Graphs of τ^p_{NR} with different values of p; (**b**) Graphs of $\tau^p_{\mathrm{S-NR}}$ with different values of p.

Proof. (a) As given in (14), $\tau^p_{\mathrm{NR}}(x) = x^p - (2x-1)^p_+$, which says

$$\begin{aligned} (\tau^p_{\mathrm{NR}})'(x) &= p\left(x^{(p-1)} - \left[\frac{(2x-1)+|2x-1|}{2}\right]^{(p-1)}(1+\mathrm{sgn}(2x-1))\right), \\ (\tau^p_{\mathrm{NR}})''(x) &= p(p-1)\left(x^{(p-2)} - \left[\frac{(2x-1)+|2x-1|}{2}\right]^{(p-2)}(1+\mathrm{sgn}(2x-1))^2\right). \end{aligned}$$

To proceed, we discuss three subcases:

Case (i): On the interval $(0, \frac{1}{2})$, we have $(1+\mathrm{sgn}(2x-1))^2 = 0$, which says $\left(\tau^p_{\mathrm{NR}}\right)''(x)$ $= p(p-1)x^{(p-2)} > 0$.

Case (ii): At the points $a = \frac{1}{2}$, we have $\left(\tau^p_{\mathrm{NR}}\right)''(\frac{1}{2}) = p(p-1)(\frac{1}{2})^{(p-2)} > 0$ as well.

Case (iii): On the interval $(\frac{1}{2}, \frac{4}{7})$, we need to show that $\left(\tau^p_{\mathrm{NR}}\right)''(x) > 0$ over $(\frac{1}{2}, \frac{4}{7})$ for all $p \geq 3$. Indeed, on the interval $(\frac{1}{2}, \frac{4}{7})$, we have $\left[\frac{(2x-1)+|2x-1|}{2}\right] = 2x-1$ and $(1+\mathrm{sgn}(2x-1))^2 = 4$. Define $g_x(p) := x^{(p-2)} - 4(2x-1)^{p-2}$. Then, our goal is to show $g_x(p) > 0$ for all $p \geq 3$ on the interval $(\frac{1}{2}, \frac{4}{7})$. When $p = 3$, we have $g_x(3) = x - 4(2x-1) = -7x+4 > 0$ on $(\frac{1}{2}, \frac{4}{7})$. In addition, note that $x > 4(2x-1)$ on the same interval. For other $p = 3+k$ with $k > 0$, we have

$$\begin{aligned} g_x(3+k) &= x^{1+k} - 4(2x-1)^{1+k} \\ &= xx^k - 4(2x-1)^{1+k} \\ &> 4(2x-1)x^k - 4(2x-1)^{1+k} \\ &= 4(2x-1)\left[x^k - (2x-1)^k\right]. \end{aligned}$$

Let $a = 1-x, b = 2x-1$. Then, the term $x^k - (2x-1)^k$ in $g_x(3+k)$ is expressed as

$$x^k - (2x-1)^k = (1-x+2x-1)^k - (2x-1)^k = (a+b)^k - b^k.$$

Since, on the interval $(\frac{1}{2}, \frac{4}{7})$ a and b are positive, we conclude that $g_x(3+k) > 0$.

To summarize, on the interval $(\frac{1}{2}, \frac{4}{7})$, the second derivative $\left(\tau^p_{\mathrm{NR}}\right)''(x) > 0$, which means that $\tau^p_{\mathrm{NR}}(x)$ is convex on this interval.

(b) As stated in (15), $\tau^p_{\text{S-NR}}(x) = \begin{cases} x^p - (2x-1)^p & \text{if } x > \frac{1}{2}, \\ (\frac{1}{2})^p & \text{if } x = \frac{1}{2}, \\ (1-x)^p - (1-2x)^p & \text{if } x < \frac{1}{2}. \end{cases}$ For $x > \frac{1}{2}$, similar to part (a), it can be verified that $\tau^p_{\text{NR}}(x)$ is convex. Therefore, $\tau^p_{\text{S-NR}}(x)$ is convex on $(\frac{1}{2}, \frac{4}{7})$. For $x < \frac{1}{2}$, due to symmetry, $\tau^p_{\text{S-NR}}(x)$ is convex on $(\frac{3}{7}, \frac{1}{2})$.

Additionally, note that $\tau^p_{\text{S-NR}}(x)$ is continuous on $(\frac{3}{7}, \frac{4}{7})$, and increasing (decreasing) on the right (left) hand side of the point $a = \frac{1}{2}$, since $\left(\tau^p_{\text{S-NR}}\right)'(1/2_+) = p(1/2)^{p-1} > 0$, $\left(\tau^p_{\text{S-NR}}\right)''(x) > 0$ on the interval $(\frac{1}{2}, \frac{4}{7})$ as well as $\left(\tau^p_{\text{S-NR}}\right)'(1/2_-) = -p(1/2)^{p-1} < 0$, $\left(\tau^p_{\text{S-NR}}\right)''(x) > 0$ on the interval $(\frac{3}{7}, \frac{1}{2})$. Hence, the point $a = \frac{1}{2}$ is the only minimizer on the interval $(\frac{3}{7}, \frac{4}{7})$. In summary, we can conclude that $\tau^p_{\text{S-NR}}(x)$ is convex on the interval $(\frac{3}{7}, \frac{4}{7})$. □

Proposition 9. *Let $\sigma^p_{\text{S-NR}}$ be defined as in (16). Then, when $p \geq 3$ and p is an odd integer, the function $\sigma^p_{\text{S-NR}}(x)$ is convex on $(-\infty, 0)$ and $(1, \infty)$. See Figure 5.*

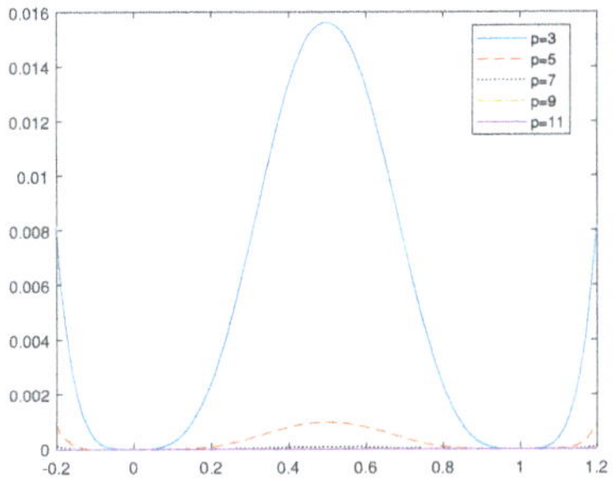

Figure 5. Graph of the function $\sigma^p_{\text{S-NR}}$ with different values of p.

Proof. As indicated in (16), $\sigma^p_{\text{S-NR}}(x) = \begin{cases} x^p(1-x)^p - (2x-1)^p(1-x)^p & \text{if } x > \frac{1}{2}, \\ (\frac{1}{2})^{2p} & \text{if } x = \frac{1}{2}, \\ x^p(1-x)^p - x^p(1-2x)^p & \text{if } x < \frac{1}{2}, \end{cases}$

where p is an odd integer and $p > 1$. Since $\sigma^p_{\text{S-NR}}(x)$ is symmetric about $x = \frac{1}{2}$, we divide it into two cases:

Cases (i): Suppose $x > 1$, the first and second derivative of this function are

$$\begin{aligned} \left(\sigma^p_{S-NR}\right)'(x) &= -p(1-x)^{p-1}[x^p - (2x-1)^p] + (1-x)^p[p(x^{p-1} - 2(2x-1)^{p-1})] \\ \left(\sigma^p_{S-NR}\right)''(x) &= f_1(x) + f_2(x) + f_3(x) \end{aligned}$$

where

$$\begin{aligned} f_1(x) &= (-2p)p[x^{p-1} - 2(2x-1)^{p-1}](1-x)^{p-1} = x^{p-1}[1 - 2(2-\frac{1}{x})^{p-1}](1-x)^{p-1}(-2p)p, \\ f_2(x) &= p(p-1)[x^{p-2} - 4(2x-1)^{p-2}](1-x)^p = x^{p-2}[1 - 4(2-\frac{1}{x})^{p-1}](1-x)^p(p-1)p, \\ f_3(x) &= p(p-1)[x^p - (2x-1)^p](1-x)^{p-2} = x^p[1 - (2-\frac{1}{x})^{p-2}](1-x)^{p-2}(p-1)p. \end{aligned}$$

Note that $\left(\sigma^p_{S-NR}\right)''(1) = 0$, we want to show that $\left(\sigma^p_{S-NR}\right)''(x)$ is positive for $p > 1$.

Because $x > 1$, we have $1 < 2 - \frac{1}{x}$, which implies $1 - 2(2-\frac{1}{x})^{p-1} < -1$. Moreover, as we have $(-2p)px^{p-1} < 0$ and $(1-x)^{p-1} > 0$, then $f_1(x) > 0$. Similarly, because $x > 1$, we have $1 < 2 - \frac{1}{x}$. Hence, $1 - 4(2 - \frac{1}{x})^{p-1} < -3$. Moreover, as we have $(p-1)px^{p-2} > 0$ and $(1-x)^p < 0$, then $f_2(x) > 0$. Finally, because $x > 1$ we have $1 < 2 - \frac{1}{x}$, which gives $1 - (2 - \frac{1}{x})^{p-2} < 0$. Moreover, we have $(p-1)px^p > 0$ and $(1-x)^{p-2} < 0$. Then, it says $f_3(x) > 0$.

To summarize, we have shown $f_1(x) + f_1(x) + f_1(x) > 0$ for $x > 1$, which says $\left(\sigma^p_{\text{S-NR}}\right)''(x) > 0$ for $x > 1$. In other words, $\sigma^p_{\text{S-NR}}(\cdot)$ is convex on $(1, \infty)$.

Cases (ii): Suppose $x < 0$, since $\sigma^p_{\text{S-NR}}(x)$ is symmetric about $x = \frac{1}{2}$. In this case, it is clear that $\sigma^p_{\text{S-NR}}(x)$ is convex on $(-\infty, 0)$.

By cases (i) and (ii), we prove that $\sigma^p_{\text{S-NR}}(x)$ is convex on $(-\infty, 0)$ and $(1, \infty)$. □

Because $\widetilde{\tau}^p_{\text{NR}}$, $\widetilde{\tau}^p_{\text{S-NR}}$ and $\widetilde{\sigma}^p_{\text{S-NR}}$ are the continuous types of τ^p_{NR}, $\tau^p_{\text{S-NR}}$ and $\sigma^p_{\text{S-NR}}$, similar to Propositions 8 and 9, we establish the next proposition.

Proposition 10. *Let $\widetilde{\tau}^p_{\text{NR}}$, $\widetilde{\tau}^p_{\text{S-NR}}$ and $\widetilde{\sigma}^p_{\text{S-NR}}$ be defined as in (17), (18), and (19), respectively. Then, the following hold. See Figure 6.*

(a) *If $p \geq 3$, then the function $\widetilde{\tau}^p_{\text{NR}}(x)$ is convex on $(0, \frac{4}{7})$.*
(b) *If $p \geq 3$, then the function $\widetilde{\tau}^p_{\text{S-NR}}(x)$ is convex on $(\frac{3}{7}, \frac{4}{7})$.*
(c) *If $p \geq 3$, then the function $\widetilde{\sigma}^p_{\text{S-NR}}(x)$ is convex on $(-\infty, 0)$ and $(1, \infty)$.*

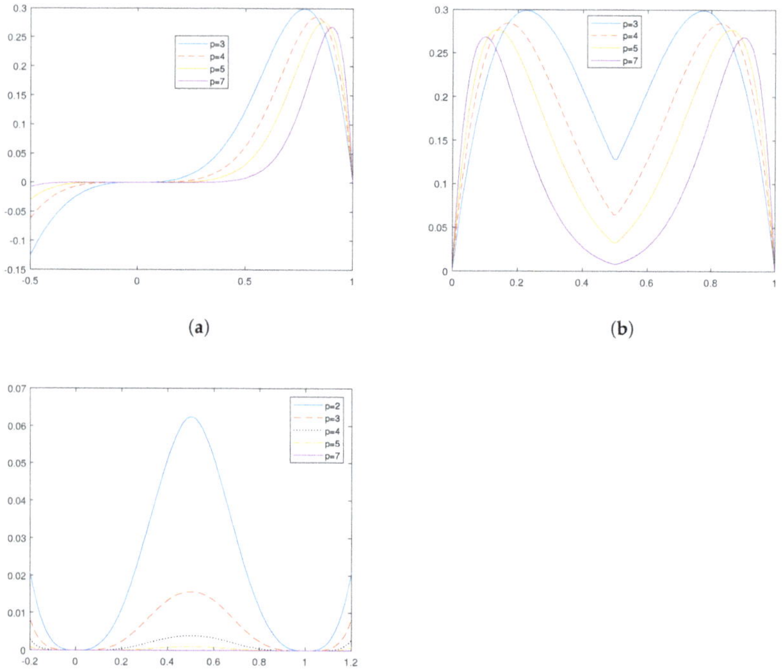

(a) (b) (c)

Figure 6. Graphs of $\widetilde{\tau}^p_{\text{NR}}(x)$, $\widetilde{\tau}^p_{\text{S-NR}}(x)$ and $\widetilde{\sigma}^p_{\text{S-NR}}$ with different values of p. (**a**) Graphs of $\widetilde{\tau}^p_{\text{NR}}(x)$ with different values of p; (**b**) Graphs of $\widetilde{\tau}^p_{\text{S-NR}}(x)$ with different values of p; (**c**) Graphs of $\widetilde{\sigma}^p_{\text{S-NR}}$ with different values of p.

The following proposition is simple but tedious. We list it here for the readers' convenience.

Proposition 11. *Let τ_{f_i,g_j} where $i = 1,2$ and $j = 1,2,3$ be defined from (20)–(28). Then, the following hold.*

(a) *The function $\tau_{f_i,g_j}(\cdot)$ for $i = 1,2$ and $j = 1,2$ is convex on $\mathbb{R}$.*

(b) *The function $\tau_{f_3,g_j}(\cdot)$ for $j = 1,2$ is convex on intervals $(-\infty, 0)$, $(0,1)$ and $(1,\infty)$.*

(c) *The function $\tau_{f_i,g_3}(\cdot)$ for $i = 1,2,3$ has inflection points, and thus is neither convex nor concave on entire $\mathbb{R}$.*

Proof. (a) As stated in (20), $\tau_{f_1,g_1}(x) = \sqrt{x^2 + (1-x)^2} - e^{(1-x)}x - e^x(1-x)$. Let $g(x) := \sqrt{x^2 + (1-x)^2}$ and $h(x) := -e^{(1-x)}x - e^x(1-x)$. Because $g(x)$ is convex on $\mathbb{R}$ according to Proposition 6(b), it suffices to show that $h(x)$ is convex. Taking the first and second derivatives of this function give

$$h'(x) = e^{(1-x)}(x-1) + e^x x, \quad \text{and} \quad h''(x) = xe^x + e^x - e^{1-x}x + 2e^{1-x}.$$

In order to verify that $h''(x) > 0$, we divide it into three cases:
Cases (i) : Suppose $x \geq 1/2$. We have $x \geq 1-x$, hence $e^x \geq e^{1-x}$. Then, we obtain $h''(x) = x(e^x - e^{1-x}) + e^x + 2e^{1-x} > 0$.
Cases (ii): Suppose $0 \leq x \leq 1/2$. We have $2 > x$, hence $2e^{1-x} > xe^{1-x}$. Then, we obtain $h''(x) = (2e^{1-x} - xe^{1-x}) + e^x + xe^x > 0$.
Cases (iii): Suppose $x \leq 0$. We have $x \leq 1-x$, hence $e^x \leq e^{1-x}$. Then, we obtain $h''(x) = x(e^x - e^{1-x}) + e^x + 2e^{1-x} > 0$.

This shows that $h''(x)$ is always positive, which indicates that $h(x)$ is convex on $\mathbb{R}$. Because $g(x)$ and $h(x)$ are convex on $\mathbb{R}$, according to Lemma 4(a), the function $\tau_{f_1,g_1}(\cdot)$ is convex on $\mathbb{R}$.

As indicated in(21), $\tau_{f1,g2}(x) = \sqrt{x^2 + (1-x)^2} - \left(\frac{\sqrt{(1-x)^2+4}+(1-x)}{2}\right)x - \left(\frac{\sqrt{x^2+4}+x}{2}\right)$ $(1-x)$. Let $h(x) := \sqrt{x^2 + (1-x)^2}$ and $g(x) := -(\frac{\sqrt{(1-x)^2+4}+(1-x)}{2})x - (\frac{\sqrt{x^2+4}+x}{2})(1-x)$. We need to verify that $g(x)$ is convex. Taking the second derivative of $g(x)$ gives

$$g''(x) = \frac{-x^3 + 3x^2 - 9x + 5}{(x^2 - 2x + 5)^{\frac{3}{2}}} + \frac{x^3 + 6x - 2}{(x^2 + 4)^{\frac{3}{2}}} + 2.$$

We want to show that that $g''(x) > 0$. The main principle of this is to check whether the minimum of the second derivative is positive. Taking the third derivative gives

$$g'''(x) = \frac{6(x+4)}{(x^2+4)^{\frac{5}{2}}} + \frac{6(x-5)}{(x^2 - 2x + 5)^{\frac{5}{2}}}$$

The critical numbers of $g''(x)$ are $x \approx \frac{1}{2}, -1.946503$, and 2.946503. Moreover, $g''(\frac{1}{2}) \approx 2.2568$, and $g''(-1.946503) = g''(2.946503) \approx 1.945045$. The intervals where it is increasing are $(-1.946503, \frac{1}{2})$ and $(2.946503, \infty)$, and the intervals where it is decreasing are $(-\infty, -1.946503)$ and $(\frac{1}{2}, 2.946503)$. Therefore, the local minimum is 1.945045, and the local maximum is 2.2568. Furthermore, we also find $\lim_{x \to \pm\infty} g''(x) = 2$. This shows that the global minimum of $g''(x)$ is positive, hence $g''(x) > 0$ on the entire $\mathbb{R}$. This implies that $g(x)$ is convex on $\mathbb{R}$. As $h(x)$ and $g(x)$ are convex on $\mathbb{R}$ according to Lemma 4(a), $\tau_{f_1,g_2}(\cdot)$ is convex on $\mathbb{R}$.

As shown in (23), $\tau_{f2,g1}(x) = \sqrt[5]{|x|^5 + |1-x|^5} - e^{(1-x)}x - e^x(1-x)$. As $\sqrt[5]{|x|^5 + |1-x|^5}$ and $-e^{(1-x)}x - e^x(1-x)$ are convex on $\mathbb{R}$ from previous discussions according to Lemma 4(a), $\tau_{f_2,g_1}(x)$ is convex on $\mathbb{R}$.

As given in (24), $\tau_{f_2,g_2}(x) = \sqrt[5]{|x|^5 + |1-x|^5} - (\frac{\sqrt{(1-x)^2+4}+(1-x)}{2})x - (\frac{\sqrt{x^2+4}+x}{2})(1-x)$. As $\sqrt[5]{|x|^5 + |1-x|^5}$ and $-(\frac{\sqrt{(1-x)^2+4}+(1-x)}{2})x - (\frac{\sqrt{x^2+4}+x}{2})(1-x)$ are convex on $\mathbb{R}$ from previous work according to Lemma 4(a), $\tau_{f_2,g_2}(x)$ is convex on $\mathbb{R}$.
(b) As shown in (26), $\tau_{f_3,g_1}(x) = \ln(e^{|x|} + e^{|1-x|} - 1) - e^{(1-x)}x - e^x(1-x)$. Let $h(x) := \ln(e^{|x|} + e^{|1-x|} - 1)$ and $g(x) := -e^{(1-x)}x - e^x(1-x)$. As $g(x)$ is convex on $\mathbb{R}$ based on the proof of the case for τ_{f_1,g_1}, the convexity of $h(x)$ is all that remains to determined. Note that $h(x)$ is not differentiable at $x = 0$ and $x = 1$, and we need to discuss three cases:
Cases (i): Suppose $0 < x < 1$. Taking the first derivative and second derivative of $h(x)$ give

$$h'(x) = \frac{\frac{xe^{|x|}}{|x|} - \frac{(1-x)e^{|1-x|}}{|1-x|}}{e^{|x|} + e^{|1-x|} - 1},$$

$$h''(x) = \frac{(e^{|x|} + e^{|1-x|})(e^{|x|} + e^{|1-x|} - 1) - (\frac{x}{|x|}e^{|x|} - \frac{(1-x)}{|1-x|}e^{|1-x|})^2}{(e^{|x|} + e^{|1-x|} - 1)^2}.$$

Since the denominator of $h''(x)$ is positive, we need to check whether the numerator is positive. The numerator is $(e^x + e^{1-x})^2 - (e^x + e^{1-x}) - (e^x - e^{1-x})^2 = 4e - (e^x + e^{1-x})$. For $0 < x < 1$, we have $1 < e^x < e$ and $1 < e^{(1-x)} < e$, which indicates that the numerator is positive. Therefore, we conclude $h''(x) > 0$, and hence $\tau_{f_3,g_1}(\cdot)$ is convex on the interval $(0, 1)$.
Cases (ii): Suppose $x > 1$, taking the second derivative of $h(x)$ gives

$$h''(x) = \frac{-\left(e^x + e^{(x-1)}\right)}{\left(e^x + e^{(x-1)} - 1\right)^2} + e^x(x+1) - e^{1-x}(x-2).$$

We want to show that $h''(x) > 0$ for $x > 1$. Taking the third derivative of $h(x)$ yields

$$h'''(x) = (\frac{(e^x + e^{x-1} + 1)(e^x + e^{x-1})}{(e^x + e^{x-1} - 1)^3}) + (e^{1-x}(x-3) + e^x(x+2)).$$

For the first term of $h'''(x)$, since $e^x + e^{x-1} > e + 1$, the denominator is positive, and hence the first term is positive. For the second term of $h'''(x)$, we have

$$e^{1-x}(x-3) + e^x(x+2) = e^{1-x}x + e^x x + 2e^x - 3e^{(1-x)} = e^{1-x}x + e^x x + 2ee^{x-1} - 3e^{(1-x)}.$$

As $2e > 3$ and $e^{x-1} > e^{1-x}$ when $x > 1$, it is also positive. Therefore, we obtain $h'''(x) > 0$. This shows that $h''(x)$ is increasing. Note also that $h''(1) = 1 + 2e - \frac{1+e}{e^2} > 0$. Then, it follows that $h''(x) > 0$. $\tau_{f_3,g_1}(x)$ is convex on the interval $(1, \infty)$.
Cases (iii): Suppose $x < 0$. As $\tau_{f_3,g_1}(x)$ is symmetric about the point $x = \frac{1}{2}$ according to case (ii), the function $\tau_{f_3,g_1}(\cdot)$ is convex on interval $(-\infty, 0)$.
As indicated in (27),

$$\tau_{f_3,g_2}(x) = \ln(e^{|x|} + e^{|1-x|} - 1) - \left(\frac{\sqrt{(1-x)^2+4} + (1-x)}{2}\right)x - \left(\frac{\sqrt{x^2+4} + x}{2}\right)(1-x).$$

Let $h(x) := \ln(e^{|x|} + e^{|1-x|} - 1)$ and $g(x) := -(\frac{\sqrt{(1-x)^2+4}+(1-x)}{2})x - (\frac{\sqrt{x^2+4}+x}{2})(1-x)$. $g(x)$ is convex on $\mathbb{R}$ according to the proof of the case for τ_{f_1,g_2} and $h(x)$ is convex on the intervals $(-\infty, 0)$, $(0, 1)$ and $(1, \infty)$ according to previous arguments. Therefore, τ_{f_3,g_2} is convex on the intervals $(-\infty, 0)$, $(0, 1)$, and $(1, \infty)$.

(c) As given in (22), $\tau_{f_1,g_3}(x) = \sqrt{x^2+(1-x)^2} - (\frac{4-e^{-(1-x)}}{1+2e^{-(1-x)}})x - (\frac{4-e^{-x}}{1+2e^{-x}})(1-x)$. Taking the second derivative of $\tau_{f_1,g_3}(x)$ gives

$$\begin{aligned}\left(\tau_{f_1,g_3}\right)''(x) &= \frac{1}{(2x^2-2x+1)^{\frac{3}{2}}} + \frac{9}{2}\left(-\frac{e(x-2)}{2e^x+e} - \frac{2e^3x}{(2e^x+e)^3}\right. \\ &\left.+\frac{e^2(3x-2)}{(2e^x+e)^2} + \frac{4e^x(x+1)-2e^{2x}(x-3)}{(e^x+2)^3}\right).\end{aligned}$$

The inflection points are $x \approx -1.986749, 2.986749, -12.999449$, and 13.99944. Then, the intervals where the curve is convex are $(-1.986749, 2.986749)$, $(-\infty, -12.999449)$ and $(13.999449, \infty)$.

As indicated in (25), we know

$$\tau_{f_2,g_3}(x) = \sqrt[5]{|x|^5+|1-x|^5} - \left(\frac{4-e^{-(1-x)}}{1+2e^{-(1-x)}}\right)x - \left(\frac{4-e^{-x}}{1+2e^{-x}}\right)(1-x).$$

Similarly, we use the second derivative to find the inflection points. The inflection points are $x \approx 3.005175, -2.005175, -11.286820$, and 12.286820. Therefore, the intervals where the curve is convex are $(-2.005175, 3.005175)$, $(12.286820, \infty)$, and $(-\infty, -11.286820)$.

As shown in (28), we know

$$\tau_{f_3,g_3}(x) = \ln(e^{|x|}+e^{|1-x|}-1) - \left(\frac{4-e^{-(1-x)}}{1+2e^{-(1-x)}}\right)x - \left(\frac{4-e^{-x}}{1+2e^{-x}}\right)(1-x).$$

Similarly, we use the second derivative to find the inflection points. The inflection points are $x \approx -1.904132$ and 2.904132. Because $\ln(e^{|x|}+e^{|1-x|}-1)$ is not differentiable at the points 0 and 1, we can only assure that the interval where the curve is convex is $(0,1)$. □

Recall that a function is called subdifferentiable at x if there exists at least one subgradient at x. Although $\tau_{f_3,g_1}(x)$ is not differentiable at the points 0 and 1, with the help of Proposition 11(b), we can still show that it is subdifferentiable thereat.

Proposition 12. (a) *The function $\tau_{f_3,g_1}(\cdot)$ is subdifferentiable at the points 0 and 1 and the subdifferential is described by*

$$\begin{aligned}\partial\tau_{f_3,g_1}(0) &= \left[\frac{(-1-e)}{e} - e, \frac{(1-e)}{e} - e\right], \\ \partial\tau_{f_3,g_1}(1) &= \left[\frac{(e-1)}{e} + e, \frac{(e+1)}{e} + e\right].\end{aligned}$$

Moreover, $\tau_{f_3,g_1}(\cdot)$ is convex on $\mathbb{R}$.

(b) *The function $\tau_{f_3,g_2}(\cdot)$ is subdifferentiable at the points 0 and 1 and the subdifferential is described by*

$$\begin{aligned}\partial\tau_{f_3,g_2}(0) &= \left[\frac{(-1-e)}{e} - \frac{\sqrt{5}}{2}, \frac{(1-e)}{e} - \frac{\sqrt{5}}{2}\right], \\ \partial\tau_{f_3,g_2}(1) &= \left[\frac{(e-1)}{e} + \frac{\sqrt{5}}{2}, \frac{(e+1)}{e} + \frac{\sqrt{5}}{2}\right].\end{aligned}$$

Moreover, $\tau_{f_3,g_2}(\cdot)$ is convex on $\mathbb{R}$.

Proof. (a) Taking the first derivative of $\tau_{f_3,g_1}(x)$ gives

$$\left(\tau_{f_3,g_1}\right)'(x) = \frac{\frac{xe^{|x|}}{|x|} - \frac{(1-x)e^{|1-x|}}{|1-x|}}{e^{|x|} + e^{|1-x|} - 1} + (e^{(1-x)}(x-1) + e^x x).$$

The right and left derivatives at the point 0 are $\left(\tau_{f_3,g_1}\right)'(0_+) = \frac{1-e}{e} - e$ and $\left(\tau_{f_3,g_1}\right)'(0_-) = \frac{-1-e}{e} - e$, respectively. Moreover, we have $\left(\tau_{f_3,g_1}\right)'(0_+) > \left(\tau_{f_3,g_1}\right)'(0_-)$. Based on the convexity of $\tau_{f_3,g_1}(x)$ on $(-\infty, 0)$ from Proposition 11(b), we have

$$\tau_{f_3,g_1}(\epsilon_- + h) - \tau_{f_3,g_1}(\epsilon_-) \geq \left(\tau_{f_3,g_1}\right)'(\epsilon_-)h$$

with small $\epsilon_- < 0$ and $h < 0$. Note here the $\tau_{f_3,g_1}(x)$ is a continuous function. Let $\epsilon_- \to 0$. Thus, we have $\tau_{f_3,g_1}(h) - \tau_{f_3,g_1}(0) \geq \left(\tau_{f_3,g_1}\right)'(0_-)h$ for $h < 0$. Similarly, according to the convexity of $\tau_{f_3,g_1}(x)$ on $(0,1)$ from Proposition 11(b), we can obtain that $\tau_{f_3,g_1}(h) - \tau_{f_3,g_1}(0) \geq \left(\tau_{f_3,g_1}\right)'(0_+)h$ where $0 < h < 1$. Therefore, we show that $\tau_{f_3,g_1}(x)$ is subdifferentiable at 0, and $\partial\tau_{f_3,g_1}(0) = \left[\frac{(-1-e)}{e} - e, \frac{(1-e)}{e} - e\right]$. Moreover based on Lemma 2.13 in [17], $\tau_{f_3,g_1}(x)$ is convex on the interval $(-\infty, 1)$, especially at the point 0. Likewise, $\partial\tau_{f_3,g_1}(1) = \left[\frac{e-1}{e} + e, \frac{e+1}{e} + e\right]$ and it is convex at the point 1. Hence, $\tau_{f_3,g_1}(x)$ is convex on entire $\mathbb{R}$.

(b) Taking the first derivative of $\tau_{f_3,g_2}(x)$ yields

$$\left(\tau_{f_3,g_2}\right)'(x) = \frac{\frac{xe^{|x|}}{|x|} - \frac{(1-x)e^{|1-x|}}{|1-x|}}{e^{|x|} + e^{|1-x|} - 1}$$
$$+\frac{1}{2}\left[(1-x)\left(\frac{-x}{\sqrt{x^2+4}} - 1\right) + \sqrt{x^2+4} - \frac{(x-1)x}{\sqrt{x(x-2)+5}} + 3x - \sqrt{x(x-2)+5} - 1\right].$$

The right derivative at the point 0 is $\left(\tau_{f_3,g_2}\right)'(0_+) = (\frac{1-e}{e}) - \frac{\sqrt{5}}{2}$ and the left derivative at the point 0 is $\left(\tau_{f_3,g_2}\right)'(0_-) = \frac{-1-e}{e} - \frac{\sqrt{5}}{2}$. Therefore, we obtain

$$\partial\tau_{f_3,g_2}(0) = \left[\frac{-1-e}{e} - \frac{\sqrt{5}}{2}, \frac{1-e}{e} - \frac{\sqrt{5}}{2}\right].$$

Similarly, $\partial\tau_{f_3,g_2}(1) = \left[\frac{e-1}{e} + \frac{\sqrt{5}}{2}, \frac{e+1}{e} + \frac{\sqrt{5}}{2}\right]$. □

5. The Local Minimum and Maximum of the Curves

After discussing the convexity and differentiability, we now work on finding the local minimum or maximum value of the curves. In addition, we shall investigate the convergent behavior of local minimum or maximum values when p becomes very large.

Proposition 13. *Let τ^p_{FB}, $\tau^p_{\mathrm{D-FB}}$ and σ^p_{FB} be defined as in (11), (13), and (12) respectively. Then, the following hold. See Figure 7.*

(a) *The function $\tau^p_{\mathrm{FB}}(x)$ has a local minimum at $x = \frac{1}{2}$ and its local minimum value converges to $-\frac{1}{2}$.*

(b) *When p is an odd integer, the function $\tau^p_{\mathrm{D-FB}}(x)$ has a local minimum at $x = \frac{1}{2}$ and its local minimum value converges to -1.*

(c) *The function $\sigma_{\mathrm{FB}}^{p}(x)$ has local minima at $x = 0$ and 1. Furthermore, it has a local maximum value at $x = \frac{1}{2}$ and its local maximum value converges to $\frac{1}{8}$.*

Proof. (a) From (11), we know that

$$\tau_{\mathrm{FB}}^{p}(x) = \sqrt[p]{|x|^p + |1-x|^p} - 1$$

where $p > 1$. The first derivative of this function is

$$(\tau_{\mathrm{FB}}^{p})'(x) = (|x|^p + |1-x|^p)^{\frac{1}{p}-1}[\mathrm{sgn}(x)|x|^{p-1} - |1-x|^{p-1}\mathrm{sgn}(1-x)].$$

Note that the first term is positive. We then investigate the second term:

$$\left[\mathrm{sgn}(x)|x|^{p-1} - |1-x|^{p-1}\mathrm{sgn}(1-x)\right].$$

Case (i): If $x > 1/2$, then $\mathrm{sgn}(x)|x|^{p-1} - |1-x|^{p-1}\mathrm{sgn}(1-x) > 0$.

Case (ii): If $x < 1/2$, then $\mathrm{sgn}(x)|x|^{p-1} - |1-x|^{p-1}\mathrm{sgn}(1-x) < 0$.

Case (iii): When $x = \frac{1}{2}$, we see that $a = \frac{1}{2}$ is the only root of $\left(\tau_{\mathrm{FB}}^{p}\right)'(x) = 0$. Moreover, $\tau_{\mathrm{FB}}^{p}(x)$ is convex on $\mathbb{R}$, which indicates $a = \frac{1}{2}$ is the only local minimizer and the value is $(\frac{1}{2})(2^{\frac{1}{p}}) - 1$. Furthermore, we observe that the local minimum value converges to $-\frac{1}{2}$ as $p \to \infty$.

(b) From (13), we know that

$$\tau_{\mathrm{D-FB}}^{p}(x) = (\sqrt{x^2 + (1-x)^2})^p - 1$$

where $p > 1$ and p is an odd integer. Taking the first derivative of this function yields

$$\left(\tau_{\mathrm{D-FB}}^{p}\right)'(x) = p(x^2 + (1-x)^2)^{\frac{p}{2}-1}(2x-1).$$

It can be verified that $a = \frac{1}{2}$ is the singular critical point. Note that $\tau_{\mathrm{D-FB}}^{p}(x)$ is convex on $\mathbb{R}$, hence $a = \frac{1}{2}$ is a local minimizer and the value is $\left(\sqrt{2(\frac{1}{2})^2}\right)^p - 1$. In addition, the local minimum value converges to -1 when $p \to \infty$.

(c) From (12), we know that

$$\sigma_{\mathrm{FB}}^{p}(x) = \frac{1}{2}|\tau_{\mathrm{FB}}^{p}(x)|^2$$

where $p > 1$. Taking the first derivative of this function gives

$$(\sigma_{\mathrm{FB}}^{p})'(x) = \tau_{\mathrm{FB}}^{p}(x)(\tau_{\mathrm{FB}}^{p})'(x).$$

We want to solve $\left(\sigma_{\mathrm{FB}}^{p}\right)'(x) = 0$, which implies $\tau_{\mathrm{FB}}^{p}(x) = 0$ or $\left(\tau_{\mathrm{FB}}^{p}\right)'(x) = 0$. If $\tau_{\mathrm{FB}}^{p}(x) = 0$, we have $x = 0$ and $x = 1$. If $\left(\tau_{\mathrm{FB}}^{p}\right)'(x) = 0$, we have $x = \frac{1}{2}$. Thus, the critical numbers are $x = 0, \frac{1}{2}, 1$. Note that 0 and 1 are the only two roots of $\tau_{\mathrm{FB}}^{p}(x) = 0$ and $\tau_{\mathrm{FB}}^{p}(x)$ is non-negative. Therefore, we see that $x = 0$ and $x = 1$ are local minimizers, and the values are both 0.

On the other hand, we know that $\iota_{\mathrm{FB}}^{p}(x)$ is decreasing (increasing) on the right (left) hand side of the point $a = \frac{1}{2}$. Hence, the point $a = \frac{1}{2}$ is a local maximizer, and the value is $\frac{1}{2}\left[(2(\frac{1}{2})^p)^{\frac{1}{p}} - 1\right]^2$. This further implies that when $p \to \infty$, the local maximum converges to $\frac{1}{8}$. □

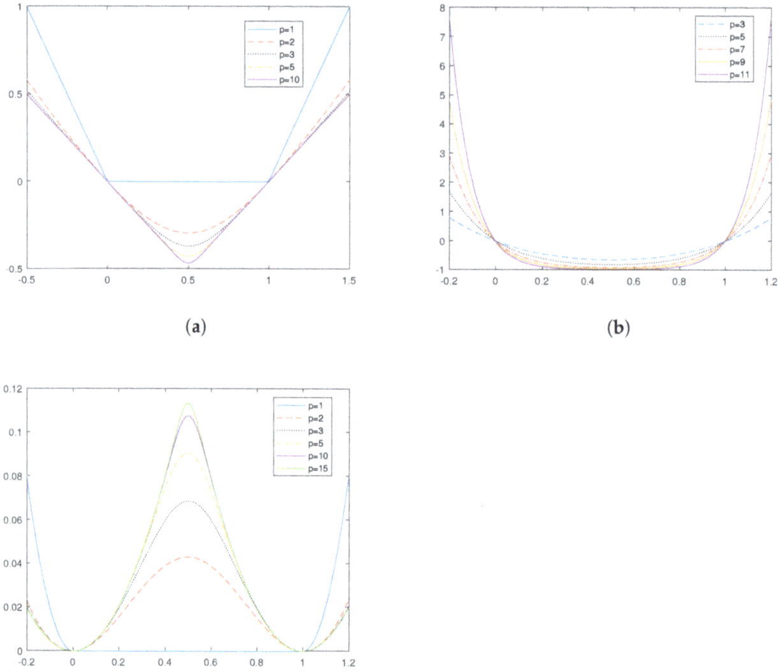

(a) (b) (c)

Figure 7. Graphs of $\tau^p_{\rm FB}(x)$, $\tau^p_{\rm D-FB}(x)$ and $\sigma^p_{\rm FB}(x)$ with different values of p. (**a**) Local minimum of $\tau^p_{\rm FB}(x)$; (**b**) Local minimum of $\tau^p_{\rm D-FB}(x)$; (**c**) Local minimum and maximum of $\sigma^p_{\rm FB}(x)$.

Proposition 14. *Let $\tau^p_{\rm NR}$ be defined as in (14) with odd integer p. Then, the function $\tau^p_{\rm NR}(\cdot)$ has a local maximum at $x = \frac{1}{2-2^{-\frac{1}{p-1}}}$. Furthermore, its minimum value converges to $\frac{1}{4}$. See Figure 8.*

Proof. From (14), we know that $\tau^p_{\rm NR}(x) = x^p - (2x-1)^p_+$ where $p > 1$ and p is an odd integer. Computing the first derivative of this function gives

$$(\tau^p_{\rm NR})'(x) = p\left(x^{(p-1)} - \left[\frac{(2x-1)+|2x-1|}{2}\right]^{(p-1)}\left(1+\frac{2x-1}{|2x-1|}\right)\right).$$

To proceed, we discuss two cases:

Cases (i): If $x < \frac{1}{2}$, then $\left(\tau^p_{\rm NR}\right)'(x) = px^{p-1} \geq 0$. Hence, $\tau^p_{\rm NR}(x)$ is increasing on $(-\infty, \frac{1}{2})$, which indicates that it does not have local minimum or maximum value.

Cases (ii): If $x > \frac{1}{2}$, then $\left(\tau^p_{\rm NR}\right)'(x) = p[x^{p-1} - 2(2x-1)^{p-1}]$. It is verified that $a = \frac{1}{2-2^{-\frac{1}{p-1}}}$ is the only root of $p[x^{p-1} - 2(2x-1)^{p-1}] = 0$ for $p > 1$. Moreover, we have that $\tau^p_{\rm NR}(x)$ is decreasing (increasing) on the right (left) hand side of the point a. Hence, a is a local maximizer and the local maximum value is $\left[\frac{1}{2-2^{-\frac{1}{p-1}}}\right]^p - \left[2(\frac{1}{2-2^{-\frac{1}{p-1}}}) - 1\right]^p$. Furthermore, the local maximum value $\left[\frac{1}{2-2^{-\frac{1}{p-1}}}\right]^p - \left[2(\frac{1}{2-2^{-\frac{1}{p-1}}}) - 1\right]^p$ converges to $\frac{1}{4}$ as $p \to \infty$. □

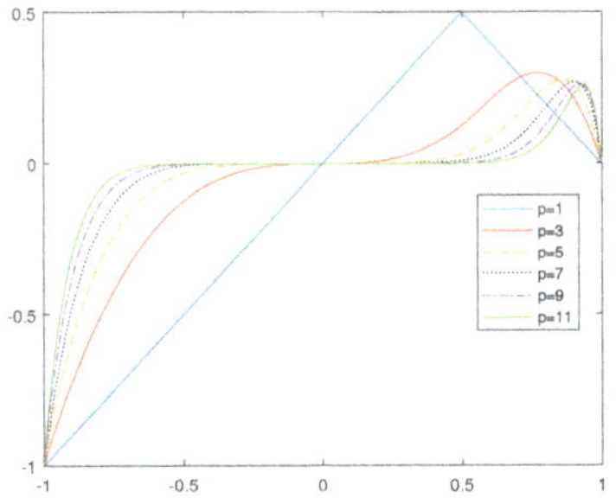

Figure 8. Local maximum of $\tau^p_{\text{NR}}(x)$ with different values of p.

Proposition 15. *Let $\tau^p_{\text{S-NR}}$ and $\sigma^p_{\text{S-NR}}$ be defined as in (15) and (16), respectively. Then, for the odd integer p, the following hold. See Figure 9.*

(a) *The function $\tau^p_{\text{S-NR}}(\cdot)$ has a local maximum at $x = 1 - \left(\frac{1}{2-2^{-\frac{1}{p-1}}}\right)$ and $\frac{1}{2-2^{-\frac{1}{p-1}}}$. Its local maximum value converges to $\frac{1}{4}$. Furthermore, it has a local minimum at $x = \frac{1}{2}$, which converges to 0.*

(b) *The function $\sigma^p_{\text{S-NR}}(\cdot)$ has a local maximum at $x = \frac{1}{2}$ and its maximum value converges to 0. In addition, it has a local minimum at $x = 0$ and $x = 1$.*

Proof. (a) From (15), we know that

$$\tau^p_{\text{S-NR}}(x) = \begin{cases} x^p - (2x-1)^p, & \text{if } x > \frac{1}{2}, \\ (\frac{1}{2})^p, & \text{if } x = \frac{1}{2}, \\ (1-x)^p - (1-2x)^p, & \text{if } x < \frac{1}{2}, \end{cases}$$

where p is an odd integer. As $\tau^p_{\text{S-NR}}(x)$ is symmetric at the point $x = \frac{1}{2}$, we consider the below two cases:

Cases (i): If $x > \frac{1}{2}$, according to Proposition 14, the local maximum point is $a = \frac{1}{2-2^{-\frac{1}{p-1}}}$ and the maximum value is $\left[\frac{1}{2-2^{-\frac{1}{p-1}}}\right]^p - [2(\frac{1}{2-2^{-\frac{1}{p-1}}}) - 1]^p$, which converges to $\frac{1}{4}$ as $p \to \infty$.

Cases (ii): If $x < \frac{1}{2}$, similar to Case (i), we obtain that $a = 1 - \left(\frac{1}{2-2^{-\frac{1}{p-1}}}\right)$ is a local maximum point and the maximum value is $\left(\frac{1}{2-2^{-\frac{1}{p-1}}}\right)^p - \left(-1 + \frac{2}{2-2^{-\frac{1}{p-1}}}\right)^p$, which converges to $\frac{1}{4}$ as $p \to \infty$.

Furthermore, because the function is increasing (decreasing) on the right (left) hand side of the point $a = \frac{1}{2}$, we can conclude $a = \frac{1}{2}$ is a local minimizer. Its the minimum value is $(\frac{1}{2})^p$, which converges to 0 when $p \to \infty$.

(b) From (16), we know that

$$\sigma^p_{\text{S-NR}}(x) = \begin{cases} x^p(1-x)^p - (2x-1)^p(1-x)^p, & \text{if } x > \frac{1}{2}, \\ (\frac{1}{2})^{2p}, & \text{if } x = \frac{1}{2}, \\ x^p(1-x)^p - x^p(1-2x)^p, & \text{if } x < \frac{1}{2}, \end{cases}$$

where p is an odd integer. Since $\sigma^p_{\text{S-NR}}(x)$ is symmetric at the point $x = \frac{1}{2}$, we divide it into two cases:

Case (i): Suppose $x \geq \frac{2}{3}$, the first derivative is

$$\left(\sigma^p_{\mathrm{S-NR}}\right)'(x) = -p(1-x)^{p-1}[x^p - (2x-1)^p] + (1-x)^p\left[p(x^{p-1} - 2(2x-1)^{p-1})\right].$$

Based on this, it is verified that $a = 1$ is a critical point. Because $\sigma^p_{\mathrm{S-NR}}(x)$ is non-negative and $\sigma^p_{\mathrm{S-NR}}(1) = 0$, we can conclude that 1 is a local minimum point and the value is 0.

Case (ii): Suppose $x \leq \frac{1}{3}$. Based on symmetry, the local minimum point is $a = 0$ and the value is 0.

Case (iii): Suppose $\frac{1}{3} < x < \frac{2}{3}$, we know that $\left(\sigma^p_{\mathrm{S-NR}}\right)'(\frac{1}{2}) = 0$ and $\sigma^p_{\mathrm{S-NR}}(x)$ is decreasing (increasing) on the right (left) side of the point $a = \frac{1}{2}$. Hence, we obtain that $a = \frac{1}{2}$ is a local maximizer and the maximum value is $(\frac{1}{2})^{2p}$ for $p \geq 3$. It clearly converges to 0 when $p \to \infty$. □

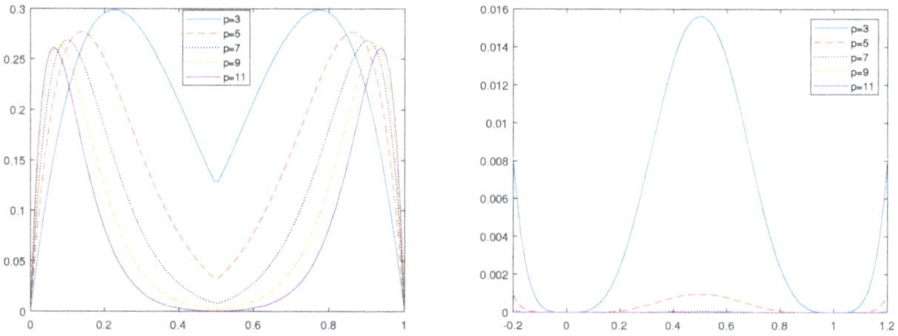

(a) (b)

Figure 9. Graphs of $\tau^p_{\mathrm{S-NR}}(x)$ and $\sigma^p_{\mathrm{S-NR}}(x)$ with different values of p. (**a**) Local minimum and maximum of $\tau^p_{\mathrm{S-NR}}(x)$; (**b**) Local minimum and maximum of $\sigma^p_{\mathrm{S-NR}}(x)$.

Due to the fact that $\widetilde{\tau}^p_{\mathrm{NR}}$, $\widetilde{\tau}^p_{\mathrm{S-NR}}$, and $\widetilde{\sigma}^p_{\mathrm{S-NR}}$ are continuous counterparts of τ^p_{NR}, $\tau^p_{\mathrm{S-NR}}$ and $\sigma^p_{\mathrm{S-NR}}$, analogous to Propositions 14 and 15, their local maximums and minimums can be obtained. We omit the proof here.

Proposition 16. *Let $\widetilde{\tau}^p_{\mathrm{NR}}(x)$, $\widetilde{\tau}^p_{\mathrm{S-NR}}$ and $\widetilde{\sigma}^p_{\mathrm{S-NR}}$ be defined as in (17), (18), and (19), respectively. Then, for $p > 1$, the following hold. See Figure 10.*

(a) *The function $\tau^p_{\mathrm{NR}}(\cdot)$ has a local maximum at $x = \frac{1}{2-2^{-\frac{1}{p-1}}}$. Furthermore its minimum value converges to $\frac{1}{4}$.*

(b) *The function $\widetilde{\tau}^p_{\mathrm{S-NR}}(\cdot)$ has a local maximum at $x = 1 - \left(\frac{1}{2-2^{-\frac{1}{p-1}}}\right)$ and $\frac{1}{2-2^{-\frac{1}{p-1}}}$ and its local maximum value converges to $\frac{1}{4}$. Furthermore, it has a local minimum at $x = \frac{1}{2}$ and converges to 0.*

(c) *The function $\widetilde{\sigma}^p_{\mathrm{S-NR}}(\cdot)$ has a local maximum at $x = \frac{1}{2}$ and its local maximum value converges to 0. In addition, it has a local minimum at $x = 0$ and $x = 1$.*

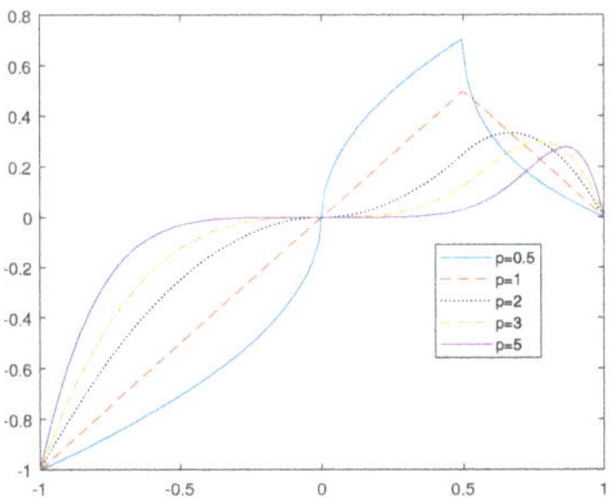

(**a**)

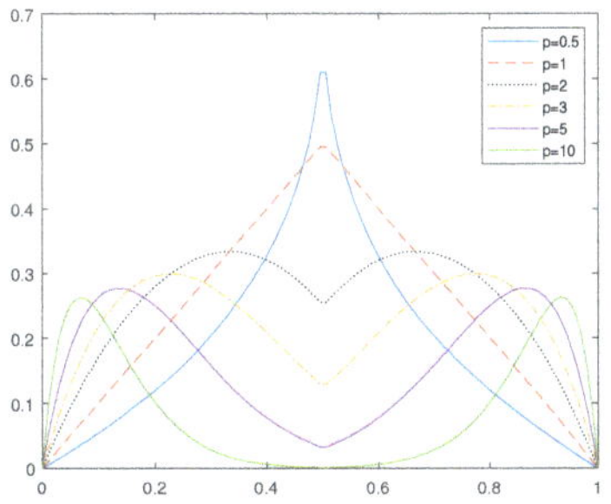

(**b**)

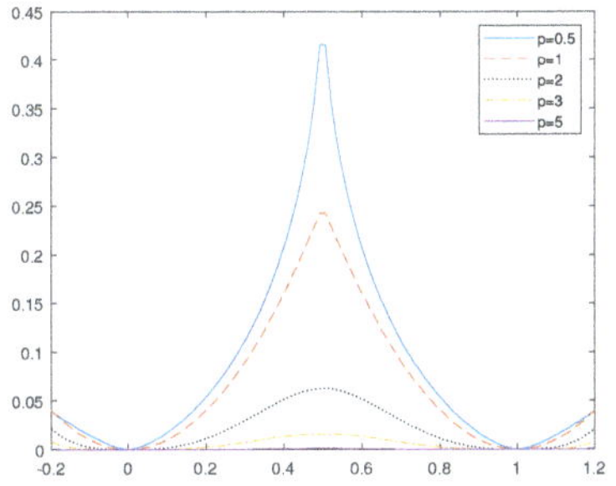

(**c**)

Figure 10. Graphs of $\widetilde{\tau}^{p}_{\mathrm{NR}}(x)$, $\widetilde{\tau}^{p}_{\mathrm{S-NR}}(x)$ and $\widetilde{\sigma}^{p}_{\mathrm{S-NR}}(x)$ with different values of p. (**a**) Local maximum of $\widetilde{\tau}^{p}_{\mathrm{NR}}(x)$; (**b**) Local minimum and maximum of $\widetilde{\tau}^{p}_{\mathrm{S-NR}}(x)$; (**c**) Local minimum and maximum of $\widetilde{\sigma}^{p}_{\mathrm{S-NR}}(x)$.

The local minimum for other $\tau_{f_i,g_i}(\cdot)$ is simple.

Proposition 17. *Let τ_{f_i,g_i} with $i = 1,2,3$ be defined as in (20)–(28). Then, the function $\tau_{f_i,g_i}(\cdot)$ has a local minimum at $x = \frac{1}{2}$. See Figure 11.*

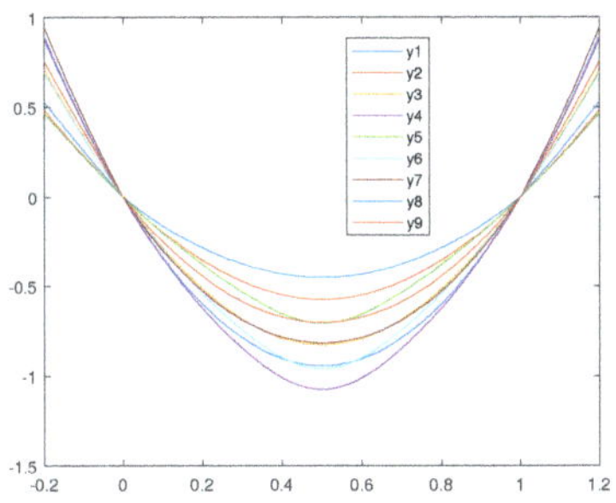

Figure 11. Local minimum of $\tau_{f_i,g_i}(x)$ for $i, j = 1,2,3$.

Proof. Because each $\tau_{f_i,g_i}(x)$ is nearly convex according to $x = \frac{1}{2}$ and $\tau_{f_i,g_i}(x)$ has a critical number at $x = \frac{1}{2}$, the local minimum at $x = \frac{1}{2}$ is confirmed and can be calculated easily. We only present the values here.

$$
\begin{aligned}
\tau_{f_1,g_1}\left(\frac{1}{2}\right) &= \frac{1}{\sqrt{2}} - \sqrt{e} \\
\tau_{f_1,g_2}\left(\frac{1}{2}\right) &= -\frac{1}{4} + \frac{1}{\sqrt{2}} - \frac{\sqrt{17}}{4} \\
\tau_{f_1,g_3}\left(\frac{1}{2}\right) &= \frac{1}{\sqrt{2}} + \frac{1-4\sqrt{e}}{2+\sqrt{e}} \\
\tau_{f_2,g_1}\left(\frac{1}{2}\right) &= \frac{1}{2^{\frac{4}{5}}} - \sqrt{e} \\
\tau_{f_2,g_2}\left(\frac{1}{2}\right) &= -\frac{1}{4} + \frac{1}{2^{\frac{4}{5}}} - \frac{\sqrt{17}}{4} \\
\tau_{f_2,g_3}\left(\frac{1}{2}\right) &= \frac{1}{2^{\frac{4}{5}}} + \frac{1-4\sqrt{e}}{2+\sqrt{e}} \\
\tau_{f_3,g_1}\left(\frac{1}{2}\right) &= \ln(2\sqrt{e}-1) - \sqrt{e} \\
\tau_{f_3,g_2}\left(\frac{1}{2}\right) &= \ln(2\sqrt{e}-1) - \frac{1}{4} - \frac{\sqrt{17}}{4} \\
\tau_{f_3,g_3}\left(\frac{1}{2}\right) &= \ln(2\sqrt{e}-1) + \frac{1-4\sqrt{e}}{2+\sqrt{e}}
\end{aligned}
$$

This completes the proof. □

6. Summary

To summarize, when comparing all the curves based on NCP functions, almost all of them are neither convex nor concave. Only the curve based on the Fischer–Burmeister function is convex due the fact that its corresponding NCP function is also convex. Nonetheless, we observe that some curves are convex whereas their corresponding NCP functions are not. For instance, the curve based on the discrete type of the Fischer–Burmeister function. This indicates that the convexity of the curves depends on the choice of vertical plane. In addition, when p is perturbed, the interval of convexity will be shrunk or stretched. For the local minimum or maximum, when p becomes very large, most of the minima and maxima converge. and the minima or maxima vary by the perturbation of p.

Author Contributions: Supervision, Y.-L.C. and J.-S.C.; writing—original draft, S.-W.L.; writing—review and editing, Y.-L.C. All authors have read and agreed to the published version of the manuscript.

Funding: National Taiwan Normal University and National Science and Technology Council, Taiwan.

Institutional Review Board Statement: Not applicable.

Informed Consent Statement: Not applicable.

Data Availability Statement: Not applicable.

Conflicts of Interest: The authors declare no conflict of interest.

References

1. Alcantara, J.H.; Chen, J.-S. A novel generalization of the natural residual function and a neural network approach for the NCP. *Neurocomputing* **2020**, *413*, 368–382. [CrossRef]
2. Chang, Y.-L.; Chen, J.-S.; Yang, C.-Y. Symmetrization of generalized natural residual function for NCP. *Oper. Res. Lett.* **2015**, *43*, 354–358. [CrossRef]
3. Chen, J.-S. On some NCP-functions based on the generalized Fischer-Burmeister function. *Asia-Pac. J. Oper. Res.* **2007**, *24*, 401–420. [CrossRef]
4. Chen, J.-S.; Ko, C.-H.; Wu, X.-R. What is the generalization of natural residual function for NCP. *Pac. J. Optim.* **2016**, *12*, 19–27.

5. Galantai, A. Properties and construction of NCP functions. *Comput. Optim. Appl.* **2012**, *52*, 805–824. [CrossRef]
6. Lee, C.-H.; Hu, C.-C.; Chen, J.-S. Using invertible functions to construct NCP functions. *Linear Nonlinear Anal.* **2020**, *6*, 347–369.
7. Ma, P.-F.; Chen, J.-S.; Huang, C.-H.; Ko, C.-H. Discovery of new complementarity functions for NCP and SOCCP. *Comput. Appl. Math.* **2018**, *37*, 5727–5749. [CrossRef]
8. Fischer, A. Solution of the monotone complementarity problem with locally Lipschitzian functions. *Math. Program.* **1997**, *76*, 513–532. [CrossRef]
9. Fischer, A. A special Newton-type optimization methods. *Optimization* **1992**, 24, 269–284. [CrossRef]
10. Tseng, P. Global behaviour of a class of merit functions for the nonlinear complementarity problem. *J. Optim. Theory Appl.* **1996**, *89*, 17–37. [CrossRef]
11. Huang, C.-H.; Weng, K.-J.; Chen, J.-S.; Chu, H.-W.; Li, M.-L. On four discrete-type families of NCP-functions. *J. Nonlinear Convex Anal.* **2019**, *20*, 283–306.
12. Alcantara, J.H.; Lee, C.-H.; Nguyen, C.T.; Chang, Y.-L.; Chen, J.-S. On construction of new NCP functions. *Oper. Res. Lett.* **2020**, *48*, 115–121. [CrossRef]
13. Tsai, H.-Y.; Chen, J.-S. Geometric views of the generalized Fischer-Burmeister function and its induced merit function. *Appl. Math. Comput.* **2014**, *237*, 31–59. [CrossRef]
14. Chen, J.-S.; Li, J.-F.; Wu, J. A continuation approach for solving binary quadratic program based on a class of NCP-functions. *Appl. Math. Comput.* **2012**, *219*, 3975–3992. [CrossRef]
15. Huang, C.-H.; Chen, J.-S.; Martinez-Legaz, J.E. Differentiability v.s. convexity for complementarity functions. *Optim. Lett.* **2017**, *11*, 209–216. [CrossRef]
16. Tuy, H. *Convex Analysis and Global Optimization*, 2nd ed.; Springer: Hanoi, Vietnam, 2016.
17. Polyak, R.A. *Introduction to Continuous Optimization*; Springer: Cham, Switzerland, 2021; Springer Optimization and Its Applications, Volume 172.

axioms

MDPI

Article

Fixed Point Theory for Multi-Valued Feng–Liu–Subrahmanyan Contractions

Claudia Luminiţa Mihiţ [1,*,†], Ghiocel Moţ [1,†] and Adrian Petruşel [2,3,†]

1 Department of Mathematics and Computer Science, "Aurel Vlaicu" University of Arad, Elena Drăgoi Street No. 2, 310330 Arad, Romania
2 Department of Mathematics, Babeş-Bolyai University Cluj-Napoca, Mihail Kogălniceanu Street No. 1, 400084 Cluj-Napoca, Romania
3 Academy of Romanian Scientists, Independenţei No. 54, 050094 Bucharest, Romania
* Correspondence: claudia.mihit@uav.ro
† These authors contributed equally to this work.

Abstract: In this paper, we consider several problems related to the so-called multi-valued Feng–Liu–Subrahmanyan contractions in complete metric spaces. Existence of the fixed points and of the strict fixed points, as well as data dependence and stability properties for the fixed point problem, are discussed. Some results are presented, under appropriate conditions, and some open questions are pointed out. Our results extend recent results given for multi-valued graph contractions and multi-valued Subrahmanyan contractions.

Keywords: complete metric space; fixed point; data dependence; Ulam–Hyers stability; Ostrowski stability

MSC: 47H10; 54H25

Citation: Mihiţ, C.L.; Moţ, G.; Petruşel, A. Fixed Point Theory for Multi-Valued Feng–Liu–Subrahmanyan Contractions. *Axioms* **2022**, *11*, 563. https://doi.org/10.3390/axioms11100563

Academic Editor: Chris Goodrich

Received: 27 July 2022
Accepted: 8 October 2022
Published: 17 October 2022

Publisher's Note: MDPI stays neutral with regard to jurisdictional claims in published maps and institutional affiliations.

Copyright: © 2022 by the authors. Licensee MDPI, Basel, Switzerland. This article is an open access article distributed under the terms and conditions of the Creative Commons Attribution (CC BY) license (https://creativecommons.org/licenses/by/4.0/).

1. Introduction and Preliminaries

Let (M,d) be a metric space. We denote by $P(M)$ the set of all nonempty subsets of M, by $P_{cl}(M)$ the set of all nonempty closed subsets of M, and by $P_{cl,b}(M)$ the set of all nonempty closed and bounded subsets of M.

The following notations are used throughout this paper:
(1) The distance between a point $m \in M$ and a set $A \in P(M)$:

$$D(m,A) := \inf\{d(m,a) \mid a \in A\}.$$

(2) The excess of A over B, where $A, B \in P(M)$:

$$e(A,B) := \sup\{D(a,B) \mid a \in A\}.$$

(3) The Hausdorff–Pompeiu distance between the sets $A, B \in P(M)$:

$$H(A,B) = \max\{e(A,B), e(B,A)\}.$$

Notice that H is a generalized metric (in the sense that it takes values in $\mathbb{R} \cup \{+\infty\}$) on $P_{cl}(M)$ and it is a metric on $P_{cl,b}(M)$.

Let (M,d) be a metric space and $S : M \to P(M)$ be a multi-valued operator with nonempty values. A fixed point of S is an element $m^* \in M$ such that $m^* \in S(m^*)$. A strict fixed point of S is an element $m^* \in M$ such that $S(m^*) = \{m^*\}$. We denote by $Fix(S)$ the fixed point set of S and by $SFix(S)$ the set of all strict fixed points of S. By $Graph(S) := \{(u,v) \mid v \in S(u)\}$, we denote the graph of S.

A multi-valued operator $S : M \to P(M)$ is said to be a multi-valued K-contraction if $K \in [0,1[$ and the following relation holds:

$$H(S(u), S(v)) \leq Kd(u,v), \text{ for all } (u,v) \in M \times M.$$

The main fixed point result for multi-valued contractions was given by Nadler in 1969; see [1]. The result was slightly improved in 1970 by Covitz and Nadler (see [2]), and it is known as the multi-valued contraction principle. It says that any multi-valued contraction on a complete metric space has at least one fixed point.

In the same context, S is called a multi-valued graph contraction with constant K if

$$H(S(u), S(v)) \leq Kd(u,v), \text{ for all } (u,v) \in Graph(S).$$

For the main fixed point result concerning multi-valued graph contractions, see [3].

Fixed point theorems for multi-valued (graph) contractions are important tools in various applications, from integral and differential inclusions to optimization and fractal theory. Moreover, strict fixed point theorems are important in the theory of generalized games (abstract economies), as well as in the study of the convergence, to the fixed point, of various iterative schemes (see [4–7]).

For fixed point results for multi-valued contractions and multi-valued graph contractions, see [3,8–10] and the references therein.

The following concept was introduced by Feng and Liu in [11].

Definition 1. *Let (M,d) be a metric space, $S : M \to P(M)$ be a multi-valued operator, $b \in]0,1[$, and $u \in M$. Consider the set*

$$I_b^u := \{v \in S(u) : bd(u,v) \leq D(u, S(u))\}.$$

Then, S is called a multi-valued K-contraction of Feng–Liu type if $K \in]0,1[$ such that for each $u \in M$ there is $v \in I_b^u$ with the property:

$$D(v, S(v)) \leq Kd(u,v).$$

It is easy to see that any multi-valued K-contraction is a multi-valued K-contraction of Feng–Liu type, but not reversely (for examples, see Remark 1 in the paper [11]). For fixed-point-results-related Feng–Liu operators, see [11–17].

The following definition was introduced in [18]. Some fixed point results for this class of multi-valued operators are given in the same paper. For the single-valued case, see [19,20].

Definition 2. *Let (M,d) be a metric space and $S : M \to P(M)$ be a multi-valued operator with nonempty values. Then, S is said to be a multi-valued Subrahmanyan contraction if there exists a function $\psi : M \to [0,1[$ such that*

(i) $H(S(u), S(v)) \leq \psi(u)d(u,v)$, for all $(u,v) \in Graph(S)$;

(ii) $\psi(v) \leq \psi(u)$, for every $(u,v) \in Graph(S)$.

In this paper, we introduce a new class of multi-valued contraction type operators by combining the above two conditions: the multi-valued contraction condition of Feng–Liu type and the multi-valued Subrahmanyan contraction. As a consequence, we present existence and stability results for the fixed point inclusion $m \in S(m), m \in M$, where (M,d) is a complete metric space and $S : M \to P(M)$ is a multi-valued Feng–Liu–Subrahmanyan contraction. The strict fixed point problem is also considered and some open questions are pointed out. Our results extend recent results given for multi-valued graph contractions and multi-valued Subrahmanyan contractions.

2. Main Results

Let (M,d) be a metric space and $S : M \to P(M)$ be a multi-valued operator. For each $(m_0, m_1) \in Graph(S)$, the sequence $\{m_n\}_{n\in\mathbb{N}}$ with the property $m_{n+1} \in S(m_n)$, $n \in \mathbb{N}$ is called the sequence of successive approximations for S starting from (m_0, m_1). We recall now the notion of multi-valued weakly Picard operator.

Definition 3 ([21]). *Let (M,d) be a metric space. Then, $S : M \to P(M)$ is called a multivalued weakly Picard operator if for each $u \in M$ and each $v \in S(u)$ there exists a sequence $\{m_n\}_{n\in\mathbb{N}}$ in M such that*

(i) $m_0 = u$, $m_1 = v$;
(ii) $m_{n+1} \in S(m_n)$, *for all* $n \in \mathbb{N}$;
(iii) $\{m_n\}_{n\in\mathbb{N}}$ *is convergent in* (M,d) *and its limit* $m^*(u,v)$ *is a fixed point of* S.

Let us recall the following important notions.

Definition 4. *Let (M,d) be a metric space and $S : M \to P(M)$ be a multi-valued weakly Picard operator. Let us consider the multi-valued operator $S^\infty : Graph(S) \to P(Fix(S))$ defined by $S^\infty(u,v) := \{m^* \in Fix(S) \mid$ there is a sequence of successive approximations of S starting from (u,v) convergent to $m^*\}$. Then, S satisfies the local retraction–displacement condition if there exists a selection s^∞ of S^∞ such that*

$$d(u, s^\infty(u,v)) \le C(u,v)d(u,v), \text{ for all } (u,v) \in Graph(S),$$

for some $C(u,v) > 0$.

When C is independent of u and v, then we say that S satisfies the retraction–displacement condition.

A similar concept is given now in our next definition.

Definition 5. *Let (M,d) be a metric space and let $S : M \to P(M)$ be a multi-valued operator such that $Fix(S) \neq \emptyset$. Then, we say that S satisfies the local strong retraction–displacement condition if there exists a set retraction $r : M \to Fix(S)$ such that*

$$d(m, r(m)) \le C(m)D(m, S(m)), \text{ for all } m \in M, \tag{1}$$

for some $C(m) > 0$.

For related notions, examples, and results, see [1,18,21–24].

We now define the central concept of this paper, i.e., a multi-valued Feng–Liu–Subrahmanyan contraction on a metric space.

Definition 6. *Let (M,d) be a metric space, $S : M \to P(M)$ be a multi-valued operator, $b \in]0,1[$, and $m \in M$. Consider the set*

$$I_b^u := \{v \in S(u) \mid bd(u,v) \le D(u, S(u))\}.$$

Then, by definition, S is a multi-valued Feng–Liu–Subrahmanyan contraction if there exists $\psi : M \to [0,b[$ such that for each $u \in M$ there is $v \in I_b^u$ with

(i) $D(v, S(v)) \le \psi(u)d(u,v)$, *for all* $(u,v) \in Graph(S)$;
(ii) $\psi(v) \le \psi(u)$, *for every* $(u,v) \in Graph(S)$.

It is obvious that any multi-valued Subrahmanyan contraction is a multi-valued Feng–Liu–Subrahmanyan contraction, but the reverse implication, in general, does not hold.

Our first main result is a fixed point theorem for a multi-valued Feng–Liu–Subrahmanyan contractions with closed graph.

Theorem 1. *Let (M, d) be a complete metric space, and consider a multi-valued Feng–Liu–Subrahmanyan contraction $S : M \to P(M)$ with closed graph. Then, the following conclusions hold:*

(a) $Fix(S) \neq \emptyset$;

(b) For every $u \in M$ there exists a sequence $\{m_n\}_{n\in\mathbb{N}}$ of successive approximations for S starting at $m_0 = u$ which converges to a fixed point $m^*(u)$ of S, and the following apriori estimation holds:

$$d(m_n, m^*(u)) \leq \left(\frac{\psi(u)}{b}\right)^n \frac{1}{b - \psi(u)} D(u, S(u)), \text{ for every } n \in \mathbb{N}.$$

(c) The following local strong retraction–displacement type condition holds:

$$d(u, m^*(u)) \leq \frac{1}{b - \psi(u)} D(u, S(u)), \text{ for all } u \in M.$$

Proof. Let $m_0 = u \in M$ be arbitrary and $b \in]0, 1[$. Then, since $S(u) \in P_{cl}(M)$, the set I_b^u is nonempty, for each $u \in M$. By Definition 6, there exist $\psi : M \to [0, b[$ and $m_1 \in I_b^u$ (i.e., $bd(u, m_1) \leq D(u, S(u))$) such that

(i) $D(m_1, S(m_1)) \leq \psi(m_0)d(m_0, m_1)$;

(ii) $\psi(m_1) \leq \psi(m_0)$.

In a similar way, there exists $m_2 \in I_b^{m_1}$ (i.e., $bd(m_1, m_2) \leq D(m_1, S(m_1))$) such that

(i) $D(m_2, S(m_2)) \leq \psi(m_1)d(m_1, m_2)$;

(ii) $\psi(m_2) \leq \psi(m_1)$.

Hence, we have

$$d(m_1, m_2) \leq \frac{1}{b} D(m_1, S(m_1)) \leq \frac{\psi(m_0)}{b} d(m_0, m_1)$$

and

$$D(m_2, S(m_2)) \leq \psi(m_1)d(m_1, m_2) \leq \frac{\psi(m_1)}{b} D(m_1, S(m_1)) \leq$$

$$\frac{\psi(m_1)}{b}\psi(m_0)d(m_0, m_1) \leq \frac{\psi(m_1)\psi(m_0)}{b^2} D(u, S(u)) \leq \left(\frac{\psi(u)}{b}\right)^2 D(u, S(u)).$$

In the next step, there exists $m_3 \in I_b^{m_2}$ (i.e., $bd(m_2, m_3) \leq D(m_2, S(m_2))$) such that

(i) $D(m_3, S(m_3)) \leq \psi(m_2)d(m_2, m_3)$;

(ii) $\psi(m_3) \leq \psi(m_2)$.

Hence, in this case, we have

$$d(m_2, m_3) \leq \frac{1}{b} D(m_2, S(m_2)) \leq \frac{\psi(m_1)}{b} d(m_1, m_2) \leq$$

$$\frac{\psi(m_1)}{b}\frac{\psi(m_0)}{b} d(m_0, m_1) \leq \left(\frac{\psi(m_0)}{b}\right)^2 d(m_0, m_1)$$

and

$$D(m_3, S(m_3)) \leq \psi(m_2)d(m_2, m_3) \leq \frac{\psi(m_2)}{b} D(m_2, S(m_2)) \leq$$

$$\frac{\psi(m_2)}{b}\frac{\psi(m_1)}{b} D(m_1, S(m_1)) \leq \left(\frac{\psi(m_1)}{b}\right)^2 D(m_1, S(m_1)) \leq \left(\frac{\psi(m_0)}{b}\right)^3 D(u, S(u)).$$

Inductively, there exists a sequence $\{m_n\}_{n\in\mathbb{N}}$ such that

(i) $D(m_{n+1}, S(m_{n+1})) \leq \psi(m_n)d(m_n, m_{n+1})$;

(ii) $\psi(m_{n+1}) \leq \psi(m_n)$;

(iii) $m_{n+1} \in I_b^{m_n}$, for $n \in \mathbb{N}$, i.e., $bd(m_n, m_{n+1}) \leq D(m_n, S(m_n))$.

Hence, we have

$$d(m_n, m_{n+1}) \leq \frac{1}{b} D(m_n, S(m_n)) \leq \frac{\psi(m_{n-1})}{b} d(m_{n-1}, m_n) \leq \cdots \leq \left(\frac{\psi(m_0)}{b}\right)^n d(m_0, m_1)$$

and

$$D(m_{n+1},S(m_{n+1}))\leq\psi(m_n)d(m_n,m_{n+1})\leq\frac{\psi(m_n)}{b}D(m_n,S(m_n))\leq\cdots\leq$$

$$\left(\frac{\psi(m_1)}{b}\right)^n D(m_1,S(m_1))\leq\left(\frac{\psi(m_0)}{b}\right)^{n+1}D(u,S(u)).$$

In order to show that the sequence $\{m_n\}_{n\in\mathbb{N}}$ is Cauchy, we can estimate

$$d(m_n,m_{n+p})\leq d(m_n,m_{n+1})+\cdots+d(m_{n+p-1},m_{n+p})\leq$$

$$\left(\frac{\psi(m_0)}{b}\right)^n d(m_0,m_1)+\cdots+\left(\frac{\psi(m_0)}{b}\right)^{n+p-1}d(m_0,m_1)=$$

$$\left(\frac{\psi(m_0)}{b}\right)^n\left[1+\frac{\psi(m_0)}{b}+\cdots+\left(\frac{\psi(m_0)}{b}\right)^{p-1}\right]d(m_0,m_1)\leq$$

$$\left(\frac{\psi(m_0)}{b}\right)^n\frac{b}{b-\psi(m_0)}d(m_0,m_1)\to 0 \; as \; n,p\to\infty.$$

We also observe that

$$d(m_n,m_{n+p})\leq\left(\frac{\psi(m_0)}{b}\right)^n\frac{b}{b-\psi(m_0)}d(m_0,m_1),\text{ for each } n,p\in\mathbb{N}^*. \tag{2}$$

It follows that $\{m_n\}_{n\in\mathbb{N}}$ is Cauchy sequence in (M,d) and, thus, there exists $m^*(u)\in M$ such that $\{m_n\}_{n\in\mathbb{N}}$ is convergent to $m^*(u)\in M$. From the condition that S has a closed graph, we deduce that $m^*(u)$ is a fixed point for S.

In addition, for $p\to+\infty$ in (2), we have

$$\begin{aligned} d(m_n,m^*(u)) &\leq \left(\frac{\psi(u)}{b}\right)^n\frac{b}{b-\psi(u)}d(u,m_1)\leq \\ & \left(\frac{\psi(u)}{b}\right)^n\frac{1}{b-\psi(u)}D(u,S(u)),\text{ for every } n\in\mathbb{N}. \end{aligned} \tag{3}$$

Taking $n=0$ in (3), it follows that $d(u,m^*(u))\leq\frac{1}{b-\psi(u)}D(u,S(u))$, for all $u\in M$. □

Example 1. *Let $S:M:=\mathbb{R}\times\mathbb{R}\to\mathbb{R}\times\mathbb{R}$ given by*

$$S(u,v)=\begin{cases}\{(u,\frac{v+|u|+v|v-|u||}{2+|v-|u||})\},\ (u,v)\in M, v=|u|\\ \{(0,1),(0,-1)\},(u,v)\in M, v\neq|u|.\end{cases} \tag{4}$$

Then, S is a multi-valued Feng–Liu–Subrahmanyan contraction with $\psi(u,v):=\frac{(v-|u|)^2+3|v-|u||+2}{(v-|u|)^2+3|v-|u||+4}$. Notice that $Fix(S)=\{(u,v)\in M: v=|u|\}$ and S is not a multi-valued Feng–Liu operator since $\sup_{(u,v)\in M}\psi(u,v)=1$.

We recall now some stability concepts for the fixed point inclusion $m\in S(m)$.

Definition 7. *Let (M,d) be a metric space and $S:M\to P(M)$ be a multi-valued operator. We say that the fixed point inclusion*

$$m\in S(m),\ m\in M \tag{5}$$

is local Ulam–Hyers stable if for any $\varepsilon > 0$ and any ε-solution u of the fixed point inclusion (5) (i.e., $u \in M$ with the property $D(u, S(u)) \leq \varepsilon$), there exist $C = C(u) > 0$ and $m^* = m^*(u) \in Fix(S)$ with

$$d(u, m^*) \leq C\varepsilon.$$

If C does not depend on u, then we say that the fixed point inclusion is Ulam–Hyers stable (see [25] for related results).

A local data dependence property is given in our next definition.

Definition 8. *Let (M, d) be a metric space and $S : M \to P(M)$ be a multi-valued operator. By definition, the fixed point inclusion*

$$m \in S(m), m \in M$$

has the local data dependence property if, for any multi-valued operator, $T : M \to P(M)$, satisfying:
(i) $Fix(T) \neq \emptyset$;
(ii) There exists $\eta > 0$ such that $H(S(m), T(m)) \leq \eta$, for all $m \in M$, the following implication holds: for each $u \in Fix(T)$ there exist $C = C(u) > 0$ and $m^* = m^*(u) \in Fix(S)$ such that $d(u, m^*) \leq C(u)\eta$.

The well-posedness of the fixed point inclusion $m \in S(m)$ is defined as follows (see [26,27]):

Definition 9. *Let (M, d) be a metric space and let $S : M \to P(M)$ be a multi-valued operator such that $Fix(S) \neq \emptyset$. Suppose there exists $r : M \to Fix(S)$, a set retraction. Then, the fixed point inclusion $m \in S(m)$ is called well-posed in the sense of Reich and Zaslavski if for each $v \in Fix(S)$ and for any sequence $\{v_n\}_{n\in\mathbb{N}} \subset r^{-1}(v)$ such that*

$$D(v_n, S(u_n)) \to 0 \text{ as } n \to \infty,$$

we have that

$$v_n \to v \text{ as } n \to \infty.$$

Finally, we recall the notion of Ostrowski stability property for a fixed point inclusion (see [23]).

Definition 10. *Let (M, d) be a metric space and let $S : M \to P(M)$ be a multi-valued operator such that $Fix(S) \neq \emptyset$. Suppose there exists $r : M \to Fix(S)$, a set retraction. Then, the fixed point inclusion $m \in S(m)$ is said to have the Ostrowski stability property if for each $m^* \in Fix(S)$ and for any sequence $\{w_n\}_{n\in\mathbb{N}} \subset r^{-1}(m^*)$ such that:*

$$D(w_{n+1}, S(w_n)) \to 0 \text{ as } n \to \infty,$$

we have that

$$w_n \to m^* \text{ as } n \to \infty.$$

Two abstract results concerning some stability properties of a multi-valued operator are given in our next results.

Theorem 2. *Let (M, d) be a metric space and let $S : M \to P(M)$ be a multi-valued operator satisfying the local strong retraction–displacement condition such that $Fix(S) \neq \emptyset$. Then, the fixed point inclusion $m \in S(m)$ has the local Ulam–Hyers stability property and satisfies the local data dependence property.*

Proof. Suppose there exists a set retraction $r : M \to Fix(S)$ such that

$$d(m, r(m)) \leq C(m)D(m, S(m)), \text{ for all } m \in M, \tag{6}$$

for some $C(m) > 0$.

Let $\varepsilon > 0$ and $u \in M$ with the property $D(u, S(u)) \leq \varepsilon$. Then, by (6), there exists $C = C(u) > 0$ such that

$$d(u, r(u)) \leq C(u)D(u, S(u)) \leq C(u)\varepsilon.$$

Thus, $m^*(u) = r(u) \in Fix(S)$ and the local Ulam–Hyers stability property is established.

For the local data dependence property, let us consider any multi-valued operator $T : M \to P(M)$ such that $Fix(T) \neq \emptyset$ and for which there exists $\eta > 0$ such that $H(S(m), T(m)) \leq \eta$, for all $m \in M$. Take $t \in Fix(T)$. Then, by (6), there exists $C = C(t) > 0$ such that

$$d(t, r(t)) \leq C(t)D(t, S(t)) \leq C(t)\eta.$$

Since $r(t) \in Fix(S)$, the local data dependence property is proven. □

By the above abstract result, we immediately obtain the following stability properties for multi-valued Feng–Liu–Subrahmanyan contractions.

Theorem 3. *Let (M, d) be a complete metric space and $S : M \to P(M)$ be a multi-valued Feng–Liu–Subrahmanyan contraction with closed graph. Then, the fixed point inclusion (5) is local Ulam–Hyers stable and satisfies the local data dependence property.*

Proof. By Theorem 1, we know that $Fix(S) \neq \emptyset$ (conclusion (a)) and S satisfies the local strong retraction–displacement condition (see conclusion (c)). The result follows by Theorem 2. □

Example 2. *Let $S : M := \mathbb{R} \times \mathbb{R} \to \mathbb{R} \times \mathbb{R}$ given by*

$$S(u,v) = \begin{cases} \{(u, \frac{v+|u|+v|v-|u||}{2+|v-|u||})\}, & (u,v) \in M, v = |u| \\ \{(0,1), (0,-1)\}, & (u,v) \in M, v \neq |u|. \end{cases} \tag{7}$$

Then, S is a multi-valued Feng–Liu–Subrahmanyan contraction with closed graph and $Fix(S) = \{(u,v) \in M : v = |u|\}$. By Theorem 2 and Theorem 3, the fixed point inclusion $m \in S(m)$ is local Ulam–Hyers stable and satisfies the local data dependence property.

Remark 1. *It is an open question to obtain the well-posedness property in the sense of Reich and Zaslavski and the Ostrowski stability property for the fixed point inclusion $m \in S(m), m \in M$ for a multi-valued Feng–Liu–Subrahmanyan contraction with closed graph defined on a complete metric space (M, d). For example, if ψ has the following property:*

$$(P) \text{ there exists } q > 0 \text{ such that } \psi(m) \leq b - q, \text{ for all } m \in M,$$

then, under the assumption given in Theorem 1, the fixed point inclusion $m \in S(m)$ has the well-posedness property in the sense of Reich and Zaslavski. Indeed, by Theorem 1 (a,b) we know that $Fix(S) \neq \emptyset$ and there exists a retraction $r : M \to Fix(S)$ given by $r(u) := \{m^*(u) :$ and there exists a sequence of successive approximations starting from u converging to $m^*(u)\}$.

If we take $v \in Fix(S)$ and any sequence $\{v_n\}_{n \in \mathbb{N}} \subset r^{-1}(v)$ such that

$$D(v_n, S(u_n)) \to 0 \text{ as } n \to \infty,$$

then, by Theorem 1 (c), we have that

$$d(v_n, v) \leq \frac{1}{b - \psi(v_n)} D(v_n, S(v_n)) \leq \frac{1}{q} D(v_n, S(v_n)) \to 0, \text{ as } n \to \infty.$$

Another open question is to obtain strict fixed point theorems for multi-valued Feng–Liu–Subrahmanyan contractions with closed graph defined on a complete metric space (M, d). For example, we have the following strict fixed point result for multi-valued Feng–Liu–Subrahmanyan contractions, which generalize some theorems in [18,28]. As a matter of fact, the conclusion of the next theorem is $Fix(S) = SFix(S) \neq \emptyset$, which is a quite a usual assumption in various iteration methods for multi-valued operators.

Theorem 4. *Let (M, d) be a complete metric space and $S : M \to P(M)$ be a multi-valued Feng–Liu–Subrahmanyan contraction with closed graph. Suppose that*

(a) $S(S(m)) \subset S(m)$, for each $m \in M$;

(b) If $A \in P_{cl}(M)$ with $S(A) = A$, then A is a singleton.

Then, $Fix(S) = SFix(S) \neq \emptyset$.

Proof. By Theorem 1, we have that $Fix(S) \neq \emptyset$. Let $m^* \in Fix(S)$. By the assumption (a) of this theorem, we obtain that $S(m^*) \subset S(S(m^*)) \subset S(m^*)$. Thus, $S(S(m^*)) = S(m^*)$, i.e., $S(m^*)$ is a fixed set for S. By the assumption (b), we obtain that $S(m^*)$ is a singleton. Hence, $S(m^*) = \{m^*\}$. We also observe that $Fix(S) \subset SFix(S)$. Thus, $Fix(S) = SFix(S) \neq \emptyset$. □

3. Conclusions

In this work, we introduced, in the context of a metric space (M, d), the class of multi-valued Feng–Liu–Subrahmanyan contractions, and we presented a fixed point theory for these kind of multi-valued operators. More precisely, if $S : M \to P(M)$ is a multi-valued Feng–Liu–Subrahmanyan contraction, we proved the following:

- An existence and approximation result for the fixed point inclusion $m \in S(m), m \in M$;
- An existence result for the strict fixed point problem $S(m) = \{m\}, m \in M$;
- The Ulam–Hyers stability property for the fixed point inclusion $m \in S(m), m \in M$;
- The data dependence property for the solution of the fixed point inclusion $m \in S(m), m \in M$;
- A partial answer for the well-posedness property in the sense of Reich and Zaslavski for the fixed point inclusion $m \in S(m), m \in M$.

Two open questions concerning the well-posedness property and the existence of the strict fixed points for multi-valued Feng–Liu–Subrahmanyan contractions are highlighted.

Author Contributions: Conceptualization, C.L.M., G.M. and A.P.; methodology, C.L.M., G.M. and A.P.; validation, C.L.M., G.M. and A.P.; investigation, C.L.M., G.M. and A.P.; writing—original draft preparation, C.L.M., G.M. and A.P.; writing—review and editing C.L.M., G.M. and A.P. All authors have read and agreed to the published version of the manuscript.

Funding: This research received no external funding.

Institutional Review Board Statement: Not applicable.

Informed Consent Statement: Not applicable.

Data Availability Statement: Not applicable.

Acknowledgments: The authors are grateful to the anonymous referees for the careful reading of the paper and for useful suggestions.

Conflicts of Interest: The authors declare no conflict of interest.

References

1. Nadler, S.B., Jr. Multi-valued contraction mappings. *Pac. J. Math.* **1969**, *30*, 475–488. [CrossRef]
2. Covitz, H.; Nadler, S.B., Jr. Multi-valued contraction mappings in generalized metric spaces. *Isr. J. Math.* **1970**, *8* , 5–11. [CrossRef]
3. Petruşel, A.; Petruşel, G.; Yao, J.-C. Multi-valued graph contraction principle with applications. *Optimization* **2020**, *69*, 1541–1556. [CrossRef]
4. He, H.; Liu, S.; Chen, R. Convergence results of multi-valued nonexpansive mappings in Banach spaces. *J. Inequal. Appl.* **2014**, *2014*, 483. [CrossRef]

5. Hussain, A.; Ali, A.; Parvaneh, V.; Aydi, H. Data dependence, strict fixed point results, and well-posedness of multivalued weakly Picard operators. *J. Math.* **2021**, *13*, 5518647. [CrossRef]
6. Rus, I.A. Strict fixed point theory. *Fixed Point Theory* **2003**, *4*, 177–183.
7. Xu, H.-K.; Alghamdi, M.A.; Shahzad, N. Remarks on iterative methods for multivalued nonexpansive mappings. *J. Nonlinear Convex Anal.* **2017**, *18*, 161–171.
8. Kumar, S.; Luambano, S. On some fixed point theorems for multivalued F-contractions in partial metric spaces. *Demonstr. Math.* **2021**, *54*, 151–161. [CrossRef]
9. Wardowski, D. Fixed points of a new type of contractive mappings in complete metric spaces. *Fixed Point Theory Appl.* **2012**, *94*, 1–6. [CrossRef]
10. Zaslavski, A.J. Asymptotic behavior of iterates of a generic cyclical nonexpansive mapping. *Numer. Funct. Anal. Optim.* **2022**, *43*, 116–125. [CrossRef]
11. Feng, Y.; Liu, S. Fixed point theorems for multi-valued contractive mappings and multi-valued Caristi type mappings. *J. Math. Anal. Appl.* **2006**, *317*, 103–112. [CrossRef]
12. Nashine, H.K.; Kadelburg, Z. Wardowski-Feng-Liu type fixed point theorems for multivalued mappings. *Fixed Point Theory* **2020**, *21*, 697–705. [CrossRef]
13. Nashine, H.K.; Dey, L.K.; Ibrahim, R.W.; Radenović, S. Feng-Liu-type fixed point result in orbital b-metric spaces and application to fractal integral equation. *Nonlinear Anal. Model. Control* **2021**, *26*, 522–533. [CrossRef]
14. Nashine, H.K.; Ibrahim, R.W.; Rhoades, B.E.; Pant, R. Unified Feng-Liu type fixed point theorems solving control problems. *Rev. R. Acad. Cienc. Exactas Fis. Nat. Ser. A Mat. RACSAM* **2021**, *115*, 17. [CrossRef]
15. Nicolae, A. Fixed point theorems for multi-valued mappings of Feng-Liu type. *Fixed Point Theory* **2011**, *12*, 145–154.
16. Sahin, H.; Aslantas, M.; Altun, I. Feng-Liu type approach to best proximity point results for multivalued mappings. *J. Fixed Point Theory Appl.* **2020**, *22*, 13. [CrossRef]
17. Altun, I.; Minak, G. On fixed point theorems for multivalued mappings of Feng-Liu type. *Bull. Korean Math. Soc.* **2015**, *52*, 1901–1910. [CrossRef]
18. Petruşel, A.; Petruşel, G. Fixed points of multi-valued Subrahmanyan contractions. *Appl.-Set-Valued Anal. Optim.* **2022**, *4*, 367–373.
19. Chaoha, P.; Atiponrat, W. Virtually stable maps and their fixed point sets. *J. Math. Anal. Appl.* **2009**, *359*, 536–542. [CrossRef]
20. Chaoha, P.; Sudprakhon, W. Fixed point sets for Subrahmanyan maps. *Linear Nonlinear Anal.* **2017**, *3*, 149–154.
21. Rus, I.A.; Petruşel, A.; Petruşel, G. *Fixed Point Theory*; Cluj University Press: Cluj-Napoca, Romania, 2008.
22. Xu, H.-K. Metric fixed point theory for multivalued mappings. *Diss. Math.* **2000**, *389*, 39. [CrossRef]
23. Petruşel, A.; Rus, I.A.; Şerban, M.A. Basic problems of the metric fixed point theory and the relevance of a metric fixed point theorem for multivalued operators. *J. Nonlinear Convex Anal.* **2014**, *15*, 493–513.
24. Reich, S. Fixed point of contractive functions. *Boll. Un. Mat. Ital.* **1972**, *5*, 26–42.
25. Petru, P.T.; Petruşel, A.; Yao, J.-C. Ulam-Hyers stability for operatorial equations and inclusions via nonself operators. *Taiwanese J. Math.* **2011**, *15*, 2195–2212. [CrossRef]
26. Reich, S.; Zaslavski, A.J. Well-posedness of fixed point problems. *Far East J. Math. Sci.* **2001**, *46*, 393–401. [CrossRef]
27. Reich, S.; Zaslavski, A.J. *Genericity in Nonlinear Analysis*; Springer: New York, NY, USA, 2014.
28. Jachymski, J. A stationary point theorem characterizing metric completeness. *Appl. Math. Lett.* **2011**, *24*, 169–171. [CrossRef]

axioms

MDPI

Article

Boundedness of Riesz Potential Operator on Grand Herz-Morrey Spaces

Babar Sultan [1], Fatima Azmi [2], Mehvish Sultan [3], Mazhar Mehmood [4] and Nabil Mlaiki [2,*]

[1] Department of Mathematics, Quaid-I-Azam University, Islamabad 45320, Pakistan
[2] Department of Mathematics and Sciences, Prince Sultan University, Riyadh 11586, Saudi Arabia
[3] Department of Mathematics, Capital University of Science and Technology, Islamabad 44000, Pakistan
[4] Department of Mathematics, Government Post Graduate College, Haripur 22620, KPK, Pakistan
* Correspondence: nmlaiki@psu.edu.sa or nmlaiki2012@gmail.com

Abstract: In this paper, we introduce grand Herz–Morrey spaces with variable exponent and prove the boundedness of Riesz potential operators in these spaces.

Keywords: Riesz potential operator; grand Herz–Morrey spaces; grand Lebesgue spaces; grand Herz spaces

MSC: Primary 46E30; Secondary 47B38

Citation: Sultan, B.; Azmi, F.; Sultan, M.; Mehmood, M.; Mlaiki, N. Boundedness of Riesz Potential Operator on Grand Herz-Morrey Spaces. *Axioms* **2022**, *11*, 583. https://doi.org/10.3390/axioms11110583

Academic Editors: Wei-Shih Du, Luigi Muglia and Adrian Petrusel

Received: 2 September 2022
Accepted: 20 October 2022
Published: 24 October 2022

Publisher's Note: MDPI stays neutral with regard to jurisdictional claims in published maps and institutional affiliations.

Copyright: © 2022 by the authors. Licensee MDPI, Basel, Switzerland. This article is an open access article distributed under the terms and conditions of the Creative Commons Attribution (CC BY) license (https://creativecommons.org/licenses/by/4.0/).

1. Introduction

In the last two decades, under the influence of some applications revealed in [1], there was a vast boom of research of the so-called variable exponent spaces, and the operator in them. For the time being, the theory of such variable exponent Lebesgue, Orlicz, Lorentz and Sobolev function spaces is widely developed, and we refer to the books [2,3] and the surveying papers [4–7]. Herz spaces with variable exponents have been recently introduced in [8–10]. In [11], variable parameters were used to define continual Herz spaces, and proved the boundedness of sublinear operators in these spaces. The boundedness of other operators such as Riesz potential operator and the Marcinkiewicz integrals was proved in [12,13].

The concept of Morrey spaces $L^{p,\lambda}$ was introduced by C. Morrey in 1938 (see [14]) in order to study regularity questions that appear in the calculus of variations. They describe local regularity more precisely than Lebesgue spaces and are widely used not just in harmonic analysis, but also in PDEs. Meskhi introduced the idea of grand Morrey spaces $L^{r),\theta,\lambda}$ and derived the boundedness of a class of integral operators (Hardy–Littlewood maximal functions, Calderón–Zygmund singular integrals and potentials) in these spaces, see ([15]). Moreover, Izuki [16] defined the Herz–Morrey spaces with a variable exponent and investigated the boundedness of fractional integrals on these spaces.

In [17], the idea of grand variable Herz spaces $\dot{K}^{\alpha,p),\theta}_{q(\cdot)}(\mathbb{R}^n)$ was introduced and proved the boundedness of sublinear operators $\dot{K}^{\alpha,p),\theta}_{q(\cdot)}(\mathbb{R}^n)$. Motivated by the concept, in this article, we introduce the concept of grand Herz–Morrey spaces, and prove the boundedness of the Riesz potential operator on grand Herz–Morrey spaces with variable exponents. There are four sections in this article; the first section is dedicated to the introduction, the second section contains some basic definitions and lemmas, we introduce the concept of grand Herz–Morrey spaces in part three, and the boundedness of the Riesz potential operator on grand variable Herz–Morrey spaces is proved in the last section.

2. Preliminaries

For this section, we refer to [2,3,9,10,18].

2.1. Lebesgue Space with Variable Exponent

Assume that $G \subseteq \mathbb{R}^n$ is an open set and $p(\cdot) : G \to [1, \infty)$ is a real-valued measurable function. Let the following condition hold:

$$1 \leq p_-(G) \leq p_+(G) < \infty, \tag{1}$$

where

(i) $p_- := \operatorname{ess}\inf_{g \in G} p(g)$

(ii) $p_+ := \operatorname{ess}\sup_{g \in G} p(g)$.

Lebesgue space $L^{p(\cdot)}(G)$ is the space of measurable functions f_1 on G such that,

$$I_{L^{p(\cdot)}}(f_1) = \int_G |f_1(g)|^{p(g)} dg < \infty,$$

norm is defined as,

$$\|f_1\|_{L^{p(\cdot)}(G)} = \operatorname{ess}\inf\left\{ \gamma > 0 : I_{L^{p(\cdot)}}\left(\frac{f_1}{\gamma}\right) \leq 1 \right\},$$

this is the Banach function space, $p'(g) = \frac{p(g)}{p(g)-1}$ denotes the conjugate exponent of $p(g)$.

Next, we will define the space $L^{p(\cdot)}_{\text{loc}}(G)$ as,

$$L^{p(\cdot)}_{\text{loc}}(G) := \left\{ \kappa : \kappa \in L^{p(\cdot)}(K) \textit{ for all compact subsets } K \subset G \right\}.$$

Now to define the log-condition,

$$|\eta(z_1) - \eta(z_2)| \leq \frac{C}{-\ln|z_1 - z_2|}, \quad |z_1 - z_2| \leq \frac{1}{2}, \quad z_1, z_2 \in G, \tag{2}$$

where $C = C(\eta) > 0$ is not dependent on z_1, z_2.

For the decay condition: let $\eta_\infty \in (1, \infty)$, such that

$$|\eta(z_1) - \eta_\infty| \leq \frac{C}{\ln(e + |z_1|)}, \tag{3}$$

$$|\eta(z_1) - \eta_0| \leq \frac{C}{\ln|z_1|}, |z_1| \leq \frac{1}{2}, \tag{4}$$

inequality (4) holds for $\eta_0 \in (1, \infty)$ in case of homogenous Herz spaces. We adopted the following notations in this paper:

(i) The Hardy–Littlewood maximal operator M for $f \in L^1_{\text{loc}}(G)$ is defined as

$$Mf(g) := \sup_{t>0} t^{-n} \int_{D(g,r)} |f(g)| dg \quad (g \in G),$$

where $D(g, t) := \{y \in G : |g - y| < t\}$.

(ii) The set $\mathcal{P}(G)$ is the collection of all $p(\cdot)$ satisfying $p_- > 1$ and $p_+ < \infty$.

(iii) $\mathcal{P}^{\log} = \mathcal{P}^{\log}(G)$ is the class of functions $p \in \mathcal{P}(G)$ satisfying (1) and (2).

(iv) When G is unbounded, $\mathcal{P}_\infty(G)$ and $\mathcal{P}_{0,\infty}(G)$ are the subsets of $\mathcal{P}(G)$ and its values lies in $[1, \infty)$ satisfying (3) and (4), respectively.

(v) In the case G is bounded, $\mathcal{P}_\infty(G)$ and $\mathcal{P}_{0,\infty}(G)$ are the subsets of $\mathcal{P}(G)$.
(vi) In the case S is unbounded, $\mathcal{P}_\infty(S)$ are the subsets of exponents in $L^\infty(S)$ and its values lies in $[1,\infty]$, which satisfy both conditions (2) and (3), respectively, and $\mathcal{P}^{\log}_\infty(S)$ is the set of exponents $p \in \mathcal{P}_\infty(S)$, satisfying condition (1).

C is a constant that is independent of the main parameters involved, and its value varies from line to line.

Lemma 1 ([11]). *Let $D > 1$ and $\eta \in \mathcal{P}_{0,\infty}(\mathbb{R}^n)$. Then,*

$$\frac{1}{k_0} t^{\frac{n}{\eta(0)}} \leq \|\chi_{R_{t,D_t}}\|_{\eta(\cdot)} \leq k_0 t^{\frac{n}{\eta(0)}}, \text{ for } 0 < t \leq 1 \tag{5}$$

and

$$\frac{1}{k_\infty} t^{\frac{n}{\eta_\infty}} \leq \|\chi_{R_{t,D_t}}\|_{\eta(\cdot)} \leq k_\infty t^{\frac{n}{\eta_\infty}}, \text{ for } t \geq 1, \tag{6}$$

respectively, where $k_0 \geq 1$ and $k_\infty \geq 1$ depend on D and do not depend on t.

Lemma 2 (Generalized Hölder's inequality [2]). *Assume that G is a measurable subset of $\mathbb{R}^n$, and $1 \leq p_-(G) \leq p_+(G) \leq \infty$. Then,*

$$\|fg\|_{L^{r(\cdot)}(G)} \leq C\|f\|_{L^{p(\cdot)}(G)}\|g\|_{L^{q(\cdot)}(G)}$$

holds, where $f \in L^{p(\cdot)}(G)$, $g \in L^{q(\cdot)}(G)$ and $\frac{1}{r(z)} = \frac{1}{p(z)} + \frac{1}{q(z)}$ for every $z \in G$.

2.2. Herz Spaces with Variable Exponent

We adopted the following notations in this subsection:

(a) $\chi_k = \chi_{R_k}$;
(b) $R_k = D_k \setminus D_{k-1}$;
(c) $D_k = D(0, 2^k) = \{x \in \mathbb{R}^n : |x| < 2^k\}$ for all $k \in \mathbb{Z}$.

Definition 1. *Let $r, s \in [1,\infty)$, $\alpha \in \mathbb{R}$, the classical versions of Herz spaces, commonly known as non-homogenous and homogenous Herz spaces, can be defined by the norms,*

$$\|g\|_{K^\alpha_{r,s}(\mathbb{R}^n)} := \|g\|_{L^r(D(0,1))} + \left\{\sum_{k\in\mathbb{N}} 2^{k\alpha s}\left(\int\limits_{R_{2^{k-1},2^k}} |g(z)|^r dz\right)^{\frac{s}{r}}\right\}^{\frac{1}{s}}, \tag{7}$$

$$\|g\|_{\dot{K}^\alpha_{r,s}(\mathbb{R}^n)} := \left\{\sum_{k\in\mathbb{Z}} 2^{k\alpha s}\left(\int\limits_{R_{2^{k-1},2^k}} |g(z)|^r dz\right)^{\frac{s}{r}}\right\}^{\frac{1}{s}}, \tag{8}$$

respectively, where $R_{t,\tau}$ stands for the annulus $R_{t,\tau} := D(0,\tau)\setminus D(0,t)$.

Definition 2. *Let $r \in [1,\infty)$, $\alpha \in \mathbb{R}$ and $s(\cdot) \in \mathcal{P}(\mathbb{R}^n)$. The homogenous Herz space $\dot{K}^{\alpha,r}_{s(\cdot)}(\mathbb{R}^n)$ is defined by*

$$\dot{K}^{\alpha,r}_{s(\cdot)}(\mathbb{R}^n) = \left\{g \in L^{s(\cdot)}{}_{\mathrm{loc}}(\mathbb{R}^n \setminus \{0\}) : \|g\|_{\dot{K}^{\alpha,r}_{s(\cdot)}(\mathbb{R}^n)} < \infty\right\}, \tag{9}$$

where

$$\|g\|_{\dot{K}^{\alpha,r}_{s(\cdot)}(\mathbb{R}^n)} = \left(\sum_{k=-\infty}^{k=\infty} \|2^{k\alpha} g\chi_k\|^r_{L^{s(\cdot)}}\right)^{\frac{1}{r}}.$$

Definition 3. *Let $r \in [1,\infty)$, $\alpha \in \mathbb{R}$ and $s(\cdot) \in \mathcal{P}(\mathbb{R}^n)$. The non-homogenous Herz space $K^{\alpha,r}_{s(\cdot)}(\mathbb{R}^n)$ is defined by*

$$K^{\alpha,r}_{s(\cdot)}(\mathbb{R}^n) = \left\{ g \in L^{s(\cdot)}_{\mathrm{loc}}(\mathbb{R}^n \setminus \{0\}) : \|g\|_{K^{\alpha,r}_{s(\cdot)}(\mathbb{R}^n)} < \infty \right\}, \quad (10)$$

where

$$\|g\|_{K^{\alpha,r}_{s(\cdot)}(\mathbb{R}^n)} = \left(\sum_{k=-\infty}^{k=\infty} \|2^{k\alpha} g\chi_k\|^r_{L^{s(\cdot)}} \right)^{\frac{1}{r}} + \|g\|_{L^{s(\cdot)}(D(0,1))}.$$

2.3. Herz–Morrey Spaces

Next, we define Herz–Morrey spaces with variable exponent.

Definition 4. *Let $\alpha \in \mathbb{R}$, $0 \le \lambda < \infty$, $0 < r < \infty$ and $s(\cdot) \in \mathcal{P}(\mathbb{R}^n)$. A Herz–Morrey spaces with variable exponent $M\dot{K}^{\alpha\lambda}_{r,s(\cdot)}(\mathbb{R}^n)$ is defined by,*

$$M\dot{K}^{\alpha\lambda}_{r,s(\cdot)}(\mathbb{R}^n) = \left\{ g \in L^{s(\cdot)}_{\mathrm{loc}}(\mathbb{R}^n \setminus \{0\}) : \|g\|_{M\dot{K}^{\alpha\lambda}_{r,s(\cdot)}(\mathbb{R}^n)} < \infty \right\},$$

where

$$\|g\|_{M\dot{K}^{\alpha\lambda}_{r,s(\cdot)}(\mathbb{R}^n)} = \sup_{k_0 \in \mathbb{Z}} 2^{-k_0\lambda} \left(\sum_{k=-\infty}^{k_0} 2^{k\alpha r} \|g\chi_k\|^r_{L^{s}(\cdot)(\mathbb{R}^n)} \right)^{\frac{1}{r}}.$$

2.4. Grand Lebesgue Sequence Space

Now, we will define the grand Lebesgue sequence space. $\mathbb{G}$ is representing one of the sets $\mathbb{N}_0, \mathbb{Z}^n, \mathbb{N}, \mathbb{Z}$ in the following definitions (see [19]).

Definition 5. *Let $r \in [1,\infty)$ and $\theta > 0$. The grand Lebesgue sequence space $l^{r)\theta}$ can be defined by the norm*

$$\begin{aligned} \|\{x_k\}_{k\in\mathbb{G}}\|_{l^{r)\theta}(\mathbb{G})} &= \|x\|_{l^{r)\theta}(\mathbb{G})} \\ &:= \sup_{\delta>0} \left(\delta^\theta \sum_{k\in\mathbb{X}} |x_k|^{r(1+\delta)} \right)^{\frac{1}{r(1+\delta)}} = \sup_{\delta>0} \delta^{\frac{\theta}{r(1+\delta)}} \|x\|_{l^{r(1+\delta)\theta}(\mathbb{G})}, \end{aligned}$$

where $x = \{x_k\}_{k\in\mathbb{G}}$. The following nesting properties hold:

$$l^{r(1-\delta)} \hookrightarrow l^r \hookrightarrow l^{r),\theta_1} \hookrightarrow l^{r),\theta_2} \hookrightarrow l^{r(1+\delta)} \quad (11)$$

for $0 < \delta < \frac{1}{r}$, $\delta > 0$ and $0 < \theta_1 \le \theta_2$.

3. Grand Variable Herz–Morrey Spaces

Grand variable Herz–Morrey spaces are introduced in this section.

Definition 6. *Let $\alpha(\cdot) \in L^\infty(\mathbb{R}^n)$, $r \in [1,\infty)$, $s : \mathbb{R}^n \to [1,\infty)$, $\theta > 0$, $0 \le \lambda < \infty$. We define the homogeneous grand variable Herz–Morrey spaces can be defined by the norm:*

$$M\dot{K}^{\alpha(\cdot),r),\theta}_{\lambda,s(\cdot)}(\mathbb{R}^n) = \left\{ g \in L^{s(\cdot)}_{\mathrm{loc}}(\mathbb{R}^n \setminus \{0\}) : \|g\|_{M\dot{K}^{\alpha(\cdot),r),\theta}_{\lambda,s(\cdot)}(\mathbb{R}^n)} < \infty \right\},$$

where

$$\|g\|_{M\dot{K}^{\alpha(\cdot),r),\theta}_{\lambda,s(\cdot)}(\mathbb{R}^n)} = \sup_{\delta>0} \sup_{k_0\in\mathbb{Z}} 2^{-k_0\lambda} \left(\delta^\theta \sum_{k\in\mathbb{Z}} 2^{k\alpha(\cdot)r(1+\delta)} \|g\chi_k\|^{r(1+\delta)}_{L^{s(\cdot)}(\mathbb{R}^n)} \right)^{\frac{1}{r(1+\delta)}}.$$

For $\lambda = 0$, the grand Herz–Morrey spaces become grand Herz spaces.

Non-homogeneous grand variable Herz–Morrey spaces can be defined in a similar way.

Theorem 1. *If $0 < r_i < \infty, 1 \le q_- \le q_+ < \infty$, $\alpha(\cdot) \in L^\infty(\mathbb{R}^n)$, $i = 1,2$, $\frac{1}{r} = \frac{1}{r_1} + \frac{1}{r_2}$, $1 = \frac{1}{q(\cdot)} + \frac{1}{q'(\cdot)}$, $\lambda = \lambda_1 + \lambda_2$ and $\alpha(\cdot) = \alpha(\cdot)_1(\cdot) + \alpha_2(\cdot)$. Then*

$$\|fg\|_{M\dot{K}^{\alpha(\cdot),r),\theta}_{\lambda,1}} \le \|f\|_{M\dot{K}^{\alpha_1(\cdot),r_1),\theta}_{\lambda,q(\cdot)}} \|g\|_{M\dot{K}^{\alpha_2(\cdot),r_2),\theta}_{\lambda,q'(\cdot)}}.$$

Proof. We have

$$\begin{aligned}
\|fg\|_{M\dot{K}^{\alpha(\cdot),),\theta}_{\lambda,1}(\mathbb{R}^n)} &= \sup_{\delta>0}\sup_{k_0\in\mathbb{Z}} 2^{-k_0\lambda}\left(\delta^\theta \sum_{k\in\mathbb{Z}} 2^{k\alpha(\cdot)r(1+\delta)} \|f\chi_k\|_{L^1}^{r(1+\delta)}\right)^{\frac{1}{r(1+\delta)}} \\
&= \sup_{\delta>0}\sup_{k_0\in\mathbb{Z}} 2^{-k_0\lambda}\left(\delta^\theta \sum_{k\in\mathbb{Z}} 2^{k\alpha(\cdot)r(1+\delta)} \left(\int_{2^k}^{2^{k+1}} |fg|\right)^{r(1+\delta)}\right)^{\frac{1}{r(1+\delta)}},
\end{aligned}$$

by using Hölder's inequality

$$\begin{aligned}
&\le C\sup_{\delta>0}\sup_{k_0\in\mathbb{Z}} 2^{-k_0\lambda}\left(\delta^\theta \sum_{k\in\mathbb{Z}} 2^{k(\alpha_1(\cdot)+\alpha_2(\cdot))r(1+\delta)} \|f\chi_k\|_{L^{q(\cdot)}}^{r(1+\delta)} \|g\chi_k\|_{L^{q'(\cdot)}}^{r(1+\delta)}\right)^{\frac{1}{r(1+\delta)}} \\
&= C\sup_{\delta>0}\sup_{k_0\in\mathbb{Z}} 2^{-k_0\lambda}\left(\delta^\theta \sum_{k\in\mathbb{Z}} 2^{k(\alpha_1(\cdot)+\alpha_2(\cdot))r(1+\delta)} \|f\chi_k\|_{L^{q(\cdot)}}^{r(1+\delta)} \|g\chi_k\|_{L^{q'(\cdot)}}^{r(1+\delta)}\right)^{\frac{1}{r(1+\delta)}} \\
&= C\sup_{\delta>0}\sup_{k_0\in\mathbb{Z}} 2^{-k_0\lambda}\left(\delta^\theta \sum_{k\in\mathbb{Z}} \left(2^{k\alpha_1(\cdot)} \|f\chi_k\|_{L^{q(\cdot)}}\right)^{r(1+\delta)} \left(2^{k\alpha_2(\cdot)} \|g\chi_k\|_{L^{q'(\cdot)}}\right)^{r(1+\delta)}\right)^{\frac{1}{r(1+\delta)}} \\
&\le C\sup_{\delta>0}\sup_{k_0\in\mathbb{Z}} 2^{-k_0\lambda}\left(\delta^\theta \sum_{k\in\mathbb{Z}} \left(2^{k\alpha_1(\cdot)} \|f\chi_k\|_{L^{q(\cdot)}(\mathbb{R}^n)}\right)^{r(1+\delta)} \left(2^{k\alpha_2(\cdot)} \|g\chi_k\|_{L^{q'(\cdot)}}\right)^{r(1+\delta)}\right)^{\frac{1}{r(1+\delta)}},
\end{aligned}$$

by using generalized Hölder's inequality

$$\begin{aligned}
&\le C\sup_{\delta>0}\sup_{k_0\in\mathbb{Z}} 2^{-k_0\lambda}\left(\delta^\theta \sum_{k\in\mathbb{Z}} \left(2^{k\alpha_1(\cdot)} \|f\chi_k\|_{L^{q(\cdot)}}\right)^{r_1(1+\delta)}\right)^{\frac{1}{r_1(1+\delta)}} \\
&\times \sup_{\delta>0}\sup_{k_0\in\mathbb{Z}} 2^{-k_0\lambda}\left(\delta^\theta \sum_{k\in\mathbb{Z}} \left(2^{k\alpha_1(\cdot)} \|f\chi_k\|_{L^{q'(\cdot)}}\right)^{r_2(1+\delta)}\right)^{\frac{1}{r_2(1+\delta)}} \\
&= C\|f\|_{M\dot{K}^{\alpha_1(\cdot),r_1),\theta}_{\lambda,q(\cdot)}} \|f\|_{M\dot{K}^{\alpha_2(\cdot),r_2),\theta}_{\lambda,q'(\cdot)}}.
\end{aligned}$$

□

4. Boundedness of the Riesz Potential Operator

Now Riesz potential operator can be defined as

$$I^{\gamma}f(z_1)=\frac{1}{\eta_n(\gamma)}\int\limits_{\mathbb{R}^n}\frac{f(z_2)}{|z_1-z_2|^{n-\gamma}}dz_2 \tag{12}$$

with the normalizing constant $\eta_n(\gamma)=2^{\gamma}\pi^{\frac{n}{2}}\frac{\Gamma(\gamma/2)}{\Gamma((n-\gamma)/2)}$.

Whenever $\gamma q_1(z_1)<n$, we can define the Sobolev conjugate of q_1 by the usual relation

$$\frac{1}{q_2(z_1)}:=\frac{1}{q_1(z_1)}-\frac{\gamma}{n}, z_1\in\mathbb{R}^n \tag{13}$$

The well-known Sobolev theorem was extended to variable exponents in [20] for bounded sets in $\mathbb{R}^n$ under the assumption that the maximal operator is bounded in $L^{p(\cdot)}(\Omega)$; for unbounded sets, proved in [21], the Sobolev theorem runs as follows.

Theorem 2. *Let $s_2\in\mathcal{P}_{\infty}^{\log}(\mathbb{R}^n)$ and $\gamma s_1^{+}<n$,*

$$\|I^{\gamma}g\|_{s_2(\cdot)}\le C\|g\|_{s_1(\cdot)}.$$

Theorem 3. *Let $1\le r<\infty$, $\alpha(\cdot),q(\cdot)\in\mathcal{P}_{\infty}^{\log}(\mathbb{R}^n)$, q_1 is sobolev conjugate defined by the relation (13) such that*

(i) $\gamma-\frac{n}{q(0)}<\alpha(0)<\frac{n}{q'(0)}$;

(ii) $\gamma-\frac{n}{q_\infty}<\alpha_\infty<\frac{n}{q'_\infty}$.

Suppose that Riesz potential operator I^{γ} is bounded on Lebesgue spaces and satisfies the size condition (12). Then, I^{γ} from $M\dot{K}^{\alpha(\cdot),r),\theta}_{q_1(\cdot)}(\mathbb{R}^n)$ to $M\dot{K}^{\alpha(\cdot),r),\theta}_{q_2(\cdot)}(\mathbb{R}^n)$.

Proof. Let $f\in M\dot{K}^{\alpha(\cdot),p),\theta}_{q_2(\cdot)}(\mathbb{R}^n)$, and $f(z_1)=\Sigma_{l=-\infty}^{\infty}f(z_1)\chi_l(z_1)=\Sigma_{l=-\infty}^{\infty}f_l(z_1)$, we have

$$\begin{aligned}
\|I^{\gamma}f\|_{M\dot{K}^{\alpha(\cdot),p,\theta}_{q_2(\cdot)}(\mathbb{R}^n)} &= \sup_{\delta>0}\sup_{k_0\in\mathbb{Z}}2^{-k_0\lambda}\left(\delta^{\theta}\sum_{k\in\mathbb{Z}}2^{k\alpha(\cdot)r(1+\delta)}\|\chi_k I^{\gamma}f\|^{r(1+\delta)}_{L^{q_2(\cdot)}(\mathbb{R}^n)}\right)^{\frac{1}{r(1+\delta)}}\\
&\le \sup_{\delta>0}\sup_{k_o\in\mathbb{Z}}2^{-k_0\lambda}\left(\delta^{\theta}\sum_{k\in\mathbb{Z}}2^{k\alpha(\cdot)r(1+\delta)}\left(\sum_{l=-\infty}^{\infty}\|\chi_k I^{\gamma}f(\chi_l)\|^{r(1+\delta)}_{L^{q_2(\cdot)}(\mathbb{R}^n)}\right)\right)^{\frac{1}{r(1+\delta)}}\\
&\le \sup_{\delta>0}\sup_{k_o\in\mathbb{Z}}2^{-k_0\lambda}\left(\delta^{\theta}\sum_{k\in\mathbb{Z}}2^{k\alpha(\cdot)r(1+\delta)}\left(\sum_{l=-\infty}^{k-2}\|\chi_k I^{\gamma}(f\chi_l)\|_{L^{q_2(\cdot)}(\mathbb{R}^n)}\right)^{r(1+\delta)}\right)^{\frac{1}{r(1+\delta)}}\\
&+ \sup_{\delta>0}\sup_{k_o\in\mathbb{Z}}2^{-k_0\lambda}\left(\delta^{\theta}\sum_{k\in\mathbb{Z}}2^{k\alpha(\cdot)r(1+\delta)}\left(\sum_{l=k-1}^{k+1}\|\chi_k I^{\gamma}(f\chi_l)\|_{L^{q_2(\cdot)}(\mathbb{R}^n)}\right)^{r(1+\delta)}\right)^{\frac{1}{r(1+\delta)}}\\
&+ \sup_{\delta>0}\sup_{k_o\in\mathbb{Z}}2^{-k_0\lambda}\left(\delta^{\theta}\sum_{k\in\mathbb{Z}}2^{k\alpha(\cdot)r(1+\delta)}\left(\sum_{l=k+2}^{\infty}\|\chi_k I^{\gamma}(f\chi_l)\|_{L^{q_2(\cdot)}(\mathbb{R}^n)}\right)^{r(1+\delta)}\right)^{\frac{1}{r(1+\delta)}}\\
&= E_1+E_2+E_3.
\end{aligned}$$

As operator I^{γ} is bounded on the Lebesgue space $L^{q_2(\cdot)}(\mathbb{R}^n)$ so for E_2,

$$\begin{aligned}
E_2 \leq & \sup_{\delta>0}\sup_{k_o\in\mathbb{Z}} 2^{-k_0\lambda}\left(\delta^{\theta}\sum_{k\in\mathbb{Z}} 2^{k\alpha(\cdot)r(1+\delta)}\left(\sum_{l=k-1}^{k+1}\|I^{\gamma}(f\chi_l)\|_{L^{q_2(\cdot)}(\mathbb{R}^n)}\right)^{r(1+\delta)}\right)^{\frac{1}{r(1+\delta)}}\\
\leq & \sup_{\delta>0}\sup_{k_o\in\mathbb{Z}} 2^{-k_0\lambda}\left(\delta^{\theta}\sum_{k=-\infty}^{-1} 2^{k\alpha(\cdot)r(1+\delta)}\left(\sum_{l=k-1}^{k+1}\|I^{\gamma}(f\chi_l)\|_{L^{q_2(\cdot)}(\mathbb{R}^n)}\right)^{r(1+\delta)}\right)^{\frac{1}{r(1+\delta)}}\\
& + \sup_{\delta>0}\sup_{k_o\in\mathbb{Z}} 2^{-k_0\lambda}\left(\delta^{\theta}\sum_{k=0}^{\infty} 2^{k\alpha(\cdot)r(1+\delta)}\left(\sum_{l=k-1}^{k+1}\|I^{\gamma}(f\chi_l)\|_{L^{q_2(\cdot)}(\mathbb{R}^n)}\right)^{r(1+\delta)}\right)^{\frac{1}{r(1+\delta)}}\\
& = E_{21} + E_{22}.
\end{aligned}$$

By using the fact $2^{k\alpha(z_1)} = 2^{k\alpha(0)}$, $k < 0$, $z_1 \in R_k$ implies that

$$\|2^{k\alpha(\cdot)}f\chi_k\|_{L^{q_1(\cdot)}(\mathbb{R}^n)} = 2^{k\alpha(0)}\|f\chi_k\|_{L^{q_1(\cdot)}(\mathbb{R}^n)},$$

$$\begin{aligned}
E_{21} \leq & \sup_{\delta>0}\sup_{k_o\in\mathbb{Z}} 2^{-k_0\lambda}\left(\delta^{\theta}\sum_{k=-\infty}^{-1} 2^{k\alpha(\cdot)r(1+\delta)}\left(\sum_{l=k-1}^{k+1}\|I^{\gamma}(f\chi_l)\|_{L^{q_2(\cdot)}(\mathbb{R}^n)}\right)^{r(1+\delta)}\right)^{\frac{1}{r(1+\delta)}}\\
\leq & C\sup_{\delta>0}\sup_{k_o\in\mathbb{Z}} 2^{-k_0\lambda}\left(\delta^{\theta}\sum_{k=-\infty}^{-1} 2^{k\alpha(0)r(1+\delta)}\left(\sum_{l=k-1}^{k+1}\|f\chi_l\|_{L^{q_1(\cdot)}(\mathbb{R}^n)}\right)^{r(1+\delta)}\right)^{\frac{1}{r(1+\delta)}}\\
\leq & C\sup_{\delta>0}\sup_{k_o\in\mathbb{Z}} 2^{-k_0\lambda}\left(\delta^{\theta}\sum_{k=-\infty}^{-1} 2^{k\alpha(0)r(1+\delta)}\|f\chi_k\|^{r(1+\delta)}_{L^{q_1(\cdot)}(\mathbb{R}^n)}\right)^{\frac{1}{r(1+\delta)}}\\
\leq & C\sup_{\delta>0}\sup_{k_o\in\mathbb{Z}} 2^{-k_0\lambda}\left(\delta^{\theta}\sum_{k\in\mathbb{Z}} 2^{k\alpha(\cdot)r(1+\delta)}\|f\chi_k\|^{r(1+\delta)}_{L^{q_1(\cdot)}(\mathbb{R}^n)}\right)^{\frac{1}{r(1+\delta)}}\\
= & C\|f\|_{M\dot{K}^{\alpha(\cdot),r),\theta}_{q_1(\cdot)}(\mathbb{R}^n)}.
\end{aligned}$$

For E_{22}, we use the fact $2^{k\alpha(z_1)} = 2^{k\alpha_\infty}$, $k \geq 0$, $z_1 \in R_k$, we obtain

$$\begin{aligned}
E_{22} \leq & \sup_{\delta>0}\sup_{k_o\in\mathbb{Z}} 2^{-k_0\lambda}\left(\delta^{\theta}\sum_{k=0}^{\infty} 2^{k\alpha(\cdot)r(1+\delta)}\left(\sum_{l=k-1}^{k+1}\|I^{\gamma}(f\chi_l)\|_{L^{q_2(\cdot)}(\mathbb{R}^n)}\right)^{r(1+\delta)}\right)^{\frac{1}{r(1+\delta)}}\\
\leq & C\sup_{\delta>0}\sup_{k_o\in\mathbb{Z}} 2^{-k_0\lambda}\left(\delta^{\theta}\sum_{k=0}^{\infty} 2^{k\alpha_\infty r(1+\delta)}\left(\sum_{l=k-1}^{k+1}\|f\chi_l\|_{L^{q_1(\cdot)}(\mathbb{R}^n)}\right)^{r(1+\delta)}\right)^{\frac{1}{r(1+\delta)}}\\
\leq & C\sup_{\delta>0}\sup_{k_o\in\mathbb{Z}} 2^{-k_0\lambda}\left(\delta^{\theta}\sum_{k=0}^{\infty} 2^{k\alpha_\infty r(1+\delta)}\|f\chi_k\|^{r(1+\delta)}_{L^{q_1(\cdot)}(\mathbb{R}^n)}\right)^{\frac{1}{r(1+\delta)}}\\
\leq & C\sup_{\delta>0}\sup_{k_o\in\mathbb{Z}} 2^{-k_0\lambda}\left(\delta^{\theta}\sum_{k\in\mathbb{Z}} 2^{k\alpha(\cdot)r(1+\delta)}\|f\chi_k\|^{r(1+\delta)}_{L^{q_1(\cdot)}(\mathbb{R}^n)}\right)^{\frac{1}{r(1+\delta)}}\\
= & C\|f\|_{M\dot{K}^{\alpha(\cdot),r),\theta}_{q_1(\cdot)}(\mathbb{R}^n)}.
\end{aligned}$$

For each $k \in \mathbb{Z}$ and $l \le k-2$ and a.e. $z_1 \in R_k, z_2 \in R_l$, we have

$$E_1 \le \sup_{\delta>0} \sup_{k_0\in\mathbb{Z}} 2^{-k_0\lambda} \left(\delta^\theta \sum_{k\in\mathbb{Z}} 2^{k\alpha(\cdot)r(1+\delta)} \left(\sum_{l=-\infty}^{k-2} \|\chi_k I^\gamma(f\chi_l)\|_{L^{q_2(\cdot)}(\mathbb{R}^n)} \right)^{r(1+\delta)} \right)^{\frac{1}{r(1+\delta)}}$$

$$\begin{aligned} |I^\gamma(f\chi_l)(z_1)| \le & \int_{R_l} |z_1 - z_2|^{\gamma-n} |f(z_2)| dz_2 \\ \le & C 2^{k(\gamma-n)} \int_{R_l} |f(z_2)| dz_2 \\ \le & C 2^{k(\gamma-n)} \|f\chi_l\|_{L^{q_1(\cdot)}(\mathbb{R}^n)} \|\chi_l\|_{L^{q_1'(\cdot)}(\mathbb{R}^n)}, \end{aligned}$$

splitting E_1 by using Minkowski's inequality we have

$$\begin{aligned} E_1 \le & \sup_{\delta>0} \sup_{k_0\in\mathbb{Z}} 2^{-k_0\lambda} \left(\delta^\theta \sum_{k=-\infty}^{-1} 2^{k\alpha(\cdot)r(1+\delta)} \left(\sum_{l=-\infty}^{k-2} \|\chi_k I^\gamma(f\chi_l)\|_{L^{q_2(\cdot)}(\mathbb{R}^n)} \right)^{r(1+\delta)} \right)^{\frac{1}{r(1+\delta)}} \\ & + \sup_{\delta>0} \sup_{k_0\in\mathbb{Z}} 2^{-k_0\lambda} \left(\delta^\theta \sum_{k=0}^{\infty} 2^{k\alpha(\cdot)r(1+\delta)} \left(\sum_{l=-\infty}^{k-2} \|\chi_k I^\gamma(f\chi_l)\|_{L^{q_2(\cdot)}(\mathbb{R}^n)} \right)^{r(1+\delta)} \right)^{\frac{1}{r(1+\delta)}} \\ = & E_{11} + E_{12}. \end{aligned}$$

By using Lemma 1, we have

$$2^{k(\gamma-n)} \|\chi_k\|_{L^{q_2(\cdot)}(\mathbb{R}^n)} \|\chi_l\|_{L^{q_1'(\cdot)}(\mathbb{R}^n)} \le C 2^{k(\gamma-n)} 2^{\frac{kn}{q_2(0)}} 2^{\frac{ln}{q_1'(0)}} \le C 2^{\frac{(l-k)n}{q_1'(0)}}, \tag{14}$$

applying above estimates to E_{11}, we can obtain

$$\begin{aligned} E_{11} \le & \sup_{\delta>0} \sup_{k_0\in\mathbb{Z}} 2^{-k_0\lambda} \left(\delta^\theta \sum_{k=-\infty}^{-1} 2^{k\alpha(\cdot)r(1+\delta)} \left(\sum_{l=-\infty}^{k-2} \|\chi_k I^\gamma(f\chi_l)\|_{L^{q_2(\cdot)}(\mathbb{R}^n)} \right)^{r(1+\delta)} \right)^{\frac{1}{r(1+\delta)}} \\ & \le C \sup_{\delta>0} \sup_{k_0\in\mathbb{Z}} 2^{-k_0\lambda} \Bigg[\delta^\theta \sum_{k=-\infty}^{-1} 2^{k\alpha(\cdot)r(1+\delta)} \Bigg(\sum_{l=-\infty}^{k-2} \|\chi_k\|_{L^{q_2(\cdot)}(\mathbb{R}^n)} 2^{k(\gamma-n)} \\ & \|f\chi_l\|_{L^{q_1(\cdot)}(\mathbb{R}^n)} \|\chi_l\|_{L^{q_1'(\cdot)}(\mathbb{R}^n)} \Bigg)^{r(1+\delta)} \Bigg]^{\frac{1}{r(1+\delta)}}, \end{aligned}$$

let $b = \frac{n}{q_1'(0)} - \alpha(0)$,

$$E_{11} \le C \sup_{\delta>0} \sup_{k_0\in\mathbb{Z}} 2^{-k_0\lambda} \left[\delta^\theta \sum_{k=-\infty}^{-1} \left(\sum_{l=-\infty}^{k-2} 2^{\alpha(0)l} \|f\chi_l\|_{L^{q_1(\cdot)}(\mathbb{R}^n)} 2^{b(l-k)} \right)^{r(1+\delta)} \right]^{\frac{1}{r(1+\delta)}}, \tag{15}$$

by using Hölder's inequality, Fubini's theorem and the inequality $2^{-r(1+\delta)} < 2^{-r}$, we obtain

$$
\begin{aligned}
E_{11} \leq & C \sup_{\delta>0} \sup_{k_o\in\mathbb{Z}} 2^{-k_0\lambda}\Bigg[\delta^\theta \sum_{k=-\infty}^{-1}\Bigg(\sum_{l=-\infty}^{k-2} 2^{\alpha(0)r(1+\delta)l}\|f\chi_l\|^{r(1+\delta)}_{L^{q_1(\cdot)}(\mathbb{R}^n)} 2^{br(1+\delta)(l-k)/2} \\
& \times \sum_{l=-\infty}^{k-2} 2^{br(1+\delta)'(l-k)/2}\Bigg)^{\frac{r(1+\delta)}{r(1+\delta)'}}\Bigg]^{\frac{1}{r(1+\delta)}} \\
= & C \sup_{\delta>0} \sup_{k_o\in\mathbb{Z}} 2^{-k_0\lambda}\Bigg(\delta^\theta \sum_{k=-\infty}^{-1}\sum_{l=-\infty}^{k-2} 2^{\alpha(0)r(1+\delta)l}\|f\chi_l\|^{r(1+\delta)}_{L^{q_1(\cdot)}(\mathbb{R}^n)} 2^{br(1+\delta)(l-k)/2}\Bigg)^{\frac{1}{r(1+\delta)}} \\
= & C \sup_{\delta>0} \sup_{k_o\in\mathbb{Z}} 2^{-k_0\lambda}\Bigg(\delta^\theta \sum_{l=-\infty}^{-1} 2^{\alpha(0)r(1+\delta)l}\|f\chi_l\|^{r(1+\delta)}_{L^{q_1(\cdot)}(\mathbb{R}^n)} \sum_{k=l+2}^{-1} 2^{br(1+\delta)(l-k)/2}\Bigg)^{\frac{1}{r(1+\delta)}} \\
< & C \sup_{\delta>0} \sup_{k_o\in\mathbb{Z}} 2^{-k_0\lambda}\Bigg(\delta^\theta \sum_{l=-\infty}^{-1} 2^{\alpha(0)r(1+\delta)l}\|f\chi_l\|^{r(1+\delta)}_{L^{q_1(\cdot)}(\mathbb{R}^n)} \sum_{k=l+2}^{-1} 2^{bp(l-k)/2}\Bigg)^{\frac{1}{r(1+\delta)}} \\
\leq & C \sup_{\delta>0} \sup_{k_o\in\mathbb{Z}} 2^{-k_0\lambda}\Bigg(\delta^\theta \sum_{l=-\infty}^{-1} 2^{\alpha(0)r(1+\delta)l}\|f\chi_l\|^{r(1+\delta)}_{L^{q_1(\cdot)}(\mathbb{R}^n)}\Bigg)^{\frac{1}{r(1+\delta)}} \\
= & C \sup_{\delta>0} \sup_{k_o\in\mathbb{Z}} 2^{-k_0\lambda}\Bigg(\delta^\theta \sum_{l\in\mathbb{Z}} 2^{\alpha(\cdot)r(1+\delta)l}\|f\chi_l\|^{r(1+\delta)}_{L^{q_1(\cdot)}(\mathbb{R}^n)}\Bigg)^{\frac{1}{r(1+\delta)}} \\
\leq & C\|f\|_{M\dot{K}^{\alpha,r),\theta}_{q_1(\cdot)}(\mathbb{R}^n)}.
\end{aligned}
$$

Now, for E_{12} using Minkowski's inequality, we have

$$
\begin{aligned}
E_{12} \leq & \sup_{\delta>0} \sup_{k_o\in\mathbb{Z}} 2^{-k_0\lambda}\left(\delta^\theta \sum_{k=0}^{\infty} 2^{k\alpha(\cdot)r(1+\delta)}\left(\sum_{l=-\infty}^{-1}\|\chi_k I^\gamma(f\chi_l)\|_{L^{q_2(\cdot)}(\mathbb{R}^n)}\right)^{r(1+\delta)}\right)^{\frac{1}{r(1+\delta)}} \\
& + \sup_{\delta>0} \sup_{k_o\in\mathbb{Z}} 2^{-k_0\lambda}\left(\delta^\theta \sum_{k=0}^{\infty} 2^{k\alpha(\cdot)r(1+\delta)}\left(\sum_{l=0}^{k-2}\|\chi_k I^\gamma(f\chi_l)\|_{L^{q_2(\cdot)}(\mathbb{R}^n)}\right)^{r(1+\delta)}\right)^{\frac{1}{r(1+\delta)}} \\
= & A_1 + A_2.
\end{aligned}
$$

The estimate for A_2 can be obtained by similar way to E_{11} by replacing $q_1'(0)$ with q_{1_∞}' and using the fact $\frac{n}{q_{1_\infty}'} - \alpha_\infty > 0$. For A_1 using Lemma 1, we obtain

$$
\begin{aligned}
2^{k(\gamma-n)}\|\chi_k\|_{L^{q_2(\cdot)}(\mathbb{R}^n)}\|\chi_l\|_{L^{q_1'(\cdot)}(\mathbb{R}^n)} & \leq C2^{k(\gamma-n)}2^{\frac{kn}{q_{2\infty}}}2^{\frac{ln}{q_1'(0)}} \\
& \leq C2^{\frac{-kn}{q_{1\infty}'}}2^{\frac{ln}{q_1'(0)}},
\end{aligned}
$$

as $\alpha_\infty - \frac{n}{q'_{1_\infty}} < 0$, we have

$$A_1 \leq C \sup_{\delta>0} \sup_{k_o\in\mathbb{Z}} 2^{-k_0\lambda}\left(\delta^\theta \sum_{k=0}^{\infty} 2^{k\alpha_\infty r(1+\delta)}\left(\sum_{l=-\infty}^{-1} \|\chi_k I^\gamma(f\chi_l)\|_{L^{q_2(\cdot)}(\mathbb{R}^n)}\right)^{r(1+\delta)}\right)^{\frac{1}{r(1+\delta)}}$$
$$\leq C \sup_{\epsilon>0}\left[\delta^\theta \sum_{k=0}^{\infty} 2^{k\alpha_\infty r(1+\delta)} \times \left(\sum_{l=-\infty}^{-1} 2^{\frac{-kn}{q_{1\infty}}} 2^{\frac{ln}{q_1'(0)}} \|f\chi_l\|_{L^{q_1(\cdot)}(\mathbb{R}^n)}\right)^{r(1+\delta)}\right]^{\frac{1}{r(1+\delta)}}$$
$$\leq C \sup_{\delta>0} \sup_{k_o\in\mathbb{Z}} 2^{-k_0\lambda}\left[\delta^\theta \sum_{k=0}^{\infty} 2^{(k\alpha - kn/q'_{1_\infty})r(1+\delta)} \times \left(\sum_{l=-\infty}^{-1} 2^{\frac{ln}{q_1'(0)}} \|f\chi_l\|_{L^{q_1(\cdot)}(\mathbb{R}^n)}\right)^{r(1+\delta)}\right]^{\frac{1}{r(1+\delta)}}$$
$$\leq C \sup_{\delta>0} \sup_{k_o\in\mathbb{Z}} 2^{-k_0\lambda}\left(\delta^\theta \left(\sum_{l=-\infty}^{-1} 2^{\frac{ln}{q'(0)}} \|f\chi_l\|_{L^{q_1(\cdot)}(\mathbb{R}^n)}\right)^{r(1+\delta)}\right)^{\frac{1}{r(1+\delta)}}$$
$$\leq C \sup_{\delta>0} \sup_{k_o\in\mathbb{Z}} 2^{-k_0\lambda}\left(\delta^\theta \left(\sum_{l=-\infty}^{-1} 2^{\frac{ln}{q_1'(0)}-\alpha(0)l} \|f\chi_l\|_{L^{q_1(\cdot)}(\mathbb{R}^n)} 2^{\alpha(0)l}\right)^{r(1+\delta)}\right)^{\frac{1}{r(1+\delta)}}.$$

Now, by using Hölder's inequality and the fact $\frac{n}{q_1'(0)} - \alpha(0) > 0$, we have

$$A_1 \leq \sup_{\delta>0} \sup_{k_o\in\mathbb{Z}} 2^{-k_0\lambda}\left(\delta^\theta \left(\sum_{l=-\infty}^{-1} 2^{\frac{ln}{q_1'(0)}-\alpha(0)l} \|f\chi_l\|_{L^{q_1(\cdot)}(\mathbb{R}^n)} 2^{\alpha(0)l}\right)^{r(1+\delta)}\right)^{\frac{1}{r(1+\delta)}}$$
$$\leq C \sup_{\delta>0} \sup_{k_o\in\mathbb{Z}} 2^{-k_0\lambda}\left[\delta^\theta \sum_{l=-\infty}^{-1} 2^{\alpha(0)lr(1+\delta)} \|f\chi_l\|^{r(1+\delta)}_{L^{q_1(\cdot)}(\mathbb{R}^n)}\right.$$
$$\left.\times \left(\sum_{l=-\infty}^{-1} 2^{(\frac{ln}{q_1'(0)}-\alpha(0)l)r(1+\delta)'}\right)^{\frac{r(1+\delta)}{r(1+\delta)'}}\right]^{\frac{1}{r(1+\delta)}}$$
$$\leq C \sup_{\delta>0} \sup_{k_o\in\mathbb{Z}} 2^{-k_0\lambda}\left(\delta^\theta \left(\sum_{l\in\mathbb{Z}} 2^{\alpha(\cdot)lr(1+\delta)} \|f\chi_l\|^{r(1+\delta)}_{L^{q_1(\cdot)}(\mathbb{R}^n)}\right)\right)^{\frac{1}{r(1+\delta)}}$$
$$\leq C\|f\|_{M\dot{K}^{\alpha(\cdot),r),\theta}_{q_1(\cdot)}(\mathbb{R}^n)}.$$

Now, we estimate E_3, for every $k \in \mathbb{Z}$ and $l \geq k+2$ and a.e. $z_1 \in R_k$; the size condition and Hölder's inequality imply

$$|I^\gamma(f\chi_l)(z-1)| \leq \int_{R_l} |z_1 - z_2|^{-n} |f(z_2)| dz_2$$
$$\leq C 2^{l(\gamma-n)} \int_{R_l} |f(z_2)| dz_2$$
$$\leq C 2^{l(\gamma-n)} \|f\chi_l\|_{L^{q_1(\cdot)}(\mathbb{R}^n)} \|\chi_l\|_{L^{q_1'(\cdot)}(\mathbb{R}^n)},$$

splitting E_3 by applying the Minkowski's inequality we have

$$
\begin{aligned}
E_3 \leq & C \sup_{\delta>0} \sup_{k_o\in\mathbb{Z}} 2^{-k_0\lambda} \left(\delta^\theta \sum_{k\in\mathbb{Z}} 2^{k\alpha(\cdot)r(1+\delta)} \left(\sum_{l=k+2}^{\infty} \|\chi_k I^\gamma(f\chi_l)\|_{L^{q_2(\cdot)}(\mathbb{R}^n)} \right)^{r(1+\delta)} \right)^{\frac{1}{r(1+\delta)}} \\
\leq & C \sup_{\delta>0} \sup_{k_o\in\mathbb{Z}} 2^{-k_0\lambda} \left(\delta^\theta \sum_{k=-\infty}^{-1} 2^{k\alpha(\cdot)r(1+\delta)} \left(\sum_{l=k+2}^{\infty} \|\chi_k I^\gamma(f\chi_l)\|_{L^{q_2(\cdot)}(\mathbb{R}^n)} \right)^{r(1+\delta)} \right)^{\frac{1}{r(1+\delta)}} \\
& + C \sup_{\delta>0} \sup_{k_o\in\mathbb{Z}} 2^{-k_0\lambda} \left(\delta^\theta \sum_{k=0}^{\infty} 2^{k\alpha(\cdot)r(1+\delta)} \left(\sum_{l=k+2}^{\infty} \|\chi_k I^\gamma(f\chi_l)\|_{L^{q_2(\cdot)}(\mathbb{R}^n)} \right)^{r(1+\delta)} \right)^{\frac{1}{r(1+\delta)}} \\
= & E_{31} + E_{32}.
\end{aligned}
$$

For E_{32} Lemma 1 yields

$$
2^{l(\gamma-n)} \|\chi_k\|_{L^{q_2(\cdot)}(\mathbb{R}^n)} \|\chi_l\|_{L^{q_1'(\cdot)}(\mathbb{R}^n)} \leq C 2^{l(\gamma-n)} 2^{\frac{kn}{q_{2\infty}}} 2^{\frac{ln}{q_{1\infty}'}} \leq C 2^{\frac{(k-l)n}{q_{1\infty}}}, \tag{16}
$$

we get

$$
\begin{aligned}
E_{32} \leq & \sup_{\delta>0} \sup_{k_o\in\mathbb{Z}} 2^{-k_0\lambda} \left(\delta^\theta \sum_{k=0}^{\infty} 2^{k\alpha(\cdot)r(1+\delta)} \left(\sum_{l=k+2}^{\infty} \|\chi_k I^\gamma(f\chi_l)\|_{L^{q_2(\cdot)}(\mathbb{R}^n)} \right)^{r(1+\delta)} \right)^{\frac{1}{r(1+\delta)}} \\
\leq & C \sup_{\delta>0} \sup_{k_o\in\mathbb{Z}} 2^{-k_0\lambda} \Bigg[\delta^\theta \sum_{k=0}^{\infty} 2^{k\alpha(\cdot)r(1+\delta)} \Bigg(\sum_{l=k+2}^{\infty} \|\chi_k\|_{L^{q_2(\cdot)}(\mathbb{R}^n)} 2^{l(\gamma-n)} \cdot \\
& \qquad \|f\chi_l\|_{L^{q_1(\cdot)}(\mathbb{R}^n)} \|\chi_l\|_{L^{q_1'(\cdot)}(\mathbb{R}^n)} \Bigg)^{r(1+\delta)} \Bigg]^{\frac{1}{r(1+\delta)}} \\
\leq & C \sup_{\delta>0} \sup_{k_o\in\mathbb{Z}} 2^{-k_0\lambda} \left(\delta^\theta \sum_{k=0}^{\infty} \left(\sum_{l=k+2}^{\infty} 2^{(\alpha_\infty)l} \|f\chi_l\|_{L^{q_1(\cdot)}(\mathbb{R}^n)} 2^{d(k-l)} \right)^{r(1+\delta)} \right)^{\frac{1}{r(1+\delta)}},
\end{aligned}
$$

where $d = \frac{n}{q_{1\infty}} + \alpha_\infty > 0$. Then, we use Hölder's theorem for series and $2^{-r(1+\delta)} < 2^{-r}$ to obtain

$$
\begin{aligned}
E_{32} \leq & C \sup_{\delta>0} \sup_{k_o\in\mathbb{Z}} 2^{-k_0\lambda} \Bigg[\delta^\theta \sum_{k=0}^{\infty} \left(\sum_{l=k+2}^{\infty} 2^{l(\alpha_\infty)r(1+\delta)} \|f\chi_l\|^{r(1+\delta)}_{L^{q_1(\cdot)}(\mathbb{R}^n)} 2^{dr(1+\delta)(k-l)/2} \right) \\
& \times \left(\sum_{l=k+2}^{\infty} 2^{dr(1+\delta)'(k-l)/2} \right)^{\frac{r(1+\delta)}{r(1+\delta)'}} \Bigg]^{\frac{1}{r(1+\delta)}} \\
\leq & C \sup_{\delta>0} \sup_{k_o\in\mathbb{Z}} 2^{-k_0\lambda} \left(\delta^\theta \sum_{k=0}^{\infty} \sum_{l=k+2}^{\infty} 2^{l(\alpha_\infty)r(1+\delta)} \|f\chi_l\|^{r(1+\delta)}_{L^{q_1(\cdot)}(\mathbb{R}^n)} 2^{dr(1+\delta)(k-l)/2} \right)^{\frac{1}{r(1+\delta)}} \\
\leq & C \sup_{\delta>0} \sup_{k_o\in\mathbb{Z}} 2^{-k_0\lambda} \left(\delta^\theta \sum_{l=0}^{\infty} 2^{l(\alpha_\infty)r(1+\delta)} \|f\chi_l\|^{r(1+\delta)}_{L^{q_1(\cdot)}(\mathbb{R}^n)} \sum_{k=0}^{l-2} 2^{dr(1+\delta)(k-l)/2} \right)^{\frac{1}{r(1+\delta)}} \\
< & C \sup_{\delta>0} \sup_{k_o\in\mathbb{Z}} 2^{-k_0\lambda} \left(\delta^\theta \sum_{l\in\mathbb{Z}} 2^{l(\alpha_\infty)r(1+\delta)} \|f\chi_l\|^{r(1+\delta)}_{L^{q_1(\cdot)}(\mathbb{R}^n)} \sum_{k=-\infty}^{l-2} 2^{dp(k-l)/2} \right)^{\frac{1}{r(1+\delta)}} \\
\leq & C \sup_{\delta>0} \sup_{k_o\in\mathbb{Z}} 2^{-k_0\lambda} \left(\delta^\theta \sum_{l\in\mathbb{Z}} 2^{\alpha(\cdot)r(1+\delta)l} \|f\chi_l\|^{r(1+\delta)}_{L^{q_1(\cdot)}(\mathbb{R}^n)} \right)^{\frac{1}{r(1+\delta)}} \\
\leq & C\|f\|_{M\dot{K}^{\alpha(\cdot),r),\theta}_{\lambda,q_1(\cdot)}(\mathbb{R}^n)}.
\end{aligned}
$$

Now, for E_{31} using Monkowski's inequality, we have

$$E_{31} \leq \sup_{\delta>0} \sup_{k_o\in\mathbb{Z}} 2^{-k_0\lambda} \left(\delta^{\theta} \sum_{k=-\infty}^{-1} 2^{k\alpha(\cdot)r(1+\delta)} \left(\sum_{l=k+2}^{-1} \|\chi_k I^{\gamma}(f\chi_l)\|_{L^{q_2(\cdot)}(\mathbb{R}^n)} \right)^{r(1+\delta)} \right)^{\frac{1}{r(1+\delta)}}$$
$$+ \sup_{\delta>0} \sup_{k_o\in\mathbb{Z}} 2^{-k_0\lambda} \left(\delta^{\theta} \sum_{k=-\infty}^{-1} 2^{k\alpha(\cdot)r(1+\delta)} \left(\sum_{l=0}^{\infty} \|\chi_k I^{\gamma}(f\chi_l)\|_{L^{q_2(\cdot)}(\mathbb{R}^n)} \right)^{r(1+\delta)} \right)^{\frac{1}{r(1+\delta)}}$$
$$= B_1 + B_2.$$

The estimate for B_1 can be obtained similar to E_{32} by replacing q_{1_∞} with $q_1(0)$ and applying the fact that $\frac{n}{q_1(0)} + \alpha(0) > 0$. For B_2 using Lemma 1, we obtain

$$2^{l(\gamma-n)} \|\chi_k\|_{L^{q_2(\cdot)}(\mathbb{R}^n)} \|\chi_l\|_{L^{q'(\cdot)}(\mathbb{R}^n)} \leq C 2^{l(\gamma-n)} 2^{\frac{kn}{q_2(0)}} 2^{\frac{ln}{q'_{1_\infty}}} \leq C 2^{\frac{kn}{q_1(0)}} 2^{\frac{l(-n)}{q_{1_\infty}}} \tag{17}$$

$$B_2 \leq C \sup_{\delta>0} \sup_{k_o\in\mathbb{Z}} 2^{-k_0\lambda} \left(\delta^{\theta} \sum_{k=\infty}^{-1} 2^{k\alpha(0)r(1+\delta)} \left(\sum_{l=0}^{\infty} \|\chi_k I^{\gamma}(f\chi_l)\|_{L^{q_2(\cdot)}(\mathbb{R}^n)} \right)^{r(1+\delta)} \right)^{\frac{1}{r(1+\delta)}}$$
$$\leq C \sup_{\delta>0} \sup_{k_o\in\mathbb{Z}} 2^{-k_0\lambda} \left(\delta^{\theta} \sum_{k=\infty}^{-1} 2^{k\alpha(0)r(1+\delta)} \times \left(\sum_{l=0}^{\infty} 2^{l(\gamma-n)} 2^{\frac{kn}{q_1(0)}} 2^{\frac{ln}{q_{1_\infty}}} \|f\chi_l\|_{L^{q_1(\cdot)}(\mathbb{R}^n)} \right)^{r(1+\delta)} \right)^{\frac{1}{r(1+\delta)}}$$
$$\leq C \sup_{\delta>0} \sup_{k_o\in\mathbb{Z}} 2^{-k_0\lambda} \left(\delta^{\theta} \sum_{k=\infty}^{-1} 2^{k\alpha(0)r(1+\delta)} \times \left(\sum_{l=0}^{\infty} 2^{\frac{kn}{q_1(0)}} 2^{\gamma l} 2^{\frac{-ln}{q_{1_\infty}}} \|f\chi_l\|_{L^{q_1(\cdot)}(\mathbb{R}^n)} \right)^{r(1+\delta)} \right)^{\frac{1}{r(1+\delta)}}$$
$$\leq C \sup_{\delta>0} \sup_{k_o\in\mathbb{Z}} 2^{-k_0\lambda} \left(\delta^{\theta} \sum_{k=\infty}^{-1} 2^{k(\alpha(0)+n)/q_1(0)r(1+\delta)} \times \left(\sum_{l=0}^{\infty} 2^{\gamma l} 2^{\frac{-ln}{q_{1_\infty}}} \|f\chi_l\|_{L^{q_1(\cdot)}(\mathbb{R}^n)} \right)^{r(1+\delta)} \right)^{\frac{1}{r(1+\delta)}}$$
$$\leq C \sup_{\delta>0} \sup_{k_o\in\mathbb{Z}} 2^{-k_0\lambda} \left(\delta^{\theta} \left(\sum_{l=0}^{\infty} 2^{\gamma l} 2^{\frac{-ln}{q_{1_\infty}}} \|f\chi_l\|_{L^{q_1(\cdot)}(\mathbb{R}^n)} \right)^{r(1+\delta)} \right)^{\frac{1}{r(1+\delta)}}$$
$$\leq C \sup_{\delta>0} \sup_{k_o\in\mathbb{Z}} 2^{-k_0\lambda} \left(\delta^{\theta} \left(\sum_{l=0}^{\infty} 2^{l(\alpha_\infty)} \|f\chi_l\|_{L^{q_1(\cdot)}(\mathbb{R}^n)} 2^{l(nq_{1_\infty}+\alpha_\infty)} \right)^{r(1+\delta)} \right)^{\frac{1}{r(1+\delta)}}.$$

Now, by using Hölder's inequality and the fact that $\frac{n}{q_\infty} + \alpha_\infty > 0$, we have

$$B_2 \leq \sup_{\delta>0} \sup_{k_o\in\mathbb{Z}} 2^{-k_0\lambda} \left(\delta^{\theta} \left(\sum_{l=0}^{\infty} 2^{2^{l(\alpha_\infty)}r(1+\delta)} \|f\chi_l\|^{r(1+\delta)}_{L^{q_1(\cdot)}(\mathbb{R}^n)} \right)^{r(1+\delta)} \right.$$
$$\left. \times \left(\sum_{l=0}^{\infty} 2^{l(nq_{1_\infty}+\alpha_\infty)r(1+\delta)} \right)^{\frac{r(1+\delta)}{r(1+\delta)'}} \right)^{\frac{1}{r(1+\delta)}}$$
$$\leq C \sup_{\delta>0} \sup_{k_o\in\mathbb{Z}} 2^{-k_0\lambda} \left(\delta^{\theta} \left(\sum_{l\in\mathbb{Z}} 2^{l(\alpha_\infty)r(1+\delta)} \|f\chi_l\|^{r(1+\delta)}_{L^{q_1(\cdot)}(\mathbb{R}^n)} \right) \right)^{\frac{1}{r(1+\delta)}}$$
$$\leq C \|f\|_{M\dot{K}^{\alpha(\cdot),r),\theta}_{\lambda,q_1(\cdot)}(\mathbb{R}^n)}$$

Combining the estimates for E_1, E_2 and E_3 yields

$$\|I^{\gamma} f\|_{M\dot{K}^{\alpha(\cdot),r),\theta}_{\lambda,q_2(\cdot)}(\mathbb{R}^n)} \leq C\|f\|_{M\dot{K}^{\alpha(\cdot),r),\theta}_{\lambda,q_1(\cdot)}(\mathbb{R}^n)}$$

□

5. Conclusions

We have defined a new type of space called variable exponents grand Herz–Morrey spaces, where we used discrete grand spaces, and we have proved the boundedness of the Riesz potential operator on these spaces.

Author Contributions: B.S.: methodology, writing—original draft; F.A.: writing—original draft, methodology; M.S.: conceptualization, supervision, writing—original draft; M.M.: conceptualization, writing–original draft; N.M.: conceptualization, supervision, writing—original draft. All authors read and approved the final manuscript.

Funding: This research received no external funding.

Institutional Review Board Statement: Not applicable.

Informed Consent Statement: Not applicable.

Data Availability Statement: Not applicable.

Acknowledgments: The authors F. Azmi and N. Mlaiki would like to thank Prince Sultan University for paying the publication fees for this work through TAS LAB.

Conflicts of Interest: The authors declare no conflict of interest.

References

1. Ruzicka, M. *Electroreological Fluids: Modeling and Mathematical Theory*; Lecture Notes in Math; Springer: Berlin/Heidelberg, Germany, 2000; Volume 1748.
2. Uribe, D.C.; Fiorenza, A. *Variable Lebesgue Space: Foundations and Harmonic Analysis*; Birkhauser: Basel, Switzerland, 2013.
3. Diening, L.; Harjulehto, P.; Hästö, P.; Ruzicka, M. *Lebesgue and Sobolev Spaces with Variable Exponents*; Springer: Berlin/Heidelberg, Germany, 2011.
4. Diening, L.; Hästö, P.; Nekvinda, A. Open Problems in Variable Exponent Lebesgue and Sobolev Spaces. *FSDONA04 Proceedings*. 2004; pp. 38–58. Available online: https://www.researchgate.net/profile/Lars-Diening/publication/228831740_Open_problems_in_variable_exponent_Lebesgue_and_Sobolev_spaces/links/0deec532c292a0b151000000/Open-problems-in-variable-exponent-Lebesgue-and-Sobolev-spaces.pdf (accessed on 1 September 2022).
5. Kokilashvili, V. On a progress in the theory of integral operators in weighted Banach function spaces. In *Function Spaces, Differential Operators and Nonlinear Analysis*; Mathematical Institute, Academy of Sciences of the Czech Republic: Praha, Czech Republic, 2004.
6. Kokilashvili, V.; Samko, S. Weighted boundedness of the maximal, singular and potential operators in variable exponent spaces, In *Analytic Methods of Analysis and Differential Equations*; Kilbas, A.A., Rogosin, S.V., Eds.; Cambridge Scientific Publishers: Cottenham, UK, 2008; pp. 139–164.
7. Samko, S. On a progress in the theory of Lebesgue spaces with variable exponent: maximal and singular operators. *Integral Transform. Spec. Funct.* **2005**, *16*, 461–482. [CrossRef]
8. Almeida, A.; Drihem, D. Maximal, potential and singular type operators on Herz spaces with variable exponents. *J. Math. Anal. Appl.* **2012**, *394*, 781–795. [CrossRef]
9. Izuki, M. Boundedness of sublinear operators on Herz spaces with variable exponent and application to wavelet characterization. *Anal. Math.* **2010**, *36*, 33–50. [CrossRef]
10. Izuki, M. Boundedness of vector-valued sublinear operators on Herz-Morrey spaces with variable exponent. *Math. Sci. Res. J.* **2009**, *13*, 243–253.
11. Samko, S. Variable exponent Herz spaces. *Mediterr. J. Math.* **2013**, *10*, 2007–2025. [CrossRef]
12. Meskhi, A.; Rafeiro, H.; Zaighum, M.A. On the boundedness of Marcinkiewicz integrals on continual variable exponent Herz spaces. *Georgian Math. J.* **2019**, *26*, 105–116. [CrossRef]
13. Rafeiro, H.; Samko, S. Riesz potential operator in continual variable eponents Herz spaces. *Math. Nachr.* **2015**, *288*, 465–475. [CrossRef]
14. Morrey, C.B. On the solutions of quasi-linear elliptic partial differential equations. *Trans. Am. Math. Soc.* **1938**, *43*, 126–166. [CrossRef]
15. Meskhi, A. Integral operators in grand Morrey spaces. *arXiv* **2010**, arXiv:1007.1186.
16. Izuki, M. Fractional integrals on Herz-Morrey spaces with variable exponent. *Hiroshima Math. J.* **2010**, *40*, 343–355. [CrossRef]
17. Nafis, H.; Rafeiro, H.; Zaighum, M.A. A note on the boundedness of sublinear operators on grand variable Herz spaces. *J. Inequal. Appl.* **2020**, *2020*, 1. [CrossRef]

18. Kováčik, O.; Rákosník, J. On spaces $L^{p(x)}$ and $W^{k,p(x)}$. *Czechoslov. Math. J.* **1991**, *41*, 592–618. [CrossRef]
19. Rafeiro, H.; Samko, S.; Umarkhadzhiev, S. Grand Lebesgue sequence spaces. *Georgian Math. J.* **2018**, *25*, 291–302. [CrossRef]
20. Samko, S.G. Convolution and potential type operators in $L^p(x)$, Integr. *Transf. Special Funct.* **1998**, *7*, 261–284. [CrossRef]
21. Capone, C.; Cruz-Uribe, D.; Fiorenza, A. The fractional maximal operator and fractional integrals on variable L^p spaces. *Rev. Mat. Iberoam.* **2007**, *23*, 743–770. [CrossRef]

axioms

MDPI

Article

Optimality Conditions and Dualities for Robust Efficient Solutions of Uncertain Set-Valued Optimization with Set-Order Relations

Yuwen Zhai [1], Qilin Wang [1,*] and Tian Tang [2]

[1] College of Mathematics and Statistics, Chongqing Jiaotong University, Chongqing 400074, China
[2] School of Mathematics and Statistics, Ningxia University, Yinchuan 750021, China
* Correspondence: 990020040623@cqjtu.edu.cn

Abstract: In this paper, we introduce a second-order strong subdifferential of set-valued maps, and discuss some properties, such as convexity, sum rule and so on. By the new subdifferential and its properties, we establish a necessary and sufficient optimality condition of set-based robust efficient solutions for the uncertain set-valued optimization problem. We also introduce a Wolfe type dual problem of the uncertain set-valued optimization problem. Finally, we establish the robust weak duality theorem and the robust strong duality theorem between the uncertain set-valued optimization problem and its robust dual problem. Several main results extend to the corresponding ones in the literature.

Keywords: uncertain set-valued optimization problems; set-based robust efficient solutions; second-order strong subdifferential; robust weak duality; robust strong duality

MSC: 49N15; 49N30; 54C60

Citation: Zhai, Y.; Wang, Q.; Tang, T. Optimality Conditions and Dualities for Robust Efficient Solutions of Uncertain Set-Valued Optimization with Set-Order Relations. *Axioms* **2022**, *11*, 648. https://doi.org/10.3390/axioms11110648

Academic Editors: Wei-Shih Du, Luigi Muglia and Adrian Petrusel

Received: 3 October 2022
Accepted: 15 November 2022
Published: 16 November 2022

Publisher's Note: MDPI stays neutral with regard to jurisdictional claims in published maps and institutional affiliations.

Copyright: © 2022 by the authors. Licensee MDPI, Basel, Switzerland. This article is an open access article distributed under the terms and conditions of the Creative Commons Attribution (CC BY) license (https://creativecommons.org/licenses/by/4.0/).

1. Introduction

Robust optimization is an important deterministic technique for studying optimization problems with data uncertainty, which is protected against data uncertainty and has grown significantly, see [1–6]. The optimization theory mainly includes multi-objective optimization and focuses on finding global optimal solutions or global efficient solutions. However, in real-world situations where the solutions are very susceptible to perturbations from the variables, we might not always be able to identify the global optimal solutions. To reduce the sensitivity to variable perturbations under these conditions, we are going to find the robust solutions.

The set-valued optimization problem:

$$(\text{SOP})\begin{cases}\min & H(z) = \{H_1(z), H_2(z), \ldots, H_k(z), \ldots, H_q(z)\}\\ \text{s.t.} & z \in M, B_j(z) \subseteq \mathbb{R}_-, j = 1, \ldots, l\end{cases}$$

has been widely studied by scholars, where M is a closed and convex subset of a real topological linear space X, $H_k : M \to 2^{\mathbb{R}}, k = 1, \ldots, q$ and $B_j : M \to 2^{\mathbb{R}}, j = 1, \ldots, l$ are given functions. Set-valued optimization is a thriving research field with numerous applications, for example in risk management [7,8], statistics [9], and others. Hamel and Heyde [7] defined set-valued (convex) measures of risk and their acceptance sets, and they gave dual representation theorems. Hamel et al. [8] defined set-valued risk measures on L_d^p with $0 \leqslant p \leqslant \infty$ for conical market models, and primal and gave dual representation results. Hamel and Kostner [9] discussed relationships to families of univariate quantile functions and to depth functions, and introduced a corresponding Value at Risk for multivariate random variables as well as stochastic orders by the set-valued approach. The vectorial criterion and the set criterion are the two different forms of solution criteria for set-valued optimization problems. Each different criterion has been studied independently. The challenge of minimizing a function, when the representation of a point is actually a set, is dealt by set-valued optimization. Since there is no way to minimize a set by a total order relation, it is necessary to give a definition for minimizing the set-valued objective function. The literature [10–12] introduced the concepts of preorders to compare sets. These preorders enable the formulation of set-valued optimization problems pertaining to the robustness of multi-objective optimization problems. Eichfelder and Jahn [10] presented different optimality notions such as minimal, weakly minimal, strongly minimal and properly minimal elements in a pre-ordered linear space and discussed the relations among these notions. Young [11] introduced the upper set less relation and lower set less relation and then used these set relations to analyze the upper and lower limits of real number sequences. Kuroiwa et al. [12] referred to the upper-type set relation and considered some duality theorems of a set optimization problem. Furthermore, six other forms of set relations [13] were also used by Kuroiwa et al. [12] to solve set optimization problems. By generalized differentiable assumptions, a separation scheme is used to construct some robust necessary conditions for uncertain optimization problems by Wei et al. [14]. By using the constraint qualification and the regularity condition, Wang et al. [15] developed weak and strong KKT robust necessary conditions for a nonconvex nonsmooth uncertain multiobjective optimization problem under the conditions of upper semi-continuity.

Rockafellar and Tyrrell [16] first introduced subdifferential concepts of convex functions. Recently, many authors have generalized subdifferentials of a vector-valued map to the one of a set-valued map [17,18]. There are two main approaches to define the subdifferential of set-valued mappings: one is to define the subdifferential by the derivative of the set-valued maps [17], the other is to define subdifferential by using algebraic forms [18–22]. Tanino [18] pioneered conjugate duality for vector optimization problems and introduced weak efficient points of a set to provide a weak subdifferential for set-valued mappings. A few characteristics of this weak subdifferential were covered by Sach [19]. By using an algebraic form, Yang [20] defined a weak subdifferential for set-valued mappings, demonstrated an extension theorem of the Hahn-Banach theorem, and talked about the existence of the weak subgradients. Chen and Jahn [21] introduced a kind of weak subdifferential, which is more powerful than the weak subdifferential [20]. By the weak subdifferential, they established a sufficient optimality condition for set-valued optimization problems. Borwein [22] introduced a strong subgradient, and proved a Lagrange multiplier theorem and a Sandwich theorem for convex maps. Peng et al. [23] proved the existence of the Borwein-strong subgradient and Yang-weak subgradient for set-valued maps and presented a new Lagrange multiplier theorem and a new Sandwich theorem for set-valued maps. Li and Guo [24] investigated the features of the weak subdifferential that was first proposed in [21], as well as the necessary and sufficient conditions for optimality in set-valued optimization problems. Hernández and Rodríguez-Marín [25] presented a new definition of the strong subgradient for set-valued mappings that were stronger than the weak subgradient of set-valued mappings introduced by Chen and Jahn [21]. Long et al. [26] obtained two existence theorems for weak subgradients of set-valued mappings described in [21]. They also deduced several features of the weak subdifferential for set-valued mappings. İnceŏglu [27] defined the second-order weak subdifferential and examined some properties of the concept.

Recently, the dual theorem in the face of data uncertainty has received a great deal of attention due to the reality of uncertainty in many real-world optimization problems. Suneja et al. [28] constructed strong/weak duality results between the primary problem and its Mond-Weir type dual problem using Clarke's generalized gradients and sufficient optimality criteria for the vector optimization problems. Chuong and Kim [29] established sufficient conditions for (weakly) efficient solutions of a nonsmooth semi-infinite multiobjective optimization problem and proposed types of Wolfe and Mond-Weir dual problems via the limiting subdifferential of locally Lipschitz functions. Moreover, they explored weak and strong duality. By means of multipliers and limiting subdifferentials of the related functions, Chuong [30] established necessary/sufficient optimality conditions for robust (weakly) Pareto solutions of a robust multiobjective optimization problem involving nonsmooth/nonconvex real-valued functions. In addition, they addressed a dual (robust) multiobjective problem to the primal one, and explored weak/strong duality. By virtue of subdifferential [31], Sun et al. [32] obtained optimality condition and established Wolfe type robust duality between the uncertain optimization problem and its uncertain dual problem under the conditions of continuity and cone-convex-concavity.

To the best of our knowledge, there are a few concepts of solutions for the uncertain set-valued optimization problem through set-order relation. Moreover, there is very little literature on the optimality condition and the dual theorem for set-based robust efficient solutions of uncertain set-valued optimization problems by terms of the second-order strong differential of a set-valued mapping. Lately, Som and Vetrivrl [33] introduced robustness for set-valued optimization to generalize some existing concepts of robustness for scalar and vector-valued optimization, and they followed the set approach for solutions to set-valued optimization problems.

To weaken the conditions of continuity and cone-convex-concavity [15,32], inspired by the subdifferential [20,22] and set-order relations [34], we introduce a new second-order strong subdifferential of set-valued mapping and define the set-based robust efficient solution for an uncertain set-valued optimization problem. Meanwhile, by using the second-order strong subdifferential of set-valued maps, we put forward Wolfe type dual problem and investigate the robust weak duality and robust strong duality of the set-based robust efficient solutions for uncertain set-valued optimization problems.

This paper is organized as follows. We quickly go through the concepts in Section 2 before introducing a brand-new second-order strong subdifferential of a set-valued map. We derive some crucial new subdifferential features in Section 3. We obtain a necessary and sufficient condition for the set-based robust efficient solutions to the uncertain set-valued optimization problem in Section 4 thanks to the concept of the second-order strong subdifferential of set-valued mappings. The robust weak duality and robust strong duality of the uncertain set-valued optimization problem are established in Section 5. Section 6 is a short conclusion of the paper.

2. Preliminaries and Definitions

Throughout the paper, let X and Y be two real topological linear spaces with their topological dual spaces X^* and Y^*, respectively. 0_X and 0_Y denote the original points of X and Y, respectively. Let $K \subseteq Y$ be a solid closed convex pointed cone. The dual cone of K is defined by

$$K^* = \{y^* \in Y^* : \langle y^*, y \rangle \geqslant 0, \quad \forall y \in K\}.$$

Let $\mathbb{N}$ be a natural number and $n, m, l \in \mathbb{N}$. Let $D \subseteq Y$ be a nonempty subset. $\mathrm{cl}D$ and $\mathrm{int}D$ denote the closure and interior of D, respectively. $\mathcal{T}(Y) := \{E \subseteq Y \mid E \text{ is nonempty}\}$.

Let M be a subset of X and $H : M \to 2^Y$ be a set-valued map. The domain, graph and epigraph of H are defined, respectively, by

$$\mathrm{dom}H := \{z \in M : H(z) \neq \emptyset\}, \mathrm{gr}H := \{(z,y) \in M \times Y : y \in H(z), z \in M\}$$

and

$$\mathrm{epi}H := \{(z,y) \in M \times Y : y \in H(z) + K\}.$$

A partial order relation($\preceq_K$) of space Y caused by the cone K as follows:

$$e \preceq_K s \text{ if and only if } s - e \in K,$$
$$e \prec_K s \text{ if and only if } s - e \in \mathrm{int}K, \quad \forall e, s \in Y.$$

Definition 1 ([34])**.** *Let $E, S \in \mathcal{T}(Y)$ be arbitrarily chosen sets.*

(i) *The lower set less order relation is defined by*

$$E \preceq_K^l S \Leftrightarrow E + K \supseteq S \Leftrightarrow \forall s \in S, \exists e \in E : e \preceq_K s,$$
$$E \prec_K^l S \Leftrightarrow E + \text{int}K \supseteq S \Leftrightarrow \forall s \in S, \exists e \in E : e \prec_K s.$$

(ii) *The upper set less order relation is defined by*

$$E \preceq_K^u S \Leftrightarrow S - K \supseteq E \Leftrightarrow \forall e \in E, \exists s \in S : e \preceq_K s,$$
$$E \prec_K^u S \Leftrightarrow S - \text{int}K \supseteq E \Leftrightarrow \forall e \in E, \exists s \in S : e \prec_K s.$$

Definition 2 ([35]). *Let $E, S \in \mathcal{T}(Y)$ be arbitrarily chosen sets. Then the certainly less order relation is defined by*

$$E \preceq_K^c S \Leftrightarrow (E = S) \text{ or } (E \neq S, \ \forall e \in E, \forall s \in S : e \preceq_K s),$$

or equivalently, $E = S$ or, $S - E \subseteq K$ whenever $E \neq S$.

Definition 3 ([31]). *Let M be a nonempty subset of X. M is said to be convex if for any $x, z \in M$ and for all $\beta \in [0,1]$,*

$$\beta x + (1-\beta) z \in M.$$

Definition 4 ([31]). *Let M be a nonempty convex subset of X. $H : M \to 2^{\mathbb{R}}$ is called K-convex if for any $x, z \in M$ and for all $\beta \in [0,1]$,*

$$\beta H(x) + (1-\beta) H(z) \subseteq H(\beta x + (1-\beta) z) + K.$$

Definition 5. *A function $H : M \to 2^{\mathbb{R}}$ has a global minimum at (x_1, y_1) if*

$$y_1 \preceq_{\mathbb{R}_+} y_2, \quad \forall x_2 \in M, y_2 \in H(x_2).$$

Definition 6 ([22]). *Let $H : M \to 2^Y$ be a set-valued map and be K-convex, $x_1 \in M, y_1 \in H(x_1)$ and $H(x_1) - y_1 \subseteq K$, the set*

$$\partial H(x_1, y_1) = \{\xi \in X^* \mid y_2 - y_1 - \langle \xi, x_2 - x_1 \rangle \in K, \quad \forall x_2 \in M, y_2 \in H(x_2)\}$$

is called the Borwein-strong subdifferential of H at (x_1, y_1).

Enlightened by the Borwein-strong subdifferential in [22,23], we put forward the new notion of second-order strong subdifferential for a set-valued map.

Definition 7. *Let $H : M \to 2^{\mathbb{R}}$ be a set-valued map, $x_1 \in M$, $y_1 \in H(x_1)$ and $H(x_1) - y_1 \subseteq \mathbb{R}_+$. Then $\xi \in X^*$ is said to be a second-order strong subgradient of H at (x_1, y_1) if*

$$y_2 - y_1 - \langle \xi, x_2 - x_1 \rangle^2 \in \mathbb{R}_+, \quad \forall x_2 \in M, y_2 \in H(x_2).$$

The set

$$\partial_s^2 H(x_1, y_1) = \{\xi \in X^* \mid y_2 - y_1 - \langle \xi, x_2 - x_1 \rangle^2 \in \mathbb{R}_+, \quad \forall x_2 \in M, y_2 \in H(x_2)\}$$

is said to be the second-order strong subdifferential of H at (x_1, y_1). If $\partial_s^2 H(x_1, y_1) \neq \emptyset$, then H is said to be second-order strong subdifferentiable at (x_1, y_1).

The following example shows Definition 7.

Example 1. *Let $H : \mathbb{R} \to 2^{\mathbb{R}}$ be a set-valued map with $H(x) = \{y \in \mathbb{R} \mid y \geq x^2\}$ for any $x \in \mathbb{R}$. Take $(x_1, y_1) = (0, 0)$. A simple calculation shows that $H(x_1) - y_1 \subseteq \mathbb{R}_+$. Then we obtain*

$$\partial_s^2 H(0,0) = \{\xi \in \mathbb{R} : \xi \in [-1,1]\}.$$

Remark 1. *Let $H : M \to 2^{\mathbb{R}}$ be a set-valued map. If the condition $H(x_1) - y_1 \subseteq \mathbb{R}_+$ is not satisfied, Definition 7 is not complete. The following example shows the case.*

Example 2. *Let $H : \mathbb{R}_+ \to 2^{\mathbb{R}}$ be a set-valued map with $H(x) = \{y \in \mathbb{R} \mid y \leq x^2\}$ for any $x \in \mathbb{R}_+$. Take $(x_1, y_1) = (1, -1)$. A simple calculation shows that $H(x_1) - y_1 \not\subseteq \mathbb{R}_+$. Then it follows from Definition 7 that ξ does not exist, i.e.,*

$$\partial_s^2 H(1,-1) = \emptyset.$$

Therefore, the condition $H(x_1) - y_1 \subseteq \mathbb{R}_+$ is necessary in Definition 7.

Remark 2. *Let $H : M \to 2^{\mathbb{R}}$ be a set-valued map. Obviously, if the second-order strong subdifferential exists, then $0 \in \partial_s^2 H(x_1, y_1)$. However, $0 \in \partial H(x_1, y_1)$ may not necessarily be true. Now we give an example to illustrate the case.*

Example 3. *Let $H : \mathbb{R}_+ \to 2^{\mathbb{R}}$ be a set-valued map, and let $H(x) = \{y \in \mathbb{R} \mid y \geq -\frac{1}{2}x\}$ for any $x \in \mathbb{R}_+$. Take $(x_1, y_1) = (0, 0)$. A simple calculation shows that $H(x_1) - y_1 \subseteq \mathbb{R}_+$. Then we have*

$$\partial_s^2 H(0,0) = \{\xi \in \mathbb{R} : \xi = 0\}.$$

and

$$\partial H(0,0) = \{\xi \in \mathbb{R} : \xi \in (-\infty, -\frac{1}{2}]\}.$$

Thus, $0 \in \partial_s^2 H(0,0)$, but $0 \notin \partial H(0,0)$.

3. Properties of a Second-Order Strong Subdifferential of Set-Valued Maps

In this section, we present some properties of a second-order strong subdifferential of set-valued maps. Firstly, we introduce the following lemma.

Lemma 1. *Let $x \in X$, $\xi, \eta \in X^*$ and $\beta \in [0,1]$. Set $h_x(\xi) := \langle \xi, x \rangle$. Then*

$$\beta h_x^2(\xi) + (1-\beta) h_x^2(\eta) \geqslant h_x^2(\beta\xi + (1-\beta)\eta).$$

Proof. Let $x \in X$, $\xi, \eta \in X^*$ and $\beta \in [0,1]$. Since $\beta^2 - \beta \leqslant 0$ and h_x is a linear function,

$$\begin{aligned} h_x^2(\beta\xi + (1-\beta)\eta) =& [h_x(\beta\xi) + h_x((1-\beta)\eta)]^2 \\ =& h_x^2(\beta\xi) + h_x^2((1-\beta)\eta) + 2h_x(\beta\xi)h_x((1-\beta)\eta) \\ =& \beta h_x^2(\xi) + (1-\beta)h_x^2(\eta) \\ &+ (\beta^2 - \beta)(h_x^2(\xi) + h_x^2(\eta) - 2h_x^2(\xi)h_x^2(\eta)) \\ \leqslant& \beta h_x^2(\xi) + (1-\beta)h_x^2(\eta). \end{aligned}$$

This proof is complete. □

Theorem 1. *Let $H : M \to 2^{\mathbb{R}}$ be a set-valued map, $x_1 \in M$, $y_1 \in H(x_1)$ and $H(x_1) - y_1 \subseteq \mathbb{R}_+$. Then the set $\partial_s^2 H(x_1, y_1)$ is convex.*

Proof. If $\partial_s^2 H(x_1, y_1) = \emptyset$, then there is nothing to be demonstrated.

Suppose $\partial_s^2 H(x_1, y_1) \neq \emptyset$. Let $\xi \in \partial_s^2 H(x_1, y_1)$, $\eta \in \partial_s^2 H(x_1, y_1)$ and $\lambda \in [0,1]$. Then,

$$y_2 - y_1 - \langle \xi, x_2 - x_1 \rangle^2 \in \mathbb{R}_+, \quad \forall x_2 \in M, y_2 \in H(x_2)$$

and

$$y_2 - y_1 - \langle \eta, x_2 - x_1 \rangle^2 \in \mathbb{R}_+, \quad \forall x_2 \in M, y_2 \in H(x_2),$$

i.e.,

$$\lambda(y_2 - y_1) - \lambda\langle \xi, x_2 - x_1 \rangle^2 \in \mathbb{R}_+, \quad \forall x_2 \in M, y_2 \in H(x_2) \tag{1}$$

and

$$(1-\lambda)(y_2 - y_1) - (1-\lambda)\langle \eta, x_2 - x_1 \rangle^2 \in \mathbb{R}_+, \quad \forall x_2 \in M, y_2 \in H(x_2). \tag{2}$$

By Lemma 1, it follows from (1) and (2) that

$$y_2 - y_1 - (\lambda\langle \xi, x_2 - x_1 \rangle^2 + (1-\lambda)\langle \eta, x_2 - x_1 \rangle^2)$$

$$\leqslant y_2 - y_1 - \langle \lambda\xi + (1-\lambda)\eta, x_2 - x_1 \rangle^2 \in \mathbb{R}_+, \quad \forall x_2 \in M, y_2 \in H(x_2).$$

Thus,

$$\lambda\xi + (1-\lambda)\eta \in \partial_s^2 H(x_1, y_1).$$

This proof is complete. □

Theorem 2. *Let $H : M \to 2^{\mathbb{R}}$ be a set-valued map, $x_1 \in M$, $y_1 \in H(x_1)$ and $H(x_1) - y_1 \subseteq \mathbb{R}_+$. Let H be second-order strong subdifferentiable at (x_1, y_1). Then H has a global minimum at (x_1, y_1) if and only if $0_{X^*} \in \partial_s^2 H(x_1, y_1)$.*

Proof. ($\Rightarrow$) Since H has a global minimum at (x_1, y_1),

$$y_2 - y_1 \in \mathbb{R}_+, \quad \forall x_2 \in M, y_2 \in H(x_2).$$

Then,

$$y_2 - y_1 - \langle 0_{X^*}, x_2 - x_1 \rangle^2 \in \mathbb{R}_+, \quad \forall x_2 \in M, y_2 \in H(x_2),$$

which implies that $0_{X^*} \in \partial_s^2 H(x_1, y_1)$.

($\Leftarrow$) Let $0_{X^*} \in \partial_s^2 H(x_1, y_1)$. Then, by Definition 7, we obtain

$$y_2 - y_1 - \langle 0_{X^*}, x_2 - x_1 \rangle^2 \in \mathbb{R}_+, \quad \forall x_2 \in M, y_2 \in H(x_2),$$

which implies that $y_2 - y_1 \in \mathbb{R}_+$ for all $x_2 \in M$, $y_2 \in H(x_2)$. Therefore, according to Definition 5, H has a global minimum at (x_1, y_1). This proof is complete. □

Theorem 3. *Let $H : M \to 2^{\mathbb{R}}$ be a set-valued map and $\alpha > 0$. Let $x_1 \in M$, $y_1 \in H(x_1)$ and $H(x_1) - y_1 \subseteq \mathbb{R}_+$. If H and αH are second-order strong subdifferentiable at (x_1, y_1) and $(x_1, \alpha y_1)$, respectively, then*

$$\partial_s^2(\alpha H)(x_1, \alpha y_1) = \sqrt{\alpha}\partial_s^2 H(x_1, y_1).$$

Proof. Let $\xi \in \partial_s^2(\alpha H)(x_1, \alpha y_1)$. Then

$$\begin{aligned}
&\alpha y_2 - \alpha y_1 - \langle \xi, x_2 - x_1 \rangle^2 \in \mathbb{R}_+, \quad \forall x_2 \in M, y_2 \in H(x_2) \\
\Leftrightarrow & y_2 - y_1 - \frac{1}{\alpha}\langle \xi, x_2 - x_1 \rangle^2 \in \mathbb{R}_+, \quad \forall x_2 \in M, y_2 \in H(x_2) \\
\Leftrightarrow & y_2 - y_1 - \langle \frac{1}{\sqrt{\alpha}}\xi, x_2 - x_1 \rangle^2 \in \mathbb{R}_+, \quad \forall x_2 \in M, y_2 \in H(x_2) \\
\Leftrightarrow & \frac{1}{\sqrt{\alpha}}\xi \in \partial_s^2 H(x_1, y_1) \\
\Leftrightarrow & \xi \in \sqrt{\alpha}\partial_s^2 H(x_1, y_1).
\end{aligned}$$

Here we finish the proof. □

Now, we provide an illustration of Theorem 3.

Example 4. *Let $H : \mathbb{R} \to 2^{\mathbb{R}}$ be a set-valued map, and let $H(x) = \{y \in \mathbb{R} \mid y \geq 3x^2\}$. Take $(x_1, y_1) = (0, 0)$. A simple calculation shows that $H(x_1) - y_1 \subseteq \mathbb{R}_+$. Then for any $\alpha > 0$, we obtain*

$$\partial_s^2(\alpha H)(0,0) = \{\xi \in \mathbb{R} : \xi \in [-\sqrt{3\alpha}, \sqrt{3\alpha}]\}$$

and

$$\sqrt{\alpha}\partial_s^2 H(0,0) = \{\xi \in \mathbb{R} : \xi \in [-\sqrt{3\alpha}, \sqrt{3\alpha}]\}.$$

Therefore, $\partial_s^2(\alpha H)(0,0) = \sqrt{\alpha}\partial_s^2 H(0,0)$.

Theorem 4. *Let H and $Q : M \to 2^{\mathbb{R}}$ be set-valued maps, $x_1 \in M$, $y_1 \in H(x_1)$, $y_2 \in Q(x_1)$, $H(x_1) - y_1 \subseteq \mathbb{R}_+$ and $Q(x_1) - y_2 \subseteq \mathbb{R}_+$. If H and Q are second-order strong subdifferentiable at (x_1, y_1) and (x_1, y_2), respectively, then*

$$\partial_s^2 H(x_1, y_1) + \partial_s^2 Q(x_1, y_2) \subseteq \sqrt{2}\partial_s^2(H+Q)(x_1, y_1 + y_2).$$

Proof. Let $\xi_1 \in \partial_s^2 H(x_1, y_1)$ and $\xi_2 \in \partial_s^2 Q(x_1, y_2)$. Then,

$$y_3 - y_1 - \langle \xi_1, x_2 - x_1 \rangle^2 \in \mathbb{R}_+, \quad \forall x_2 \in M, y_3 \in H(x_2)$$

and

$$y_4 - y_2 - \langle \xi_2, x_2 - x_1 \rangle^2 \in \mathbb{R}_+, \quad \forall x_2 \in M, y_4 \in Q(x_2),$$

i.e.,

$$\frac{1}{2}(y_3 - y_1) - \frac{1}{2}\langle \xi_1, x_2 - x_1 \rangle^2 \in \mathbb{R}_+, \quad \forall x_2 \in M, y_3 \in H(x_2) \tag{3}$$

and

$$\frac{1}{2}(y_4 - y_2) - \frac{1}{2}\langle \xi_2, x_2 - x_1 \rangle^2 \in \mathbb{R}_+, \quad \forall x_2 \in M, y_4 \in Q(x_2). \tag{4}$$

According to Lemma 1, it follows from (3) and (4) that

$$\begin{aligned}
&\frac{1}{2}[(y_3 - y_1) + (y_4 - y_2)] - [\frac{1}{2}\langle \xi_1, x_2 - x_1 \rangle^2 + \frac{1}{2}\langle \xi_2, x_2 - x_1 \rangle^2] \\
\leqslant &\frac{1}{2}[(y_3 + y_4) - (y_1 + y_2)] - \langle \frac{1}{2}\xi_1 + \frac{1}{2}\xi_2, x_2 - x_1 \rangle^2 \in \mathbb{R}_+, \\
&\qquad \forall x_2 \in M, y_3 + y_4 \in (H+Q)(x_2).
\end{aligned}$$

Thus,

$$\frac{\sqrt{2}}{2}\xi_1 + \frac{\sqrt{2}}{2}\xi_2 \in \partial_s^2(H+Q)(x_1, y_1 + y_2),$$

i.e.,

$$\xi_1 + \xi_2 \in \sqrt{2}\partial_s^2(H+Q)(x_1, y_1 + y_2).$$

Therefore, $\partial_s^2 H(x_1, y_1) + \partial_s^2 Q(x_1, y_2) \subseteq \sqrt{2}\partial_s^2(H+Q)(x_1, y_1 + y_2)$. This proof is complete. □

Corollary 1. *Let $H_i : M \to 2^{\mathbb{R}}$ be set-valued maps, $i = 1, \ldots, m$, $x_1 \in M$, $y_i \in H_i(x_1)$ and $H_i(x_1) - y_i \subseteq \mathbb{R}_+$. If H_i is second-order strong subdifferentiable at (x_1, y_i), $i = 1, \ldots, m$, then*

$$\sum_{i=1}^{m} \partial_s^2 H_i(x_1, y_i) \subseteq \sqrt{m}\partial_s^2 \sum_{i=1}^{m} H_i(x_1, \sum_{i=1}^{m} y_i).$$

Remark 3. *Let H and $Q : M \to 2^{\mathbb{R}}$ be set-valued maps. If H and Q are strong subdifferentiable at (x_1, y_1) and (x_1, y_2), respectively, then*

$$\partial H(x_1, y_1) + \partial Q(x_1, y_2) \subseteq \partial(H + Q)(x_1, y_1 + y_2).$$

However, $\sqrt{2}$ can not be omitted in Theorem 4.

We take into consideration the following examples to demonstrate Theorem 4 and Remark 3.

Example 5. *Let H and $Q : \mathbb{R} \to 2^{\mathbb{R}}$ be set-valued maps with $H(x) = \{y \in \mathbb{R} \mid y \geq x^2\}$ and $Q(x) = \{y \in \mathbb{R} \mid y \geq 4x^2\}$. Take $x_1 = 1$, $y_1 = 1 \in H(x_1)$ and $y_2 = 4 \in Q(x_1)$. A simple calculation shows that $H(x_1) - y_1 \subseteq \mathbb{R}_+$ and $Q(x_1) - y_2 \subseteq \mathbb{R}_+$. Then we obtain*

$$\partial_s^2 H(1,1) = \{\xi_1 \in \mathbb{R} : \xi_1 \in [-1,1]\}$$

and

$$\partial_s^2 Q(1,4) = \{\xi_2 \in \mathbb{R} : \xi_2 \in [-2,2]\},$$

so,

$$\partial_s^2 H(1,1) + \partial_s^2 Q(1,4) = \{\xi_1 + \xi_2 \in \mathbb{R} : \xi_1 + \xi_2 \in [-3,3]\}.$$

Moreover,

$$\partial_s^2 (H + Q)(1,5) = \{\xi_3 \in \mathbb{R} : \xi_3 \in [-\sqrt{5}, \sqrt{5}]\}.$$

and

$$\sqrt{2}\partial_s^2 (H + Q)(1,5) = \{\sqrt{2}\xi_3 \in \mathbb{R} : \sqrt{2}\xi_3 \in [-\sqrt{10}, \sqrt{10}]\}.$$

In fact, $3 \nless \sqrt{5}$ and $3 < \sqrt{10}$. Therefore, $\partial_s^2 H(x_1, y_1) + \partial_s^2 Q(x_1, y_2) \nsubseteq \partial_s^2 (H + Q)(x_1, y_1 + y_2)$ and $\partial_s^2 H(x_1, y_1) + \partial_s^2 Q(x_1, y_2) \subseteq \sqrt{2}\partial_s^2 (H + Q)(x_1, y_1 + y_2)$.

Example 6. *Let H and $Q : \mathbb{R} \to 2^{\mathbb{R}}$ be set-valued maps, and let $H(x) = \{y \in \mathbb{R} \mid y \geq x\}$, $Q(x) = \{y \in \mathbb{R} \mid y \geq 4x\}$. Take $(x_1, y_1) = (0,0) = (x_1, y_2)$. A simple calculation shows that $H(x_1) - y_1 \subseteq \mathbb{R}_+$ and $Q(x_1) - y_2 \subseteq \mathbb{R}_+$. Then we obtain*

$$\partial H(0,0) = \{\xi_1 \in \mathbb{R} : \xi_1 \leqslant 1\}$$

and

$$\partial Q(0,0) = \{\xi_2 \in \mathbb{R} : \xi_2 \leqslant 4\},$$

so,

$$\partial H(0,0) + \partial Q(0,0) = \{\xi_1 + \xi_2 \in \mathbb{R} : \xi_1 + \xi_2 \leqslant 5\}.$$

Moreover,

$$\partial (H + Q)(0,0) = \{\xi_3 \in \mathbb{R} : \xi_3 \leqslant 5\}.$$

Therefore, $\partial H(x_1, y_1) + \partial Q(x_1, y_2) \subseteq \partial(H + Q)(x_1, y_1 + y_2)$.

4. The Optimality Condition for the Uncertain Set-Valued Optimization Problem

Problem (SOP) has been studied extensively without taking into account data uncertainty. However, in most real-world practical applications, there are more uncertainties in optimization problems. To define an uncertain set-valued optimization problem (USOP), we assume that uncertainties in the objective function are given as scenarios from a known uncertainty set $U = \{u_1, u_2, \ldots, u_m\} \subseteq \mathbb{R}^m$, where u_i is an uncertain parameter, $i = 1, \ldots, m$. The following uncertain set-valued optimization problem (USOP) can be used to describe the problem (SOP) when there is data uncertainty for both the objectives and the constraints:

$$\text{(USOP)}\begin{cases} \min & H(z,u_i) = \{H_1(z,u_i), H_2(z,u_i), \ldots, H_k(z,u_i), \ldots, H_q(z,u_i)\} \\ \text{s.t.} & z \in M, u_i \in U, B_j(z,v_j) \subseteq \mathbb{R}_-, \forall v_j \in V_j, j = 1, \ldots, l, \end{cases}$$

where $H_k : M \times \mathbb{R}^m \to 2^{\mathbb{R}}, k = 1, \ldots, q$ and $B_j : M \times \mathbb{R}^l \to 2^{\mathbb{R}}$, $j = 1, \ldots, l$ are given functions, and the uncertain parameter v_j belongs to a compact and convex uncertainty set $V_j \subseteq \mathbb{R}^l$.

Let $G : M \times U \to 2^{\mathbb{R}}$ be a set-valued map, $\max\limits_{u_i \in U} G(z,u_i)$ is defined as follows:

$$G(z,u_i) \preceq^l_{\mathbb{R}_+} \max_{u_i \in U} G(z,u_i), \quad \forall i = 1, \ldots, m.$$

In this paper, we investigate problem (USOP) using a robust approach. As we all know, there is no proper method to directly solve problem (USOP), so it is necessary to replace problem (USOP) by the deterministic version, that is, the robust counterpart of problem (USOP). By this means, various concepts of robustness have been proposed on the basis of different robust counterparts to describe the preferences of decision makers.

The most celebrated and researched robustness concept is called worst-case robustness (also known as min-max robustness or strict robustness in the literature). The idea is to minimize the worst possible objective function value, and search for a solution that is good enough in the worst case. Meanwhile, the constraints should be satisfied for every parameter $v_j \in V_j, j = 1, \ldots, l$. Worst-case robustness is a conservative concept and reveals the pessimistic attitude of a decision maker. Then, the robust (worst-case) counterpart of problem (USOP) is as follows :

$$\text{(URSOP)}\begin{cases} \min & \max\limits_{u_i \in U} H(z,u_i) = \{\max\limits_{u_i \in U} H_1(z,u_i), \max\limits_{u_i \in U} H_2(z,u_i), \ldots, \max\limits_{u_i \in U} H_k(z,u_i), \\ & \qquad \ldots, \max\limits_{u_i \in U} H_q(z,u_i)\} \\ \text{s.t.} & z \in M, B_j(z,v_j) \subseteq \mathbb{R}_-, \forall v_j \in V_j, j = 1, \ldots, l. \end{cases}$$

Definition 8. *The robust feasible set of problem (USOP) is defined by*

$$A := \{z \in M \mid B_j(z,v_j) \subseteq \mathbb{R}_-, \forall v_j \in V_j, j = 1, \ldots, m\}.$$

We assume that $A \neq \emptyset$. Obviously, the set of all robust feasible solutions to problem (USOP) is the same as the set of all feasible solutions to problem (URSOP).

Definition 9. *$\check{z} \in A$ is said to be a $\preceq^l_{\mathbb{R}_+}$-robust efficient solution to problem (USOP) if $\check{z}$ is a $\preceq^l_{\mathbb{R}_+}$-efficient solution to problem (URSOP), i.e., for all $z \in A$ such that*

$$\max_{u_i \in U} H_k(\check{z},u_i) \preceq^l_{\mathbb{R}_+} \max_{u_i \in U} H_k(z,u_i).$$

In this part, we create a necessary and sufficient optimality condition of the $\preceq^l_{\mathbb{R}_+}$-robust efficient solution to problem (USOP).

Theorem 5. *Let $H_k : M \times \mathbb{R}^m \to 2^{\mathbb{R}}, k = 1, \ldots, q$ and $B_j : M \times \mathbb{R}^l \to 2^{\mathbb{R}}$, $j = 1, \ldots, l$ be set-valued maps, $\check{z} \in M$, $\check{y} \in \bigcap_{u_i \in U} H_k(\check{z},u_i)$ and $\check{y}_j \in \bigcap_{v_j \in V_j} B_j(\check{z},v_j)$. Assume that the following conditions hold:*

(i) H_k is bounded on $M \times U$;

(ii) $\max\limits_{u_i \in U} H_k(z,u_i)$ exists for all $z \in M$;

(iii) for any i, j and k, $H_k(\check{z},u_i) - \check{y} \subseteq \mathbb{R}_+$ and $B_j(\check{z},v_j) - \check{y}_j \subseteq \mathbb{R}_+$;

(iv) *for any j and k, H_k, B_j is second-order strong subdifferentiable at $(\check{z}, \check{y})$ and $(\check{z}, \check{y}_j)$, respectively.*

Then $\check{z}$ is a $\preceq^l_{\mathbb{R}_+}$-robust efficient solution to problem (USOP) *if and only if for any i, j and k, there exist $\check{u}_i \in U, \check{v}_j \in V_j$ and $\check{\mu}_j \in \mathbb{R}_+$ such that*

$$0 \in \partial_s^2 H_k(\cdot, \check{u}_i)(\check{z}, \check{y}) + \sum_{j=1}^{l} \check{\mu}_j \partial_s^2 B_j(\cdot, \check{v}_j)(\check{z}, \check{y}_j),$$

$$(\check{\mu}_j B_j)(\check{z}, \check{v}_j) = \{0\}$$

and

$$H_k(\check{z}, \check{u}_i) = \max_{u_i \in U} H_k(\check{z}, u_i).$$

Proof. $(\Rightarrow)$ Let $\check{z}$ be a $\preceq^l_{\mathbb{R}_+}$-robust efficient solution to problem (USOP). Then $\check{z} \in A$. Hence, for all $v_j \in V_j$, we have $B_j(\check{z}, v_j) \subseteq \mathbb{R}_-$. Thus, take $\check{v}_j \in V_j$ such that

$$B_j(\check{z}, \check{v}_j) \subseteq \mathbb{R}_-.$$

Moreover, for any j, there exists $\check{\mu}_j \in \mathbb{R}_+$ such that

$$(\check{\mu}_j B_j)(\check{z}, \check{v}_j) = \{0\}. \tag{5}$$

In fact, there are two cases to illustrate (5) as follows:

(i) If $B_j(\check{z}, \check{v}_j) = \{0\}$, then take arbitrary $\check{\mu}_j > 0$, we get $(\check{\mu}_j B_j)(\check{z}, \check{v}_j) = \{0\}$.

(ii) If $B_j(\check{z}, \check{v}_j) \subseteq \mathbb{R}_- \setminus \{0\}$, then take $\check{\mu}_j = 0$, we can easily get that $(\check{\mu}_j B_j)(\check{z}, \check{v}_j) = \{0\}$.

Since U is a finite set and H_k is bounded, there exists $\check{u}_i \in U$ such that

$$H_k(\check{z}, \check{u}_i) = \max_{u_i \in U} H_k(\check{z}, u_i).$$

According to the definition of the second-order strong subdifferential, one obtains

$$0 \in \partial_s^2 H_k(\cdot, \check{u}_i)(\check{z}, \check{y}) \text{ and } 0 \in \sum_{j=1}^{l} \check{\mu}_j \partial_s^2 B_j(\cdot, \check{v}_j)(\check{z}, \check{y}_j).$$

Therefore, we get

$$0 \in \partial_s^2 H_k(\cdot, \check{u}_i)(\check{z}, \check{y}) + \sum_{j=1}^{l} \check{\mu}_j \partial_s^2 B_j(\cdot, \check{v}_j)(\check{z}, \check{y}_j).$$

$(\Leftarrow)$ Assume that for any i, j and k, there exist $\check{z} \in A, \check{u}_i \in U, \check{v}_j \in V_j$ and $\check{\mu}_j \in \mathbb{R}_+$ such that

$$0 \in \partial_s^2 H_k(\cdot, \check{u}_i)(\check{z}, \check{y}) + \sum_{j=1}^{l} \check{\mu}_j \partial_s^2 B_j(\cdot, \check{v}_j)(\check{z}, \check{y}_j),$$

$$(\check{\mu}_j B_j)(\check{z}, \check{v}_j) = \{0\}$$

and

$$H_k(\check{z}, \check{u}_i) = \max_{u_i \in U} H_k(\check{z}, u_i). \tag{6}$$

By Theorem 3 and Corollary 1, we get

$$\begin{aligned}\partial_s^2 H_k(\cdot,\breve{u}_i)(\breve{z},\breve{y})+&\sum_{j=1}^{l}\breve{\mu}_j\partial_s^2 B_j(\cdot,\breve{v}_j)(\breve{z},\breve{y}_j)\\ &=\partial_s^2 H_k(\cdot,\breve{u}_i)(\breve{z},\breve{y})+\sum_{j=1}^{l}\partial_s^2(\breve{\mu}_j^2 B_j)(\cdot,\breve{v}_j)(\breve{z},\breve{\mu}_j^2\breve{y}_j)\\ &\subseteq\sqrt{l+1}\partial_s^2(H_k(\cdot,\breve{u}_i)+\sum_{j=1}^{l}(\breve{\mu}_j^2 B_j)(\cdot,\breve{v}_j))(\breve{z},\breve{y}+\sum_{j=1}^{l}\breve{\mu}_j^2\breve{y}_j).\end{aligned}$$

Since $0\in\partial_s^2 H_k(\cdot,\breve{u}_i)(\breve{z},\breve{y})+\sum_{j=1}^{l}\breve{\mu}_j\partial_s^2 B_j(\cdot,\breve{v}_j)(\breve{z},\breve{y}_j)$, one has

$$0\in\sqrt{l+1}\partial_s^2(H_k(\cdot,\breve{u}_i)+\sum_{j=1}^{l}(\breve{\mu}_j^2 B_j)(\cdot,\breve{v}_j))(\breve{z},\breve{y}+\sum_{j=1}^{l}\breve{\mu}_j^2\breve{y}_j).$$

Therefore,

$$0\in\partial_s^2(H_k(\cdot,\breve{u}_i)+\sum_{j=1}^{l}(\breve{\mu}_j^2 B_j)(\cdot,\breve{v}_j))(\breve{z},\breve{y}+\sum_{j=1}^{l}\breve{\mu}_j^2\breve{y}_j).$$

Obviously, $\breve{y}\in H_k(\breve{z},\breve{u}_i),\breve{y}_j\in B_j(\breve{z},\breve{v}_j)$. Then by Definition 7, we get

$$y-\breve{y}+\sum_{j=1}^{l}\breve{\mu}_j^2 y_j-\sum_{j=1}^{l}\breve{\mu}_j^2\breve{y}_j\in\mathbb{R}_+,\quad\forall z\in A,y\in H_k(z,\breve{u}_i),y_j\in B_j(z,\breve{v}_j).\tag{7}$$

Since $(\breve{\mu}_j B_j)(\breve{z},\breve{v}_j)=\{0\}$ for any j, we calculate that $\sum_{j=1}^{l}(\breve{\mu}_j^2 B_j)(\breve{z},\breve{v}_j)=\{0\}$, i.e., for the preceding element $\breve{y}_j\in B_j(\breve{z},\breve{v}_j)$, we have $\sum_{j=1}^{l}\breve{\mu}_j^2\breve{y}_j=0$. Together with $\sum_{j=1}^{l}(\breve{\mu}_j^2 B_j)(z,\breve{v}_j)\subseteq\mathbb{R}_-$ for all $z\in A$, i.e., $\sum_{j=1}^{l}\breve{\mu}_j^2 y_j\in\mathbb{R}_-$ for all $z\in A$ and $y_j\in B_j(z,\breve{v}_j)$, it follows from (7) that

$$y-\breve{y}\in\mathbb{R}_+,\quad\forall z\in A,y\in H_k(z,\breve{u}_i),$$

i.e.,

$$H_k(\breve{z},\breve{u}_i)\preceq^l_{\mathbb{R}_+}H_k(z,\breve{u}_i),\quad\forall z\in A.$$

Moreover, by the transitivity of $\preceq^l_{\mathbb{R}_+}$ set-order relation, it follows from (6) and $H_k(z,\breve{u}_i)\preceq^l_{\mathbb{R}_+}\max_{u_i\in U}H_k(z,u_i)$, one has

$$\max_{u_i\in U}H_k(\breve{z},u_i)\preceq^l_{\mathbb{R}_+}\max_{u_i\in U}H_k(z,u_i),\quad\forall z\in A.$$

Thus, $\breve{z}$ is a $\preceq^l_{\mathbb{R}_+}$-robust efficient solution to problem (USOP). This proof is complete. □

Remark 4.

(i) *We extend the uncertain scalar optimization problem in [32] (Theorem 3.1) to the uncertain set-valued optimization problem (USOP) in Theorem 5.*

(ii) *Ref. [32] (Theorem 3.1) is established under the conditions of continuity and cone-convex-concavity, [15] (Corollaries 3.1 and 3.2) are established under the conditions of upper semi-continuity, it is under the conditions of existence of the maximum and boundedness that we obtain Theorem 5. Since bounded functions may not be continuous, our result in Theorem 5 extends [32] (Theorem 3.1) and [15] (Corollaries 3.1 and 3.2).*

5. Wolfe Type Robust Duality of Problem (USOP)

The robust weak duality and the robust strong duality are covered in this section, which begin by introducing a Wolfe type dual problem (DSOP_W) for the uncertain set-valued optimization problem (USOP).

We now consider the Wolfe type dual problem (DSOP_W) of problem (USOP):

$$\begin{cases} \max & (H_1(z,u_i)+\sum_{j=1}^{l}(\mu_jB_j)(z,v_j),\ldots,H_q(z,u_i)+\sum_{j=1}^{l}(\mu_jB_j)(z,v_j)) \\ \text{s.t.} & 0\in \partial_s^2 H_k(\cdot,u_i)(z,y)+\sum_{j=1}^{l}\mu_j\partial_s^2 B_j(\cdot,v_j)(z,y_j), \\ & (\mu_jB_j)(z,v_j)\subseteq \mathbb{R}_-, j=1,\ldots,l, \\ & u_i\in U, i=1,\ldots,m, v_j\in V_j, \mu_j\in\mathbb{R}_+, \\ & z\in A, y\in H_k(z,u_i), y_j\in B_j(z,v_j), k=1,\ldots,q. \end{cases}$$

Definition 10. *The robust feasible solution set P of problem* (DSOP_W) *is defined by*

$$\begin{aligned} P := \{(z,\mu_j,u_i,v_j)\ | 0\in \partial_s^2 H_k(\cdot,u_i)(z,y)+\sum_{j=1}^{l}\mu_j\partial_s^2 B_j(\cdot,v_j)(z,y_j), \\ (\mu_jB_j)(z,v_j)\subseteq \mathbb{R}_-, v_j\in V_j, \mu_j\in\mathbb{R}_+, j=1,\ldots,l, \\ u_i\in U, i=1,\ldots,m, z\in A, y\in H_k(z,u_i), \\ y_j\in B_j(z,v_j), k=1,\ldots,q\}. \end{aligned}$$

In this section, we suppose that $P\neq\emptyset$.

Definition 11. $(\check{x},\check{\mu}_j,\check{u}_i,\check{v}_j)\in P$ *is said to be a* $\prec^u_{\mathbb{R}_+}$*-robust efficient solution to problem* (DSOP_W) *if there is no feasible solution* $(z,\mu_j,u_i,v_j)\in P$ *other than* $(\check{x},\check{\mu}_j,\check{u}_i,\check{v}_j)$ *such that*

$$H_k(\check{x},\check{u}_i)-\sum_{j=1}^{l}(\check{\mu}_jB_j)(\check{x},\check{v}_j)\prec^u_{\mathbb{R}_+} H_k(z,u_i)-\sum_{j=1}^{l}(\mu_jB_j)(z,v_j),$$
$$i=1,\ldots,m, k=1,\ldots,q.$$

Theorem 6. (Robust weak duality) *If for any k,* H_k *is bounded and closed, and* $\max_{u_i\in U} H_k(x,u_i)$ *exists for all* $x\in M$*, then for any feasible solution x to problem* (URSOP) *and any feasible solution* (z,μ_j,u_i,v_j) *to problem* (DSOP_W)*, we have*

$$\max_{u_p\in U} H_k(x,u_p)\nprec^u_{\mathbb{R}_+} H_k(z,u_i)+\sum_{j=1}^{l}(\mu_jB_j)(z,v_j),\quad i=1,\ldots,m, k=1,\ldots,q. \tag{8}$$

Proof. Let x be a feasible solution to problem (URSOP) and (z,μ_j,u_i,v_j) be a feasible solution to problem (DSOP_W).

To the contrary, suppose that (8) does not hold. Then, there exist $\check{x},\check{z}\in A$, $\check{u}_i\in U$, $\check{v}_j\in V_j$ and $\check{\mu}_j\in\mathbb{R}_+$ such that

$$\max_{u_p\in U} H_k(\check{x},u_p)\prec^u_{\mathbb{R}_+} H_k(\check{z},\check{u}_i)+\sum_{j=1}^{l}(\check{\mu}_jB_j)(\check{z},\check{v}_j). \tag{9}$$

From $\sum_{j=1}^{l}(\check{\mu}_jB_j)(\check{x},\check{v}_j)\subseteq\mathbb{R}_-$, we have

$$\max_{u_p\in U} H_k(\check{x},u_p)+\sum_{j=1}^{l}(\check{\mu}_jB_j)(\check{x},\check{v}_j)\prec^u_{\mathbb{R}_+} H_k(\check{z},\check{u}_i)+\sum_{j=1}^{l}(\check{\mu}_jB_j)(\check{z},\check{v}_j).$$

Then, for all $\mathring{y} \in \max_{u_p \in U} H_k(\check{x}, u_p)$ and $y_j \in B_j(\check{x}, \breve{v}_j)$, there exist $\breve{y} \in H_k(\check{z}, \breve{u}_i)$ and $\breve{y}_j \in B_j(\check{z}, \breve{v}_j)$ such that

$$\mathring{y} + \sum_{j=1}^{l} \breve{\mu}_j y_j \prec_{\mathbb{R}_+} \breve{y} + \sum_{j=1}^{l} \breve{\mu}_j \breve{y}_j,$$

i.e.,

$$(\mathring{y} + \sum_{j=1}^{l} \breve{\mu}_j y_j) - (\breve{y} + \sum_{j=1}^{l} \breve{\mu}_j \breve{y}_j) \in \text{int}\mathbb{R}_-. \tag{10}$$

Due to $H_k(\check{x}, \breve{u}_i) \preceq^c_{\mathbb{R}_+} \max_{u_p \in U} H_k(\check{x}, u_p)$, we can conclude that $H_k(\check{x}, \breve{u}_i) \neq \max_{u_p \in U} H_k(\check{x}, u_p)$. In fact, suppose that $H_k(\check{x}, \breve{u}_i) = \max_{u_p \in U} H_k(\check{x}, u_p)$. Then, it follows from (9) that

$$H_k(\check{x}, \breve{u}_i) \prec^u_{\mathbb{R}_+} H_k(\check{x}, \breve{u}_i) + \sum_{j=1}^{l} (\breve{\mu}_j B_j)(\check{x}, \breve{v}_j).$$

Since H_k is bounded and closed, and $\sum_{j=1}^{l} (\breve{\mu}_j B_j)(\check{x}, \breve{v}_j) \subseteq \mathbb{R}_-$, we obtain

$$\max_{u_p \in U} H_k(\check{x}, u_p) \prec^u_{\mathbb{R}_+} H_k(\check{x}, \breve{u}_i) + \sum_{j=1}^{l} (\breve{\mu}_j B_j)(\check{x}, \breve{v}_j),$$

which is impossible. Thus, $H_k(\check{x}, \breve{u}_i) \neq \max_{u_p \in U} H_k(\check{x}, u_p)$. And then, by the definition of $\preceq^c_{\mathbb{R}_+}$ set-order relationship, one has

$$y \preceq_{\mathbb{R}_+} \mathring{y}, \quad \forall y \in H_k(\check{x}, \breve{u}_i), \mathring{y} \in \max_{u_p \in U} H_k(\check{x}, u_p). \tag{11}$$

It follows from $0 \in \partial^2_s H_k(\cdot, \breve{u}_i)(\check{z}, \breve{y})$ and (11) that

$$y - \breve{y} - \langle 0, x - \check{z} \rangle^2 \in \mathbb{R}_+, \quad \forall x \in A, y \in H_k(x, \breve{u}_i),$$

i.e.,

$$\mathring{y} - \breve{y} - \langle 0, x - \check{z} \rangle^2 \in \mathbb{R}_+, \quad \forall x \in A, \mathring{y} \in \max_{u_p \in U} H_k(x, u_p). \tag{12}$$

Moreover, it follows from $0 \in \sum_{j=1}^{l} \mu_j \partial^2_s B_j(\cdot, \breve{v}_j)(\check{z}, \breve{y}_j)$, one has

$$\sum_{j=1}^{l} \breve{\mu}_j y_j - \sum_{j=1}^{l} \breve{\mu}_j \breve{y}_j - \langle 0, x - \check{z} \rangle^2 \in \mathbb{R}_+, \quad \forall x \in A, y_j \in B_j(x, \breve{v}_j). \tag{13}$$

Thus, it follows from (12) and (13) that

$$(\mathring{y} + \sum_{j=1}^{l} \breve{\mu}_j y_j) - (\breve{y} + \sum_{j=1}^{l} \breve{\mu}_j \breve{y}_j) \in \mathbb{R}_+, \quad \forall \mathring{y} \in \max_{u_p \in U} H_k(\check{x}, u_p), y_j \in B_j(\check{x}, \breve{v}_j),$$

which contradicts (10). Therefore, for any feasible solution x to problem (URSOP) and any feasible solution (z, μ_j, u_i, v_j) to problem (DSOP_W), we have

$$\max_{u_p \in U} H_k(x, u_p) \nprec^u_{\mathbb{R}_+} H_k(z, u_i) + \sum_{j=1}^{l} (\mu_j B_j)(z, v_j), \quad i = 1, \ldots, m, k = 1, \ldots, q.$$

We complete the proof. □

Theorem 7 (Robust strong duality). *Let $H_k : M \times \mathbb{R}^m \to 2^{\mathbb{R}}, k = 1, \ldots, q$ and $B_j : M \times \mathbb{R}^l \to 2^{\mathbb{R}}$, $j = 1, \ldots, l$ be set-valued maps, $\breve{x} \in M$, $\breve{y} \in \bigcap_{u_i \in U} H_k(\breve{x}, u_i)$ and $\breve{y}_j \in \bigcap_{v_j \in V_j} B_j(\breve{x}, v_j)$. Assume that the following conditions hold:*

(i) H_k is bounded on $M \times U$ for any k;
(ii) $\max_{u_i \in U} H_k(x, u_i)$ exists for all $x \in M$ and k;
(iii) for any i, j and k, $H_k(\breve{x}, u_i) - \breve{y} \subseteq \mathbb{R}_+$ and $B_j(\breve{x}, v_j) - \breve{y}_j \subseteq \mathbb{R}_+$;
(iv) for any j and k, H_k and B_j are second-order strong subdifferentiable at $(\breve{x}, \breve{y})$ and $(\breve{x}, \breve{y}_j)$, respectively;
(v) $\breve{x} \in A$ is a $\preceq^l_{\mathbb{R}_+}$-robust efficient solution to problem (USOP).

Then for any i, j, k, there exist $\breve{u}_i \in U, \breve{v}_j \in V_j$ and $\breve{\mu}_j \in \mathbb{R}_+$ such that $(\breve{x}, \breve{\mu}_j, \breve{u}_i, \breve{v}_j)$ is a $\prec^u_{\mathbb{R}_+}$-robust efficient solution to problem (DSOP_W).

Proof. Let $\breve{x}$ be a $\preceq^l_{\mathbb{R}_+}$-robust efficient solution to problem (USOP). By Theorem 5, we know that for any i, j and k, there exist $\breve{u}_i \in U, \breve{v}_j \in V_j$ and $\breve{\mu}_j \in \mathbb{R}_+$ such that

$$0 \in \partial^2_s H_k(\cdot, \breve{u}_i)(\breve{x}, \breve{y}) + \sum_{j=1}^{l} \breve{\mu}_j \partial^2_s B_j(\cdot, \breve{v}_j)(\breve{x}, \breve{y}_j),$$

$$(\breve{\mu}_j B_j)(\breve{x}, \breve{v}_j) = \{0\} \tag{14}$$

and

$$H_k(\breve{x}, \breve{u}_i) = \max_{u_i \in U} H_k(\breve{x}, u_i), \quad k = 1, 2, \ldots, q. \tag{15}$$

Therefore, $(\breve{x}, \breve{\mu}_j, \breve{u}_i, \breve{v}_j)$ is a feasible solution to problem (DSOP_W). Then, for any feasible solution (z, μ_j, u_i, v_j) to problem (DSOP_W), it follows from (14) and (15) and Theorem 6 that

$$\begin{aligned} H_k(\breve{x}, \breve{u}_i) - \sum_{j=1}^{l} (\breve{\mu}_j B_j)(\breve{x}, \breve{v}_j) &= \max_{u_i \in U} H_k(\breve{x}, u_i) \\ &\not\subseteq H_k(z, u_i) + \sum_{j=1}^{l} (\mu_j B_j)(z, v_j) - \text{int}\mathbb{R}_+. \end{aligned}$$

Hence, $(\breve{x}, \breve{\mu}_j, \breve{u}_i, \breve{v}_j)$ is a $\prec^u_{\mathbb{R}_+}$-robust efficient solution to problem (DSOP_W). This proof is complete. □

Remark 5. *Theorems 10 and 11 generalize Theorems 4.1 and 4.2 in [32] from a scalar case to a set-valued one, respectively.*

6. Conclusions

In this paper, we introduce a new second-order strong subdifferential of the set-valued maps and the robust efficient solutions for set approach of the uncertain set-valued optimization problems, and then a necessary and sufficient optimality condition is derived for set-based robust efficient solutions of the uncertain set-valued optimization problem. Finally, we demonstrate robust strong duality and robust weak duality for the dual problem of the uncertain set-valued optimization problem. Our discussion makes it desirable to investigate optimality conditions and the duality theorem of a set-valued optimization problem, and the main results can be applied to risk management.

Author Contributions: Conceptualization, Y.Z. and Q.W.; methodology Y.Z., Q.W. and T.T.; writing—original draft Y.Z.; writing-review and editing Y.Z., Q.W. and T.T. All authors have read and agreed to the published version of the manuscript.

Funding: This research was partially supported by the National Natural Science Foundation of China (No. 11971078), the Group Building Project for Scientifc Innovation for Universities in Chongqing (CXQT21021), and the Graduate Student Science and Technology Innovation Project (2021ST004).

Data Availability Statement: Not applicable.

Conflicts of Interest: The author declares no conflict of interest.

References

1. Beck, A.; Ben-Tal, A. Duality in robust optimization: Primal worst equals dual best. *Oper. Res. Lett.* **2009**, *37*, 1–6. [CrossRef]
2. Ben-Tal, A.; Nemirovski, A. Robust optimization–methodology and applications. *Math. Program.* **2002**, *92*, 453–480. [CrossRef]
3. Jeyakumar, V.; Li, G.Y. Strong duality in robust convex programming: Complete characterizations. *SIAM J. Optim.* **2010**, *20*, 3384–3407. [CrossRef]
4. Jeyakumar, V.; Li, G.; Lee, G.M. Robust duality for generalized convex programming problems under data uncertainty. *Nonlinear Anal.* **2012**, *75*, 1362–1373. [CrossRef]
5. Jeyakumar, V.; Lee, G.M.; Li, G. Characterizing robust solution sets of convex programs under data uncertainty. *J. Optim. Theory Appl.* **2015**, *164*, 407–435. [CrossRef]
6. Clarke, F.H. *Optimization and Nonsmooth Analysis*; Society for Industrial and Applied Mathematics: Philadelphia, PA, USA, 1990.
7. Hamel, A.H.; Heyde, F. Duality for set-valued measures of risk. *SIAM J. Financ. Math.* **2010**, *1*, 66–95. [CrossRef]
8. Hamel, A.H.; Heyde, F.; Rudloff, B. Set-valued risk measures for conical market models. *Math. Financ. Econ.* **2011**, *5*, 1–28. [CrossRef]
9. Hamel, A.H.; Kostner, D. Cone distribution functions and quantiles for multivariate random variables. *J. Multivar. Anal.* **2018**, *167*, 97–113. [CrossRef]
10. Eichfelder, G.; Jahn, J. Vector optimization problems and their solution concepts. In *Recent Developments in Vector Optimization*; Springer: Berlin/Heidelberg, Germany, 2012; pp. 1–27.
11. Young, R.C. The algebra of many-valued quantities. *Math. Ann.* **1931**, *104*, 260–290. [CrossRef]
12. Kuroiwa, D. Some duality Theorems of set-valued optimization. *RIMS Kokyuroku* **1999**, *1079*, 15–19.
13. Kuroiwa, D.; Tanaka, T.; Ha, T. On cone convexity of set-valued maps. *Nonlinear Anal.* **1997**, *30*, 1487–1496. [CrossRef]
14. Wei, H.Z.; Chen, C.R.; Li, S.J. Necessary optimality conditions for nonsmooth robust optimization problems. *Optimization* **2022**, *71*, 1817–1837. [CrossRef]
15. Wang, J.; Li, S.J.; Feng, M. Unified robust necessary optimality conditions for nonconvex nonsmooth uncertain multiobjective optimization. *J. Optim. Theory Appl.* **2022**, *195*, 226–248. [CrossRef] [PubMed]
16. Rockafellar, R.T. Convex Functions and Dual Extremum Problems. Ph.D. Thesis, Harvard University, Cambridge, MA, USA, 1963.
17. Song, W. Weak subdifferential of set-valued mappings. *Optimization* **2003**, *52*, 263–276. [CrossRef]
18. Tanino, T. Conjugate duality in vector optimization. *J. Math. Anal. Appl.* **1992**, *167*, 84–97. [CrossRef]
19. Sach, P.H. Moreau–Rockafellar Theorems for nonconvex set-valued maps. *J. Optim. Theory Appl.* **2007**, *133*, 213–227. [CrossRef]
20. Yang, X.Q. A Hahn-Banach Theorem in ordered linear spaces and its applications. *Optimization* **1992**, *25*, 1–9. [CrossRef]
21. Chen, G.Y.; Jahn, J. Optimality conditions for set-valued optimization problems. *Math. Methods Oper. Res.* **1998**, *48*, 187–200. [CrossRef]
22. Borwein, J.M. A Lagrange multiplier Theorem and a sandwich Theorem for convex relations. *Math. Scand.* **1981**, *48*, 189–204. [CrossRef]
23. Peng, J.W.; Lee, H.W.J.; Rong, W.D.; Yang, X.M. Hahn-Banach Theorems and subgradients of set-valued maps. *Math. Methods Oper. Res.* **2005**, *61*, 281–297. [CrossRef]
24. Li, S.J.; Guo, X.L. Weak subdifferential for set-valued mappings and its applications. *Nonlinear Anal.* **2009**, *71*, 5781–5789. [CrossRef]
25. Hernández, E.; Rodríguez-Marín, L. Weak and strong subgradients of set-valued maps. *J. Optim. Theory Appl.* **2011**, *149*, 352–365. [CrossRef]
26. Long, X.J.; Peng, J.W.; Li, X.B. Weak subdifferentials for set-valued mappings. *J. Optim. Theory Appl.* **2014**, *162*, 1–12. [CrossRef]
27. İnceoğlu, G. Some properties of second-order weak subdifferentials. *Turkish J. Math.* **2021**, *45*, 955–960.
28. Suneja, S.K.; Khurana, S.; Bhatia, M. Optimality and duality in vector optimization involving generalized type I functions over cones. *J. Glob. Optim.* **2011**, *49*, 23–35. [CrossRef]
29. Chuong, T.D.; Kim, D.S. Nonsmooth semi-infinite multiobjective optimization problems. *J. Optim. Theory Appl.* **2014**, *160*, 748–762. [CrossRef]
30. Chuong, T.D. Optimality and duality for robust multiobjective optimization problems. *Nonlinear Anal.* **2016**, *134*, 127–143. [CrossRef]
31. Rockafellar, R.T. *Convex Analysis*; Princeton University Press: Princeton, NJ, USA, 1970.

32. Sun, X.K.; Peng, Z.Y.; Guo, X.L. Some characterizations of robust optimal solutions for uncertain convex optimization problems. *Optim. Lett.* **2016**, *10*, 1463–1478. [CrossRef]
33. Som, K.; Vetrivel, V. On robustness for set-valued optimization problems. *J. Glob. Optim.* **2021**, *79*, 905–925. [CrossRef]
34. Kuroiwa, D. The natural criteria in set-valued optimization research on nonlinear analysis and convex analysis. *Surikaisekik-Enkyusho Kokyuroku* **1998**, *1031*, 85–90.
35. Chiriaev, A.; Walster, G.W. Interval Arithmetic Specification; Technical Report. 1998. Available online: http://www.mscs.mu.edu/globsol/walster-papers.html (accessed on 2 October 2022).

axioms

MDPI

Article

Second-Ordered Parametric Duality for the Multi-Objective Programming Problem in Complex Space

Chia-Yu Hsu † and Tone-Yau Huang *,†

Department of Applied Mathematics, Feng Chia University, Taichung 407102, Taiwan
* Correspondence: huangty@fcu.edu.tw
† These authors contributed equally to this work.

Abstract: We introduced and discussed a second-ordered parametric dual model of a complex multi-objective programming problem (P). Moreover, the authors constructed and proved the weak, strong and strictly converse duality theorems by the second-ordered generalized Θ-bonvexity.

Keywords: multi-objective programming; efficient solutions; generalized convexity; duality problem

MSC: 49K35; 90C29; 26A51; 90C46

1. Introduction

The complex optimization problem has been applied in many fields in electrical engineering, such as minimal entropy or maximum kurtosis. Levinson published their study on complex linear programming in 1966 [1]. Since then, case studies on complex nonlinear, fractional, and duality programming problems have been discussed [2–4]. Duca formulated the vectorial optimization problem in complex space and obtained the necessary and sufficient conditions [5–8]. Datta and Bhatia started their study on a complex minimax problem in 1984 [9]. Lai and Huang constructed various cases of complex minimax optimal problems. Following that, Huang et. al. constructed several types of second-order duality models for complex fractional and nonfractional minimax programming problems, and also derived the duality theorems under second-order generalized Θ-bonvexity [10–12].

All of the above, the complex optimal problems were focused on the real parts of complex objective functions. Youness and Elbrolosy considered the general case with both real and imaginary parts [13,14]. The complex extended programming problem is formulated as follows.

$$(\mathrm{P}_0) \qquad \min \quad f(z,\overline{z}) \quad \text{such that} \quad X = \{(z,\overline{z}) \in Q \mid -g(z,\overline{z}) \in S\},$$

where S is a polyhedral cone in $\mathbb{C}^m$, $f : \mathbb{C}^{2n} \to \mathbb{C}$ and $g : \mathbb{C}^{2n} \to \mathbb{C}^m$ are analytic in $\mathbf{z} = (z,\overline{z}) \in Q$, and the set $Q = \{(z,\overline{z}) \mid z \in \mathbb{C}^n\} \subset \mathbb{C}^{2n}$ is a linear manifold over real field. Elbrolosy extended the complex multi-objective vector optimization problem (P), and also defined the concept of optimal efficient solutions and established the optimality conditions of the problem (P) by using the scalarization techniques as follows [15].

$$(\mathrm{P}) \qquad \min \quad f(\mathbf{z}) = (f_1(\mathbf{z}),\ldots,f_p(\mathbf{z})) \quad \text{such that} \quad \mathbf{z} = (z,\overline{z}) \in X = \{\mathbf{z} \in Q \mid -g(\mathbf{z}) \in S\},$$

where $S \subset \mathbb{C}^q$ is a polyhedral cone, and $f : \mathbb{C}^{2n} \to \mathbb{C}^p$, $g : \mathbb{C}^{2n} \to \mathbb{C}^q$ are analytic in $\mathbf{z} = (z,\overline{z}) \in Q = \{(z,\overline{z}) \mid z \in \mathbb{C}^n\} \subset \mathbb{C}^{2n}$.

Recently, Huang and Tanaka established the sufficient optimality conditions of problem (P), formulated the parametric dual problem and proved their duality theorems under

Citation: Hsu, C.-Y.; Huang, T.-Y. Second-Ordered Parametric Duality for the Multi-Objective Programming Problem in Complex Space. *Axioms* **2022**, *11*, 717. https://doi.org/10.3390/axioms11120717

Academic Editor: Gustavo Olague

Received: 31 October 2022
Accepted: 9 December 2022
Published: 11 December 2022

Publisher's Note: MDPI stays neutral with regard to jurisdictional claims in published maps and institutional affiliations.

Copyright: © 2022 by the authors. Licensee MDPI, Basel, Switzerland. This article is an open access article distributed under the terms and conditions of the Creative Commons Attribution (CC BY) license (https://creativecommons.org/licenses/by/4.0/).

the generalized convexities [16]. Usually, the objective function in the complex programming problem was focused on the real part only. The novelty of this paper is extended the case of objective function from the real part to the case of both real and imaginary parts. Moreover, we would formulate the second-ordered parametric dual problem (D) with respect to the problem (P) and prove their duality theorems under the second-ordered generalized Θ-bonvexity.

2. Notations and Preliminary

Given $z \in \mathbb{C}^p$, the notations $\overline{z}$, z^T and z^H are the conjugate, transpose and conjugate transpose of z. Let $T = \{z \in \mathbb{C}^p \mid \mathrm{Re}(Kz) \geq 0\} \subset \mathbb{C}^p$ be a polyhedral cone with matrix $K \in \mathbb{C}^{k\times p}$ where k is a positive integer. The dual cone T^* of the convex cone T is defined by

$$T^* = \{\eta \in \mathbb{C}^p \mid \mathrm{Re}\langle z, \eta\rangle \geq 0 \text{ for all } z \in T\},$$

where $\langle z, \eta\rangle = \eta^H z$ is defined to be the inner product of z and η in complex spaces. For $z_0 \in T$, the set $T(z_0)$ is the intersection of those closed half spaces that includes z_0 in their boundaries. Thus, if $z_0 \in \mathrm{int}(T)$, $T(z_0)$ is the whole space $\mathbb{C}^p$.

Let $T \subset \mathbb{C}^p$ be a pointed, closed convex cone. For any $y, y_0 \in \mathbb{C}^p$, the ordered relation notation "$\leq_T$" with respect to cone T is defined as:

$$y_0 \leq_T y \;\Leftrightarrow\; y - y_0 \in T.$$

Note that for a nonzero vector $\mu \in T^*$,

$$y_0 \leq_T y \;\Rightarrow\; \mathrm{Re}[\mu^H(y - y_0)] \geq 0.$$

Definition 1 (Duca [8], Definition 3.3.1 (Optimal efficient solution)). *Let X be a nonempty subset of $Q = \{\mathbf{z} = (z, \overline{z}) \in \mathbb{C}^{2n} \mid z \in \mathbb{C}^n\} \subset \mathbb{C}^{2n}$, $T \subset \mathbb{C}^p$ be a pointed and closed convex cone, and $f : X \to \mathbb{C}^p$ be a map from X to $\mathbb{C}^p$.*

(1) *The point $\mathbf{z}_0 = (z_0, \overline{z_0}) \in X$ is a minimal efficient (or Pareto-minimal) solution of f with respect to T if there exists no other feasible point $\mathbf{z} = (z, \overline{z}) \in X$ such that $f(\mathbf{z}_0) - f(\mathbf{z}) \in T \setminus \{0\}$.*

(2) *The point $\mathbf{z}_0 = (z_0, \overline{z_0}) \in X$ is a maximal efficient (or Pareto-maximal) solution of f with respect to T if there exists no other feasible point $\mathbf{z} = (z, \overline{z}) \in X$ such that $f(\mathbf{z}) - f(\mathbf{z}_0) \in T \setminus \{0\}$.*

Note that $\mathbf{z}_0 \in X$ is a minimal efficient solution of f with respect to T if $(f(X) - f(\mathbf{z}_0)) \cap (-T) = \{0\}$; analogously, $\mathbf{z}_0 \in X$ is a maximal efficient solution of f with respect to T if $(f(\mathbf{z}_0) - f(X)) \cap (-T) = \{0\}$. The minimal efficient solution or maximal efficient solution of f with respect to T in a multi-objective programming problem is called the optimal efficient solution of f with respect to T.

In order to establish the optimality conditions and duality properties, we re-called the gradient expression and second-order gradient expression of the complex functions. Given $\mathbf{z} = (z, \overline{z}) \in \mathbb{C}^{2n}$ and a twice differentiable analytic function $f : \mathbb{C}^{2n} \to \mathbb{C}$, the gradient expression $\nabla f(\mathbf{z})$ is denoted by

$$\nabla f(\mathbf{z}) = \left(\nabla_z f(\mathbf{z}), \nabla_{\overline{z}} f(\mathbf{z})\right) \in \mathbb{C}^{p\times 2n}$$

with $\nabla_z f(\mathbf{z}) = \begin{pmatrix} \frac{\partial}{\partial z_1} f_1(\mathbf{z}) & \cdots & \frac{\partial}{\partial z_n} f_1(\mathbf{z}) \\ \vdots & \ddots & \\ \frac{\partial}{\partial z_1} f_p(\mathbf{z}) & \cdots & \frac{\partial}{\partial z_n} f_p(\mathbf{z}) \end{pmatrix}$, $\nabla_{\bar{z}} f(\mathbf{z}) = \begin{pmatrix} \frac{\partial}{\partial \bar{z}_1} f_1(\mathbf{z}) & \cdots & \frac{\partial}{\partial \bar{z}_n} f_1(\mathbf{z}) \\ \vdots & \ddots & \\ \frac{\partial}{\partial \bar{z}_1} f_p(\mathbf{z}) & \cdots & \frac{\partial}{\partial \bar{z}_n} f_p(\mathbf{z}) \end{pmatrix} \in \mathbb{C}^{p\times n}$.
The second-order gradient expression $\nabla^2 f_k(\mathbf{z}), k = 1\ldots,p$ is denoted by

$$\nabla^2 f_k(\mathbf{z}) = \begin{pmatrix} \nabla_{zz} f_k(\mathbf{z}), \ \nabla_{z\bar{z}} f_k(\mathbf{z}) \\ \nabla_{\bar{z}z} f_k(\mathbf{z}), \ \nabla_{\bar{z}\bar{z}} f_k(\mathbf{z}) \end{pmatrix} \in \mathbb{C}^{2n\times 2n}$$

with

$$\nabla_{zz} f_k(\mathbf{z}) = \left(\frac{\partial^2}{\partial z_i z_j} f_k(\mathbf{z})\right)_{n\times n}, i, j = 1,\ldots n, \quad \nabla_{\bar{z}z} f_k(\mathbf{z}) = \left(\frac{\partial^2}{\partial \bar{z}_i z_j} f_k(\mathbf{z})\right)_{n\times n}, i, j = 1,\ldots n,$$
$$\nabla_{z\bar{z}} f_k(\mathbf{z}) = \left(\frac{\partial^2}{\partial z_i \bar{z}_j} f_k(\mathbf{z})\right)_{n\times n}, i, j = 1,\ldots n, \quad \nabla_{\bar{z}\bar{z}} f_k(\mathbf{z}) = \left(\frac{\partial^2}{\partial \bar{z}_i \bar{z}_j} f_k(\mathbf{z})\right)_{n\times n}, i, j = 1,\ldots n.$$

We express the differential form of a complex function by using the gradient representations as the following lemma.

Lemma 1. *Given* $\mathbf{z} = (z, \bar{z}), \mathbf{z}_0 = (z_0, \overline{z_0}) \subset \mathbb{C}^{2n}$ *and* $(v, \bar{v}) = (z - z_0, \overline{z - z_0})$. *Suppose that* $f(\cdot) : \mathbb{C}^{2n} \to \mathbb{C}^p, \tau = (\tau_1, \ldots, \tau_p) \in \mathbb{C}^p$ *and* $\Phi(\mathbf{z}) = \langle f(\mathbf{z}), \tau\rangle = \tau^H f(\mathbf{z})$. *Then*
(a) *-ok*

$$\mathrm{Re}[\Phi'(\mathbf{z}_0)(\mathbf{z} - \mathbf{z}_0)] = \mathrm{Re}\Big\langle z - z_0, \ \tau^T \overline{\nabla_z f(\mathbf{z}_0)} + \tau^H \nabla_{\bar{z}} f(\mathbf{z}_0) \Big\rangle.$$

(b)

$$\begin{aligned}(\mathbf{z} - \mathbf{z}_0)^T \nabla^2 \Phi(\mathbf{z}_0)(\mathbf{z} - \mathbf{z}_0) &= \Big\langle v, v^H[\tau^T \overline{\nabla_{zz} f(\mathbf{z}_0)}] \Big\rangle + \Big\langle v^H[\tau^H \nabla_{\bar{z}\bar{z}} f(\mathbf{z}_0)], vs. \Big\rangle \\ &+ \Big\langle v, v^T[\tau^T \overline{\nabla_{\bar{z}z} f(\mathbf{z}_0)}] \Big\rangle + \Big\langle v^T[\tau^H \nabla_{z\bar{z}} f(\mathbf{z}_0)], vs. \Big\rangle.\end{aligned}$$

The real part of Equation (b) is equal to

$$\mathrm{Re}\Big\langle v, v^H\Big[\tau^T \overline{\nabla_{zz} f(\mathbf{z}_0)} + \tau^H \nabla_{\bar{z}\bar{z}} f(\mathbf{z}_0)\Big] + v^T\Big[\tau^T \overline{\nabla_{\bar{z}z} f(\mathbf{z}_0)} + \tau^H \nabla_{z\bar{z}} f(\mathbf{z}_0)\Big] \Big\rangle.$$

Proof.

(a) Since $\langle x, y\rangle = y^H x$ is the inner product in complex space,

$$\begin{aligned}\Phi'(\mathbf{z}_0)(\mathbf{z} - \mathbf{z}_0) &= \langle f'(\mathbf{z}_0)(\mathbf{z} - \mathbf{z}_0), \tau\rangle \\ &= \Big\langle (\nabla_z f(\mathbf{z}_0), \nabla_{\bar{z}} f(\mathbf{z}_0)) \begin{pmatrix} v \\ \bar{v} \end{pmatrix}, \tau \Big\rangle \\ &= \Big\langle \nabla_z f(\mathbf{z}_0) v + \nabla_z f(\mathbf{z}_0)\bar{v}, \tau \Big\rangle \\ &= \tau^H \nabla_z f(\mathbf{z}_0) v + \tau^H \nabla_{\bar{z}} f(\mathbf{z}_0) \bar{v} \\ &= \sum_{j=1}^{p}\sum_{i=1}^{n} \overline{\tau_j} \frac{\partial}{\partial z_i} f_j(\mathbf{z}_0)\, v_i + \sum_{j=1}^{p}\sum_{i=1}^{n} \overline{\tau_j} \frac{\partial}{\partial \overline{z_i}} f_j(\mathbf{z}_0)\, \overline{v_i} \\ &= \sum_{j=1}^{p}\sum_{i=1}^{n} \overline{\left(\tau_j \cdot \overline{\frac{\partial}{\partial z_i} f_j(\mathbf{z}_0)}\right)} \cdot v_i + \sum_{j=1}^{p}\sum_{i=1}^{n} \overline{v_i} \cdot \left(\overline{\tau_j} \cdot \frac{\partial}{\partial \overline{z_i}} f_j(\mathbf{z}_0)\right) \\ &= \Big\langle v, \tau^T \overline{\nabla_z f(\mathbf{z}_0)} \Big\rangle + \Big\langle \tau^H \nabla_{\bar{z}} f(\mathbf{z}_0), v \Big\rangle.\end{aligned}$$

We obtain

$$\Phi'(\mathbf{z}_0)(\mathbf{z} - \mathbf{z}_0) = \Big\langle z - z_0, \tau^T \overline{\nabla_z f(\mathbf{z}_0)} \Big\rangle + \Big\langle \tau^H \nabla_{\bar{z}} f(\mathbf{z}_0), z - z_0 \Big\rangle.$$

Moreover, since Re $[\langle x,y\rangle] = \mathrm{Re}[\overline{\langle y,x\rangle}] = \mathrm{Re}[\langle y,x\rangle]$, we have

$$\begin{aligned}
\mathrm{Re}\,[\Phi'(\mathbf{z}_0)(\mathbf{z}-\mathbf{z}_0)] &= \mathrm{Re}\left\{ \left\langle z-z_0, \tau^T\overline{\nabla_z f(\mathbf{z}_0)} \right\rangle + \overline{\left\langle \tau^H \nabla_{\overline{z}} f(\mathbf{z}_0), z-z_0 \right\rangle} \right\} \\
&= \mathrm{Re}\left\langle z-z_0, \tau^T\overline{\nabla_z f(\mathbf{z}_0)} \right\rangle + \mathrm{Re}\left\langle z-z_0,\ \overline{\tau^H \nabla_{\overline{z}} f(\mathbf{z}_0)} \right\rangle \\
&= \mathrm{Re}\left\langle z-z_0, \tau^T\overline{\nabla_z f(\mathbf{z}_0)} \right\rangle + \mathrm{Re}\left\langle z-z_0,\ \tau^H \nabla_{\overline{z}} f(\mathbf{z}_0) \right\rangle \\
&= \mathrm{Re}\left\langle z-z_0, \tau^T\overline{\nabla_z f(\mathbf{z}_0)} + \tau^H \nabla_{\overline{z}} f(\mathbf{z}_0) \right\rangle.
\end{aligned}$$

(b) Let $\Phi(\mathbf{z}) = \langle f(\mathbf{z}), \tau\rangle = \sum_{k=1}^{p} \overline{\tau_k} f_k(\mathbf{z}_0) = \overline{\tau_1} f_1(\mathbf{z}_0) + \cdots + \overline{\tau_p} f_p(\mathbf{z}_0)$, where $f_k(\mathbf{z}_0)$ is the mapping from $\mathbb{C}^{2n}$ to $\mathbb{C}^1$ for $k = 1, \ldots, p$. Then

$$\begin{aligned}
&(\mathbf{z}-\mathbf{z}_0)^T \nabla^2 \langle f(\mathbf{z}_0), \tau\rangle (\mathbf{z}-\mathbf{z}_0) \\
&\quad = (\mathbf{z}-\mathbf{z}_0)^T \overline{\tau_1} \nabla^2 f_1(\mathbf{z}_0)(\mathbf{z}-\mathbf{z}_0) + \cdots + (\mathbf{z}-\mathbf{z}_0)^T \overline{\tau_p} \nabla^2 f_p(\mathbf{z}_0)(\mathbf{z}-\mathbf{z}_0). \quad (1)
\end{aligned}$$

For $j = 1, \ldots, p$, and $\mathbf{z}-\mathbf{z}_0 = (z-z_0, \overline{z-z_0}) = (v, \overline{v})$,

$$(\mathbf{z}-\mathbf{z}_0)^T \overline{\tau_j} \nabla^2 f_j(\mathbf{z}_0)(\mathbf{z}-\mathbf{z}_0) = (v,\overline{v}) \begin{pmatrix} \overline{\tau_j}\nabla_{zz} f_j(\mathbf{z}_0), & \overline{\tau_j}\nabla_{z\overline{z}} f_j(\mathbf{z}_0) \\ \overline{\tau_j}\nabla_{\overline{z}z} f_j(\mathbf{z}_0), & \overline{\tau_j}\nabla_{\overline{z}\overline{z}} f_j(\mathbf{z}_0) \end{pmatrix} \begin{pmatrix} v \\ \overline{v} \end{pmatrix}$$

$$\begin{aligned}
&= \sum_{l=1}^{n}\left[\sum_{k=1}^{n} v_k \overline{\tau_j} \frac{\partial^2 f_j(\mathbf{z}_0)}{\partial z_k \partial z_l}\right] v_l + \sum_{l=1}^{n}\left[\sum_{k=1}^{n} \overline{v_k \tau_j} \frac{\partial^2 f_j(\mathbf{z}_0)}{\partial \overline{z_k} \partial z_l}\right] v_l + \sum_{l=1}^{n}\left[\sum_{k=1}^{n} v_k \overline{\tau_j} \frac{\partial^2 f_j(\mathbf{z}_0)}{\partial z_k \partial \overline{z_l}}\right] \overline{v_l} + \sum_{l=1}^{n}\left[\sum_{k=1}^{n} \overline{v_k \tau_j} \frac{\partial^2 f_j(\mathbf{z}_0)}{\partial \overline{z_k} \partial \overline{z_l}}\right] \overline{v_l} \\
&= \sum_{l=1}^{n}\left[\sum_{k=1}^{n} \overline{v_k} \tau_j \frac{\overline{\partial^2 f_j(\mathbf{z}_0)}}{\partial z_k \partial z_l}\right] v_l + \sum_{l=1}^{n}\left[\sum_{k=1}^{n} v_k \tau_j \frac{\overline{\partial^2 f_j(\mathbf{z}_0)}}{\partial \overline{z_k} \partial z_l}\right] v_l + \sum_{l=1}^{n} \overline{v_l}\left[\sum_{k=1}^{n} v_k \overline{\tau_j} \frac{\partial^2 f_j(\mathbf{z}_0)}{\partial z_k \partial \overline{z_l}}\right] + \sum_{l=1}^{n} \overline{v_l}\left[\sum_{k=1}^{n} \overline{v_k \tau_j} \frac{\partial^2 f_j(\mathbf{z}_0)}{\partial \overline{z_k} \partial \overline{z_l}}\right] \\
&= \left\langle v, v^H[\tau_j \overline{\nabla_{zz} f_j(\mathbf{z}_0)}] \right\rangle + \left\langle v^T[\overline{\tau_j}\nabla_{z\overline{z}} f_j(\mathbf{z}_0)], vs. \right\rangle + \left\langle v, v^T[\tau_j \overline{\nabla_{\overline{z}z} f_j(\mathbf{z}_0)}] \right\rangle + \left\langle v^H[\overline{\tau_j}\nabla_{\overline{z}\overline{z}} f_j(\mathbf{z}_0)], vs. \right\rangle.
\end{aligned}$$

By formula above, Equation (1) implies that

$$\begin{aligned}
(\mathbf{z}-\mathbf{z}_0)^T \nabla^2 \langle f(\mathbf{z}_0), \tau\rangle (\mathbf{z}-\mathbf{z}_0) &= \left\langle v, v^H[\tau^T \overline{\nabla_{zz} f(\mathbf{z}_0)}] \right\rangle + \left\langle v^T[\tau^H \nabla_{z\overline{z}} f(\mathbf{z}_0)], vs. \right\rangle \\
&\quad + \left\langle v, v^T[\tau^T \overline{\nabla_{\overline{z}z} f(\mathbf{z}_0)}] \right\rangle + \left\langle v^H[\tau^H \nabla_{\overline{z}\overline{z}} f(\mathbf{z}_0)], vs. \right\rangle,
\end{aligned}$$

and the real part of the above identity is equal to

$$\mathrm{Re}\left(\left\langle v, v^H\left[\tau^T\overline{\nabla_{zz} f(\mathbf{z}_0)} + \tau^H \nabla_{\overline{z}\overline{z}} f(\mathbf{z}_0)\right] + v^T\left[\tau^T\overline{\nabla_{\overline{z}z} f(\mathbf{z}_0)} + \tau^H \nabla_{z\overline{z}} f(\mathbf{z}_0)\right] \right\rangle\right).$$

□

3. Optimality Conditions

We would like to find the minimum efficient solutions to the complex multi-objective programming problem (P). The scalarization technique is going to be applied to the multi-objective programming problem. We would obtain the existence of minimum efficient solutions of problem (P) above by scalarized programming problem (P_τ) below, and the lemmas followed will be stated [15,16].

Given a nonzero vector $\tau \in \mathbb{C}^p$, we consider the scalarized programming problem with respect to problem (P) as follows.

$$\begin{array}{lll}
(\mathrm{P}_\tau) & \min & \mathrm{Re}[\tau^H f(\mathbf{z})] \\
 & \text{such that} & X = \{\zeta = (z,\overline{z}) \in Q \mid -g(\mathbf{z}) \in S\}.
\end{array}$$

Lemma 2 (Elbrolosy [15], Theorem 4.4). *Let $T \subset \mathbb{C}^p$ be a pointed, closed and convex cone and $f(X)$ be a convex set. If point $\mathbf{z}_0$ is a minimal efficient solution of (P) with respect to T, then there exists a nonzero vector $\tau \in T^*$ such that $\mathbf{z}_0$ is an optimal solution of (P_τ).*

Lemma 3 (Elbrolosy [15], Theorem 4.6). *Let $T \subset \mathbb{C}^p$ be a pointed, closed and convex cone, and $\tau \in T^*$ with $\tau \neq 0$. Assume that $\mathbf{z}_0$ is an optimal solution of (P_τ), and anyone of the following conditions holds,*
(1) nonzero vector $\tau \in int(T^*)$,
(2) point $\mathbf{z}_0$ is the unique optimal solution of (P_τ).
Then $\mathbf{z}_0$ is the minimal efficient solution of (P) with respect to T.

Elbrolosy [15] established the Kuhn-Tucker necessary optimality conditions of problem (P) by using the scalarization techniques, we described as follows.

Definition 2 (Lai and Huang [12], Definition 3). *The problem (P) is said to satisfy the* **constraint qualification**
at a point $\mathbf{z}_0 = (z_0, \overline{z_0})$, if for any nonzero $\mu \in S^* \subset \mathbb{C}^q$,

$$\langle\, g'_{\mathbf{z}}(\mathbf{z}_0)(\mathbf{z} - \mathbf{z}_0), \mu \,\rangle \neq 0, \text{ for } \mathbf{z} \neq \mathbf{z}_0.$$

Under the gradient expression as in Lemma 1, the constraint qualification can be expressed by

$$\mu^T \overline{\nabla_z g(\mathbf{z}_0)} + \mu^H \nabla_{\bar{z}} g(\mathbf{z}_0) \neq 0, \ \text{ for } \mu \neq 0 \text{ in } S^*,$$

where $\mu^H = \overline{\mu^T}$.

Theorem 1 (Elbrolosy [15], Theorem 4.9 (Necessary optimality conditions)). *Let $T \subset \mathbb{C}^p$ be a pointed, closed and convex cone, S be a polyhedral cone in $\mathbb{C}^q$ and $f(X)$ be a convex set. Suppose that the mappings $f(\cdot) : \mathbb{C}^{2n} \to \mathbb{C}^p$ and $g(\cdot) : \mathbb{C}^{2n} \to \mathbb{C}^q$ are analytic on $X \subseteq Q$, and $\mathbf{z}_0$ is a minimal efficient solution of (P) with respect to T. If problem (P) possesses the constraint qualification at $\mathbf{z}_0$, there are nonzero vectors $\tau \in T^* \subset \mathbb{C}^p$ and $\mu \in S^* \subset \mathbb{C}^q$ satisfying the following conditions:*

$$\tau^T \overline{\nabla_z f(\mathbf{z}_0)} + \tau^H \nabla_{\bar{z}} f(\mathbf{z}_0) + \mu^T \overline{\nabla_z g(\mathbf{z}_0)} + \mu^H \nabla_{\bar{z}} g(z_0) = 0, \tag{2}$$

$$\text{Re } \mu^H g(\mathbf{z}_0) = 0. \tag{3}$$

In order to formulate the sufficient optimality conditions and duality theorems, we introduce the generalized convexity in complex spaces as follows.

Definition 3 (Lai and Huang [12], Definition 1). *The real part of an analytic function $f(\cdot)$ is said to be:*

(i) *convex (strictly) at $\mathbf{z}_0 \in Q \subset \mathbb{C}^{2n}$ if for all $\mathbf{z} \in Q$,*
$$\text{Re } [f(\mathbf{z}) - f(\mathbf{z}_0)] \ \geq (>) \text{ Re } [f'(\mathbf{z}_0)(\mathbf{z} - \mathbf{z}_0)],$$
(ii) *pseudoconvex (strictly) at $\mathbf{z}_0 \in Q$ if for all $\mathbf{z} \in Q$,*
$$\text{Re } [f'(\mathbf{z}_0)(\mathbf{z} - \mathbf{z}_0)] \geq 0 \Rightarrow \text{Re } [f(\mathbf{z}) - f(\mathbf{z}_0)] \ \geq 0 (> 0),$$
(iii) *quasiconvex at $\mathbf{z}_0 \in Q$ if for all $\mathbf{z} \in Q$,*
$$\text{Re } [f(\mathbf{z}) - f(\mathbf{z}_0)] \leq 0 \Rightarrow \text{Re } [f'(\mathbf{z}_0)(\mathbf{z} - \mathbf{z}_0)] \leq 0.$$

Huang and Tanaka [16] established the sufficient optimality conditions below.

Theorem 2 ([16], Theorem 3.6 (Sufficient optimality conditions)). *Let $T \subset \mathbb{C}^p$ be a pointed, closed and convex cone, S be a polyhedral cone in $\mathbb{C}^q$, and $f(\cdot) : \mathbb{C}^{2n} \to \mathbb{C}^p$ and $g(\cdot) : \mathbb{C}^{2n} \to \mathbb{C}^q$ be two analytic mappings on $X \subseteq Q$, where $Q \subset \mathbb{C}^{2n}$. Suppose that $\mathbf{z}_0$ is a feasible solution of (P), and there are nonzero vectors $\tau \in T^* \subset \mathbb{C}^p$ and $\mu \in S^* \subset \mathbb{C}^q$ satisfying conditions* (2) *and* (3) *in Theorem 1. If any one of the following conditions (i)–(iii) holds:*

(i) *Either of* $\text{Re}[\tau^H f(\cdot)]$ *or* $\text{Re}[\mu^H g(\cdot)]$ *is strictly convex and the other is convex at $\mathbf{z}_0 \in Q$, or both are strictly convex at $\mathbf{z}_0 \in Q$,*
(ii) $\text{Re}[\tau^H f(\cdot)]$ *is quasiconvex at $\mathbf{z}_0 \in Q$ and* $\text{Re}[\mu^H g(\cdot)]$ *is strictly pseudoconvex at $\mathbf{z}_0 \in Q$,*

(iii) $\mathrm{Re}[\tau^H f(\cdot) + \mu^H g(\cdot)]$ *is strictly pseudoconvex at* $\mathbf{z}_0 \in Q$,
then $\mathbf{z}_0$ *is the minimal efficient solution of (P) with respect to* T.

4. The Second-Order Parametric Duality Model

We would like to use the following differential notations to simplify the expression. Let $\mathbf{u} = (u, \overline{u}) \in \mathbb{C}^{2n}$, $\tau \in \mathbb{C}^p$, $\mu \in \mathbb{C}^q$, and $f : \mathbb{C}^{2n} \to \mathbb{C}^p$, $g : \mathbb{C}^{2n} \to \mathbb{C}^q$ are analytic mappings:

$$F^{(1)}(\mathbf{u},\tau) = \tau^T \overline{\nabla_z f(\mathbf{u})} + \tau^H \nabla_{\overline{z}} f(\mathbf{u});$$
$$F_1^{(2)}(\mathbf{u},\tau) = \tau^T \overline{\nabla_{zz} f(\mathbf{u})} + \tau^H \nabla_{\overline{z}\overline{z}} f(\mathbf{u}); \quad F_2^{(2)}(\mathbf{u},\tau) = \tau^T \overline{\nabla_{\overline{z}z} f(\mathbf{u})} + \tau^H \nabla_{z\overline{z}} f(\mathbf{u}).$$
$$G^{(1)}(\mathbf{u},\mu) = \mu^T \overline{\nabla_z g(\mathbf{u})} + \mu^H \nabla_{\overline{z}} g(\mathbf{u});$$
$$G_1^{(2)}(\mathbf{u},\mu) = \mu^T \overline{\nabla_{zz} g(\mathbf{u})} + \mu^H \nabla_{\overline{z}\overline{z}} g(\mathbf{u}); \quad G_2^{(2)}(\mathbf{u},\mu) = \mu^T \overline{\nabla_{\overline{z}z} g(\mathbf{u})} + \mu^H \nabla_{z\overline{z}} g(\mathbf{u}).$$

The second-order parametric dual problem of problem (P) is considered as the following form.

$$(\mathrm{D}) \quad \max_{\mathcal{F}_D} \quad \gamma = (\gamma_1, \ldots, \gamma_p),$$

where $\mathcal{F}_D$ is the set of all feasible solutions $(\tau, \mathbf{u}, \mu, \nu, \gamma)$ satisfied the following conditions: For $\mathbf{u} = (u, \overline{u}) \in Q$, $\tau \in \mathbb{C}^p$, $\nu \in \mathbb{C}^n$ and $\mu \in S^*$,

$$[F^{(1)}(\mathbf{u},\tau) + G^{(1)}(\mathbf{u},\mu)] + \nu^H [F_1^{(2)}(\mathbf{u},\tau) + G_1^{(2)}(\mathbf{u},\mu)] + \nu^T [F_2^{(2)}(\mathbf{u},\tau) + G_2^{(2)}(\mathbf{u},\mu)] = 0, \quad (4)$$

$$\mathrm{Re}\,\langle f(\mathbf{u}) - \gamma, \tau \rangle \geq \frac{1}{2} \mathrm{Re} \left\langle \nu \,,\, \nu^H F_1^{(2)}(\mathbf{u},\tau) + \nu^T F_2^{(2)}(\mathbf{u},\tau) \right\rangle, \quad (5)$$

$$\mathrm{Re}\,\langle g(\mathbf{u}), \mu \rangle \geq \frac{1}{2} \mathrm{Re} \left\langle \nu \,,\, \nu^H G_1^{(2)}(\mathbf{u},\mu) + \nu^T G_2^{(2)}(\mathbf{u},\mu) \right\rangle. \quad (6)$$

We introduce the second-ordered generalized Θ-bonvexity as follows.

Definition 4 (Huang [10], Definition 4.1). *The real part of an analytic function* $f(\cdot)$ *is called,*

(i) **Θ-bonvex (strictly)** *at* $\mathbf{z}_0 \in Q \subset \mathbb{C}^{2n}$ *if there exists a suitable mapping* $\Theta : \mathbb{C}^{2n} \times \mathbb{C}^{2n} \to \mathbb{C}^{2n}$ *such that for any* $\mathbf{z} \in Q$,
$$\mathrm{Re}\left\{ f(\mathbf{z}) - f(\mathbf{z}_0) + \frac{1}{2}(\mathbf{z} - \mathbf{z}_0)^T \nabla^2 f(\mathbf{z}_0)(\mathbf{z} - \mathbf{z}_0) \right\}$$
$$\geq (>) \ \mathrm{Re}\left\{ [\nabla f(\mathbf{z}_0) + (\mathbf{z} - \mathbf{z}_0)^T \nabla^2 f(\mathbf{z}_0)] \Theta(\mathbf{z}, \mathbf{z}_0) \right\},$$

(ii) **Θ-pseudobonvex (strictly)** *at* $\mathbf{z}_0 \in Q \subset \mathbb{C}^{2n}$ *if there exists a suitable mapping* $\Theta : \mathbb{C}^{2n} \times \mathbb{C}^{2n} \to \mathbb{C}^{2n}$ *such that for any* $\mathbf{z} \in Q$,
$$\mathrm{Re}\left\{ [\nabla f(\mathbf{z}_0) + (\mathbf{z} - \mathbf{z}_0)^T \nabla^2 f(\mathbf{z}_0)] \Theta(\mathbf{z}, \mathbf{z}_0) \right\} \geq 0$$
$$\Rightarrow \mathrm{Re}\left\{ f(\mathbf{z}) - f(\mathbf{z}_0) + \frac{1}{2}(\mathbf{z} - \mathbf{z}_0)^T \nabla^2 f(\mathbf{z}_0)(\mathbf{z} - \mathbf{z}_0) \right\} \geq 0 \ (> 0),$$

(iii) **Θ-quasibonvex** *at* $\mathbf{z}_0 \in Q$ *if there exists a suitable mapping* $\Theta : \mathbb{C}^{2n} \times \mathbb{C}^{2n} \to \mathbb{C}^{2n}$ *such that for any* $\mathbf{z} \in Q$,
$$\mathrm{Re}\left\{ f(\mathbf{z}) - f(\mathbf{z}_0) + \frac{1}{2}(\mathbf{z} - \mathbf{z}_0)^T \nabla^2 f(\mathbf{z}_0)(\mathbf{z} - \mathbf{z}_0) \right\} \leq 0$$
$$\Rightarrow \mathrm{Re}\left\{ [\nabla f(\mathbf{z}_0) + (\mathbf{z} - \mathbf{z}_0)^T \nabla^2 f(\mathbf{z}_0)] \Theta(\mathbf{z}, \mathbf{z}_0) \right\} \leq 0.$$

Using the generalized Θ-bonvexities, we could obtain the weak, strong and strictly converse duality theorem of dual problem (D) with respect to primary problem (P).

Theorem 3 (Weak Duality). *Let* $\mathbf{z} = (z, \overline{z})$ *be (P)-feasible solution, and* $(\tau, \mathbf{u}, \mu, \nu, \gamma)$ *be (D)-feasible solution. Suppose that any one of the conditions holds:*

(i) *Either one of* $\mathrm{Re}[\tau^H f(\cdot)]$ *or* $\mathrm{Re}[\mu^H g(\cdot)]$ *is strictly* Θ*-bonvex and the other is* Θ*-bonvex at* $\mathbf{u} \in Q$*, or both are strictly* Θ*-bonvex at* $\mathbf{u} \in Q$*,*

(ii) $\mathrm{Re}[\tau^H f(\cdot)]$ *is* Θ*-quasibonvex at* $\mathbf{u} \in Q$ *and* $\mathrm{Re}[\mu^H g(\cdot)]$ *is strictly* Θ*-pseudobonvex at* $\mathbf{u} \in Q$*,*

(iii) $\mathrm{Re}[\tau^H f(\cdot) + \mu^H g(\cdot)]$ *is strictly* Θ*-pseudoconvex at* $\mathbf{u} \in Q$*.*

Then

$$f(\mathbf{z}) \nless_T \gamma.$$

Proof. Suppose on the contrary that

$$\gamma - f(\mathbf{z}) \in T \setminus \{0\}. \tag{7}$$

We could pick a nonzero vector $\tau \in T^*$, such that $\mathrm{Re}\langle \gamma - f(\mathbf{z}), \tau \rangle \geq 0$, or

$$\mathrm{Re}\langle f(\mathbf{z}) - \gamma, \tau \rangle \leq 0.$$

By inequality (5), then

$$\mathrm{Re}\langle f(\mathbf{z}) - \gamma, \tau \rangle \leq 0 \leq \mathrm{Re}\langle f(\mathbf{u}) - \gamma, \tau \rangle - \frac{1}{2}\mathrm{Re}\left\langle \nu\ ,\ \nu^H F_1^{(2)}(\mathbf{u}, \tau) + \nu^T F_2^{(2)}(\mathbf{u}, \tau) \right\rangle.$$

That is

$$\mathrm{Re}\langle f(\mathbf{z}) - f(\mathbf{u}), \tau \rangle + \frac{1}{2}\mathrm{Re}\left\langle \nu\ ,\ \nu^H F_1^{(2)}(\mathbf{u}, \tau) + \nu^T F_2^{(2)}(\mathbf{u}, \tau) \right\rangle \leq 0. \tag{8}$$

Since the feasibility of $\mathbf{z}$ for problem (P) and the inequality (6),

$$\mathrm{Re}\ \langle g(\mathbf{z}), \mu \rangle \leq 0 \leq \mathrm{Re}\langle g(\mathbf{u}), \mu \rangle - \frac{1}{2}\mathrm{Re}\ \langle\ \nu\ ,\ \nu^H G_1^{(2)}(\mathbf{u}, \mu) + \nu^T G_2^{(2)}(\mathbf{u}, \mu)\ \rangle.$$

We get the following inequality

$$\mathrm{Re}\ \langle g(\mathbf{z}) - g(\mathbf{u}), \mu \rangle + \frac{1}{2}\mathrm{Re}\ \langle\ \nu\ ,\ \nu^H G_1^{(2)}(\mathbf{u}, \mu) + \nu^T G_2^{(2)}(\mathbf{u}, \mu)\ \rangle \leq 0. \tag{9}$$

(a) If hypothesis (i) holds, without loss of generality, assume that $\mathrm{Re}[\tau^H f(\cdot)]$ is strictly Θ-bonvex and $\mathrm{Re}[\mu^H g(\cdot)]$ is Θ-bonvex at $\mathbf{u} \in Q$, and let $(\nu, \overline{\nu}) = \mathbf{z} - \mathbf{u}$.
From inequality (8) and $\mathrm{Re}[\tau^H f(\cdot)]$ is strictly Θ-bonvex at $\mathbf{u} \in Q$, then there is a mapping $\Theta : \mathbb{C}^{2n} \times \mathbb{C}^{2n} \to \mathbb{C}^{2n}$ such that

$$\mathrm{Re}\left\{[\nabla \tau^H f(\mathbf{u}) + (\nu, \overline{\nu})^T \nabla^2 \tau^H f(\mathbf{u})]\Theta(\mathbf{z}, \mathbf{u})\right\} < 0. \tag{10}$$

From inequality (9) and $\mathrm{Re}[\mu^H g(\cdot)]$ is Θ-bonvex at $\mathbf{u} \in Q$, then there is a mapping $\Theta : \mathbb{C}^{2n} \times \mathbb{C}^{2n} \to \mathbb{C}^{2n}$ such that

$$\mathrm{Re}\left\{[\nabla \mu^H g(\mathbf{u}) + (\nu, \overline{\nu})^T \nabla^2 \mu^H g(\mathbf{u})]\Theta(\mathbf{z}, \mathbf{u})\right\} \leq 0. \tag{11}$$

Combine inequalities (10) and (11), then

$$\mathrm{Re}\left\{\nabla[\tau^H f(\mathbf{u}) \mu^H g(\mathbf{u})] + (\nu, \overline{\nu})^T \nabla^2 [\tau^H f(\mathbf{u}) + \mu^H g(\mathbf{u})]\right\}\Theta(\mathbf{z}, \mathbf{u}) < 0.$$

This implies that

$$\left[F^{(1)}(\mathbf{u}, \tau) + G^{(1)}(\mathbf{u}, \mu)\right] + \nu^H \left[F_1^{(2)}(\mathbf{u}, \tau) + G_1^{(2)}(\mathbf{u}, \mu)\right] + \nu^T \left[F_2^{(2)}(\mathbf{u}, \tau) + G_2^{(2)}(\mathbf{u}, \mu)\right] \neq 0, \tag{12}$$

this contradicts the equality (4).

(b) If hypothesis (ii) holds, $\mathrm{Re}[\tau^H f(\cdot)]$ is Θ-quasibonvex at $\mathbf{u}$ and according to inequality (8), then there is a mapping $\Theta : \mathbb{C}^{2n} \times \mathbb{C}^{2n} \to \mathbb{C}^{2n}$ such that

$$\mathrm{Re}\left\{[\nabla \tau^H f(\mathbf{u}) + (\nu, \overline{\nu})^T \nabla^2 \tau^H f(\mathbf{u})]\Theta(\mathbf{z}, \mathbf{u})\right\} \leq 0.$$

By inequality (9) and $\mathrm{Re}[\mu^H g(\cdot)]$ is strictly Θ-pesudobonvex at $\mathbf{u} \in Q$, then there is a mapping $\Theta : \mathbb{C}^{2n} \times \mathbb{C}^{2n} \to \mathbb{C}^{2n}$ such that

$$\mathrm{Re}\left\{[\nabla \mu^H g(\mathbf{u}) + (\nu, \overline{\nu})^T \nabla^2 \mu^H g(\mathbf{u})]\Theta(\mathbf{z}, \mathbf{u})\right\} < 0.$$

We obtain inequality (12) by summing up the two inequalities above, and then this contradicts the equality of (4).

(c) Combine inequalities (8) and (9), and since $\mathrm{Re}[\tau^H f(\cdot) + \mu^H g(\cdot)]$ is strictly Θ-pseudoconvex at $\mathbf{u} \in Q$, then we get the same inequality (12), which contradicts the equality (4).
Therefore, the result of theorem is proved.

□

Theorem 4 (Strong Duality). *Let $T \subset \mathbb{C}^p$ is a pointed, closed and convex cone. Suppose that $\mathbf{z}_0$ is a minimal efficient solution of (P) with respect to T, and the problem (P) satisfies the constraint qualification at $\mathbf{z}_0$. Then there exists $(\tau, \mathbf{z}_0, \mu, \nu, \gamma)$ a feasible solution of the dual problem (D). Moreover, if the hypotheses of Theorem 3 are fulfilled, then $(\tau, \mathbf{z}_0, \mu, \nu, \gamma)$ is also an optimal solution of (D) with respect to T, and the two problems (P) and (D) have the same optimal values.*

Proof. Let $\mathbf{z}_0 = (z_0, \overline{z_0}) \in Q$ is a minimal efficient solution of problem (P) with optimal value γ, and take $\nu = z_0 - z_0 = 0$. By using Theorem 1 (Necessary optimality conditions), there exist $\tau \in T^* \subset \mathbb{C}^p$ and $\mu \in S^* \subset \mathbb{C}^q$ such that

$$\begin{aligned}&\tau^T \overline{\nabla_z f(\mathbf{z}_0)} + \tau^H \nabla_{\overline{z}} f(\mathbf{z}_0) + \mu^T \overline{\nabla_z g(\mathbf{z}_0)} + \mu^H \nabla_{\overline{z}} g(\mathbf{z}_0) = 0,\\ &\mathrm{Re}[\mu^H g(\mathbf{z}_0)] = 0,\end{aligned}$$

then conditions (4) and (6) of dual problem (D) are hold. Because γ is the optimal value of problem (P), that is $\gamma = \min f(\mathbf{z}) = f(\mathbf{z}_0)$. It implies that $\mathrm{Re}\langle f(\mathbf{z}_0) - \gamma, \tau\rangle = 0$, the condition (5) of problem (D) holds. Hence, $(\tau, \mathbf{z}_0, \mu, \nu = 0, \gamma)$ is a feasible solution of the dual problem (D). From Theorem 3, the optimality of the feasible solution $(\tau, \mathbf{z}_0, \mu, \nu, \gamma)$ for (D) reduces to be the optimal value of (D). Indeed, if there exists a feasible solution $(\tau, \mathbf{z}', \mu, \nu, \gamma')$ of (D) such that $\gamma' - \gamma \in T \setminus \{0\}$. Since $\gamma = f(\mathbf{z}_0)$ is the optimal value of problem (P), we obtain

$$\gamma' - f(\mathbf{z}_0) \in T \setminus \{0\},$$

which contradicts to Theorem 3. □

Theorem 5 (Strictly Converse Duality). *Let $T \subset \mathbb{C}^p$ is a pointed, closed and convex cone. Suppose that $\widehat{\mathbf{z}}$ and $(\tau, \widehat{\mathbf{u}}, \mu, \nu, \gamma)$ are optimal efficient solutions of (P) and (D) with respect to T, respectively, and assume that the assumptions of Theorem 4 are fulfilled. Meanwhile, if $\mathrm{Re}[\tau^H f(\cdot)]$ is strictly Θ-pseudobonvex at $\widehat{\mathbf{u}} \in Q$ and $\mathrm{Re}[\mu^H g(\cdot)]$ is Θ-quasibonvex at $\widehat{\mathbf{u}} \in Q$, then $\widehat{\mathbf{z}} = \widehat{\mathbf{u}}$, and the problems of (P) and (D) with the same optimal values.*

Proof. We assume that $\widehat{\mathbf{z}} \neq \widehat{\mathbf{u}}$. Since $\widehat{\mathbf{z}}$ is an optimal efficient solution of (P) with optimal value γ, and from Theorem 4, then

$$\gamma = \min f(\widehat{\mathbf{z}}) = \big(f_1(\widehat{\mathbf{z}}), \dots, f_p(\widehat{\mathbf{z}})\big).$$

So, we get $\mathrm{Re}\langle f(\widehat{\mathbf{z}})-\gamma,\tau\rangle = 0$ for nonzero $\tau \in T^*$. By condition (5) and the above inequality,

$$\mathrm{Re}\langle f(\widehat{\mathbf{z}})-\gamma,\tau\rangle = 0 \le \mathrm{Re}\,\langle f(\widehat{\mathbf{u}})-\gamma,\tau\rangle - \frac{1}{2}\mathrm{Re}\left\langle \nu\,,\, \nu^H F_1^{(2)}(\widehat{\mathbf{u}},\tau)+\nu^T F_2^{(2)}(\widehat{\mathbf{u}},\tau)\right\rangle.$$

That is,

$$\mathrm{Re}\langle f(\widehat{\mathbf{z}})-f(\widehat{\mathbf{u}}),\tau\rangle + \frac{1}{2}\mathrm{Re}\left\langle \nu\,,\, \nu^H F_1^{(2)}(\widehat{\mathbf{u}},\tau)+\nu^T F_2^{(2)}(\widehat{\mathbf{u}},\tau)\right\rangle \le 0. \tag{13}$$

Using the feasibility of $\widehat{\mathbf{z}}$ of (P) with $\mu \in S^*$, and inequality (6),

$$\mathrm{Re}[\mu^H g(\widehat{\mathbf{z}})] \le 0 \le \mathrm{Re}[\mu^H g(\widehat{\mathbf{u}})] - \frac{1}{2}\mathrm{Re}\left\langle \nu\,,\, \nu^H G_1^{(2)}(\mathbf{u},\mu)+\nu^T G_2^{(2)}(\mathbf{u},\mu)\right\rangle.$$

Then

$$\mathrm{Re}[\mu^H g(\widehat{\mathbf{z}}) - \mu^H g(\widehat{\mathbf{u}})] + \frac{1}{2}\mathrm{Re}\left\langle \nu\,,\, \nu^H G_1^{(2)}(\mathbf{u},\mu)+\nu^T G_2^{(2)}(\mathbf{u},\mu)\right\rangle \le 0. \tag{14}$$

If $\mathrm{Re}[\tau^H f(\cdot)]$ is strictly Θ-pseudobonvex at $\widehat{\mathbf{u}} \in Q$ and by inequality (13), there is a mapping $\Theta : \mathbb{C}^{2n} \times \mathbb{C}^{2n} \to \mathbb{C}$ such that

$$\mathrm{Re}\,\left\{[\nabla \tau^H f(\mathbf{u}) + (\nu,\overline{\nu})^T \nabla^2 \tau^H f(\mathbf{u})]\Theta(\mathbf{z},\mathbf{u})\right\} < 0. \tag{15}$$

If $\mathrm{Re}[\mu^H g(\cdot)]$ is Θ-quasibonvex at $\widehat{\mathbf{u}} \in Q$ and by inequality (14), there is a mapping $\Theta : \mathbb{C}^{2n} \times \mathbb{C}^{2n} \to \mathbb{C}$ such that

$$\mathrm{Re}\,\left\{[\nabla \mu^H g(\mathbf{u}) + (\nu,\overline{\nu})^T \nabla^2 \mu^H g(\mathbf{u})]\Theta(\mathbf{z},\mathbf{u})\right\} \le 0. \tag{16}$$

By considering inequalities (15) and (16), we could obtain the following inequality:

$$\left[F^{(1)}(\widehat{\mathbf{u}},\tau)+G^{(1)}(\widehat{\mathbf{u}},\mu)\right] + \nu^H\left[F_1^{(2)}(\widehat{\mathbf{u}},\tau)+G_1^{(2)}(\widehat{\mathbf{u}},\mu)\right] + \nu^T\left[F_2^{(2)}(\widehat{\mathbf{u}},\tau)+G_2^{(2)}(\widehat{\mathbf{u}},\mu)\right] \ne 0,$$

which contradicts the equality (4). This completed the proof. □

5. Conclusions

In this paper, we state the necessary and sufficient optimality conditions of (P), establish the second-ordered parameter dual model (D) with respect to problem (P), and discuss their duality theorems.

Author Contributions: Writing original draft, C.-Y.H. and T.-Y.H. Both authors contributed equally to the manuscript. All authors have read and agreed to the published version of the manuscript.

Funding: This paper is partially supported by Grant No. MOST 111-2115-M-035-002 of the Ministry of Science and Technology of the Republic of China.

Institutional Review Board Statement: Not applicable.

Informed Consent Statement: Not applicable.

Data Availability Statement: Not applicable.

Acknowledgments: The authors wish to express their hearty thanks to the anonymous referees for their valuable suggestions and comments.

Conflicts of Interest: The authors declare no conflict of interest.

References

1. Levinson, N. Linear programming in complex space. *J. Math. Anal. Appl.* **1966**, *14*, 44–62. [CrossRef]
2. Abrams, R.A.; Ben-Israel, A. Nonlinear programming in complex space: Necessary conditions. *SIAM J. Control.* **1971**, *9*, 606–620. [CrossRef]
3. Abrams, R.A. Nonlinear Programming in complex space: Sufficient conditions and duality. *J. Math. Anal. Appl.* **1972**, *38*, 619–632. [CrossRef]
4. Mond, B.; Craven, B.D. A class of nondifferentiable complex programming problems. *J. Math. Oper. Stat.* **1975**, *6*, 581–591.
5. Duca, D.I. On vectorial programming problem in complex space. *Stud. Univ. Babes-Bolya Math.* **1979**, *24*, 51–56.
6. Duca, D.I. Proper Efficiency in the Complex Vectorial Programing. *Stud. Univ. Babes-Bolyai Math.* **1980**, *25*, 73–80.
7. Duca, D.I. Efficiency Criteria in Vectorial Programming in Complex Space without Convexity. *Cah. Cent. Etudes Rech. Oper.* **1984**, *26*, 217–226.
8. Duca, D.I. *Multicriteria Optimization in Complex Spaces*; Casa du Cartii de Stiinta: Cluj-Napoca, Romania , 2005.
9. Datta, N.; Bhatia, D. Duality for a class of nondifferentiable mathematical programming problems in complex space. *J. Math. Anal. Appl.* **1984**, *101*, 1–11. [CrossRef]
10. Huang, T.Y. Second-order duality for a non-differentiable minimax programming in complex spaces. *Int. J. Comput. Math.* **2017**, *94*, 2508–2519. [CrossRef]
11. Huang, T.Y. Second-order parametric free dualities for complex minimax fractional programming. *Mathematics* **2020**, 8, 67. [CrossRef]
12. Lai, H.C.; Huang, T.Y. Optimality Conditions for a Nondifferentiable Minimax Programming in Complex Spaces. *Nonlinear Anal.* **2009**, *71*, 1205–1212. [CrossRef]
13. Youness, E.A.; Elbrolosy, M.E. Extension to necessary optimality conditions in complex programming. *J. Appl. Math. Comput.* **2004**, *154*, 229–237. [CrossRef]
14. Youness, E.A.; Elbrolosy, M.E. Extension to sufficient optimality conditions in complex programming. *J. Math. Stat.* **2005**, *1*, 40–48. [CrossRef]
15. Elbrolosy, M.E. Efficiency for a generalized form of vector optimization problems in complex space. *Optimization* **2016**, *65*, 1245–1257. [CrossRef]
16. Huang, T.Y.; Tanaka, T. Optimality and duality for complex multi-objective programming. *Numer. Anal. Control Optim.* **2022**, *12*, 121–134. [CrossRef]

axioms

MDPI

Article

The Asymptotic Behavior for Generalized Jiřina Process

You Lv [1,*] and Huaping Huang [2]

[1] College of Science, Donghua University, Shanghai 201620, China;
[2] School of Mathematics and Statistics, Chongqing Three Gorges University, Wanzhou 404020, China
* Correspondence: lvyou@dhu.edu.cn

Abstract: As the classic branching process, the Galton-Watson process has obtained intensive attentions in the past decades. However, this model has two idealized assumptions–discrete states and time-homogeneity. In the present paper, we consider a branching process with continuous states, and for any given $n \in \mathbb{N}$, the branching law of every particle in generation n is determined by the population size of generation n. We consider the case that the process is extinct with Probability 1 since in this case the process will be substantially different from the size-dependent branching process with discrete states. We give the extinction rate in the sense of L^2 and almost surely by the form of harmonic moments, that is to say, we show how fast $\{Z_n^{-1}\}$ grows under a group of sufficient conditions. From the result of the present paper, we observe that the extinction rate will be determined by an asymptotic behavior of the mean of the branching law. The results obtained in this paper have the more superiority than the counterpart from the existing literature.

Keywords: size-dependent Jiřina process; L^2-convergence; extinction

MSC: 60J80

Citation: Lv, Y.; Huang, H. The Asymptotic Behavior for Generalized Jiřina Process. *Axioms* **2023**, *12*, 13. https://doi.org/10.3390/axioms12010013

Academic Editor: Behzad Djafari-Rouhani

Received: 17 November 2022
Revised: 17 December 2022
Accepted: 19 December 2022
Published: 23 December 2022

Copyright: © 2022 by the authors. Licensee MDPI, Basel, Switzerland. This article is an open access article distributed under the terms and conditions of the Creative Commons Attribution (CC BY) license (https://creativecommons.org/licenses/by/4.0/).

1. Introduction and Preliminaries

Branching process is an important class of Markov processes, which describes the survival and extinction of a particle system. The most classical branching process is called the Galton-Watson process (see [1]). For a chosen family, Galton and Watson [1] used this process to record the number of males in each generation. For a Galton-Watson process $\{Z_n\}$,, we usually set $Z_0 = 1$, which means that there is a male ancestor in the family. The relationship between Z_{n+1} and Z_n is written by

$$Z_{n+1} = \mathbf{1}_{Z_n \geq 1} \sum_{i=1}^{Z_n} \eta_{n,i},$$

where $\eta_{n,i}$ presents the number of boys whose father (in generation n) is indexed by i. In a Galton-Watson process, the random array $\{\eta_{n,i}\}_{n,i \in \mathbb{N}}$ is set to be i.i.d. Hence, Galton-Watson process is a time homogeneous Markov chains with discrete state. There are two idealized assumptions in this model: one is the discrete state space, the other is the property of time homogeneous. In other words, there are two directions to extend this model.

Jiřina process (see [2–5]) is the continuous version of the Galton-Watson process, which stresses that the role of $\eta_{n,i}$ can take value in $\mathbb{R}^+$ ($\mathbb{R}^+ := [0, +\infty)$) instead of $\mathbb{N}$. Since the state space of this process is a subset of $\mathbb{R}^+$, we use the Laplace transform to describe the relationship between the number of particles in generation n and $n+1$, which is described by

$$\mathbb{E}(\mathrm{e}^{-sZ_{n+1}} | Z_n = x) = \mathrm{e}^{-xF(s)}, \;\; x \in \mathbb{R}^+,$$

where $F(s)$ is a cumulate generate function of a certain infinitely divisible distribution G. G can be observed as the common branching mechanism (i.e., the law of $\eta_{1,1}$) of each particle.

It should be noted that in the above equality, $F(s)$ is independent of n, thus, we see that the Jiřina process is still time-homogeneous.

To break the feature of time homogeneous, several time-inhomogeneous branching processes have been studied over the past decades. There are different motivations to construct the time-inhomogeneous property for a branching process, one of which assumes that the common law of $\eta_{n,1}, \eta_{n,2}, \ldots$ is depending on Z_n, and $\eta_{n,i}$ takes value in $\mathbb{N}$ for every n, i. We call this a time-inhomogeneous branching process as the size-dependent branching process (with discrete time and discrete state). This assumption (the law of $\eta_{n,1}$ depends on Z_n) has a strong practical background; for example, when a country is overpopulated, the government may promote family planning, while if a country faces the problem of population scarcity, the government will encourage childbearing. This model has been investigated in [6–8] and some other papers.

In the present paper, the model we consider is the continuous version of the size-dependent branching process, which is also called the generalized Jiřina process (for short, GJP). This model was introduced in [9], where the model is defined by the Laplace transform as

$$\mathbb{E}(\mathrm{e}^{-Z_{n+1}\tau}|Z_n = x) = \mathrm{e}^{-xF(x,s)}, \quad x \in \mathbb{R}^+, \tag{1}$$

where $F(x,s)$ is called a reproduction cumulative function (for short, r.c.f.) and it has the following representation:

$$F(x,s) = r(x)\tau + \int_{0^+}^{+\infty} (1 - \mathrm{e}^{-us})v(x, \mathrm{d}u). \tag{2}$$

We can refer to [9] on how to obtain (2). On the other hand, ref. [9] also explains that $r(x)$ is a non-negative Borel function, and $(1 \wedge u)v(x, \mathrm{d}u)$ is a bounded kernel from $\mathbb{R}^+$ to $(0, +\infty)$. That is to say,

$$\forall x \geq 0, \quad \int_{0^+}^{+\infty} (1 \wedge u)v(x, \mathrm{d}u) < +\infty.$$

Hence, we see that the r.c.f. $F(x,\tau)$ is determined by $r(x)$ and $v(x, \mathrm{d}u)$. Obviously, if there exist a constant r and a measure v on $(0, +\infty)$ such that

$$r(x) \equiv r, \qquad v(x, \mathrm{d}u) \equiv v(\mathrm{d}u),$$

then GJP will degenerate to the Jiřina process. Moreover, from (1) one can see

$$\mathbb{E}(Z_{n+1}|Z_n = x) = -\frac{\partial \mathrm{e}^{-xF(x,s)}}{\partial s}\Big|_{s=0^+}.$$

Note that

$$\lim_{s \to 0^+} F(x,s) = 0$$

and

$$\lim_{s \to 0^+} \frac{\partial F(x,s)}{\partial s} = r(x) + \int_{0^+}^{+\infty} uv(x, \mathrm{d}u).$$

Actually, we have set that $(1 \wedge u)v(x, \mathrm{d}u)$ is a bounded kernel. Denote

$$m(x) := r(x) + \int_{0^+}^{+\infty} uv(x, \mathrm{d}u),$$

then we have

$$\mathbb{E}(Z_{n+1}|Z_n = x) = xm(x),$$

which means that $m(x)$ presents the expectation of the children reproduced by unit parent when the generation of the parent contains x particle(s). The above equality is equivalent to

$$\mathbb{E}(Z_{n+1}|Z_n) = Z_n m(Z_n).$$

Denote

$$\sigma^2(x) := \int_{0^+}^{+\infty} u^2 v(x, \mathrm{d}u) = \frac{\partial^2 \mathrm{e}^{-xF(x,s)}}{\partial^2 s}\Big|_{s=0^+}.$$

By a direct calculation we obtain

$$\mathbb{E}(Z_{n+1}^2|Z_n) = \sigma^2(Z_n)Z_n + Z_n^2 m^2(Z_n).$$

For a branching process $\{Z_n\}$, a very important topic, which is usually considered first, is the limit behavior of Z_n and the distribution of the limit (if it exists). For example, the celebrated Kesten-Stigum theorem (see [1], Chapter 1) for the Galton-Watson process and various generalized Kesten-Stigum theorem for different types of branching processes (see [3,7,10]). In summary, the Kesten-Stigum theorem and its various of generalized versions demonstrate that $\{Z_n\}$ converges to 0 with Probability p_0 and to $+\infty$ with Probability $1 - p_0$ and p_0 depends on the branching mechanism (reproduction law) of the branching process. Ref. [11] showed that the asymptotic behavior of GJP also behaves as

$$\mathbb{P}\Big(\lim_{n\to\infty} Z_n \in \{0, +\infty\}\Big) = 1$$

and $p_0 := \mathbb{P}(Z_n \to 0)$ is depending on some properties of $F(x,s)$. The author of [11] also pointed out that it is as similar as the asymptotic behavior of size-dependent branching process for the case $\{Z_n \to +\infty\}$. The most interesting and worth investigating is the case that $\{Z_n \to 0\}$, since when the state space is $\mathbb{N}$, then $Z_n \to 0$ means that there exists a finite generation n such that $Z_n = 0$ but Z_n can always be positive even though $Z_n \to 0$ when the state space is $\mathbb{R}^+$. Under some mild assumptions, ref. [10] gave the extinction rate of Z_n in the sense of almost surely when $\mathbb{P}(Z_n \to 0) = 1$. The idea to deal with the extinction rate is to consider the growth rate of Z_n^{-1}, then, the method to show the growth rate of the size-dependent branching process $\{X_n\}$ when $\mathbb{P}(X_n \to +\infty) = 1$ can be referred. Ref. [12] gave a sufficient condition to ensure that the extinction rate in the sense of it almost surely is also the extinction rate in the sense of L^2. In the present paper, we obtain a new extinction rate, which is easier to understanding by the definition of the mean function $m(\cdot)$ (see Section 3 for detail). Combining with the result in [12], we can observe that an extinct GJP may have different extinction rates under different conditions.

In this paper, we consider the rate of Z_n in the sense of almost surely and L^2 when the GJP behaves as $\mathbb{P}(Z_n \to 0) = 1$. We will give another group of sufficient conditions to ensure that there exists a constant sequence $\{c_n\}$ such that $\{c_n/Z_n\}$ has a limit in the sense of almost surely and L^2. Compared with the previous results, our results have more values for applications.

The GJP has a strong connection with reality. We can use GJP to model a number of chemical reactions and biological situations. For instance, it is proper to describe the trend of the concentration by GJP for some bacteria or virus whose reproduction depend on their concentration in the medium. For more examples, we recommend [7] and the references therein.

2. Main Results

For the sake of presenting our results, first of all, we give some basic assumptions as follows.

(A1) $r := \lim_{x\to 0^+} m(x)$, where $0 < r < 1$.

(A2) There exits a function $\bar{m}(x) \geq m(x)$ for all $x \geq 0$ which satisfies that $\inf_{x \geq 0} \bar{m}(x) \geq r$ and

$$p(x) := |\bar{m}(1/x) - r| (= \bar{m}(1/x) - r)$$

is non-increasing, $xp(x)$ is non-decreasing and concave, and

$$\int_1^{+\infty} \frac{p(x)}{x} \mathrm{d}x < +\infty.$$

(A3) For any $x \geq 0$, it satisfies $rx \int_0^{+\infty} \mathrm{e}^{-xF(x,s)} \mathrm{d}s \leq 1$.

(A4) $xp(\sqrt{x})$ is non-decreasing, concave and $xp^2(\sqrt{x})$ is concave.

(A5) For any $x \geq 0$, it satisfies $r^2 x^2 \int_0^{+\infty} s\mathrm{e}^{-xF(x,s)} \mathrm{d}s \leq 1$.

We remind that if $p''(x)$ exists on $(0, +\infty)$, then (A2) implies (A4). Denote

$$Y_n := \frac{1}{Z_n}, \quad q := \frac{1}{r}, \quad S_n := \frac{Y_n}{q^n} = \frac{r^n}{Z_n}.$$

First, we give some lemmas and results which will be used during, as we prove our main theorems.

Lemma 1. *Suppose that $h(x)$ is a positive and non-increasing function, then for any $t > 1, \epsilon > 0$, the following propositions are equivalent:*

(1) $\int_1^{+\infty} \frac{h(x)}{x} \mathrm{d}x < +\infty$;

(2) $\sum_{n=1}^{\infty} h(\epsilon t^n) < +\infty$.

Proof. See ([6], p. 42). □

Lemma 2. *Let $h(x)$ be a positive and non-increasing real function defined on $[0, +\infty)$. Assume that $xh(x)$ is non-decreasing and $\int_1^{+\infty} \frac{h(x)}{x} \mathrm{d}x < +\infty$. Let $\{c_n\}$ be a positive sequence and there exists a $t > 1$ such that for any n, it satisfies*

$$|c_{n+1} - c_n| \leq c_n h(c_n t^n),$$

then $\{c_n\}$ exists a finite non-negative limit. Moreover, there exists a constant $\tilde{c}$ depending on $h(x)$ and t such that, $\lim_{n \to \infty} c_n > 0$ only if the first term $c_0 > \tilde{c}$.

Proof. See ([6], p. 45). □

It is worth mentioning that the method from this paper is mainly concentrating on the martingale convergence theorems listed below.

Theorem 1. *(Martingale convergence theorem, (ref. [13], p. 270)) If $\{\xi_n\}$ is a sub-martingale and $\sup_n \mathbb{E}|\xi_n| < +\infty$, then there exists a random variable (denoted by $\xi_{+\infty}$) satisfying that*

$$\lim_{n \to \infty} \xi_n = \xi_{+\infty}, \text{ a.s.}, \quad \mathbb{P}(\xi_{+\infty} < +\infty) = 1, \quad \mathbb{E}|\xi_{+\infty}| < +\infty.$$

Theorem 2. *(Martingale L^p convergence theorem, (ref. [14], p. 60)) If $\{\xi_n\}$ is a sub-martingale and $\sup\limits_n \mathbb{E}|\xi_n^p| < +\infty$ for some $p > 1$, then, there exists a random variable (denoted by $\xi_{+\infty}$) satisfying that*

$$\lim_{n\to\infty} \xi_n = \xi_{+\infty}, \text{ a.s., } L^p, \quad \mathbb{P}(\xi_{+\infty} < +\infty) = 1, \quad \mathbb{E}|\xi_{+\infty}^p| < +\infty.$$

Now, we give our main results as follows:

Theorem 3. *Let $\{Z_n\}$ be a GJP, if Assumptions (A1)–(A3) hold and $\mathbb{P}(Z_0 = z_0) = 1$, where z_0 is a positive constant, then there exist a constant $\gamma \in (0, +\infty)$ and a random variable S (both depending on z_0) such that*

$$\gamma = \lim_{n\to\infty} \mathbb{E}(S_n | Z_0 = z_0),$$
$$S = \lim_{n\to\infty} S_n, \text{ a.s.},$$

and

$$\mathbb{E}S < +\infty.$$

Proof. Let $\mathcal{F}_n$ be the σ-algebra field, which is generated by $Z_0, Z_1, \ldots, Z_n$. Recalling that $Z_n := \frac{1}{Y_n}$, which means that

$$\begin{aligned}
\mathbb{E}(Y_{n+1}|\mathcal{F}_n) &= \mathbb{E}\left(\frac{1}{Z_{n+1}}|\mathcal{F}_n\right) \\
&= \mathbb{E}\left(\int_0^{+\infty} e^{-sZ_{n+1}} ds \Big| Z_n\right) \\
&= \int_0^{+\infty} \mathbb{E}(e^{-sZ_{n+1}}|Z_n) ds \\
&= \int_0^{+\infty} e^{-Z_n F(Z_n, s)} ds \\
&= \int_0^{+\infty} e^{-\frac{1}{Y_n} F(\frac{1}{Y_n}, s)} ds \\
&:= h(Y_n).
\end{aligned} \tag{3}$$

The second equality above is due to $c\int_0^{+\infty} e^{-cs} ds = 1$, where $c > 0$ is a constant. By Taylor's expansion we can observe

$$F(x, s) \leq m(x)s. \tag{4}$$

Assumption (A3) and (4) imply that

$$\int_0^{+\infty} e^{-x\bar{m}(x)s} ds \leq \int_0^{+\infty} e^{-xm(x)s} ds \leq \int_0^{+\infty} e^{-xF(x,s)} ds \leq \frac{1}{rs} = \int_0^{+\infty} e^{-xrs} ds.$$

By the smoothing property of conditional expectation and (3), we obtain that

$$\begin{aligned}
&|\mathbb{E}S_n - \mathbb{E}S_{n+1}| \\
&= \frac{1}{q^{n+1}} |\mathbb{E}(qY_n) - \mathbb{E}(h(Y_n))| \\
&= \frac{1}{q^{n+1}} \left| \mathbb{E}\int_0^{+\infty} e^{-\frac{s}{qY_n}} ds - \mathbb{E}\int_0^{+\infty} e^{-\frac{1}{Y_n}F(\frac{1}{Y_n}, s)} ds \right| \\
&\leq \frac{1}{q^{n+1}} \left| \mathbb{E}\int_0^{+\infty} (e^{-rsZ_n} - e^{-Z_n \bar{m}(Z_n)s}) ds \right|.
\end{aligned}$$

According to the mean value theorem, there exists a constant $\vartheta \in [0,1]$ such that

$$\begin{aligned}
&\left|\mathbb{E}\int_0^{+\infty}(\mathrm{e}^{-rsZ_n}-\mathrm{e}^{-Z_n\bar{m}(Z_n)s})\mathrm{d}s\right| \\
&=\left|\mathbb{E}\int_0^{+\infty}(\mathrm{e}^{-(rsZ_n+\vartheta(Z_n\bar{m}(Z_n)s-rsZ_n))})(sZ_n\bar{m}(Z_n)-rsZ_n)\mathrm{d}s\right| \\
&\leq\left|\mathbb{E}\int_0^{+\infty}\mathrm{e}^{-rsZ_n}(\bar{m}(Z_n)sZ_n-rsZ_n)\mathrm{d}s\right| \\
&=\left|(\bar{m}(Z_n)-r)Z_n\mathbb{E}\int_0^{+\infty}\mathrm{e}^{-rsZ_n}s\mathrm{d}s\right|.
\end{aligned}$$

Hence, we have

$$\begin{aligned}
&|\mathbb{E}S_n-\mathbb{E}S_{n+1}| \\
&\leq\frac{1}{q^{n+1}}\left|\mathbb{E}\left(\frac{(\bar{m}(Z_n)-r)Z_n}{r^2Z_n^2}\right)\right| \\
&\leq\left|\mathbb{E}\left(\frac{(\bar{m}(Z_n)-r)Y_n}{r^2q^{n+1}}\right)\right| \\
&=\frac{1}{r}\mathbb{E}(S_n|(\bar{m}(Z_n)-r)|).
\end{aligned}$$

From Assumption (A2), i.e., the concavity of $p(x)$, we have

$$|\mathbb{E}S_{n+1}-\mathbb{E}S_n|=\frac{1}{r}\mathbb{E}(p(Y_n)S_n)\leq\frac{1}{r}p(\mathbb{E}Y_n)\mathbb{E}(S_n)=\frac{1}{r}p(q^n\mathbb{E}S_n)\mathbb{E}(S_n).$$

Note that $q>1$, hence by applying Lemma 2, it follows that $\lim_{n\to\infty}\mathbb{E}S_n$ exists and

$$b:=\lim_{n\to\infty}\mathbb{E}S_n<+\infty.$$

Note that b lies on the starting state Z_0. Since $\mathbb{P}(Z_0=z_0)=1$, then by using Lemma 2 it is easy to observe that $b>0$ if $\mathbb{E}S_0=1/z_0$ large enough. Therefore, by a similar argument as stated in [12], we can observe $b>0$ only if $z_0>0$.

On the other hand, noting that

$$S_n-\mathbb{E}(S_{n+1}|\mathcal{F}_n)=\int_0^{+\infty}\frac{1}{t^{n+1}}(\mathrm{e}^{-rsZ_n}-\mathrm{e}^{-Z_nF(Z_n,s)})\mathrm{d}s>0,$$

we declare that $\{S_n,\mathcal{F}_n\}$ is a non-negative super martingale. Using Theorem 1 we speculate that there exists a random variable S such that

$$\lim_{n\to\infty}S_n=S,\ \text{a.s.}.$$

By Fatou's Lemma we claim that

$$\mathbb{E}S\leq\lim_{n\to\infty}\mathbb{E}S_n<+\infty.$$

Accordingly, we complete the proof. □

Theorem 4. *Let $\{Z_n\}$ be a GJP, Assumptions (A1)–(A5) hold and $\mathbb{P}(Z_0=z_0)=1$. Then,*

$$S=\lim_{n\to\infty}S_n,\ \text{in}\ L^2,$$

and

$$\mathbb{P}(S>0)>0.$$

Proof. Recall a simple calculation

$$c^2 \int_0^{+\infty} s e^{-cs} ds = 1, \quad c > 0.$$

First, we observe that

$$\begin{aligned}
\mathbb{E}(Y_{n+1}^2 | \mathcal{F}_n) &= \mathbb{E}\left(\frac{1}{Z_{n+1}^2} | \mathcal{F}_n \right) \\
&= \mathbb{E}\left(\int_0^{+\infty} s e^{-sZ_{n+1}} ds | Z_n \right) \\
&= \int_0^{+\infty} s \mathbb{E}(e^{-sZ_{n+1}} | Z_n) ds \\
&= \int_0^{+\infty} s e^{-Z_n F(Z_n, s)} ds \\
&= \int_0^{+\infty} s e^{-\frac{1}{Y_n} F(\frac{1}{Y_n}, s)} ds.
\end{aligned}$$

Hence, one sees that

$$\begin{aligned}
& |\mathbb{E}S_n^2 - \mathbb{E}S_{n+1}^2| \\
= & \frac{1}{q^{2n+2}} \left| \mathbb{E} \int_0^{+\infty} s e^{-\frac{s}{qY_n}} ds - \mathbb{E} \int_0^{+\infty} s e^{-\frac{1}{Y_n} F(\frac{1}{Y_n}, s)} ds \right| \\
\leq & \frac{1}{q^{2n+2}} \left| \mathbb{E}\left(\int_0^{+\infty} s(e^{-rsZ_n} - e^{-Z_n \bar{m}(Z_n) s}) ds \right) \right|. \qquad (5)
\end{aligned}$$

By the mean-value theorem, there exists a constant $\vartheta \in [0, 1]$ such that

$$\begin{aligned}
& \left| \mathbb{E}\left(\int_0^{+\infty} s(e^{-rsZ_n} - e^{-Z_n \bar{m}(Z_n) s}) ds \right) \right| \\
= & \left| \mathbb{E} \int_0^{+\infty} s(e^{-(rsZ_n + \vartheta(Z_n \bar{m}(Z_n) s - rsZ_n))} (Z_n \bar{m}(Z_n) s - rsZ_n)) ds \right| \\
\leq & \left| \mathbb{E} \int_0^{+\infty} s^2 Z_n e^{-rsZ_n} (\bar{m}(Z_n) - r) ds \right| \\
\leq & \mathbb{E} \frac{2|\bar{m}(Z_n) - r| Z_n}{r^3 Z_n^3}. \qquad (6)
\end{aligned}$$

Based on (5) and (6) we obtain

$$|\mathbb{E}S_n^2 - \mathbb{E}S_{n+1}^2| \leq \frac{1}{q^{2n}} \mathbb{E} \frac{2|\bar{m}(Z_n) - r|}{r Z_n^2} = \frac{2}{rq^{2n}} \mathbb{E}(Y_n^2 p(Y_n)).$$

By the concavity of $l(x) := xp(\sqrt{x})$, we have

$$\begin{aligned}
|\mathbb{E}S_n^2 - \mathbb{E}S_{n+1}^2| &= \frac{2}{rq^{2n}} \mathbb{E}(l(Y_n^2)) \\
&\leq \frac{2}{rq^{2n}} l(\mathbb{E}Y_n^2) \\
&= \frac{2}{r} \mathbb{E}S_n^2 p\left(\sqrt{\mathbb{E}(S_n^2)} q^n \right).
\end{aligned}$$

Since $p(x)$ is non-increasing, we obtain

$$|\mathbb{E}S_n^2 - \mathbb{E}S_{n+1}^2| \leq \frac{2}{r} \mathbb{E}S_n^2 p(q^n \mathbb{E}S_n).$$

According to the conclusion in Theorem 1 we obtain $b^* := \inf_n \mathbb{E}S_n > 0$. Hence, ones have

$$|\mathbb{E}S_n^2 - \mathbb{E}S_{n+1}^2| \leq \frac{2}{r}\mathbb{E}S_n^2 p(q^n b^*).$$

That is to say, we arrive at

$$\mathbb{E}S_{n+1}^2 \leq \frac{2}{r}\mathbb{E}S_n^2(1 + p(q^n b^*)).$$

From Lemma 1 we have $\sum_{n=1}^{\infty} p(b^* q^n) < +\infty$, which means that

$$\sup_n \mathbb{E}S_n^2 < +\infty$$

and thus the limit $\beta := \lim_{n\to\infty} \mathbb{E}S_n^2$ exists. Now, we construct a martingale as

$$U_n := S_n + V_n,$$

where

$$V_n := \sum_{k=0}^{n-1} \int_0^{+\infty} \frac{1}{q^{k+1}} (\mathrm{e}^{-rsZ_k} - \mathrm{e}^{-Z_k F(Z_k,s)}) \mathrm{d}s.$$

Denote $\|X\|$ as the L^2-norm of the random variable X, hence, it is clear that

$$\|U_n\| \leq \|S_n\| + \|V_n\|.$$

Define

$$Q_k = \int_0^{+\infty} \frac{1}{q^{k+1}} (\mathrm{e}^{-rsZ_k} - \mathrm{e}^{-Z_k F(Z_k,s)}) \mathrm{d}s.$$

It is obvious that for any n, one has

$$\|V_n\| \leq \sum_{k=0}^{\infty} \|Q_k\|.$$

Moreover, from the estimate in the proof of Theorem 3, we have

$$|Q_n| \leq \frac{1}{q^{n+1}} \int_0^{+\infty} \mathrm{e}^{-Z_n s} |rsZ_n - F(Z_n,s)Z_n| \mathrm{d}s \leq \frac{1}{qr^2} \frac{|r - m(Z_n)|}{S_n}.$$

Since $xp^2(\sqrt{x})$ is a concave function (see Assumption (A4)), we can obtain that

$$\begin{aligned}\sum_{k=0}^{\infty} \|Q_k\| &\leq \sum_{k=0}^{\infty} \sqrt{\mathbb{E}\left[\left(\frac{1}{qr^2} S_k p(S_k q^k)\right)^2\right]} \\ &\leq \sum_{k=0}^{\infty} \frac{1}{r} \sqrt{\mathbb{E}(S_k^2) p^2(q^k \mathbb{E}S_k)}.\end{aligned}$$

Since $\alpha^2 := \sup_n ES_n^2 < +\infty$, then it follows that

$$\sup_n \|V_n\| \leq \sum_{k=0}^{\infty} \frac{\alpha}{r} p(\mathbb{E}S_k q^k).$$

Thus, by utilizing Lemma 1, it is not hard to verify that

$$\sum_{k=0}^{\infty} p(\mathbb{E}S_k q^k) \leq \sum_{k=0}^{\infty} p(b^* q^k) < +\infty,$$

then

$$\sup_n \|V_n\| \le \sum_{k=0}^{\infty} \|Q_k\| < +\infty,$$

which establishes that

$$\sup_n \|U_n\| \le \sup_n \|S_n\| + \sup_n \|V_n\| \le \alpha^2 + \sup_n \|V_n\| < +\infty.$$

Combining the above inequality with the fact that $\{U_n, \mathcal{F}_n\}$ is a martingale, we claim that $\{U_n\}$ has a limit in the sense of L^2 from the martingale L^p convergence theorem. On the other hand, we observe that $\{V_n\}$ also has the L^2 limit since $\left\{ \sum_{k=0}^{n} \|Q_k\| \right\}$ is a Cauchy sequence. Recall that $S_n = U_n - V_n$ and we have shown that $\{S_n\}$ has the limit S in the sense of almost surely, then we have

$$S_n \to S, \text{ a.s., } L^2,$$

and

$$\lim_{n\to\infty} \mathbb{E}S_n^2 = \mathbb{E}S^2.$$

Moreover, $\lim_{n\to\infty} \mathbb{E}S_n = \mathbb{E}S > 0$, thus, $\mathbb{P}(S > 0) > 0$. That is to say, S is non-degenerate. □

3. Conclusions

Compared with the results in [12], the assumptions in the present paper do not need that $\inf_{x\ge0} r(x) > 0$. We also even do not require that $\inf_{x\ge0} m(x) > 0$. Intuitively, $\inf_{x\ge0} m(x) = 0$ will make the process more likely to be extinct. Hence, $\inf_{x\ge0} r(x) > 0$ is not a natural enough condition under the case $\mathbb{P}(Z_n \to 0) = 1$, which we consider. Moreover, the extinction rate may be different between in [12] and in this paper, since under the assumption in [12] the rate will be $\lim_{x\to0^+} r(x)$ (if it exists). One can see that there are many cases (for example, the case that $v(x, du)$ is not depending on x) in which $\lim_{x\to0^+} r(x) < \lim_{x\to0^+} m(x)$. We remind that the rate in our paper $\lim_{x\to0^+} m(x)$ appears reasonable because of $m(x) = x^{-1}\mathbb{E}(Z_{n+1}|Z_n = x)$, and further, we consider the case that the process is extinct.

Throughout our paper, under the Assumptions (A1)–(A5), we obtain an extinction rate for a GJP in the sense of almost surely and L^2, which enriches the limit theory of GJP process. Therefore, our results have potential values in applications.

Author Contributions: Y.L. designed the research, wrote the paper and gave the support of funding acquisition. H.H. made some revisions to the paper. All authors have read and agreed to the published version of the manuscript.

Funding: The first author acknowledges the Fundamental Research Funds for the Central Universities (No. 2232021D-30). The second author acknowledges the financial support from the Natural Science Foundation of Chongqing of China (No. cstc2020jcyj-msxmX0762), and the Initial Funding of Scientific Research for High-level Talents of Chongqing Three Gorges University of China (No. 2104/09926601).

Institutional Review Board Statement: Not applicable.

Informed Consent Statement: Not applicable.

Data Availability Statement: The data presented in this study are available upon request from the corresponding author.

Acknowledgments: The authors thank the editor and the referees for their valuable comments and suggestions, which improved greatly the quality of this paper.

Conflicts of Interest: The authors declare no conflict of interest.

References

1. Athreya, K.B.; Ney, P. *Branching Processes;* Springer: Berlin/Heidelberg, Germany, 1972.
2. Jiřina, M. Stochastic branching processes with continuous state space. *Czechoslovak. Math. J.* **1958**, *83*, 292–313. [CrossRef]
3. Seneta, E.; Vere-Jones, D. On the asymptotic behaviour of subcritical branching processes with continuous state space. *Z. Wahrsch. Verw. Gebiete.* **1968**, *10*, 212–225. [CrossRef]
4. Seneta, E.; Vere-Jones, D. On a problem of M.Jiřina concerning continuous state branching processes. *Czechoslovak. Math. J.* **1969**, *94*, 277–283. [CrossRef]
5. Pakes, A.G. Some limit theorems for Jiřina processes. *Period. Math. Hungar.* **1979**, *10*, 55–66. [CrossRef]
6. Klebaner, F.C. Geometric rate of growth in population-size-dependent branching processes. *J. Appl. Probab.* **1984**, *21*, 40–49. [CrossRef]
7. Klebaner, F.C. On population-size-dependent branching processes. *Adv. Appl. Probab.* **1984**, *22*, 30–55. [CrossRef]
8. Klebaner, F.C. A limit theorem for population-size-dependent branching processes. *J. Appl. Probab.* **1985**, *22*, 48–57. [CrossRef]
9. Li, Y. On a continuous-state population-size-dependent branching processes and its extinction. *J. Appl. Probab.* **2006**, *43*, 195–207. [CrossRef]
10. Li, Y. The speed of extinction for some generalized Jiřina processes. *Adv. Appl. Probab.* **2009**, *41*, 576–599. [CrossRef]
11. Li, Y. Limit theorems for generalized Jiřina process. *Statat. Probab. Lett.* **2009**, *79*, 158–164. [CrossRef]
12. Lv, Y.; Li, Y. L^2 limits of generalized Jiřina process. *Statat. Probab. Lett.* **2017**, *129*, 588–596. [CrossRef]
13. Bass, R.F. *Real Analysis for Graduate Students*, 2nd ed.; CreateSpace Independent Publishing Platform: Charleston, SC, USA, 2013.
14. Loeve, M. *Probability Theory*, 2nd ed.; Springer: New York, NY, USA, 1978.

Disclaimer/Publisher's Note: The statements, opinions and data contained in all publications are solely those of the individual author(s) and contributor(s) and not of MDPI and/or the editor(s). MDPI and/or the editor(s) disclaim responsibility for any injury to people or property resulting from any ideas, methods, instructions or products referred to in the content.

MDPI
St. Alban-Anlage 66
4052 Basel
Switzerland
www.mdpi.com

Axioms Editorial Office
E-mail: axioms@mdpi.com
www.mdpi.com/journal/axioms

Disclaimer/Publisher's Note: The statements, opinions and data contained in all publications are solely those of the individual author(s) and contributor(s) and not of MDPI and/or the editor(s). MDPI and/or the editor(s) disclaim responsibility for any injury to people or property resulting from any ideas, methods, instructions or products referred to in the content.

www.ingramcontent.com/pod-product-compliance
Lightning Source LLC
LaVergne TN
LVHW070443100526
838202LV00014B/1655
* 9 7 8 3 7 2 5 8 1 0 4 0 6 *